If you are frequently puzzled by the complexities of English spelling and pronunciation, then this handy reference work is what you have been waiting for. It contains more than 23,000 entries with special emphasis on:

MAJOR PRONUNCIATION ERRORS

☐ Improper enunciation
☐ Wrong accent
☐ Accent shifts

MAJOR SPELLING ERRORS

☐ When to drop the final "e"
☐ When to double final letters
☐ When to use a hyphen
☐ When to use a compound word
☐ Correct abbreviations
☐ Proper nouns and foreign phrases

If you can spell the word but ~~cannot pro~~nounce it correctly, or if ~~~~ but cannot spell it ~~~~ by both points, th~~~~ will enable you to ~~~~ and for all time.

Words
Most Often
Misspelled
and Mis-
pronounced

Ruth Gleeson Gallagher
and James Colvin

POCKET BOOKS

New York   London   Toronto   Sydney   Tokyo   Singapore

The system of indicating pronunciation is used
by permission. From THE NEW MERRIAM-
WEBSTER DICTIONARY, copyright © 1964
by C. & C. Merriam Company, publishers of the
Merriam-Webster Dictionaries.

POCKET BOOKS, a division of Simon & Schuster Inc.
1230 Avenue of the Americas, New York, NY 10020

ISBN: 0-671-64874-8

First Pocket Books printing August 1963

31   30   29

POCKET and colophon are trademarks of
Simon & Schuster Inc.

Printed in the U.S.A.

PREFACE

Words Most Often Misspelled and Mispronounced is a quick reference guide to the trickiest words in the English language. Ours being a problem-laden language, the list is long—over 23,000 words. These are the words likeliest to be looked up by the student, secretary, businessman, and writer—in fact, anyone to whom correct spelling and pronunciation are vital in social and business life.

Keep this book handy. A quick reference guide will do little good on a high shelf. *Words Most Often Misspelled and Mispronounced* is compact enough to keep in your desk drawer. Use it every time you have a word question, until "looking it up" is an engrained habit. Never let yourself get away with a sloppy guess. The most important single aid in improving your word skills is the habit of looking up words *as you use them, as questions arise.*

You might find it helpful to circle words you have to look up. Unless your memory is better than most, you will probably be looking up the same word again. When you write the word, look at it for a second or two. You might even jot it down a couple of times on a scratch pad. Next time you have to refer to this word it will come more easily; soon it will be a confident part of your vocabulary.

For pronunciations the same general idea applies. Say the word a time or two; get the sound of it in your ear. This will lead you into the habit of correct usage, so that in future conversation the right pronunciation comes naturally, without doubts or fumbling.

USING THIS BOOK

This book has been designed to clear up everyday problems in spelling and pronunciation and to make it quick and easy to find words.

Problems in Spelling and Pronunciation

Endings. Misspellings commonly result from changes in the root word with the addition of suffixes. For example, *cause* loses its final *e* when the final *-ing* is added; thus:

cause, causing

A word like *block* does not alter the spelling of its root when *-ing* is added:

block, blocking

Obviously, this isn't a problem. But a few endings cause questions even though the root remains the same:

canoe, canoeing

Words like this are considered problems; consequently, the suffixes have been included in the book. The concern here is to leave no question in the user's mind.

Other examples in this category are words in which the final consonant is doubled with the addition of suffixes:

essential, essentially
occur, occurring

. . . or changes that occur in the plural of nouns:

ability, abilities

As in many traditional dictionaries, the simplest endings (*-ed*, *-ing*, and *-ies*) are picked up at the last unchanged syllable and immediately follow the main entry. Other derivatives follow:

> accumulate
>   -lating
>   accumulable
>   accumulation
>   accumulative
>   accumulator

But even the simplest endings are never broken between double letters. Thus, instead of *accede, -ceding,* the word *acceding* is written out in full. This is done to avoid careless omission of the second *c*.

Pronunciations. The major pronunciation errors of English speakers are the result of improper enunciation or accent. This work uses the standard phonetic symbols of the Merriam-Webster Dictionaries. See page x for the list of these symbols.

Both primary and secondary accents are shown:

> primary: ′
> secondary: ′
> Example: **aberration** (ab′er • a′shun)

When the accent shifts as a result of a change in the word's form, the editors have included this face in the sub-entry:

> **apocalypse** (a • pok′a • lips)
> **apocalyptic** (a • pok′a • lip′tik)

When the accent has been omitted from one of the sub-entries (for example, *abnormally*), the user should assume the accent is that of the original entry (ab • nor′mal).

Hyphen problems. "Is it one word, two words, or hyphenated?"

In an attempt to answer this question, extended lists of word compounds and combinations are included. Such lists show the preferred form of compounds in commonest usage. Very often these words are so simple there is no other reason for including them. For example:

> good-bye
> goodhearted
> good-humored
> good will

Confusing similarities. Brief definitions and cross references are included for words often mistaken for each other, like *disperse-disburse, serge-surge* and *bouillon-bullion.* For example:

> **bouillon** (soup; see *bullion*)

These definitions are intended as quick reference hints. For your knottier word problems, consult a dictionary.

Places, people, brands, and foreign phrases. State names are listed, along with the preferred abbreviations and correct terms for state residents. For example, a native of Michigan may correctly be called a *Michiganite* or a *Michigander.* Town, city, or river names are included if they are sources of spelling or pronunciation difficulties. Also provided are a selected list of world figures like *Khrushchev, Macmillan,* and *Mao Tse-tung;* brand names that are a part of the language like *Kodachrome;* and common foreign phrases like *coup d'état.*

Choice of words to be included in this book. The editors didn't include words so simple you'd never look them up— words like *man, fan,* and *ran;* nor the blockbusters used to stump the experts, like *cuproiodargyrite.* This left room for words that people do look up and for endings that cause questions.

Some of the words may seem much too simple for a "problem list," but consider the following hardy perennials among the most commonly misspelled words in the language:

> there, their
> receive
> exist, existence, existent
> separate, separation
> occur, occurred, occurring, occurrence
> occasion
> definite, definitely
> definition
> believe, belief

Ease of Finding Words

Have you ever hunted up and down a dictionary page for a word you weren't quite sure of? Sometimes a word and its derivatives are widely separated alphabetically. Many reference works put the derivatives with the main entry; others list them alphabetically. For example, *drier* is a long way from *dry*, and it is a derivative that has considerable importance of its own. In this book, the word *drier* is listed both in straight alphabetical order, and under *dry*. This way, you'll find it whichever place you look first.

Ease of finding main entries is further enhanced by the modern system of syllabifying by centered dots, omitting accent marks. Words are less "broken up" this way and more quickly spotted on the page. If you wish to know the correct accent or a word, it is included in the pronunciation that follows the word.

Fast identification is aided by including the context of certain specialized words. Thus, rather than *sleight*, the entry is *sleight of hand*.

The dominating editorial principle of this book has been the ease with which it could be used, still maintaining a maximum of information. Where the user desires further information on the meanings and uses of words he is referred to the Merriam-Webster series of dictionaries.

The concept of this book originated with James Colvin and the late Frederick Gleeson. They saw the need for a convenient reference work that would clarify two of the greatest irregularities in the English language: *spelling* and *pronunciation*. Both Mr. Colvin and Mr. Gleeson were closely associated with the National Spelling Bee, which is administered by the Scripps-Howard Newspapers. When Mr. Gleeson died, his widow completed the book. She had been his research teammate and has since become a faculty member of St. John College of Cleveland.

—The Publisher

KEY TO THE SYMBOLS
USED IN THE RESPELLING
FOR PRONUNCIATION

The system of indication pronunciation used throughout this book is taken from the 1964 *Merriam-Webster Dictionary*.

ā,   *as in* āle, fāte, lā′bor, chā′os.

à,   *as in* chȧ·ot′ic, fȧ·tal′i·ty, in·an′·i·māte.

â,   *as in* câre, pâr′ent, com·pâre′, beâr, âir.

ă,   *as in* ădd, ăm, făt, ăc·cept′.

ȧ,   *as in* ȧc·count′. in′fȧnt, guid′-dȧnce.

ä,   *as in* ärm, fär, fä′ther, pälm.

à,   *as in* àsk, gràss, dànce, stàff, päth.

ȧ,   *as in* so′fȧ, i·de′ȧ, ȧ·bound′, di′ȧ·dem.

b,   *as in* ba′by, be, bit, bob, but.

ch,   *as in* chair, much; *also for* tch *as in* match; *for* ti *as in* ques′tion; *for* te as in right′eous.

d,   *as in* day, add′ed; *also for* ed *as in* robbed.

dụ: *for* du *as in* ver′dure; *for* deu *as in* gran′deur.

ē,   *as in* ēve, mēte, se·rēne′.

ẹ,   *as in* hẹre, fẹar, wẹird, deer (dẹr).

ê,   *as in* ê·vent′, dê·pend′, crê·ate′.

ĕ,   *as in* ĕnd, ĕx·cuse′, ĕf·face′.

ĕ,   *as in* si′lĕnt, pru′dĕnce, nov′ĕl.

ē,   *as in* mak′ēr, pēr·vert′, in′fēr·ence.

f,   *as in* fill, feel; *for* ph *as in* tri′umph; *for* gh *as in* laugh.

g,   (*always* "*hard*"), *as in* go, be·gin′; *also for* gu *as in* guard; *for* gue *as in* plague; *for* gh *as in* ghost.

gz: *for* x *as in* ex·ist′, ex·am′ple.

h,   *as in* hat, hot, hurt, a·head′.

hw: *for* wh *as in* what, why, where.

ī,   *as in* īce, sīght, in·spīre′, Ī·de′a.

ĭ,   *as in* ĭll, ad·mĭt′, hab′ĭt, pit′y (pĭt′ĭ).

ĭ,   *as in* char′i·ty, pos′si·ble, di·rect′, A′prĭl.

j,   *as in* joke, jol′ly; *also for* "*soft*" g, *as in* gem, gi′ant; *for* gi *and* ge *as in* re·li′gion, pi′geon; *for* di *as in* sol′dier; *for* dg(e) *as in* edge, judg′ment.

k,   *as in* keep; *also for* "*hard*" ch, *as in* cho′rus; *for* "*hard*" c, *as in* cube; *for* ck, *as in* pack; *for* qu *as in* con′quer; *for* que *as in* pique.

ĸ,   (*small capital*): *for* ch *as in* German ich, ach, *etc.*

ks: *for* x *as in* vex, ex′e·cute, per·plex′.

kw: *for* qu *as in* queen, quit, qual′i·ty.

l,   *as in* late, leg, lip, hol′ly.

m,   *as in* man, mine, hum, ham′mer.

n,   *as in* no, man, man′ner; *also for* gn *as in* sign.

N,   (*small capital*): *without sound of its own indicates the nasal tone* (*as in French or Portuguese*) *of the preceding vowel, as in* bon (bôN)

ng,   *as in* sing, long, sing′er; *also for* ngue, *as in* tongue; *for* n *before the sound of* k *or* "*hard*" g, *as in* bank, junc′tion, lin′ger.

ō,   *as in* ōld, nōte, cal′i·cō.

ô,   *as in* ô·bey′, a·nat′ô·my, prô·pose′.

ô,   *as in* ôrb, lôrd, ôr·dain′; law (lô), bought (bôt), caught (kôt). all (ôl).

ŏ,   *as in* ŏdd, nŏt, tŏr′rid, fŏr′est.

ŏ,   *as in* sŏft, dŏg, clŏth, lŏss, cŏst.

ô,   *as in* cŏn·nect′, ŏc·cur′, co′lŏn, cŏm·bine′.

oi,   *as in* oil, nois′y, a·void′, goi′ter.

ōō, *as in* fōōd, fōōl, nōōn; rude (rōōd), ru'mor (rōō'mẽr).

ŏŏ, *as in* fŏŏt, wŏŏl; put (pŏŏt), pull (pŏŏl).

ou, *as in* out, thou, de·vour'.

p, *as in* pa'pa, pen, pin, put.

r, *as in* rap, red, rip, hor'rid; *also for* rh *as in* rho'do·den'dron.

s (*always voiceless, or* "*sharp*"), *as in* so, this, haste; *also for* "*soft*" c, *as in* cell, vice; *for* sc *as in* scene, sci'ence; *for* ss *as in* hiss.

sh, *as in* she, ship, shop; *also for* ch *as in* ma·chine'; *for* ce *as in* o'cean; *for* ci *as in* so'cial; *for* sci *as in* con'scious; *for* s *as in* sure; *for* se *as in* nau'seous; *for* si *as in* pen'sion; *for* ss *as in* is'sue; *for* ssi *as in* pas'sion; *for* ti *as in* na'tion.

t, *as in* time, talk; *also for* ed *as in* baked; *for* th *as in* Thom'as.

th (*voiced*): *for* th *as in* then, though, this, smooth, breathe.

th (*voiceless*), *as in* thin, through, wealth, worth, width.

tū: *for* tu *as in* na'ture, cul'ture, pic'ture.

ū, *as in* cūbe, pūre, tūne, lūte, dū'ty.

û, *as in* û·nite', for'mū·late, hû·mane'.

û, *as in* ûrn, fûrl, con·cûr'; her (hûr), fern (fûrn), fir (fûr); *for* German ö, oe, *as in* schön (shûn), Goe'the (gû'tĕ); *for* French eu, *as in* jeu (zhû), seul (sûl).

ŭ, *as in* ŭp, tŭb, stŭd'y, ŭn'der.

u, *as in* cir'cŭs, dā'tŭm, cir'cŭm·stance, de'mon (-mŭn), na'tion (-shŭn).

ü: *for* German ü, *as in* grün; *for* French u, *as in* me·nu' (mĕ·nü').

v, *as in* van, vote, re·vise'; *also for* f *as in* of.

w, *as in* want, win; *also for* u *as in* per·suade' (-swād') *or* o *as in* choir (kwīr).

y, *as in* yet, be·yond'; *also for* i *as in* un'ion (-yŭn).

z, *as in* zone, haze; *also for voiced* ("*soft*") s, *as in* is, lives, wise, mu'sic, ears; *for* x *as in* xy'lo·phone.

zh: *for* z *as in* az'ure; *for* zi *as in* bra'zier; *for* s *as in* pleas'ure, u'su·al; *for* si *as in* vi'sion; *for* ssi *as in* re·scis'sion; *for* g *as in* rouge, mi·rage'.

' *as in* par'don (pär'd'n), eat'en (ēt''n), e'vil (ē'v'l), *indicates that the following consonant is syllabic.*

SYMBOLS FOR PHONETIC RESPELLING USED IN WEBSTER'S *THIRD INTERNATIONAL DICTIONARY*

Webster's Third International Dictionary, published in 1967, uses a new system of symbols for indicating pronunciation. That system is reproduced on the following page for your convenience in using any dictionary in conjunction with WORDS MOST COMMONLY MISSPELLED AND MISPRONOUNCED.

ə .... alone, silent, capital, collect, suppose

ˈə, ˌə .. humdrum, abut

ᵊ .... (in ᵊl, ᵊn) battle, cotton; (in lᵊ, mᵊ, rᵊ) French table, prisme, titre

ər .... operation, further

a .... map, patch

ā .... day, fate

ä .... bother, cot, father

à .... a sound between \a\ and \ä\, as in an Eastern New England pronunciation of aunt, ask

aú ... now, out

b .... baby, rib

ch .... chin, catch

d .... did, adder

e .... set, red

ē .... beat, nosebleed, easy

f .... fifty, cuff

g .... go, big

h .... hat, ahead

hw ... whale

i .... tip, banish

ī .... site, buy

j .... job, edge

k .... kin, cook

ḵ .... loch as commonly pronounced in Scotland (it is \k\ without actual contact between tongue and palate)

l . .lily, cool

m . .murmur, dim

n .... nine, own

ⁿ .... indicates that a preceding vowel or diphthong is pronounced through both nose and mouth, as in French bon \bōⁿ\

ŋ .... sing, singer, finger, ink

ō .... bone, hollow

ò .... saw, cork

œ .... \e\ with lip rounding, as in French bœuf, German Hölle

œ̄ .... \ā\ with lip rounding, as in French feu, German Höhle

òi .... toy, sawing

p .... pepper, lip

r .... rarity

s .... source, less

sh .. shy, mission

t .... tie, attack

th .... thin, ether

t͟h .... then, either

ü .... boot, few \ˈfyü\

ú .... put, pure \ˈpyúr\

ue ... \i\ with lip rounding, as in German füllen

ū̄ .... \ē\ with lip rounding, as in French rue, German fühlen

v .... vivid, give

w .... we, away

y .... yard, cue \ˈkyü\

ʸ .... indicates that a preceding \l\, \n\, or \w\ is modified by the placing of the tongue tip against the lower front teeth, as in French digne \dēnʸ\

z .... zone, raise

zh ... vision pleasure

\ .... slant line used in pairs to mark the beginning and end of a transcription: \ˈpen\

ˈ .... mark at the beginning of a syllable that has primary (strongest) stress: \ˈpen-mən-ˌship\

ˌ .... mark at the beginning of a syllable that has secondary (next-strongest) stress: \ˈpen-mən-ˌship\

- .... mark of syllable division in pronunciations (the mark of syllable division in entries is a centered dot •)

( ) .... indicate that what is symbolized between sometimes occurs and sometimes does not occur in the pronunciation of the word: factory \ˈfak-t(ə-)rē\ = \ˈfak-tə-rē, ˈfak-trē\

WORDS MOST OFTEN
MISSPELLED
AND MISPRONOUNCED

ABBREVIATIONS USED IN THIS BOOK

abbr.	abbreviated, abbreviation	n.	noun
adj.	adjective	N.C.	North Carolina
&	and	N. Dak.	North Dakota
Afr.	Africa	N. Mex.	New Mexico
Calif.	California	N.Y.	New York
Can.	Canada	O.	Ohio
Cen. Am.	Central America	Pa.	Pennsylvania
coll.	college	pl.	plural
fem.	feminine	riv.	river
Fla.	Florida	S. Afr.	South Africa
Ga.	Georgia	S. Amer.	South America
Ia.	Iowa	sing.	singular
Ill.	Illinois	St.	Saint
Ind.	Indiana	Tenn.	Tennessee
is.	island, islands	Tex.	Texas
Kans.	Kansas	Turk.	Turkey
masc.	masculine	univ. or U.	university
Md.	Maryland	v.	verb
Me.	Maine	Va.	Virginia
Mex.	Mexico	Wash.	Washington
Minn.	Minnesota	Wyo.	Wyoming
mt(s)	mount(s), mountain(s)		

A

ab·a·cus　(ăb′ ȧ·kŭs)
　pl. ab·a·ci　(-sī)
a·ban·don　(ȧ·băn′ dŭn)
　a·ban·don·ment
a·base　(ȧ·bās′)
　-bas·ing　a·base·ment
a·bate　(ȧ·bāt′)
　-bat·ing　a·bat·a·ble
　a·bate·ment
ab·bey　(ăb′ ĭ)
ab·bre·vi·ate　(ȧ·brē′ vĭ·āt)
　-at·ing
　ab·bre·vi·a·tion
　　　　(ȧ·brē′ vĭ·ā′ shŭn)
ab·di·cate　(ăb′ dĭ·kāt)
　-cat·ing
　ab·di·ca·tion　(ăb′ dĭ·kā′ shŭn)
ab·do·men　(ăb·dō′ měn)
　ab·dom·i·nal　(ăb·dŏm′ ĭ·năl)
　-nal·ly
ab·duct　(ăb·dŭkt′)
　ab·duc·tion　ab·duc·tor
ab·er·rant　(ăb·ĕr′ ănt)
　ab·er·rance
　ab·er·ra·tion　(ăb′ ĕr·ā′ shŭn)
a·bet　(ȧ·bĕt′)
　-bet·ted　-bet·ting
　a·bet·tor
a·bey·ance　(ȧ·bā′ ăns)
ab·hor　(ăb·hôr′)
　-horred　-hor·ring
　ab·hor·rence　ab·hor·rent
a·bide　(ȧ·bīd′)
　-bid·ing
a·bil·i·ty　(ȧ·bĭl′ ĭ·tĭ)
　-ties
ab·ject　(ăb′ jĕkt)
a·ble　(ā′ b'l)
　a·ble-bod·ied　a·bly

ab·nor·mal　(ăb·nôr′ măl)
　ab·nor·mal·i·ty
　　　　(ăb′ nôr·măl′ ĭ·tĭ)
　-ties　ab·nor·mal·ly
a·board　(ȧ·bōrd′)
a·bode　(ȧ·bōd′)
a·bol·ish　(ȧ·bŏl′ ĭsh)
　a·bol·ish·a·ble
　a·bol·ish·ment
ab·o·li·tion　(ăb′ ō·lĭsh′ ŭn)
　ab·o·li·tion·ist
A-bomb　(ā′ bŏm′)
a·bom·i·na·ble　(ȧ·bŏm′ ĭ·nȧ·b'l)
　a·bom·i·na·bly
　a·bom·i·na·tion
　　　　(ȧ·bŏm′ ĭ·nā′ shŭn)
ab·o·rig·i·nes　(ăb′ ō·rĭj′ ĭ·nēs)
a·bor·tion　(ȧ·bôr′ shŭn)
　a·bor·tive
a·bout-face　(ȧ·bout′ fās′)
a·bove　(ȧ·bŭv′)
　a·bove-board　a·bove-cit·ed
　a·bove-ground
　a·bove-men·tioned
　a·bove-named　a·bove-said
ab·ra·sion　(ăb·rā′ zhŭn)
a·breast　(ȧ·brĕst′)
a·bridge　(ȧ·brĭj′)
　-bridg·ing　a·bridg·ment
a·broad　(ȧ·brôd′)
ab·ro·gate　(ăb′ rō·gāt)
　-gat·ing
　ab·ro·ga·tion　(ăb′ rō·gā′ shŭn)
　ab·ro·ga·tor
ab·rupt　(ăb·rŭpt′)
ab·scess　(ăb′ sĕs)
ab·scond　(ăb·skŏnd′)
ab·sent　(ăb′ sĕnt)
　ab·sence
　ab·sen·tee　(ăb′ sĕn·tē′)
　ab·sent-mind·ed

1

ab·so·lute (ăb′ sŏ·lūt)
  ab·so·lute·ly
  ab·so·lut·ism (ăb′ sŏ·lūt·ĭz′m)
ab·solve (ăb·sŏlv′)
  -solv·ing
  ab·so·lu·tion (ăb′ sŏ·lū′ shŭn)
ab·sorb (ăb·sôrb′)
  ab·sorb·a·bil·i·ty
    (ăb·sôrb′ à·bĭl′ ĭ·tĭ)
  ab·sorb·a·ble
  ab·sorb·en·cy -ent
  ab·sorp·tion (ăb·sôrp′ shŭn)
ab·stain (ăb·stān′)
ab·ste·mi·ous (ăb·stē′ mĭ·ŭs)
ab·sten·tion (ăb·stĕn′ shŭn)
ab·sti·nence (ăb′ stĭ·nĕns)
  -nent
ab·stract (ăb′ străkt)
    adj., n.
    (ăb·străkt′) v.
  ab·strac·tion (ăb·străk′ shŭn)
ab·struse (ăb·strōōs′)
ab·surd (ăb·sûrd′)
  ab·surd·i·ty (ăb·sûr′ dĭ·tĭ)
a·bun·dance (à·bŭn′ dăns)
  -dant
a·buse (à·būz′) v.
    (à·būs′) n.
  -bus·ing
  a·bu·sive (à·bū′ sĭv)
a·but (à·bŭt′)
  -but·ted -but·ting
  a·but·ment
a·bys·mal (à·bĭz′ măl)
  a·bys·mal·ly
a·byss (à·bĭs′)
ac·a·dem·ic (ăk′ à·dĕm′ ĭk)
  ac·a·dem·i·cal·ly
  a·cad·e·mi·cian
    (à·kăd′ ĕ·mĭsh′ ăn)
  a·cad·e·my (à·kăd′ ĕ·mĭ)
  -mies
ac·cede (ăk·sēd′)
  (to agree; see exceed)
  ac·ced·ing
ac·cel·er·ate (ăk·sĕl′ ĕr·āt)
  -at·ing
  ac·cel·er·a·tion
    (ăk·sĕl′ ĕr·ā′ shŭn)
  ac·cel·er·a·tor
ac·cent (ăk′ sĕnt)
ac·cen·tu·ate (ăk·sĕn′ tū·āt)
  -at·ing
  ac·cen·tu·a·tion
    (ăk·sĕn′ tū·ā′ shŭn)

ac·cept (ăk·sĕpt′)
  ac·cept·a·bil·i·ty
    (ăk·sĕp′ tá·bĭl′ ĭ·tĭ)
  ac·cept·a·ble ac·cept·ance
ac·cess (ăk′ sĕs)
  ac·ces·si·bil·i·ty
    (ăk·sĕs′ ĭ·bĭl′ ĭ·tĭ)
  ac·ces·si·ble (ăk·sĕs′ ĭ·b′l)
ac·ces·sion (ăk·sĕsh′ ŭn)
ac·ces·so·ry (ăk·sĕs′ ŏ·rĭ)
  -ries
ac·ci·dent (ăk′ sĭ·dĕnt)
  ac·ci·den·tal (ăk′ sĭ·dĕn′ tăl)
  -tal·ly
ac·claim (à·klām′)
  ac·cla·ma·tion
    (ăk′ là·mā′ shŭn)
  (applause; see acclimation)
ac·cli·mate (à·klī′ mĭt)
  -mat·ing
  ac·cli·ma·tion (ăk′ lĭ·mā′ shŭn)
  (of climate; see acclamation)
  ac·cli·ma·tize -tiz·ing
ac·co·lade (ăk′ ŏ·lād′)
ac·com·mo·date
    (à·kŏm′ ŏ·dāt)
  -dat·ing
  ac·com·mo·da·tion
    (à·kŏm′ ŏ·dā′ shŭn)
ac·com·pa·ny (à·kŭm′ pá·nĭ)
  -nied -ny·ing
  ac·com·pa·ni·ment
  ac·com·pa·nist
ac·com·plice (à·kŏm′ plĭs)
ac·com·plish (à·kŏm′ plĭsh)
  ac·com·plish·a·ble
  ac·com·plish·ment
ac·cord (à·kôrd′)
  ac·cord·ance ac·cord·ing·ly
ac·cor·di·on (à·kôr′ dĭ·ŭn)
ac·cost (à·kŏst′)
ac·count (à·kount′)
  ac·count·a·bil·i·ty
    (à·koun′ tá·bĭl′ ĭ·tĭ)
  ac·count·a·ble ac·count·ing
  ac·count·ant (à·koun′ tănt)
  -an·cy
ac·cred·it (à·krĕd′ ĭt)
  -it·ed -it·ing
ac·crete (à·krēt′)
  ac·cret·ing
  ac·cre·tion (à·krē′ shŭn)
ac·crue (à·krōō′)
  ac·cru·ing ac·cru·al

ac·cu·mu·late (ă·kū′ mŭ·lāt)
  -lat·ing
ac·cu·mu·la·ble
ac·cu·mu·la·tion
    (ă·kū′ mŭ·lā′ shŭn)
ac·cu·mu·la·tive
    (ă·kū′ mŭ·lā′ tĭv)
ac·cu·mu·la·tor
ac·cu·rate (ăk′ û·rĭt)
ac·cu·ra·cy ac·cu·rate·ly
ac·cuse (ă·kūz′)
  ac·cus·ing ac·cus·al
ac·cu·sa·tion (ăk′ û·zā′ shŭn)
ac·cu·sa·to·ry (ă·kū′ zá·tō′ rĭ)
ac·cus·tom (ă·kŭs′ tŭm)
  -tomed
ace·e·tate (ăs′ ê·tāt)
a·ce·tic (ă·sē′ tĭk)
ace·e·tone (ăs′ ê·tōn)
a·cet·y·lene (ă·sĕt′ ĭ·lēn)
ache (āk)
  ach·ing
a·chieve (ă·chēv′)
  -chiev·ing a·chiev·a·ble
  a·chieve·ment a·chiev·er
A·chil·les′ ten·don
    (ă·kĭl′ ēz)
ac·id (ăs′ ĭd)
  ac·id-form·ing
a·cid·ic (ă·sĭd′ ĭk)
a·cid·i·fy (ă·sĭd′ ĭ·fī)
a·cid·i·ty (ă·sĭd′ ĭ·tĭ)
ac·i·do·sis (ăs′ ĭ·dō′ sĭs)
a·cid·u·lous (ă·sĭd′ û·lŭs)
ac·knowl·edge (ăk·nŏl′ ĕj)
  -edg·ing ac·knowl·edge·a·ble
  ac·knowl·edg·ment
ac·me (ăk′ mē)
ac·ne (ăk′ nē)
ac·o·lyte (ăk′ ō·līt)
a·cous·tics (ă·kōōs′ tĭks)
  a·cous·ti·cal -cal·ly
ac·quaint (ă·kwānt′)
  ac·quaint·ance
ac·qui·esce (ăk′ wĭ·ĕs′)
  -esc·ing ac·qui·es·cence
ac·quire (ă·kwīr′)
  -quir·ing ac·quir·a·ble
  ac·quire·ment
ac·qui·si·tion (ăk′ wĭ·zĭsh′ ŭn)
ac·quis·i·tive (ă·kwĭz′ ĭ·tĭv)
  ac·quis·i·tive·ness
ac·quit (ă·kwĭt′)
  -quit·ted -quit·ting
ac·quit·tal ac·quit·tance

a·cre (ā′ kĕr)
a·cre·age (ā′ kĕr·ĭj)
ac·rid (ăk′ rĭd)
ac·ri·mo·ni·ous
    (ăk′ rĭ·mō′ nĭ·ŭs)
ac·ri·mo·ny (ăk′ rĭ·mō′ nĭ)
ac·ro·bat (ăk′ rō·băt)
ac·ro·bat·ic (ăk′ rō·băt′ ĭk)
a·cross (ă·krôs′)
ac·tion (ăk′ shŭn)
ac·tion·a·ble
ac·ti·vate (ăk′ tĭ·vāt)
  -vat·ing
ac·ti·va·tion (ăk′ tĭ·vā′ shŭn)
ac·tive (ăk′ tĭv)
ac·tive·ly
ac·tiv·i·ty (ăk·tĭv′ ĭ·tĭ)
ac·tor (ăk′ tĕr)
ac·tress
ac·tu·al (ăk′ tŭ·ăl)
ac·tu·al·ly
ac·tu·al·i·ty (ăk′ tŭ·ăl′ ĭ·tĭ)
  -ties
ac·tu·ar·y (ăk′ tŭ·ĕr′ ĭ)
  -ar·ies
ac·tu·ar·i·al (ăk′ tŭ·âr′ ĭ·ăl)
ac·tu·ate (ăk′ tŭ·āt)
  -at·ing
a·cu·i·ty (ă·kū′ ĭ·tĭ)
  -ties
a·cu·men (ă·kū′ mĕn)
a·cute (ă·kūt′)
  a·cute·ly
ad·age (ăd′ ĭj)
a·da·gio (ă·dā′ jō)
ad·a·mant (ăd′ á·mănt)
a·dapt (ă·dăpt′)
  (adjust; see adept, adopt)
  a·dapt·a·bil·i·ty
    (ă·dăp′ tá·bĭl′ ĭ·tĭ)
a·dapt·a·ble
ad·ap·ta·tion (ăd′ ăp·tā′ shŭn)
a·dapt·er a·dap·tive
ad·den·dum (ă·dĕn′ dŭm)
  pl. ad·den·da
ad·der (ăd′ ĕr)
ad·dict (ăd′ ĭkt) n.
    (ă·dĭkt′) v.
ad·dict·ed (ă·dĭk′ tĕd)
ad·dic·tion (ă·dĭk′ shŭn)
ad·di·tion (ă·dĭsh′ ŭn)
ad·di·tion·al -al·ly
ad·di·tive (ăd′ ĭ·tĭv)
ad·dle·brained (ăd′·l brānd′)

ad·dress (ă·drĕs')
  ad·dress·ee ad·dress·er
  Ad·dres·so·graph
ad·duce (ă·dūs')
  ad·duc·ing ad·duc·i·ble
ad·e·noid (ăd' ĕ·noid)
a·dept (ă·dĕpt')
  (expert; see *adapt, adopt*)
ad·e·quate (ăd' ĕ·kwit)
  ad·e·qua·cy (-kwá·sǐ)
  ad·e·quate·ly
ad·here (ăd·hēr')
  -her·ing
  ad·her·ence -ent
ad·he·sion (ăd·hē' shŭn)
  ad·he·sive (ăd·hē' sǐv)
ad hoc (ăd hŏk')
a·dieu (á·dū')
Ad·i·ron·dack (ăd' ĭ·rŏn' dăk)
  (mts.)
ad·ja·cent (ă·jā' sĕnt)
  -cen·cy
ad·jec·tive (ăj' ĕk·tǐv)
  ad·jec·ti·val (ăj' ĕk·tī' văl)
ad·join·ing (ă·join' ǐng)
ad·journ (ă·jûrn')
  ad·journ·ment
ad·judge (ă·jŭj')
  -judg·ing
ad·ju·di·cate (ă·jōō' dǐ·kāt)
  -cat·ing
  ad·ju·di·ca·tion
    (ă·jōō' dǐ·kā' shŭn)
  ad·ju·di·ca·tor
ad·junct (ăj' ŭngkt)
ad·jure (ă·jōōr')
  -jur·ing
ad·just (ă·jŭst')
  ad·just·a·ble ad·just·er
  ad·just·ment
ad·ju·tant (ăj' ŏŏ·tănt)
ad-lib (ăd' lĭb')
  -libbed -lib·bing
ad·min·is·ter (ăd·mĭn' ĭs·tĕr)
  ad·min·is·tra·ble
ad·min·is·trate (ăd·mĭn' ĭs·trāt)
  -trat·ing
  ad·min·is·tra·tion
    (ăd·mĭn' ĭs·trā' shŭn)
  ad·min·is·tra·tive (-trā' tǐv)
  ad·min·is·tra·tor (-trā' tĕr)
ad·mi·ra·ble (ăd' mĭ·rá·b'l)
ad·mi·ral (ăd' mĭ·răl)
  ad·mi·ral·ty

ad·mire (ăd·mīr')
  -mir·ing
  ad·mi·ra·tion (ăd' mĭ·rā' shŭn)
  ad·mir·er
ad·mis·si·ble (ăd·mĭs' ĭ·b'l)
ad·mis·sion (ăd·mĭsh' ŭn)
ad·mit (ăd·mĭt')
  -mit·ted -mit·ting
  ad·mit·tance ad·mit·ted·ly
ad·mix·ture (ăd·mĭks' tŭr)
ad·mon·ish (ăd·mŏn' ĭsh)
  ad·mo·ni·tion (ăd' mō·nĭsh'ŭn)
  ad·mon·i·to·ry
    (ăd·mŏn' ĭ·tō' rǐ)
ad nau·se·am (ăd nô' shē·ăm)
a·do (á·dōō')
a·do·be (á·dō' bǐ)
ad·o·les·cent (ăd' ô·lĕs' ĕnt)
  -cence
a·dopt (á·dŏpt')
  (to choose; see *adapt, adept*)
  a·dopt·a·ble a·dop·tion
  a·dop·tive
a·dore (á·dōr')
  -dor·ing a·dor·a·ble
  ad·o·ra·tion (ăd' ô·rā' shŭn)
a·dorn·ment (á·dôrn' mĕnt)
ad·re·nal (ăd·rē' năl)
ad·ren·al·ine (ăd·rĕn' ăl·ĭn)
A·dri·at·ic (ā' drǐ·ăt' ǐk)
a·droit (á·droit')
ad·u·la·tion (ăd' û·lā' shŭn)
a·dult (á·dŭlt')
a·dul·ter·ant (á·dŭl' tĕr·ănt)
a·dul·ter·ate (á·dŭl' tĕr·āt)
  -at·ing
  a·dul·ter·a·tion
    (á·dŭl' tĕr·ā' shŭn)
a·dul·ter·y (á·dŭl' tĕr·ǐ)
  a·dul·ter·ess *n.*
  a·dul·ter·er
  a·dul·ter·ous *adj.*
ad·va·lo·rem (ăd·vá·lō' rĕm)
ad·vance (ăd·văns')
  -vanc·ing ad·vance·ment
ad·van·tage (ăd·văn' tǐj)
  ad·van·ta·geous
    (ăd' văn·tā' jŭs)
ad·ven·ture (ăd·věn' tŭr)
  ad·ven·ture·some
  ad·ven·tur·ess *n.*
  ad·ven·tur·ous *adj.*
ad·verb (ăd' vûrb)
  ad·ver·bi·al (ăd·vûr' bǐ·ăl)

ad·ver·sar·y   (ăd′ vĕr·sĕr′ ĭ)
 -sar·ies
ad·verse   (ăd·vûrs′)
 ad·verse·ly
ad·ver·si·ty   (ăd·vûr′ sĭ·tĭ)
 -ties
ad·ver·tise   (ăd′ vĕr·tīz)
 -tis·ing
ad·ver·tise·ment
       (ăd·vûr′ tĭz·mĕnt)
 ad·ver·tis·er
ad·vice   (ăd·vīs′) n.
 (recommendation)
ad·vise   (ăd·vīz′) v.
 (give advice to)
 -vis·ing
ad·vis·a·bil·i·ty
       (ăd·vīz′ à·bĭl′ ĭ·tĭ)
 ad·vis·a·ble   ad·vis·ed·ly
 ad·vise·ment   ad·vis·er
 ad·vi·so·ry
ad·vo·cate   (ăd′ vô·kāt) n.
       (-kāt) v.
 -cat·ing
 ad·vo·ca·cy   (ăd′ vô·kà·sĭ)
Ae·ge·an   (ê·jē′ ăn)
ae·gis   (ē′ jĭs)
a·er·ate   (ā′ ĕr·āt)
 -at·ing
 a·er·a·tion   (ā′ ĕr·ā′ shŭn)
 a·er·a·tor
a·e·ri·al   (à·ēr′ ĭ·đl)
a·er·i·fy   (ā′ ĕr·ĭ·fĭ)
 -fied   -fy·ing
a·er·o·dy·nam·ics
       (ā′ ĕr·ô·đi·năm′ ĭks)
a·er·o·nau·tics   (ā′ ĕr·ô·nô′ tĭks)
a·er·o·sol   (ā′ ĕr·ô·sŏl′)
Aes·chy·lus   (ĕs′ kĭ·lŭs)
Ae·sop   (ē′ sŏp)
aes·thete   (ĕs′ thēt)
 aes·thet·ic   (ĕs·thĕt′ ĭk)
 (of beauty; see *ascetic*)
 aes·thet·i·cism
       (ĕs·thĕt′ ĭ·sĭz′m)
af·fa·ble   (ăf′ à·b′l)
 af·fa·bil·i·ty   (ăf′ à·bĭl′ ĭ·tĭ)
af·fair   (à·fâr′)
af·fect   (à·fĕkt′) v.
 (assume; see *effect*)
 af·fec·ta·tion   (ăf′ ĕk·tā′ shŭn)
 af·fect·ed·ly
af·fec·tion   (à·fĕk′ shŭn)
 af·fec·tion·ate (-ĭt)
 -ate·ly

af·fi·da·vit   (ăf′ ĭ·dā′ vĭt)
af·fil·i·ate   (à·fĭl′ ĭ·āt) v.
 -at·ing   (-ăt) n.
 af·fil·i·a·tion   (à·fĭl′ ĭ·ā′ shŭn)
af·fin·i·ty   (à·fĭn′ ĭ·tĭ)
 -ties
af·firm   (à·fûrm′)
 af·firm·a·ble
 af·fir·ma·tion   (ăf′ ĕr·mā′ shŭn)
af·firm·a·tive   (à·fûr′ mà·tĭv)
 -tive·ly
af·fix   (à·fĭks′)
af·flict   (à·flĭkt′)
 af·flic·tion   (à·flĭk′ shŭn)
af·flu·ence   (ăf′ lù·ĕns)
 -ent
af·ford   (à·fōrd′)
af·fray   (à·frā′)
af·front   (à·frŭnt′)
Af·ghan·i·stan   (ăf·găn′ ĭ·stăn)
a·field   (à·fēld′)
a·float   (à·flōt′)
a·fore·said   (à·fōr′ sĕd′)
a·fore·thought   (à·fōr′ thôt′)
 (malice aforethought)
a·fraid   (à·frād′)
Af·ri·can   (ăf′ rĭ·kăn)
aft·er   (ăf′ tĕr)
 aft·er·burn·er
 aft·er·din·ner speech
 aft·er·ef·fect   aft·er·math
 aft·er·noon   aft·er·taste
 aft·er·thought   aft·er·ward
a·gain   (à·gĕn′)
a·gainst   (à·gĕnst′)
ag·ate   (ăg′ ĭt)
age   (āj)
 ag·ing   age·less
 age·long
a·gen·da   (à·jĕn′ đà)
a·gent   (ā′ jĕnt)
 a·gen·cy   -cies
ag·glom·er·ate   (à·glŏm′ ĕr·āt)
 -at·ing
 ag·glom·er·a·tion
       (à·glŏm′ ĕr·ā′ shŭn)
ag·gran·dize·ment
       (à·grăn′ dĭz·mĕnt)
ag·gra·vate   (ăg′ rà·vāt)
 -vat·ing
 ag·gra·va·tion   (ăg′ rà·vā′ shŭn)
ag·gre·gate   (ăg′ rê·gāt) adj.
       (-gāt) v.
 -gat·ing
 ag·gre·ga·tion   (ăg′ rê·gā′ shŭn)

ag·gres·sive (ă·grĕs′ ĭv)
  ag·gres·sion   ag·gres·sor
ag·grieved (ă·grēvd′)
a·ghast (ă·găst′)
ag·ile (ăj′ ĭl)
  ag·ile·ly
  a·gil·i·ty (ă·jĭl′ ĭ·tĭ)
ag·i·tate (ăj′ ĭ·tāt)
  -tat·ing
  ag·i·ta·tion (ăj′ ĭ·tā′ shŭn)
  ag·i·ta·tor
ag·nos·tic (ăg·nŏs′ tĭk)
  ag·nos·ti·cism (-tĭ·sĭz′m)
ag·o·nize (ăg′ ô·nīz)
  -niz·ing
ag·o·ny (ăg′ ô·nĭ)
  -nies
a·grar·i·an (ă·grâr′ ĭ·ăn)
a·gree (ă·grē′)
  a·gree·a·bil·i·ty
              (ă·grē′ ă·bĭl′ ĭ·tĭ)
  a·gree·a·ble   a·gree·ment
ag·ri·cul·ture (ăg′ rĭ·kŭl′ tŭr)
  ag·ri·cul·tur·al
              (ăg′ rĭ·kŭl′ tŭr·ăl)
  ag·ri·cul·tur·ist
           (ăg′ rĭ·kŭl′ tŭr·ĭst)
a·gron·o·my (ă·grŏn′ ô·mĭ)
  a·gron·o·mist
a·hoy (ă·hoi′)
aid (ād) v.
  (to help)
aide (ād) n.
  (assistant)
  aide-de-camp (ād′ dē·kămp′)
ail·ment (āl′ mĕnt)
air (âr)
  air base   air-borne
  air-con·di·tion
  air-con·di·tioned
  air-con·di·tion·er
  air-con·di·tion·ing
  air-cooled   air·craft
  air-dried   air drill
  air-driv·en   air·field
  air-filled   air fil·ter
  air force   air·lift
  air·line   air·mail
  air·man   air-mind·ed
  air·plane   air·port
  air·proof   air raid
  air·strip   air·tight
Aire·dale (âr′ dāl′)
aisle (īl)
  (of a church; see isle)

a·jar (ă·jär′)
a·kim·bo (ă·kĭm′ bō)
a·kin (ă·kĭn′)
Al·a·bam·a (ăl′ ă·băm′ ă)
  abbr. Ala.
  Al·a·bam·i·an (ăl′ ă·băm′ ĭ·ăn)
al·a·bas·ter (ăl′ ă·băs′ tĕr)
à la carte (ă lä kärt′)
a·lac·ri·ty (ă·lăk′ rĭ·tĭ)
A·lad·din (ă·lăd′ ĭn)
a·la·mode (ä′ lă·mōd′)
a·larm·ist (ă·lär′ mĭst)
A·las·ka (ă·lăs′ kă)
  A·las·kan
al·ba·tross (ăl′ bă·trŏs)
al·be·it (ôl·bē′ ĭt)
al·bi·no (ăl·bī′ nō)
  -nos
al·bum (ăl′ bŭm)
al·bu·men (ăl·bū′ mĕn)
Al·bu·quer·que,
  N. Mex. (ăl′ bŭ·kûr′ kê)
al·che·my (ăl′ kê·mĭ)
  al·che·mist (-mĭst)
al·co·hol (ăl′ kô·hŏl)
  al·co·hol·ic (ăl′ kô·hŏl′ ĭk)
  al·co·hol·ism (ăl′ kô·hŏl·ĭz′m)
al·cove (ăl′ kŏv)
al·der·man (ôl′ dĕr·măn)
A·leu·tian (ă·lū′ shăn)
al·fal·fa (ăl·făl′ fă)
al·ga (ăl′ gă)
  pl. al·gae (-jē)
al·ge·bra (ăl′ jê·bră)
  al·ge·bra·ic (ăl′ jê·brā′ ĭk)
a·li·as (ā′ lĭ·ăs)
al·i·bi (ăl′ ĭ·bī)
  -bis
al·ien (āl′ yĕn)
  al·ien·a·ble   al·ien·ate
  al·ien·a·tion (āl′ yĕn·ā′ shŭn)
a·lign (ă·līn′)
  a·lign·ment
al·i·men·ta·ry (ăl′ ĭ·mĕn′ tă·rĭ)
al·i·mo·ny (ăl′ ĭ·mô′ nĭ)
al·ka·li (ăl′ kă·lī)
  -lies
  al·ka·line (ăl′ kă·lĭn)
  al·ka·lin·i·ty (ăl′ kă·lĭn′ ĭ·tĭ)
  al·ka·loid (ăl′ kă·loid)
all (ôl)
  all-A·mer·i·can
  all-out ef·fort
  all·o·ver pat·tern
  all right (not alright)

al·lay (å·lā′)
al·le·ga·tion (ăl′ ĕ·gā′ shŭn)
al·lege (å·lĕj′)
al·leg·ing
al·leg·ed·ly (å·lĕj′ ĕd·lĭ)
Al·le·ghe·ny (ăl′ ĕ·gā′ nĭ)
(mts.) -nies
al·le·giance (å·lē′ jåns)
al·le·go·ry (ăl′ ĕ·gō′ rĭ)
-ries
al·le·gor·i·cal (ăl′ ĕ·gŏr′ ĭ·kål)
al·ler·gy (ăl′ ĕr·jĭ)
-gies
al·ler·gic (å·lûr′ jĭk)
al·le·vi·ate (å·lē′ vĭ·āt)
-at·ing
al·le·vi·a·tion (å·lē′ vĭ·ā′ shŭn)
al·ley (ăl′ ĭ)
al·leys al·ley·way
al·li·ance (å·lī′ åns)
al·lied (å·līd′)
al·li·ga·tor (ăl′ ĭ·gā′ tĕr)
al·lit·er·a·tion (å·lĭt′ ĕr·ā′ shŭn)
al·lo·cate (ăl′ ō·kāt)
-cat·ing
al·lo·ca·tion (ăl′ ō·kā′ shŭn)
al·lot (å·lŏt′)
al·lot·ted al·lot·ting
al·lot·ment
al·low (å·lou′)
al·low·a·ble al·low·ance
al·loy (å·loi′)
all right (ôl rīt)
all·spice (ôl′ spīs′)
al·lude (å·lūd′)
(to refer; see elude)
al·lud·ing
al·lure (å·lūr′)
al·lur·ing al·lure·ment
al·lu·sion (å·lū′ zhŭn)
(indirect reference; see illusion)
al·lu·sive
al·lu·vi·al (å·lū′ vĭ·ål)
al·ly (å·lī′)
al·lied al·ly·ing
Al·ma Ma·ter (ăl′ må mā′ tĕr)
al·ma·nac (ôl′ må·năk)
al·might·y (ôl·mīt′ ĭ)
al·might·i·ly
al·mond (ä′ mŭnd)
al·most (ôl′ mōst)
alms·house (ämz′ hous′)
a·lo·ha (ä·lō′ hä)
a·long·side (å·lŏng′ sīd′)
a·loof (å·lōōf′)

a·loud (å·loud′)
al·pac·a (ăl·păk′ å)
al·pha·bet (ăl′ få·bĕt)
al·pha·bet·ic (ăl′ få·bĕt′ ĭk)
al·pha·bet·ize -iz·ing
al·read·y (ôl·rĕd′ ĭ)
(Already means previously: "He had already arrived"; all ready means prepared.)
Al·sace-Lor·raine (ăl′ săs lŏ·rān′)
Al·sa·tian (ăl·sā′ shăn)
al·tar (ôl′ tĕr)
(in church)
al·tar·piece
al·ter (ôl′ tĕr)
(to modify)
al·ter·a·tion (ôl′ tĕr·ā′ shŭn)
al·ter·a·ble
al·ter·ca·tion (ôl′ tĕr·kā′ shŭn)
(quarrel)
al·ter e·go (ăl′ tĕr ē′ gō)
al·ter·nate (ôl′ tĕr·nĭt) adj.
(-nāt) v.
-nat·ing
al·ter·nate·ly (ôl′ tĕr·nĭt·lĭ)
al·ter·na·tion (ôl′ tĕr·nā′ shŭn)
al·ter·na·tive (ôl·tûr′ nå·tĭv)
al·ter·na·tive·ly
al·though (ôl·thō′)
al·tim·e·ter (ăl·tĭm′ ĕ·tĕr)
al·ti·tude (ăl′ tĭ·tūd)
al·to·geth·er (ôl′ tōō·gĕth′ ĕr)
al·tru·ism (ăl′ trōō·ĭz′m)
al·tru·ist
al·tru·is·tic (ăl′ trōō·ĭs′ tĭk)
al·um (ăl′ ŭm)
a·lu·mi·num (å·lū′ mĭ·nŭm)
a·lum·na (å·lŭm′ nå) ; fem.
pl. a·lum·nae (-nē)
a·lum·nus (å·lŭm′ nŭs)
masc.; pl. a·lum·ni (-nī)
al·ways (ôl′ wăz)
a·mal·gam·ate (å·măl′ gå·māt)
-at·ing
a·mal·gam·a·tion (å·măl′ gå·mā′ shŭn)
a·mass (å·măs′)
am·a·teur (ăm′ å·tûr′)
am·a·teur·ish
am·a·to·ry (ăm′ å·tō′ rĭ)
a·maze (å·māz′)
-maz·ing a·maz·ed·ly
a·maze·ment

Am·a·zon   (ăm′ ȧ·zŏn)
Am·a·zo·ni·an
                (ăm′ ȧ·zō′ nĭ·ȧn)
am·bas·sa·dor   (ăm·băs′ ȧ·dēr)
am·bas·sa·do·ri·al
                (ăm·băs′ ȧ·dō′ rĭ·ăl)
am·ber   (ăm′ bēr)
am·bi·dex·trous
                (ăm′ bĭ·dĕk′ strŭs)
am·bi·gu·i·ty   (ăm′ bĭ·gū′ ĭ·tĭ)
  -ties
am·big·u·ous   (ăm·bĭg′ û·ŭs)
am·bi·tion   (ăm·bĭsh′ ŭn)
  am·bi·tious
am·biv·a·lence (ăm·bĭv′ ȧ·lĕns)
  -lent
am·ble   (ăm′ b′l)
  -bling
am·bro·si·a   (ăm·brō′ zhĭ·ȧ)
  am·bro·si·al
am·bu·lance   (ăm′ bû·lăns)
am·bu·la·tory   (ăm′ bû·là·tō′ rĭ)
am·bush   (ăm′ bŏŏsh)
a·mel·io·rate   (ȧ·mēl′ yō·rāt)
  -rat·ing
  a·mel·io·ra·tion
                (ȧ·mēl′ yō·rā′ shŭn)
a·men   (ā′ měn′)
a·me·na·ble   (ȧ·mē′ nȧ·b′l)
a·mend   (ȧ·měnd′)
  a·mend·ment
a·men·i·ty   (ȧ·měn′ ĭ·tĭ)
  -ties
A·mer·i·ca·na (ȧ·měr′ ĭ·kā′ nȧ)
A·mer·i·can·ism
                (ȧ·měr′ ĭ·kȧn·ĭz′m)
am·e·thyst   (ăm′ ē·thĭst)
Am·herst (coll.) (ăm′ ērst)
a·mi·a·ble   (ā′ mĭ·ȧ·b′l)
  -bly
  a·mi·a·bil·i·ty
                (ā′ mĭ·ȧ·bĭl′ ĭ·tĭ)
am·i·ca·ble   (ăm′ ĭ·kȧ·b′l)
  -bly
a·mid   (ȧ·mĭd′)
  a·midst   (ȧ·mĭdst′)
a·miss   (ȧ·mĭs′)
am·i·ty   (ăm′ ĭ·tĭ)
  (friendship; see enmity)
  -ties
am·mo·ni·a   (ă·mō′ nĭ·ȧ)
am·mu·ni·tion (ăm′ û·nĭsh′ ŭn)
am·ne·si·a   (ăm·nē′ zhĭ·ȧ)
am·nes·ty   (ăm′ něs·tĭ)

a·moe·ba   (ȧ·mē′ bȧ)
  pl. a·moe·bae (-bē)
  a·moe·bic
a·mong   (ȧ·mŭng′)
  a·mongst
a·mor·al   (ā·mŏr′ ăl)
  a·mo·ral·i·ty (ā′ mō·răl′ ĭ·tĭ)
am·o·rous   (ăm′ ō·rŭs)
a·mor·phous   (ȧ·môr′ fŭs)
am·or·tize   (ăm′ ēr·tīz)
  -tiz·ing
  am·or·ti·za·tion
                (ăm′ ēr·tĭ·zā′ shŭn)
a·mount   (ȧ·mount′)
am·phib·ian   (ăm·fĭb′ ĭ·ȧn)
  am·phib·i·ous
am·phi·the·a·ter
                (ăm′ fĭ·thē′ ȧ·tēr)
am·ple   (ăm′ p′l)
  -ply
am·pli·fy   (ăm′ plĭ·fī)
  -fied   -fy·ing
  am·pli·fi·ca·tion
                (ăm′ plĭ·fĭ·kā′ shŭn)
  am·pli·fi·er
am·pu·tate   (ăm′ pû·tāt)
  -tat·ing
  am·pu·ta·tion (ăm′ pû·tā′ shŭn)
  am·pu·tee   (ăm′ pû·tē′)
a·muck   (ȧ·mŭk′)
am·u·let   (ăm′ û·lĕt)
a·muse   (ȧ·mūz′)
  -mus·ing   a·mus·a·ble
  a·muse·ment
a·nach·ro·nism
                (ȧ·năk′ rō·nĭz′m)
  a·nach·ro·nis·tic
                (ȧ·năk′ rō·nĭs′ tĭk)
an·a·con·da   (ăn′ ȧ·kŏn′ dȧ)
an·al·ge·si·a (ăn′ ăl·jē′ zĭ·ȧ)
  an·al·ge·sic (-jē′ sĭk)
an·a·logue   (ăn′ ȧ·lŏg)
  com·put·er
a·nal·o·gy   (ȧ·năl′ ō·jĭ)
  -gies
  an·a·log·i·cal (ăn′ ȧ·lŏj′ ĭ·kăl)
  a·nal·o·gous (ȧ·năl′ ō·gŭs)
a·nal·y·sis   (ȧ·năl′ ĭ·sĭs)
  pl. a·nal·y·ses (-sēz)
  an·a·lyst   (ăn′ ȧ·lĭst)
  an·a·lyt·ic   (ăn′ ȧ·lĭt′ ĭk)
  an·a·lyze   (ăn′ ȧ·līz)
  -lyz·ing
  an·a·lyz·a·ble (ăn′ ȧ·līz·ȧ·b′l)

an·arch·y (ăn′ ăr·kĭ)
-arch·ies   an·arch·ism
an·arch·ist
a·nath·e·ma (à·năth′ ĕ·mà)
a·nat·o·my (à·năt′ ō·mĭ)
-mies
an·a·tom·i·cal
(ăn′ à·tŏm′ ĭ·kăl)
an·ces·tor (ăn′ sĕs′ tēr)
an·ces·tral (ăn·sĕs′ trăl)
an·ces·try (ăn′ sĕs′ trĭ)
an·chor (ăng′ kēr)
an·chor·age (-ĭj)
an·cho·vy (ăn·chō′ vĭ)
-vies
an·cient (ăn′ shĕnt)
an·cil·lar·y (ăn′ sĭ·lĕr′ ĭ)
an·ec·dote (ăn′ ĕk·dōt)
(story; see antidote)
an·ec·do·tal (-dō′ tăl)
a·nem·o·ne (à·nĕm′ ō·nē)
an·es·the·si·a (ăn′ ĕs·thē′ zhĭ·à)
an·es·thet·ic (-thĕt′ ĭk)
an·es·the·tist (ăn·ĕs′ thē·tĭst)
an·es·thet·i·za·tion
(ăn′ ĕs·thĕt′ ĭ·zā′ shŭn)
an·es·the·tize (ăn·ĕs′ thē·tīz)
-tiz·ing
an·gel (ăn′ jĕl)
an·gel·ic (ăn·jĕl′ ĭk)
an·ger (ăng′ gēr)
an·gle (ăng′ g′l)
-gling   an·gler
an·gle·worm
An·gli·can (ăng′ glĭ·kăn)
An·glo-Sax·on (ăng′ glō·săk′ s′n)
An·go·la, Afr. (ăng·gō′ là)
An·go·ra (ăng·gō′ rà)
an·gry (ăng′ grĭ)
an·gri·er   -gri·est
-gri·ly   -gri·ness
an·guish (ăng′ gwĭsh)
an·gu·lar (ăng′ gû·lēr)
an·gu·lar·i·ty (ăng′gû·lăr′ĭ·tĭ)
an·i·mal (ăn′ ĭ·măl)
an·i·mal·i·ty (ăn′ ĭ·măl′ ĭ·tĭ)
an·i·mate (ăn′ ĭ·māt) v.
(-măt) adj.
-mat·ing
an·i·ma·tion (ăn′ ĭ·mā′ shŭn)
an·i·mos·i·ty (ăn′ ĭ·mŏs′ ĭ·tĭ)
-ties
an·ise (ăn′ ĭs)
an·i·seed
An·ka·ra, Turk. (ăng′ kà·rà)

an·kle (ăng′ k′l)
an·kle·bone   an·klet
an·nals (ăn′ dlz)
An·nap·o·lis, (à·năp′ ō·lĭs)
Md.
an·neal (à·nēl′)
an·neal·ing
an·nex (à·nĕks′) v.
(ăn′ ĕks) n.
an·nex·a·tion (ăn′ ĕk·sā′ shŭn)
an·ni·hi·late (à·nī′ ĭ·lāt)
-lat·ing
an·ni·hi·la·tion
(à·nī′ ĭ·lā′ shŭn)
an·ni·hi·la·tor
an·ni·ver·sa·ry (ăn′ ĭ·vûr′ sà·rĭ)
-sar·ies
an·no·tate (ăn′ ō·tāt)
-tat·ing
an·no·ta·tion (ăn′ ō·tā′ shŭn)
an·nounce (à·nouns′)
an·nounc·ing
an·nounce·ment
an·nounc·er
an·noy (à·noi′)
an·noy·ance
an·nu·al (ăn′ û·ăl)
an·nu·al·ly
an·nu·i·ty (à·nū′ ĭ·tĭ)
-ties
an·nul (à·nŭl′)
an·nulled   an·nul·ling
an·nul·la·ble   an·nul·ment
an·nun·ci·a·tion
(à·nŭn′ sĭ·ā′ shŭn)
an·ode (ăn′ ōd)
a·noint (à·noint′)
a·noint·ment
a·nom·a·ly (à·nŏm′ à·lĭ)
-lies
a·nom·a·lous (-lŭs)
a·non (à·nŏn′)
a·non·y·mous (à·nŏn′ ĭ·mŭs)
an·o·nym·i·ty (ăn′ ō·nĭm′ ĭ·tĭ)
an·oth·er (à·nŭth′ ēr)
an·swer (ăn′ sēr)
an·swer·a·ble
an·tag·o·nize (ăn·tăg′ ō·nīz)
-niz·ing
an·tag·o·nism an·tag·o·nist
an·tag·o·nis·tic
(ăn·tăg′ ō·nĭs′ tĭk)
Ant·arc·ti·ca (ănt·ärk′ tĭ·kà)
an·te- (ăn′ tē)
(prefix meaning before)

an·te·bel·lum   an·te·cham·ber
an·te·date
an·te·di·lu·vi·an (-dǐ·lū′ vǐ·ăn)
an·te me·rid·i·em (*abbr.* a.m.)
   (-mē·rǐd′ ǐ·ĕm)
an·te·room
an·te·ced·ence (ăn′ tê·sēd′ ĕns)
-ent
an·te·lope (ăn′ tê·lōp)
an·ten·na (ăn·tĕn′ ȧ)
an·te·ri·or (ăn·tēr′ ǐ·ẽr)
an·them (ăn′ thĕm)
an·thol·o·gy (ăn·thŏl′ ô·jǐ)
-gies
an·thra·cite (ăn′ thrȧ·sīt)
an·thro·poid (ăn′ thrô·poid)
an·thro·pol·o·gy
   (ăn′ thrô·pŏl′ ô·jǐ)
an·thro·pol·o·gist
an·thro·po·mor·phize
   (ăn′ thrô·pô·môr′ fīz)
-phiz·ing
an·ti·air·craft (ăn′ tǐ·âr′ krȧft′)
an·ti·bi·ot·ic (ăn′ tǐ·bī·ŏt′ ǐk)
an·ti·bod·y (ăn′ tǐ·bŏd′ ǐ)
-bod·ies
an·tic (ăn′ tǐk)
an·tic·i·pate (ăn·tǐs′ ǐ·pāt)
-pat·ing
an·tic·i·pa·tion
   (ăn·tǐs′ ǐ·pā′ shŭn)
an·tic·i·pa·to·ry
   (ăn·tǐs′ ǐ·pȧ·tō′ rǐ)
an·ti·cli·max (ăn′ tǐ·klī′ măks)
an·ti·cli·mac·tic
   (-klǐ·măk′ tǐk)
an·ti·dote (ăn′ tǐ·dōt)
(remedy; see *anecdote*)
an·ti·freeze (ăn′ tǐ·frēz′)
an·ti·his·ta·mine
   (ăn′ tǐ·hǐs′ tȧ·mēn)
an·ti·ma·cas·sar
   (ăn′ tǐ·mȧ·kăs′ ẽr)
an·ti·pa·sto (ăn′ tê·päs′ tô)
an·tip·a·thy (ăn·tǐp′ ȧ·thǐ)
-thies
an·ti·quar·i·an
   (ăn′ tǐ·kwâr′ ǐ·ăn)
an·ti·quat·ed (ăn′ tǐ·kwāt′ ĕd)
an·tique (ăn·tēk′)
an·tiq·ui·ty (ăn·tǐk′ wǐ·tǐ)
-ties
an·ti·Sem·i·tism
   (ăn′ tǐ·sĕm′ ǐ·tǐz′m)

an·ti·Se·mit·ic
   (ăn′ tǐ·sê·mǐt′ ǐk)
an·ti·sep·tic (ăn′ tǐ·sĕp′ tǐk)
an·ti·sep·ti·cize (-tǐ·sīz)
-ciz·ing
an·tith·e·sis (ăn·tǐth′ ê·sǐs)
an·ti·tox·in (ăn′ tǐ·tŏk′ sǐn)
an·ti·trust (ăn′ tǐ·trŭst′)
an·vil (ăn′ vǐl)
anx·i·e·ty (ăng·zī′ ĕ·tǐ)
-ties
anx·ious (ăngk′ shŭs)
anx·ious·ly
an·y (ĕn′ ǐ)
an·y·bod·y   an·y·how
an·y·more   an·y·one
an·y·thing   an·y·way
an·y·where
a·or·ta (ā·ôr′ tȧ)
a·part·heid (ȧ·pärt′ hāt)
a·part·ment (ȧ·pärt′ mĕnt)
ap·a·thy (ăp′ ȧ·thǐ)
ap·a·thet·ic (ăp′ ȧ·thĕt′ ǐk)
a·pé·ri·tif (ȧ′ pā′ rē′ tēf′)
ap·er·ture (ăp′ ẽr·tûr)
a·pex (ā′ pĕks)
aph·o·rism (ăf′ ô·rǐz′m)
aph·ro·dis·i·ac (ăf′ rô·dǐz′ ǐ·ăk)
a·pi·ar·y (ā′ pǐ·ĕr′ ǐ)
-ar·ies
a·piece (ȧ·pēs′)
ap·ish (ăp′ ǐsh)
a·plomb (ȧ·plŏm′)
a·poc·a·lypse (ȧ·pŏk′ ȧ·lǐps)
a·poc·a·lyp·tic
   (ȧ·pŏk′ ȧ·lǐp′ tǐk)
a·poc·ry·phal (ȧ·pŏk′ rǐ·fȧl)
a·pol·o·gy (ȧ·pŏl′ ô·jǐ)
-gies
a·pol·o·get·ic (ȧ·pŏl′ ô·jĕt′ ǐk)
-i·cal·ly
a·pol·o·gist
a·pol·o·gize (-gǐz·ing)
ap·o·plex·y (ăp′ ô·plĕk′ sǐ)
ap·o·plec·tic (ăp′ ô·plĕk′ tǐk)
a·pos·tle (ȧ·pŏs′ 'l)
ap·os·tol·ic (ăp′ ŏs·tŏl′ ǐk)
a·pos·tro·phe (ȧ·pŏs′ trô·fê)
a·poth·e·car·y (ȧ·pŏth′ ê·kĕr′ ǐ)
a·poth·e·car·ies′ meas·ure
ap·o·thegm (ăp′ ô·thĕm)
a·poth·e·o·sis (ȧ·pŏth′ ê·ō′ sǐs)
pl. a·poth·e·o·ses (-sēz)
Ap·pa·la·chian (ăp′ ȧ·lā′ chăn)
(mts.)
ap·pall (ȧ·pôl′)

ap·pa·ra·tus   (ăp′ à·rā′ tŭs)
  n. sing. & pl.
ap·par·el   (à·păr′ ĕl)
-eled,   -el·ing
ap·par·ent   (à·păr′ ĕnt)
ap·pa·ri·tion   (ăp′ à·rĭsh′ ŭn)
ap·peal   (à·pēl′)
  ap·peal·ing
ap·pear   (à·pēr′)
  ap·pear·ance
ap·pease   (à·pēz′)
  ap·peas·ing   ap·pease·ment
  ap·peas·er
ap·pel·late   (à·pĕl′ ăt)
ap·pel·la·tion   (ăp′ ĕ·lā′ shŭn)
ap·pend   (à·pĕnd′)
  ap·pend·age   (à·pĕn′ dĭj)
ap·pen·dec·to·my
     (ăp′ ĕn·dĕk′ tô·mĭ)
  ap·pen·di·ci·tis
     (à·pĕn′ dĭ·sī′ tĭs)
ap·pen·dix   (à·pĕn′ dĭks)
  -dix·es
ap·per·tain   (ăp′ ẽr·tān′)
ap·pe·tite   (ăp′ ê·tīt)
  ap·pe·tiz·er   ap·pe·tiz·ing
Ap·pi·an Way   (ăp′ ĭ·ăn)
ap·plaud   (à·plôd′)
ap·plause   (à·plôz′)
ap·ple   (ăp′ ′l)
  ap·ple·sauce
ap·pli·ance   (à·plī′ ăns)
ap·pli·ca·ble   (ăp′ lĭ·kà·b′l)
  ap·pli·ca·bil·i·ty
     (ăp′ lĭ·kà·bĭl′ ĭ·tĭ)
ap·pli·cant   (ăp′ lĭ·kănt)
ap·pli·ca·tion   (ăp′ lĭ·kā′ shŭn)
ap·pli·ca·tor   (ăp′ lĭ·kā′ tẽr)
ap·pli·ca·to·ry   (ăp′ lĭ·kà·tō′ rĭ)
ap·pli·qué   (ăp′ lĭ·kā′)
ap·ply   (à·plī′)
  ap·plied   ap·ply·ing
  ap·pli·er
ap·point   (à·point′)
  ap·point·ee   (à·poin′ tē′)
  ap·poin·tive   ap·point·ment
Ap·po·mat·tox,   (ăp′ ô·măt′ ŭks)
  Va.
ap·por·tion   (à·pōr′ shŭn)
  ap·por·tion·ment
ap·praise   (à·prāz′)
  (to judge; see apprise)
  ap·prais·ing   ap·prais·al
  ap·praise·ment   ap·prais·er

ap·pre·ci·a·ble   (à·prē′shĭ·à·b′l)
  -bly
ap·pre·ci·ate   (à·prē′ shĭ·āt)
  -at·ing
ap·pre·ci·a·tion
     (à·prē′ shĭ·ā′ shŭn)
ap·pre·ci·a·tive
     (à·prē′ shĭ·ā′ tĭv)
ap·pre·ci·a·to·ry
     (-à·tō′ rĭ)
ap·pre·hend   (ăp′ rê·hĕnd′)
ap·pre·hen·si·ble   (-hĕn′ sĭ·b′l)
ap·pre·hen·sion   (-hĕn′ shŭn)
ap·pre·hen·sive   (-hĕn′ sĭv)
ap·pren·tice   (à·prĕn′ tĭs)
  -tic·ing   ap·pren·tice·ship
ap·prise   (à·prīz′)
  (to inform; see appraise)
  ap·pris·ing
ap·proach   (à·prōch′)
  ap·proach·a·ble
ap·pro·ba·tion   (ăp′ rô·bā′ shŭn)
ap·pro·pri·ate   (à·prō′ prĭ·ĭt)
  adj.
  (-āt) v.
  -at·ing
ap·pro·pri·a·tion
     (à·prō′ prĭ·ā′ shŭn)
ap·prove   (à·prōōv′)
  ap·prov·ing   ap·prov·a·ble
  ap·prov·al
ap·prox·i·mate   (à·prŏk′ sĭ·mĭt)
  adj.
  (-māt) v.
  -mat·ing
ap·prox·i·mate·ly
     (à·prŏk′ sĭ·mĭt·lĭ)
ap·prox·i·ma·tion
     (à·prŏk′ sĭ·mā′ shŭn)
ap·pur·te·nance
     (à·pûr′ tê·nåns)
a·pri·cot   (ā′ prĭ·kŏt)
a pri·o·ri   (ā′ prĭ·ô′ rĭ)
a·pron   (ā′ prŭn)
ap·ro·pos   (ăp′ rô·pō′)
ap·ti·tude   (ăp′ tĭ·tūd)
apt·ly   (ăpt′ lĭ)
aq·ua   (ăk′ wå)
  aq·ua·cade   aq·ua·lung
  aq·ua·ma·rine But: aq·ue·duct
a·quar·i·um   (à·kwâr′ ĭ·ŭm)
a·quat·ic   (à·kwăt′ ĭk)
aq·ue·duct   (ăk′ wê·dŭkt)
a·que·ous   (ā′ kwê·ŭs)
aq·ui·line   (ăk′ wĭ·lĭn)

A·qui·nas, (á·kwī′ nás)
St. Thom·as
ar·a·besque (ăr′ á·běsk′)
A·ra·bi·an (á·rā′ bĭ·án)
Ar·a·bic (ăr′ á·bĭk)
ar·a·ble (ăr′ á·b′l)
ar·a·bil·i·ty (ăr′ á·bĭl′ ĭ·tĭ)
ar·bi·ter (ăr′ bĭ·tẽr)
ar·bi·tral
ar·bit·ra·ment (ăr·bĭt′ rá·měnt)
ar·bi·trar·y (ăr′ bĭ·trĕr′ ĭ)
ar·bi·trar·i·ly -i·ness
ar·bi·trate (ăr′ bĭ·trāt)
-trat·ing
ar·bi·tra·tion (ăr′ bĭ·trā′ shŭn)
ar·bi·tra·tor
ar·bor (ăr′ bẽr)
ar·bo·re·al (ăr· bō′ rē·ál)
ar·bo·re·tum (ăr′ bō· rē′ tŭm)
ar·bor·vi·tae (ăr′ bōr· vī′ tē)
ar·bu·tus (ăr· bū′ tŭs)
arc (ărk)
(bowlike curve; see ark)
arced
ar·cade (ăr· kād′)
arch (ärch)
arch·bish·op arch·dea·con
arch·di·o·cese arch·duke
arch·duch·ess arch·en·e·my
But: ar·che·type
ar·chae·ol·o·gy
(ăr′ kē·ŏl′ ō·jĭ)
-gist
ar·cha·ic (ăr· kā′ ĭk)
arch·an·gel (ărk′ ăn′ jěl)
arch·er·y (ăr′ chĕr·ĭ)
ar·che·type (ăr′ kē·tīp)
Ar·chi·me·des (ăr′ kĭ· mē′ dēz)
Ar·chi·me·de·an
(ăr′ kĭ· mē′ dē·ăn)
ar·chi·pel·a·go (ăr′ kĭ· pěl′ á·gō)
-goes
ar·chi·tect (ăr′ kĭ· těkt)
ar·chi·tec·tur·al
(ăr′ kĭ· těk′ tür·ál)
ar·chi·tec·ture (ăr′ kĭ· těk′ tür)
ar·chives (ăr′ kīvz)
arc·tic (ărk′ tĭk)
(frigid)
Arc·tic (ărk′ tĭk)
(Ocean, Circle, zone)
ar·dent (ăr′ děnt)
-den·cy
ar·dor (ăr′ dẽr)
ar·du·ous (ăr′ dụ·ŭs)

a·re·a (ā′ rē·á)
(flat surface; see aria)
a·re·a·way
a·re·na (á·rē′ ná)
aren't (ărnt)
ar·go·sy (ăr′ gō·sĭ)
-sies
ar·gue (ăr′ gū)
-gu·ing ar·gu·a·ble
ar·gu·er
ar·gu·ment (ăr′ gū·měnt)
ar·gu·men·ta·tion
(ăr′ gū·měn·tā′ shŭn)
ar·gu·men·ta·tive
(ăr′ gū·měn′ tá·tĭv)
a·ri·a (ā′ rĭ·á)
(melody; see area)
ar·id (ăr′ ĭd)
a·rid·i·ty (á·rĭd′ ĭ·tĭ)
a·ris·to·crat (á·rĭs′ tō·krăt)
ar·is·toc·ra·cy (ăr′ ĭs·tŏk′ rá·sĭ)
-cies
a·ris·te·crat·ic
(á·rĭs′ tō·krăt′ ĭk)
Ar·is·toph·a·nes
(ăr′ ĭs·tŏf′ á·nēz)
Ar·is·tot·le (ăr′ ĭs·tŏt′ ′l)
Ar·is·to·te·li·an
(ăr′ ĭs·tō·tē′ lĭ·ăn)
a·rith·me·tic (á·rĭth′ mě·tĭk)
ar·ith·met·i·cal
(ăr′ ĭth·mět′ ĭ·kál)
a·rith·me·ti·cian
(á·rĭth′ mě·tĭsh′ ăn)
Ar·i·zo·na (ăr′ ĭ·zō′ ná)
abbr. Ariz.
Ar·i·zo·nan or Ar·i·zo·ni·an
(-nĭ·ăn)
ark (ărk)
(ship; see arc)
Ar·kan·sas (ăr′ kăn·sô)
abbr. Ark.
Ar·kan·san (ăr·kăn′ zăn)
ar·ma·da (ăr·mä′ dä)
ar·ma·dil·lo (ăr′ má·dĭl′ ō)
ar·ma·ment (ăr′ má·měnt)
ar·ma·ture (ăr′ má·tür)
arm·ful (ärm′ fŏŏl)
ar·mi·stice (ăr′ mĭ·stĭs)
ar·mor (ăr′ mẽr)
ar·mor·y (ăr′ mẽr·ĭ)
-mor·ies
ar·my (ăr′ mĭ)
-mies
a·ro·ma (á·rō′ má)

ar·o·mat·ic (ăr′ ô·măt′ ĭk)
-i·cal·ly
a·round (á·round′)
a·rouse (á·rouz′)
-rous·ing
ar·peg·gio (är·pĕj′ ô)
ar·raign (á·rān′)
ar·raign·ment
ar·range (á·rānj′)
ar·rang·ing
ar·range·ment ar·rang·er
ar·rant (ăr′ ánt)
(notorious; see *errant*)
ar·ray (á·rā′)
ar·rears (á·rērz′)
ar·rest (á·rĕst′)
ar·rive (á·rīv′)
ar·riv·ing ar·riv·al
ar·ro·gance (ăr′ ô·găns)
-gant
ar·ro·gate (ăr′ ô·gāt)
-gat·ing
ar·ro·ga·tion (ăr′ ô·gā′ shŭn)
ar·row (ăr′ ô)
ar·row·head
ar·se·nal (ăr′ sĕ·năl)
ar·se·nic (ăr′ sĕ·nĭk)
ar·son (ăr′ s'n)
ar·son·ist
ar·te·ri·al (ăr·tēr′ ĭ·ăl)
ar·te·ri·o·scle·ro·sis
(ăr·tē′ ri·ô·sklĕ·rō′ sĭs)
ar·ter·y (ăr′ tēr·ĭ)
-ter·ies
ar·te·sian well (ăr·tē′ zhăn)
art·ful (ärt′ fŏŏl)
-ful·ly -ful·ness
ar·thri·tis (ăr·thrī′ tĭs)
ar·thrit·ic (-thrĭt′ ĭk)
ar·ti·choke (ăr′ tĭ·chŏk)
ar·ti·cle (ăr′ tĭ·k'l)
ar·tic·u·late (ăr·tĭk′ û·lāt)
adj.
(-lăt) *v.*
-lat·ing
ar·tic·u·late·ly (-lăt·lĭ)
ar·tic·u·la·tion
(ăr·tĭk′ û·lā′ shŭn)
ar·tic·u·la·tive (-lā′ tĭv)
ar·tic·u·la·tor (-lā′ tēr)
ar·ti·fact (ăr′ tĭ·făkt)
ar·ti·fice (ăr′ tĭ·fĭs)
ar·ti·fi·cial (ăr′ tĭ·fĭsh′ ăl)
ar·ti·fi·ci·al·i·ty
(ăr′ tĭ·fĭsh′ ĭ·ăl′ ĭ·tĭ)

ar·ti·fi·cial·ly
ar·til·ler·y (ăr·tĭl′ ĕr·ĭ)
ar·til·ler·y·man
ar·ti·san (ăr′ tĭ·zăn)
art·ist (är′ tĭst)
ar·tis·tic (är·tĭs′ tĭk)
art·ist·ry
art·less (ärt′ lĕs)
Ar·y·an (âr′ ĭ·ăn)
as·bes·tos (ăs·bĕs′ tôs)
as·cend (á·sĕnd′)
as·cend·ance (á·sĕn′ dăns)
-an·cy -ant
as·cen·sion (á·sĕn′ shŭn)
as·cent (á·sĕnt′)
(rise; see *assent*)
as·cer·tain (ăs′ ĕr·tān′)
as·cer·tain·a·ble
as·cer·tain·ment
as·cet·ic (á·sĕt′ ĭk)
(self-denying; see *aesthetic*)
as·cet·i·cism (-ĭ·sĭz'm)
as·cot tie (ăs′ kŏt)
as·cribe (ăs·krīb′)
-crib·ing as·crib·a·ble
as·crip·tion (ăs·krĭp′ shŭn)
a·sep·tic (á·sĕp′ tĭk)
ash (ăsh)
ash·en ash·es
a·shamed (á·shāmd′)
a·sham·ed·ly (á·shăm′ ĕd·lĭ)
A·sian (ā·zhăn)
A·si·at·ic (ā′ zhĭ·ăt′ ĭk)
a·side (á·sīd′)
as·i·nine (ăs′ ĭ·nīn)
as·i·nin·i·ty (ăs′ ĭ·nĭn′ ĭ·tĭ)
a·skance (á·skăns′)
a·skew (á·skū′)
a·sleep (á·slēp′)
as·par·a·gus (ăs·păr′ á·gŭs)
as·pect (ăs′ pĕkt)
as·pen (ăs′ pĕn)
as·per·i·ty (ăs·pĕr′ ĭ·tĭ)
-ties
as·per·sion (ăs·pûr′ shŭn)
as·phalt (ăs′ fŏlt)
as·phyx·i·ate (ăs·fĭk′ sĭ·āt)
-at·ing as·phyx·i·a
as·phyx·i·a·tion
(ăs·fĭk′ sĭ·ā′ shŭn)
as·pic (ăs′ pĭk)
as·pir·ant (ăs·pīr′ ănt)
as·pi·rate (ăs′ pĭ·rĭt) *n.*
-rat·ing (-rāt) *v.*
as·pi·ra·tion (ăs′ pĭ·rā′ shŭn)

as·pire (ăs·pīr′)
-pir·ing
as·pi·rin (ăs′ pĭ·rĭn)
as·sail (ă·sāl′)
as·sail·a·ble as·sail·ant
as·sas·sin (ă·săs′ ĭn)
as·sas·si·nate
as·sault (ă·sôlt′)
as·sault·er
as·say (ă·sā′)
as·say·er
as·sem·ble (ă·sĕm′ b'l)
-bling
as·sem·blage (-blĭj)
as·sem·bly (ă·sĕm′ blĭ)
-blies as·sem·bly line
as·sem·bly·man
as·sent (ă·sĕnt′)
(agree; see ascent)
as·sent·or
as·sert (ă·sûrt′)
as·ser·tion as·ser·tive·ness
as·sess (ă·sĕs′)
as·sess·a·ble as·sess·ment
as·ses·sor
as·set (ăs′ ĕt)
as·sid·u·ous (ă·sĭd′ ū·ŭs)
as·si·du·i·ty (ăs′ ĭ·dū′ ĭ·tĭ)
as·sign (ă·sīn′)
as·sign·a·ble
as·sign·ee (ăs′ ĭ·nē′)
as·sign·er as·sign·ment
as·sig·na·tion (ăs′ ĭg·nā′ shŭn)
as·sim·i·late (ă·sĭm′ ĭ·lāt)
-lat·ing
as·sim·i·la·ble (-lă·b'l)
as·sim·i·la·tion
(ă·sĭm′ ĭ·lā′ shŭn)
as·sim·i·la·tive (-lā′ tĭv)
as·sim·i·la·to·ry (-lă·tō′ rĭ)
as·sist (ă·sĭst′)
as·sist·ance as·sist·ant
as·so·ci·ate (ă·sō′ shĭ·āt) v.
-at·ing (-ăt) n., adj.
as·so·ci·a·ble (-shĭ·ă·b'l)
as·so·ci·a·tion (ă·sō′ sĭ·ā′ shŭn)
-tion·al
as·so·ci·a·tive (-shĭ·ă′ tĭv)
as·so·nance (ăs′ ŏ·năns)
as·sort (ă·sôrt′)
as·sort·ment
as·suage (ă·swāj′)
as·suag·ing as·suage·ment
as·sua·sive

as·sume (ă·sūm′)
as·sum·ing
as·sump·tion (ă·sŭmp′ shŭn)
as·sure (ă·shoor′)
as·sur·ing as·sur·ance
as·sur·ed·ly as·sur·ed·ness
as·ter (ăs′ tēr)
as·ter·isk (ăs′ tēr·ĭsk)
as·ter·oid (ăs′ tēr·oid)
asth·ma (ăz′ mă)
asth·mat·ic (ăz·măt′ ĭk)
a·stig·ma·tism (ă·stĭg′ mă·tĭz'm)
as·tig·mat·ic (ăs′ tĭg·măt′ ĭk)
as·ton·ish (ăs·tŏn′ ĭsh)
as·ton·ish·ment
as·tound·ing (ăs·tound′ ĭng)
as·tral (ăs′ trăl)
a·stride (ă·strīd′)
as·trin·gent (ăs·trĭn′ jĕnt)
as·trin·gen·cy
as·trol·o·gy (ăs·trŏl′ ŏ·jĭ)
as·tro·log·i·cal
(ăs′ trŏ·lŏj′ ĭ·kăl)
as·tro·naut (ăs′ trŏ·nôt)
as·tron·o·my (ăs·trŏn′ ŏ·mĭ)
as·tron·o·mer
as·tro·nom·i·cal
(ăs′ trŏ·nŏm′ ĭ·kăl)
as·tro·phys·ics (ăs′ trŏ·fĭz′ ĭks)
as·tute (ăs·tūt′)
as·tute·ness
a·sun·der (ă·sŭn′ dēr)
a·sy·lum (ă·sī′ lŭm)
a·sym·me·try (ă·sĭm′ ĕ·trĭ)
-tries
at·a·vism (ăt′ ă·vĭz'm)
a·the·ist (ā′ thē·ĭst)
a·the·is·tic (ā′ thē·ĭs′ tĭk)
ath·lete (ăth′ lēt)
ath·let·ic (ăth·lĕt′ ĭk)
At·lan·tic (ăt·lăn′ tĭk)
at·las (ăt′ lăs)
at·mos·phere (ăt′ mŏs·fēr)
at·mos·pher·ic (ăt′ mŏs·fĕr′ ĭk)
at·oll (ăt′ ŏl)
at·om (ăt′ ŭm)
a·tom·ic (ă·tŏm′ ĭk)
at·om·ize (ăt′ ŭm·īz)
-iz·ing
a·tone (ă·tōn′)
-ton·ing a·tone·ment
a·tro·cious (ă·trō′ shŭs)
a·troc·i·ty (ă·trŏs′ ĭ·tĭ)
at·ro·phy (ăt′ rŏ·fĭ)
-phied -phy·ing

at·tach   (á·tăch´)
  at·tach·a·ble   at·tach·ment
at·ta·ché   (ăt´ à·shā´)
at·tack   (á·tăk´)
at·tain   (ă·tān´)
  at·tain·a·ble   at·tain·ment
at·tain·der   (á·tān´ dĕr)
  (bill of)
at·tar   (ăt´ ĕr)
at·tempt   (á·tĕmpt´)
  at·tempt·a·ble
at·tend   (á·tĕnd´)
  at·tend·ance   -ant
at·ten·tion   (á·tĕn´ shŭn)
at·ten·tive   (á·tĕn´ tĭv)
  at·ten·tive·ness
at·ten·u·ate   (á·tĕn´ û·āt)
  -at·ing
  at·ten·u·a·tion
           (á·tĕn´ û·ā´ shŭn)
at·test   (á·tĕst´)
  at·tes·ta·tion   (ăt´ ĕs·tā´ shŭn)
at·tic   (ăt´ ĭk)
at·tire   (á·tīr´)
  at·tir·ing   at·tire·ment
at·ti·tude   (ăt´ ĭ·tūd)
at·tor·ney   (á·tûr´ nĭ)
  -neys
at·tract   (á·trăkt´)
  at·tract·a·ble
  at·trac·tion   (á·trăk´ shŭn)
  at·trac·tive   (á·trăk´ tĭv)
  at·trac·tor
at·trib·ute   (á·trĭb´ ût) v.
  -ut·ing
at·tri·bute   (ăt´ rĭ·būt) n.
  at·trib·ut·a·ble
           (á·trĭb´ ût·á·b´l)
  at·tri·bu·tion   (ăt´ rĭ·bū´ shŭn)
  at·trib·u·tive   (á·trĭb´ û·tĭv)
at·tri·tion   (á·trĭsh´ ŭn)
at·tune   (á·tūn´)
  at·tun·ing
au·burn   (ô´ bĕrn)
Auck·land,   (ôk´ lănd)
  New Zea·land
auc·tion   (ôk´ shŭn)
  auc·tion·eer   (ôk´ shŭn·ēr´)
au·da·cious   (ô·dā´ shŭs)
  au·dac·i·ty   (ô·dăs´ ĭ·tĭ)
au·di·ble   (ô´ dĭ·b´l)
  au·di·bil·i·ty   (ô´ dĭ·bĭl´ ĭ·tĭ)
au·di·ence   (ô´ dĭ·ĕns)
au·di·o·vis·u·al
           (ô´ dĭ·ô·vĭzh´ û·ál)

au·dit   (ô´ dĭt)
  -dit·ed   -dit·ing
  au·dit·or
au·di·tion   (ô·dĭsh´ ŭn)
au·di·to·ri·um   (ô´ dĭ·tō´ rĭ·ŭm)
au·di·to·ry   (ô´ dĭ·tō´ rĭ)
au·ger   (ô´ gĕr)
  (tool; see augur)
aught   (ôt)
  (cipher; see ought)
aug·ment   (ôg·mĕnt´)
  aug·ment·a·ble
  aug·men·ta·tion
           (ôg´ mĕn·tā´ shŭn)
au gra·tin   (ō´ grä´ tăn´)
au·gur   (ô´ gĕr)
  (foretell; see auger)
  au·gu·ry
au·gust   (ô·gŭst´)
  (stately; see August)
Au·gust   (ô´ gŭst)
  (month; see august)
auld lang syne   (ôld lăng sīn)
aunt   (ănt)
au·ral   (ô´ rál)
  (of the ear; see oral)
au·re·o·my·cin   (ô´ rē·ô·mī´ sĭn)
au re·voir   (ō´ rĕ·vwär´)
au·ro·ra bo·re·a·lis
           (ô·rō´ rá bō´ rē·ā´ lĭs)
aus·pi·ces   (ôs´ pĭ·sĕs)
aus·pi·cious   (ôs·pĭsh´ ŭs)
aus·tere   (ôs·tēr´)
  aus·tere·ly
  aus·ter·i·ty   (ôs·tĕr´ ĭ·tĭ)
Aus·tra·lia   (ôs·trāl´ yá)
au·then·tic   (ô·thĕn´ tĭk)
  au·then·ti·cal·ly
  au·then·ti·cate   -cat·ing
  au·then·tic·i·ty
           (ô´ thĕn·tĭs´ ĭ·tĭ)
au·thor   (ô´ thĕr)
  au·thor·ess
au·thor·i·tar·i·an
           (ô·thŏr´ ĭ·târ´ ĭ·ăn)
au·thor·i·ty   (ô·thŏr´ ĭ·tĭ)
  -ties
  au·thor·i·ta·tive
  au·thor·ize   (ô´ thĕr·īz)
  -iz·ing
  au·thor·i·za·tion
           (ô´ thĕr·ĭ·zā´ shŭn)
au·to·bi·og·ra·phy
           (ô´ tô·bĭ·ŏg´ rá·fĭ)
  -phies

au·to·bi·o·graph·i·cal
  (ô' tô· bī' ô· grăf' ĭ· kăl)
au·to·crat (ô' tô· krăt)
au·toc·ra·cy (ô· tŏk' rá· sĭ)
au·to·crat·ic (ô' tô· krăt' ĭk)
au·to·graph (ô' tô· grăf)
au·to·mat (ô' tô· măt)
au·to·mat·ic (ô' tô· măt' ĭk)
au·to·mat·i·cal·ly
au·to·ma·tion (ô' tô· mā' shŭn)
au·tom·a·ton (ô· tŏm' á· tŏn)
au·to·mo·bile (ô' tô· mô· bēl')
au·to·mo·tive (ô' tô· mō' tĭv)
au·ton·o·my (ô· tŏn' ô· mĭ)
au·ton·o·mous
au·top·sy (ô' tŏp· sĭ)
-sies
au·to·sug·ges·tion
  (ô' tô· sŭg· jĕs' chŭn)
au·tumn (ô' tŭm)
au·tum·nal (ô· tŭm' năl)
aux·il·ia·ry (ôg· zĭl' yá· rĭ)
-ries
a·vail·a·ble (á· vāl' á· b'l)
a·vail·a·bil·i·ty
  (á· vāl' á· bĭl' ĭ· tĭ)
av·a·lanche (ăv' á· lănch)
a·vant-garde (ă· vänt' gärd')
av·a·rice (ăv' á· rĭs)
av·a·ri·cious (ăv' á· rĭsh' ŭs)
a·venge (á· vĕnj')
-veng·ing a·veng·er
av·e·nue (ăv' ĕ· nū)
a·ver (á· vûr')
-verred -ver·ring
av·er·age (ăv' ĕr· ĭj)
a·verse (á· vûrs')
a·verse·ly
a·ver·sion (á· vûr' zhŭn)
a·vert (á· vûrt')
a·vert·i·ble
a·vi·ar·y (ā' vĭ· ĕr' ĭ)
-ar·ies
a·vi·a·tion (ā' vĭ· ā' shŭn)
a·vi·a·tor (ā' vĭ· ā' tĕr)
a·vi·a·trix (ā' vĭ· ā' trĭks)
av·id (ăv' ĭd)
a·vid·i·ty (á· vĭd' ĭ· tĭ)
av·o·ca·do (ăv' ô· kä' dō)
-dos
av·o·ca·tion (ăv' ô· kā' shŭn)
a·void (á· void')
a·void·a·ble a·void·ance
av·oir·du·pois (ăv' ĕr· dŭ· poiz')

a·vow (á· vou')
a·vow·al
a·wak·en (á· wăk' ĕn)
a·ware·ness (á· wâr' nĕs)
awe (ô)
awe·some awe-strick·en
aw·ing
a·weigh (á· wā')
aw·ful (ô' fŏŏl)
-ful·ly -ful·ness
awk·ward (ôk' wĕrd)
awl (ôl)
awn·ing (ôn' ĭng)
a·wry (á· rī')
ax (ăks)
ax·es
ax·i·al (ăk' sĭ· ăl)
ax·i·om (ăk' sĭ· ŭm)
ax·i·o·mat·ic (ăk' sĭ· ô· măt' ĭk)
ax·is (ăk' sĭs)
pl. ax·es (-sēz)
ax·le (ăk' s'l)
a·zal·ea (á· zăl' yá)
az·ure (ăzh' ĕr)

B

bab·ble (băb' 'l)
bab·bling
ba·boon (bă· bōōn')
ba·bush·ka (bá· bŏŏsh' ká)
ba·by (bā' bĭ)
-bies ba·bies'-breath
ba·by·hood ba·by·ish
ba·by-sit ba·by sit·ter
Bab·y·lon (băb' ĭ· lŏn)
Bab·y·lo·ni·an
  (băb' ĭ· lō' nĭ· ăn)
bac·ca·lau·re·ate
  (băk' á· lô' rē· ăt)
bach·e·lor (băch' ĕ· lĕr)
ba·cil·lus (bá· sĭl' ŭs)
pl. ba·cil·li (-ī)
back (băk)
back·bite back·bone
back·gam·mon back·ground
back·hand·ed back·log
back·stairs back·stop
back·stroke back talk
back·ward back·wa·ter
back·woods
back·woods·man
ba·con (bā' kŭn)

bac·te·ri·a   (băk·tēr′ ĭ·ȧ)
   sing. bac·te·ri·um
   bac·te·ri·al
bac·te·ri·ol·o·gy
         (băk·tēr′ ĭ·ŏl′ ô·jĭ)
   bac·te·ri·ol·o·gist
badg·er   (băj′ ēr)
bad·i·nage   (băd′ ĭ·näzh′)
bad·min·ton   (băd′ mĭn′ t'n)
baf·fle   (băf′ 'l)
   baf·fling   baf·fle·ment
bag·a·telle   (băg′ ȧ·tĕl′)
bag·gage   (băg′ ĭj)
bag·gy   (băg′ĭ)
Bagh·dad, I·raq   (băg′ dăd)
ba·guette   (bȧ·gĕt′)
Ba·ha·ma Is.   (bȧ·hä′ mȧ)
   Ba·ha·mi·an   (-mĭ·ȧn)
bail   (bāl)
   (set free; see *bale*)
bail·iff   (bāl′ ĭf)
bail·i·wick   (bāl′ ĭ·wĭk)
bait   (bāt)
   (a lure; see *bate*)
bak·er·y   (bāk′ ēr·ĭ)
   -er·ies
bal·ance   (băl′ ăns)
   -anc·ing
bal·co·ny   (băl′ kô·nĭ)
   -nies
bald-head·ed   (bôld′ hĕd′ ĕd)
bale   (bāl)
   (bundle; see *bail*)
   bal·ing
bale·ful   (bāl′ fŏŏl)
Bal·e·ar·ic (is.)   (băl′ ê·ăr′ ĭk)
Ba·li   (bä′ lê)
   Ba·li·nese   (bä′ lê·nēz′)
balk·y   (bôk′ ĭ)
ball   (bôl)
   ball-and-sock·et joint
   ball bear·ing   ball-point pen
   ball·room
bal·lad   (băl′ ȧd)
bal·last   (băl′ ȧst)
bal·le·ri·na   (băl′ ê·rē′ nȧ)
bal·let   (băl′ ā)
bal·lis·tic   (bȧ·lĭs′ tĭk)
bal·loon   (bȧ·lŏŏn′)
bal·lot   (băl′ ŭt)
bal·ly·hoo   (băl′ ĭ·hŏŏ)
balm   (bäm)
   balm·i·ness
bal·sa   (bôl′ sȧ)
bal·sam   (bôl′ săm)

bal·us·trade   (băl′ ŭs·trād′)
bam·boo   (băm·bŏŏ′)
bam·boo·zle   (băm·bŏŏ′ z'l)
   -zling
ba·nal   (bā′ năl)
   ba·nal·i·ty   (bȧ·năl′ ĭ·tĭ)
   ba·nal·ly
ba·nan·a   (bȧ·năn′ ȧ)
band·age   (băn′ dĭj)
   -ag·ing
ban·dan·na   (băn·dăn′ ȧ)
ban·deau   (băn·dō′)
ban·dit   (băn′ dĭt)
   ban·dit·ry
band·stand   (bănd′ stănd′)
ban·dy   (băn′ dĭ)
   -died   -dy·ing
   ban·dy-leg·ged
bane·ful   (bān′ fŏŏl)
Banff, Can.   (bămf)
Bang·kok,   (băng′ kŏk)
   Thai·land
ban·ish   (băn′ ĭsh)
ban·is·ter   (băn′ ĭs·tēr)
ban·jo   (băn′ jō)
   -jos
bank·rupt   (băngk′ rŭpt)
   bank·rupt·cy   (-rŭpt·sĭ)
ban·ner   (băn′ ēr)
ban·quet   (băng′ kwĕt)
   -quet·ed
ban·shee   (băn′ shē)
ban·tam   (băn′ tăm)
   ban·tam·weight
ban·ter·ing   (băn′ tēr·ĭng)
bap·tism   (băp′ tĭz'm)
   bap·tis·mal   (băp·tĭz′ măl)
   Bap·tist   bap·tize
Bar·ba·dos (is.)   (bär·bā′ dōz)
bar·bar·i·an   (bär·bâr′ ĭ·ȧn)
   bar·bar·ic   (bär·bâr′ ĭk)
   bar·ba·rism   (bär′ bȧ·rĭz'm)
   bar·bar·i·ty   (bär·băr′ ĭ·tĭ)
   -ties
   bar·ba·rous   (bär′ bȧ·rŭs)
bar·be·cue   (bär′ bê·kū)
   -cu·ing
bar·ber   (bär′ bēr)
bar·bi·tu·rate   (bär′ bĭ·tū′ rāt)
bar·ca·role   (bär′ kȧ·rōl)
bare   (bâr)
   bar·ing   bare·ly
   bare·back   bare-head·ed
bar·gain   (bär′ gĭn)
   bar·gain·er

barge (bärj)
barg·ing
bar·i·tone (bär′ ĭ·tōn)
bar·keep·er (bär′ kēp′ ēr)
bar·ley (bär′ lĭ)
bar·na·cle (bär′ nȧ·k′l)
ba·rom·e·ter (bȧ·rŏm′ ê·tēr)
bar·o·met·ric (bär′ ô·mĕt′ rĭk)
bar·on (bär′ ŭn)
(nobleman; see *barren*)
bar·on·age (-ĭj)
bar·on·ess
ba·ro·ni·al (bȧ·rō′ nĭ·ȧl)
ba·roque (bȧ·rōk′)
bar·racks (bär′ ȧks)
bar·ra·cu·da (bär′ ȧ·kōō′ dȧ)
n. *sing. & pl.*
bar·rage (bȧ·räzh′)
bar·rel (bär′ ĕl)
bar·reled   bar·rel chair
bar·rel house   bar·rel or·gan
bar·ren (bär′ ĕn)
(sterile; see *baron*)
bar·ren·ness
bar·ri·cade (bär′ ĭ·kād′)
-cad·ing
bar·ri·er (bär′ ĭ·ēr)
bar·ris·ter (bär′ ĭs·tēr)
bar·room (bär′ rōōm′)
bar·tend·er (bär′ tĕn′ dēr)
bar·ter (bär′ tēr)
bas·al me·tab·o·lism
(bās′ȧl mē·tăb′ô·lĭz′m)
ba·salt (bȧ·sôlt′)
ba·sal·tic (bȧ·sôl′ tĭk)
base (bās)
bas·ing   base·ball
base·board   base·less
base·ly   base·ment
base-mind·ed
bash·ful (băsh′ fōōl)
bash·ful·ly   -ful·ness
bas·ic (bās′ ĭk)
bas·i·cal·ly
bas·il (băz′ ĭl)
ba·sil·i·ca (bȧ·sĭl′ ĭ·kȧ)
ba·sin (bā′ s′n)
ba·sis (bā′ sĭs)
pl. ba·ses (-sēz)
bas·ket (băs′ kĕt)
bas·ket·ball   bas·ket·ful
bas·ket·ry
bas-re·lief (bä′ rê·lēf′)
bass (bās)
bass clef   bass drum

bass vi·ol
bas·set hound (băs′ ĕt)
bas·si·net (băs′ ĭ·nĕt′)
bas·so (bás′ ō)
bas·soon (bȧ·sōōn′)
bas·tard (băs′ tērd)
baste (bāst)
bast·ing
bas·tille (băs·tēl′)
bas·tion (băs′ chŭn)
batch (băch)
bate (bāt)
(to reduce; see *bait*)
bat·ing
bathe (bāth) v.
bath·ing
ba·tiste (bȧ·tēst′)
ba·ton (bȧ·tŏn′)
Bat·on Rouge, (băt′ 'n rōōzh′)
La.
bat·tal·ion (bȧ·tăl′ yŭn)
bat·ten (băt′ 'n)
bat·ter·y (băt′ ēr·ĭ)
bat·ter·ies
bat·tle (băt′ 'l)
bat·tling   bat·tle-ax
bat·tle cruis·er bat·tle cry
bat·tle·field   bat·tle·ground
bat·tle·ship
bau·ble (bô′ b′l)
baux·ite (bôks′ ĭt)
bawd (bôd)
bawd·i·ness   bawd·y
bawl·ing (bôl′ ĭng)
bay·o·net (bā′ ô·nĕt)
bay·ou (bī′ ōō)
ba·zaar (bȧ·zär′)
(market; see *bizarre*)
ba·zoo·ka (bȧ·zōō′ kȧ)
beach (bēch)
(seashore; see *beech*)
beach·comb·er beach·head
beach wag·on
bea·con (bē′ kŭn)
bead·y (bēd′ ĭ)
bea·gle (bē′ g′l)
bear·a·ble (bâr′ ȧ·b′l)
beard (bērd)
beast·ly (bēst′ lĭ)
bes·tial (bĕst′ yȧl)
be·at·i·fy (bê·ăt′ ĭ·fī)
(canonize)
-fied   -fy·ing
be·at·i·fi·ca·tion
(bê·ăt′ ĭ·fĭ·kā′ shŭn)

beau   (bō)
  pl. beaux   (bōz)
beau·ty   (bū′ tĭ)
  -ties
  beau·te·ous   (bū′ tĕ·ŭs)
  beau·ti·cian   (bū·tĭsh′ ăn)
  beau·ti·ful   -ful·ly
  beau·ti·fy   -fied, -fy·ing
beaux-arts   (bō′ zár′)
bea·ver   (bē′ vĕr)
be·calm   (bē· kăm)
be·cause   (bē· kôz′)
Bech·u·a·na·land
    (bĕch′ ŏŏ·ä′ nȧ·lănd′)
beck·on·ing   (bĕk′ ŭn·ĭng)
be·come   (bē· kŭm′)
  -com·ing
bed   (bĕd)
  bed·ded   bed·ding
  bed·bug   bed·clothes
  bed·fel·low   bed lamp
  bed lin·en   bed pad
  bed·post   bed·rid·den
  bed·roll   bed·room
  bed sheet   bed·side
  bed·spread   bed·stead
  bed·time   bed warm·er
be·daub   (bē· dôb′)
bed·lam   (bĕd′ lăm)
Bed·ou·in   (bĕd′ ŏŏ·ĭn)
be·drag·gled   (bē· drăg′ ld)
beech   (bēch)
  (tree; see *beach*)
beef·steak   (bēf′ stāk′)
bee·hive   (bē′ hīv′)
bee·keep·ing   (bē′ kēp′ ĭng)
Be·el·ze·bub   (bē· ĕl′ zē·bŭb)
beet   (bēt)
  (vegetable)
Bee·tho·ven,   (vän bā′ tō′ vĕn)
  Lud·wig van
bee·tle   (bē′ t′l)
  bee·tle-browed
be·fit   (bē·fĭt′)
  -fit·ted   -fit·ting
be·fore·hand   (bē· fôr′ hănd′)
be·fud·dle   (bē· fŭd′ ′l)
  -fud·dling   be·fud·dle·ment
beg·gar   (bĕg′ ẽr)
be·gin   (bē· gĭn′)
  -gan   -gin·ning
  be·gin·ner
be·go·ni·a   (bē· gō′ nĭ·ȧ)
be·grudge   (bē· grŭj′)
  -grudg·ing

be·guile   (bē· gīl′)
  -guil·ing   be·guile·ment
be·half   (bē· hȧf′)
be·have   (bē· hāv′)
  -hav·ing
be·hav·ior   (bē· hāv′ yẽr)
be·hest   (bē· hĕst′)
be·hind   (bē· hīnd′)
be·hold·en   (bē· hōl′ d′n)
be·hoove   (bē· hōōv′)
  -hoov·ing
beige   (bāzh)
be·ing   (bē′ ĭng)
Bei·rut,   (bā· rōōt′)
  Leb·a·non
be·la·bor   (bē· lā′ bẽr)
be·lat·ed·ly   (bē· lāt′ ĕd·lĭ)
belch   (bĕlch)
be·lea·guer   (bē· lē′ gẽr)
bel·fry   (bĕl′ frĭ)
  -fries
Bel·gium   (bĕl′ jŭm)
  Bel·gian   (bĕl′ jăn)
be·lie   (bē· lī′)
  -lied   -ly·ing
be·lief   (bē· lēf′)
be·lieve   (bē· lēv′)
  -liev·ing   be·liev·a·ble
  be·liev·er
be·lit·tle   (bē· lĭt″ l)
  -lit·tling   be·lit·tle·ment
bel·la·don·na   (bĕl′ ȧ·dŏn′ ȧ)
belles-let·tres   (bĕl′ lĕt′ r′)
bell·hop   (bĕl′ hŏp′)
bel·li·cose   (bĕl′ ĭ·kōs)
bel·lig·er·ence   (bē· lĭj′ ẽr·ĕns)
  -en·cy   -ent
bel·lows   (bĕl′ ōz)
bell·weth·er   (bĕl′ wĕth′ ẽr)
be·long·ing   (bē· lŏng′ ĭng)
be·lov·ed   (bē· lŭv′ ĕd)
be·low   (bē· lō′)
be·muse   (bē· mūz′)
  -mus·ing
be·neath   (bē· nēth′)
Ben·e·dic·tine   (bĕn′ ē·dĭk′ tĭn)
  (pron. -tēn when referring to the
  drink of this name.)
ben·e·dic·tion   (bĕn′ ē·dĭk′ shŭn)
  ben·e·dic·to·ry
ben·e·fac·tor   (bĕn′ ē·făk′ tẽr)
  ben·e·fac·tress
be·nef·i·cence   (bē· nĕf′ ĭ·sĕns)
  -cent

ben·e·fi·cial (bĕn' ê·fĭsh' ăl)
-cial·ly
ben·e·fi·ci·ar·y
    (bĕn' ê·fĭsh' ĭ·ĕr' ĭ)
-ar·ies
ben·e·fit (bĕn' ê·fĭt)
-fit·ed   -fit·ing .
be·nev·o·lence (bĕ·nĕv' ô·lĕns)
-lent
Ben-Gur·ion, (bĕn' goŏr·yŏn')
Da·vid
be·nign (bĕ·nīn')
be·nig·nant (bĕ·nĭg' nănt)
-nan·cy
be·nig·ni·ty (bĕ·nĭg' nĭ·tĭ)
-ties
be·numb (bĕ·nŭm')
-numbed
Ben·zed·rine (bĕn·zĕd' rēn)
ben·zine (bĕn' zēn)
  (cleaning fluid)
be·queath (bĕ·kwēth')
be·quest (bĕ·kwĕst')
be·rate (bĕ·rāt')
-rat·ing
be·reave (bĕ·rēv')
-reav·ing   be·reave·ment
be·ret (bĕ·rā')
ber·i·ber·i (bĕr' ĭ·bĕr' ĭ)
Be·ring (strait) (bĕr' ĭng)
Berke·ley, Calif. (bûrk' lĭ)
ber·ry (bĕr' ĭ)
ber·ries
ber·serk (bûr' sûrk)
berth (bûrth)
  (a bunk; see birth)
be·seech·ing (bĕ·sēch' ĭng)
be·set (bĕ·sĕt')
-set·ting
be·side (bĕ·sīd')
be·siege (bĕ·sēj')
-sieg·ing
be·smear (bĕ·smēr')
be·smirch (bĕ·smûrch')
be·speak (bĕ·spēk')
best (bĕst)
  best-known   best-liked
  best man   best sel·ler
  best-sell·ing
bes·tial (bĕst' yăl)
bes·ti·al·i·ty (bĕs' tĭ·ăl' ĭ·tĭ)
be·stow (bĕ·stō')
be·ta ray (bā' tá)
Be·thes·da, Md. (bĕ·thĕz' dá)
Beth·le·hem, Pa. (bĕth' lê·ĕm)

be·tide (bĕ·tīd')
be·tray (bĕ·trā')
-trayed   -tray·ing
be·tray·al   be·tray·er
be·troth (bĕ·trŏth')
be·troth·al
bet·ter·ment (bĕt' ĕr·mĕnt)
be·tween (bĕ·twēn')
be·twixt (bĕ·twĭkst')
bev·el (bĕv' ĕl)
-eled   -el·ing
bev·er·age (bĕv' ĕr·ĭj)
Bev·er·ly Hills, (bĕv' ĕr·lĭ)
Calif.
bev·y (bĕv' ĭ)
bev·ies
be·wail (bĕ·wāl')
-wailed   -wail·ing
be·ware (bĕ·wâr')
be·wil·der·ing (bĕ·wĭl' dĕr·ĭng)
be·witch·ing (bĕ·wĭch' ĭng)
be·yond (bĕ·yŏnd')
bi·an·nu·al (bī·ăn' û·ăl)
  (occurring twice a year; see
  biennial)
bi·an·nu·al·ly
bi·as (bī' ás)
bi·ased
Bi·ble (bī' b'l)
Bib·li·cal (bĭb' lĭ·kăl)
bib·li·og·ra·phy
    (bĭb' lĭ·ŏg' rá·fĭ)
-phies
bib·li·o·graph·i·cal
    (bĭb' lĭ·ô·grăf' ĭ·kăl)
bib·u·lous (bĭb' û·lŭs)
  (tippling; see bilious)
bi·cam·er·al (bī·kăm' ĕr·ăl)
bi·car·bon·ate (bī·kär' bŏn·āt)
bi·cen·ten·ni·al (bī' sĕn·tĕn' ĭ·ăl)
bi·ceps (bī' sĕps)
bick·er·ing (bĭk' ĕr·ĭng)
bi·cy·cle (bī' sĭk'l)
bi·cy·cling   bi·cy·clist
bid (bĭd)
bid·ding   bid·da·ble
bid·den
bide (bīd)
bid·ing
bi·en·ni·al (bī·ĕn' ĭ·ăl)
  (once in two years; see biannual)
bi·en·ni·al·ly   bi·en·ni·um
bier (bĕr)
  (coffin)
bi·fo·cal (bī·fō' kăl)

big·a·my (bĭg′ ȧ·mĭ)
  big·a·mist   big·a·mous
big·ot (bĭg′ ŭt)
  -ot·ed   big·ot·ry
big·wig (bĭg′ wĭg′)
bi·ki·ni (bĭ·kē′ nĭ)
bi·lat·er·al (bĭ·lăt′ ĕr·ȧl)
  -al·ly
bilge wa·ter (bĭlj)
bi·lin·e·ar (bĭ·lĭn′ ė·ẽr)
bi·lin·gual (bĭ·lĭng′ gwȧl)
  bi·lin·guist
bil·ious (bĭl′ yŭs)
  (ill-tempered; see *bibulous*)
bilk (bĭlk)
bill·board (bĭl′ bôrd′)
bil·let (bĭl′ ĕt)
  bil·let·ed
bil·let-doux (bĭl′ȧ·dōō′)
bill·fold (bĭl′ fōld′)
bil·liards (bĭl′ yẽrdz)
bil·lion (bĭl′ yŭn)
bill of: (bĭl ŏv)
  bill of fare   bill of lad·ing
  bill of rights   bill of sale
bil·low (bĭl′ ō)
bi·me·tal·lic (bī′ mė·tăl′ ĭk)
bi·month·ly (bī·mŭnth′ lĭ)
  (once in two months)
bi·na·ry (bī′ nȧ·rĭ)
bin·au·ral (bĭn·ô′ rȧl)
bind·er·y (bīn′ dẽr·ĭ)
  -er·ies
bin·oc·u·lars (bĭn·ŏk′ û·lẽrz)
bi·o·chem·is·try
       (bī′ ō·kĕm′ ĭs·trĭ)
  bi·o·chem·ist
bi·og·ra·phy (bī·ŏg′ rȧ·fĭ)
  -phies
  bi·o·graph·i·cal
       (bī′ ō·grăf′ ĭ·kȧl)
bi·ol·o·gy (bī·ŏl′ ō·jĭ)
  bi·o·log·i·cal (bī′ ō:lŏj′ ĭ·kȧl)
  -cal·ly
bi·o·syn·the·sis
       (bī′ ō·sĭn′ thė·sĭs)
bi·par·ti·san·ship
       (bī·pär′ tĭ·zȧn·shĭp′)
bi·par·tite (bī·pär′ tīt)
bi·po·lar (bī·pō′ lẽr)
  bi·po·lar·i·ty (bī′ pō·lăr′ ĭ·tĭ)
birch (bûrch)
bird (bûrd)
  bird dog   bird·house

bird of par·a·dise
bird of prey   bird's-eye view
bird watch·er
bird·ie (bûr′ dĭ)
  (golf term)
birth (bûrth)
  (origin; see *berth*)
  birth·day   birth·mark
  birth·place   birth rate
  birth·right   birth·stone
Bis·cayne Bay, (bĭs′kān)
  Fla.
bis·cuit (bĭs′ kĭt)
bi·sect (bī′ sĕkt′)
  bi·sec·tion·al (bī·sĕk′ shŭn·ȧl)
bi·sex·u·al (bī·sĕk′ shŏŏ·ȧl)
bish·op (bĭsh′ ŭp)
  bish·op·ric
Bis·marck, (bĭz′ märk)
  N. Dak.
bi·son (bī′ s'n)
bisque (bĭsk)
bite (bīt)
  bit·ing
  bit·ten (bĭt′ 'n)
bit·ter (bĭt′ ẽr)
  bit·ter·ness   bit·ter·sweet
bi·tu·mi·nous (bĭ·tū′ mĭ·nŭs)
  coal
biv·ouac (bĭv′ wăk)
  -ouacked   -ouack·ing
bi·week·ly (bī·wēk′ lĭ)
bi·zarre (bī·zär′)
  (odd; see *bazaar*)
  bi·zarre·ly
black (blăk)
  black·ball   black·ber·ry
  black·board   Black Death
  black·ened
  black-eyed Su·san
  black·head   black-list *v.*
  black mag·ic   black·mail
  black mar·ket·eer
  black·out   black sheep
  black·smith
blad·der (blăd′ ẽr)
blame (blām)
  blam·ing   blam·a·ble
  blame·less
  blame·wor·thi·ness
blan·dish·ment (blăn′ dĭsh·mĕnt)
blan·ket (blăng′ kĕt)
  -ket·ed   -ket·ing
blar·ney (blär′ nĭ)
bla·sé (blä·zā′)

blas·phe·my (blăs′ fê·mĭ)
-mies
blas·phem·er (blăs·fēm′ ẽr)
blas·phe·mous (blăs′ fê·mŭs)
bla·tant (blā′ tănt)
-tan·cy
blaz·er (blāz′ ẽr)
bla·zon (blā′ z′n)
bla·zon·ry
bleach (blēch)
bleach·ers (blēch′ ẽrs)
bleak (blēk)
blear·y (blĭr′ ĭ)
bleat (blēt)
bleed (blēd)
blem·ish (blĕm′ ĭsh)
bless (blĕs)
bless·ed·ness
blight (blīt)
blind (blīnd)
blind·fold
blind·man's buff
blink·er (blĭngk′ ẽr)
bliss (blĭs)
blis·ter (blĭs′ tẽr)
blithe (blīth)
blithe·ly
blitz·krieg (blĭts′ krēg′)
bliz·zard (blĭz′ ẽrd)
bloat (blōt)
bloc (blŏk)
(political group)
block (blŏk)
block·bust·er block·head
block·house
block·ade (blŏk·ād′)
block·ade-run·ner
blond (blŏnd)
adj. & n. masc.
blonde (blŏnd) n. fem.
blood (blŭd)
blood·cur·dling
blood·hound blood·ied
blood·i·est blood pres·sure
blood·shed
blood·thirst·i·ness
blood ves·sel
bloom·er (blōōm′ ẽr)
blos·som (blŏs′ ŭm)
blot (blŏt)
blot·ting blot·ter
blotch (blŏch)
blotch·es blotch·y
blow (blō)

blow·gun blow·out
blow·pipe blow·up
blown (blōn)
blowz·y (blous′ ĭ)
blub·ber (blŭb′ ẽr)
bludg·eon (blŭj′ ŭn)
blue (blōō)
blue·ber·ry blue·bird
blue blood blue·bon·net
blue book blue chip
blue-eyed blue·grass
blue jay blue laws
blue-pen·cil v. blue·print
bluff (blŭf)
blu·ing (blōō′ ĭng)
blun·der·buss (blŭn′ dẽr·bŭs)
blur (blûr)
blurred blur·ry
blurb (blûrb)
blurt (blûrt)
boa con·stric·tor (bō′ á)
boar (bōr)
(hog; see bore)
board·er (bōr′ dẽr)
(one who boards; see border)
board·ing·house
board·ing school
boast (bōst)
boast·ful -ful·ly
boat·swain (bō′ s′n)
bob·bin (bŏb′ ĭn)
bob·by-sox (bŏb′ ĭ·sŏks′)
bobby-sox·er
bob·o·link (bŏb′ ô·lĭngk)
bob·sled (bŏb′ slĕd′)
bob·tail (bŏb′ tāl′)
Bo·ca Ra·ton, (bō′ ká rá·tōn′)
Fla.
bock beer (bŏk)
bode (bōd)
bod·ing
bod·ice (bŏd′ ĭs)
bod·y (bŏd′ ĭ)
bod·ies bod·ied
bod·i·less
bod·i·ly (bŏd′ ĭ·lĭ)
bod·y·guard
Boer (bōōr)
bo·gey (bō′ gĭ)
(golf term) -geys
bog·gle (bŏg′ ′l)
bog·gling
bo·gus (bō′ gŭs)
bo·gy (bō′ gĭ)
(goblin) -gies

Bo·he·mi·an (bȯ·hē′ mĭ·ản)
boil·er (boil′ ẽr)
bois·ter·ous (bois′ tẽr·ŭs)
bold-faced (bōld′ fāst′)
bo·le·ro (bȯ·lâr′ ō)
Bo·liv·i·a (bȯ·lĭv′ ĭ·ȧ)
boll wee·vil (bōl)
bo·lo·ney (bȯ·lō′ nĭ)
　(also baloney)
Bol·she·vik (bŏl′ shĕ·vĭk)
bol·ster (bōl′ stẽr)
bomb (bŏm)
　bomb·proof　bomb·shell
　bomb shel·ter　bomb·sight
bom·bard (bŏm·bärd′)
bom·bard·ier (bŏm′bẽr·dẽr′)
bom·bast (bŏm′ băst)
　bom·bas·tic (bŏm·băs′ tĭk)
bo·na fi·de (bō′ nȧ fī′ dē)
bo·nan·za (bȯ·năn′ zȧ)
Bo·na·parte, Na·po·le·on
　　(bō′ nȧ·pärt, nȧ·pō′ lē·ŭn)
bond (bŏnd)
　bond·hold·er　bond·man
　bond ser·vant
bond·age (bŏn′ dĭj)
bon·fire (bŏn′ fīr′)
bon·net (bŏn′ ĕt)
　bon·net·ed
bon·ny (bŏn′ ĭ)
bo·nus (bō′ nŭs)
　-nus·es
bon voy·age (bôN′ vwȧ′ yȧzh′)
bon·y (bŏn′ ĭ)
　bon·i·ness
boob·y trap (bōō′ bĭ)
book (bŏŏk)
　book·bind·er　book·case
　book end　book·keep·er
　book·keep·ing　book·let
　book·lov·er
　book·mak·er　(bookie)
　book·mark　book·mo·bile
　book re·view　book·shelf
　book·store　book val·ue
　book·worm
boom·er·ang (bōōm′ ẽr·ăng)
boon·dog·gle (bōōn′ dŏg′′ l)
　-dog·gling
boor·ish (bŏŏr′ ĭsh)
boost·er (bōōs′ tẽr)
boot (bōōt)
　boot·black　boot·leg
　boot·leg·ger　boot·lick·er

boot·ee (bōō′ tē′)
　(baby's boot)
boo·ty (bōō′ tĭ)
　(plunder)
booze (bōōz)
bo·rax (bō′ răks)
Bor·deaux (bôr′ dō′)
bor·del·lo (bôr·dĕl′ ō)
bor·der (bôr′ dẽr)
　(edge: see boarder)
　bor·der·line adj.
bore (bōr)
　(dull person; see boar)
　bor·ing　bore·dom
bo·ric acid (bō′ rĭk)
born (bôrn)
　(given birth)
borne (bôrn)
　(carried)
bo·ron (bō′ rŏn)
bor·ough (bûr′ ō)
　(town)
bor·row (bŏr′ ō)
borsch (bôrsh)
bos·om (bŏŏz′ ŭm)
boss·y (bŏs′ ĭ)
　boss·i·ness
bot·a·ny (bŏt′ ȧ·nĭ)
　bo·tan·i·cal (bȯ·tăn′ ĭ·kȧl)
　bot·a·nist (bŏt′ ȧ·nĭst)
botch (bŏch)
　botch·er·y
both·er·some (bŏth′ ẽr·sŭm)
bot·tle (bŏt′ ′l)
　bot·tling　bot·tle·fed
　bot·tle·neck　bot·tle wash·er
bot·tom (bŏt′ ŭm)
bot·u·lism (bŏt′ û·lĭz′m)
bou·clé (bōō′ klā′)
bou·doir (bōō′ dwär)
bough (bou)
bought (bôt)
bouil·la·baise (bōō(l)′ yȧ·bās′)
bouil·lon (bōō′ yŏn′)
　(soup; see bullion)
boul·der (bōl′ dẽr)
bou·le·vard (bōō′ lė·värd)
bounce (bouns)
　bounc·ing　bounc·er
bound·a·ry (boun′ dȧ·rĭ)
　-ries
bound·less (bound′ lĕs)
boun·te·ous (boun′ tė·ŭs)
boun·ty (boun′ tĭ)
　-ties

boun·ti·ful -ful·ly
bou·quet (bōō·kā')
bour·bon (bŏŏr' bŭn)
bour·geois (bŏŏr·zhwă')
  bour·geoi·sie (bŏŏr' zhwá' zē')
bou·ton·niere (bōō' tŏ·nyär')
bo·vine (bō' vĭn)
bowd·ler·ize (boud' lēr·ĭz)
  -iz·ing
Bow·doin (coll.) (bō' d'n)
bow·el (bou' ĕl)
bow·er (bou' ĕr)
bow·er·y (bou' ĕr·ĭ)
  -er·ies
bow·ie knife (bō' ĭ)
bow·knot (bō' nŏt')
bow·leg·ged (bō' lĕg' ĕd)
bowl·ing al·ley (bōl' ĭng)
bow·string (bō' strĭng')
box (bŏks)
  box·car   box eld·er
  box·ing glove   box kite
  box of·fice   box spring
boy·cott (boi' kŏt)
boy·sen·ber·ry (boi' s'n·bĕr' ĭ)
  -ber·ries
brace·let (brās' lĕt)
brac·ing (brās' ĭng)
brack·et (brăk' ĕt)
  -et·ed   -et·ing
brack·ish (brăk' ĭsh)
brag (brăg)
  brag·ging
  brag·ga·do·ci·o
    (brăg' à·dō' shĭ·ō)
  brag·gart
Brahms, Jo·han·nes
    (brämz, yō·hän' ĕs)
braid (brād)
Braille (brāl)
brain (brān)
  brain·i·ness   brain·less
  brain storm   brain·wash·ing
  brain·y
brake (brāk)
  (to slow down; see break)
  brak·ing   brake·man
bram·ble (brăm' b'l)
bran·dish (brăn' dĭsh)
brand-new (brănd' nū')
bran·dy (brăn' dĭ)
  -died
Bra·si·lia, (brà·zēl' yà)
  Bra·zil
bras·sière (brà·zēr')

brass·y (brăs' ĭ)
  brass·i·ness
bra·va·do (brà·vä' dō)
brav·er·y (brăv' ĕr·ĭ)
bra·vo (brä' vō)
  -voes
bra·vu·ra (brà·vū' rà)
brawl (brôl)
  brawl·er
brawn·y (brôn' ĭ)
  brawn·i·ness
bra·zen (brä' z'n)
  bra·zen·ness
Bra·zil·ian (brà·zĭl' yăn)
breach (brēch)
  (violation; see breech)
bread·bas·ket (brĕd' băs' kĕt)
breadth (brĕdth)
  (width)
break (brāk)
  (burst; see brake)
  break·a·ble   break·age (-ĭj)
  break·down   break·through
  break·up   break·wa·ter
break·fast (brĕk' făst)
breast·bone (brĕst' bōn')
breath (brĕth)
  breath·less   breath-tak·ing
breathe (brēth) v.
  breath·ing
breech (brēch)
  (rear; see breach)
breech·es (brĭch' ĕz)
breed·ing (brēd' ĭng)
breeze (brēz)
  breeze·way   breez·y
  breez·i·er   -i·est
  -i·ly   -i·ness
breth·ren (brĕth' rĕn)
bre·vet (brĕ·vĕt')
  -vet·ted   -vet·ting
bre·vi·ar·y (brē' vĭ·ĕr' ĭ)
  -ar·ies
brev·i·ty (brĕv' ĭ·tĭ)
brew·er·y (brōō' ĕr·ĭ)
  -er·ies
bribe (brĭb)
  brib·ing   brib·a·ble
  brib·er·y   -er·ies
bric-a-brac (brĭk' à·brăk')
brick (brĭk)
  brick·bat   brick·lay·er
  brick-red adj.   brick·yard
bride (brĭd)
  brid·al (of a wedding; see bridle)

bride·groom   brides·maid
bridge   (brĭj)
   bridg·ing   bridge·a·ble
   bridge·work
bri·dle   (brī′ d'l)
   (harness; see *bridal*)
   -dling   bri·dle path
brief   (brēf)
   brief case   brief·ly
bri·er   (brī′ ẽr)
brig   (brĭg)
bri·gade   (brĭ·gād′)
brig·a·dier   (brĭg′ á·dẽr′)
   gen·er·al
brig·and   (brĭg′ ănd)
bright   (brīt)
   bright·en   bright-eyed
Brigh·ton,   (brī′ t'n)
   Eng·land
bril·liance   (brĭl′ yăns)
brim   (brĭm)
   brimmed   brim·ming
   brim·ful   brim·stone
brine   (brīn)
   brin·ish   brin·y
bri·quet   (brĭ·kĕt′)
bris·ket   (brĭs′ kĕt)
bris·tle   (brĭs′ 'l)
   -tling
Bris·tol,   (brĭs′ t'l)
   Eng·land
Brit·ain   (brĭt′ 'n)
Brit·ish   (brĭt′ ĭsh)
Brit·on   (brĭt′ ŭn)
   (native of Britain)
Brit·ta·ny   (brĭt′ 'n·ĭ)
   (region of France)
brit·tle   (brĭt′ 'l)
   brit·tle·ness
broach   (brōch)
   (to utter first; see *brooch*)
broad   (brôd)
   broad·ax   broad·cast
   broad·cloth   broad·en·ing
   broad-gauge   broad jump
   broad-mind·ed   broad·side
   broad·sword   broad·tail
bro·cade   (brō·kād′)
broc·co·li   (brŏk′ ô·lĭ)
bro·chure   (brō·shŏŏr′)
brogue   (brōg)
broil   (broil)
   broil·er
bro·ken   (brō′ kĕn)
   bro·ken·heart·ed

bro·ker·age   (brō′ kẽr·ĭj)
bro·mide   (brō′ mĭd)
bron·chi·al   (brŏng′ kĭ·ăl)
   bron·chi·tis   (brŏn·kī′ tĭs)
   bron·chit·ic   (brŏn·kĭt′ ĭk)
bron·co·bust·er
            (brŏng′ kō·bŭs′ tẽr)
bron·to·sau·rus
            (brŏn′ tô·sô′ rŭs)
bronze   (brŏnz)
brooch   (brōch)
   (jewelry; see *broach*)
brood   (brōōd)
brook·let   (brŏŏk′ lĕt)
Brook·line,   (brŏŏk′ līn)
   Mass.
Brook·lyn,   (brŏŏk′ lĭn)
   N.Y.
broom·stick   (brōōm′ stĭk′)
broth   (brŏth)
broth·el   (brŏth′ ĕl)
broth·er   (brŭth′ ẽr)
   broth·er·hood   broth·er-in-law
   broth·ers-in-law
   broth·er·ly
brought   (brôt)
brow·beat   (brou′ bĕt′)
brown   (broun)
   brown Bet·ty   brown·ie
   brown·stone   brown sug·ar
browse   (brouz)
   brows·ing
bruise   (brōōz)
   bruis·ing
bru·nette   (brōō·nĕt′)
brush-off   (brŭsh′ ôf′)
brusque   (brŭsk)
   brusque·ly
Brus·sels,   (brŭs′ 'lz)
   Bel·gium
   Brus·sels lace
   Brus·sels sprouts
bru·tal   (brōō′ tăl)
   bru·tal·i·ty   (brōō·tăl′ ĭ tĭ)
   bru·tal·ize   -iz·ing
   bru·tal·ly
brute   (brōōt)
   brut·ish
Bryn Mawr   (brĭn′ mär′)
   (coll.)
bub·ble   (bŭb′ 'l)
   bub·bling   bub·ble gum
   bub·bly
bu·bon·ic   (bû·bŏn′ ĭk)
   plague

buc·ca·neer (bŭk′ å·nẽr′)
Bu·cha·rest, (boo′ kå·rĕst)
  Ro·ma·nia
buck (bŭk)
  buck·board   buck pri·vate
  buck·saw   buck·shot
  buck·skin   buck·tail
  buck·tooth   buck·wheat
buck·a·roo (bŭk′å·roo′)
buck·et (bŭk′ ĕt)
  buck·et·ful   buck·et seat
buck·le (bŭk′ ′l)
  -ling
buck·ram (bŭk′ răm)
bu·col·ic (bû·kŏl′ ĭk)
Bud·dha (bood′ å)
  Bud·dhism   Bud·dhist
budge (bŭj)
  budg·ing
budg·et (bŭj′ ĕt)
  -et·ed   -et·ing
  budg·et·ar·y
Bue·nos Ai·res, (bwā′ nŭs âr′ ĕz)
  Ar·gen·ti·na
buf·fa·lo (bŭf′ å·lō)
  -loes   buf·fa·lo fish
buff·er state (bŭf′ ẽr)
buf·fet (bŭf′ ĕt)
  (slap)
buf·fet (boo·fā′)
  (sideboard)
buf·foon·er·y (bŭ foon′ ẽr·ĭ)
  -er·ies
bug·a·boo (bŭg′ å·boo′)
bug·gy (bŭg′ ĭ)
  bug·gies
bu·gle (bû′ g′l)
  -gling   bu·gler
build (bĭld)
  build·ing   build-up
  built
bulb (bŭlb)
  bulb·ar (bŭl′ bẽr)
  bulb·ous
bulge (bŭlj)
  bulg·ing
bulk·head (bŭlk′ hĕd′)
bulk·y (bŭl′ kĭ)
  bulk·i·ness
bull (bool)
  bull·dog   bull·doz·er
  bull·fight   bull·finch
  bull·frog   bull·head·ed
  bull pen   bull's-eye
  bull ter·ri·er   bull·whip

bul·let (bool′ ĕt)
  bul·let·proof
bul·le·tin (bool′ ĕ·tĭn)
bul·lion (bool′ yŭn)
  (gold or silver; see bouillon)
bul·rush (bool′ rŭsh′)
bul·wark (bool′ wẽrk)
bum·ble·bee (bŭm′ b′l·bē′)
bump·kin (bŭmp′ kĭn)
bump·tious (bŭmp′ shŭs)
bun·dle (bŭn′ d′l)
  -dling
bun·ga·low (bŭng′ gå·lō)
bun·gle (bŭng′ g′l)
  -gling   bun·gler
bun·ion (bŭn′ yŭn)
bunk·house (bŭngk′ hous′)
Bun·sen burn·er
  (bŭn′ s′n)
bun·ting (bŭn′ tĭng)
buoy (boo′ ĭ)
  buoy·ant (boo′ yånt)
  -an·cy
bur (bûr)
  (weed; see burr)
bur·den (bûr′ d′n)
  bur·den·some
bu·reau (bû′ rō)
bu·reauc·ra·cy (bû·rŏk′ rå·sĭ)
  -cies
  bu·reau·crat·ic
  (bû′ rō·krăt′ ĭk)
bu·rette (bû·rĕt′)
bur·geon·ing (bûr′ jŭn·ĭng)
burgh·er (bûr′ gẽr)
bur·glar (bûr′ glẽr)
  bur·glar·ize   -iz·ing
  bur·gla·ry   -ries
bur·i·al (bĕr′ ĭ·ål)
bur·lap (bûr′ lăp)
bur·lesque (bûr·lĕsk′)
bur·ley (bûr′ lĭ)
  (tobacco)
bur·ly (bûr′ lĭ)
  (brawny)
  bur·li·ness
Bur·mese (bûr′ mēz′)
bur·nish (bûr′ nĭsh)
burnt (bûrnt)
burp (bûrp)
burr (bûr)
  (roughness or accent; see bur)
bur·ro (bûr′ ō)
  (donkey)
  bur·ros

bur·row (bûr′ ō)
  (to dig)
bur·sar (bûr′ sēr)
burst (bûrst)
bur·y (bĕr′ ĭ)
  bur·ied   bur·y·ing
  bur·i·al
bus (bŭs)
  bus·es   bus boy
bush·el (bŏŏsh′ ĕl)
  -eled   -el·ing
bush·y (bŏŏsh′ ĭ)
  bush·i·ness
busi·ness (bĭz′ nĕs)
  busi·ness·like   busi·ness·man
bus·tle (bŭs′ ′l)
  -tling
bus·y (bĭz′ ĭ)
  bus·ied   bus·y·ing
  bus·i·er, -i·est, -i·ly, -i·ness
  bus·y·bod·y
butch·er (bŏŏch′ ēr)
  butch·er·y
but (bŭt)
  (prep., conj.; see butt)
butt (bŭt)
  (end)
butte (bŭt)
  (hill)
but·ter (bŭt′ ēr)
  but·ter·cup   but·ter·fat
  but·ter·fin·gered
  but·ter·fly   -flies
  but·ter·milk   but·ter·scotch
but·tock (bŭt′ ŭk)
but·ton (bŭt′ ′n)
  but·ton·hole
but·tress (bŭt′ rĕs)
buy·er (bī′ ēr)
buz·zard (bŭz′ ērd)
by (bī)
  by-and-by   by·gone
  by·law   by-line
  by·name   by·pass
  by·path   by-prod·uct
  by·stand·er   by·street
  by·way   by·word
By·zan·tine (bī·zăn′ tĭn)

C

ca·bal (kȧ·băl′)
  cab·a·lis·tic (kăb′ ȧ·lĭs′ tĭc)
cab·a·ret (kăb′ ȧ·rā′)

cab·bage (kăb′ ĭj)
cab·in (kăb′ ĭn)
  cab·in class   cab·in cruis·er
cab·i·net (kăb′ ĭ·nĕt)
  cab·i·net·mak·er
ca·ble (kā′ b′l)
  -bling   ca·ble car
  ca·ble·gram
ca·boose (kȧ·bōōs′)
cache (kăsh)
ca·chet (kă·shā′)
cack·le (kăk′ ′l)
  -ling
ca·coph·o·ny (kȧ·kŏf′ ō·nĭ)
cac·tus (kăk′ tŭs)
  pl. cac·ti (-tī)
ca·dav·er (kȧ·dăv′ ēr)
  ca·dav·er·ous
cad·die (kăd′ ĭ)
  cad·died   cad·dy·ing
cad·dish (kăd′ ĭsh)
ca·dence (kā′ dĕns)
  -dent
ca·det (kȧ·dĕt′)
Cad·il·lac (kăd′ ′l·ăk)
Cae·sar·e·an (sē·zâr′ ē·ȧn)
  (also spelled Cesarean)
ca·fé (kȧ′ fā′)
caf·e·te·ri·a (kăf′ ē·tēr′ ĭ·ȧ)
caf·fe·ine (kăf′ ē·ĭn)
cage·y (kāj′ ĭ)
  cag·i·ness
Cai·ro, E·gypt (kī′ rō)
Cai·ro, Ill. (kâr′ ō)
cais·son (kā′ sŭn)
ca·jole (kȧ·jōl′)
  -jol·ing   ca·jole·ment
  ca·jol·er·y
cake (kāk)
  cake·box   cake pan
  cake·walk
cal·a·boose (kăl′ ȧ·bōōs)
cal·a·mine (kăl′ ȧ·mīn)
ca·lam·i·ty (kȧ·lăm′ ĭ·tĭ)
  -ties   ca·lam·i·tous
cal·ci·fy (kăl′ sĭ·fī)
  -fied   -fy·ing
  cal·ci·fi·ca·tion
           (kăl′ sĭ·fĭ·kā′ shŭn)
cal·ci·mine (kăl′ sĭ·mĭn)
cal·ci·um (kăl′ sĭ·ŭm)
cal·cu·late (kăl′ kū·lāt)
  -lat·ing   cal·cu·la·ble
  cal·cu·la·tion (kăl′ kū·lā′ shŭn)
  cal·cu·la·tor

cal·cu·lus (kăl′ kû·lŭs)
  pl. cal·cu·li (-lī)
Cal·cut·ta, (kăl·kŭt′ á)
  In·di·a
cal·dron (kôl′ drŭn)
cal·en·dar (kăl′ ĕn·dĕr)
calf (kăf)
  calves calf·skin
Cal·ga·ry, (kăl′ gá·rĭ)
  Can.
cal·i·ber (kăl′ ĭ·bĕr)
cal·i·co (kăl′ ĭ·kō)
  -coes
Cal·i·for·nia (kăl′ ĭ·fôrn′ yá)
  abbr. Calif. *or* Cal.
  Cal·i·for·nian
ca·liph (kā′ lĭf)
cal·is·then·ics (kăl′ ĭs·thĕn′ ĭks)
calk (kôk)
cal·lig·ra·phy (ká·lĭg′ rá·fĭ)
cal·lous (kăl′ ŭs) *adj.*
  (unfeeling)
cal·low (kăl′ ō)
cal·lus (kăl′ ŭs) s.
  (thickened skin)
calm (kăm)
  calm·ly
cal·o·rie (kăl′ ô·rĭ)
ca·lor·ic (ká·lŏr′ ĭk)
cal·um·ny (kăl′ ŭm·nĭ)
  -nies
Cal·va·ry (kăl′ vá·rĭ)
Cal·vin·ist (kăl′ vĭn·ĭst)
ca·lyp·so (ká·lĭp′ sō)
ca·ma·ra·de·rie
  (kä′ má·rä′ dĕ·rē)
cam·el (kăm′ ĕl)
ca·mel·li·a (ká·mĕl′ ĭ·á)
cam·e·o (kăm′ ĕ·ō)
cam·er·a (kăm′ ĕr·á)
cam·i·sole (kăm′ ĭ·sōl)
cam·o·mile tea (kăm′ ô·mīl)
cam·ou·flage (kăm′ ŏŏ·fläsh)
  -flag·ing
cam·paign (kăm·pān′)
camp·fire (kămp′ fīr′)
cam·phor (kăm′ fĕr)
  cam·phor·at·ed
cam·pus (kăm′ pŭs)
Can·a·da (kăn′ á·dá)
  Ca·na·di·an (ká·nā′ dĭ·ăn)
ca·nal (ká·năl′)
  -nalled -nal·ling
  ca·nal·boat

can·a·pé (kăn′ á·pā)
ca·nard (ká·närd′)
ca·nar·y (ká·nâr′ ĭ)
  -nar·ies
ca·nas·ta (ká·năs′ tá)
Ca·nav·er·al, (ká·năv′ ĕr·ál)
  Cape
Can·ber·ra, (kăn′ bĕr·á)
  Aus·tra·lia
can·can (kăn′ kăn)
can·cel (kăn′ sĕl)
  -celed -cel·ing
  can·cel·er
  can·cel·la·tion (kăn′ sĕ·lā′ shŭn)
can·cer (kăn′ sĕr)
  can·cer·ous
can·de·la·brum
  (kăn′ dĕ·lä′ brŭm)
  pl. can·de·la·bra
can·des·cence (kăn·dĕs′ ĕns)
  -cent
can·did (kăn′ dĭd)
can·di·date (kăn′ dĭ·dāt)
  can·di·da·cy (kăn′ dĭ·dá·sĭ)
  can·di·da·ture (kăn′ dĭ·dá·tûr)
can·died (kăn′ dĭd)
can·dle (kăn′ d′l)
  can·dle·light can·dle pow·er
  can·dle·stick
  can·dle·wick bed·spread
can·dor (kăn′ dĕr)
can·dy (kăn′ dĭ)
  -dies, -died, -dy·ing
ca·nine (kā′ nīn)
can·is·ter (kăn′ ĭs·tĕr)
can·ker (kăng′ kĕr)
  can·ker·ous can·ker sore
  can·ker·worm
can·ner·y (kăn′ ĕr·ĭ)
  can·ner·ies
Cannes, France (kăn)
can·ni·bal (kăn′ ĭ·băl)
  can·ni·bal·ism
  can·ni·bal·is·tic
  (kăn′ ĭ·băl·ĭs′ tĭk)
can·ning (kăn′ ĭng)
can·non (kăn′ ŭn)
  (gun; see *canon*)
  can·non·ade (kăn′ ŭn·ād′)
  can·non ball
  can·non·eer (kăn′ ŭn·ĕr′)
can·not (kăn′ nŏt)
can·ny (kăn′ ĭ)
  can·ni·ness

ca·noe   (ká·nōō′)
  -noed   -noe·ing
  ca·noe·ist
can·on   (kăn′ ŭn)
  (decree; see *cannon*)
  ca·non·i·cal   (ká·nŏn′ ĭ·kál)
  ca·non·ize   -iz·ing
  can·on law
can·o·py   (kăn′ ŏ·pĭ)
  -pies
can't   (kănt)
can·ta·loupe   (kăn′ tá·lōp)
can·tan·ker·ous
                  (kăn·tăng′ kĕr·ŭs)
can·ta·ta   (kán·tä′ tá)
can·teen   (kăn·tēn′)
can·ter   (kăn′ tĕr)
  (light gallop; see *cantor*)
Can·ter·bur·y   (kăn′ tĕr·bĕr·ĭ)
can·ti·cle   (kăn′ tĭ·k'l)
can·ti·le·ver   (kăn′ tĭ·lĕ′ vĕr)
can·to   (kăn′ tō)
  -tos
can·ton   (kăn′ tŏn)
Can·ton·ese   (kăn′ tŏn·ēz′)
can·tor   (kăn′ tōr)
  (singer; see *canter*)
can·vas   (kăn′ vás)
  (cloth)
  can·vas·back duck
can·vass   (kăn′ vás)
  (to solicit)   can·vass·er
can·yon   (kăn′ yŭn)
ca·pa·ble   (kā′ pá·b'l)
  -bly
  ca·pa·bil·i·ty (kā′ pá·bĭl′ ĭ·tĭ)
ca·pa·cious   (ká·pā′ shŭs)
ca·pac·i·ty   (ká·păs′ ĭ·tĭ)
  -ties
ca·per   (kā′ pĕr)
cape·skin   (kāp′ skĭn′)
cap·il·lar·y   (kăp′ ĭ·lĕr′ ĭ)
  -il·lar·ies
cap·i·tal   (kăp′ ĭ·tál)
  (property)
  cap·i·tal cit·y
  cap·i·tal goods
  cap·i·tal·ism   -ist
  cap·i·tal·i·za·tion
                  (kăp′ ĭ·tál·ĭ·zā′ shŭn)
  cap·i·tal·ize   -iz·ing
  cap·i·tal lev·y
  cap·i·tal stock
cap·i·tol   (kăp′ ĭ·tŏl)
  (statehouse)

ca·pit·u·late   (ká·pĭt′ û·lāt)
  -lat·ing
  ca·pit·u·la·tion
                  (ká·pĭt′ û·lā′ shŭn)
ca·pon   (kā′ pŏn)
ca·price   (ká·prēs′)
  ca·pri·cious   (ká·prĭsh′ ŭs)
cap·size   (kăp·sīz′)
  -siz·ing
cap·sule   (kăp′ sŭl)
cap·tain   (kăp′ tĭn)
  cap·tain·cy
cap·tion   (kăp′ shŭn)
cap·tious   (kăp′ shŭs)
cap·ti·vate   (kăp′ tĭ·vāt)
  -vat·ing
  cap·ti·va·tion
                  (kăp′ tĭ·vā′ shŭn)
  cap·ti·va·tor
cap·tive   (kăp′ tĭv)
  cap·tiv·i·ty   (kăp·tĭv′ ĭ·tĭ)
cap·tor   (kăp′ tĕr)
cap·ture   (kăp′ tûr)
  -tur·ing
car·a·mel   (kăr′ á·mĕl)
car·at   (kăr′ ăt)
  (unit of weight; see *caret*, *carrot*)
car·a·van   (kăr′ á·văn)
car·a·way seeds   (kăr′ á·wā)
car·bide   (kär′ bĭd)
car·bine   (kär′ bĭn)
car·bo·hy·drate   (kär′ bō·hī′ drāt)
car·bol·ic ac·id (kär·bŏl′ ĭk)
car·bon   (kär′ bŏn)
  car·bo·na·ceous
                  (kär′ bō·nā′ shŭs)
  car·bo·nat·ed
  car·bon·a·tion
                  (kär′ bŏn·ā′ shŭn)
  car·bon bi·sul·fide
  car·bon black
  car·bon cop·y
  car·bon di·ox·ide
  car·bon di·sul·fide
  car·bon·ic   (kär·bŏn′ ĭk)
  car·bon·if·er·ous
                  (kär′ bŏn·ĭf′ ĕr·ŭs)
  car·bon mon·ox·ide
  car·bon pa·per
  car·bon proc·ess
  car·bon tet·ra·chlo·ride
car·bun·cle   (kär′ bŭng·k'l)
car·bu·ret·or   (kär′ bû·rā′ tĕr)
car·cass   (kär′ kás)
  -cass·es

car·ci·no·ma (kär′ sĭ·nō′ má)
  pl. car·ci·no·ma·ta (-má·tá)
car·da·mom (kär′ dá·mŭm)
card·board (kärd′ bōrd′)
car·di·ac (kär′ dĭ′·ăk)
car·di·gan (kär′ dĭ·găn)
car·di·nal (kär′ dĭ·nȧl)
oar·di·o·gram (kär′ dĭ·ȯ·grăm′)
  car·di·o·graph
  car·di·ol·o·gy (kär′ dĭ·ŏl′ ȯ·jĭ)
card·sharp (kärd′ shärp′)
care (kâr)
  car·ing   care·free
  care·ful, -ful·ly, -ful·ness
  care·less   -less·ly
  care·tak·er   care·worn
ca·reen (ká·rēn′)
  -reen·ing
ca·reer (ká·rēr′)
ca·ress (ká·rĕs′)
  ca·ress·ing·ly
car·et (kăr′ ĕt)
  (proofreaders′ mark; see *carat,*
  carrot)
car·go (kär′ gō)
  -goes
Car·ib·be·an (kär′ ĭ·bē′ ȧn)
  (sea)
car·i·bou (kär′ ĭ·bōō)
  n. sing. & pl.
car·i·ca·ture (kär′ ĭ·ká·tụ̆r)
car·i·es (kâr′ ĭ·ēz)
  (tooth decay)
car·il·lon (kär′ ĭ·lŏn)
car·mine (kär′ mĭn)
car·nage (kär′ nĭj)
car·nal (kär′ nȧl)
  car·nal·i·ty (kär·năl′ ĭ·tĭ)
  car·nal·ly
car·na·tion (kär·nā′ shŭn)
car·ni·val (kär′ nĭ·vȧl)
car·ni·vore (kär′ nĭ·vōr)
  car·niv·o·rous (kär·nĭv′ ȯ·rŭs)
car·ol (kär′ ŭl)
  -oled   -ol·ing
car·om shot (kär′ ŭm)
ca·rous·al (ká·rouz′ ȧl)
  (drunken revel; see *carrousel*)
  ca·rouse   -rous·ing
car·pen·ter (kär′ pĕn·tĕr)
  car·pen·try
car·pet (kär′ pĕt)
  -pet·ed   -pet·ing
  car·pet·bag·ger
  car·pet bee·tle

carp·ing (kär′ pĭng)
car·port (kär′ pōrt′)
car·riage (kär′ ĭj)
car·ri·er pi·geon
        (kär′ ĭ·ĕr)
car·ri·on (kär′ ĭ·ŭn)
car·rot (kär′ ŭt)
  (vegetable; see *carat, caret*)
car·rou·sel (kär′ ŏŏ·zĕl′)
  (merry-go-round; see *carousal*)
car·ry (kär′ ĭ)
  car·ried   car·ry·ing
  car·ri·er   car·ry·all
  car·ry·o·ver
cart·age (kär′ tĭj)
carte blanche (kärt′ blänsh′)
car·tel (kär·tĕl′)
Car·te·sian (kär·tē′ zhȧn)
car·ti·lage (kär′ tĭ·lĭj)
  car·ti·lag·i·nous
      (kär′ tĭ·lăj′ ĭ·nŭs)
car·tog·ra·phy (kär·tŏg′ rá·fĭ)
  car·to·graph·i·cal
      (kär′ tȯ·grăf′ ĭ·kȧl)
car·ton (kär′ tŏn)
  (box)
car·toon (kär·tōōn′)
  (drawing)   car·toon·ist
car·tridge (kär′ trĭj)
ca·sa·ba mel·on
        (ká·sä′ bá)
Cas·a·blan·ca, (kăs′ á·blăng′ ká)
  Mo·roc·co
cas·cade (kăs·kād′)
  -cad·ing
cas·car·a (kăs·kâr′ á)
ca·se·in (kā′ sē·ĭn)
case·ment (kās′ mĕnt)
case·work·er (kās′ wûrk′ ĕr)
cash (kăsh)
  n. sing. & pl.
  cash·book
  cash reg·is·ter
ca·shew nut (ká·shōō′)
cash·ier (kăsh·ēr′)
  cash·ier′s check
cash·mere (kăsh′ mẽr)
ca·si·no (ká·sē′ nō)
  (gambling place; see *cassino*)
  -nos
cas·ket (kăs′ kĕt)
Cas·san·dra (kȧ·săn′ drȧ)
cas·se·role (kăs′ ĕ·rōl)
cas·si·a (kăsh′ ĭ·á)

cas·si·no (kȧ·sē′ nō)
  (card game; see *casino*)
Cas·si·o·pe·ia's Chair
                (kăs′ ĭ·ō·pē′ yȧz)
cas·sock (kăs′ ŭk)
cast (kȧst)
  (throw; see *caste*)
cas·ta·net (kăs′ tȧ·nĕt′)
cast·a·way (kȧst′ ȧ·wā′)
caste (kȧst)
  (social class; see *cast*)
cast·er (kȧs′ tẽr)
  (wheel; see *castor*)
cas·ti·gate (kăs′ tĭ·gāt)
  -gat·ing
  cas·ti·ga·tion (kăs′ tĭ·gā′ shŭn)
  cas·ti·ga·tor
cas·tile soap (kăs′ tēl)
cas·tle (kăs′ 'l)
cast·off (kȧst′ ôf′)
cas·tor (kȧs′ tẽr)
  (oil; see *caster*)
cas·trate (kăs′ trāt)
  -trat·ing
  cas·tra·tion (kăs·trā′ shŭn)
Cas·tro, Fi·del (kăs′ trō)
cas·u·al (kăzh′ ū·ȧl)
  cas·u·al·ly cas·u·al·ness
cas·u·al·ty (kăzh′ ū·ȧl·tĭ)
  -ties
cas·u·ist (kăzh′ ū·ĭst)
  cas·u·ist·ry (kăzh′ ū·ĭs·trĭ)
cat (kăt)
  cat·bird cat·boat
  cat·call cat·fish
  cat·gut cat nap
  cat·nip cat-o′-nine-tails
  cat's-eye cat's-paw
  cat·tail cat·walk
cat·a·clysm (kăt′ ȧ·klĭz′m)
  cat·a·clys·mal (kăt′ ȧ·klĭz′ mȧl)
  cat·a·clys·mic (kăt′ ȧ·klĭz′ mĭk)
cat·a·comb (kăt′ ȧ·kōm)
cat·a·lep·sy (kăt′ ȧ·lĕp′ sĭ)
  cat·a·lep·tic (kăt′ ȧ·lĕp′ tĭk)
cat·a·log (kăt′ ȧ·lŏg)
  -loged -log·ing
  cat·a·log·er cat·a·log·ist
ca·tal·pa (kȧ·tăl′ pȧ)
cat·a·lyst (kăt′ ȧ·lĭst)
cat·a·ma·ran (kăt′ ȧ·mȧ·răn′)
cat·a·pult (kăt′ ȧ·pŭlt)
cat·a·ract (kăt′ ȧ·răkt)
  (waterfall, eye defect)
ca·tarrh (kȧ·tär′)

ca·tas·tro·phe (kȧ·tăs′ trō·fē)
  cat·a·stroph·ic (kăt′ ȧ·strŏf′ ĭk)
cat·a·ton·ic (kăt′ ȧ·tŏn′ ĭk)
Ca·taw·ba (kȧ·tô′ bȧ)
catch (kăch)
  catch·all catch·er
  catch·ment catch·word
  catch·y
cat·e·chism (kăt′ ê·kĭz′m)
cat·e·chize (kăt′ ê·kīz)
  -chiz·ing
cat·e·chu·men (kăt′ ê·kū′ mĕn)
cat·e·go·ry (kăt′ ê·gō′ rĭ)
  -ries
cat·e·go·ri·cal
                (kăt·ê·gŏr′ ĭ·kȧl)
  -cal·ly
ca·ter (kā′ tẽr)
  -tered -ter·ing
  ca·ter·er ca·ter·ess
cat·er-cor·nered
                (kăt′ ẽr·kôr′ nẽrd)
cat·er·pil·lar (kăt′ ẽr·pĭl′ ẽr)
ca·thar·sis (kȧ·thär′ sĭs)
  ca·thar·tic
ca·the·dral (kȧ·thē′ drȧl)
cath·e·ter (kăth′ ê·tẽr)
  cath·e·ter·ize -iz·ing
ca·thex·is (kȧ·thĕk′ sĭs)
  ca·thec·tic (kȧ·thĕk′ tĭk)
cath·ode (kăth′ ōd)
cath·o·lic (kăth′ ô·lĭk)
  (universal)
  ca·tho·lic·i·ty (kăth′ ô·lĭs′ ĭ·tĭ)
Cath·o·lic (kăth′ ô·lĭk)
  (church)
  Ca·thol·i·cism
                (kȧ·thŏl′ ĭ·sĭz′m)
cat·sup (kăt′ sŭp)
cat·tle (kăt′ 'l)
  cat·tle·man
cat·ty (kăt′ ĭ)
  cat·ti·ly cat·ti·ness
Cau·ca·sian (kô·kā′ zhȧn)
cau·cus (kô′ kŭs)
  -cused -cus·ing
cau·dal (kô′ dȧl)
caught (kôt)
cau·li·flow·er (kô′ lĭ·flou′ ẽr)
caus·al (kôz′ ȧl)
  cau·sal·i·ty (kô·zăl′ ĭ·tĭ)
  caus·al·ly
cause (kôz)
  caus·ing caus·a·ble
  cau·sa·tion (kô·sā′ shŭn)

caus·a·tive (kôz′ a·tĭv)
cause·less cause·way
caus·tic (kôs′ tĭk)
cau·ter·ize (kô′ tẽr·īz)
-iz·ing
cau·tion (kô′ shŭn)
cau·tion·ar·y (kô′ shŭn·ẽr′ ĭ)
cau·tious (kô′ shŭs)
cav·al·cade (kăv′ ăl·kād′)
cav·a·lier (kăv′ a·lẽr′)
cav·al·ry·man (kăv′ ăl·rĭ·măn)
cave (kăv)
cav·ing cave-in
cave man
cav·ern (kăv′ ẽrn)
cav·ern·ous
cav·i·ar (kăv′ ĭ·är)
cav·il (kăv′ ĭl)
-iled -il·ing
cav·i·ty (kăv′ ĭ·tĭ)
-ties
ca·vort (ka·vôrt′)
cay·enne pep·per
(kī·ĕn′)
cease (sēs)
ceas·ing cease·less
ce·dar (sē′ dẽr)
cede (sēd)
(yield)
ced·ing
ces·sion (sĕsh′ ŭn)
ceil·ing (sēl′ ĭng)
Cel·a·nese (sĕl′ a·nēs)
cel·e·brate (sĕl′ ê·brāt)
-brat·ing cel·e·brant
cel·e·bra·tion (sĕl′ ê·brā′ shŭn)
cel·e·bra·tor
ce·leb·ri·ty (sê·lĕb′ rĭ·tĭ)
-ties
ce·ler·i·ty (sê·lĕr′ ĭ·tĭ)
cel·er·y (sĕl′ ẽr·ĭ)
ce·les·tial (sê·lĕs′ chăl)
cel·i·bate (sĕl′ ĭ·bât)
cel·i·ba·cy (sĕl′ ĭ·ba·sĭ)
cel·lar (sĕl′ ẽr)
cel·lo (chĕl′ ō)
cel·list
cel·lo·phane (sĕl′ ō·fān)
cel·lu·lar (sĕl′ û·lẽr)
cel·lu·loid (sĕl′ û·loid)
cel·lu·lose (sĕl′ û·lōs)
ce·ment (sê·mĕnt′)
ce·ment·er
cem·e·ter·y (sĕm′ ê·tẽr′ ĭ)
-ter·ies

cen·sor (sĕn′ sẽr)
(examiner)
cen·so·ri·al (sĕn·sō′ rĭ·ăl)
cen·so·ri·ous (sĕn·sō′ rĭ·ŭs)
cen·sor·ship
cen·sure (sĕn′ shẽr)
(criticize)
-sur·ing
cen·sur·a·bil·i·ty
(sĕn′ shẽr·a·bĭl′ ĭ·tĭ)
cen·sur·a·ble
cen·sus (sĕn′ sŭs)
cen·taur (sĕn′ tôr)
cen·te·nar·y (sĕn′ tê·nẽr′ ĭ)
cen·te·nar·i·an
(sĕn′ tê·nâr′ ĭ·ăn)
cen·ten·ni·al (sĕn·tĕn′ ĭ·ăl)
cen·ter (sĕn′ tẽr)
cen·ter·piece
cen·ti- (sĕn′ tĭ-)
cen·ti·grade cen·ti·gram
cen·ti·me·ter cen·ti·pede
cen·tral (sĕn′ trăl)
cen·tral·i·za·tion
(sĕn′ trăl·ĭ·zā′ shŭn)
cen·tral·ize -iz·ing
cen·tral·ly
cen·trif·u·gal (sĕn·trĭf′ û·găl)
(going away from center)
cen·trip·e·tal (sĕn·trĭp′ ê·tăl)
(going toward center)
cen·tu·ri·on (sĕn·tū′ rĭ·ŭn)
cen·tu·ry (sĕn′ tû·rĭ)
-ries
ce·phal·ic (sê·făl′ ĭk)
ce·ram·ics (sê·răm′ ĭks)
ce·re·al (sẽr′ ê·ăl)
(grain; see serial)
cer·e·bel·lum (sẽr′ ê·bĕl′ ŭm)
cer·e·bral pal·sy
(sẽr′ ê·brăl)
cer·e·brum (sẽr′ ê·brŭm)
cer·e·mo·ny (sẽr′ ê·mō′ nĭ)
-nies
cer·e·mo·ni·al (sẽr′ ê·mō′ nĭ·ăl)
cer·e·mo·ni·ous
(sẽr′ ê·mō′ nĭ·ŭs)
ce·rise (sê·rēz′)
cer·tain (sûr′ tĭn)
cer·tain·ly cer·tain·ty, -ties
cer·tif·i·cate (sẽr·tĭf′ ĭ·kĭt)
cer·ti·fy (sûr′ tĭ·fĭ)
-fied -fy·ing
cer·ti·fi·a·ble (sûr′ tĭ·fĭ′ a·b'l)

cer·ti·fi·ca·tion
      (sûr′ tĭ·fĭ·kā′ shŭn)
cer·ti·fi·er
cer·ti·o·ra·ri   (sûr′ shĭ·ô·rā′ rĭ)
cer·ti·tude   (sûr′ tĭ·tūd)
ce·ru·le·an   (sĕ·rōō′ lê·ăn)
cer·vix   (sûr′ vĭks)
  pl. cer·vi·ces   (sûr·vī′ sēz)
cer·vi·cal
Ce·sar·e·an   (sĕ·zâr′ ê·ăn)
ces·sa·tion   (sĕ·sā′ shŭn)
  (a stop)
ces·sion   (sĕsh′ ŭn)
  (yielding; see session)
cess·pool   (sĕs′ pōōl′)
Cey·lon   (sĕ·lŏn′)
Cé·zanne, Paul   (sā′ zán′)
Cha·blis wine   (shä′ blē′)
chafe   (chāf)
  chaf·ing
chaff   (cháf)
cha·grin   (shá·grĭn′)
  -grined   -grin·ing
chain   (chān)
  chain gang   chain let·ter
  chain mail
  chain-re·act·ing pile
  chain re·ac·tion
  chain re·ac·tor
  chain stitch   chain store
chair·man   (châr′ mán)
  chair·man·ship
  chair·wom·an
chaise longue   (shāz′ lôŋg′)
chal·ced·o·ny   (kăl·sĕd′ ô·nĭ)
cha·let   (shă·lā′)
chal·ice   (chăl′ ĭs)
chalk   (chôk)
  chalk·stone   chalk·y
chal·lenge   (chăl′ ĕnj)
  chal·leng·ing   chal·lenge·a·ble
  chal·leng·er
chal·lis   (shăl′ ĭ)
cham·ber   (chăm′ bĕr)
  cham·ber con·cert
  cham·ber·maid
  cham·ber mu·sic
  cham·ber of com·merce
cham·ber·lain   (chăm′ bĕr·lĭn)
cham·bray   (shăm′ brā)
cha·me·le·on   (ká·mē′ lê·ŭn)
cham·fer   (chăm′ fĕr)
cham·ois   (shăm′ ĭ)
  n. sing. & pl.
cham·pagne   (shăm·pān′)

Cham·paign, Ill.   (shăm·pān′)
cham·pi·on   (chăm′ pĭ·ŭn)
  cham·pi·on·ship
Cham·plain,   (shăm·plān′)
  Lake, N.Y.
Champs É·ly·sées
      (shän′ -sā′ lē′ zā′)
chance   (cháns)
  chanc·ing   chance·ful
  chanc·y   chanc·i·ness
chan·cel   (chán′ sĕl)
chan·cel·lor   (chán′ sĕ·lĕr)
  chan·cel·ler·y   -cel·ler·ies
  chan·cel·lor of the ex·cheq·uer
chan·cer·y   (chán′ sĕr·ĭ)
  -cer·ies
chan·de·lier   (shăn′ dĕ·lĕr′)
change   (chānj)
  chang·ing
  change·a·bil·i·ty
  change·a·ble   change·ful
  change·less   change·ling
chan·nel   (chăn′ ĕl)
  chan·neled   chan·nel·ing
chan·teuse   (shän′ tûz′)
chant·ey   (shán′ tĭ)
  -eys
chan·ti·cleer   (chăn′ tĭ·klĕr)
cha·os   (kā′ ŏs)
cha·ot·ic   (ká·ŏt′ ĭk)
chap·ar·ral   (shăp′ ă·răl′)
cha·peau   (shá′ pō′)
  pl. cha·peaux   (-pōz′)
chap·el   (chăp′ ĕl)
chap·er·on   (shăp′ ĕr·ŏn)
  chap·er·on·age
chap·lain   (chăp′ lĭn)
  chap·lain·cy
chap·ter   (chăp′ tĕr)
char·ac·ter   (kăr′ ăk·tĕr)
  char·ac·ter·is·tic
      (kăr′ ăk·tĕr·ĭs′ tĭk)
  -ti·cal·ly
  char·ac·ter·i·za·tion
      (kăr′ ăk·tĕr·ĭ·zā′ shŭn)
  char·ac·ter·ize   -iz·ing
cha·rade   (shá·rād′)
char·coal   (chär′ kŏl′)
charge   (chärj)
  charg·ing   charge·a·ble
char·gé d'af·faires
      (shär′ zhā′ dá·fâr′)
char·i·ot   (chăr′ ĭ·ŭt)
char·i·ot·eer   (chăr′ ĭ·ŭt·ēr′)
cha·ris·ma   (ká·rĭz′ má)

char·is·mat·ic (kăr′ ĭz·măt′ ĭk)
char·i·ty (chăr′ ĭ·tĭ)
  -ties   char·i·ta·ble
  char·i·ta·ble·ness
cha·ri·va·ri (shä′ rĕ·vä′ rĕ or shĭv′ á·rē)
char·la·tan (shär′ lá·tăn)
  char·la·tan·ry
Char·le·magne (shär′ lĕ·män)
Char·ley horse (chär′ lĭ)
char·lotte russe (shär′ lŏt rōōs′)
charm·ing (chärm′ ĭng)
char·nel (chär′ nĕl)
char·ter (chär′ tēr)
char·treuse (shär·trōōz′)
char·wom·an (chär′ wŏŏm′ ăn)
char·y (chăr′ ĭ)
  char·i·ly
chasm (kăz′m)
chas·sis (shăs′ ĭ)
  pl. chas·sis (shăs′ ĭz)
chaste (chăst)
  chaste·ly
  chas·ten (chăs′ ′n)
chas·tise (chăs·tīz′)
  -tis·ing
  chas·tise·ment (chăs′ tĭz·mĕnt)
chas·ti·ty (chăs′ tĭ·tĭ)
châ·teau (shă·tō′)
  pl. châ·teaux (-tōz′)
chat·e·laine (shăt′ ĕ·lān)
Chat·ta·noo·ga, (chăt′ á·nōō′ gá)
  Tenn.
chat·tel mort·gage (chăt′ ′l)
chat·ter·box (chăt′ ēr·bŏks′)
chat·ty (chăt′ĭ)
  chat·ti·ness
chauf·feur (shō·fûr′)
chau·vin·ism (shō′ vĭn·ĭz′m)
  chau·vin·is·tic (shō′ vĭn·ĭs′ tĭk)
cheap (chēp)
  cheap·en   cheap·skate
cheat·er (chēt′ ēr)
check (chĕk)
  check·book   check·mate
  check·room
check·er (chĕk′ ēr)
  check·er·board
  check·ered
Ched·dar cheese (chĕd′ ēr)
cheek (chēk)
cheer (chēr)
  cheer·ful, -ful·ly, -ful·ness

cheer·y   cheer·i·er
  -i·est, -i·ly, -i·ness
cheese (chēz)
  cheese·cake   cheese·cloth
  chees·y
chee·tah (chē′ tá)
chef (shĕf)
chef·-d′oeu·vre (shĕ′ dŭ′ vr′)
Che·khov, An·ton (chĕ′ xŭf)
chem·i·cal (kĕm′ ĭ·kál)
  chem·i·cal·ly
che·mise (shĕ·mēz′)
chem·ist (kĕm′ ĭst)
  chem·is·try
che·nille (shĕ·nĕl′)
cher·chez la femme (shĕr′ shā′ lá fäm′)
cher·ish (chĕr′ ĭsh)
Cher·o·kee (chĕr′ ō·kē′)
che·root (shĕ·rōōt′)
cher·ry (chĕr′ ĭ)
  cher·ries
cher·ub (chĕr′ ŭb)
  che·ru·bic (chĕ·rōō′ bĭk)
  pl. cher·u·bim or cher·ubs
cher·vil (chûr′ vĭl)
Ches·a·peake (bay) (chĕs′ á·pēk)
Chesh·ire cat (chĕsh′ ēr)
chess·board (chĕs′ bŏrd′)
ches·ter·field coat (chĕs′ tēr·fēld)
chest·nut (chĕs′ nŭt)
chev·a·lier (shĕv′ á·lēr′)
chev·ron (shĕv′ rŭn)
Chey·enne, Wyo. (shī·ĕn′)
Chi·an·ti wine (kĭ·ăn′ tĭ)
chic (shēk)
  chic·quer   -quest
chi·can·er·y (shĭ·kăn′ ēr·ĭ)
chick·a·dee (chĭk′ á·dē)
chick·en (chĭk′ ĕn)
  chick·en·heart·ed
  chick·en pox
chick·pea (chĭk′ pē′)
chic·le (chĭk′ ′l)
chic·o·ry (chĭk′ ō·rĭ)
chide (chīd)
  chid·ing
chief (chēf)
  chief·ly
  chief·tain (chēf′ tĭn)
  chief·tain·cy

chif·fon	(shĭ·fŏn´)
chif·fo·nier	(shĭf´ ô·nẽr´)
chig·ger	(chĭg´ ẽr)
chi·gnon	(shēn´ yŏn)
Chi·hua·hua	(chè·wä´ wä)
chil·blain	(chĭl´ blān´)
child	(chīld)
child·bear·ing	child·birth
child·hood	child·like
chil·dren	(chĭl´ drĕn)
Chil·e	(chĭl´ è)
Chil·e·an	(chĭl´ è·ăn)
chil·i	(chĭl´ ĭ)
chil·i con car·ne	
	(chĭl´ ĭ kŏn kär´ nè)
chil·i sauce	
chill·y	(chĭl´ ĭ)
chill·i·ness	
chime	(chīm)
chim·ing	
chi·me·ra	(kĭ·mẽr´ å)
chi·mer·i·cal	(kĭ·mẽr´ ĭ·kål)
chim·ney	(chĭm´ nĭ)
-neys	
chim·pan·zee	(chĭm´ păn·zē´)
chi·na	(chī´ nå)
chi·na·ber·ry	Chi·na·town
chi·na·ware	
chinch bug	(chĭnch)
chin·chil·la	(chĭn·chĭl´ å)
Chi·nese	(chī´ nēz´)
Chi·nook	(shĭ·nŏŏk´)
chintz	(chĭnts)
chip·munk	(chĭp´ mŭngk)
Chip·pen·dale	(chĭp´ ĕn·dāl)
Chip·pe·wa	(chĭp´ ĕ·wä)
chi·rop·o·dy	(kĭ·rŏp´ ô·dĭ)
chi·rop·o·dist	
chi·ro·prac·tor	(kī´ rô·prăk´ tẽr)
chi·ro·prac·tic	(kī´ rô·prăk´ tĭk)
chis·el	(chĭz´ ´l)
-eled	-el·ing
chis·el·er	
chi-square	(kī´ skwâr´)
chit·chat	(chĭt´ chăt´)
chat·ted	chat·ting
chit·ter·lings	(chĭt´ ẽr·lĭngz)
chiv·al·ry	(shĭv´ ål·rĭ)
chiv·al·ric	chiv·al·rous
chlo·rine	(klō´ rēn)
chlo·rin·ate	(klō´ rĭ·nāt)
-nat·ing	
chlo·rate	(klō´ rāt)
chlo·ride	(klō´ rīd)
chlo·rite	(klō´ rīt)

chlo·ro·form	(klō´ rô·fôrm)
chlo·ro·phyll	(klō´ rô·fĭl)
chock-full	(chŏk´ fŏŏl´)
choc·o·late	(chŏk´ ô·lĭt)
choice	(chois)
choir	(kwīr)
choir·boy	choir loft
choir·mas·ter	
choke	(chōk)
chok·ing	choke·cher·ry
chok·er	
chol·er·a	(kŏl´ ẽr·å)
chol·er·ic	(kŏl´ ẽr·ĭk)
cho·les·ter·ol	(kô·lĕs´ tẽr·ōl)
choose	(chŏŏz)
choos·ing	choos·i·ness
choos·y	
chop	(chŏp)
chopped	chop·ping
chop·house	chop·py
chop·stick	chop su·ey
cho·ral	(kō´ rål)
cho·ral·ly	
chord	(kôrd)
(music; see *cord*)	
chore	(chōr)
cho·re·og·ra·phy	
	(kō´ rē·ŏg´ rå·fĭ)
cho·re·og·ra·pher	
chor·tle	(chôr´ t´l)
-tling	
cho·rus	(kō´ rŭs)
chose	(chōz)
cho·sen	
Chou En-lai	(jō´ ĕn´ lī´)
chow·der	(chou´ dẽr)
chow mein	(chou´ mān´)
chris·ten	(krĭs´ ´n)
-ten·ing	
Chris·ten·dom	(krĭs´ ´n·dŭm)
Chris·tian	(krĭs´ chån)
Chris·ti·an·i·ty	
	(krĭs´ chĭ·ăn´ ĭ·tĭ)
Chris·tian·ize	-iz·ing
Christ·like	(krīst´ līk´)
Christ·mas	(krĭs´ más)
chro·mat·ic	(krô·măt´ ĭk)
chrome	(krōm)
chro·mi·um	(krō´ mĭ·ŭm)
chron·ic	(krŏn´ ĭk)
chron·i·cal·ly	
chron·i·cle	(krŏn´ ĭ·k´l)
-cling	

chron·o·log·i·cal
    (krŏn′ ô·lŏj′ ĭ·kăl)
  -cal·ly
chro·nol·o·gy (krŏ·nŏl′ ô·jĭ)
  -gies
chrys·a·lis (krĭs′ á·lĭs)
chrys·an·the·mum
    (krĭs·ăn′ thê·măm)
chub·by (chŭb′ ĭ)
  chub·bi·ness
chuck·le (chŭk′ 'l)
  -ling
chum·my (chŭm′ ĭ)
  chum·mi·ness
Chung·king, Chi·na
    (chŏŏng′ kĭng′)
chunk·y (chŭngk′ ĭ)
church (chûrch)
  church·go·er church·ly
  church·yard
Church·ill, Win·ston
    (chûrch′ ĭl)
churl·ish (chûr′ lĭsh)
churn (chûrn)
chute (shŏŏt)
chut·ney (chŭt′ nĭ)
ci·ca·da (sĭ·kā′ dá)
ci·der (sī′ dēr)
ci·gar (sĭ·gär′)
cig·a·rette (sĭg′ á·rĕt′)
cinch (sĭnch)
Cin·cin·nat·i, O.
    (sĭn′ sĭ·năt′ ĭ)
cin·der (sĭn′ dēr)
Cin·der·el·la (sĭn′ dēr·ĕl′ á)
cin·e·ma (sĭn′ ê·má)
  cin·e·mat·ic (sĭn′ ê·măt′ ĭk)
  cin·e·ma·tog·ra·phy
    (sĭn′ ê·má·tŏg′ rá·fĭ)
cin·na·bar (sĭn′ á·bär)
cin·na·mon (sĭn′ á·măn)
ci·pher (sī′ fēr)
cir·ca (sûr′ ká)
  abbr. c.
cir·cle (sûr′ k'l)
  -cling cir·clet
cir·cuit (sûr′ kĭt)
  -cuit·ed -cuit·ing
  cir·cu·i·tous (sēr·kū′ ĭ·tŭs)
cir·cu·lar (sûr′ kū·lēr)
  cir·cu·lar·i·ty (sûr′ kū·lăr′ ĭ·tĭ)
  cir·cu·lar·ly
  cir·cu·lar·ize -iz·ing
cir·cu·late (sûr′ kū·lāt)
  -lat·ing

cir·cu·la·tion (sûr′ kū·lā·shŭn)
cir·cu·la·to·ry (sûr′ kū·lá·tō′rĭ)
cir·cum·cise (sûr′ kŭm·sīz)
  -cis·ing
cir·cum·ci·sion
    (sûr′ kŭm·sĭzh′ ŭn)
cir·cum·fer·ence
    (sēr·kŭm′ fēr·ĕns)
cir·cum·flex (sûr′ kŭm·flĕks)
cir·cum·lo·cu·tion
    (sûr′ kŭm·lô·kū′ shŭn)
cir·cum·scribe (sûr′ kŭm·skrīb′)
  -scrib·ing
cir·cum·scrip·tion
    (sûr′ kŭm·skrĭp′ shŭn)
cir·cum·spect (sûr′ kŭm·spĕkt)
cir·cum·stance (sûr′ kŭm·stăns)
cir·cum·stan·tial
    (sûr′ kŭm·stăn′ shăl)
cir·cum·stan·ti·ate
    (sûr′ kŭm·stăn′ shĭ·āt)
  -at·ing
cir·cum·vent (sûr′ kŭm·vĕnt′)
cir·cum·ven·tion
    (-vĕn′ shŭn)
cir·cus (sûr′ kŭs)
cir·rho·sis (sĭ·rō′ sĭs)
cir·ro·cu·mu·lus
    (sĭr′ ô·kū′ mū·lŭs)
cir·ro·stra·tus (sĭr′ ô·strā′ tŭs)
cir·rus (sĭr′ ŭs)
cis·tern (sĭs′ tērn)
cit·a·del (sĭt′ á·dĕl)
ci·ta·tion (sī·tā′ shŭn)
cite (sīt)
  (quote; see *site*, *sight*)
  cit·ing cit·a·ble
cit·i·zen (sĭt′ ĭ·zĕn)
  cit·i·zen·ry
cit·ric ac·id (sĭt′ rĭk)
cit·ron (sĭt′ rŭn)
cit·ron·el·la (sĭt′ rŭn·ĕl′ á)
cit·rus fruit (sĭt′ rŭs)
cit·y (sĭt′ ĭ)
  cit·ies
cit·i·fied (sĭt′ ĭ·fīd)
cit·y-born cit·y-folk
civ·et (sĭv′ ĕt)
civ·ic (sĭv′ ĭk)
civ·il (sĭv′ ĭl)
  civ·il en·gi·neer
  civ·il law civ·il·ly
  civ·il rights civ·il serv·ice
ci·vil·ian (sĭ·vĭl′ yăn)

ci·vil·i·ty   (sĭ·vĭl′ ĭ·tĭ)
 -ties
civ·i·lize   (sĭv′ ĭ·līz)
 -liz·ing   civ·i·liz·a·ble
 civ·i·li·za·tion
                   (sĭv′ ĭ·lĭ·zā′ shŭn)
claim·ant   (klām′ ănt)
clair·voy·ance   (klâr·voi′ ăns)
 -ant
clam·bake   (klăm′ bāk′)
clam·ber   (klăm′ bĕr)
clam·my   (klăm′ ĭ)
 clam·mi·ness
clam·or   (klăm′ ĕr)
 clam·or·ous
clan   (klăn)
 clan·nish   clans·man
clan·des·tine   (klăn·dĕs′ tĭn)
 -tine·ly
clang·or   (klăng′ ĕr)
 clang·or·ous
clap·board   (klăb′ ĕrd)
clap·per   (klăp′ ĕr)
claque   (klăk)
 (paid applauders)
clar·et   (klăr′ ĕt)
clar·i·fy   (klăr′ ĭ·fī)
 -fied,   -fy·ing
 clar·i·fi·ca·tion
                   (klăr′ ĭ·fĭ·kā′ shŭn)
 clar·i·fi·er   (-fī′ ĕr)
clar·i·net   (klăr′ ĭ·nĕt′)
 clar·i·net·ist
clar·i·on   (klăr′ ĭ·ŭn)
clar·i·ty   (klăr′ ĭ·tĭ)
class   (klăs)
 class·a·ble   class-con·scious
 class·mate   class·room
clas·sic   (klăs′ ĭk)
 clas·si·cal   -cal·ly
 clas·si·cism   (klăs′ ĭ·sĭz′m)
clas·si·fy   (klăs′ ĭ·fī)
 -fied,   -fy·ing
 clas·si·fi·a·ble   (-fī′ á·b'l)
 clas·si·fi·ca·tion
                   (klăs′ ĭ·fĭ·kā′ shŭn)
clat·ter   (klăt′ ĕr)
clause   (klôz)
claus·tro·pho·bi·a
                   (klôs′ trŏ·fō′ bĭ·á)
clav·i·chord   (klăv′ ĭ·kôrd)
clav·i·cle   (klăv′ ĭ·k'l)
clay   (klā)
 clay·ey   clay pi·geon

clean   (klēn)
 clean·a·ble   clean-cut
 clean·er
 clean·li·ness   (klĕn′ lĭ·nĕs)
 clean·ly   (klĕn′ lĭ)
 clean·ness
cleanse   (klĕnz)
 cleans·ing   cleans·er
clear   (klēr)
 clear-cut   clear-eyed
 clear·head·ed   clear·ing·house
 clear-sight·ed
 clear·ance   (klēr′ăns)
cleat   (klēt)
cleave   (klēv)
 cleav·ing
 cleav·age   (-ĭj)
 cleav·ers
clef   (klĕf)
 (musical notation; see cliff)
cleft pal·ate   (klĕft)
clem·en·cy   (klĕm′ ĕn·sĭ)
 -ent
clench   (klĕnch)
Cle·o·pat·ra   (klē′ ŏ·păt′ rá)
cler·gy·man   (klûr′ jĭ′ măn)
cler·ic   (klĕr′ ĭk)
 cler·i·cal
clev·er   (klĕv′ ĕr)
cli·ché   (klē·shā′)
cli·ent   (klī′ ĕnt)
 cli·en·tele   (klī′ ĕn·tĕl′)
cliff   (klĭf)
 (rock; see clef)
cli·mate   (klī′ mĭt)
 cli·mat·ic   (klī·măt′ ĭk)
cli·max   (klī′ măks)
 cli·mac·tic   (klī·măk′ tĭk)
climb   (klīm)
cling·stone   (klĭng′ stŏn′)
clin·ic   (klĭn′ ĭk)
 clin·i·cal   -cal·ly
 cli·ni·cian   (klĭ·nĭsh′ ăn)
clip·per   (klĭp′ ĕr)
clique   (klēk)
 cli·quish
clob·ber   (klŏb′ ĕr)
cloche   (klōsh)
clock·wise   (klŏk′ wīz′)
clod·dish   (klŏd′ ĭsh)
cloi·son·né   (kloi′ zŏ·nā′)
clois·ter   (klois′ tĕr)
close   (klōs) adj
 close-fist·ed   close·ly
 close-up

close (klōz) v.
  clos·ing
clos·et (klŏz′ ĕt)
  -et·ed   -et·ing
clo·sure (klō′ zhẽr)
cloth (klŏth) n.
clothe (klōth) v.
  cloth·ing
clothes (klōthz)
  clothes·bas·ket
  clothes·brush   clothes·line
cloth·ier (klōth′ yẽr)
cloud·burst (kloud′ bûrst′)
cloud·y (kloud′ ĭ)
  cloud·i·est   -i·ness
clout (klout)
clo·ver-leaf (klō′ vẽr-lēf′)
  adj.
clown·ish (kloun′ ĭsh)
cloy·ing (kloi′ ĭng)
club (klŭb)
  clubbed   club·bing
  club car   club chair
  club·foot·ed   club·room
  club steak
clue (klōō)
  clu·ing
clum·sy (klŭm′ zĭ)
  clum·si·er   -si·est
  -si·ly   -si·ness
clus·ter (klŭs′ tẽr)
clutch (klŭch)
clut·ter (klŭt′ ẽr)
coach·man (kōch′ măn)
co·ag·u·late (kō·ăg′ û·lāt)
  -lat·ing   co·ag·u·lant
  co·ag·u·la·tion
       (kō·ăg′ û·lā′ shŭn)
  co·ag·u·la·tor
coal (kōl)
  coal·bin   coal gas
  coal mine   coal tar
  coal·yard
co·a·lesce (kō′ ȧ·lĕs′)
  -lesc·ing   co·a·les·cence,
  -cent
co·a·li·tion (kō′ ȧ·lĭsh′ ŭn)
coarse (kōrs)
  (rough; see *course*)
  coars·en   coarse·ness
coast (kōst)
  coast·al   coast ar·til·ler·y
  coast·er   coast guard
  coast·ward
co·au·thor (kō·ô′ thẽr)

coax (kōks)
co·ax·i·al ca·ble
       (kō·ăk′ sĭ·ȧl)
cob·bler (kŏb′ lẽr)
cob·ble·stone (kŏb′ 'l·stōn′)
co·bra (kō′ brȧ)
cob·web (kŏb′ wĕb′)
  cob·web·by
co·caine (kō·kān′)
coc·cyx (kŏk′ sĭks)
  pl. coc·cy·ges (kŏk·sī′ jēz)
  coc·cyg·e·al (kŏk·sĭj′ ē·ȧl)
cock·a·too (kŏk′ ȧ·tōō′)
cock·er span·iel
       (kŏk′ ẽr)
cock·eyed (kŏk′ ĭd′)
cock·le·shell (kŏk′ 'l·shĕl′)
cock·ney (kŏk′ nĭ)
cock·pit (kŏk′ pĭt′)
cock·roach (kŏk′ rōch′)
cock·sure (kŏk′ shoor′)
cock·tail (kŏk′ tāl′)
cock·y (kŏk′ ĭ)
  cock·i·er   -i·est
  -i·ly   -i·ness
co·co mat·ting (kō′ kō)
co·coa (kō′ kō)
co·co·nut (kō′ kō·nŭt′)
co·coon (kō·kōōn′)
cod·dle (kŏd′ 'l)
  cod·dling
co·de·fend·ant (kō′ dē·fĕn′ dȧnt)
co·de·ine (kō′ dē·ēn)
cod·fish (kŏd′ fĭsh′)
codg·er (kŏj′ ẽr)
cod·i·cil (kŏd′ ĭ·sĭl)
cod·i·fy (kŏd′ ĭ·fī)
  -fied   -fy·ing
  cod·i·fi·ca·tion
       (kŏd′ ĭ·fĭ·kā′ shŭn)
cod-liv·er oil (kŏd′ lĭv′ ẽr)
co·ed (kō′ ĕd′)
  co·ed·u·ca·tion·al
       (kō′ ĕd·u·kā′ shŭn·ȧl)
co·ef·fi·cient (kō′ ĕ·fĭsh′ ĕnt)
co·e·qual (kō·ē′ kwȧl)
co·erce (kō·ûrs′)
  -erc·ing
co·er·ci·ble (kō·ûr′ sĭ·b'l)
co·er·cion (-shŭn)
co·er·cive (-sĭv)
co·es·sen·tial (kō′ ĕ·sĕn′ shȧl)
co·ex·ec·u·tor
  n. masc. (kō′ ĕg·zĕk′ û·tẽr)
  co·ex·ec·u·trix (-trĭks) n. fem.

co·ex·ist	(kō′ ĕg·zĭst′)
co·ex·ist·ence	
cof·fee	(kôf′ ĭ)
cof·fee·house	cof·fee·pot
cof·fee shop	cof·fee ta·ble
cof·fers	(kôf′ ērz)
cof·fin	(kôf′ ĭn)
co·gent	(kō′ jĕnt)
co·gen·cy	
cog·i·tate	(kŏj′ ĭ·tāt)
-tat·ing	
cog·i·ta·tion	(kŏj′ ĭ·tā′ shŭn)
cog·i·ta·tive	(kŏj′ ĭ·tā′ tĭv)
cog·i·ta·tor	(kŏj′ ĭ·tā′ tĕr)
co·gnac	(kō′ nyăk)
cog·nate	(kŏg′ nāt)
cog·ni·tion	(kŏg·nĭsh′ ŭn)
cog·ni·zant	(kŏg′ nĭ·zdnt)
-zance	
cog·no·men	(kŏg·nō′ mĕn)
cog·wheel	(kŏg′ hwēl′)
co·hab·it	(kō·hăb′ ĭt)
co·hab·i·ta·tion	
	(kō·hăb′ ĭ·tā′ shŭn)
co·here	(kō·hēr′)
-her·ing	co·her·ence,
-ent	
co·he·sion	(kō·hē′ zhŭn)
co·he·sive	-sive·ly
co·hort	(kō′ hôrt)
coif	(koif)
coif·fure	(kwä·fūr′)
coin	(koin)
coin·age	(-ĭj)
co·in·cide	(kō′ ĭn·sīd′)
-cid·ing	
co·in·ci·dence	(kō·ĭn′ sĭ·dĕns)
co·in·ci·dent·al	
	(kō·ĭn′ sĭ·dĕn′ tǎl)
co·in·her·it·ance	
	(kō′ ĭn·hĕr′ ĭ·tǎns)
co·in·sure	(kō′ ĭn shōōr′)
co·i·tion	(kō·ĭsh′ ŭn)
co·i·tus	(kō′ ĭ·tŭs)
col·an·der	(kŭl′ ǎn·dĕr)
cold	(kōld)
cold-blood·ed	cold cream
cold sore	cold war
cole·slaw	(kōl′ slô′)
col·ic	(kŏl′ ĭk)
col·i·se·um	(kŏl′ ĭ·sē′ ŭm)
(any stadium; see *Colosseum*)	
co·li·tis	(kō·lī′ tĭs)
col·lab·o·rate	(kō·lăb′ ō·rāt)
-rat·ing	

col·lab·o·ra·tion	
	(kō·lăb′ ō·rā′ shŭn)
col·lab·o·ra·tive	
	(kō·lăb′ ō·rā′ tĭv)
col·lab·o·ra·tor	
	(kō·lăb′ ō·rā′ tĕr)
col·lapse	(kō′ lăps′)
col·laps·ing	col·laps·i·ble
col·lar	(kŏl′ ĕr)
col·lar·band	col·lar·bone
col·lar but·ton	
col·late	(kō·lāt′)
col·lat·ing	
col·la·tion	(-lā′ shŭn)
col·lat·er·al	(kō·lăt′ ĕr·ǎl)
-al·ly	
col·league	(kŏl′ ēg)
col·lect	(kō·lĕkt′)
col·lect·i·ble	col·lec·tion
col·lec·tive	-tive·ly
col·lec·tiv·ism	
col·lec·tiv·i·ty	
	(kŏl′ ĕk·tĭv′ ĭ·tĭ)
col·lec·tiv·ize	-iz·ing
col·lec·tor	
col·lege	(kŏl′ ĕj)
col·le·gi·an	(kō·lē′ jĭ·ǎn)
col·le·gi·ate	(kō·lē′ jĭ·ĭt)
col·lide	(kō·līd′)
col·lid·ing	
col·li·sion	(kō·lĭzh′ ŭn)
col·lie	(kŏl′ ĭ)
col·lier·y	(kŏl′ yēr·ĭ)
col·lier·ies	
col·li·sion	(kō·lĭzh′ ŭn)
col·lo·di·on	(kō·lō′ dĭ·ŭn)
col·loid	(kŏl′ oid)
col·loi·dal	(kō·loi′ dǎl)
col·lo·qui·al	(kō·lō′ kwĭ·ǎl)
-al·ly	
col·lo·qui·al·ism	
col·lo·quy	(kŏl′ ō·kwĭ)
-quies	
col·lude	(kō·lūd′)
col·lud·ing	col·lu·sion
co·logne	(kō·lōn′)
Co·lom·bi·a,	(kō·lŭm′ bĭ·ǎ)
S. Amer.	
(see *Columbia*)	
co·lon	(kō′ lŏn)
colo·nel	(kûr′ nĕl)
colo·nel·cy	
col·on·nade	(kŏl′ ō·nād′)
col·o·ny	(kŏl′ ō·nĭ)
-nies	

co·lo·ni·al (kô·lō′ nǐ·ăl)
col·o·nist
col·o·ni·za·tion
       (kŏl′ ô·nǐ·zā′ shŭn)
col·o·nize   -niz·ing
col·o·phon (kŏl′ ô·fŏn)
col·or (kŭl′ ĕr)
col·or·a·tion (kŭl′ ĕr·ā′ shŭn)
col·or-blind   col·or·ful,
-ful·ly   -ful·ness
col·or·less   -less·ness
Col·o·ra·do (kŏl′ ô·rä′ dō)
abbr. Colo.
Col·o·ra·dan (-rä′ d′n)
col·o·ra·tu·ra so·pran·o
       (kŭl′ ĕr·à·tū′ rà)
co·los·sal (kô·lŏs′ ăl)
co·los·sal·ly
Col·os·se·um (kŏl′ ô·sē′ ŭm)
(Roman amphitheater; see
coliseum)
co·los·sus (kô·lŏs′ ŭs)
Co·lum·bi·a (kô·lŭm′ bǐ·à)
(University, River, District of;
see Colombia)
col·um·bine (kŏl′ ŭm·bīn)
Co·lum·bus (kô·lŭm′ bŭs)
col·umn (kŏl′ ŭm)
co·lum·nar (kô·lŭm′ nĕr)
col·um·nist
co·ma (kō′ mà)
(trance; see comma)
com·bat (kŏm′ băt) n.
com·bat (kŏm·băt′) v.
-bat·ing   com·bat·a·ble
com·bat·ant (kŏm′ bà·tănt)
com·bat·ive
com·bine (kŏm′ bīn) n.
com·bine (kŏm·bīn′) v.
-bin·ing   com·bin·a·ble
com·bi·na·tion
       (kŏm′ bǐ·nā′ shŭn)
com·bus·tion (kŏm·bŭs′ chŭn)
com·bus·ti·ble
com·bus·tive   com·bus·tor
come·back (kŭm′ băk′)
co·me·di·an (kô·mē′ dǐ·ăn)
co·me·di·enne (kô·mē′ dǐ·ĕn′)
n. fem.
come·down (kŭm′ doun′)
com·e·dy (kŏm′ ĕ·dǐ)
-dies
come·ly (kŭm′ lǐ)
come·li·er   -li·est
-li·ness

com·et (kŏm′ ĕt)
come·up·pance
       (kŭm·ŭp′ ăns)
com·fort (kŭm′ fĕrt)
com·fort·a·ble
com·ic (kŏm′ ĭk)
com·i·cal   -cal·ly
com·ing (kŭm′ ĭng)
com·ma (kŏm′ à)
(punctuation; see coma)
com·mand (kô·mánd′)
com·mand·er   com·mand·ment
com·man·dant (kŏm′ ăn·dănt′)
com·man·deer (kŏm′ ăn·dĕr′)
com·man·do (kô·mán′ dō)
-dos
com·mem·o·rate
       (kô·mĕm′ ô·rāt)
-rat·ing
com·mem·o·ra·tion
       (kô·mĕm′ ô·rā′ shŭn)
com·mem·o·ra·tive
       (kô·mĕm′ ô·rā′ tǐv)
com·mence (kô·mĕns′)
com·menc·ing
com·mence·ment
com·mend (kô·mĕnd′)
com·mend·a·ble
com·mend·a·tion
       (kŏm′ ĕn·dā′ shŭn)
com·mend·a·tory
com·men·su·rate
       (kô·mĕn′ shŏŏ·rǐt)
com·men·su·ra·ble
com·men·su·rate·ly
com·men·su·ra·tion
       (kô·mĕn′ shŏŏ·rā′ shŭn)
com·ment (kŏm′ ĕnt)
com·men·tar·y
       (kŏm′ ĕn·tĕr′ ǐ)
-tar·ies
com·men·ta·tor (-tā′ tĕr)
com·merce (kŏm′ ûrs)
com·mer·cial (kô·mûr′ shăl)
com·mer·cial·ism
com·mer·cial·i·za·tion
       (kô·mûr′ shăl·ǐ·zā′ shŭn)
com·mer·cial·ize
-iz·ing   com·merc·ial·ly
com·min·gle (kô·mĭng′ g′l)
-gling
com·mis·er·ate
       (kô·mĭz′ ĕr·āt)
-at·ing

com·mis·er·a·tion
    (kŏ·mĭz′ ĕr·ā′ shŭn)
com·mis·sar   (kŏm′ ĭ·sär′)
  com·mis·sar·i·at
      (kŏm′ ĭ·sär′ ĭ·ăt)
com·mis·sar·y   (kŏm′ ĭ·sĕr′ ĭ)
  com·mis·sar·ies
com·mis·sion   (kŏ·mĭsh′ ŭn)
  com·mis·sioned of·fi·cer
com·mit   (kŏ·mĭt′)
  com·mit·ted   com·mit·ting
  com·mit·ment com·mit·tal
com·mit·tee   (kŏ·mĭt′ ĭ)
  com·mit·tee·man
com·mode   (kŏ·mōd′)
com·mod·i·ous
    (kŏ·mō′ dĭ·ŭs)
com·mod·i·ty   (kŏ·mŏd′ ĭ·tĭ)
  -ties
com·mo·dore   (kŏm′ ō·dōr′)
com·mon   (kŏm′ ŭn)
  com·mon de·nom·i·na·tor
  com·mon·er
  com·mon-law mar·riage
  com·mon·ly   com·mon·ness
  com·mon·place
  com·mon sense n.
  com·mon-sense adj.
  com·mon stock
  com·mon·weal
  com·mon·wealth
com·mo·tion   (kŏ·mō′ shŭn)
com·mu·nal   (kŏm′ û·ndl)
  com·mu·nal·ly
com·mune   (kŏ·mūn′) v.
  com·mun·ing   (kŏm′ ûn) n.
com·mu·ni·cate
    (kŏ·mū′ nĭ·kāt)
  -cat·ing
  com·mu·ni·ca·ble
      (-kd′ b'l)
  com·mu·ni·cant
      (-kănt)
  com·mu·ni·ca·tion
      (kŏ·mū′ nĭ·kā′ shŭn)
  com·mu·ni·ca·tive
      (-kā′ tĭv)
  com·mu·ni·ca·tor
      (-kā′ tĕr)
com·mun·ion   (kŏ·mūn′ yŭn)
com·mu·ni·qué   (kŏ·mū′ nĭ·kā′)
com·mu·nist   (kŏm′ û·nĭst)
  com·mu·nism
  com·mu·nis·tic
    (kŏm′ û·nĭs′ tĭk)

com·mu·nize   -niz·ing
Com·mu·nist   kŏm′ û·nĭst)
  (specific political party)
com·mu·ni·ty   (kŏ·mū′ nĭ·tĭ)
  -ties
com·mute   (kŏ·mūt′)
  com·mut·ing
  com·mu·ta·tion
      (kŏm′ û·tā′ shŭn)
  com·mut·er
com·pact   (kŏm·păkt′) adj.
      (kŏm′ păkt) n.
com·pan·ion   (kŏm·păn′ yŭn)
  com·pan·ion·a·bil·i·ty
    (kŏm·păn′ yŭn·á·bĭl′ ĭ·tĭ)
  com·pan·ion·a·ble
  com·pan·ion·ate
      (-ăt)
  com·pan·ion·ship
com·pa·ny   (kŭm′ pá·nĭ)
  -nies
com·pare   (kŏm·pâr′)
  -par·ing
  com·pa·ra·bil·i·ty
    (kŏm′ pá·rá·bĭl′ ĭ·tĭ)
  com·pa·ra·ble (kŏm′ pá·rá·b'l)
  com·par·a·tive
      (kŏm·păr′ á·tĭv)
  -tive·ly
  com·pa·ri·son (kŏm·păr′ ĭ·sŭn)
com·part·ment   (kŏm·pärt′ mĕnt)
com·pass   (kŭm′ pás)
com·pas·sion   (kŏm·păsh′ ŭn)
  com·pas·sion·ate (-ĭt)
com·pat·i·ble   (kŏm·păt′ ĭ·b'l)
  com·pat·i·bil·i·ty
    (kŏm·păt′ ĭ·bĭl′ ĭ·tĭ)
com·pa·tri·ot   (kŏm·pā′ trĭ·ŭt)
com·pel   (kŏm·pĕl′)
  -pelled   -pel·ling
com·pen·di·ous
    (kŏm·pĕn′ dĭ·ŭs)
com·pen·di·um
    (kŏm·pĕn′ dĭ·ŭm)
com·pen·sate   (kŏm′ pĕn·sāt)
  -sat·ing
  com·pen·sa·tion
    (kŏm′ pĕn·sā′ shŭn)
  com·pen·sa·tive
    (kŏm′ pĕn·sā′ tĭv)
  com·pen·sa·to·ry
    (kŏm·pĕn′ sá·tō′ rĭ)
com·pete   (kŏm·pēt′)
  -pet·ing

com·pe·tence (kŏm′ pĕ·tĕns)
-ten·cy, -tent
com·pe·ti·tion
    (kŏm′ pĕ·tĭsh′ ŭn)
  com·pet·i·tive
    (kŏm·pĕt′ ĭ·tĭv)
-tive·ly
com·pet·i·tor (kŏm·pĕt′ ĭ·tĕr)
com·pile (kŏm·pīl′)
-pil·ing
com·pi·la·tion
    (kŏm′ pĭ·lā′ shŭn)
com·pla·cent (kŏm·plā′ sĕnt)
(self-satisfied; see *complaisant*)
  com·pla·cence
com·plain (kŏm·plān′)
  com·plain·ant com·plaint
com·plai·sant (kŏm·plā′ zănt)
(obliging; see *complacent*)
  com·plai·sance
com·plect·ed (kŏm·plĕk′ tĕd)
com·ple·ment (kŏm′ plĕ·mĕnt)
(that which completes; see
compliment)
  com·ple·men·tal
  com·ple·men·ta·ry
    (kŏm′ plĕ·mĕn′ tȧ·rĭ)
com·plete (kŏm·plēt′)
-plet·ing com·plete·ly
-plete·ness
com·ple·tion (-plē′ shŭn)
com·plex (kŏm·plĕks′) adj
    (kŏm′ plĕks) n.
  com·plex·i·ty (kŏm·plĕk′ sĭ·tĭ)
com·plex·ion (kŏm·plĕk′ shŭn)
  com·plex·ioned
com·pli·ant (kŏm·plī′ ănt)
-ance
com·pli·cate (kŏm′ plĭ·kāt)
-cat·ing
com·pli·ca·tion
    (kŏm′ plĭ·kā′ shŭn)
com·plic·i·ty (kŏm·plĭs′ ĭ·tĭ)
com·pli·ment (kŏm′ plĭ·mĕnt)
(flattery; see *complement*)
  com·pli·men·ta·ry
    (kŏm′ plĭ·mĕn′ tȧ·rĭ)
com·ply (kŏm·plī′)
-plied -ply·ing
com·pli·a·ble (kŏm·plī′ ȧ·b'l)
com·po·nent (kŏm·pō′ nĕnt)
com·port (kŏm·pōrt′)
com·pose (kŏm·pōz′)
-pos·ing com·posedly
com·pos·er

com·pos·ite (kŏm·pŏz′ ĭt)
com·po·si·tion
    (kŏm′ pō·zĭsh′ ŭn)
comp·os·i·tor (kŏm·pŏz′ ĭ·tĕr)
com·pos·ure (kŏm·pō′ zhĕr)
com·pote (kŏm′ pōt)
com·pound (kŏm·pound′) v.
    (kŏm′ pound) n.,
    adj.
  com·pound·a·ble
    (kŏm·pound′ ȧ·b'l)
  com·pound in·ter·est
    (kŏm′ pound)
com·pre·hend (kŏm′ prĕ·hĕnd′)
  com·pre·hen·si·ble
    (-hĕn′ sĭ·b'l)
  com·pre·hen·sion
    (-hĕn′ shŭn)
  com·pre·hen·sive
    (hĕn′ sĭv)
com·press (kŏm·prĕs′) v.
    (kŏm′ prĕs) n.
  com·press·i·ble
    (kŏm·prĕs′ ĭ·b'l)
  com·pres·sion (kŏm·prĕsh′ ŭn)
  com·pres·sor (kŏm·prĕs′ ĕr)
com·prise (kŏm·prīz′)
-pris·ing
com·pro·mise (kŏm′ prō·mīz)
-mis·ing com·pro·mis·er
Comp·tom·e·ter
    (kŏmp·tŏm′ ê·tĕr)
comp·trol·ler (kŏn·trōl′ ĕr)
com·pul·sion (kŏm·pŭl′ shŭn)
  com·pul·sive (-sĭv)
  com·pul·so·ry (-sō·rĭ)
  com·pul·so·ri·ly
com·punc·tion
    (kŏm·pŭngk′ shŭn)
com·pute (kŏm·pūt′)
-put·ing com·put·a·ble
com·pu·ta·tion
    (kŏm′ pû·tā′ shŭn)
com·put·er
com·rade (kŏm′ răd)
  com·rade·ship
con·cave (kŏn′ kāv)
  con·cav·i·ty (kŏn·kăv′ ĭ·tĭ)
con·ceal (kŏn·sēl′)
-cealed -ceal·ing
  con·ceal·a·ble con·ceal·ment
con·cede (kŏn·sēd′)
-ced·ing
con·ceit (kŏn·sēt′)
-ceit·ed

con·ceive   (kŏn·sēv′)
  -ceiv·ing   con·ceiv·able,
  -bly
con·cen·trate   (kŏn′sĕn·trāt)
  -trat·ing
  con·cen·tra·tion
    (kŏn′sĕn·trā′shŭn)
  con·cen·tra·tor
con·cen·tric   (kŏn·sĕn′trĭk)
con·cept   (kŏn′sĕpt)
  con·cep·tion   (kŏn·sĕp′shŭn)
  con·cep·tu·al (kŏn·sĕp′tū·ăl)
con·cern   (kŏn·sûrn′)
  -cern·ing
con·cert   (kŏn·sûrt′) v.
    (kŏn′sûrt) n.
con·cer·ti·na   (kŏn′sĕr·tē′nà)
con·cer·to   (kŏn·chĕr′tō)
  -tos
con·ces·sion   (kŏn·sĕsh′ŭn)
  con·ces·sion·aire
    (kŏn·sĕsh′ŭn·âr′)
  con·ces·sion·ar·y
    (kŏn·sĕsh′ŭn·ĕr′ĭ)
conch shell   (kŏngk)
con·cil·i·ate   (kŏn·sĭl′ĭ·āt)
  -at·ing
  con·cil·i·a·tion
    (kŏn·sĭl′ĭ·ā′shŭn)
  con·cil·i·a·tor (kŏn·sĭl′ĭ·ā′tĕr)
  con·cil·i·a·to·ry
    (kŏn·sĭl′ĭ·à·tō′rĭ)
con·cise   (kŏn·sīs′)
  -cise·ly
con·clave   (kŏn′klāv)
con·clude   (kŏn·klōōd′)
  -clud·ing
  con·clu·sion   (-klōō′zhŭn)
  con·clu·sive   -sive·ly
con·coct   (kŏn·kŏkt′)
  con·coc·tion   (kŏn·kŏk′shŭn)
con·com·i·tant
    (kŏn·kŏm′ĭ·tănt)
  -tance
con·cord   (kŏn′kôrd)
  con·cord·ance (kŏn·kôr′dăns)
con·course   (kŏn′kōrs)
con·crete   (kŏn′krēt)
  -crete·ness
con·cu·bine   (kŏng′kū·bĭn)
  con·cu·bi·nage
    (kŏn·kū′bĭ·nĭj)
con·cu·pis·cent
    (kŏn·kū′pĭ·sĕnt)
  -cence

con·cur   (kŏn·kûr′)
  -curred   -cur·ring
  con·cur·rence -cur·rent
con·cus·sion   (kŏn·kŭsh′ŭn)
con·demn   (kŏn·dĕm′)
  con·dem·na·ble
  con·dem·na·tion
    (kŏn′dĕm·nā′shŭn)
  con·dem·na·to·ry
    (kŏn·dĕm′nà·tō′rĭ)
  con·demn·er   (-dĕm′ĕr)
con·dense   (kŏn·dĕns′)
  -dens·ing   con·den·sa·ble
  con·den·sa·tion
    (kŏn′dĕn·sā′shŭn)
  con·dens·er
con·de·scend   (kŏn′dē·sĕnd′)
  con·de·scend·ing·ly
  con·de·scen·sion
    (-sĕn′shŭn)
con·di·ment   (kŏn′dĭ·mĕnt)
con·di·tion   (kŏn·dĭsh′ŭn)
  con·di·tion·al -al·ly
con·dole   (kŏn·dōl′)
  -dol·ing
  con·do·lence   (-dō′lĕns)
con·done   (kŏn·dōn′)
  -don·ing
con·dor   (kŏn′dĕr)
con·duce   (kŏn·dūs′)
  -duc·ing
  con·du·cive   (-dū′sĭv)
con·duct   (kŏn′dŭkt) n.
con·duct   (kŏn·dŭkt′) v.
  con·duct·i·ble con·duc·tion
  con·duc·tive   con·duc·tor
con·duit   (kŏn′dwĭt)
Co·ney Is.   (kō′nĭ)
con·fec·tion   (kŏn·fĕk′shŭn)
  con·fec·tion·er, -er·y
con·fed·er·a·cy
    (kŏn·fĕd′ĕr·à·sĭ)
  -cies
  con·fed·er·ate (-ĭt)
  con·fed·er·a·tion
    (kŏn·fĕd′ĕr·ā′shŭn)
con·fer   (kŏn·fûr′)
  -ferred   -fer·ring
  con·fer·ee   (kŏn′fĕr·ē′)
  con·fer·ence   (kŏn′fĕr·ĕns)
  con·fer·ra·ble
con·fess   (kŏn·fĕs′)
  con·fessed·ly
  con·fes·sion   (kŏn·fĕsh′ŭn)
  -fes·sion·al   con·fes·sor

con·fet·ti (kŏn·fĕt′ ĭ)
con·fi·dant (kŏn′ fĭ·dănt′)
  n. masc., (friend)
  con·fi·dante (kŏn′ fĭ·dănt′)
  n. fem.
con·fide (kŏn·fīd′)
  -fid·ing
con·fi·dent (kŏn′ fĭ·dĕnt)
  (sure)
  con·fi·dence con·fi·dent·ly
con·fi·den·tial (kŏn′ fĭ·dĕn′ shăl)
  -tial·ly
con·fig·u·ra·tion
    (kŏn·fĭg′ û·rā′ shŭn)
con·fine (kŏn·fīn′) *v.*
  -fin·ing con·fin·a·ble
  con·fine·ment
con·fines (kŏn′ fīnz) *n.*
con·firm (kŏn·fûrm′)
  con·firm·a·ble
  con·fir·ma·tion
    (kŏn′ fĕr·mā′ shŭn)
  con·firm·a·to·ry
    (kŏn·fûr′ má·tō′ rĭ)
con·fis·cate (kŏn′ fĭs·kāt)
  -cat·ing
  con·fis·ca·tion
    (kŏn′ fĭs·kā′ shŭn)
  con·fis·ca·to·ry
    (kŏn·fĭs′ ká·tō′ rĭ)
con·fla·gra·tion
    (kŏn′ flá·grā′ shŭn)
con·flict (kŏn′ flĭkt′) *v.*
    (kŏn′ flĭkt) *n.*
con·flu·ence (kŏn′ flŏŏ·ĕns)
con·form (kŏn·fôrm′)
  con·form·able
  con·for·ma·tion
    (kŏn′ fôr·mā′ shŭn)
  con·form·ist con·form·ity
con·found (kŏn·found′)
  con·found·ed·ly
con·frere (kŏn′ frâr)
con·front (kŏn·frŭnt′)
  con·fron·ta·tion
    (kŏn′ frŭn·tā′ shŭn)
Con·fu·cius (kŏn·fū′ shŭs)
  Con·fu·cian·ism
    (kŏn·fū′ shăn·ĭz′m)
con·fuse (kŏn·fūz′)
  -fus·ing con·fus·ed·ly
  con·fu·sion (-fū′ zhŭn)
con·fute (kŏn·fūt′)
  -fut·ing

con·fu·ta·tion
    (kŏn′ fû·tā′ shŭn)
con·ga (kŏng′ gá)
con·geal (kŏn·jēl′)
  -gealed -geal·ing
  con·geal·a·ble con·geal·ment
con·gen·ial (kŏn·jēn′ yăl)
  (compatible)
  con·ge·ni·al·i·ty
    (kŏn·jē′ nĭ·ăl′ ĭ·tĭ)
  con·gen·ial·ly
con·gen·i·tal (kŏn·jĕn′ ĭ·tăl)
  (inborn) con·gen·i·tal·ly
  con·gen·i·tal id·i·ot
con·gest (kŏn·jĕst′)
  con·ges·tion (-jĕs′ chŭn)
con·glom·er·ate
    (kŏn·glŏm′ ĕr·ĭt) *adj.*
  -at·ing (-āt) *v.*
  con·glom·er·a·tion
    (kŏn·glŏm′ ĕr·ā′ shŭn)
con·grat·u·late
    (kŏn·grăt′ û·lāt)
  -lat·ing
  con·grat·u·la·tion
    (kŏn·grăt′ û·lā′ shŭn)
  con·grat·u·la·tor (-lā′ tĕr)
  con·grat·u·la·to·ry (-lá·tō′ rĭ)
con·gre·gate (kŏng′ grĕ·gāt)
  -gat·ing
  con·gre·ga·tion
    (kŏng′ grĕ·gā′ shŭn)
Con·gre·ga·tion·al·ist
    (kŏng′ grĕ·gā′ shŭn·ăl·ĭst)
con·gress (kŏng′ grĕs)
  con·gres·sion·al
    (kŏn·grĕsh′ ŭn·ăl)
  con·gress·man
con·gru·ent (kŏng′ grŏŏ·ĕnt)
  -ence
  con·gru·ity (kŏng·grŏŏ′ ĭ·tĭ)
  con·gru·ous (kŏng′ grŏŏ·ŭs)
con·ic (kŏn′ ĭk)
  con·i·cal
co·ni·fer (kō′ nĭ·fĕr)
  co·nif·er·ous (kō·nĭf′ ĕr·ŭs)
con·jec·ture (kŏn·jĕk′ tûr)
  con·jec·tur·al
con·ju·gal (kŏn′ jŏŏ·găl)
con·ju·gate (kŏn′ jŏŏ·gāt)
  -gat·ing
  con·ju·ga·tion
    (kŏn′ jŏŏ·gā′ shŭn)
con·junc·tion (kŏn·jŭngk′ shŭn)
  con·junc·tive con·junc·ture

con·jure (kŭn′ jẽr)
　-jur·ing
　con·ju·ra·tion
　　　　　(kŏn′ jōō·rā′ shŭn)
　con·jur·er (kŭn′ jẽr·ẽr)
con·nect (kŏ·nĕkt′)
　con·nect·ed·ly con·nec·tion
　con·nec·tive con·nec·tor
Con·nect·i·cut (kŏ·nĕt′ ĭ·kŭt)
　abbr. Conn.
con·nip·tion fit (kŏ·nĭp′ shŭn)
con·nive (kŏ·nīv′)
　con·niv·ing con·niv·ance
　con·niv·er
con·nois·seur (kŏn′ ĭ·sûr′)
con·note (kŏ·nōt′)
　con·not·ing
　con·no·ta·tion (kŏn′ ō·tā′ shŭn)
　con·not·a·tive (kŏ·nōt′ ȧ·tĭv)
con·nu·bi·al (kŏ·nū′ bĭ·ăl)
con·quer (kŏng′ kẽr)
　con·quer·a·ble con·quer·or
con·quest (kŏng′ kwĕst)
con·quis·ta·dor
　　　　　(kŏn·kwĭs′ tȧ·dôr)
con·san·guin·i·ty
　　　　　(kŏn′ săng·gwĭn′ ĭ·tĭ)
　con·san·guin·e·ous (-ē·ŭs)
con·science (kŏn′ shĕns)
　con·science·less
con·sci·en·tious
　　　　　(kŏn′ shĭ·ĕn′ shŭs)
con·scious (kŏn′ shŭs)
　con·scious·ness
con·script (kŏn′ skrĭpt)
　　　　　adj., n.
　　　　　(kŏn·skrĭpt′) *v.*
　con·scrip·tion (kŏn·skrĭp′ shŭn)
con·se·crate (kŏn′ sĕ·krāt)
　-crat·ing
　con·se·cra·tion
　　　　　(kŏn′ sĕ·krā′ shŭn)
　con·se·cra·tor
con·sec·u·tive (kŏn·sĕk′ ū·tĭv)
　-tive·ly
con·sen·sus (kŏn·sĕn′ sŭs)
　con·sen·su·al (-shū·ăl)
con·sent (kŏn·sĕnt′)
con·se·quence (kŏn′ sĕ·kwĕns)
　con·se·quent, -quent·ly
　con·se·quen·tial
　　　　　(kŏn′ sĕ·kwĕn′ shăl)
　-tial·ly

con·serv·a·to·ry
　　　　　(kŏn·sûr′ vȧ·tō′ rĭ)
　-ries
con·serve (kŏn·sûrv′)
　-serv·ing
　con·ser·va·tion
　　　　　(kŏn′ sẽr·vā′ shŭn)
　-tion·al
　con·serv·a·tism
　　　　　(kŏn·sûr′ vȧ·tĭz′m)
　con·serv·a·tive (-tĭv)
　-tive·ly
con·sid·er (kŏn·sĭd′ ẽr)
　con·sid·er·a·ble, -bly
　con·sid·er·ate (-ĭt)
　-ate·ly
　con·sid·er·a·tion
　　　　　(kŏn·sĭd′ ẽr·ā′ shŭn)
con·sign (kŏn·sīn′)
　con·sign·ee (kŏn′ sī·nē′)
　con·sign·ment con·sign·or
con·sist (kŏn·sĭst′)
　con·sist·ent (kŏn·sĭs′ tĕnt)
　con·sist·en·cy con·sist·ent·ly
con·sole (kŏn·sōl′) *v.*
　-sol·ing
　con·so·la·tion
　　　　　(kŏn′ sō·lā′ shŭn)
　con·so·ler
con·sole ta·ble (kŏn′ sōl)
con·sol·i·date (kŏn·sŏl′ ĭ·dāt)
　-dat·ing
　con·sol·i·da·tion
　　　　　(kŏn·sŏl′ ĭ·dā′ shŭn)
con·som·mé (kŏn′ sŏ·mā′)
con·so·nance (kŏn′ sō·năns)
　-nant
con·sort (kŏn′ sôrt) *n.*
　　　　　(kŏn·sôrt′) *v.*
con·spic·u·ous (kŏn·spĭk′ û·ŭs)
con·spir·a·cy (kŏn·spĭr′ ȧ·sĭ)
　-cies
con·spir·a·tor (kŏn·spĭr′ ȧ·tẽr)
　con·spir·a·to·ri·al
　　　　　(kŏn·spĭr′ ȧ·tō′ rĭ·ăl)
con·spire (kŏn·spīr′)
　-spir·ing
con·sta·ble (kŭn′ stȧ·b'l)
con·stab·u·lar·y
　　　　　(kŏn·stăb′ û·lẽr′ ĭ)
　-lar·ies
con·stant (kŏn′ stănt)
　-stan·cy
con·stel·la·tion
　　　　　(kŏn′ stĕ·lā′ shŭn)

con·ster·na·tion
    (kŏn′ stĕr·nā′ shŭn)
con·sti·pat·ed (kŏn′ stĭ·pāt′ ĕd)
  con·sti·pa·tion
    (kŏn′ stĭ·pā′ shŭn)
con·stit·u·en·cy
    (kŏn·stĭt′ û·ĕn·sĭ)
 -ent
con·sti·tute (kŏn′ stĭ·tūt)
 -tut·ing
con·sti·tu·tion (kŏn′ stĭ·tū′ shŭn)
 con·sti·tu·tion·al, -al·ism,
 -al·ly
 con·sti·tu·tion·al·i·ty
    (kŏn′ stĭ·tū′ shŭn·ăl′ ĭ·tĭ)
con·strain (kŏn·strān′)
 con·strain·ed·ly
    (-strān′ ĕd·lĭ)
 con·straint
con·strict (kŏn·strĭkt′)
 con·stric·tion (-strĭk′ shŭn)
 con·stric·tive con·stric·tor
con·struct (kŏn·strŭkt′)
 con·struc·ter
 con·struc·tion (-strŭk′ shŭn)
 con·struc·tive -tive·ly
con·strue (kŏn·strōō′)
 -stru·ing
con·sul (kŏn′ sŭl)
 (diplomat; see *council, counsel*)
 con·su·lar (kŏn′ sŭ·lẽr)
 con·su·late (kŏn′ sŭ·lăt)
con·sult (kŏn·sŭlt′)
 con·sult·ant (-tănt)
 con·sul·ta·tion
    (kŏn′ sŭl·tā′ shŭn)
 con·sul·tive (-tĭv)
con·sume (kŏn·sūm′)
 -sum·ing con·sum·a·ble
 con·sum·ers′ goods
con·sum·mate (kŏn·sŭm′ ĭt)
 adj. (perfect)
con·sum·mate (kŏn′ sŭ·māt) *v.*
 (to complete)
 -sum·mat·ing
 con·sum·ma·tion
    (kŏn′ sŭ·mā′ shŭn)
con·sump·tion (kŏn·sŭmp′ shŭn)
con·sump·tive (kŏn·sŭmp′ tĭv)
con·tact (kŏn′ tăkt)
 con·tact lens con·tact print
con·ta·gion (kŏn·tā′ jŭn)
 con·ta·gious (-jŭs)
con·tain (kŏn·tān′)
 con·tain·a·ble con·tain·er

con·tam·i·nate (kŏn·tăm′ ĭ·nāt)
 -nat·ing
 con·tam·i·na·tion
    (kŏn·tăm′ ĭ·nā′ shŭn)
 con·tam·i·na·tor
con·tem·plate (kŏn′ tĕm·plāt)
 -plat·ing
 con·tem·pla·tion
    (kŏn′ tĕm·plā′ shŭn)
 con·tem·pla·tive
    (kŏn·tĕm′ plá·tĭv)
con·tem·po·rar·y
    (kŏn·tĕm′ pô·rĕr′ ĭ)
 -rar·ies
 con·tem·po·ra·ne·ous
    (-tĕm′ pô·rā′ nē·ŭs)
con·tempt (kŏn·tĕmpt′)
 con·tempt·i·ble
 con·temp·tu·ous
    (-tĕmp′ tū·ŭs)
con·tend (kŏn·tĕnd′)
 con·tend·er
con·tent (kŏn′ tĕnt) *n.*
con·tent (kŏn·tĕnt′) *adj.*
 con·tent·ed con·tent·ment
con·ten·tion (kŏn·tĕn′ shŭn)
con·ten·tious (kŏn·tĕn′ shŭs)
con·ter·mi·nous
    (kŏn·tûr′ mĭ·nŭs)
con·test (kŏn′ tĕst) *n.*
con·test (kŏn·tĕst′) *v.*
 con·test·a·ble con·test·ant
con·text (kŏn′ tĕkst)
con·tig·u·ous (kŏn·tĭg′ û·ŭs)
 con·ti·gu·i·ty (kŏn′ tĭ·gū′ ĭ·tĭ)
con·ti·nence (kŏn′ tĭ·nĕns)
 -nen·cy
con·ti·nent (kŏn′ tĭ·nĕnt)
 con·ti·nen·tal (kŏn·tĭ·nĕn′ tăl)
con·tin·gent (kŏn·tĭn′ jĕnt)
 -gen·cy
con·tin·ue (kŏn·tĭn′ ū)
 -u·ing
 con·tin·u·al -al·ly
 con·tin·u·ance
 con·tin·u·a·tion
    (kŏn·tĭn′ û·ā′ shŭn)
 con·tin·u·ous
con·ti·nu·i·ty (kŏn′ tĭ·nū′ ĭ·tĭ)
 -ties
con·tort (kŏn·tôrt′)
 con·tor·tion·ist
    (-tôr′ shŭn·ĭst)
con·tour (kŏn′ tōōr)
con·tra·band (kŏn′ trá·bănd)

con·tra·cep·tion
(kŏn′ trȧ·sĕp′ shŭn)
con·tra·cep·tive
con·tract (kŏn′ trăkt) n.
con·trac·tor
con·tract (kŏn·trăkt′) v.
con·tract·i·ble
con·trac·tion (-trăk′ shŭn)
con·trac·tu·al (-trăk′ tụ·ăl)
con·tra·dict (kŏn′ trȧ·dĭkt′)
con·tra·dic·tion (-dĭk′ shŭn)
con·tra·dic·to·ry (-dĭk′ tô·rĭ)
con·tra·dis·tinc·tion
(kŏn′ trȧ·dĭs·tĭngk′ shŭn)
con·tral·to (kŏn·trăl′ tō)
-tos
con·tra·ry (kŏn′ trĕr·ĭ)
con·tra·ri·ly (-trĕr·ĭ·lĭ)
con·tra·ri·ness (-ĭ·nĕs)
con·tra·ri·wise (ĭ·wīz′)
con·trast (kŏn·trăst′) v.
con·trast·a·ble
con·trast (kŏn′ trăst) n.
con·tra·vene (kŏn′ trȧ·vēn′)
-ven·ing
con·tra·ven·tion
(kŏn′ trȧ·vĕn′ shŭn)
con·trib·ute (kŏn·trĭb′ ūt)
-but·ing
con·trib·ut·a·ble
con·tri·bu·tion
(kŏn′ trĭ·bū′ shŭn)
con·trib·u·tor
con·trib·u·to·ry
(-trĭb′ ū·tō′ rĭ)
con·trite (kŏn′ trīt)
-trite·ly
con·tri·tion (kŏn·trĭsh′ ŭn)
con·trive (kŏn·trīv′)
-triv·ing
con·triv·ance (kŏn·trīv′ ȧns)
con·trol (kŏn·trōl′)
-trolled -trol·ling
con·trol·la·ble con·trol·ler
con·tro·ver·sy (kŏn′ trō·vûr′ sĭ)
-sies
con·tro·ver·sial
(kŏn′ trō·vûr′ shăl)
-sial·ly
con·tro·vert (kŏn′ trō·vûrt)
con·tu·ma·cious
(kŏn′ tū·mā′ shŭs)
con·tu·ma·cy (kŏn′ tū·mȧ·sĭ)
con·tu·sion (kŏn·tū′ zhŭn)
co·nun·drum (kō·nŭn′ drŭm)

con·va·lesce (kŏn′ vȧ·lĕs′)
-lesc·ing
con·va·les·cent, -cence
con·vec·tion (kŏn·vĕk′ shŭn)
con·vec·tive (-vĕk′ tĭv)
con·vene (kŏn·vēn′)
-ven·ing
con·ven·ience (kŏn·vēn′ yĕns)
-ient
con·vent (kŏn′ vĕnt)
con·ven·tion (kŏn·vĕn′ shŭn)
con·ven·tion·al, -al·ly
con·ven·tion·al·i·ty
(kŏn·vĕn′ shŭn·ăl′ ĭ·tĭ)
con·verge (kŏn·vûrj′)
-verg·ing
con·ver·gence (-vûr′ jĕns)
-gent
con·verse (kŏn·vûrs′) v.
-vers·ing
con·ver·sance (kŏn′ vĕr·sȧns)
-sant
con·ver·sa·tion
(kŏn′ vĕr·sā′ shŭn)
-tion·al
con·verse (kŏn′ vûrs)
adj., n.
con·ver·sion (kŏn·vûr′ shŭn)
con·vert (kŏn·vûrt′) v.
con·vert·i·ble (-vûr′ tĭ·b′l)
con·vert (kŏn′ vûrt) n.
con·vex (kŏn′ vĕks)
con·vex·i·ty (kŏn·vĕk′ sĭ·tĭ)
con·vey (kŏn·vā′)
con·vey·ance (kŏn·vā′ ȧns)
con·vey·er
con·vict (kŏn′ vĭkt) n.
con·vict (kŏn·vĭkt′) v.
con·vic·tion (-vĭk′ shŭn)
con·vince (kŏn·vĭns′)
-vinc·ing con·vin·ci·ble
con·vinc·ing·ly
con·viv·i·al (kŏn·vĭv′ ĭ·ăl)
con·viv·i·al·i·ty
(kŏn·vĭv′ ĭ·ăl′ ĭ·tĭ)
con·viv·i·al·ly
con·vo·ca·tion
(kŏn′ vō·kā′ shŭn)
con·voke (kŏn·vōk′)
-vok·ing
con·vo·lu·tion (kŏn′ vō·lū′ shŭn)
con·voy (kŏn·voi′) v.
(kŏn′ voi) n.
con·vulse (kŏn·vŭls′)
-vuls·ing

con·vul·sion (-vŭl′ shŭn)
con·vul·sive (-vŭl′ sĭv)
cook·book (kŏŏk′ bŏŏk′)
cook·er·y (kŏŏk′ ĕr·ĭ)
cook·y (kŏŏk′ ĭ)
cook·ies
cool (kŏŏl)
cool·ant (kŏŏl′ ănt)
cool·er cool·ly
cool·ness
coo·lie (kŏŏ′ lĭ)
(laborer; see coulee)
coop·er·age (kŏŏp′ ĕr·ĭj)
co·op·er·ate (kŏ·ŏp′ ĕr·āt)
-at·ing
co·op·er·a·tion
(kŏ·ŏp′ ĕr·ā′ shŭn)
co·op·er·a·tive
(kŏ·ŏp′ ĕr·ā′ tĭv)
-tive·ness
co·opt (kŏ·ŏpt′)
co·op·ta·tion (cŏ′ ŏp·tā′ shŭn)
co·or·di·nate (kŏ·ôr′ dĭ·nāt) v.
-nat·ing (-ăt) n., adj.
co·or·di·na·tion
(kŏ·ôr′ dĭ·nā′ shŭn)
co·part·ner (kŏ·pärt′ nĕr)
Co·pen·ha·gen (kŏ′ pĕn·hā′ gĕn)
Den·mark
Co·per·ni·cus (kŏ·pûr′ nĭ·kŭs)
Co·per·ni·can (kŏ·pûr′ nĭ·kăn)
cop·ing saw (kŏp′ ĭng)
co·pi·ous (kŏ′ pĭ·ŭs)
cop·per (kŏp′ ĕr)
cop·per·head cop·per·plate
cop·per·smith
cop·u·late (kŏp′ û·lāt)
-lat·ing
cop·u·la·tion (kŏp′ û·lā′ shŭn)
cop·y (kŏp′ ĭ)
cop·ies cop·y·book
cop·y·cat cop·y·hol·der
cop·y·ist cop·y·right
co·quette (kŏ·kĕt′)
co·quet·ry (kŏ′ kĕ·trĭ)
co·quet·tish
cor·al (kŏr′ ăl)
(as in coral reef; see corral)
cord (kŏrd)
(string; see chord)
cord·age (kŏr′ dĭj)
cor·dial (kŏr′ jăl)
cor·dial·i·ty (kŏr·jăl′ ĭ·tĭ)
cor·dial·ly
cor·don (kŏr′ dŏn)

cor·do·van (kŏr′ dŏ·văn)
cor·du·roy (kŏr′ dŭ·roi)
co·re·spond·ent
(kŏ′ rĕ·spŏn′ dĕnt)
(legal term; see correspondent)
co·ri·an·der (kŏ′ rĭ·ăn′ dĕr)
cork·screw (kôrk′ skrŏŏ′)
cor·mo·rant (kŏr′ mŏ·rănt)
corn (kôrn)
corn bor·er corn bread
corn·cake corn·cob
corn·flow·er corn pone
corn sir·up corn starch
corn sug·ar
cor·ne·a (kŏr′ nê·à)
cor·ne·al
cor·ner (kŏr′ nĕr)
cor·ner·stone
cor·net (kŏr′ nĕt)
(horn; see coronet)
cor·net·ist (kŏr·nĕt′ ĭst)
cor·nice (kŏr′ nĭs)
cor·nu·co·pi·a (kŏr′ nŭ·kŏ′ pĭ·à)
cor·ol·lar·y (kŏr′ ŏ·lĕr′ ĭ)
-ol·lar·ies
co·ro·na (kŏ·rŏ′ nà)
cor·o·nar·y throm·bo·sis
(kŏr′ ŏ·nĕr′ ĭ)
cor·o·na·tion (kŏr′ ŏ·nā′ shŭn)
cor·o·ner (kŏr′ ŏ·nĕr)
cor·o·net (kŏr′ ŏ·nĕt)
(crown; see cornet)
cor·po·ral (kŏr′ pŏ·răl)
cor·po·rate (kŏr′ pŏ·rĭt)
cor·po·ra·te·ly
cor·po·ra·tion (kŏr′ pŏ·rā′ shŭn)
cor·po·ra·tive (kŏr′ pŏ·rā′ tĭv)
cor·po·re·al (kŏr·pŏ′ rê·ăl)
corps (kŏr)
corps·man (kŏr′ măn)
cor·pu·lent (kŏr′ pû·lĕnt)
-lence
Cor·pus Chris·ti,
Tex. (kŏr′ pŭs krĭs′ tĭ)
cor·pus·cle (kŏr′ pŭs·′l)
cor·ral (kŏ·răl′)
(stockade; see coral)
cor·ralled
cor·rect (kŏ·rĕkt′)
cor·rec·tion·al (-rĕk′ shŭn·ăl)
cor·rec·tive cor·rec·tor
cor·re·late (kŏr′ ĕ·lāt)
-lat·ing
cor·re·la·tion (kŏr′ ĕ·lā′ shŭn)
cor·rel·a·tive (kŏ·rĕl′ à·tĭv)

cor·re·spond   (kŏr′ ê·spŏnd′)
cor·re·spond·ent
        (kŏr′ ê·spŏn′ dĕnt)
  (letter writer; see *coresspondent*)
cor·re·spond·ence
cor·ri·dor   (kŏr′ ĭ·dôr)
cor·rob·o·rate   (kŏ·rŏb′ ô·rāt)
  -rat·ing
cor·rob·o·ra·tion
    (kŏ·rŏb′ ô·rā′ shŭn)
cor·rob·o·ra·tive (-rā′ tĭv)
cor·rode   (kŏ·rōd′)
cor·rod·ing
cor·ro·sion   (kŏ·rō′ zhŭn)
cor·ro·sive (-sĭv)
cor·ru·gat·ed i·ron
    (kŏr′ û·gāt′ ĕd)
cor·ru·ga·tion (kŏr′ û·gā′ shŭn)
cor·rupt   (kŏ·rŭpt′)
cor·rupt·er   cor·rupt·i·ble
cor·rup·tion   cor·rup·tive
cor·sage   (kŏr·säzh′)
cor·sair   (kŏr′ sâr)
cor·set   (kŏr′ sĕt)
cor·tege   (kŏr·tĕzh′)
cor·tex   (kŏr′ tĕks)
  pl. cor·ti·ces (-tĭ·sēz)
cor·ti·cal (-tĭ·kăl)
cor·ti·sone   (kŏr′ tĭ·sōn)
Cor·vette   (kŏr·vĕt′)
cos·met·ic   (kŏs·mĕt′ ĭk)
cos·met·i·cal·ly
cos·mic   (kŏz′ mĭk)
cos·mi·cal·ly   cos·mic dust
cos·mic ray
cos·mol·o·gy (kŏz·mŏl′ ô·jĭ)
  -gies
cos·mo·log·i·cal
    (kŏz′ mŏ·lŏj′ ĭ·kăl)
cos·mo·pol·i·tan
    (kŏz′ mŏ·pŏl′ ĭ·tăn)
cos·mop·o·lite (kŏz·mŏp′ ô·līt)
cos·mos   (kŏz′ mŏs)
Cos·sack   (kŏs′ ăk)
Cos·ta Ri·ca (kŏs′ tá rē′ ká)
cost·ly   (kŏst′ lĭ)
cost·li·ness
cos·tume   (kŏs′ tūm)
co·te·rie   (kō′ tĕ·rĭ)
co·til·lion   (kŏ·tĭl′ yŭn)
cot·tage   (kŏt′ ĭj)
cot·ter pin   (kŏt′ ẽr)
cot·ton   (kŏt′ 'n)
  cot·ton belt   cot·ton flan·nel
  cot·ton gin   cot·ton·mouth

cot·ton·seed   cot·ton·tail
cot·ton·wood
couch   (kouch)
cou·gar   (kōō′ gẽr)
cough   (kŏf)
could   (kŏŏd)
cou·lee   (kōō′ lĭ)
  (deep valley; see *coolie*)
coun·cil   (koun′ sĭl)
  (assembly; see *consul, counsel*)
coun·cil·man
coun·sel   (koun′ sĕl)
  (advice; see *council, consul*)
-seled   -sel·ing
coun·se·lor
count   (kount)
count·a·ble   count·less
coun·te·nance (koun′ tĕ·năns)
coun·ter   (koun′ tẽr-)
coun·ter·act
coun·ter·bal·ance
coun·ter·charge, -charg·ing
coun·ter·claim
coun·ter·clock·wise
coun·ter·cur·rent
coun·ter·es·pi·o·nage
coun·ter·feit, -feit·er
coun·ter·in·tel·li·gence
coun·ter·ir·ri·tant
coun·ter·mand
coun·ter·of·fen·sive
coun·ter·part
coun·ter·prop·a·gan·da
coun·ter·rev·o·lu·tion
coun·ter·sign
coun·ter·vail·ing
count·ess   (koun′ tĕs)
coun·try   (kŭn′ trĭ)
  -tries
coun·tri·fied (kŭn′ trĭ·fīd)
coun·try·bred   coun·try·man
coun·try·side   coun·try·style
coun·ty   (koun′ tĭ)
  -ties
coup d'é·tat   (kōō dā′ tá′)
cou·pé   (kōō′ pā′)
cou·ple   (kŭp′ 'l)
  -pling
cou·plet   (kŭp′ lĕt)
cou·pon   (kōō′ pŏn)
cour·age   (kûr′ ĭj)
cou·ra·geous (kŭ·rā′ jŭs)
cour·i·er   (kŏŏr′ ĭ·ẽr)
course   (kōrs)
  (path; see *coarse*)

court (kōrt)
  court·house   court-mar·tial
  court·room   court·ship
  court·yard
cour·te·ous (kûr′ tē·ŭs)
cour·te·san (kōr′ tē·zăn)
cour·te·sy (kûr′ tē·sĭ)
  -sies
court·ly (kōrt′ lĭ)
  court·li·ness
cous·in (kŭz′ 'n)
cou·tu·rier (kōō′ tū·ryā′)
  n. masc.
  cou·tu·rière (kōō′ tū·ryâr′)
  n. fem.
cov·e·nant (kŭv′ ĕ·nănt)
cov·er·age (kŭv′ ĕr·ĭj)
cov·er·let (kŭv′ ĕr·lĕt)
cov·ert (kŭv′ ĕrt)
cov·et (kŭv′ ĕt)
  -et·ed   -et·ing
cov·et·ous (kŭv′ ĕ·tŭs)
cov·ey (kŭv′ ĭ)
  (flock)
cow (kou)
  cow·bell   cow·bird
  cow·boy   cow·hide
  cow·man
cow·ard (kou′ ĕrd)
  cow·ard·ice (kou′ ĕr·dĭs)
  cow·ard·li·ness
cow·lick (kou′ lĭk′)
co-work·er (kō·wûr′ kĕr)
cox·swain (kŏk′ s'n)
coy·ness (koi′ nĕs)
coy·ote (kī′ ōt)
co·zy (kō′ zĭ)
  co·zi·er   -zi·est
  -zi·ly   -zi·ness
crab (krăb)
  crab ap·ple   crab·by
  crab grass
crack (krăk)
  crack·down   crack·pot
  crack-up
crack·er (krăk′ ĕr)
crack·le (krăk′ 'l)
  -ling   crack·ly
cra·dle (krā′ d'l)
  -dling
craft (krăft)
  crafts·man·ship
  craft·y   craft·i·er
  ·i·est, -i·ly, -i·ness

crag (krăg)
  crag·gi·ness   crag·gy
cram·pon (krăm′ pŏn)
cran·ber·ry (krăn′ bĕr′ ĭ)
  -ber·ries
cra·ni·al (krā′ nĭ·ăl)
  -al·ly
cra·ni·um (krā′ nĭ·ŭm)
crank (krăngk)
  crank·case   crank·pin
  crank·shaft   crank·y
cran·ny (krăn′ ĭ)
  cran·nied
crap·pie (krăp′ ĭ)
crass (krăs)
crate (krāt)
  crat·ing
cra·ter (krā′ tĕr)
cra·vat (krá·văt′)
crave (krāv)
  crav·ing
cra·ven (krā′ vĕn)
  cra·ven·ly   cra·ven·ness
crawl (krôl)
cray·fish (krā′ fĭsh)
cray·on (krā′ ŏn)
cra·zy (krā′ zĭ)
  cra·zi·er, -zi·est, -zi·ly, -zi·ness
  cra·zy bone   cra·zy quilt
creak (krēk)
  (sound; see *creek*)
  creak·i·ness   creak·y
cream·er·y (krēm′ ĕr·ĭ)
  -er·ies
crease (krēs)
  creas·ing
cre·ate (krē·āt′)
  -at·ing   cre·a·tion
  cre·a·tive   cre·a·tor
crea·ture (krē′ tûr)
crèche (krāsh)
cre·dence (krē′ dĕns)
cre·den·tial (krē·dĕn′ shăl)
cred·i·ble (krĕd′ ĭ·b'l)
  cred·i·bil·i·ty (krĕd′ ĭ·bĭl′ ĭ·tĭ)
cred·it (krĕd′ ĭt)
  -it·ed   -it·ing
  cred·it·a·ble   cred·i·tor
cre·do (krē′ dō)
  -dos
cre·du·li·ty (krē·dū′ lĭ·tĭ)
cred·u·lous (krĕd′ ū·lŭs)
creek (krēk)
  (stream; see *creek*)

creep   (krēp)
  crept   (krĕpt)
cre·mate   (krē′ māt)
  -mat·ing
  cre·ma·tion   (krė·mā′ shŭn)
  crem·a·to·ri·um
                         (krĕm′ á·tō′ rĭ·ŭm)
cre·ole   (krē′ ōl)
cre·o·sol   (krē′ ō·sōl)
cre·o·sote   (krē′ ō·sōt)
crepe   (krāp)
  crepe pa·per n.
  crepe-pa·per adj.
  crepe rub·ber
  crepe su·zette   (krāp′ sōō·zĕt′)
cre·scen·do   (krĕ·shĕn′ dō)
  -dos
cres·cent   (krĕs′ ĕnt)
crest·fall·en   (krĕst′ fôl′ ĕn)
cre·tin   (krē′ tĭn)
cre·tonne   (krė·tŏn′)
cre·vasse   (krė·văs′)
crev·ice   (krĕv′ ĭs)
crib·bage   (krĭb′ ĭj)
crick·et   (krĭk′ ĕt)
cried   (krīd)
  cri·er   (krī′ ẽr)
crim·i·nal   (krĭm′ ĭ·nǎl)
  -nal·ly
  crim·i·nal·i·ty
                         (krĭm′ ĭ·nǎl′ ĭ·tĭ)
  crim·i·nol·o·gy
                         (krĭm′ ĭ·nŏl′ ō·jĭ)
crim·son   (krĭm′ z′n)
cringe   (krĭnj)
  cring·ing
crin·kle   (krĭng′ k′l)
  -kling
crin·o·line   (krĭn′ ō·lĭn)
crip·ple   (krĭp′ ′l)
  crip·pling   crip·pler
cri·sis   (crī′ sĭs)
  pl. cri·ses   (-sēz)
crisp·y   (krĭs′ pĭ)
criss·cross   (krĭs′ krŏs′)
cri·te·ri·on   (krī·tẽr′ ĭ·ŭn)
  pl. cri·te·ri·a
crit·ic   (krĭt′ ĭk)
  crit·i·cal   -cal·ly
  crit·i·cism   (krĭt′ ĭ·sĭz′m)
  crit·i·cize   (-sīz)
  -ciz·ing
cri·tique   (krĭ·tēk′)
croak   (krōk)

cro·chet   (krō·shā′)
  -chet·ing
crock·er·y   (krŏk′ ẽr·ĭ)
croc·o·dile   (krŏk′ ō·dĭl)
cro·cus   (krō′ kŭs)
  -cus·es
Croe·sus   (krē′ sŭs)
Cro-Ma·gnon   (krō·măn′ yŏn)
cro·ny   (krō′ nĭ)
  -nies
crook·ed   (krŏŏk′ ĕd)
cro·quet   (krō·kā′)
  (game)
cro·quette   (krō·kĕt′)
  (food)
cross   (krŏs)
  cross·bar   cross·bow
  cross·bred   cross-coun·try
  cross·cut   cross-ex·am·ine
  cross-eyed
  cross-fer·ti·li·za·tion
  cross fire   cross-grained
  cross in·dex n. cross-in·dex v.
  cross·o·ver
  cross-pol·li·na·tion
  cross-ques·tion
  cross ref·er·ence
  cross·road   cross·ruff
  cross sec·tion cross-stitch
  cross·walk   cross·wise
  cross·word puz·zle
crotch·et·y   (krŏch′ ĕ·tĭ)
  crotch·et·i·ness
crouch   (krouch)
croup   (krōōp)
crou·pi·er   (krōō′ pĭ·ẽr)
crou·ton   (krōō·tŏN′)
crow·bar   (krō′ bär′)
crowd   (kroud)
cru·cial   (krōō′ shǎl)
  -cial·ly
cru·ci·ble   (krōō′ sĭ·b′l)
cru·ci·fix   (krōō′ sĭ·fĭks)
  cru·ci·fix·ion
                         (krōō′ sĭ·fĭk′ shŭn)
cru·ci·fy   (krōō′ sĭ·fī)
  -fied   -fy·ing
crude   (krōōd)
  crude·ly
  cru·di·ty   (krōō′ dĭ·tĭ)
cru·el   (krōō′ ĕl)
  cru·el·ly   cru·el·ty
cru·et   (krōō′ ĕt)
cruise   (krōōz)
  cruis·ing   cruis·er

crul·ler (krŭl′ ĕr)
crum·ble (krŭm′ b'l)
  -bling
crum·ple (krŭm′ p'l)
  -pling
cru·sade (krōō·sād′)
  -sad·ing cru·sad·er
crus·ta·cean (krŭs·tā′ shăn)
  crus·ta·ceous (-shŭs)
crust·y (krŭs′ tĭ)
  crust·i·ness
crutch (krŭch)
crux (krŭks)
cry (krī)
  cried cry·ing
  cri·er cries
crypt (krĭpt)
  cryp·tic (krĭp′ tĭk)
  cryp·tog·ra·phy
    (krĭp·tŏg′ rá·fĭ)
crys·tal (krĭs′ tăl)
  crys·tal·line (krĭs′ tăl·ĭn)
  crys·tal·li·za·tion
    (krĭs′ tăl·ĭ·zā′ shŭn)
  crys·tal·lize (krĭs′ tăl·īz)
  -tal·liz·ing
cu·bic (kū′ bĭk)
cu·bi·cal (kū′ bĭ·kăl)
  (cube-shaped)
cu·bi·cle (kū′ bĭ·k'l)
  (compartment)
cuck·old (kŭk′ ŭld)
cuck·oo (kŏŏk′ ōō)
cu·cum·ber (kū′ kŭm·bĕr)
cud·dle (kŭd′ 'l)
  cud·dling cud·dle·some
  cud·dly
cudg·el (kŭj′ ĕl)
  -geled -gel·ing
cue (kū)
  (hint; see *queue*)
cue ball (kū)
cuff (kŭf)
cui·rass (kwē·răs′)
cui·sine (kwē·zēn′)
cul-de-sac (kŏŏl′ dē·săk′)
cu·li·nar·y (kū′ lĭ·nĕr′ ĭ)
cul·mi·nate (kŭl′ mĭ·nāt)
  -nat·ing
  cul·mi·na·tion
    (kŭl′ mĭ·nā′ shŭn)
cu·lottes (kū·lŏts′)
cul·pa·ble (kŭl′ pá·b'l)
  cul·pa·bil·i·ty (kŭl′ pá·bĭl′ ĭ·tĭ)
cul·prit (kŭl′ prĭt)

cult·ist (kŭl′ tĭst)
cul·ti·vate (kŭl′ tĭ·vāt)
  -vat·ing
  cul·ti·va·ble (kŭl′ tĭ·vá·b'l)
  cul·ti·va·tion (kŭl′ tĭ·vā′ shŭn)
  cul·ti·va·tor
cul·ture (kŭl′ tŭr)
  cul·tur·al
cum·ber·some (kŭm′ bĕr·sŭm)
cum·brous (kŭm′ brŭs)
cum·in (kŭm′ ĭn)
cum lau·de (kŭm lō′ dĕ)
cum·mer·bund (kŭm′ ĕr·bŭnd)
cu·mu·la·tive (kū′ mū·lă′ tĭv)
cu·mu·lus (kū′ mū·lŭs)
cu·ne·i·form (kū·nē′ ĭ·fôrm)
cun·ning (kŭn′ ĭng)
cup·board (kŭb′ ĕrd)
cup·ful (kŭp′ fŏŏl)
  -fuls
cu·pid·i·ty (kū·pĭd′ ĭ·tĭ)
cu·po·la (kū′ pŏ·lá)
cu·ra·çao (kū′ rá·sō′)
cu·rate (kū′ răt)
  cu·ra·cy (kū′ rá·sĭ)
  cu·ra·tor (kū·rā′ tĕr)
curb·stone (kûrb′ stōn′)
cur·dle (kûr′ d'l)
  -dling
cure (kūr)
  cur·ing cur·a·ble
  cure-all
cu·rette (kū·rĕt′)
cur·few (kûr′ fū)
cu·ri·ous (kū′ rĭ·ŭs)
  cu·ri·os·i·ty (kū′ rĭ·ŏs′ ĭ·tĭ)
  -ties
curl·i·cue (kûr′ lĭ·kū)
curl·y (kûr′ lĭ)
  curl·i·ness
cur·mudg·eon (kĕr·mŭj′ ŭn)
cur·rant (kûr′ ănt)
  (fruit)
cur·rent (kûr′ ĕnt)
  (timely)
  cur·ren·cy
cur·ric·u·lum (kŭ·rĭk′ û·lŭm)
cur·ry (kûr′ ĭ)
  cur·ried cur·ry·ing
curse (kûrs)
  curs·ing
cur·so·ry (kûr′ sō·rĭ)
curt (kûrt)
cur·tail·ment (kûr·tāl′ mĕnt)
cur·tain (kûr′ tĭn)

curt·sy   (kûrt′ sĭ)
  -sied   -sy·ing
curve   (kûrv)
  curv·ing
  cur·va·ceous   (kûr·vā′ shŭs)
  cur·va·ture   (kûr′ vá·t̶u̶r)
cush·ion   (kŏŏsh′ ŭn)
cus·pi·dor   (kŭs′ pĭ·dôr)
cuss·ed·ness   (kŭs′ ĕd·nĕs)
cus·tard   (kŭs′ tērd)
cus·to·dy   (kŭs′ tô·dĭ)
  -dies
  cus·to·di·al   (kŭs·tô′ dĭ·ăl)
  cus·to·di·an   (kŭs·tô′ dĭ·ăn)
cus·tom   (kŭs′ tŭm)
  cus·tom·ar·i·ly   (-ĕr′ ĭ·lĭ)
  cus·tom·ar·y   (-ĕr′ ĭ)
  cus·tom·house
cus·tom·er   (kŭs′ tŭm·ēr)
cut   (kŭt)
  cut·ting   cut·a·way
  cut·back   cut·off
  cut·out   cut·o·ver
  cut-rate   cut·throat
cu·ta·ne·ous   (kû·tā′ nĕ·ŭs)
cute   (kŭt)
  cute·ness
cu·ti·ole   (kū′ tĭ·k′l)
cut·lass   (kŭt′ lás)
cut·ler·y   (kŭt′ lēr·ĭ)
cut·let   (kŭt′ lĕt)
cy·an·am·ide   (sĭ′ ăn·ăm′ ĭd)
cy·a·nide   (sĭ′ á·nĭd)
cy·cle   (sĭ′ k′l)
  cy·cli·cal   (sĭ′ klĭ·kăl)
  cy·clist   (sĭ′ klĭst)
cy·cloid   (sĭ′ kloid)
cy·clom·e·ter   (sĭ·klŏm′ ê·tēr)
cy·clone   (sĭ′ klŏn)
cy·clo·pe·di·a   (sĭ′ klô·pē′ dĭ·á)
cy·clo·tron   (sĭ′ klô·trŏn)
cyg·net   (sĭg′ nĕt)
cyl·in·der   (sĭl′ ĭn·dēr)
  cy·lin·dri·cal   (sĭ·lĭn′ drĭ·kăl)
cym·bal   (sĭm′ băl)
  (musical instrument; see *symbol*)
  cym·bal·ist
cyn·ic   (sĭn′ ĭk)
  cyn·i·cal   -cal·ly
  cyn·i·cism   (sĭn′ ĭ·sĭz'm)
cy·press   (sĭ′ prĕs)
Cy·prus (is.)   (sĭ′ prŭs)
cyst   (sĭst)
  cyst·ic
cy·tol·o·gy   (sĭ·tŏl′ ô·jĭ)

czar   (zär)
Czech·o·slo·va·ki·a
                           (chĕk′ ô·slô·vä′ kĭ·á)

D

dab·ble   (dăb′ ′l)
  dab·bling
Dachs·hund   (däks′ hŏŏnt′)
Da·cron   (dā′ krŏn)
daf·fo·dil   (dăf′ ô·dĭl)
dag·ger   (dăg′ ĕr)
da·guerre·o·type
                           (dá·gĕr′ ô·tĭp)
dahl·ia   (dăl′ yá)
Da·ho·mey,   (dá·hō′ mĭ)
  Re·pub·lic of
dai·ly   (dā′ lĭ)
  -lies
dain·ty   (dān′ tĭ)
  dain·ti·ly
dair·y   (dâr′ ĭ)
  dair·ies   dair·y cat·tle
  dair·y·ing   dair·y·man
da·is   (dā′ ĭs)
dai·sy   (dā′ zĭ)
  -sies
Da·lai La·ma   (dä·lī′ lä′ má)
dal·ly   (dăl′ ĭ)
  dal·lied   dal·ly·ing
  dal·li·ance   (dăl′ ĭ·dns)
Dal·ma·tian dog   (dăl·mā′ shǎn)
dam   (dăm)
  (water barrier; see *damn*)
  dammed
dam·age   (dăm′ ĭj)
  -ag·ing   dam·age·able
dam·ask   (dăm′ ásk)
damn   (dăm)
  (to condemn; see *dam*)
  dam·na·ble   (dăm′ ná·b′l)
  dam·na·tion   (dăm·nā′ shǔn)
dam·sel   (dăm′ zĕl)
dan·de·li·on   (dăn′ dê·lĭ′ ǔn)
dan·druff   (dăn′ drǔf)
dan·ger·ous   (dăn′ jĕr·ǔs)
dan·gle   (dăng′ g′l)
  -gling
Dan·ish   (dăn′ ĭsh)
dap·per   (dăp′ ĕr)
dap·pled   (dăp′ ′ld)
Dar·da·nelles   (där′ d'n·ĕlz′)
dare·dev·il   (dâr′ dĕv′ ′l)
dar·ing   (dâr′ ĭng)

dar·ling (där′ lĭng)
Dar·win·i·an (där·wĭn′ ĭ·ăn)
dash·board (dăsh′ bōrd′)
das·tard·ly (dăs′ tẽrd·lĭ)
da·ta (dā′ tȧ) n. pl.
  sing. da·tum
da·tive (dā′ tĭv)
daub (dôb)
daugh·ter-in-law (dô′ tẽr·ĭn·lô′)
  pl. daugh·ters-in-law
daunt·less (dônt′ lĕs)
dau·phin (dô′ fĭn)
dav·en·port (dăv′ ĕn·pōrt)
Da·vy Jones's lock·er
  (dā′ vĭ jōnz′ zĭz)
daw·dle (dô′ d′l)
  -dling
dawn (dôn)
day (dā)
  day bed day·break
  day·dream day let·ter
  day·light sav·ing
  day·time
daze (dāz)
  daz·ing daz·ed·ly
daz·zle (dăz′ 'l)
  daz·zling
DDT (dē′ dē′ tē′)
dea·con (dē′ kŭn)
  dea·con·ess
dead (dĕd)
  dead·en·ing dead·line
  dead·lock
  dead·ly, -li·er, -li·est, -li·ness
  dead weight dead·wood
deaf (dĕf)
  deaf-and-dumb al·pha·bet
  deaf·en deaf-mute
deal·er (dē′ lẽr)
dearth (dûrth)
death (dĕth)
  death·bed death war·rant
de·ba·cle (dē·bä′ k'l)
de·bar (dē·bär′)
  -barred -bar·ring
  de·bar·ment
de·bar·ka·tion (dē′ bär·kā′ shŭn)
de·base·ment (dē·bās′ mĕnt)
de·bate (dē·bāt′)
  -bat·ing de·bat·a·ble
  de·bat·er
de·bauch (dē·bôch′)
  de·bauch·er·y
de·ben·ture (dē·bĕn′ tụr)

de·bil·i·tate (dē·bĭl′ ĭ·tāt)
  -tat·ing
  de·bil·i·ta·tion
  (dē·bĭl′ ĭ·tā′ shŭn)
de·bil·i·ty -ties
deb·it (dĕb′ ĭt)
deb·o·nair (dĕb′ ō·nâr′)
de·bris (dē·brē′)
debt·or (dĕt′ ẽr)
de·bunk (dē·bŭngk′)
de·but (dā′ bū)
deb·u·tante (dĕb′ ū·tänt′)
dec·ade (dĕk′ ād)
de·ca·dence (dē·kā′ dĕns)
  -dent
de·cal (dē′ kăl)
de·cant·er (dē·kăn′ tẽr)
de·cap·i·tate (dē·kăp′ ĭ·tāt)
  -tat·ing
  de·cap·i·ta·tion
  (dē·kăp′ ĭ·tā′ shŭn)
de·cath·lon (dē·kăth′ lŏn)
de·cay (dē·kā′)
  -cayed
de·ceased (dē·sēst′)
  de·ce·dent (dē·sē′ dĕnt)
de·ceit (dē·sēt′)
  de·ceit·ful, -ful·ly, -ful·ness
de·ceive (dē·sēv′)
  -ceiv·ing de·ceiv·a·ble
  de·ceiv·er
de·cel·er·ate (dē·sĕl′ ẽr·āt)
  -at·ing
De·cem·ber (dē·sĕm′ bẽr)
de·cent (dē′ sĕnt)
  de·cen·cy
de·cen·tral·ize (dē·sĕn′ trăl·īz)
  -iz·ing
de·cep·tion (dē·sĕp′ shŭn)
  de·cep·tive -tive·ly
dec·i·bel (dĕs′ ĭ·bĕl)
de·cide (dē·sīd′)
  -cid·ing de·cid·ed·ly
de·cid·u·ous (dē·sĭd′ ū·ŭs)
dec·i·mal (dĕs′ ĭ·măl)
dec·i·mate (dĕs′ ĭ·māt)
  -mat·ing
de·ci·pher (dē·sī′ fẽr)
  de·ci·pher·a·ble
de·ci·sion (dē·sĭzh′ ŭn)
de·ci·sive (dē·sī′ sĭv)
  -sive·ness
dec·la·ma·tion
  (dĕk′ lȧ·mā′ shŭn)

de·clare   (dē·klâr′)
  -clar·ing
  dec·lar·a·tion   (dĕk′ lá·rā′ shŭn)
  de·clar·a·tive   (dē·klăr′ á·tĭv)
  -to·ry
de·clen·sion   (dē·klĕn′ shŭn)
de·cline   (dē·klīn′)
  -clin·ing
de·cliv·i·ty   (dē·klĭv′ Ĭ·tĭ)
  -ties
de·code   (dē·kōd′)
  -cod·ing
dé·col·le·té   (dā′ kŏl′ ĕ·tā′)
  dé·col·le·tage   (dā′ kŏl′ ĕ·tāzh′)
de·com·pose   (dē′ kŏm·pōz′)
  -pos·ing
  de·com·po·si·tion
       (dē′ kŏm·pô·zĭsh′ ŭn)
de·com·press   (dē′ kŏm·prĕs′)
  de·com·pres·sion   (-prĕsh′ ŭn)
de·con·tam·i·nate
       (dē′ kŏn·tăm′ Ĭ·nāt)
  -nat·ing
  de·con·tam·i·na·tion
       (dē′ kŏn·tăm′ Ĭ·nā′ shŭn)
dé·cor   (dā′ kôr′)
dec·o·rate   (dĕk′ ô·rāt)
  -rat·ing
  dec·o·ra·tion   (dĕk′ ô·rā′ shŭn)
  dec·o·ra·tive   (-rā′ tĭv)
  dec·o·ra·tor
dec·o·rous   (dĕk′ ô·rŭs)
de·co·rum   (dē·kō′ rŭm)
de·coy   (dē·koi′)
de·crease   (dē·krēs′) v.
  -creas·ing   (dē′ krēs) n.
de·cree   (dē·krē′)
de·crep·it   (dē·krĕp′ Ĭt)
  de·crep·i·tude   (dē·krĕp′ Ĭ·tūd)
de·cry   (dē·krī′)
  -cried   -cry·ing
ded·i·cate   (dĕd′ Ĭ·kāt)
  -cat·ing
  ded·i·ca·tion   (dĕd′ Ĭ·kā′ shŭn)
  ded·i·ca·to·ry   (dĕd′ Ĭ·ká·tō′ rĬ)
de·duce   (dē·dūs′)
  -duc·ing   de·duc·i·ble
de·duct   (dē·dŭkt′)
  de·duct·i·ble   de·duc·tion
  de·duc·tive
deem   (dēm)
deep   (dēp)
  deep·en   Deep·freeze
  deep-root·ed   deep-sea div·er
  deep-seat·ed

deer·skin   (dēr′ skĭn′)
de·face   (dē·fās′)
  -fac·ing   de·face·ment
de·fame   (dē·fām′)
  -fam·ing
  def·a·ma·tion   (dĕf′ á·mā′ shŭn)
  de·fam·a·to·ry
       (dē·făm′ á·tō′ rĬ)
de·fault   (dē·fôlt′)
de·feat   (dē·fēt′)
  de·feat·ism   -ist
def·e·cate   (dĕf′ ē·kāt)
  -cat·ing
  def·e·ca·tion   (dĕf′ ē·kā′ shŭn)
de·fect   (dē·fĕkt′)
  de·fec·tion   de·fec·tive
de·fend   (dē·fĕnd′)
  de·fend·ant
de·fense   (dē·fĕns′)
  de·fense·less   de·fen·si·ble
  de·fen·sive   -sive·ly
de·fer   (dē·fûr′)
  -ferred   -fer·ring
  de·fer·ment   de·fer·ra·ble
  def·er·ence   (dĕf′ ēr·ĕns)
  def·er·en·tial   (dĕf′ ēr·ĕn′ shăl)
de·fi·ance   (dē·fī′ ăns)
  -ant
de·fi·cien·cy   (dē·fĭsh′ ĕn·sĬ)
  -cies   de·fi·cient
def·i·cit   (dĕf′ Ĭ·sĭt)
de·file   (dē·fīl′)
  -fil·ing   de·file·ment
de·fine   (dē·fīn′)
  -fin·ing   de·fin·a·ble
def·i·nite   (dĕf′ Ĭ·nĭt)
  def·i·nite·ly   -nite·ness
def·i·ni·tion   (dĕf′ Ĭ·nĭsh′ ŭn)
de·fin·i·tive   (dē·fĭn′ Ĭ·tĭv)
de·flate   (dē·flāt′)
  -flat·ing
  de·fla·tion   (dē·flā′ shŭn)
  de·fla·tion·ary
de·flect   (dē·flĕkt′)
  de·flec·tion
de·flow·er   (dē·flou′ ēr)
de·form   (dē·fôrm′)
  de·for·ma·tion
       (dē′ fôr·mā′ shŭn)
  de·formed
  de·form·i·ty   (dē·fôr′ mĬ·tĬ)
  -ties
de·fraud   (dē·frôd′)
de·fray   (dē·frā′)
  de·fray·ment

de·frost (dē·frôst′)
deft (dĕft)
de·funct (dē·fŭngkt′)
de·fy (dē·fī′)
-fied -fy·ing
de Gaulle, Charles
(dĕ·gōl′)
de·gen·er·ate (dē·jĕn′ĕr·ĭt)
adj., n.
(-āt) v.
-at·ing
de·gen·er·a·cy (-ȧ·sĭ)
de·gen·er·a·tion
(dē′jĕn·ĕr·ā′shŭn)
de·grade (dē·grād′)
-grad·ing
deg·ra·da·tion
(dĕg′rȧ·dā′shŭn)
de·gree (dē·grē′)
de·hu·man·ize (dē·hū′mȧn·īz)
-iz·ing
de·hu·man·i·za·tion
(dē·hū′mȧn·ĭ·zā′shŭn)
de·hu·mid·i·fy (dē′hū·mĭd′ĭ·fī)
-fied -fy·ing
de·hu·mid·i·fi·er
de·hy·drate (dē·hī′drāt)
-drat·ing
de·i·fy (dē′ĭ·fī)
-fied -fy·ing
deign (dān)
de·i·ty (dē′ĭ·tĭ)
-ties
de·is·tic (dē·ĭs′tĭk)
de·ject (dē·jĕkt′)
de·jec·tion (-jĕk′shŭn)
Del·a·ware (dĕl′ȧ·wâr)
abbr. Del.
Del·a·war·e·an
(dĕl′ȧ·wâr′ē·ȧn)
de·lay (dē·lā′)
de·lec·ta·ble (dē·lĕk′tȧ·b'l)
de·lec·ta·tion (dē′lĕk·tā′shŭn)
del·e·gate (dĕl′ē·gāt)
-gat·ing
del·e·ga·tion (dĕl′ē·gā′shŭn)
de·lete (dē·lēt′)
-let·ing
de·le·tion (dē·lē′shŭn)
del·e·te·ri·ous (dĕl′ē·tēr′ĭ·ŭs)
delft·ware (dĕlft′wâr′)
de·lib·er·ate (dē·lĭb′ĕr·ĭt)
adj.
-ate·ly
-at·ing (-āt) v.

de·lib·er·a·tion
(dē·lĭb′ĕr·ā′shŭn)
del·i·cate (dĕl′ĭ·kĭt)
-cate·ly
del·i·ca·cy (-kȧ·sĭ)
de·li·cious (dē·lĭsh′ŭs)
de·light (dē·līt′)
de·light·ed·ly de·light·ful
-ful·ly -ful·ness
de·lim·it (dē·lĭm′ĭt)
-it·ed -it·ing
de·lim·i·ta·tion
(dē·lĭm′ĭ·tā′shŭn)
de·lin·e·ate (dē·lĭn′ē·āt)
-at·ing de·lin·e·a·tor
de·lin·quen·cy (dē·lĭng′kwĕn·sĭ)
de·lin·quent
de·lir·i·ous (dē·lĭr′ĭ·ŭs)
de·lir·i·um (dē·lĭr′ĭ·ŭm)
de·lir·i·um tre·mens
(trē′mĕnz)
de·liv·er (dē·lĭv′ĕr)
de·liv·er·a·ble de·liv·er·ance
de·liv·er·y
del·phin·i·um (dĕl·fĭn′ĭ·ŭm)
de·lude (dē·lūd′)
-lud·ing
de·lu·sion (-lū′zhŭn)
del·uge (dĕl′ūj)
-ug·ing
de luxe (dē·lŏŏks′)
delve (dĕlv)
delv·ing
de·mag·net·ize (dē·măg′nĕ·tīz)
-iz·ing
dem·a·gogue (dĕm′ȧ·gŏg)
dem·a·gog·uer·y (-gŏg′ĕr·ĭ)
dem·a·gog·ic (dĕm′ȧ·gŏj′ĭk)
de·mand (dē·mȧnd′)
de·mand·a·ble
de·mar·cate (dē·mär′kāt)
-cat·ing
de·mar·ca·tion
(dē′mär·kā′shŭn)
de·mean (dē·mēn′)
de·mean·or (dē·mēn′ĕr)
de·ment·ed (dē·mĕn′tĕd)
de·men·ti·a prae·cox
(dē·mĕn′shĭ·ȧ prē′kŏks)
de·mer·it (dē·mĕr′ĭt)
de·mesne (dē·mān′)
de·mil·i·ta·rize (dē·mĭl′ĭ·tȧ·rīz)
-riz·ing
de·mil·i·ta·ri·za·tion
(dē·mĭl′ĭ·tȧ·rĭ·zā′shŭn)

de·mise   (dē·mīz′)
dem·i·tasse   (dĕm′ ĭ·tăs)
dem·i·urge   (dĕm′ ĭ·ûrj)
de·mo·bi·lize   (dē·mō′ bĭ·līz)
  -liz·ing
de·mo·bi·li·za·tion
      (dē·mō′ bĭ·lĭ·zā′ shŭn)
de·moc·ra·cy   (dē·mŏk′ rá·sĭ)
  -cies
dem·o·crat   (dĕm′ ô·krăt)
dem·o·crat·ic   (dĕm′ ô·krăt′ ĭk)
de·moc·ra·tize   (dē·mŏk′ rá·tīz)
  -tiz·ing
de·mol·ish   (dē·mŏl′ ĭsh)
dem·o·li·tion   (dĕm′ ô·lĭsh′ ŭn)
de·mon   (dē′ mŭn)
de·mo·ni·a·cal
      (dē′ mô·nī′ á·kál)
de·mon·ic   (dē·mŏn′ ĭk)
de·mon·e·tize   (dē·mŏn′ ê·tīz)
  -tis·ing
dem·on·strate   (dĕm′ ŭn·strāt)
  -strat·ing
de·mon·stra·ble
      (dē·mŏn′ strá·b′l)
dem·on·stra·tion
      (dĕm′ ŭn·strā′ shŭn)
de·mon·stra·tive
      (dē·mŏn′ strá·tĭv)
dem·on·stra·tor
de·mor·al·ize   (dē·mŏr′ ăl·īz)
  -iz·ing
de·mor·al·i·za·tion
      (dē·mŏr′ ăl·ĭ·zā′ shŭn)
de·mote   (dē·mōt′)
  -mot·ing
de·mo·tion   (dē·mō′ shŭn)
de·mur   (dē·mûr′)
  (delay)
  -murred
  -mur·ring   de·mur·rer
de·mure   (dē·mūr′)
  (modest)   de·mure·ly
de·na·tion·al·ize
      (dē·năsh′ ŭn·ál·īz)
  -iz·ing
de·nat·u·ral·ize
      (dē·năt′ û·rál·īz)
  -iz·ing
de·na·ture   (dē·nā′ tûr)
  -tur·ing
den·drite   (dĕn′ drīt)
de·ni·al   (dē·nī′ ăl)
den·i·grate   (dĕn′ ĭ·grāt)
  -grat·ing

den·im   (dĕn′ ĭm)
den·i·zen   (dĕn′ ĭ·zĕn)
de·nom·i·na·tion·al
      (dē·nŏm′ ĭ·nā′ shŭn·ăl)
de·nom·i·na·tor
      (dē·nŏm′ ĭ·nā′ tĕr)
de·note   (dē·nōt′)
  -not·ing
de·noue·ment   (dā·nōō′ mäɴ)
de·nounce   (dē·nouns′)
  -nounc·ing   de·nounce·ment
dense   (dĕns)
  dense·ly
den·si·ty   (dĕn′ sĭ·tĭ)
den·tal   (dĕn′ tăl)
den·ti·frice   (dĕn′ tĭ·frĭs)
den·tist   (dĕn′ tĭst)
den·ture   (dĕn′ tûr)
de·nude   (dē·nūd′)
  -nud·ing
de·nun·ci·ate   (dē·nŭn′ shĭ·āt)
  -at·ing
de·nun·ci·a·tion
      (dē·nŭn′ sĭ·ā′ shŭn)
de·nun·ci·a·to·ry
      (-nŭn′ shĭ·á·tō′ rĭ)
de·ny   (dē·nī′)
  -nied   -ny·ing
de·ni·al   de·ni·er
de·o·dor·ant   (dē·ō′ dēr·ănt)
de·o·dor·ize   -iz·ing
de·ox·i·dize   (dē·ŏk′ sĭ·dīz)
  -diz·ing
de·part   (dē·pärt′)
de·par·ture   (dē·pär′ tûr)
de·part·ment   (dē·pärt′ mĕnt)
de·part·men·tal
      (dē′ pärt·mĕn′ tăl)
De Paul (univ.)   (dĕ pôl′)
De·Pauw (univ.)   (dĕ·pô′)
de·pend   (dē·pĕnd′)
de·pend·a·bil·i·ty
      (dē·pĕn′ dá·bĭl′ ĭ·tĭ)
de·pend·a·ble   (dē·pĕn′ dá·b′l)
de·pend·ence   (dē·pĕn′ dĕns)
  -en·cy   -ent
de·pict   (dē·pĭkt′)
de·pic·tion   (dē·pĭk′ shŭn)
de·pil·a·to·ry   (dē·pĭl′ á·tō′ rĭ)
  -tor·ies
de·plete   (dē·plēt′)
  -plet·ing
de·ple·tion   (dē·plē′ shŭn)
de·plore   (dē·plōr′)
  -plor·ing   de·plor·a·ble

de·ploy·ment (dĕ·ploi′ mĕnt)
de·po·lar·ize (dē·pō′ lēr·īz)
  -iz·ing
de·pop·u·late (dē·pŏp′ û·lāt)
  -lat·ing
de·port (dē·pōrt′)
  de·por·ta·tion
    (dē′ pōr·tā′ shŭn)
  de·por·tee (dē′ pōr·tē′)
  de·port·ment
de·pose (dē·pōz′)
  -pos·ing de·pos·al
de·pos·it (dē·pŏz′ ĭt)
  -it·ed -it·ing
de·pos·i·tor (dē·pŏz′ ĭ·tēr)
de·pos·i·to·ry (dē·pŏz′ ĭ·tō′ rĭ)
dep·o·si·tion (dĕp′ ô·zĭsh′ ŭn)
de·pot (dē′ pō)
dep·ra·va·tion (dĕp′ rá·vā′ shŭn)
  (corruption; see *deprivation*)
de·praved (dē·prāvd′)
  de·prav·i·ty (dē·prăv′ ĭ·tĭ)
  -ties
dep·re·cate (dĕp′ rê·kāt)
  -cat·ing
  dep·re·ca·tion
    (dĕp′ rê·kā′ shŭn)
de·pre·ci·ate (dē·prē′ shĭ·āt)
  -at·ing
  de·pre·ci·a·ble
    (-á·b′l)
  de·pre·ci·a·tion
    (dē·prē′ shĭ·ā′ shŭn)
dep·re·da·tion (dĕp′ rê·dā′ shŭn)
de·press (dē·prĕs′)
  de·pres·sant de·pres·sive
  de·pres·sor
de·pres·sion (dē·prĕsh′ ŭn)
dep·ri·va·tion (dĕp′ rĭ·vā′ shŭn)
  (loss; see *depravation*)
depth (dĕpth)
dep·u·ta·tion (dĕp′ û·tā′ shŭn)
dep·u·ty (dĕp′ û·tĭ)
  -ties
  dep·u·tize (dĕp′ û·tīz)
de·ranged (dē·rānjd′)
  de·range·ment
der·e·lict (dĕr′ ĕ·lĭkt)
  der·e·lic·tion (dĕr′ ĕ·lĭk′ shŭn)
de·ride (dē·rīd′)
  -rid·ing
  de·ri·sion (dē·rĭzh′ ŭn)
  de·ri·sive (dē·rī′ sĭv)
de·rive (dē·rīv′)
  -riv·ing

der·i·va·tion (dĕr′ ĭ·vā′ shŭn)
de·riv·a·tive (dē·rĭv′ á·tĭv)
der·ma·ti·tis (dûr′ má·tī′ tĭs)
der·ma·tol·o·gy
    (dûr′ má·tŏl′ ô·jĭ)
der·o·gate (dĕr′ ô·gāt)
  -gat·ing
  der·o·ga·tion (dĕr′ ô·gā′ shŭn)
de·rog·a·tive (dē·rŏg′ á·tĭv)
de·rog·a·to·ry (dē·rŏg′ á·tō′ rĭ)
der·rick (dĕr′ ĭk)
der·ring-do (dĕr′ ĭng·dōō′)
der·vish (dûr′ vĭsh)
des·cant (dĕs·kănt′)
de·scend (dē·sĕnd′)
  de·scend·ant (dē·sĕn′ dănt)
  de·scent (dē·sĕnt′)
  (ancestry; see *dissent*)
de·scribe (dē·skrīb′)
  -scrib·ing de·scrib·a·ble
  de·scrip·tion (dē·skrĭp′ shŭn)
  de·scrip·tive (dē·skrĭp′ tĭv)
des·e·crate (dĕs′ ê·krāt)
  -crat·ing
  des·e·cra·tion (dĕs′ ê·krā′ shŭn)
de·seg·re·gate (dē·sĕg′ rê·gāt)
  -gat·ing
  de·seg·re·ga·tion
    (dē·sĕg′ rê·gā′ shŭn)
de·sen·si·tize (dē·sĕn′ sĭ·tīz)
  -tiz·ing
des·ert (dĕz′ ērt)
  (arid region)
de·sert (dē·zûrt′)
  (to abandon; see *dessert*)
  de·sert·er
  de·ser·tion (dē·zûr′ shŭn)
de·serve (dē·zûrv′)
  -serv·ing
  de·serv·ed·ly (-zûr′ vĕd·lĭ)
des·ic·cate (dĕs′ ĭ·kāt)
  -ic·cat·ing
de·sid·er·a·tum
    (dē·sĭd′ ēr·ā′ tŭm)
  pl. de·sid·er·a·ta
de·sign (dē·zīn′)
  de·sign·er
des·ig·nate (dĕz′ ĭg·nāt)
  -nat·ing
  des·ig·na·tion (dĕz′ ĭg·nā′ shŭn)
de·sire (dē·zīr′)
  -sir·ing
  de·sir·a·bil·i·ty
    (dē·zīr′ á·bĭl′ ĭ·tĭ)

de·sir·a·ble   de·sir·ous
de·sist   (dĕ·zĭst')
Des Moines, Ia.   (dĕ moin')
des·o·late   (dĕs' ŏ·lĭt) *adj.*
  -lat·ing   (-lāt) *v.*
  des·o·late·ly   (-lĭt·lĭ)
  des·o·la·tion   (dĕs' ŏ·lā' shŭn)
de·spair   (dĕ·spâr')
  de·spair·ing·ly
des·per·a·do   (dĕs' pĕr·ā' dō)
  -does
des·per·ate   (dĕs' pĕr·ĭt)
  (without hope; see *disparate*)
  des·per·ate·ly
  des·per·a·tion
                  (dĕs' pĕr·ā' shŭn)
des·pi·ca·ble   (dĕs' pĭ·kȧ·b'l)
de·spise   (dĕ·spīz')
  -spis·ing
de·spite   (dĕ·spīt')
de·spoil   (dĕ·spoil')
  de·spoil·er
de·spond·ence   (dĕ·spŏn' dĕns)
  -enc·y   -ent
des·pot   (dĕs' pŏt)
  des·pot·ic   (dĕs·pŏt' ĭk)
  -i·cal·ly
  des·pot·ism   (dĕs' pŏt·ĭz'm)
des·sert   (dĭ·zûrt')
  (sweets; see *desert*)
des·ti·ny   (dĕs' tĭ·nĭ)
  -nies
  des·ti·na·tion (dĕs' tĭ·nā' shŭn)
  des·tined
des·ti·tute   (dĕs' tĭ·tūt)
  des·ti·tu·tion (dĕs' tĭ·tū' shŭn)
de·stroy   (dĕ·stroi')
  de·stroy·er
de·struc·tion   (dĕ·strŭk' shŭn)
  de·struct·i·ble
  de·struc·tive   -tive·ness
des·ue·tude   (dĕs' wē·tūd)
des·ul·to·ry   (dĕs' ŭl·tō' rĭ)
  des·ul·to·ri·ness
de·tach   (dĕ·tăch')
  de·tach·a·ble   de·tach·ment
de·tail   (dĕ·tāl')
  de·tailed
de·tain   (dĕ·tān')
  de·tain·ment
de·tect   (dĕ·tĕkt')
  de·tect·a·ble
  de·tec·tion   (dĕ·tĕk' shŭn)
  de·tec·tor
de·tec·tive   (dĕ·tĕk' tĭv)

de·ten·tion   (dĕ·tĕn' shŭn)
de·ter   (dĕ·tûr')
  -terred   -ter·ring
  de·ter·ment   de·ter·rent
de·ter·gent   (dĕ·tûr' jĕnt)
de·te·ri·o·rate   (dĕ·tĕr' ĭ·ŏ·rāt)
  -rat·ing
  de·te·ri·o·ra·tion
                  (dĕ·tĕr' ĭ·ŏ·rā' shŭn)
de·ter·mine   (dĕ·tûr' mĭn)
  -min·ing
  de·ter·mi·nant
                  (-mĭ' nȧnt)
  de·ter·mi·na·tion
                  (dĕ·tûr' mĭ·nā' shŭn)
  de·ter·mined·ly
                  (-mĭnd·lĭ)
  de·ter·min·ism
                  (-mĭn·ĭz'm)
de·ter·rent   (dĕ·tûr' ĕnt)
  -ter·rence
de·test   (dĕ·tĕst')
  de·test·a·ble
de·throne   (dĕ·thrōn')
  -thron·ing   de·throne·ment
det·o·nate   (dĕt' ŏ·nāt)
  -nat·ing
  det·o·na·tion   (dĕt·ŏ·nā' shŭn)
de·tour   (dē' tōōr)
de·tract   (dĕ·trăkt')
  de·trac·tion   (dĕ·trăk' shŭn)
  de·trac·tor
det·ri·ment   (dĕt' rĭ·mĕnt)
  det·ri·men·tal (dĕt' rĭ·mĕn' tȧl)
deuce   (dūs)
de·val·u·ate   (dĕ·văl' ū·āt)
  -at·ing
  de·val·u·a·tion
                  (dĕ·văl' ū·ā' shŭn)
dev·as·tate   (dĕv' ȧs·tāt)
  -tat·ing
  dev·as·ta·tion
                  (dĕv' ȧs·tā' shŭn)
  dev·as·ta·tor
de·vel·op   (dĕ·vĕl' ŭp)
  -oped   -op·ing
  de·vel·op·er   de·vel·op·ment
  de·vel·op·men·tal
                  (dĕ·vĕl' ŭp·mĕn' tȧl)
de·vi·ate   (dē' vĭ·āt)
  -at·ing
  de·vi·ant   (dē' vĭ·ȧnt)
  de·vi·a·tion   (dē' vĭ·ā' shŭn)
de·vice   (dĕ·vīs') *n.*
  (a scheme)

dev·il	(dĕv′ ′l)
dev·il·ish	dev·il·ment
dev·il·try	
de·vi·ous	(dē′ vĭ·ŭs)
de·vise	(dē·vīz′) v.
(to invent)	-vis·ing
de·vi·tal·ize	(dē·vī′ tăl·ĭz)
-iz·ing	
de·void	(dē·void′)
de·volve	(dē·vŏlv′)
-volv·ing	
de·vote	(dē·vōt′)
-vot·ing	de·vot·ed·ly
dev·o·tee	(dĕv′ ō·tē′)
de·vo·tion	(dē·vō′ shŭn)
-tion·al	
de·vour	(dē·vour′)
de·vout	(dē·vout′)
dew·drop	(dū′ drŏp′)
dew·y	(dū′ ĭ)
dew·i·ness	
dex·ter·i·ty	(dĕks·tĕr′ ĭ·tĭ)
dex·ter·ous	(dĕk′ stĕr·ŭs)
dex·trose	(dĕks′ trōs)
di·a·be·tes	(dī′ à·bē′ tēz)
di·a·bet·ic	(-bĕt′ ĭk)
di·a·bol·ic	(dī′ à·bŏl′ ĭk)
di·a·bol·i·cal	(-ĭ·kăl)
di·a·crit·i·cal mark	
	(dī′ à·krĭt′ ĭ·kăl)
di·a·dem	(dī′ à·dĕm)
di·ag·nose	(dī′ ăg·nōs′)
-nos·ing	
di·ag·no·sis	(dī′ ăg·nō′ sĭs)
pl. -no·ses	(-sēz)
di·ag·nos·tic	(dī′ ăg·nŏs′ tĭk)
di·ag·nos·ti·cian	
	(dī′ ăg·nŏs·tĭsh′ ăn)
di·ag·o·nal	(dī·ăg′ ō·năl)
di·ag·o·nal·ly	
di·a·gram	(dī′ à·grăm)
-gramed	-gram·ing
di·a·gram·mat·ic	
	(dī′ à·grà·măt′ ĭk)
di·al	(dī′ ăl)
di·aled	di·al·ing
di·a·lect	(dī′ à·lĕkt)
di·a·lec·tic	(dī′ à·lĕk′ tĭk)
di·a·lec·ti·cal ma·te·ri·al·ism	
di·a·logue	(dī′ à·lŏg)
di·am·e·ter	(dī·ăm′ ē·tēr)
di·a·met·ric	(dī′ à·mĕt′ rĭk)
di·a·met·ri·cal·ly	
di·a·mond	(dī′ à·mŭnd)
di·a·per	(dī′ à·pēr)

di·aph·a·nous	(dī·ăf′ à·nŭs)
di·a·phragm	(dī′ à·frăm)
di·ar·rhe·a	(dī′ à·rē′ à)
di·ar·rhet·ic	(-rĕt′ ĭk)
di·a·ry	(dī′ à·rĭ)
-ries	
di·a·ther·my	(dī′ à·thŭr′ mĭ)
di·a·tribe	(dī′ à·trīb)
dice	(dīs) n. pl.
sing. die	
di·chot·o·my	(dī·kŏt′ ō·mĭ)
-mies	di·chot·o·mize
-miz·ing	
dick·ey	(dĭk′ ĭ)
-eys	
Dic·ta·phone	(dĭk′ tà·fōn)
dic·tate	(dĭk′ tāt)
-tat·ing	
dic·ta·tion	(dĭk·tā′ shŭn)
dic·ta·tor	
dic·ta·to·ri·al	(dĭk′ tà·tō′ rĭ·ăl)
dic·tion	(dĭk′ shŭn)
dic·tion·ar·y	(dĭk′ shŭn·ĕr′ ĭ)
-ar·ies	
dic·tum	(dĭk′ tŭm)
pl. dic·ta	
di·dac·tic	(dī·dăk′ tĭk)
di·dac·ti·cal	
die	(dī)
died	dy·ing
die·sel en·gine	(dē′ zĕl)
di·et	(dī′ ĕt)
di·e·tar·y	(dī′ ĕ·tĕr′ ĭ)
di·e·tet·ic	(dī′ ĕ·tĕt′ ĭk)
di·e·ti·tian	(dī′ ĕ·tĭsh′ ăn)
dif·fer	(dĭf′ ĕr)
dif·fer·ence	(dĭf′ ĕr·ĕns)
-ent	
dif·fer·en·tial	(dĭf′ ĕr·ĕn′ shăl)
dif·fer·en·ti·ate	
	(dĭf′ ĕr·ĕn′ shĭ·āt)
-at·ing	
dif·fer·en·ti·a·tion	
	(dĭf′ ĕr·ĕn′ shĭ·ā′ shŭn)
dif·fi·cult	(dĭf′ ĭ·kŭlt)
dif·fi·cul·ty	
dif·fi·dence	(dĭf′ ĭ·dĕns)
-dent	
dif·fract	(dĭ·frăkt′)
dif·frac·tion	(dĭ·frăk′ shŭn)
dif·fuse	(dĭ·fūs′) adj.
	(-fūz′) v.
dif·fus·ing	
dif·fu·sion	(dĭ·fū′ zhŭn)
di·gest	(dī′ jĕst) n.

di·gest   (dǐ·jěst′) v.
  di·gest·ant   (-jěs′ tᴗnt)
  di·gest·i·bil·i·ty
                   (dǐ·jěst′ ǐ·bǐl′ ǐ·tǐ)
  di·gest·i·ble   di·ges·tive
dig·it   (dǐj′ ǐt)
  dig·it·al com·pu·ter
                   (dǐj′ ǐ·tᴗl)
dig·i·tal·is   (dǐj′ ǐ·tǎl′ ǐs)
dig·ni·fy   (dǐg′ nǐ·fī)
  -fied,   -fy·ing
dig·ni·tar·y   (dǐg′ nǐ·těr′ ǐ)
  -tar·ies
dig·ni·ty   (dǐg′ nǐ·tǐ)
  -ties
di·gress   (dǐ·grěs′)
  di·gres·sion   (dǐ·grěsh′ ŭn)
dike   (dǐk)
di·lap·i·dat·ed
                   (dǐ·lǎp′ ǐ·dǎt′ ěd)
  di·lap·i·da·tion
                   (dǐ·lǎp′ ǐ·dā′ shŭn)
di·late   (dǐ·lāt′)
  -lat·ing
  di·la·tion   (dǐ·lā′ shŭn)
dil·a·to·ry   (dǐl′ ᴗ·tō′ rǐ)
  dil·a·to·ri·ness
di·lem·ma   (dǐ·lěm′ ᴗ)
dil·et·tan·te   (dǐl′ ě·tän′ tē)
  dil·et·tant·ism
                   (-tän′ tǐz′m)
dil·i·gence   (dǐl′ ǐ·jěns)
  -gent
dil·ly·dal·ly   (dǐl′ ǐ·dǎl′ ǐ)
  -dal·lied   -dal·ly·ing
di·lute   (dǐ·lūt′)
  -lut·ing
  di·lu·tion   (dǐ·lū′ shŭn)
di·men·sion   (dǐ·měn′ shŭn)
  di·men·sion·al
di·min·ish   (dǐ·mǐn′ ǐsh)
dim·i·nu·tion   (dǐm′ ǐ·nū′ shŭn)
di·min·u·tive   (dǐ·mǐn′ û·tǐv)
dim·i·ty   (dǐm′ ǐ·tǐ)
dim·ple   (dǐm′ p'l)
din·er   (dǐn′ ěr)
din·ette   (dǐ·nět′)
din·ghy   (dǐng′ gǐ)
  (rowboat)   -ghies
din·gy   (dǐn′ jǐ)
  (grimy)
  din·gi·ness
din·ing room   (dǐn′ ǐng)
din·ner   (dǐn′ ěr)
di·no·saur   (dī′ nô·sôr)

di·o·cese   (dī′ ô·sēs)
  di·oc·e·san   (dī·ǒs′ ê·sǎn)
Di·og·e·nes   (dī·ǒj′ ê·nēz)
di·o·ra·ma   (dī′ ô·rä′ mᴗ)
di·ox·ide   (dī·ǒk′ sīd)
diph·the·ri·a   (dǐf·thēr′ ǐ·ᴗ)
diph·thong   (dǐf′ thŏng)
di·plo·ma   (dǐ·plō′ mᴗ)
di·plo·ma·cy   (dǐ·plō′ mᴗ·sǐ)
  dip·lo·mat   (dǐp′ lô·mǎt)
  dip·lo·mat·ic   (dǐp′ lô·mǎt′ ǐk)
dip·per   (dǐp′ ěr)
dip·so·ma·ni·a
                   (dǐp′ sô·mā′ nǐ·ᴗ)
  dip·so·ma·ni·ac
                   (-ǎk)
dire   (dīr)
  dire·ness   dir·est
di·rect   (dǐ·rěkt′)
  di·rec·tion   (dǐ·rěk′ shŭn)
  -tion·al   di·rec·tive
  di·rec·tor
  di·rec·to·rate   (dǐ·rěk′ tô·rǐt)
  di·rec·to·ry   (dǐ·rěk′ tô·rǐ)
  -ries
dirge   (dûrj)
dir·i·gi·ble   (dǐr′ ǐ·jǐ·b'l)
dirn·dl   (dûrn′ d'l)
dirt·y   (dûr′ tǐ)
  dirt·ied   dirt·y·ing
dis·a·bil·i·ty   (dǐs′ ᴗ·bǐl′ ǐ·tǐ)
  -ties
dis·a·ble   (dǐs·ā′ b'l)
  -bling   dis·a·ble·ment
dis·ad·van·tage
                   (dǐs′ ǎd·vǎn′ tǐj)
dis·af·fec·tion   (dǐs′ ᴗ·fěk′ shŭn)
dis·a·gree   (dǐs′ ᴗ·grē′)
  dis·a·gree·a·ble
  dis·a·gree·ment
dis·al·low   (dǐs′ ᴗ·lou′)
dis·ap·pear   (dǐs′ ᴗ·pēr′)
  dis·ap·pear·ance
dis·ap·point   (dǐs′ ᴗ·point′)
  dis·ap·point·ed
  dis·ap·point·ment
dis·ap·pro·ba·tion
                   (dǐs′ ǎp·rô·bā′ shŭn)
dis·ap·prove   (dǐs′ ᴗ·proōv′)
  -ap·prov·ing   dis·ap·prov·al
dis·ar·ma·ment
                   (dǐs·är′ mᴗ·měnt)
dis·arm·ing   (dǐs·ärm′ ǐng)
dis·ar·range   (dǐs′ ᴗ·rānj′)
  -ar·rang·ing

dis·ar·ray (dǐs′ ȧ·rā′)
dis·as·sem·ble (dǐs′ ȧ·sĕm′ b'l)
  -bling
dis·as·so·ci·ate (dǐs′ ȧ·sō′ shǐ·āt)
  -at·ing
dis·as·ter (dǐ·zǎs′ tēr)
  dis·as·trous (-trŭs)
dis·a·vow (dǐs′ ȧ·vou′)
  dis·a·vowal
dis·band (dǐs·bǎnd′)
dis·bar (dǐs·bär′)
  -barred   -bar·ring
  dis·bar·ment
dis·be·lief (dǐs′ bê·lēf′)
  dis·be·lieve -liev·ing
dis·burse (dǐs·bûrs′)
  (to pay out; see *disperse*)
  -burs·ing dis·burs·a·ble
  dis·burse·ment
disc (dǐsk)
  disc jock·ey
dis·card (dǐs·kärd′) v.
(dǐs′ kärd) n.
dis·cern (dǐ·zûrn′)
  dis·cern·i·ble dis·cern·ment
dis·charge (dǐs·chärj′)
  -charg·ing
dis·ci·ple (dǐ·sī′ p'l)
dis·ci·pline (dǐs′ ǐ·plǐn)
  dis·ci·pli·nar·i·an
(dǐs′ ǐ·plǐ·nâr′ ǐ·ȧn)
  dis·ci·pli·nar·y
(dǐs′ ǐ·plǐ·nĕr′ ǐ)
dis·claim·er (dǐs·klām′ ēr)
dis·close (dǐs·klōz′)
  -clos·ing
  dis·clo·sure (-klō′ zhēr)
dis·col·or (dǐs·kŭl′ ēr)
  dis·col·or·a·tion
(dǐs·kŭl′ ēr·ā′ shŭn)
dis·com·fit (dǐs·kŭm′ fǐt)
  (embarrass)
  dis·com·fi·ture (-fǐ·tūr)
dis·com·fort (dǐs·kŭm′ fērt)
dis·com·po·sure
(dǐs′ kŏm·pō′ zhēr)
dis·con·cert·ing
(dǐs′ kŏn·sûrt′ ǐng)
dis·con·nect (dǐs′ kǒ·nĕkt′)
  dis·con·nect·ed·ly
dis·con·so·late (dǐs·kŏn′ sŏ·lǐt)
  -late·ly
dis·con·tent·ed
(dǐs′ kŏn·tĕn′ tĕd)

dis·con·tin·ue (dǐs′ kŏn·tǐn′ ū)
  -u·ing
  dis·con·tin·u·a·tion
(-tǐn′ ū·ā′ shŭn)
  dis·con·ti·nu·i·ty
(-tǐ·nū′ ǐ·tǐ)
  dis·con·tin·u·ous
(-tǐn′ ū·ŭs)
dis·cor·dant (dǐs·kôr′ dȧnt)
  -dance
dis·count (dǐs′ kount)
dis·cour·age (dǐs·kûr′ ĭj)
  -ag·ing
  dis·cour·age·ment
dis·course (dǐs·kōrs′)
dis·cour·te·ous (dǐs·kûr′ tê·ŭs)
  dis·cour·te·sy (dǐs·kûr′ tê·sǐ)
  -sies
dis·cov·er·a·ble
(dǐs·kŭv′ ēr·ȧ·b'l)
dis·cov·er·y (dǐs·kŭv′ ēr·ǐ)
  -er·ies
dis·cred·it (dǐs·krĕd′ ǐt)
  -it·ed   -it·ing
  dis·cred·it·a·ble
dis·creet (dǐs·krēt′)
  (prudent)
  dis·cre·tion (dǐs·krĕsh′ ŭn)
dis·crep·an·cy (dǐs·krĕp′ ȧn·sǐ)
dis·crete (dǐs·krēt′)
  (separate)
  dis·cre·tion (dǐs·krĕsh′ ŭn)
dis·crim·i·nate
(dǐs·krǐm′ ǐ·nāt) v.
  -nat·ing
  dis·crim·i·na·tion
(dǐs·krǐm′ ǐ·nā′ shŭn)
  dis·crim·i·na·to·ry
(dǐs·krǐm′ ǐ·nȧ·tō′ rǐ)
dis·cur·sive (dǐs·kûr′ sǐv)
dis·cus (dǐs′ kŭs)
  (athletic device)
dis·cuss (dǐs·kŭs′)
  (to debate)
  dis·cus·sion (-kŭsh′ ŭn)
dis·dain·ful (dǐs·dān′ fŏŏl)
  -ful·ly   -ful·ness
dis·ease (dǐ·zēz′)
dis·em·bark (dǐs′ ĕm·bärk′)
  dis·em·bar·ka·tion
(dǐs·ĕm′ bär·kā′ shŭn)
dis·em·bod·y (dǐs′ ĕm·bŏd′ ǐ)
  -bodied   -bodying
dis·em·bow·el (dǐs′ ĕm·bou′ ĕl)
  -eled   -eling

dis·en·chant·ment
           (dĭs′ ĕn·chánt′ mĕnt)
dis·en·cum·ber
           (dĭs′ ĕn·kŭm′ bĕr)
dis·en·fran·chise
           (dĭs′ ĕn·frăn′ chīz)
  -chis·ing
  dis·en·fran·chise·ment
dis·en·gage   (dĭs′ ĕn·gāj′)
  -gag·ing
  dis·en·gage·ment
dis·en·tan·gle·ment
           (dĭs′ ĕn·tăng′ g'l·mĕnt)
dis·es·teem   (dĭs′ ĕs·tēm′)
dis·fa·vor   (dĭs·fā′ vĕr)
dis·fig·ure·ment
           (dĭs·fĭg′ ûr·mĕnt)
dis·fran·chise   (dĭs·frăn′ chīz)
  chis·ing
dis·gorge   (dĭs·gôrj′)
  -gorg·ing
dis·grace·ful   (dĭs·grās′ fŏŏl)
  -ful·ly   -ful·ness
dis·grun·tled   (dĭs·grŭn′ t'ld)
dis·guise   (dĭs·gīz′)
  -guis·ing
dis·gust·ing   (dĭs·gŭs′ tĭng)
dis·ha·bille   (dĭs′ à·bēl′)
dis·har·mo·ni·ous
           (dĭs′ här·mō′ nĭ·ŭs)
dis·heart·en   (dĭs·här′ t'n)
di·shev·eled   (dĭ·shĕv′ ĕld)
  di·shev·el·ment
dis·hon·es·ty   (dĭs·ŏn′ ĕs·tĭ)
  -ties
dis·hon·or·a·ble
           (dĭs·ŏn′ ĕr·à·b'l)
dis·il·lu·sion   (dĭs′ ĭ·lū′ zhŭn)
  (to free from illusion; see *dis-*
  solution)
dis·in·clined   (dĭs′ ĭn·klīnd′)
  dis·in·cli·na·tion
           (dĭs·ĭn′ klĭ·nā′ shŭn)
dis·in·fect   (dĭs′ ĭn·fĕkt′)
  dis·in·fect·ant dis·in·fec·tion
dis·in·gen·u·ous
           (dĭs′ ĭn·jĕn′ û·ŭs)
dis·in·her·it   (dĭs·ĭn·hĕr′ ĭt)
  -it·ed   -it·ing
  dis·in·her·it·ance
dis·in·te·grate (dĭs·ĭn′ tê·grāt)
  -grat·ing
  dis·in·te·gra·tion
           (dĭs·ĭn′ tê·grā′ shŭn)

dis·in·ter·est·ed
           (dĭs·ĭn′ tĕr·ĕs·tĕd)
dis·joint·ed   (dĭs·join′ tĕd)
dis·junc·tion   (dĭs·jŭngk′ shŭn)
disk   (dĭsk)
  (platelike object; also *disc*)
dis·like   (dĭs·līk′)
  -lik·ing
dis·lo·ca·tion   (dĭs′ lô·kā′ shŭn)
dis·loy·al   (dĭs·loi′ ăl)
  dis·loy·al·ty
dis·mal   (dĭz′ măl)
  dis·mal·ly
dis·man·tle   (dĭs·măn′ t'l)
  -tling
dis·may   (dĭs·mā′)
dis·mem·ber·ment
           (dĭs·mĕm′ bĕr·mĕnt)
dis·miss   (dĭs·mĭs′)
  dis·mis·sal
dis·mount   (dĭs·mount′)
dis·o·be·di·ence
           (dĭs′ ô·bē′ dĭ·ĕns)
dis·o·bey   (dĭs′ ô·bā′)
dis·o·blig·ing (dĭs′ ô·blīj′ ĭng)
dis·or·dered   (dĭs·ôr′ dĕrd)
  dis·or·der·ly -li·ness
dis·or·gan·ized
           (dĭs·ôr′ găn·īzd)
dis·o·ri·ent·ed (dĭs·ô′ rĭ·ĕnt·ĕd)
dis·own   (dĭs·ōn′)
dis·par·age   (dĭs·păr′ ĭj)
  -ag·ing
  dis·par·age·ment
dis·pa·rate   (dĭs′ pà·răt)
  (dissimilar; see *desperate*)
  dis·par·i·ty   (dĭs·păr′ ĭ·tĭ)
dis·pas·sion·ate
           (dĭs·păsh′ ŭn·ĭt)
dis·patch   (dĭs·păch′)
dis·pel   (dĭs·pĕl′)
  -pelled   -pel·ling
dis·pen·sa·ble (dĭs·pĕn′ sà·b'l)
  dis·pen·sa·bil·i·ty
           (dĭs·pĕn′ sà·bĭl′ ĭ·tĭ)
dis·pen·sa·ry   (dĭs·pĕn′ sà·rĭ)
  -ries
dis·pen·sa·tion
           (dĭs′ pĕn·sā′ shŭn)
dis·pens·er   (dĭs·pĕn′ sĕr)
dis·perse   (dĭs·pûrs′)
  (to scatter; see *disburse*)
  -pers·ing
dis·per·sal   (-pûr′ săl)
dis·per·sion   (-pûr′ shŭn)

dis·pir·it·ed (dĭs·pĭr′ ĭt·ĕd)
dis·place (dĭs·plās′)
 -plac·ing
 dis·placed per·son
 dis·place·ment
dis·play (dĭs·plā′)
dis·please (dĭs·plēz′)
 -pleas·ing
 dis·pleas·ure (dĭs·plĕzh′ ẽr)
dis·pose (dĭs·pōz′)
 -pos·ing dis·pos·al
 dis·po·si·tion (dĭs′ pŏ·zĭsh′ ŭn)
dis·pos·sess (dĭs′ pŏ·zĕs′)
dis·pro·por·tion
  (dĭs′ prŏ·pôr′ shŭn)
 dis·pro·por·tion·ate
  (-ĭt)
dis·prove (dĭs·prōōv′)
 -prov·ing
dis·pute (dĭs·pūt′)
 -put·ing dis·pu·ta·ble
 dis·pu·tant (dĭs′ pū·tănt)
 dis·pu·ta·tion (dĭs′ pū·tā′ shŭn)
 dis·pu·ta·tious
  (dĭs′ pū·tā′ shŭs)
dis·qual·i·fy (dĭs·kwŏl′ ĭ·fī)
 -fied -fy·ing
 dis·qual·i·fi·ca·tion
  (dĭs·kwŏl′ ĭ·fī·kā′ shŭn)
dis·qui·et·ing (dĭs·kwī′ ĕt·ĭng)
dis·re·gard (dĭs′ rĕ·gärd′)
dis·re·pair (dĭs′ rĕ·pâr′)
dis·re·pute (dĭs′ rĕ·pūt′)
 dis·rep·u·ta·ble
  (dĭs·rĕp′ ū·tá·b'l)
dis·re·spect (dĭs′ rĕ·spĕkt′)
dis·rupt (dĭs·rŭpt′)
 dis·rup·tion (dĭs·rŭp′ shŭn)
 dis·rup·tive (-tĭv)
dis·sat·is·fy (dĭs·săt′ ĭs·fī)
 -fied, -fy·ing
 dis·sat·is·fac·tion
  (dĭs′ săt·ĭs·făk′ shŭn)
dis·sect (dĭ·sĕkt′)
 dis·sec·tion (dĭ·sĕk′ shŭn)
dis·sem·ble (dĭ·sĕm′ b'l)
 -bling
dis·sem·i·nate (dĭ·sĕm′ ĭ·nāt)
 -nat·ing
 dis·sem·i·na·tion
  (dĭ·sĕm′ ĭ·nā′ shŭn)
dis·sen·sion (dĭ·sĕn′ shŭn)
dis·sent (dĭ·sĕnt′)
 (disagree; see descent)
 dis·sen·ter

dis·sen·tient (dĭ·sĕn′ shĕnt)
dis·ser·ta·tion (dĭs′ ẽr·tā′ shŭn)
dis·serv·ice (dĭs·sûr′ vĭs)
dis·si·dence (dĭs′ ĭ·dĕns)
 -dent
dis·sim·i·lar (dĭ·sĭm′ ĭ·lẽr)
 dis·sim·i·lar·i·ty
  (dĭ·sĭm′ ĭ·lăr′ ĭ·tĭ)
dis·sim·u·late (dĭ·sĭm′ û·lāt)
 -lat·ing
dis·si·pate (dĭs′ ĭ·pāt)
 -pat·ing
 dis·si·pa·tion (dĭs′ ĭ·pā′ shŭn)
 dis·si·pa·tor
dis·so·ci·ate (dĭ·sō′ shĭ·āt)
 -at·ing
 dis·so·ci·a·tion
  (dĭ·sō′ sĭ·ā′ shŭn)
dis·so·lute (dĭs′ ŏ·lūt)
 dis·so·lute·ness
dis·so·lu·tion (dĭs′ ŏ·lū′ shŭn)
  (disintegration; see disillusion)
dis·solve (dĭ·zŏlv′)
 dis·solv·ing dis·sol·vent
dis·so·nance (dĭs′ ŏ·nŏns)
 -nant
dis·suade (dĭ·swād′)
 dis·suad·ing
 dis·sua·sion (dĭ·swā′ zhŭn)
 dis·sua·sive (-sĭv)
dis·sym·me·try
  (dĭs·sĭm′ ĕ·trĭ)
dis·taff (dĭs′ tȧf)
dis·tance (dĭs′ tăns)
dis·taste (dĭs·tāst′)
 dis·taste·ful -ful·ly
 -ful·ness
dis·tem·per (dĭs·tĕm′ pẽr)
dis·tend (dĭs·tĕnd′)
dis·till (dĭs·tĭl′)
 dis·til·la·tion (dĭs′ tĭ·lā′ shŭn)
 dis·til·ler·y (dĭs·tĭl′ ẽr·ĭ)
 -til·ler·ies
dis·tinct (dĭs·tĭngkt′)
 dis·tinc·tion (dĭs·tĭngk′ shŭn)
 dis·tinc·tive (-tĭngk′ tĭv)
dis·tin·guished (dĭs·tĭng′ gwĭsht)
 dis·tin·guish·a·ble
dis·tort (dĭs·tôrt′)
 dis·tor·tion (-tôr′ shŭn)
dis·tract (dĭs·trăkt′)
 dis·tract·ed·ly dis·tract·i·ble
 dis·trac·tion (-trăk′ shŭn)
dis·traught (dĭs·trôt′)

dis·tress (dĭs·trĕs′)
  dis·tress·ful dis·tress·ing·ly
dis·trib·ute (dĭs·trĭb′ ŭt)
  -ut·ing dis·trib·ut·a·ble
  dis·tri·bu·tion
      (dĭs′·trĭ·bū′ shŭn)
  dis·trib·u·tor
dis·trict at·tor·ney
      (dĭs′ trĭkt)
dis·trust·ful (dĭs·trŭst′ fŏŏl)
dis·turb·ance (dĭs·tûr′ bǎns)
dis·un·ion (dĭs·ūn′ yŭn)
dis·use (dĭs·ūs′) n.
ditch (dĭch)
dit·to (dĭt′ ō)
dit·ty (dĭt′ ĭ)
  dit·ties
di·ur·nal (dī·ûr′ nǎl)
  -nal·ly
di·van (dī′ vǎn)
dive bomb·er (dīv)
di·verge (dĭ·vûrj′)
  -verg·ing di·ver·gence,
  -gent
di·vers (dī′ vĕrz)
  (several)
di·verse (dĭ·vûrs′)
  (different)
  di·verse·ly
di·ver·si·fy (dĭ·vûr′ sĭ·fī)
  -fied, -fy·ing
di·ver·si·ty (dĭ·vûr′ sĭ·tĭ)
  -ties
di·ver·sion (dĭ·vûr′ shŭn)
  di·ver·sion·ar·y
di·vert·ing (dĭ·vûrt′ ĭng)
di·vest (dĭ·vĕst′)
di·vide (dĭ·vīd′)
  -vid·ing di·vid·a·ble
div·i·dend (dĭv′ ĭ·dĕnd)
div·i·na·tion (dĭv′ ĭ·nā′ shŭn)
di·vine (dĭ·vīn′)
di·vin·i·ty (dĭ·vĭn′ ĭ·tĭ)
  -ties
di·vis·i·ble (dĭ·vĭz′ ĭ·b′l)
di·vi·sion (dĭ·vĭzh′ ŭn)
  di·vi·sion·al
di·vi·sive (dĭ·vī′ sĭv)
di·vi·sor (dĭ·vī′ zēr)
di·vorce (dĭ·vōrs′)
  -vorc·ing
  di·vor·cee (dĭ·vōr′ sē′)
div·ot (dĭv′ ŭt)
di·vulge (dĭ·vŭlj′)
  -vulg·ing di·vul·gence

Dix·ie (dĭk′ sĭ)
diz·zy (dĭz′ ĭ)
  diz·zi·ness
Do·ber·man pin·scher
    (dō′ bĕr·mǎn pĭn′ shĕr)
doc·ile (dŏs′ ĭl)
  doc·ile·ly
  do·cil·i·ty (dō·sĭl′ ĭ·tĭ)
dock·et (dŏk′ ĕt)
  -et·ed, -et·ing
dock·yard (dŏk′ yärd′)
doc·tor (dŏk′ tēr)
  doc·tor·al (dŏk′ tēr·ǎl)
  doc·tor·ate (dŏk′ tēr·ĭt)
doc·trine (dŏk′ trĭn)
  doc·tri·naire (dŏk′ trĭ·nâr′)
  doc·tri·nal (dŏk′ trĭ·nǎl).
doc·u·ment (dŏk′ ū·mĕnt)
  doc·u·men·ta·ry
      (dŏk′ ū·mĕn′ tà·rĭ)
  -ries
  doc·u·men·ta·tion
      (dŏk′ ū·mĕn·tā′ shŭn)
dod·der·ing (dŏd′ ĕr·ĭng)
dodge (dŏj)
  dodg·ing
do·er (dōō′ ĕr)
doe·skin (dō′ skĭn′)
does·n't (dŭz′ ĕnt)
dog (dŏg)
  dog days dog-eared
  dog·fight dog-ged·ly
  dog·house dog-tired
  dog·watch dog·wood
dog·ger·el (dŏg′ ĕr·ĕl)
dog·ma (dŏg′ mà)
  dog·mat·ic (dŏg·mǎt′ ĭk)
  dog·ma·tism (dŏg′ mà·tĭz′m)
do-good·er (dōō′ gŏŏd′ ĕr)
doi·ly (doi′ lĭ)
  -lies
dol·drums (dŏl′ drŭmz)
dole·ful (dōl′ fŏŏl)
  -ful·ly -ful·ness
dol·lar (dŏl′ ĕr)
dol·lop (dŏl′ ŭp)
dol·man sleeve (dŏl′ mǎn)
dol·or·ous (dŏl′ ĕr·ŭs)
dol·phin (dŏl′ fĭn)
dolt·ish (dōlt′ ĭsh)
do·main (dō·mǎn′)
do·mes·tic (dō·mĕs′ tĭk)
  do·mes·ti·cate (dō·mĕs′ tĭ·kāt)
  -cat·ing

do·mes·tic·i·ty
(dō′ mĕs·tĭs′ ĭ·tĭ)
dom·i·cile (dŏm′ ĭ·sĭl)
dom·i·nant (dŏm′ ĭ·nănt)
-nance
dom·i·nate (dŏm′ ĭ·nāt)
-nat·ing
dom·i·na·tion
(dŏm′ ĭ·nā′ shŭn)
dom·i·neer·ing
(dŏm′ ĭ·nēr′ ĭng)
Do·min·i·can (dō·mĭn′ ĭ·kăn)
Re·pub·lic
do·min·ion (dō·mĭn′ yŭn)
dom·i·no (dŏm′ ĭ·nō)
-noes
do·nate (dō′ nāt)
-nat·ing
do·na·tion (dō·nā′ shŭn)
Don Juan (dŏn hwän′)
don·key (dŏng′ kĭ)
-keys
do·nor (dō′ nĕr)
Don Quix·ote (dŏn kē·hō′ tā)
don't (dōnt)
doo·dle (dōō′ d'l)
-dling
dooms·day (dōōmz′ dā′)
door (dōr)
door·keep·er door·nail
door·step door·way
dope fiend (dōp)
dope·y (dōp′ ĭ)
dor·mant (dôr′ mănt)
-man·cy
dor·mer win·dow
(dôr′ mēr)
dor·mi·to·ry (dôr′ mĭ·tō′ rĭ)
-ries
dor·sal (dôr′ săl)
do·ry (dō′ rĭ)
-ries
dos·age (dōs′ ĭj)
dos·si·er (dŏs′ ĭ·ā)
Do·sto·ev·ski, Fyo·dor
(dŏs′ tŭ·yĕv′ skĭ, fyô′ dēr)
dote (dōt)
dot·ing
dot·age (dōt′ ĭj)
do·tard (dō′ tērd)
dot·ted swiss (dŏt′ ĕd)
dou·ble (dŭb′ 'l)
-bly
dou·ble-breast·ed
dou·ble-deal·ing

dou·ble-deck·er
dou·ble-en·ten·dre
dou·ble-head·er
dou·ble-take dou·ble talk
dou·ble time
doubt (dout)
doubt·er doubt·ful
-ful·ly -ful·ness
doubt·less
douche (dōōsh)
dough·boy (dō′ boi′)
dough·nut (dō′ nŭt′)
dour (dōōr)
douse (dous)
dous·ing
dove·tail (dŭv′ tāl′)
-tailed -tail·ing
dow·a·ger (dou′ á·jēr)
dow·dy (dou′ dĭ)
dow·di·ness
dow·el (dou′ ĕl)
dow·el·ing
down (doun)
down·beat down·cast
down·fall down·heart·ed
down·pour down·stairs
down·town down·trod·den
down·ward down·y
dow·ry (dou′ rĭ)
-ries
dox·ol·o·gy (dŏks·ŏl′ ŏ·jĭ)
-gies
doze (dōz)
doz·ing
doz·en (dŭz′ 'n)
drach·ma (drăk′ má)
draft (drăft)
drafts·man
drag·net (drăg′ nĕt′)
drag·on·fly (drăg′ ŭn·flī′)
-flies
drain (drān)
drain·age (drān′ ĭj)
drain·pipe
dra·ma (drä′ má)
dra·mat·ic (drá·măt′ ĭk)
-i·cal·ly
dram·a·tist (drăm′ á·tĭst)
dram·a·ti·za·tion
(drăm′ á·tĭ·zā′ shŭn)
dra·per·y (drā′ pēr·ĭ)
-per·ies
dras·tic (drăs′ tĭk)
-ti·cal·ly
draw·back (drô′ băk′)

draw·bridge (drô′ brĭj′)
draw·er (drô′ ĕr)
drawl (drôl)
drawn (drôn)
dray·age (drā′ ĭj)
dread·ful (drĕd′ fŏŏl)
  -ful·ly   -ful·ness
dread·nought (drĕd′ nôt′)
dream·land (drēm′ lănd′)
dream·y (drēm′ ĭ)
  dream·i·ness
drear·y (drēr′ ĭ)
  drear·i·ly   drear·i·some
dredge (drĕj)
  dredg·ing
dregs (drĕgz)
drench (drĕnch)
dress·mak·er (drĕs′ māk′ ĕr)
dres·sy (drĕs′ ĭ)
drib·ble (drĭb′ l)
  drib·bling
dri·er (drī′ ĕr)
drift·wood (drĭft′ wŏŏd′)
drill·mas·ter (drĭl′ măs′ tĕr)
drink·a·ble (drĭngk′ á·b′l)
drive (drīv)
  driv·ing   drive-in
  drive·way
driv·el (drĭv′ ′l)
  -eled   -el·ing
driz·zle (drĭz′ ′l)
  driz·zling
droll (drōl)
  droll·er·y (drōl′ ĕr·ĭ)
drom·e·dar·y (drŏm′ ĕ·dĕr′ ĭ)
drone (drōn)
  dron·ing
droop·y (drŏŏp′ ĭ)
  droop·i·ness
drop (drŏp)
  dropped   drop·ping
  drop-forge   drop leaf *n.*
  drop-leaf *adj.*   drop·let
drop·sy (drŏp′ sĭ)
  drop·si·cal
drought (drout)
  (dryness; also *drouth*)
drown (droun)
  drowned   (dround)
drow·sy (drou′ zĭ)
  drow·si·er   -si·est
  -si·ly   -si·ness
drudge (drŭj)
  drudg·er·y

drug (drŭg)
  drugged   drug·ging
  drug·gist   drug·less
  drug·store
dru·id (drŏŏ′ ĭd)
drum (drŭm)
  drum·head
  drum ma·jor·ette
  drum·mer   drum·ming
  drum·stick
drunk·ard (drŭngk′ ĕrd)
drunk·en (drŭngk′ ĕn)
  drunk·en·ly   drunk·en·ness
dry (drī)
  dried   dry·ing
  dri·er   dri·est
  dry-clean   dry clean·ing
  dry goods   dry·ly
  dry·ness   dry rot
du·al (dū′ ăl)
  (double; see *duel*)
  du·al·ism
  du·al·i·ty (dû·ăl′ ĭ·tĭ)
  du·al·ly   du·al-pur·pose
du·bi·ous (dū′ bĭ·ŭs)
du·cal (dū′ kăl)
duc·at (dŭk′ ăt)
duch·ess (dŭch′ ĕs)
duch·y (dŭch′ ĭ)
  duch·ies
duck·ling (dŭk′ lĭng)
duc·tile (dŭk′ tĭl)
  duc·til·i·ty (dŭk·tĭl′ ĭ·tĭ)
duct·less gland (dŭkt′ lĕs)
dude ranch (dūd)
dudg·eon (dŭj′ ŭn)
du·el (dū′ ĕl)
  (fight; see *dual*)
  du·eled   du·el·ing
  du·el·ist
du·en·na (dû·ĕn′ á)
du·et (dû·ĕt′)
duf·fel bag (dŭf′ ĕl)
duf·fer (dŭf′ ĕr)
dug·out (dŭg′ out′)
duke·dom (dūk′ dŭm)
dul·cet (dŭl′ sĕt)
dul·ci·mer (dŭl′ sĭ·mĕr)
dull (dŭl)
  dull·ard (dŭl′ ĕrd)
  dull·ness
  dul·ly
du·ly (dū′ lĭ)
  (in due manner)

dumb·bell (dŭm′ bĕl′)
dum·found (dŭm′ found′)
dum·my (dŭm′ ĭ)
  dum·mies
dump·ling (dŭmp′ lĭng)
Dun·can Phyfe (dŭng′ kăn fīf′)
dun·ga·rees (dŭng′ gå·rēz′)
dun·geon (dŭn′ jŭn)
du·o·de·num (dū′ ô·dē′ nŭm)
dupe (dūp)
  dup·ing
du·plex (dū′ plĕks)
du·pli·cate (dū′ plĭ·kăt)
  adj., n.
  (-kāt) v.
-cat·ing
đu·pli·ca·tion
    (dū′ plĭ·kā′ shŭn)
đu·pli·ca·tor (-kā′ tẽr)
du·plic·i·ty (dû·plĭs′ ĭ·tĭ)
-ties
du·ra·ble (dū′ rå·b′l)
  du·ra·bil·i·ty (dū′ rå·bĭl′ ĭ·tĭ)
du·ra·tion (dū·rā′ shŭn)
du·ress (dū′ rĕs)
dur·ing (dūr′ ĭng)
dusk·y (dŭs′ kĭ)
dust (dŭst)
  dust·bin   dust bowl
  dust·pan
Dutch ov·en (dŭch)
du·ty (dū′ tĭ)
-ties
du·te·ous (dū′ tê·ŭs)
du·ti·ful, -ful·ly, -ful·ness
dwarf (dwôrf)
dwell·ing (dwĕl′ ĭng)
dwin·dle (dwĭn′ d′l)
-dling
dye (dī)
  dyed   dye·ing
  dye·stuff
dy·ing (dī′ ĭng)
  (expiring)
dy·nam·ic (dī·năm′ ĭk)
  dy·nam·i·cal·ly
dy·na·mism (dī′ nå·mĭz′m)
dy·na·mite (dī′ nå·mīt)
dy·na·mo (dī′ nå·mō)
-mos
dy·nas·ty (dī′ nås·tĭ)
-ties
  dy·nas·tic (dī·năs′ tĭk)
dys·en·ter·y (dĭs′ ĕn·tĕr′ ĭ)
dys·func·tion (dĭs·fŭngk′ shŭn)

dys·pep·sia (dĭs·pĕp′ shå)
  dys·pep·tic (dĭs·pĕp′ tĭk)
dys·tro·phy (dĭs′ trô·fĭ)

E

ea·ger (ē′ gẽr)
ea·gle (ē′ g′l)
  ea·glet (ē′ glĕt)
ear (ẽr)
  ear·ache   ear·drum
  ear·phone   ear·ring
  ear·shot
earl·dom (ûrl′ dŭm)
ear·ly (ûr′ lĭ)
  ear·li·er, -li·est, -li·ness
ear·nest (ûr′ nĕst)
earn·ing (ûr′ nĭng)
earth (ûrth)
  earth·en·ware earth·ling
  earth·ly   -li·ness
  earth·quake earth·y
ease (ēz)
  eas·ing
ea·sel (ē′ z′l)
East·er (ēs′ tẽr)
east·ern·er (ēs′ tẽr·nẽr)
east·ward (ēst′ wẽrd)
eas·y (ēz′ ĭ)
  eas·i·er   eas·i·est
  eas·i·ly   eas·i·ness
  eas·y·go·ing
Eau de Co·logne
    (ō đē kô·lōn′)
eaves·drop·per (ēvz′ drŏp′ ẽr)
ebb tide (ĕb tīd)
eb·on·y (ĕb′ ŭn·ĭ)
e·bul·li·ence (ê·bŭl′ ĭ·ĕns)
  e·bul·li·ent
ec·cen·tric (ĕk·sĕn′ trĭk)
  ec·cen·tric·i·ty
    (ĕk′ sĕn·trĭs′ ĭ·tĭ)
Ec·cle·si·as·tes (ê·klē′ zĭ·ăs′ tēz)
ec·cle·si·as·ti·cal
    (ê·klē′ zĭ·ăs′ tĭ·kăl)
ech·e·lon (ĕsh′ ê·lŏn)
ech·o (ĕk′ o)
-oed   -o·ing
  ech·oes
é·clair (å·klâr′)
ec·lec·tic (ĕk·lĕk′ tĭk)
  ec·lec·ti·cism (-tĭ·sĭz′m)
e·clipse (ê·klĭps′)
-clips·ing

ec·logue (ĕk′ lŏg)
e·col·o·gy (ĕ·kŏl′ ð·jǐ)
e·col·o·gist (ĕ·kŏl′ ð·jǐst)
e·con·o·my (ĕ·kŏn′ ð·mǐ)
  -mies
e·co·nom·ic (ē′ kð·nŏm′ ǐk)
e·co·nom·i·cal
                (ē′ kð·nŏm′ ǐ·kðl)
e·con·o·mist (ĕ·kŏn′ ð·mǐst)
e·con·o·mize (ĕ·kŏn′ ð·mǐz)
  -miz·ing
ec·ru (ĕk′ rōō·)
ec·sta·sy (ĕk′ stá·sǐ)
  -sies
ec·stat·ic (ĕk·stǎt′ ǐk)
  -i·cal·ly
ec·to·plasm (ĕk′ tð·plǎz′m)
  ec·to·plas·mic
                (ĕk′ tð·plǎz′ mǐk)
Ec·ua·dor (ĕk′ wá·dôr)
ec·u·men·i·cal
                (ĕk′ û·mĕn′ ǐ·kðl)
ec·ze·ma (ĕk′ sĕ·má)
E·dam cheese (ē′ dǎm)
ed·dy (ĕd′ ǐ)
  ed·died ed·dy·ing
  ed·dies
e·del·weiss (ā′ dĕl·vīs)
E·den (ē′ d′n)
edge (ĕj)
  edg·ing edge·wise
  edg·y
ed·i·ble (ĕd′ ǐ·b′l)
  ed·i·bil·i·ty (ĕd′ ǐ·bǐl′ ǐ·tǐ)
e·dict (ē′ dǐkt)
ed·i·fice (ĕd′ ǐ·fǐs)
ed·i·fy (ĕd′ ǐ·fī)
  -fied -fy·ing
  ed·i·fi·ca·tion
                (ĕd′ ǐ·fǐ·kā′ shǔn)
ed·it (ĕd′ ǐt)
  -it·ed -it·ing
  e·di·tion (ĕ·dǐsh′ ǔn)
  ed·i·tor
  ed·i·to·ri·al (ĕd′ ǐ·tô′ rǐ·ðl)
  -al·ly
ed·u·cate (ĕd′ û·kāt)
  -cat·ing
  ed·u·ca·ble (ĕd′ û·ká·b′l)
  ed·u·ca·tion (ĕd′ û·kā′ shǔn)
  -tion·al
  ed·u·ca·tive (ĕd′ û·kā′ tǐv)
  ed·u·ca·tor (ĕd′ û·kā′ tēr)
e·duce (ĕ·dūs′)
  -duc·ing e·duc·i·ble

ee·rie (ē′ rǐ)
  ee·ri·ly -i·ness
ef·face (ĕ·fās′)
  ef·fac·ing ef·face·ment
ef·fect (ĕ·fĕkt′)
  (result; see affect)
  ef·fec·tive
ef·fec·tu·al (ĕ·fĕk′ tû·ðl)
  ef·fec·tu·ate (-āt)
  -at·ing
ef·fem·i·nate (ĕ·fĕm′ ǐ·nǐt)
  ef·fem·i·na·cy (-ná·sǐ)
ef·fer·vesce (ĕf′ ēr·vĕs′)
  -vesc·ing ef·fer·ves·cence
ef·fete (ĕ·fēt′)
ef·fi·ca·cy (ĕf′ ǐ·ká·sǐ)
  ef·fi·ca·cious (ĕf′ ǐ·kā′ shǔs)
ef·fi·cient (ĕ·fǐsh′ ĕnt)
  ef·fi·cien·cy
ef·fi·gy (ĕf′ ǐ·jǐ)
  -gies
ef·fort (ĕf′ ērt)
  ef·fort·less·ly
ef·fron·ter·y (ĕ·frǔn′ tēr·ǐ)
  -ter·ies
ef·fu·sion (ĕ·fū′ zhǔn)
ef·fu·sive (ĕ·fū′ sǐv)
e·gal·i·tar·i·an
                (ĕ·gǎl′ ǐ·târ′ ǐ·ðn)
egg·head (ĕg′ hĕd′)
egg·nog (ĕg′ nŏg′)
e·go (ē′ gō)
  e·go·cen·tric (ē′ gō·sĕn′ trǐk)
  e·go·ism (ē′ gō·ǐz′m)
  -ist
  e·go·tism (ē′ gō·tǐz′m)
  -tist
  e·go·tis·ti·cal (ē′ gō·tǐs′ tǐ·kðl)
e·gre·gious (ĕ·grē′ jǔs)
e·gress (ē′ grĕs)
e·gret (ē′ grĕt)
E·gypt (ē′ jǐpt)
  E·gyp·tian (ĕ·jǐp′ shðn)
ei·der down (ī′ dēr)
eight·een (ā′ tēn′)
eight·y (ā′ tǐ)
  eight·ies eight·i·eth
Ein·stein the·o·ry
                (īn′ stīn)
Ei·sen·how·er, Dwight D.
                (ī′ s′n·hou′ ēr)
ei·ther (ē′ thēr)
e·jac·u·late (ĕ·jǎk′ û·lāt)
  -lat·ing

e·jac·u·la·tion
    (ê·jăk′ û·lā′ shŭn)
e·jac·u·la·tor
e·ject   (ê·jĕkt′)
  e·jec·tion   (-jĕk′ shŭn)
  e·jec·tor
eke   (ēk)
  ek·ing
e·lab·o·rate   (ê·lăb′ ô·rĭt)
    adj.
    (-rāt) *v.*
  -rat·ing
  e·lab·o·rate·ly   (-rĭt·lĭ)
  e·lab·o·ra·tion
    (ê·lăb′ ô·rā′ shŭn)
é·*lan*   (ā′ läN′)
e·lapse   (ê·lăps′)
  -laps·ing
e·las·tic   (ê·lăs′ tĭk)
  e·las·tic·i·ty   (ê·lăs′ tĭs′ ĭ·tĭ)
e·late   (ê·lāt′)
  -lat·ing   e·lat·ed·ly
  e·la·tion
el·bow   (ĕl′ bō)
  el·bow·room
el·der·ber·ry   (ĕl′ dēr·bĕr′ ĭ)
  -ber·ries
eld·er·ly   (ĕl′ dēr·lĭ)
El Do·ra·do   (ĕl dô·rä′ dō)
e·lect   (ê·lĕkt′)
  e·lec·tion   (ê·lĕk′ shŭn)
  e·lec·tive   e·lec·tor
  e·lec·tor·al col·lege
    (ê·lĕk′ tēr·ăl)
  e·lec·tor·ate   (ê·lĕk′ tēr·ĭt)
e·lec·tric   (ê·lĕk′ trĭk)
  e·lec·tri·cal
  e·lec·tri·cian   (ê·lĕk′ trĭsh′ ăn)
  e·lec·tric·i·ty   (ê·lĕk′ trĭs′ ĭ·tĭ)
e·lec·tri·fy   (ê·lĕk′ trĭ·fī)
  -fied   -fy·ing
  e·lec·tri·fi·ca·tion
    (ê·lĕk′ trĭ·fĭ·kā′ shŭn)
e·lec·tro·car·di·o·gram
    (ê·lĕk′ trô·kär′ dĭ·ô·grăm′)
e·lec·tro·cute   (ê·lĕk′ trô·kūt)
  -cut·ing
  e·lec·tro·cu·tion
    (ê·lĕk′ trô·kū′ shŭn)
e·lec·trode   (ê·lĕk′ trōd)
e·lec·tro·dy·nam·ics
    (ê·lĕk′ trô·dī·năm′ ĭks)
e·lec·trol·y·sis   (ê·lĕk′ trŏl′ ĭ·sĭs)
e·lec·tro·lyt·ic   (ê·lĕk′ trô·lĭt′ ĭk)

e·lec·tro·mag·net·ic
    (ê·lĕk′ trô·măg·nĕt′ ĭk)
e·lec·tron   (ê·lĕk′ trŏn)
  e·lec·tron·ic   (ê·lĕk′ trŏn′ ĭk)
e·lec·tro·plate   (ê·lĕk′ trô·plāt′)
  -plat·ing
e·lec·tro·ther·a·py
    (ê·lĕk′ trô·thĕr′ á·pĭ)
el·ee·mos·y·nar·y
    (ĕl′ ê·mŏs′ ĭ·nĕr′ ĭ)
el·e·gance   (ĕl′ ê·gáns)
  -gant
el·e·gy   (ĕl′ ê·jĭ)
  -gies
el·e·gi·ac   (ĕl′ ê·jī′ ăk)
el·e·gize   (ĕl′ ê·jīz)
  -giz·ing
el·e·ment   (ĕl′ ê·mĕnt)
  el·e·men·tal   (ĕl′ ê·mĕn′ tál)
  el·e·men·ta·ry   (ĕl′ ê·mĕn′ tá·rĭ)
el·e·phant   (ĕl′ ê·fánt)
  el·e·phan·tine   (ĕl′ ê·făn′ tĭn)
el·e·vate   (ĕl′ ê·vāt)
  -vat·ing
  el·e·va·tion   (ĕl′ ê·vā′ shŭn)
  el·e·va·tor   (ĕl′ ê·vā′ tēr)
e·lev·en   (ê·lĕv′ ĕn)
elf·in   (ĕl′ fĭn)
e·lic·it   (ê·lĭs′ ĭt)
  (to draw forth; see *illicit*)
  -it·ed   -it·ing
e·lide   (ê·līd′)
  -lid·ing
  e·li·sion   (ê·lĭzh′ ŭn)
el·i·gi·ble   (ĕl′ ĭ·jĭ·b′l)
  el·i·gi·bil·i·ty   (ĕl′ ĭ·jĭ·bĭl′ ĭ·tĭ)
e·lim·i·nate   (ê·lĭm′ ĭ·nāt)
  -nat·ing
  e·lim·i·na·tion
    (ê·lĭm′ ĭ·nā′ shŭn)
e·li·sion   (ê·lĭzh′ ŭn)
e·lite   (â·lēt′)
e·lix·ir   (ê·lĭk′ sēr)
E·liz·a·be·than   (ê·lĭz′ á·bē′ thán)
el·lipse   (ê·lĭps′)
  el·lip·sis   el·lip·tic
  -ti·cal
el·o·cu·tion   (ĕl′ ô·kū′ shŭn)
e·lon·gate   (ê·lŏng′ gāt)
  -gat·ing
  e·lon·ga·tion
    (ê·lŏng′ gā′ shŭn)
e·lope   (ê·lōp′)
  -lop·ing   e·lope·ment

el·o·quence (ĕl' ō·kwĕns)
  -quent
else·where (ĕls' hwâr)
e·lu·ci·date (ê·lū' sĭ·dāt)
  -dat·ing
  e·lu·ci·da·tion
    (ê·lū' sĭ·dā' shŭn)
e·lude (ê·lūd')
  (evade; see *allude*)
  -lud·ing
  e·lu·sion (ê·lū' zhŭn)
e·lu·sive (ê·lū' sĭv)
  (baffling; see *illusive*)
e·ma·ci·ate (ê·mā' shĭ·āt)
  (to make thin)
  -at·ing
  e·ma·ci·a·tion
    (ê·mā' sĭ·ā·shŭn)
em·a·nate (ĕm' á·nāt)
  (to flow)
  -nat·ing
  em·a·na·tion (ĕm' á·nā' shŭn)
e·man·ci·pate (ê·măn' sĭ·pāt)
  (to free)
  -pat·ing
  e·man·ci·pa·tion
    (ê·măn' sĭ·pā' shŭn)
e·mas·cu·late (ê·măs' kū·lāt)
  -lat·ing
  e·mas·cu·la·tion
    (ê·măs' kū·lā' shŭn)
em·balm (ĕm·bäm')
em·bank·ment (ĕm·băngk' mĕnt)
em·bar·go (ĕm·bär' gō)
  -goes
em·bark (ĕm·bärk')
  em·bar·ka·tion
    (ĕm' bär·kā' shŭn)
  em·bark·ment
em·bar·rass (ĕm·băr' ăs)
  em·bar·rass·ment
em·bas·sy (ĕm' bă·sĭ)
  -bas·sies
em·bat·tle (ĕm·băt' 'l)
  -bat·tling
em·bed (ĕm·bĕd')
  -bed·ded -bed·ding
em·bel·lish (ĕm·bĕl' ĭsh)
em·ber (ĕm' bēr)
em·bez·zle (ĕm·bĕz' 'l)
  -bez·zling
  em·bez·zle·ment
  em·bez·zler
em·bit·ter (ĕm·bĭt' ēr)
em·bla·zon (ĕm·blā' z'n)

em·blem (ĕm' blĕm)
  em·blem·at·ic (ĕm' blĕ·măt' ĭk)
em·bod·y (ĕm·bŏd' ĭ)
  -bod·ied -bod·y·ing
  em·bod·i·ment
    (ĕm·bŏd' ĭ·mĕnt)
em·bold·en (ĕm·bōl' dĕn)
em·boss (ĕm·bŏs')
em·brace (ĕm·brās')
  -brac·ing
em·broi·der (ĕm·broi' dēr)
  em·broi·der·y
em·broil (ĕm·broil')
em·bry·o (ĕm' brĭ·ō)
  -os
  em·bry·o·log·i·cal
    (ĕm' brĭ·ô·lŏj' ĭ·kăl)
  em·bry·ol·o·gy
    (ĕm' brĭ·ŏl' ô·jĭ)
  em·bry·on·ic (ĕm' brĭ·ŏn' ĭk)
em·cee (ĕm' sē')
e·mend (ê·mĕnd')
  e·men·da·tion
    (ē' mĕn·dā' shŭn)
em·er·ald (ĕm' ēr·ăld)
  Em·er·ald Isle
e·merge (ê·mûrj')
  -merg·ing e·mer·gent,
  -gence
e·mer·gen·cy (ê·mûr' jĕn·sĭ)
  -cies
e·mer·i·tus (ê·mĕr' ĭ·tŭs)
e·merse (ê·mûrs')
  -mers·ing
  e·mer·sion (ê·mûr' shŭn)
em·er·y (ĕm' ēr·ĭ)
e·met·ic (ê·mĕt' ĭk)
em·i·grate (ĕm' ĭ·grāt)
  (to leave one's homeland; see
  immigrate) -grat·ing
  em·i·grant (-grănt)
  em·i·gra·tion (ĕm' ĭ·grā' shŭn)
  é·mi·gré (ā' mē' grā')
em·i·nence (ĕm' ĭ·nĕns)
  em·i·nent do·main
em·is·sar·y (ĕm' ĭ·sĕr' ĭ)
  em·is·sar·ies
e·mis·sion (ê·mĭsh' ŭn)
e·mit (ê·mĭt')
  -mit·ted -mit·ting
e·mol·li·ent (ê·mŏl' ĭ·ĕnt)
  (lotion)
e·mol·u·ment (ê·mŏl' ủ·mĕnt)
  (wages)

e·mo·tion (ê·mō′ shŭn)
  e·mo·tion·al -al·ly
e·mo·tive (ê·mō′ tĭv)
em·pa·thy (ĕm′ pà·thĭ)
em·per·or (ĕm′ pĕr·ẽr)
em·pha·sis (ĕm′ fá·sĭs)
  pi. em·pha·ses (-sēz)
  em·pha·size -siz·ing
em·phat·ic (ĕm·făt′ ĭk)
  -i·cal·ly
em·pire (ĕm′ pīr)
em·pir·ic (ĕm·pĭr′ ĭk)
  em·pir·i·cal
  em·pir·i·cism (-ĭ·sĭz′m)
em·place·ment (ĕm·plās′ mĕnt)
em·ploy (ĕm·ploi′)
  em·ploy·a·ble em·ploy·ee
  em·ploy·er em·ploy·ment
em·po·ri·um (ĕm·pō′ rĭ·ŭm)
em·pow·er (ĕm·pou′ ẽr)
emp·ty (ĕmp′ tĭ)
  -tied -ty·ing
  emp·ti·ly -ti·ness
em·py·re·an (ĕm′ pĭ·rē′ ăn)
em·u·late (ĕm′ û·lāt)
  -lat·ing
  em·u·la·tion (ĕm′ û·lā′ shŭn)
  em·u·la·tive (ĕm′ û·lā′ tĭv)
  em·u·la·tor (ĕm′ û·lā′ tẽr)
e·mul·si·fy (ê·mŭl′ sĭ·fī)
  -fied -fy·ing
  e·mul·si·fi·ca·tion
    (ê·mŭl′ sĭ·fĭ·kā′ shŭn)
e·mul·sion (ê·mŭl′ shŭn)
en·a·ble (ĕn·ā′ b'l)
  -bling
en·act·ment (ĕn·ăkt′ mĕnt)
en·am·el (ĕn·ăm′ ĕl)
  -eled -el·ing
en·am·ored (ĕn·ăm′ ẽrd)
en·camp·ment (ĕn·kămp′ mĕnt)
en·ceph·a·lo·gram
    (ĕn·sĕf′ à·lò·grăm′)
en·chant (ĕn·chánt′)
  en·chant·ress
en·cir·cle (ĕn·sûr′ k'l)
  -cling en·cir·cle·ment
en·clasp (ĕn·klásp′)
en·clave (ĕn′ klāv)
en·close (ĕn·klōz′)
  -clos·ing
  en·clo·sure (ĕn·klō′ zhẽr)
en·co·mi·um (ĕn·kō′ mĭ·ŭm)
en·com·pass (ĕn·kŭm′ pás)
en·core (äng′ kōr)

en·coun·ter (ĕn·koun′ tẽr)
en·cour·age (ĕn·kûr′ ĭj)
  -ag·ing
  en·cour·age·ment
en·croach (ĕn·krōch′)
en·crust (ĕn·krŭst′)
en·cum·ber (ĕn·kŭm′ bẽr)
  en·cum·brance
en·cyc·li·cal (ĕn·sĭk′ lĭ·kál)
en·cy·clo·pe·di·a
    (ĕn·sī′ klò·pē′ dĭ·à)
  en·cy·clo·pe·dic
en·dan·ger (ĕn·dăn′ jẽr)
en·dear·ing (ĕn·dẽr′ ĭng)
en·deav·or (ĕn·dĕv′ ẽr)
en·dem·ic (ĕn·dĕm′ ĭk)
  en·dem·i·cal·ly
en·dive (ĕn′ dĭv)
end·less·ly (ĕnd′ lĕs·lĭ)
en·do·crine (ĕn′ dò·krĭn)
  en·do·cri·nol·o·gy
    (ĕn′ dò·krĭ·nŏl′ ò·jĭ)
en·dorse (ĕn·dôrs′)
  -dors·ing en·dors·a·ble
  en·dor·see (ĕn′ dôr·sē′)
  en·dorse·ment
en·dow·ment (ĕn·dou′ mĕnt)
en·due (ĕn·dū′)
  -du·ing
en·dure (ĕn·dūr′)
  -dur·ing en·dur·a·ble
  en·dur·ance
en·e·ma (ĕn′ ê·mà)
en·e·my (ĕn′ ê·mĭ)
  -mies
en·er·gy (ĕn′ ẽr·jĭ)
  -gies
  en·er·get·ic (ĕn′ ẽr·jĕt′ ĭk)
  -i·cal·ly
  en·er·gize (ĕn′ ẽr·jīz)
  -giz·ing
en·er·vate (ĕn′ ẽr·vāt)
  (to deprive of nerve; see *innervate*)
  -vat·ing
  en·er·va·tion (ĕn′ ẽr·vā′ shŭn)
en·fee·ble (ĕn·fē′ b'l)
  -fee·bling
en·force (ĕn·fōrs′)
  -forc·ing en·force·a·ble
  en·force·ment
en·fran·chise (ĕn·frăn′ chīz)
  -chis·ing
  en·fran·chise·ment
en·gage (ĕn·gāj′)
  -gag·ing en·gage·ment

en·gen·der	(ĕn·jĕn′ dĕr)
en·gine	(ĕn′ jĭn)
en·gi·neer	(ĕn′ jĭ·nẽr′)
en·gi·neer·ing	
Eng·lish·man	(ĭng′ glĭsh·mǎn)
en·grave	(ĕn·grāv′)
-grav·ing	en·grav·er
en·gross	(ĕn·grōs′)
en·gulf	(ĕn·gŭlf′)
en·hance	(ĕn·hăns′)
-hanc·ing	en·hance·ment
e·nig·ma	(ê·nĭg′ mä)
e·nig·mat·ic	(ê′ nĭg·măt′ ĭk)
-i·cal·ly	
en·join	(ĕn·join′)
en·joy	(ĕn·joi′)
en·joy·a·ble	en·joy·ment
en·large	(ĕn·lärj′)
-larg·ing	en·large·ment
en·light·en·ment	
	(ĕn·līt′ 'n·mĕnt)
en·list	(ĕn·lĭst′)
en·list·ment	
en·liv·en	(ĕn·lĭv′ ĕn)
en masse	(ĕn mäs′)
en·mesh	(ĕn·mĕsh′)
en·mi·ty	(ĕn′ mĭ·tĭ)
(ill will; see *amity*)	
-ties	
en·no·ble	(ê·nō′ b'l)
-bling	
en·nui	(än′ wê)
e·nor·mous	(ê·nôr′ mŭs)
e·nor·mi·ty	(ê·nôr′ mĭ·tĭ)
e·nough	(ê·nŭf′)
en·plane	(ĕn·plān′)
-plan·ing	
en·rage	(ĕn·rāj′)
-rag·ing	
en·rap·ture	(ĕn·răp′ tûr)
-tur·ing	
en·rich	(ĕn·rĭch′)
en·roll	(ĕn·rōl′)
en·roll·ment	
en route	(än rōōt′)
en·sconce	(ĕn·skŏns′)
-sconc·ing	
en·sem·ble	(än·sŏm′ b'l)
en·shrine	(ĕn·shrīn′)
-shrin·ing	
en·shroud	(ĕn·shroud′)
en·sign	(ĕn′ sīn)
en·slave·ment	(ĕn·slāv′ mĕnt)
en·sue	(ĕn·sū′)
-su·ing	

en·tail	(ĕn·tāl′)
en·tan·gle	(ĕn·tăng′ g'l)
-gling	en·tan·gle·ment
en·tente cor·diale	
	(än′ tänt′ kôr′ dyäl′)
en·ter	(ĕn′ tẽr)
en·trant	
en·ter·prise	(ĕn′ tẽr·prīz)
-pris·ing	
en·ter·tain	(ĕn′ tẽr·tān′)
en·ter·tain·ing·ly	
en·ter·tain·ment	
en·thrall	(ĕn·thrôl′)
en·throne	(ĕn·thrōn′)
-thron·ing	en·throne·ment
en·thu·si·asm	(ĕn·thū′ zĭ·ăz'm)
en·thu·si·ast	(ĕn·thū′ zĭ·ăst)
en·thu·si·as·tic	
	(ĕn·thū′ zĭ·ăs′ tĭk)
-ti·cal·ly	
en·tice	(ĕn·tīs′)
-tic·ing	en·tice·ment
en·tire·ty	(ĕn·tīr′ tĭ)
en·ti·tle	(ĕn·tī′ t'l)
-ti·tling	
en·ti·ty	(ĕn′ tĭ·tĭ)
-ties	
en·to·mol·o·gy	(ĕn′ tô·mŏl′ ô·jĭ)
en·tou·rage	(än·tŏō·räzh′)
en·trails	(ĕn′ trālz)
en·trance	(ĕn′ trŭns) *n.*
en·trance	(ĕn·träns′) *v.*
-tranc·ing	
en·trant	(ĕn′ trănt)
en·treat	(ĕn·trēt′)
en·treat·ing·ly	
en·treat·y	-treat·ies
en·tree	(än′ trā)
en·trench·ment	
	(ĕn·trĕnch·mĕnt)
en·tre·pre·neur	
	(än′ trĕ·prĕ·nûr′)
en·trust	(ĕn·trŭst′)
en·try	(ĕn′ trĭ)
-tries	en·try·way
en·twine	(ĕn·twīn′)
-twin·ing	
e·nu·mer·ate	(ê·nū′ mĕr·āt)
-at·ing	
e·num·er·a·tion	
	(ê·nū′ mĕr·ā′ shŭn)
e·nun·ci·ate	(ê·nŭn′ shĭ·āt)
-at·ing	
e·nun·ci·a·tion	
	(ê·nŭn′ sĭ·ā′ shŭn)

en·vel·op (ĕn·vĕl′ ŭp) v.
(to wrap up)
-oped -op·ing
en·vel·op·ment
en·ve·lope (ĕn′ vĕ·lōp) n.
(letter container)
en·ven·om (ĕn·vĕn′ ŭm)
en·vi·a·ble (ĕn′ vĭ·à·b′l)
en·vi·ous (ĕn′ vĭ·ŭs)
en·vi·ron·ment
(ĕn·vī′ rŭn·mĕnt)
en·vi·ron·men·tal
(ĕn·vī′ rŭn·mĕn′ tăl)
en·vi·rons (ĕn·vī′ rŭnz)
en·vis·age (ĕn·vĭz′ ĭj)
-ag·ing
en·vi·sion (ĕn·vĭzh′ ŭn)
en·voy (ĕn′ voi)
en·vy (ĕn′ vĭ)
-vied -vy·ing
en·wrap (ĕn·răp′)
-wrapped -wrap·ping
en·zyme (ĕn′ zīm)
e·on (ē′ ŏn)
ep·au·let (ĕp′ ô·lĕt)
e·phem·er·al (ě·fĕm′ ĕr·ăl)
ep·ic (ĕp′ ĭk)
ep·i·cure (ĕp′ ĭ·kūr)
ep·i·cu·re·an (ĕp′ ĭ·kū·rē′ ăn)
ep·i·dem·ic (ĕp′ ĭ·dĕm′ ĭk)
ep·i·der·mis (ĕp′ ĭ·dûr′ mĭs)
ep·i·gram (ĕp′ ĭ·grăm)
ep·i·gram·mat·ic
(ĕp′ ĭ·grà·măt′ ĭk)
ep·i·lep·sy (ĕp′ ĭ·lĕp′ sĭ)
ep·i·lep·tic (ĕp′ ĭ·lĕp′ tĭk)
ep·i·logue (ĕp′ ĭ·lôg)
E·piph·a·ny (ě·pĭf′ à·nĭ)
E·pis·co·pa·li·an
(ě·pĭs′ kō·pā′ lĭ·ăn)
ep·i·sode (ĕp′ ĭ·sōd)
e·pis·tle (ě·pĭs′ ′l)
ep·i·taph (ĕp′ ĭ·tăf)
(tomb inscription)
ep·i·thet (ĕp′ ĭ·thĕt)
(nickname)
e·pit·o·me (ě·pĭt′ ô·mē)
e·pit·o·mize (ě·pĭt′ ô·mīz)
-miz·ing
ep·och (ĕp′ ŏk)
ep·och·al
eq·ua·ble (ĕk′ wà·b′l)
e·qual (ē′ kwăl)
-qualed -qual·ing
e·qual·i·ty (ê·kwŏl′ ĭ·tĭ)

e·qual·ize -iz·ing
e·qual·ly
e·qua·nim·i·ty (ē′ kwà·nĭm′ ĭ·tĭ)
e·quate (ê·kwāt′)
-quat·ing
e·qua·tion (ê·kwā′ zhŭn)
e·qua·tor (ê·kwā′ tẽr)
e·qua·to·ri·al (ē′ kwà·tō′ rĭ·ăl)
e·ques·tri·an (ê·kwĕs′ trĭ·ăn)
e·qui·dis·tant (ē′ kwĭ·dĭs′ tănt)
e·qui·lat·er·al (ē′ kwĭ·lăt′ ĕr·ăl)
-al·ly
e·qui·li·bra·tion
(ē′ kwĭ·lĭ·brā′ shŭn)
e·qui·lib·ri·um
(ē′ kwĭ·lĭb′ rĭ·ŭm)
e·quine (ē′ kwīn)
e·qui·nox (ē′ kwĭ·nŏks)
e·qui·noc·tial
(ē′ kwĭ·nŏk′ shăl)
e·quip (ê·kwĭp′)
-quipped -quip·ping
eq·ui·page (ĕk′ wĭ·pĭj)
e·quip·ment
eq·ui·ta·ble (ĕk′ wĭ·tà·b′l)
eq·ui·ty (ĕk′ wĭ·tĭ)
-ties
e·quiv·a·lent (ê·kwĭv′ à·lĕnt)
-lence
e·quiv·o·cal (ê·kwĭv′ ô·kăl)
-cal·ly
e·quiv·o·cate (ê·kwĭv′ ô·kāt)
-cat·ing
e·quiv·o·ca·tion
(ê·kwĭv′ ô·kā′ shŭn)
e·ra (ē′ rà)
e·rad·i·cate (ê·răd′ ĭ·kāt)
-cat·ing
e·rad·i·ca·ble (ê·răd′ ĭ·kà·b′l)
e·rad·i·ca·tion
(ê·răd′ ĭ·kā′ shŭn)
e·rad·i·ca·tor (ê·răd′ ĭ·kā′ tẽr)
e·rase (ê·rās′)
-ras·ing e·ras·a·ble
e·ras·er
e·ra·sure (ê·rā′ zhẽr)
e·rect (ê·rĕkt′)
e·rect·er
e·rec·tile (ê·rĕk′ tĭl)
e·rec·tion
er·go (ûr′ gō)
er·mine (ûr′ mĭn)
e·rode (ê·rōd′)
-rod·ing
e·ro·sion (ê·rō′ zhŭn)

e·rot·ic   (ē·rŏt′ ĭk)
err   (ûr)
er·rand   (ĕr′ ănd)
er·rant   (ĕr′ ănt)
   (wandering; *see* arrant)
er·rat·ic   (ĕ·răt′ ĭk)
   -i·cal·ly
er·ra·tum   (ĕ·rā′ tŭm)
   pl. er·ra·ta
er·ro·ne·ous   (ĕ·rō′ nē·ŭs)
er·ror   (ĕr′ ẽr)
er·satz   (ĕr·zäts′)
erst·while   (ûrst′ hwīl′)
er·u·dite   (ĕr′ ŏŏ·dīt)
er·u·di·tion   (ĕr′ ŏŏ·dĭsh′ ŭn)
e·rupt   (ĕ·rŭpt′)
   e·rup·tion   e·rup·tive
es·ca·la·tor   (ĕs′ kà·lā′ tẽr)
es·ca·pade   (ĕs′ kà·pād′)
es·cape   (ĕs·kāp′)
   -cap·ing   es·cap·a·ble
   es·cape·ment   es·cap·ism, -ist
es·ca·role   (ĕs′ kà·rōl)
es·carp·ment   (ĕs·kärp′ mĕnt)
es·chew   (ĕs·chŏŏ′)
es·cort   (ĕs′ kôrt) *n.*
                        (ĕs·kôrt′) *v.*
es·crow   (ĕs′ krō′)
es·cutch·eon   (ĕs·kŭch′ ŭn)
Es·ki·mo   (ĕs′ kĭ·mō)
   -mos
es·o·ter·ic   (ĕs′ ō·tĕr′ ĭk)
es·pe·cial   (ĕs·pĕsh′ ăl)
   es·pe·cial·ly
Es·pe·ran·to   (ĕs′ pĕ·rän′ tō)
es·pi·o·nage   (ĕs′ pĭ·ō·nĭj)
es·pla·nade   (ĕs′ plà·nād′)
es·pouse   (ĕs·pouz′)
   -pous·ing   es·pous·al
es·prit de corps
                       (ĕs′ prē′ dē kôr′)
es·py   (ĕs·pī′)
   -pied   -py·ing
es·quire   (ĕs·kwīr′)
es·say   (ĕ·sā′) *v.*
                 (ĕs′ ā) *n.*
es·sence   (ĕs′ ĕns)
es·sen·tial   (ĕ·sĕn′ shăl)
   -tial·ly
es·tab·lish   (ĕs·tăb′ lĭsh)
es·tate   (ĕs·tāt′)
es·teem   (ĕs·tēm′)
es·ti·ma·ble   (ĕs′ tĭ·mà·b′l)
es·ti·mate   (ĕs′ tĭ·māt) *n.*
   -mat·ing   (-māt) *v.*

es·ti·ma·tion   (ĕs′ tĭ·mā′ shŭn)
es·top   (ĕs·tŏp′)
   -topped   -top·ping
   es·top·page
es·trange   (ĕs·trānj′)
   -trang·ing   es·trange·ment
es·tro·gen   (ĕs′ trō·jĕn)
   es·tro·gen·ic   (ĕs′ trō·jĕn′ ĭk)
es·tu·ar·y   (ĕs′ tū·ĕr′ ĭ)
   -ar·ies
et cet·er·a   (ĕt sĕt′ ĕr·à)
etch·ing   (ĕch′ ĭng)
e·ter·nal   (ĕ·tûr′ năl)
   -nal·ly
e·ter·ni·ty   (ĕ·tûr′ nĭ·tĭ)
e·ther   (ē′ thĕr)
e·the·re·al   (ē·thēr′ ē·ăl)
eth·ics   (ĕth′ ĭks)
   eth·i·cal
eth·nic   (ĕth′ nĭk)
e·thos   (ē′ thŏs)
eth·yl   (ĕth′ ĭl)
e·ti·ol·o·gy   (ē′ tĭ·ŏl′ ō·jĭ)
et·i·quette   (ĕt′ ĭ·kĕt)
E·ton jack·et   (ē′ t′n)
E·trus·can   (ē·trŭs′ kăn)
é·tude   (ā′ tūd)
et·y·mol·o·gy   (ĕt′ ĭ·mŏl′ ō·jĭ)
   et·y·mol·o·gist
eu·ca·lyp·tus   (ū′ kà·lĭp′ tŭs)
Eu·cha·rist   (ū′ kà·rĭst)
eu·chre   (ū′ kẽr)
Eu·clid   (ū′ klĭd)
   Eu·clid·e·an   (û·klĭd′ ē·ăn)
eu·gen·ic   (û·jĕn′ ĭk)
eu·lo·gy   (ū′ lō·jĭ)
   -gies
   eu·lo·gis·tic   (ū′ lō·jĭs′ tĭk)
   eu·lo·gize   (ū′ lō·jīz)
   -giz·ing
eu·nuch   (ū′ nŭk)
eu·phe·mism   (ū′ fē·mĭz′m)
   eu·phe·mis·tic   (ū′ fē·mĭs′ tĭk)
   -ti·cal·ly
eu·phon·ic   (û·fŏn′ ĭk)
eu·pho·ri·a   (û·fō′ rĭ·à)
eu·re·ka   (û·rē′ kà)
Eu·ro·pe·an   (ū′ rō·pē′ ăn)
Eu·sta·chi·an tube
                   (û·stā′ kĭ·ăn)
eu·tha·na·si·a   (ū′ thà·nā′ zhĭ·à)
e·vac·u·ate   (ē·văk′ û·āt)
   -at·ing
   e·vac·u·a·tion
                   (ē·văk′ û·ā′ shŭn)

e·vac·u·ee (ĕ·văk′ û·ē′)
e·vade (ĕ·vād′)
 -vad·ing
e·val·u·ate (ă·văl′ û·āt)
 -at·ing
e·val·u·a·tion
    (ĕ·văl′ û·ā′ shŭn)
ev·a·nes·cent (ĕv′ á·nĕs′ ĕnt)
 -cence
e·van·gel·i·cal
    (ā′ văn·jĕl′ ĭ·kđl)
e·van·ge·list (ĕ·văn′ jĕ·list)
e·vap·o·rate (ĕ·văp′ ô·rāt)
 -rat·ing
e·vap·o·ra·tion
    (ĕ·văp′ ô·rā′ shŭn)
e·va·sion (ĕ·vā′ zhŭn)
e·va·sive -sive·ly
e·ven (ē′ vĕn)
e·ven·ly e·ven·ness
eve·ning (ēv′ nĭng)
e·vent (ĕ·vĕnt′)
e·vent·ful, -ful·ly, -ful·ness
e·ven·tide (ē′ vĕn·tīd′)
e·ven·tu·al (ĕ·vĕn′ tû·đl)
e·ven·tu·al·i·ty
    (ĕ·vĕn′ tû·ăl′ ĭ·tĭ)
e·ven·tu·al·ly
ev·er (ĕv′ ĕr)
 the Ev·er·glades
ev·er·green ev·er·last·ing
ev·er·more
ev·er·y (ĕv′ ĕr·ĭ)
ev·er·y·bod·y
ev·er·y·day adj.
ev·er·y·one pron.
ev·er·y·thing ev·er·y·where
e·vict (ĕ·vĭkt′)
e·vic·tion (ĕ·vĭk′ shŭn)
ev·i·dence (ĕv′ ĭ·dĕns)
ev·i·dent·ly
e·vil (ē′ v′l)
e·vil·do·er -do·ing
e·vil·ly e·vil-mind·ed
e·vince (ĕ·vĭns′)
 -vinc·ing e·vin·ci·ble
e·vis·cer·ate (ĕ·vĭs′ ĕr·āt)
 -at·ing
e·vis·cer·a·tion
    (ĕ·vĭs′ ĕr·ā′ shŭn)
e·voke (ĕ·vōk′)
 -vok·ing
ev·o·ca·tion (ĕv′ ô·kā′ shŭn)
e·voc·a·tive (ĕ·vŏk′ á·tĭv)

ev·o·lu·tion (ĕv′ ô·lū′ shŭn)
ev·o·lu·tion·ar·y
e·volve (ĕ·vŏlv′)
 -volv·ing
ex·ac·er·bate (ĕg·zăs′ ĕr·bāt)
 -bat·ing
ex·ac·er·ba·tion
    (ĕg·zăs′ ĕr·bā′ shŭn)
ex·act (ĕg·zăkt′)
ex·act·ing ex·ac·tion
ex·ag·ger·ate (ĕg·zăj′ ĕr·āt)
 -at·ing ex·ag·ger·a·tor
ex·ag·ger·a·tion
    (ĕg·zăj′ ĕr·ā′ shŭn)
ex·alt (ĕg·zôlt′)
ex·al·ta·tion (ĕg′ zôl·tā′ shŭn)
ex·am·ine (ĕg·zăm′ ĭn)
 -in·ing
ex·am·i·na·tion
    (ĕg·zăm′ ĭ·nā′ shŭn)
ex·am·ple (ĕg·zăm′ p'l)
ex·as·per·ate (ĕg·zăs′ pĕr·āt)
 -at·ing
ex·as·per·a·tion
    (ĕg·zăs′ pĕr·ā′ shŭn)
Ex·cal·i·bur (ĕks·kăl′ ĭ·bĕr)
ex·ca·vate (ĕks′ ká·vāt)
 -vat·ing
ex·ca·va·tion
    (ĕks′ ká·vā′ shŭn)
ex·ca·va·tor
ex·ceed (ĕk·sēd′)
 (to surpass; see accede)
ex·ceed·ing·ly
ex·cel (ĕk·sĕl′)
 -celled -cel·ling
ex·cel·lent (ĕk′ sĕ·lĕnt)
 -cel·lence
ex·cel·si·or (ĕk·sĕl′ sĭ·ôr)
ex·cept (ĕk·sĕpt′)
ex·cep·tion
ex·cep·tion·a·ble
ex·cep·tion·al, -al·ly
ex·cerpt (ĕk·sûrpt′) v.
    (ĕk′ sûrpt) n.
ex·cess (ĕk·sĕs′)
ex·ces·sive
ex·change (ĕks·chānj′)
ex·change·a·ble
ex·cheq·uer (ĕks·chĕk′ ĕr)
ex·cise (ĕk′ sīz) n.
 -cis·ing (ĕk·sīz′) v.
ex·ci·sion (ĕk·sĭzh′ ŭn)
ex·cite (ĕk·sīt′)
 -cit·ing

ex·cit·a·bil·i·ty
    (ĕk·sīt′ à·bĭl′ ĭ·tĭ)
ex·cit·a·ble
ex·ci·ta·tion   (ĕk′ sĭ·tā′ shŭn)
ex·cit·ed·ly   ex·cite·ment
ex·claim   (ĕks·klām′)
  ex·cla·ma·tion
    (ĕks′ klá·mā′ shŭn)
  ex·clam·a·to·ry
    (ĕks·klăm′ à·tō′ rĭ)
ex·clude   (ĕks·klōōd′)
  -clud·ing   ex·clu·sion
  ex·clu·sive   -sive·ly
ex·com·mu·ni·cate
    (ĕks′ kŏ·mū′ nĭ·kāt)
  -cat·ing
ex·co·ri·ate   (ĕks·kō′ rĭ·āt)
  -at·ing
ex·cre·ment   (ĕks′ krē·mĕnt)
ex·cres·cence   (ĕks·krĕs′ ĕns)
ex·crete   (ĕks·krēt′)
  -cret·ing   ex·cre·tion
  ex·cre·to·ry   (ĕks′ krē·tō′ rĭ)
ex·cru·ci·at·ing
    (ĕks·krōō′ shĭ·āt′ ĭng)
  ex·cru·ci·a·tion
    (ĕks·krōō′ shĭ·ā′ shŭn)
ex·cur·sion   (ĕks·kûr′ zhŭn)
ex·cuse   (ĕks·kūz′) v.
  -cus·ing   (ĕks·kūs′) n.
  ex·cus·a·ble   (ĕks·kūz′ à·b'l)
ex·e·cra·ble   (ĕk′ sē·krá·b'l)
ex·e·cute   (ĕk′ sē·kūt)
  -cut·ing
  ex·e·cu·tion   (ĕk′ sē·kū′ shŭn)
ex·ec·u·tive   (ĕg·zĕk′ û·tĭv)
ex·ec·u·tor   (ĕg·zĕk′ û·tēr)
  n. masc.
  ex·ec·u·trix   (-trĭks) n. fem.
ex·e·ge·sis   (ĕk′ sē·jē′ sĭs)
  pl. -ses   (sēz)
ex·em·pla·ry   (ĕg·zĕm′ plá·rĭ)
ex·em·pli·fy   (ĕg·zĕm′ plĭ·fī)
  -fied   -fy·ing
  ex·em·pli·fi·ca·tion
    (ĕg·zĕm′ plĭ·fĭ·kā′ shŭn)
ex·empt   (ĕg·zĕmpt′)
  ex·empt·i·ble   ex·emp·tion
ex·er·cise   (ĕk′ sēr·sīz)
  -cis·ing
ex·ert   (ĕg·zûrt′)
  ex·er·tion
ex·hale   (ĕks·hāl′)
  -hal·ing   ex·hal·ant
  ex·ha·la·tion   (ĕks′ há·lā′ shŭn)

ex·haust   (ĕg·zôst′)
  ex·haust·i·ble   ex·haus·tion
  ex·haus·tive
ex·hib·it   (ĕg·zĭb′ ĭt)
  -it·ed   -it·ing
  ex·hib·i·tor
ex·hi·bi·tion   (ĕk′ sĭ·bĭsh′ ŭn)
  -tion·ist
ex·hil·a·rate   (ĕg·zĭl′ à·rāt)
  -rat·ing
  ex·hil·a·ra·tion
    (ĕg·zĭl′ à·rā′ shŭn)
ex·hort   (ĕg·zôrt′)
  ex·hor·ta·tion   (ĕg′ zôr·tā′ shŭn)
ex·hume   (ĕks·hūm′)
  -hum·ing
ex·i·gen·cy   (ĕk′ sĭ·jĕn·sĭ)
ex·ig·u·ous   (ĕg·zĭg′ û·ŭs)
ex·ile   (ĕk′ sīl)
ex·ist   (ĕg·zĭst′)
  ex·ist·ence   -ent
ex·is·ten·tial·ism
    (ĕg′ zĭs·tĕn′ shăl·ĭs′m)
ex·it   (ĕg′ sĭt)
ex·o·dus   (ĕk′ sŏ·dŭs)
ex·on·er·ate   (ĕg·zŏn′ ĕr·āt)
  -at·ing
  ex·on·er·a·tion
    (ĕg·zŏn′ ĕr·ā′ shŭn)
ex·o·ra·ble   (ĕk′ sŏ·rá·b'l)
ex·or·bi·tant   (ĕg·zôr′ bĭ·tănt)
  -tance
ex·or·cise   (ĕk′ sôr·sīz)
  (to expel)   -cis·ing
ex·ot·ic   (ĕks·ŏt′ ĭk)
ex·pand   (ĕks·pănd′)
  ex·pand·a·ble
ex·panse   (ĕks·păns′)
  ex·pan·sion   ex·pan·sive
ex·pa·tri·ate   (ĕks·pā′ trĭ·āt)
ex·pect·ant   (ĕks·pĕk′ tănt)
  ex·pect·an·cy
  ex·pec·ta·tion
    (ĕks′ pĕk·tā′ shŭn)
ex·pec·to·rate   (ĕks·pĕk′ tô·rāt)
  -rat·ing   ex·pec·to·rant
  ex·pec·to·ra·tion
    (ĕks·pĕk′ tô·rā′ shŭn)
ex·pe·di·ent   (ĕks·pē′ dĭ·ĕnt)
  ex·pe·di·en·cy
ex·pe·dite   (ĕks′ pē·dīt)
  -dit·ing   ex·pe·dit·er
ex·pe·di·tion   (ĕks′ pē·dĭsh′ ŭn)
  ex·pe·di·tion·ar·y
ex·pe·di·tious   (ĕks′ pē·dĭsh′ ŭs)

ex·pel (ĕks·pĕl′)
-pelled -pel·ling
ex·pend·a·ble (ĕks·pĕn′ dá·b′l)
ex·pend·i·ture (ĕks·pĕn′ dĭ·tûr)
ex·pense (ĕks·pĕns′)
ex·pen·sive -sive·ly
ex·pe·ri·ence (ĕks·pēr′ ĭ·ĕns)
ex·per·i·ment (ĕks·pĕr′ ĭ·mĕnt)
ex·per·i·men·tal
(ĕks·pĕr′ ĭ·mĕn′ tǎl)
ex·per·i·men·ta·tion
(ĕks·pĕr′ ĭ·mĕn·tā′ shŭn)
ex·pert (ĕks′ pûrt′) adj.
(ĕks′ pûrt) n.
ex·pi·ate (ĕks′ pĭ·āt)
-at·ing
ex·pi·a·tion (ĕks′ pĭ·ā′ shŭn)
ex·pi·ra·tion (ĕk′ spĭ·rā′ shŭn)
ex·plain (ĕks·plān′)
ex·plain·a·ble
ex·pla·na·tion
(ĕks·plá·nā′ shŭn)
ex·plan·a·to·ry
(ĕks·plăn′ á·tō′ rĭ)
ex·ple·tive (ĕks′ plē·tĭv)
ex·pli·ca·to·ry (ĕks′ plĭ·ká·tō′ rĭ)
ex·plic·it (ĕks·plĭs′ ĭt)
ex·ploit (ĕks′ ploit) n.
(ĕks·ploit′) v.
ex·ploi·ta·tion
(ĕks′ ploi·tā′ shŭn)
ex·plore (ĕks·plōr′)
-plor·ing
ex·plo·ra·tion
(ĕks′ plŏ·rā′ shŭn)
ex·plor·a·to·ry
(ĕks·plōr′ á·tō′ rĭ)
ex·plor·er
ex·plo·sion (ĕks·plō′ zhŭn)
ex·plo·sive
ex·po·nent (ĕks·pō′ nĕnt)
ex·port (ĕks·pōrt′) v.
(ĕks′ pōrt) n.
ex·por·ta·tion
(ĕks′ pŏr·tā′ shŭn)
ex·pose (ĕks·pōz′) v.
-pos·ing
ex·po·sé (ĕks′ pŏ·zā′) n.
ex·po·si·tion (ĕks′ pŏ·zĭsh′ ŭn)
ex post fac·to (ĕks pŏst făk′ tō)
ex·pos·tu·late (ĕks·pŏs′ tṵ·lāt)
-lat·ing
ex·pos·tu·la·tion
(ĕks·pŏs′ tṵ·lā′ shŭn)
ex·po·sure (ĕks·pō′ zhĕr)

ex·pound (ĕks·pound′)
ex·press (ĕks·prĕs′)
ex·press·i·ble ex·pres·sion
ex·pres·sive ex·press·way
ex·pro·pri·ate (ĕks·prō′ prĭ·āt)
-at·ing
ex·pro·pri·a·tion
(ĕks·prō′ prĭ·ā′ shŭn)
ex·pul·sion (ĕks·pŭl′ shŭn)
ex·punge (ĕks·pŭnj′)
-pung·ing
ex·pur·gate (ĕks′ pĕr·gāt)
-gat·ing
ex·pur·ga·tion
(ĕks′ pĕr·gā′ shŭn)
ex·qui·site (ĕks′ kwĭ·zĭt)
ex·qui·site·ly
ex·tant (ĕks′ tănt)
(in existence; see *extent*)
ex·tem·po·ra·ne·ous
(ĕks·tĕm′ pŏ·rā′ nē·ŭs)
ex·tem·po·rize (ĕks·tĕm′ pŏ·rīz)
-riz·ing
ex·ten·sion (ĕks·tĕn′ shŭn)
ex·ten·sive (ĕks·tĕn′ sĭv)
-sive·ly
ex·tent (ĕks·tĕnt′)
(degree; see *extant*)
ex·ten·u·ate (ĕks·tĕn′ ṵ·āt)
-at·ing
ex·te·ri·or (ĕks·tēr′ ĭ·ẽr)
ex·ter·mi·nate (ĕks·tûr′ mĭ·nāt)
-nat·ing -na·tor
ex·ter·mi·na·tion
(ĕks·tûr′ mĭ·nā′ shŭn)
ex·ter·nal (ĕks·tûr′ nǎl)
ex·ter·nal·ly
ex·tinct (ĕks·tĭngkt′)
ex·tinc·tion
ex·tin·guish (ĕks·tĭng′ gwĭsh)
ex·tin·guish·a·ble
ex·tin·guish·er
ex·tir·pate (ĕk′ stĕr·pāt)
-pat·ing
ex·tol (ĕks·tŏl′)
-tolled -tol·ling
ex·tort (ĕks·tôrt′)
ex·tor·tion -tion·ist
ex·tract (ĕks′ trăkt) n.
ex·tract (ĕks·trăkt′) v.
ex·trac·tion ex·trac·tive
ex·trac·tor
ex·tra·cur·ric·u·lar
(ĕks′ trá·kŭ·rĭk′ û·lẽr)

ex·tra·dite   (ĕks′ trȧ·dīt)
   -dit·ing
   ex·tra·di·tion
           (ĕks′ trȧ·dĭsh′ ŭn)
ex·tra·mar·i·tal
           (ĕks′ trȧ·măr′ ĭ·tȧl)
ex·tra·ne·ous   (ĕks·trā′ nē·ŭs)
ex·traor·di·nar·y
           (ĕks·trôr′ dĭ·nĕr′ ĭ)
   ex·traor·di·nar·i·ly
           (ĕks·trôr′ dĭ·nĕr′ ĭ·lĭ)
ex·trap·o·late   (ĕks·trăp′ ȏ·lāt)
   -lat·ing
ex·tra·sen·so·ry perception
           (ĕks′ trȧ·sĕn′ sȏ·rĭ)
ex·tra·ter·ri·to·ri·al
           (ĕks′ trȧ·tĕr′ ĭ·tȏ′ rĭ·ȧl)
ex·trav·a·gance
           (ĕks·trăv′ ȧ·gȧns)
ex·treme   (ĕks·trēm′)
   ex·treme·ly   ex·trem·ism
   ex·trem·ist
   ex·trem·i·ty   (ĕks·trĕm′ ĭ·tĭ)
ex·tri·cate   (ĕks′ trĭ·kāt)
   -cat·ing
   ex·tri·ca·ble   (ĕks′ trĭ·kȧ·b′l)
ex·trin·sic   (ĕks·trĭn′ sĭk)
ex·tro·vert   (ĕks′ trȏ·vûrt)
   ex·tro·ver·sion
           (ĕks′ trȏ·vûr′ shŭn)
ex·tru·sion   (ĕks·trōō′ zhŭn)
ex·u·ber·ant   (ĕg·zū′ bēr·ȧnt)
   -ance
ex·ude   (ĕks·ūd′)
   -ud·ing
ex·ult   (ĕg·zŭlt′)
   ex·ult·an·cy   ex·ult·ant
   ex·ul·ta·tion   (ĕk′ sŭl·tā′ shŭn)
eye   (ī)
   eye·brow   eye·cup
   eye·let   eye·lid
   eye·shot   eye·strain
   eye·tooth   eye·wit·ness

F

fa·ble   (fā′ b′l)
fab·ric   (făb′ rĭk)
fab·ri·cate   (făb′ rĭ·kāt)
   -ca·ting
   fab·ri·ca·tion   (făb′ rĭ·kā′shŭn)
   fab·ri·ca·tor
fab·u·lous   (făb′ û·lŭs)
fa·çade   (fȧ·säd′)

face   (fās)
   fac·ing   face card
   face val·ue   fa·cial
fac·et   (făs′ ĕt)
   -et·ed
fa·ce·tious   (fȧ·sē′ shŭs)
   (joking; see *factious*)
fa·cial   (fā′ shȧl)
fac·ile   (făs′ ĭl)
fa·cil·i·tate   (fȧ·sĭl′ ĭ·tāt)
   (help; see *felicitate*)
   -tat·ing
fa·cil·i·ty   (fȧ·sĭl′ ĭ·tĭ)
   -ties
fac·sim·i·le   (făk·sĭm′ ĭ·lĕ)
fac·tion   (făk′ shŭn)
   fac·tion·al
fac·tious   (făk′ shŭs)
   (dissenting; see *facetious*)
fac·tor   (făk′ tēr)
fac·to·ry   (făk′ tȏ·rĭ)
   -ries
fac·to·tum   (făk·tō′ tŭm)
fac·tu·al   (făk′ tû·ȧl)
   -al·ly
fac·ul·ty   (făk′ ŭl·tĭ)
   -ties
fad·dist   (făd·ĭst)
fag·ot   (făg′ ŭt)
   fag·ot·ing
Fahr·en·heit   (făr′ ĕn·hīt)
fail·ure   (fāl′ ûr)
faint   (fānt)
   (lose consciousness; see *feint*)
   faint·heart·ed
fair   (fâr)
   fair and square
   fair-mind·ed   fair-sized
   fair-trade a·gree·ment
   fair·way
fair·y   (fâr′ ĭ)
   fair·ies   fair·y·land
   fair·y tale
fait ac·com·pli (fĕ′ tȧ′ kôn′ plē′)
faith   (fāth)
   faith·ful, -ful·ly, -ful·ness
   faith·less
fak·er   (fāk′ ēr)
   (fraud)
fa·kir   (fȧ·kēr′)
   (yogi)
fal·con   (fôl′ kŭn)
fal·la·cy   (făl′ ȧ·sĭ)
   -cies
   fal·la·cious   (fȧ·lā′ shŭs)

fall·en   (fôl′ ĕn)
fal·li·ble   (făl′ ĭ·b'l)
  fal·li·bil·i·ty   (făl′ ĭ·bĭl′ ĭ·tĭ)
Fal·lo·pi·an tube
        (fă·lō′ pĭ·ăn)
fall-out   (fôl′ out′)
fal·low   (făl′ ō)
false   (fôls)
  false·heart·ed   false·hood
  false·ly
fal·set·to   (fôl·sĕt′ ō)
fal·si·fy   (fôl′ sĭ·fī)
  -fied   -fy·ing
fal·si·ty   (fôl′ sĭ·tĭ)
  -ties
Fal·staff·i·an   (fôl·stăf′ ĭ·ăn)
fal·ter·ing   (fôl′ tēr·ĭng)
fa·mil·iar   (fá·mĭl′ yēr)
  fa·mil·i·ar·i·ty
        (fá·mĭl′ ĭ·ăr′ ĭ·tĭ)
  fa·mil·iar·ize, -iz·ing
fam·i·ly   (făm′ ĭ·lĭ)
  -lies
  fa·mil·ial   (fá·mĭl′ yăl)
  fam·i·ly cir·cle
  fam·i·ly name
fam·ine   (făm′ ĭn)
fam·ish   (făm′ ĭsh)
fa·mous   (fā′ mŭs)
fa·nat·ic   (fá·năt′ ĭk)
  fa·nat·i·cal   -cal·ly
  fa·nat·i·cism
fan·cy   (făn′ sĭ)
  -cied   -cy·ing
  fan·cier
  fan·ci·ful, -ful·ly, -ful·ness
  fan·cy dress   fan·cy-free
  fan·cy·work
fan·dan·go   (făn·dăng′ gō)
fan·fare   (făn′ fâr)
fan·tas·tic   (făn·tăs′ tĭk)
  -ti·cal·ly
fan·ta·sy   (făn′ tá·sĭ)
  -sies
far   (fär)
  far·a·way   Far East
  far·fetched   far-flung
  far-off adj.   far-reach·ing
  far·see·ing   far·sight·ed
farce   (färs)
  far·ci·cal   (făr′ sĭ·kăl)
fare·well   (fâr′ wĕl′)
fa·ri·na   (fá·rē′ ná)
farm   (färm)
  farm hand   farm·house

farm·yard
far·ther   (fär′ thēr)
  (refers only to spatial distance;
  see further)   far·thest
fas·ci·nate   (făs′ ĭ·nāt)
  -nat·ing
  fas·ci·na·tion   (făs′ ĭ·nā′ shŭn)
fas·cism   (făsh′ ĭz'm)
  fas·cist
fash·ion   (făsh′ ŭn)
  fash·ion·a·ble   fash·ion plate
fas·ten·ing   (făs′ 'n·ĭng)
fas·tid·i·ous   (făs·tĭd′ ĭ·ŭs)
fa·tal   (fā′ tăl)
  fa·tal·i·ty   (fá·tăl′ ĭ·tĭ)
  -ties   fa·tal·is·tic
  fa·tal·ly
fate   (fāt)
  fate·ful   -ful·ly
fa·ther   (fä′ thēr)
  fa·ther-in-law   fa·thers-in-law
  fa·ther·land   fa·ther·less
  Fa·ther's Day
fath·om   (făth′ ŭm)
  fath·om·a·ble   fath·om·less
fa·tigue   (fá·tēg′)
  -tigued   -ti·guing
  fa·ti·ga·ble
fat·ten   (făt′ 'n)
fat·u·ous   (făt′ û·ŭs)
  fa·tu·i·ty   (fá·tū′ ĭ·tĭ)
fau·cet   (fô′ sĕt)
fault   (fôlt)
  fault·find·ing   fault·y
faun   (fôn)
  (wood sprite; see fawn)
faux pas   (fō′ pä′)
fa·vor   (fā′ vēr)
  fa·vor·a·ble
  fa·vor·ite   (fā′ vēr·ĭt)
  fa·vor·it·ism
fawn   (fôn)
  (young deer; see faun)
faze   (fāz)
  (disconcert; see phase)
  faz·ing
fear   (fēr)
  fear·ful, -ful·ly, -ful·ness
  fear·some
fea·si·ble   (fē′ zĭ·b'l)
  fea·si·bil·i·ty   (fē′ zĭ·bĭl′ ĭ·tĭ)
feat   (fēt)
  (deed; see fete)
feath·er   (fĕth′ ēr)
  feath·er·bed   -bed·ding

feath·er·weight
fea·ture (fē′ tūr)
  -tur·ing   fea·ture·less
Feb·ru·ar·y (fĕb′ rŏŏ·ĕr′ĭ)
feck·less (fĕk′ lĕs)
fe·cund (fē′ kŭnd)
  fe·cun·di·ty (fĕ·kŭn′ dĭ·tĭ)
fed·er·al (fĕd′ ĕr·ăl)
  fed·er·al·ist   fed·er·al·ly
fed·er·ate (fĕd′ ĕr·āt)
  -at·ing
  fed·er·a·tion (fĕd′ ĕr·ā′ shŭn)
fee·ble (fē′ b′l)
  fee·ble-mind·ed
  fee·ble·ness
  fee·bler, -blest, -bly
feed·back (fēd′ băk′)
feign (fān)
feint (fānt)
  (trick; see *faint*)
fe·lic·i·tate (fĕ·lĭs′ ĭ·tāt)
  (make happy; see *facilitate*)
  -tat·ing
  fe·lic·i·ta·tion
          (fĕ·lĭs′ ĭ·tā′ shŭn)
fe·lic·i·ty (fĕ·lĭs′ ĭ·tĭ)
  -ties   fe·lic·i·tous
fe·line (fē′ līn)
fel·low (fĕl′ ō)
  fel·low·ship
  fel·low trav·el·er
fel·on (fĕl′ ŭn)
  fe·lo·ni·ous (fĕ·lō′ nĭ·ŭs)
  fel·o·ny   -nies
fe·male (fē′ māl)
fem·i·nine (fĕm′ ĭ·nĭn)
  fem·i·nin·i·ty (fĕm′ ĭ·nĭn′ ĭ·tĭ)
fence (fĕns)
  fenc·ing   fence·less
fend·er (fĕn′ dĕr)
fen·nel (fĕn′ ĕl)
fe·ral (fēr′ ăl)
fer-de-lance (fâr′ dĕ·lăns′)
fer·ment (fûr′ mĕnt) n.
fer·ment (fĕr·mĕnt′) v.
  fer·men·ta·tion
         (fûr′ mĕn·tā′ shŭn)
fe·ro·cious (fĕ·rō′ shŭs)
  fe·roc·i·ty (fĕ·rŏs′ ĭ·tĭ)
fer·ret (fĕr′ ĕt)
Fer·ris wheel (fĕr′ ĭs)
fer·rous (fĕr′ ŭs)
fer·ry (fĕr′ ĭ)
  fer·ried   fer·ry·ing
  fer·ry·boat

fer·tile (fûr′ tĭl)
  fer·tile·ly
  fer·til·i·ty (fĕr·tĭl′ ĭ·tĭ)
fer·ti·lize (fûr′ tĭ·līz)
  -liz·ing
  fer·ti·li·sa·tion
         (fûr′ tĭ·lĭ·zā′ shŭn)
  fer·ti·liz·er
fer·vent (fûr′ vĕnt)
  -ven·cy
fer·vid (fûr′ vĭd)
fer·vor (fûr′ vĕr)
fes·ti·val (fĕs′ tĭ·văl)
fes·tive (fĕs′ tĭv)
  fes·tiv·i·ty (fĕs·tĭv′ ĭ·tĭ)
  -ties
fes·toon (fĕs·tōōn′)
fetch (fĕch)
fete (fāt)
  (festival; see *feat*)
fet·id (fĕt′ ĭd)
fe·tish (fē′ tĭsh)
fet·ter (fĕt′ ĕr)
fe·tus (fē′ tŭs)
  -tus·es
feud (fūd)
feu·dal (fū′ dăl)
fe·ver (fē′ vĕr)
  fe·ver·ish   fe·ver·rid·den
fi·an·cé (fē′ än·sā′)
  n. masc.
fi·an·cée (fē′ än·sā′) *n. fem.*
fi·as·co (fē·ăs′ kō)
fi·at (fī′ ăt)
fi·ber (fī′ bĕr)
  fi·ber·board   Fi·ber·glas
  fi·brous
fick·le (fĭk′ ′l)
  fick·le·ness
fic·tion (fĭk′ shŭn)
  fic·tion·al   -al·ly
fic·ti·tious (fĭk·tĭsh′ ŭs)
fid·dle (fĭd′ ′l)
  fid·dling   fid·dle-fad·dle
  fid·dle·sticks
fi·del·i·ty (fĭ·dĕl′ ĭ·tĭ)
fidg·et (fĭj′ ĕt)
  -et·ed   -et·ing
fi·du·ci·ar·y (fĭ·dū′ shĭ·ĕr′ ĭ)
field (fēld)
fiend (fēnd)
  fiend·ish
fierce (fērs)
fi·er·y (fī′ rĭ)
  fi·er·i·er, -i·est, -i·ness

fi·es·ta (fǐ·ĕs′ tà)
fif·teen (fǐf′ tēn′)
  fif·teenth
fifth (fǐfth)
  fifth col·um·nist
fif·ty (fǐf′ tǐ)
  -ties
  fif·ty·fold
fight·er (fīt′ ĕr)
fig·ment (fǐg′ mĕnt)
fig·ure (fǐg′ ûr)
  -ur·ing
  fig·u·ra·tion (fǐg′ û·rā′ shŭn)
  fig·ur·a·tive (fǐg′ ûr·à·tǐv)
  fig·ure·head
  fig·u·rine (fǐg′ û·rēn′)
fil·a·ment (fǐl′ à·mĕnt)
fil·bert (fǐl′ bĕrt)
fil·i·al (fǐl′ ǐ·ăl)
fil·i·bus·ter (fǐl′ ǐ·bŭs′ tĕr)
fil·i·gree (fǐl′ ǐ·grē)
Fil·i·pi·no (fǐl′ ǐ·pē′ nō)
  -nos
  But: Phil·ip·pine Is·lands
fil·let (fǐl′ ĕt)
fil·ly (fǐl′ ǐ)
  fil·lies
film (fǐlm)
  film·i·er, -i·est, -i·ness
  film·strip   film·y
fil·ter (fǐl′ tĕr)
  (porous article; see *philter*)
  fil·ter·a·bil·i·ty
         (fǐl′ tĕr·à·bǐl′ ǐ·tǐ)
  fil·ter·a·ble
  fil·tra·tion (fǐl·trā′ shŭn)
filth·y (fǐl′ thǐ)
  filth·i·er, -i·est, -i·ly, -i·ness
fi·na·gler (fǐ·nā′ glĕr)
fi·nal (fī′ năl)
  fi·nal·i·ty (fī·năl′ ǐ·tǐ)
  fi·nal·ly
fi·na·le (fè·nä′ là)
fi·nance (fǐ·năns′)
  -nanc·ing
fi·nan·cial (fǐ·năn′ shǎl)
fin·an·cier (fǐn′ ăn·sēr′)
fine (fīn)
  fine arts   fin·er·y
  fine·spun   fine-tooth comb
fi·nesse (fǐ·nĕs′)
fin·ger (fǐng′ gĕr)
  fin·ger bowl   fin·ger·nail
  fin·ger·print
fin·ick·y (fǐn′ ǐ·kǐ)

fi·nis (fī′ nǐs)
fin·ish (fǐn′ ǐsh)
fi·nite (fī′ nīt)
Fin·land (fǐn′ lǎnd)
  Finn   Finn·ish
fiord (fyôrd)
fire (fīr)
  fir·ing   fire·arm
  fire·bug   fire·brand
  fire·crack·er   fire-eat·er
  fire en·gine   fire es·cape
  fire ex·tin·guish·er
  fire·man   fire·place
  fire·plug   fire·pow·er
  fire·proof   fire·side
  fire·trap   fire·ward·en
  fire·wood   fire·works
fir·ma·ment (fûr′ mà·mĕnt)
first (fûrst)
  first aid   first base
  first-born   first class *n.*
  first-class *adj.*   first·hand
  first-rate
fis·cal (fǐs′ kǎl)
fish (fǐsh)
  fish·er·man   fish·er·y, -er·ies
  fish·hook   fish meal
  fish mon·ger
fis·sion (fǐsh′ ŭn)
  fis·sion·a·ble   fis·sion bomb
fis·sure (fǐsh′ ĕr)
fist·ic (fǐs′ tǐk)
  fist·i·cuffs
fit·ful (fǐt′ fŏŏl)
  -ful·ly   -ful·ness
five·fold (fīv′ fōld′)
fix·a·tion (fǐks·ā′ shŭn)
fix·ture (fǐks′ tûr)
fiz·zle (fǐz′ ′l)
  fiz·zling
flab·ber·gast (flăb′ ĕr·găst)
flab·by (flăb′ ǐ)
  flab·bi·ness
flac·cid (flăk′ sǐd)
flag (flăg)
  flagged   flag·ging
  flag·pole   flag·ship
  flag stop
flag·el·late (flăj′ ĕ·lāt)
  -el·lat·ing   flag·el·lant
flag·on (flăg′ ŭn)
fla·grant (flā′ grănt)
  -gran·cy
flair (flâr)
  (aptitude; see *flare*)

flake (flāk)
  flak·y   flak·i·er
  -i·est, -i·ly, -i·ness
flam·boy·ant (flăm·boi′ ănt)
  -an·cy
flame (flām)
  flam·ing   flame·proof
  flame throw·er
fla·min·go (flå·mĭng′ gō)
  -gos
flam·ma·ble (flăm′ å·b′l)
  flam·ma·bil·ity
        (flăm′ å·bĭl′ ĭ·tĭ)
flap·per (flăp′ ẽr)
flare (flâr)
  (blaze; see *flair*)
  flare-up   flar·ing
flash (flăsh)
  flash·back   flash flood
  flash·light   flash·y,
  flash·i·er, -i·est, -i·ly, -i·ness
flat (flăt)
  flat·boat   flat·car
  flat-foot·ed
  Flat·head In·di·an
  flat·i·ron   flat·tened
  flat·top   flat·ware
flat·ter·y (flăt′ ẽr·ĭ)
  flat·ter·ies   flat·ter·er
flaunt (flônt)
fla·vor (flā′ vẽr)
  fla·vor·ful
flax·en (flăk′ s′n)
flea (flē)
  (insect)
  flea·bite
  flea-bit·ten
fledg·ling (flĕj′ lĭng)
flee (flē)
  (escape)
fleece (flēs)
fleet (flēt)
Flem·ish (flĕm′ ĭsh)
flesh·y (flĕsh′ ĭ)
  flesh·i·ness
fleur-de-lis (flûr′ dē·lē′)
flex·i·ble (flĕk′ sĭ·b′l)
  flex·i·bil·i·ty (flĕk′ sĭ·bĭl′ ĭ·tĭ)
flib·ber·ti·gib·bet
      (flĭb′ ẽr·tĭ·jĭb′ ĕt)
flick·er (flĭk′ ẽr)
fli·er (flī′ ẽr)
flight (flīt)
  flight·y   flight·i·er
  -i·est, -i·ly, -i·ness

flim·sy (flĭm′ zĭ)
  flim·si·er, -si·est, -si·ly, -si·ness
flint·lock (flĭnt′ lŏk′)
flip·pant (flĭp′ ănt)
  flip·pan·cy
flir·ta·tion (flûr·tā′ shŭn)
flir·ta·tious (flûr·tā′ shŭs)
float (flōt)
flo·ta·tion (flō·tā′ shŭn)
floc·cu·late (flŏk′ û·lāt)
  -lat·ing
  floc·cu·la·tion (flŏk′ û·lā′ shŭn)
flog·ging (flŏg′ ĭng)
flood (flŭd)
  flood·gate   flood·light
  flood tide
floor (flōr)
  floor lead·er   floor show
  floor·walk·er
flop·house (flŏp′ hous′)
flop·py (flŏp′ ĭ)
flo·ral (flō′ răl)
flo·ri·cul·ture (flō′ rĭ·kŭl′ tụr)
flor·id (flŏr′ ĭd)
Flor·i·da (flŏr′ ĭ·då)
  abbr. Fla.
  Flo·rid·i·an (flō·rĭd′ ĭ·ăn)
flo·rist (flō′ rĭst)
flo·ta·tion (flō·tā′ shŭn)
flo·til·la (flō·tĭl′ å)
flot·sam (flŏt′ săm)
flounce (flouns)
  flounc·ing
floun·der (floun′ dẽr)
flour·ish (flûr′ ĭsh)
flow·age (flō′ ĭj)
flow·er (flou′ ẽr)
  flow·er·i·ness   flow·er·pot
  flow·er·y
flown (flōn)
flu (flōō)
  (influenza)
fluc·tu·ate (flŭk′ tụ·āt)
  -at·ing
  fluc·tu·a·tion (flŭk′tụ·ā′ shŭn)
flue (flōō)
  (chimney)
flu·ent (flōō′ ĕnt)
  -en·cy
flu·id (flōō′ ĭd)
  flu·id·i·ty (flōō·ĭd′ ĭ·tĭ)
fluke (flōōk)
flum·mox (flŭm′ ŭks)
flunk·y (flŭngk′ ĭ)
  flunk·ies

flu·o·res·cent   (flōō′ ô·rĕs′ ĕnt)
-cence

flu·o·ri·date   (flōō′ ô·rĭ·dāt)
-dat·ing
flu·o·ri·da·tion
     (flōō′ ô·rĭ·dā′ shŭn)

flu·o·ri·nate   (flōō′ ô·rĭ·nāt)
-nat·ing
flu·o·ri·na·tion
     (flōō′ ô·rĭ·nā′ shŭn)

flu·o·ro·scope   (flōō′ ô·rŏ·skŏp)

flur·ry   (fûr′ ĭ)
flur·ries

flute   (flōōt)
flut·ist

flut·ter   (flŭt′ ĕr)

flux   (flŭks)

fly   (flī)
flew   fly·ing
flies   fly-by-night
fly·ing fish   fly·ing sau·cer
fly·leaf   fly·pa·per
fly·speck   fly·wheel

fo·cal   (fō′ kăl)

fo·cus   (fō′ kŭs)
-cused   -cus·ing

fod·der   (fŏd′ ĕr)

fog·gy   (fŏg′ ĭ)
fog·gi·ness

fo·gy   (fō′ gĭ)
("old fogy")   -gies

foi·ble   (foi′ b′l)

foist   (foist)

fo·li·age   (fō′ lĭ·ĭj)

fo·li·o   (fō′ lĭ·ō)

folk   (fōk)
folk dance   folk·lore
folk mu·sic   folk tale
folk·way

fol·li·cle   (fŏl′ ĭ·k′l)

fol·low   (fŏl′ ō)
fol·low-through
fol·low-up

fol·ly   (fŏl′ ĭ)
fol·lies

fo·ment   (fō·mĕnt′)
fo·men·ta·tion
     (fō′ mĕn·tā′ shŭn)

fon·dant   (fŏn′ dănt)

fon·dle   (fŏn′ d′l)
-dling

fon·due   (fŏn·dōō′)

fool   (fōōl)
fool·er·y   -er·ies
fool·har·dy   -di·ness

fool·proof   fool's gold
fool's par·a·dise

foot   (fŏŏt)
foot·age   (fŏŏt′ ĭj)
foot·ball   foot brake
foot·bridge   foot-can·dle
foot·fall   foot·hill
foot·hold   foot·lights
foot·loose   foot·man
foot·note   foot·print
foot·rest   foot sol·dier
foot·step   foot·stool
foot·work

fop·per·y   (fŏp′ ĕr·ĭ)

for·age   (fôr′ ĭj)
-ag·ing

for·ay   (fôr′ ā)
-ay·ing

for·bear   (fôr·bâr′)
for·bear·ance   for·borne

for·bid   (fôr·bĭd′)
-bid·ding
for·bade   (fôr·băd′)
for·bid·den   for·bid·ding·ly

force   (fôrs)
forc·ing   force·ful
-ful·ly   -ful·ness
for·ci·ble

for·ceps   (fôr′ sĕps)

Ford·ham (univ.)   (fôr′ dăm)

fore-   (fôr-)
fore·arm
fore·bode   -bod·ing
fore·cast   fore·close
fore·clo·sure   fore·fa·thers
fore·fin·ger   fore·go
fore·gone con·clu·sion
fore·hand   fore·man
fore·most   fore·noon
fore·or·dain   fore·quar·ter
fore·run·ner   fore·see·a·ble
fore·shad·ow   fore·stall
fore·tell

for·eign   (fôr′ ĭn)

fo·ren·sic   (fô·rĕn′ sĭk)

for·est   (fôr′ ĕst)
for·est·a·tion   (fôr′ ĕs·tā′ shŭn)

for·ev·er   (fôr·ĕv′ ĕr)

for·feit   (fôr′ fĭt)
-feit·ed   -feit·ing
for·feit·a·ble   for·fei·ture

forge   (fôrj)
forg·ing

for·ger·y   (fôr′ jĕr·ĭ)
-ger·ies

for·get (fŏr·gĕt′)
  -get·ting   for·get·ful
  -ful·ly   -ful·ness
  for·get-me-not for·get·ta·ble
for·give (fŏr·gĭv′)
  -giv·ing   for·giv·a·ble
  for·give·ness
for·go (fŏr·gō′)
for·got (fŏr·gŏt′)
  for·got·ten
for·lorn (fŏr·lôrn′)
  for·lorn·ly   for·lorn·ness
for·mal (fôr′mǎl)
  for·mal·ism   for·mal·ly
  for·mal·i·ty (fôr·mǎl′ĭ·tĭ)
form·al·de·hyde
          (fôr·mǎl′dě·hīd)
for·mal·ize fôr′mǎl·īz)
  -iz·ing
  for·mal·i·za·tion
        (fôr′mǎl·ĭ·zā′shŭn)
for·mat (fôr′mǎt)
for·ma·tion (fôr·mā′shŭn)
form·a·tive (fôr′mǎ·tĭv)
for·mi·da·ble (fôr′mĭ·dǎ·b′l)
For·mo·sa (fôr·mō′sá)
  (also: Taiwan)
for·mu·la (fôr′mū·lá)
  pl. -las or -lae (-lē)
for·mu·late (fôr′mū·lāt)
  -lat·ing
  for·mu·la·tion
        (fôr′mū·lā′shŭn)
  for·mu·la·tor
for·sake (fŏr·sāk′)
  -sak·ing   for·sak·en
for·syth·i·a (fŏr·sĭth′ĭ·á)
forth (fôrth)
  forth·com·ing forth·right
  forth·with
for·ti·eth (fôr′tĭ·ĕth)
for·ti·fy (fôr′tĭ·fī)
  -fied   -fy·ing
  for·ti·fi·ca·tion
        (fôr′tĭ·fĭ·kā′shŭn)
for·tis·si·mo (fŏr·tĭs′ĭ·mō)
for·ti·tude (fôr′tĭ·tūd)
Fort Lau·der·dale,
  Fla.   (fôrt lô′dĕr·dāl)
fort·night (fôrt′nīt)
for·tress (fôr′trĕs)
for·tu·i·tous (fŏr·tū′ĭ·tŭs)
  for·tu·i·ty
for·tu·nate (fôr′tû·nĭt)
  -nate·ly

for·tune (fôr′tûn)
  for·tune hunt·er
  for·tune·tell·er
for·ty (fôr′tĭ)
  -ties   for·ti·eth
  for·ty·fold for·ty·nin·er
fo·rum (fō′rŭm)
for·ward (fôr′wĕrd)
fos·sil (fŏs′ĭl)
  fos·sil·ized (fŏs′ĭ·līzd)
fought (fôt)
foul (foul)
  (dirty; see fowl)
  foul·mouthed foul play
found (found)
foun·da·tion (foun·dā′shŭn)
found·ry (foun′drĭ)
  -ries
foun·tain (foun′tĭn)
  foun·tain·head foun·tain pen
four (fôr)
  four-di·men·sion·al
  four-flush·er four-in-hand
  four-post·er four·score
  four·some four·square
  four-wheeled
four·teen (fôr′tēn′)
fowl (foul)
  (poultry; see foul)
fox (fŏks)
  fox·glove fox·hole
  fox·hound fox·tail
  fox ter·ri·er fox·trot
  fox·y
foy·er (foi′ĕr)
fra·cas (frā′kás)
frac·tion (frǎk′shŭn)
  frac·tion·al -al·ly
frac·ture (frǎk′tûr)
frag·ile (frǎj′ĭl)
  -ile·ly
  fra·gil·i·ty (frá·jĭl′ĭ·tĭ)
frag·ment (frǎg′mĕnt)
  frag·men·tar·y
  frag·men·ta·tion
        (frǎg′mĕn·tā′shŭn)
fra·grant (frā′grǎnt)
  -grance
frail (frāl)
  frail·ty   -ties
frame-up (frām′ŭp′)
frame·work (frām′wûrk′)
fran·chise (frǎn′chīz)
  fran·chise·ment

Fran·co, Fran·cis·co
 (fräng′ kō,
 frän·thēs′ kō)
Fran·co·phile (fräng′ kō·fil)
Frank·en·stein (frăngk′ ĕn·stīn)
frank·furt·er (frăngk′ fẽr·tẽr)
frank·in·cense (frăngk′ ĭn·sĕns)
fran·tic (frăn′ tĭk)
 fran·ti·cal·ly
frap·pé (frá′ pā′)
fra·ter·nal (frá·tûr′ năl)
 -nal·ly fra·ter·nal·ism
fra·ter·ni·ty (frá·tûr′ nĭ·tĭ)
 -ties
frat·er·nize (frăt′ ẽr·nīz)
 -niz·ing
 frat·er·ni·za·tion
  (frăt′ ẽr·nĭ·zā′ shŭn)
fraud (frôd)
 fraud·u·lent -lence
fraught (frôt)
Fräu·lein (froi′ līn)
freak·ish (frēk′ ĭsh)
freck·le (frĕk′ 'l)
 -ling
Fred·er·icks·burg ,Va.
 (frĕd′ rĭks·bûrg)
free (frē)
 fre·er
 free on board (f.o.b.)
 free·born free-for-all
 free·hand *adj.*
 free-lance *adj. & v.*
 Free·ma·son free-think·er
 free·way
 free-will of·fer·ing
free·dom (frē′ dŭm)
freez·er (frēz′ ẽr)
freight (frāt)
 freight·age freight·er
fren·zy (frĕn′ zĭ)
 -zied -zy·ing
fre·quent (frē′ kwĕnt)
 -quen·cy
fres·co (frĕs′ kō)
 -coes
fresh (frĕsh)
 fresh·en fresh-water *adj.*
 fresh·man
fret (frĕt)
 fret·ted fret·ting
 fret·ful, -ful·ly, -ful·ness
Freud·i·an (froid′ ĭ·ăn)
fri·ar (frī′ ẽr)
 (churchman; see *fryer*)

fric·as·see (frĭk′ á·sē′)
fric·tion (frĭk′ shŭn)
Fri·day (frī′ dĭ)
fried (frīd)
friend·ly (frĕnd′ lĭ)
 friend·li·er, -li·est, -li·ness
frieze (frēz)
 (ornamented band)
frig·ate (frĭg′ ĭt)
fright (frīt)
 -ful·ly -ful·ness
 fright·en fright·ful
frig·id (frĭj′ ĭd)
 fri·gid·i·ty (frĭ·jĭd′ ĭ·tĭ)
fri·jole (frē′ hōl)
fringe (frĭnj)
 fring·ing
frip·per·y (frĭp′ ẽr·ĭ)
 frip·per·ies
frisk·y (frĭs′ kĭ)
 frisk·i·er, -i·est, -i·ly, -i·ness
frit·ter (frĭt′ ẽr)
friv·o·lous (frĭv′ ô·lŭs)
 fri·vol·i·ty (frĭ·vŏl′ ĭ·tĭ)
 -ties
frog·man (frŏg′ măn)
frol·ic (frŏl′ ĭk)
 frol·ick·er frol·ick·y
 frol·ic·some
front·age (frŭn′ tĭj)
fron·tal (frŭn′ tăl)
 -tal·ly
fron·tiers·man (frŭn·tẽrz′ măn)
fron·tis·piece (frŭn′ tĭs·pēs)
frost·bite (frŏst′ bīt′)
 frost·bit·ten (-bĭt′ 'n)
froth·y (frŏth′ ĭ)
 froth·i·ness
frown (froun)
fro·zen (frō′ z'n)
fru·gal (frōō′ găl)
 fru·gal·i·ty (frōō·găl′ ĭ·tĭ)
 fru·gal·ly
fruit (frōōt)
 -ful·ly -ful·ness
 fruit·cake fruit·ful
 fruit·less
fru·i·tion (frōō·ĭsh′ ŭn)
frus·trate (frŭs′ trāt)
 -trat·ing
 frus·tra·tion (frŭs·trā′ shŭn)
fry (frī)
 fried fry·ing
 fry·er (chicken; see *friar*)
fuch·sia (fū′ shá)

fu·el   (fū′ ĕl)
  -eled   -el·ing
fu·gi·tive   (fū′ jĭ·tĭv)
fugue   (fūg)
ful·crum   (fŭl′ krŭm)
ful·fill   (fŏŏl·fĭl′)
  ful·fill·ment
full   (fŏŏl)
  full·back   full-blood·ed
  full-blown   full-fledged
  full-sized   ful·ly
ful·some   (fŏŏl′ sŭm)
fum·ble   (fŭm′ b'l)
  -bling
fu·mi·gate   (fū′ mĭ·gāt)
  -gat·ing
  fu·mi·ga·tion   (fū′ mĭ·gā′ shŭn)
  fu·mi·ga·tor
func·tion   (fŭngk′ shŭn)
  func·tion·al   -al·ly
  func·tion·ar·y
fun·da·men·tal
                       (fŭn′ dȧ·men′ tȧl)
  -tal·ly
fu·ner·al   (fū′ nĕr·ȧl)
fu·ne·re·al   (fū·nēr′ ē·ȧl)
fun·gus   (fŭng′ gŭs)
  pl. fun·gi   (fŭn′ jī)
fun·nel   (fŭn′ ĕl)
  fun·neled   fun·nel·ing
fun·ny   (fŭn′ ĭ)
  fun·ni·est
fur   (fûr)
  fur·ry
fur·bish   (fûr′ bĭsh)
fu·ri·ous   (fū′ rĭ·ŭs)
furl   (fûrl)
fur·long   (fûr′ lông)
fur·lough   (fûr′ lō)
fur·nace   (fûr′ nĭs)
fur·nish·ings   (fûr′ nĭsh·ĭngz)
fur·ni·ture   (fûr′ nĭ·tụr)
fu·ror   (fū′ rôr)
fur·ri·er   (fûr′ ĭ·ẽr)
fur·row   (fûr′ ō)
fur·ther   (fûr′ thẽr)
  (more distant in time, degree, or
  quantity; see farther)
  fur·ther·ance   fur·ther·more
  fur·ther·most   fur·thest
fur·tive   (fûr′ tĭv)
fu·ry   (fū′ rĭ)
  -ries
fuse   (fūz)
  fus·ing

fu·se·lage   (fū′ zĕ·läzh′)
fu·sel oil   (fū′ zĕl)
fu·si·ble   (fū′ zĭ·b'l)
fu·sil·lade   (fū′ zĭ·lād′)
fu·sion bomb   (fū′ zhŭn)
fus·sy   (fŭs′ ĭ)
  fuss·i·ly   -i·ness
fu·tile   (fū′ tĭl)
  fu·tile·ly
  fu·til·i·ty   (fū·tĭl′ ĭ·tĭ)
fu·ture   (fū′ tụr)
  fu·tu·ri·ty   (fū·tū′ rĭ·tĭ)
fuz·zy   (fŭz′ ĭ)

                    G

gab·ar·dine   (găb′ ẽr·dēn′)
gad·a·bout   (găd′ ȧ·bout′)
gad·fly   (găd′ fīr′)
  -flies
gadg·et   (găj′ ĕt)
Gael·ic   (gāl′ ĭk)
  (Irish; see Gallic)
gai·e·ty   (gā′ ĕ·tĭ)
  -ties
gai·ly   (gā′ lĭ)
gain·ful   (gān′ fŏŏl)
  -ful·ly   -ful·ness
gain·say   (gān′ sā′)
gait   (gāt)
  (manner of walking; see gate)
gal·ax·y   (găl′ ȧk·sĭ)
  -ax·ies
  ga·lac·tic   (gȧ·lăk′ tĭk)
Gal·i·lee   (găl′ ĭ·lē)
  Gal·i·le·an   (găl′ ĭ·lē′ ȧn)
gal·lant   (găl′ ȧnt)
  gal·lant·ry   -ries
gal·le·on   (găl′ ē·ŭn)
gal·ler·y   (găl′ ẽr·ĭ)
  gal·ler·ies
gal·ley   (găl′ ĭ)
Gal·lic   (găl′ ĭk)
  (French; see Gaelic)
gal·lon   (găl′ ŭn)
  abbr. gal.
gal·lop   (găl′ ŭp)
  gal·loped   gal·lop·ing
gall·stone   (gôl′ stōn′)
Gal·lup poll   (găl′ ŭp)
ga·lore   (gȧ·lōr′)
ga·losh   (gȧ·lŏsh′)
  (overshoe; see goulash)

gal·va·nize (găl′ vá·nīz)
 -niz·ing
 gal·van·ic (găl·văn′ ĭk)
 gal·va·ni·za·tion
  (găl′ vá·nĭ·zā′ shŭn)
Gal·ves·ton, Tex.
  (găl′ vĕs·tŭn)
gam·bit (găm′ bĭt)
gam·ble (găm′ b′l)
 (bet) -bling
gam·bol (găm′ bŭl)
 (frolic) -boled, -bol·ing
game (găm)
 game bird game dog
 game fish game·keep·er
 game laws game·ster
 game ward·en gam·y
gam·ma (găm′ á)
 gam·ma glob·u·lin
 gam·ma rays
gam·ut (găm′ ŭt)
Gan·dhi, Mo·han·das
  (găn′ dē,
  mō′ hän·däs)
 title: Ma·hat·ma (má·hăt′ má)
gan·gling (găng′ glĭng)
gang·plank (găng′ plăngk′)
gan·grene (găng′ grēn)
 gan·gre·nous (-grē·nŭs)
gang·ster (găng′ stĕr)
ga·rage (gá·räzh′)
gar·bage (gär′ bĭj)
gar·den·er (gär′ d′n·ĕr)
gar·de·ni·a (gär·dē′ nĭ·á)
gar·gle (gär′ g′l)
 -gling
gar·goyle (gär′ goil)
gar·ish (gâr′ ĭsh)
gar·land (gär′ lănd)
gar·lic (gär′ lĭk)
 gar·lick·y
gar·nish·ee (gär′ nĭsh·ē′)
gar·ri·son (gär′ ĭ·sŭn)
gar·ru·lous (găr′ û·lŭs)
 gar·ru·li·ty (gá·rōō′ lĭ·tĭ)
gas (găs)
 gas·e·ous (găs′ ē·ŭs)
 gas·light gas·o·line
 gas·sing gas sta·tion
gas·ket (găs′ kĕt)
gas·tric (găs′ trĭk)
gas·tron·o·my (găs·trŏn′ ō·mĭ)
 gas·tro·nom·ic
  (găs′ trō·nŏm′ ĭk)

gate (găt)
 (fence opening; see gait)
 gate·house gate·keep·er
 gate·way
gath·er·ing (găth′ ĕr·ĭng)
gauche (gōsh)
 gauche·ly
 gau·che·rie (gō′ shē·rē′)
gaud·y (gôd′ ĭ)
 gaud·i·er, -i·est, -i·ly, -i·ness
gauge (gāj)
 gaug·ing
Gau·guin, Paul (gō′ găn′)
gaunt (gônt)
gaunt·let (gônt′ lĕt)
gauze (gôz)
 gauz·y
gav·el (găv′ ĕl)
gawk·y (gôk′ ĭ)
 gawk·i·ness
ga·zelle (gá·zĕl′)
ga·zette (gá·zĕt′)
 gaz·et·teer (găz′ ĕ·tēr′)
gear·shift (gēr′ shĭft′)
Gei·ger count·er
  (gī′ gēr)
gei·sha (gā′ shá)
gel·a·tin (jĕl′ á·tĭn)
 ge·lat·i·nous (jē·lăt′ ĭ·nŭs)
gen·darme (zhän·därm′)
gen·e·al·o·gy (jĕn′ ē·ăl′ ō·jĭ)
 gen·e·al·o·gist
gen·er·al (jĕn′ ēr·ăl)
 gen·er·al·is·si·mo
  (jĕn′ ēr·ăl·ĭs′ ĭ·mō)
 gen·er·al·i·sa·tion
  (jĕn′ ēr·ăl·ĭ·zā′ shŭn)
 gen·er·al·ly
gen·er·ate (jĕn′ ēr·āt)
 -at·ing
 gen·er·a·tion (jĕn′ ēr·ā′ shŭn)
 gen·er·a·tive (jĕn′ ēr·ā′ tĭv)
 gen·er·a·tor
ge·ner·ic (jē·nĕr′ ĭk)
gen·er·ous (jĕn′ ēr·ŭs)
 gen·er·os·i·ty (jĕn′ ēr·ŏe′ ĭ·tĭ)
 -ties
gen·e·sis (jĕn′ ē·sĭs)
ge·net·ics (jē·nĕt′ ĭks)
 ge·net·i·cist (jē·nĕt′ ĭ·sĭst)
Gen·ghis Khan (jĕng′ gĭs kän′)
gen·ial (jĕn′ yăl)
 -ial·ly
 ge·ni·al·i·ty (jē′ nĭ·ăl′ ĭ·tĭ)
gen·i·tal (jĕn′ ĭ·tăl)

gen·i·tive (jĕn′ ĭ·tĭv)
gen·ius (jĕn′ yŭs)
gen·o·cide (jĕn′ ō·sīd)
gen·re (zhäN′ r′)
gen·teel (jĕn·tēl′)
  -teel·ly
gen·tian (jĕn′ shăn)
gen·tile (jĕn′ tīl)
gen·til·i·ty (jĕn·tĭl′ ĭ·tĭ)
gen·tle (jĕn′ t′l)
  gen·tle·man   gen·tle·ness
  gen·tlest   gen·tly
gen·try (jĕn′ trĭ)
gen·u·flect (jĕn′ û·flĕkt)
  gen·u·flec·tion
    (jĕn′ û·flĕk′ shŭn)
gen·u·ine (jĕn′ û·ĭn)
ge·nus (jē′ nŭs)
  pl. gen·er·a (jĕn′ ĕr·à)
ge·o·det·ic (jē′ ō·dĕt′ ĭk)
ge·og·ra·phy (jē·ŏg′ rà·fĭ)
  ge·og·ra·pher
  ge·o·graph·i·cal
    (jē′ ō·grăf′ ĭ·kăl)
ge·ol·o·gy (jē·ŏl′ ō·jĭ)
  ge·o·log·ic (jē′ ō·lŏj′ ĭk)
  ge·ol·o·gist (jē·ŏl′ ō·jĭst)
ge·om·e·try (jē·ŏm′ ē·trĭ)
  ge·o·met·ric (jē′ ō·mĕt′ rĭk)
  ge·o·met·ri·cal
    (jē′ ō·mĕt′ rĭ·kăl)
ge·o·phys·ics (jē′ ō·fĭz′ ĭks)
ge·o·po·lit·i·cal
    (jē′ ō·pō·lĭt′ ĭ·kăl)
Geor·gia (jôr′ já)
  abbr. Ga.
  Geor·gi·an (jôr′ jĭ·ăn)
ge·ra·ni·um (jē·rā′ nĭ·ŭm)
ger·i·at·rics (jĕr′ ĭ·ăt′ rĭks)
ger·mane (jŭr·mān′)
ger·mi·cide (jŭr′ mĭ·sīd)
ger·mi·nal (jŭr′ mĭ·năl)
ger·mi·na·tion (jŭr′ mĭ·nā′ shŭn)
germ·proof (jŭrm′ prōōf′)
ger·ry·man·der (gĕr′ ĭ·măn′ dĕr)
ger·und (jĕr′ ŭnd)
Ge·sta·po (gĕ·stä′ pō)
ges·ta·tion (jĕs·tā′ shŭn)
ges·tic·u·late (jĕs·tĭk′ û·lāt)
  -lat·ing
  ges·tic·u·la·tion
    (jĕs·tĭk′ û·lā′ shŭn)
ges·ture (jĕs′ tụr)
Ge·sund·heit (gĕ·zōōnt′ hīt)
get·a·way (gĕt′ à·wā′)

get·ting (gĕt′ ĭng)
gey·ser (gī′ zĕr)
Gha·na (gä′ nó)
  Gha·na·ian (gä′ nó·yăn)
ghast·ly (găst′ lĭ)
  ghast·li·er, -li·est, -li·ness
ghet·to (gĕt′ ō)
  ghet·tos
ghost (gōst)
  ghost·like   ghost·li·ness
  ghost·ly   ghost writ·er
  ghost·writ·ten
ghoul·ish (gōōl′ ĭsh)
GI (jē′ ī′)
  pl. GIs
gi·ant (jī′ ănt)
gib·ber·ish (jĭb′ ĕr·ĭsh)
gibe (jīb)
  (also jibe)   gib·ing
gib·let (jĭb′ lĕt)
Gi·bral·tar (jĭ·brôl′ tĕr)
gid·dy (gĭd′ ĭ)
  gid·di·ness
gi·gan·tic (jī·găn′ tĭk)
gig·gle (gĭg′ ′l)
  gig·gling   gig·gly
gig·o·lo (jĭg′ ō·lō)
  -los
gild (gĭld)
  (plate with gold; see guild)
  gilt-edged
gim·mick (gĭm′ ĭk)
gin·ger (jĭn′ jĕr)
  gin·ger ale   gin·ger·bread
  gin·ger·snap
ging·ham (gĭng′ ăm)
gin·gi·vi·tis (jĭn′ jĭ·vī′ tĭs)
gin rum·my (jĭn′ rŭm′ ĭ)
gi·raffe (jĭ·răf′)
gird·er (gûr′ dĕr)
gir·dle (gûr′ d′l)
  -dling
girth (gûrth)
gist (jĭst)
give (gĭv)
  giv·ing   give-and-take
  give·a·way
giz·zard (gĭz′ ĕrd)
gla·cier (glā′ shĕr)
  gla·cial (glā′ shăl)
  gla·ci·a·tion (glā′ sĭ·ā′ shŭn)
glad (glăd)
  glad·den   glad·dest
  glad·ly
glad·i·a·tor (glăd′ ĭ·ā′ tĕr)

glad·i·o·la (glăd' ĭ·ō' lá)
glam·our (glăm' ẽr)
  glam·or·ize -iz·ing
  glam·or·ous
glance (glăns)
  glanc·ing
glan·du·lar (glăn' dụ·lẽr)
glar·ing (glâr' ĭng)
Glas·gow, Scot·land
  (glăs' kō)
glass (glás)
  glass blow·er glass·ful
  glass·ware
gleam·ing (glēm' ĭng)
glee club (glē)
glee·ful (glē' fŏŏl)
glib·ness (glĭb' nĕs)
glide (glīd)
  glid·ing
glim·mer (glĭm' ẽr)
glimpse (glĭmps)
  glimps·ing
glis·ten (glĭs' 'n)
gloat·ing (glōt' ĭng)
glob·al (glōb' ăl)
  -al·ly
glob·u·lar (glŏb' ụ·lẽr)
gloom·y (glōōm' ĭ)
  gloom·i·er, -i·est, -i·ly, -i·ness
glo·ri·fy (glô' rĭ·fĭ)
  -fied -fy·ing
  glo·ri·fi·ca·tion
    (glô' rĭ·fĭ·kā' shŭn)
glo·ri·ous (glô' rĭ·ŭs)
glos·sa·ry (glŏs' á·rĭ)
  -ries
glos·sy (glŏs' ĭ)
  gloss·i·ness
Glouces·ter, Mass.
  (glŏs' tẽr)
glow·worm (glō' wûrm')
glu·cose (glōō' kōs)
glue (glōō)
  glue·y glu·ing
glum·ly (glŭm' lĭ)
glut·ton (glŭt' 'n)
  glut·ton·ous (glŭt' 'n·ŭs)
  glut·ton·y
glyc·er·in (glĭs' ẽr·ĭn)
gnarl (närl)
gnash (năsh)
gnat (năt)
gnaw (nô)
gnome (nōm)
goad (gōd)

goal (gōl)
  goal·ee (gōl' ė)
gob·let (gŏb' lĕt)
gob·lin (gŏb' lĭn)
god (gŏd)
  god·child god·daugh·ter
  god·dess god·fa·ther
  god·send
Goe·the, Jo·hann von
    (fôn gụ̈' tẽ, yō' hän)
go-get·ter (gō' gĕt' ẽr)
gog·gles (gŏg' lz)
  gog·gle-eyed
Gogh, Vin·cent van
    (vän kŏk', vĭn·sĕnt')
gold (gōld)
  gold·brick v. gold dig·ger
  gold·fish
gold·en·rod (gōl' dĕn·rŏd')
golf (gŏlf)
  (game; see *gulf*)
  golf club
Go·li·ath (gō·lī' áth)
Go·mor·rah (gō·mŏr' á)
gon·do·la (gŏn' dō·lá)
gon·or·rhe·a (gŏn' ō·rē' á)
good (gŏŏd)
  good-bye good-heart·ed
  good-hu·mored good will
goose (gōōs)
  goose·ber·ry goose pim·ple
  goose step
go·pher (gō' fẽr)
gor·geous (gôr' jŭs)
go·ril·la (gō·rĭl' á)
  (ape; see *guerrilla*)
gos·pel (gŏs' pĕl)
gos·sa·mer (gŏs' á·mẽr)
gos·sip (gŏs' ĭp)
  gos·sip·ing gos·sip·y
Go·tham (gŏth' ăm)
Goth·ic (gŏth' ĭk)
got·ten (gŏt' 'n)
gouge (gouj)
  goug·ing
gou·lash (gōō' läsh)
  (Hungarian dish; see *galosh*)
gourd (gōrd)
gour·met (gŏŏr' mā)
gout (gout)
  gout·y
gov·ern·a·ble (gŭv' ẽr·ná·b'l)
gov·ern·ess (gŭv' ẽr·nĕs)

gov·ern·ment (gŭv' ẽrn·mĕnt)
  gov·ern·men·tal
         (gŭv' ẽrn·mĕn' tằl)
  -tal·ly
gov·er·nor (gŭv' ẽr·nẽr)
  gov·er·nor gen·er·al
  gov·er·nor·ship
gown (goun)
grace (grās)
  grace·ful, -ful·ly, -ful·ness
  grace·less
gra·cious (grā' shŭs)
gra·da·tion (grā·dā' shŭn)
  (series)
gra·di·ent (grā' dĭ·ĕnt)
grad·u·al (grăd' û·ăl)
  -al·ly -al·ness
grad·u·ate (grăd' û·āt)
  -at·ing
  grad·u·a·tion (grăd' û·ā' shŭn)
  (commencement)
grain·y (grān' ĭ)
  grain·i·ness
gram (grăm)
gram·mar (grăm' ẽr)
  gram·mar·i·an (grŏ·mâr' ĭ·ăn)
  gram·mat·i·cal
         (grŏ·măt' ĭ·kăl)
  -cal·ly
gran·a·ry (grăn' à·rĭ)
  -ries
grand (grănd)
  grand·child grand·dad
  grand·daugh·ter
  grand·duke grand·par·ent
  grand·son grand·stand
gran·deur (grăn' dũr)
gran·dil·o·quence
      (grăn·dĭl' ō·kwĕns)
gran·di·ose (grăn' dĭ·ōs)
  -ose·ly
gran·ite (grăn' ĭt)
grant-in-aid (grănt' ĭn·ād')
  grants-in-aid
gran·u·late (grăn' û·lāt)
  -lat·ing
gran·u·lar (grăn' û·lẽr)
grape (grāp)
  grape·fruit grape juice
  grape·shot grape·vine
graph·ic (grăf' ĭk)
  graph·i·cal·ly
graph·ite (grăf' ĭt)
grap·ple (grăp' 'l)
  grap·pling hook

grass·hop·per (grăs' hŏp' ẽr)
grate (grāt)
  grat·ing
grate·ful (grāt' fŏŏl)
  grate·ful·ly -ful·ness
grat·i·fy (grăt' ĭ·fī)
  -fied -fy·ing
  grat·i·fi·ca·tion
      (grăt' ĭ·fĭ·kā' shŭn)
grat·i·tude (grăt' ĭ·tūd)
gra·tu·i·ty (grŏ·tū' ĭ·tĭ)
  -ties
gra·tu·i·tous (grŏ·tū' ĭ·tŭs)
grav·el (grăv' ĕl)
  -el·ly
grav·en im·age (grăv' ĕn)
grave·stone (grāv' stōn')
grav·i·ty (grăv' ĭ·tĭ)
gra·vy (grā' vĭ)
  -vies
gray (grā)
  gray·beard gray·ness
grease (grēs)
  greas·ing greas·i·ness
  greas·y
great (grāt)
  great-grand·fa·ther
  Great Lakes
  Great Smok·y Mts.
Gre·cian (grē' shŭn)
Gre·co, El (ĕl grā' kō)
greed·y (grēd' ĭ)
  greed·i·er, -i·est, -i·ly, -i·ness
green (grēn)
  green·er·y green-eyed
  green·gage green·horn
  green·house
Green·wich Vil·lage
      (grĕn' ĭch)
greet·ing (grēt' ĭng)
gre·gar·i·ous (grē·gâr' ĭ·ŭs)
Gre·go·ri·an cal·en·dar
      (grē·gō' rĭ·ăn)
grem·lin (grĕm' lĭn)
gre·nade (grē·nād')
gren·a·dier (grĕn' à·dẽr')
gren·a·dine (grĕn' à·dēn')
Gresh·am's law (grĕsh' ămz)
grey·hound (grā' hound')
grid·dle·cake (grĭd' 'l·kāk')
grid·i·ron (grĭd' ĭ·ẽrn)
grief-strick·en (grēf' strĭk' ĕn)
grieve (grēv)
  griev·ing
  griev·ance (grēv' ăns)

griev·ous (grēv′ ŭs)
grill (grĭl)
  (to broil)
grille (grĭl)
  (a grating)
grim (grĭm)
  grim·mest grim·ly
gri·mace (grĭ·mās′)
  -mac·ing
grime (grīm)
  grim·i·ness grim·y
grin (grĭn)
  grinned grin·ning
grind·stone (grīnd′ stōn′)
grip (grĭp)
  gripped grip·ping
gripe (grīp)
  grip·ing
gris·ly (grĭz′ lĭ)
  gris·li·est gris·li·ness
gris·tle (grĭs′ ′l)
grist·mill (grĭst′ mĭl′)
griz·zly bear (grĭz′ lĭ)
gro·cer (grō′ sĕr)
  gro·cer·y -cer·ies
grog·gy (grŏg′ ĭ)
  grog·gi·ness
grom·met (grŏm′ ĕt)
gros·beak (grōs′ bĕk′)
gros·grain rib·bon
  (grō′ grān′)
gro·tesque (grō·tĕsk′)
  -tesque·ly
grot·to (grŏt′ ō)
grouch·y (grouch′ ĭ)
  grouch·i·ness
ground (ground)
  ground floor ground hog
  ground·work
grouse (grous)
grov·el (grŏv′ ′l)
  -eled -el·ing
grown·up (grōn′ ŭp′) n.
growth (grōth)
grub (grŭb)
  grub·bi·ness grub·by
  grub·stake
grudge (grŭj)
  grudg·ing·ly
gru·el (grōō′ ĕl)
  gru·el·ing
grue·some (grōō′ sŭm)
grum·ble (grŭm′ b′l)
  -bling

Gua·da·lupe (gwŏd′ ′l·ōōp)
  Riv. & Mt., Tex.
Gua·de·loupe Is.,
  West In·dies (gwŏd′ ′l·ōōp)
Guan·tá·na·mo
  (gwän·tä′ nä·mô)
guar·an·tee (găr′ ăn·tē′)
  -tee·ing
  guar·an·tor (găr′ ăn·tôr)
guar·an·ty (găr′ ăn·tĭ)
  -ties
guard (gärd)
guard·i·an (gär′ dĭ·ăn)
Gua·te·ma·la (gwä′ tĕ·mä′ lă)
Gua·ya·quil, (gwä′ yä·kēl′)
  Ec·ua·dor
gu·ber·na·to·ri·al
  (gū′ bĕr·ná·tô′ rĭ·ál)
Guern·sey (gûrn′ zĭ)
  -seys
guer·ril·la (gĕ·rĭl′ á)
  (irregular warrior; see gorilla)
guess·work (gĕs′ wûrk′)
guest (gĕst)
guf·faw (gŭ·fô′)
Gui·a·na (gĕ·ä′ ná)
  (S. Amer. region)
guide (gīd)
  guid·ing guid·a·ble
  guid·ance guide·book
  guide·post guid·ed mis·sile
guild (gĭld)
  (association; see gild)
guile (gīl)
  guile·less
guil·lo·tine (gĭl′ ô·tēn)
guilt·y (gĭl′ tĭ)
  guilt·i·ly
Guin·ea, Afr. (gĭn′ ĭ)
guin·ea pig (gĭn′ ĭ)
guise (gīz)
gui·tar (gĭ·tär′)
gulf (gŭlf)
  (separation; see golf)
gul·li·ble (gŭl′ ĭ·b′l)
gul·ly (gŭl′ ĭ)
  gul·lies
gum·bo (gŭm′ bō)
gun (gŭn)
  gun·man gun·ner
  gun·ner·y gun play
  gun pow·der gun·shot
gur·gle (gûr′ g′l)
  -gling
gus·to (gŭs′ tō)

gust·y   (gŭs′ tĭ)
  gust·i·ness
gut·ter·snipe   (gŭt′ ĕr·snĭp′)
gut·tur·al   (gŭt′ ĕr·ăl)
  -al·ly
guz·zle   (gŭz′ 'l)
  guz·zling
gym·na·si·um   (jĭm·nā′ zĭ·ŭm)
gym·nast   (jĭm′ năst)
  gym·nas·tic   (jĭm·năs′ tĭk)
gyn·e·col·o·gy   (jĭn′ ê·kŏl′ ô·jĭ)
  gyn·e·co·log·i·cal
                (jĭn′ ê·kô·lŏj′ ĭ·kăl)
gyp   (jĭp)
  gypped   gyp·ping
gyp·sum   (jĭp′ sŭm)
gyp·sy   (jĭp′ sĭ)
  -sies
gy·rate   (jī′ rāt)
  -rat·ing
gy·ra·tion   (jī·rā′ shŭn)
  gy·ra·tor
gy·ro·scope   (jī′ rŏ·skōp)

H

ha·be·as cor·pus
                (hā′ bê·ás kôr′ pŭs)
hab·er·dash·er·y
                (hăb′ ĕr·dăsh′ ĕr·ĭ)
hab·it   (hăb′ ĭt)
  hab·it·a·ble   hab·i·tat
  hab·i·ta·tion   (hăb′ ĭ·tā′ shŭn)
  ha·bit·u·al   (há·bĭt′ û·ăl)
  -al·ly
  ha·bit·u·a·tion
                (há·bĭt′ û·ā′ shŭn)
  ha·bit·u·é   (há·bĭt′ û·ā′)
ha·ci·en·da   (hās′ ĭ·ĕn′ dá)
hack·neyed   (hăk′ nĭd)
had·dock   (hăd′ ŭk)
Ha·des   (hā′ dēz)
hag·gard   (hăg′ ĕrd)
hag·gle   (hăg′ 'l)
  hag·gling
Hague, The, Neth·er·lands
                (hāg)
hail   (hāl)
  hail·stone   hail·storm
hair   (hâr)
  hair·breadth   hair·dress·er
  hair·split·ter   hair·spring
  hair trig·ger   hair·y

Hai·ti   (hā′ tĭ)
  Hai·ti·an   (hā′ tĭ·ăn)
hal·cy·on   (hăl′ sĭ·ŭn)
hale   (hāl)
  (and hearty)
half   (hăf)
  pl. halves   half-and-half
  half·back   half-baked
  half·breed   half broth·er
  half·caste   half dol·lar
  half·heart·ed   half-hour
  half life   half-mast
  half-moon   half nel·son
  half sis·ter   half-tim·bered
  half·way   half-wit·ted
hal·i·but   (hăl′ ĭ·bŭt)
hal·i·to·sis   (hăl′ ĭ·tō′ sĭs)
hal·le·lu·jah   (hăl′ ê·lōō′ yá)
hall·mark   (hôl′ märk′)
hal·lowed ground
                (hăl′ ōd)
Hal·low·een   (hăl′ ô·ēn′)
hal·lu·ci·na·tion
                (há·lū′ sĭ·nā′ shŭn)
ha·lo   (hā′ lō)
  -los
hal·ter   (hôl′ tĕr)
halt·ing   (hôl′ tĭng)
halve   (hăv)
  halv·ing
hal·yard   (hăl′ yĕrd)
ham·burg·er   (hăm′ bûr·gĕr)
Ham·let   (hăm′ lĕt)
ham·mer and sick·le
                (hăm′ ĕr ănd sĭk′ 'l)
ham·mer·head shark
                (hăm′ ĕr·hĕd′)
ham·mock   (hăm′ ŭk)
ham·per   (hăm′ pĕr)
ham·ster   (hăm′ stĕr)
ham·string   (hăm′ strĭng′)
hand   (hănd)
  hand·bag   hand·bill
  hand·cuff   hand·ful
  hand gre·nade   hand·made
  hand-me-down   hand·out
  hand·spring   hand-to-mouth
  hand·writ·ing
hand·i·cap   (hăn′ dĭ·kăp)
  -capped   -cap·ping
hand·i·craft   (hăn′ dĭ·kráft)
hand·i·work   (hăn′ dĭ·wûrk′)
han·dle   (hăn′ d'l)
  -dling

hand·some (hăn′ sŭm)
  -some·ly
hand·y (hăn′ dĭ)
  hand·i·ly   hand·y man
hang (hăng)
  hang·nail   hang·out
  hang-o·ver
hang·ar (hăng′ ẽr)
  (for aircraft)
hang·er (hăng′ ẽr)
  (for clothes)
han·ker·ing (hăng′ kẽr·ĭng)
han·som cab (hăn′ sŭm)
Ha·nuk·kah (hä′ nŏŏ·kä)
hap·haz·ard (hăp′ hăz′ ẽrd)
hap·pen·ing (hăp′ ĕn·ĭng)
hap·py (hăp′ ĭ)
  hap·pi·er   hap·pi·est
  hap·pi·ly   hap·pi·ness
  hap·py-go-luck·y
har·a·kir·i (här′ á·kĭr′ ĭ)
ha·rangue (há·răng′)
  -rangu·ing
har·ass (hăr′ ás)
  har·ass·ment
har·bin·ger (här′ bĭn·jẽr)
har·bor (här′ bẽr)
hard (härd)
  hard-bit·ten   hard-boiled
  hard·en   hard·head·ed
  hard·heart·ed   hard·ship
  hard·tack   hard·ware
har·dy (här′ dĭ)
  har·di·ness
hare·brained (hâr′ brānd′)
hare·lip (hâr′ lĭp′)
ha·rem (hā′ rĕm)
hark·en (här′ kĕn)
Har·le·quin (här′ lĕ·kwĭn)
har·lot (här′ lŏt)
harm·ful (härm′ fŏŏl)
  -ful·ly   -ful·ness
har·mon·i·ca (här·mŏn′ ĭ·ká)
har·mo·ny (här′ mō·nĭ)
  -nies
  har·mon·ic (här·mŏn′ ĭk)
  har·mo·ni·ous (här·mō′ nĭ·ŭs)
  har·mo·niz·ing
             (här′ mō·nĭz·ĭng)
har·ness (här′ nĕs)
har·poon (här·pōōn′)
harp·si·chord (härp′ sĭ·kôrd)
har·row·ing (här′ ō·ĭng)
har·ry (hăr′ ĭ)
  har·ried   har·ry·ing

Har·vard (univ.) (här′ vẽrd)
har·vest·er (här′ vĕs·tẽr)
has-been (hăz′ bĭn′)
ha·sen·pfef·fer (hä′ zĕn(p)fĕf′ ẽr)
has·sock (hăs′ ŭk)
haste (hāst)
  has·ten (hās′ ′n)
  hast·y
hatch (hăch)
  hatch·er·y (hăch′ ẽr·ĭ)
hatch·et (hăch′ ĕt)
  hatch·et-faced
hate·ful (hāt′ fŏŏl)
  -ful·ly   -ful·ness
ha·tred (hā′ trĕd)
Hat·ter·as, Cape, (hăt′ ẽr·ás)
  N.C.
haugh·ty (hô′ tĭ)
  haugh·ti·er   -ti·est
  -ti·ly   -ti·ness
haul (hôl)
haunch (hônch)
haunt (hônt)
Ha·van·a, Cu·ba
             (há·văn′ á)
ha·ven (hā′ vĕn)
hav·er·sack (hăv′ ẽr·săk)
hav·oc (hăv′ ŭk)
Ha·wai·i (há·wī′ ê)
  Ha·wai·ian (há·wī′ ăn)
hawk-eyed (hôk′ īd′)
haw·thorn (hô′ thôrn)
hay (hā)
  hay fe·ver   hay·fork
  hay·loft   hay·seed
  hay·stack   hay·wire
haz·ard·ous (hăz′ ẽr·dŭs)
haze (hāz)
  ha·zy
ha·zel·nut (hā′ z′l·nŭt′)
H-bomb (āch′ bŏm′)
head (hĕd)
  head·ache   head·dress
  head·first   head·gear
  head-hunt·er   head·light
  head·line   head·long
  head·mas·ter
  head-on col·li·sion
  head·phone   head·piece
  head·quar·ters head·strong
  head·wait·er   head wind
heal (hēl)
  (cure)
health·ful (hĕlth′ fŏŏl)
  -ful·ly   -ful·ness

health·y (hĕl' thĭ)
  health·i·ness
hear·say ev·i·dence
            (hĕr' sā')
hearse (hûrs)
heart (härt)
  heart·ache   heart·break·ing
  heart·burn   heart dis·ease
  heart·en·ing   heart·felt
  heart·less   heart-rend·ing
  heart-to-heart
hearth (härth)
heat·er (hēt' ēr)
hea·then (hē' thĕn)
  hea·then·ish
heath·er (hĕth' ēr)
heave (hēv)
  heav·ing
heav·en (hĕv' ĕn)
  heav·en·ward
heav·y (hĕv' ĭ)
  heav·i·er, -i·est, -i·ly, -i·ness
  heav·y-du·ty   heav·y·heart·ed
  heav·y·weight
He·bra·ic (hē·brā' ĭk)
heck·le (hĕk' 'l)
  -ling
hec·tic (hĕk' tĭk)
  hec·ti·cal·ly
hec·to·graph (hĕk' tô·grăf)
hedge (hĕj)
  hedge·hog   hedge·row
he·don·ism (hē' dŏn·ĭz'm)
  he·don·ist
heed (hēd)
  heed·ful, -ful·ly, -ful·ness
  heed·less
heel (hēl)
  (foot part)
heft·y (hĕf' tĭ)
  heft·i·ness
He·ge·li·an (hā·gā' lĭ·ăn)
he·gem·o·ny (hē·jĕm' ô·nĭ)
heif·er (hĕf' ēr)
heigh-ho (hī' hō')
height (hīt)
  height·en (hīt' 'n)
hei·nous (hā' nŭs)
heir (âr)
  heir ap·par·ent
  heir·ess   heir·loom
hel·i·cal (hĕl' ĭ·kăl)
hel·i·cop·ter (hĕl' ĭ·kŏp' tēr)
he·li·o·trope (hē' lĭ·ô·trōp)
he·li·um (hē' lĭ·ŭm)

hell (hĕl)
  hell·cat   hell-div·er
  hell-fire
Hel·len·ic (hĕ·lĕn' ĭk)
helm (hĕlm)
hel·met (hĕl' mĕt)
  -met·ed
help (hĕlp)
  help·ful, -ful·ly, -ful·ness
  help·less   help·mate
hel·ter-skel·ter (hĕl' tēr·skĕl' tēr)
hem·i·sphere (hĕm' ĭ·sfēr)
  hem·i·spher·ic (hĕm' ĭ·sfĕr' ĭk)
hem·lock (hĕm' lŏk)
he·mo·glo·bin (hē' mô·glō' bĭn)
he·mo·phil·i·a (hē' mô·fĭl' ĭ·ȧ)
  he·mo·phil·i·ac (-fĭl' ĭ·ăk)
hem·or·rhage (hĕm' ô·rĭj)
hem·or·rhoid (hĕm' ô·roid)
hence·forth (hĕns' fôrth')
  hence·for·ward
hench·man (hĕnch' măn)
hen·na (hĕn' ȧ)
  hen·naed   hen·na·ing
hen-pecked (hĕn' pĕkt')
hep·a·ti·tis (hĕp' ȧ·tī' tĭs)
Hep·ple·white (hĕp' 'l·hwīt)
her·ald (hĕr' ȧld)
  he·ral·dic (hĕ·răl' dĭk)
  her·ald·ry (hĕr' ȧld·rĭ)
herb (ûrb)
  her·ba·ceous (hûr·bā' shŭs)
  herb·age (ûr' bĭj)
  her·biv·o·rous (hûr·bĭv' ô·rŭs)
her·cu·le·an (hûr·kū' lē·ăn)
herds·man (hûrdz' măn)
here (hēr)
  here·a·bout   here·aft·er
  here·at   here·by
  here·in   here·in·aft·er
  here·to·fore   here·unto
  here·up·on   here·with
he·red·i·tar·y (hē·rĕd' ĭ·tĕr' ĭ)
he·red·i·ty (hē·rĕd' ĭ·tĭ)
Her·e·ford cat·tle
            (hĕr' ĕ·fērd)
her·e·sy (hĕr' ĕ·sĭ)
  -sies
  her·e·tic (hĕr' ĕ·tĭk)
  he·ret·i·cal (hĕ·rĕt' ĭ·kăl)
her·it·age (hĕr' ĭ·tĭj)
her·met·ic (hûr·mĕt' ĭk)
  her·met·i·cal·ly sealed
her·mit (hûr' mĭt)
  her·mit·age (hûr' mĭ·tĭj)

her·ni·a (hûr′ nǐ·à)
he·ro (hēr′ ō)
-roes
he·ro·ic (hē·rō′ ǐk)
he·ro·i·cal·ly
her·o·ine (hěr′ ō·ǐn)
her·o·ism (hěr′ ō·ǐz′m)
her·o·in (hěr′ ō·ǐn)
(drug)
her·on (hěr′ ŭn)
(bird)
her·ring·bone (hěr′ ǐng·bōn′)
her·self (hûr·sělf′)
hes·i·tate (hěz′ ǐ·tāt)
-tat·ing
hes·i·tan·cy (hěz′ ǐ·tǎn·sǐ)
hes·i·tant (hěz′ ǐ·tǎnt)
hes·i·ta·tion (hěz′ ǐ·tā′ shǔn)
Hes·sian (hěsh′ ǎn)
het·er·o·dox (hět′ ěr·ō·dǒks)
het·er·o·ge·ne·ous
(hět′ ěr·ō·jē′ nē·ǔs)
het·er·o·ge·ne·i·ty
(-jē·ně′ ǐ·tǐ)
het·er·o·sex·u·al
(hět′ ěr·ō·sěk′ shŏŏ·ǎl)
heu·ris·tic (hū·rǐs′ tǐk)
hew (hū)
(cut; see hue)
hewn (hūn)
hex·a·gon (hěk′ sà·gǒn)
hex·ag·o·nal (hěks·ǎg′ ō·nǎl)
hex·am·e·ter (hěks·ǎm′ ě·tēr)
hey·day (hā′ dā′)
hi·a·tus (hī·ā′ tǔs)
Hi·a·wa·tha (hī′ à·wô′ thà)
hi·ber·nate (bī′ běr·nāt)
-nat·ing
hi·ber·na·tion
(hī′ běr·nā′ shǔn)
hi·bis·cus (hī·bǐs′ kǔs)
hic·cup (hǐk′ ŭp)
hick·o·ry (hǐk′ ō·rǐ)
hid·den (hǐd′ 'n)
hide·bound (hīd′ bound′)
hid·e·ous (hǐd′ ē·ǔs)
hie (hī)
hied
hy·ing
hi·er·arch·y (hī′ ěr·är′ kǐ)
-arch·ies
hi·er·o·glyph·ic
(hī′ ěr·ō·glǐf′ ǐk)
hi-fi (hī′ fī′)
high (hī)
high·ball   high·born

high·brow
high-flown
high jump
high school
high-spir·it·ed
high-ten·sion
hi·jack (hī′ jǎk)
hi·lar·i·ous (hǐ·lâr′ ǐ·ǔs)
hi·lar·i·ty (hǐ·lǎr′ ǐ·tǐ)
hill·bil·ly (hǐl′ bǐl′ ǐ)
Hi·ma·la·ya (mts.)
(hǐ·mä′ là·yà)
him·self (hǐm·sělf′)
hind·quar·ter (hīnd′ kwôr′ tēr)
hin·drance (hǐn′ drǎns)
hind·sight (hīnd′ sīt′)
Hin·du (hǐn′ dōō)
Hin·du·ism (hǐn′ dōō·ǐz'm)
Hin·du·sta·ni (hǐn′ dōō·stä′ nē)
hinge (hǐnj)
hing·ing
hin·ter·land (hǐn′ tēr·lǎnd′)
Hip·po·crat·ic oath
(hǐp′ ō·krǎt′ ǐk)
hip·po·drome (hǐp′ ō·drōm)
hip·po·pot·a·mus
(hǐp′ ō·pǒt′ à·mǔs)
-mus·es
hir·a·ble (hīr′ à·b'l)
hire·ling (hīr′ lǐng)
Hi·ro·hi·to (hē′ rō·hē′ tō)
hir·sute (hûr′ sūt)
his·ta·mine (hǐs′ tà·mēn)
his·tol·o·gy (hǐs·tǒl′ ō·jǐ)
his·to·ry (hǐs′ tō·rǐ)
-ries
his·to·ri·an (hǐs·tō′ rǐ·ǎn)
his·tor·ic (hǐs·tŏr′ ǐk)
his·tor·i·cal (hǐs·tŏr′ ǐ·kǎl)
-cal·ly
his·to·ri·og·ra·pher
(hǐs·tō′ rǐ·ǒg′ rà·fēr)
his·tri·on·ic (hǐs′ trǐ·ǒn′ ǐk)
hit-and-run (hǐt′ ǎnd rǔn′)
hitch·hike (hǐch′ hīk′)
-hik·ing
hith·er·to (hǐth′ ěr·tōō′)
hives (hīvz)
hoard (hōrd)
hoar·frost (hōr′ frŏst′)
hoarse (hōrs)
hoarse·ly
hoar·y (hōr′ ǐ)
hoar·i·ness
hoax (hōks)

high fi·del·i·ty
high-fre·quen·cy
high·light
high-sound·ing
high-strung
high·way

hob·ble   (hŏb′ 'l)
   hob·bling
hob·by   (hŏb′ ĭ)
   hob·bies   hob·by·horse
hob·gob·lin   (hŏb′ gŏb′ lĭn)
hob·nail   (hŏb′ nāl′)
hob·nob   (hŏb′ nŏb′)
   -nobbed   -nob·bing
ho·bo   (hō′ bō)
   -boes
hock·ey   (hŏk′ ĭ)
ho·cus-po·cus   (hō′ kŭs·pō′ kŭs)
hod car·ri·er   (hod)
hodge·podge   (hŏj′ pŏj′)
hoe   (hō)
   hoe·ing
hog·wash   (hŏg′ wŏsh′)
hoi pol·loi   (hoi′ pŏ·loi′)
hoist   (hoist)
ho·kum   (hō′ kŭm)
hold·up   (hōld′ ŭp′)
hol·i·day   (hŏl′ ĭ·dā)
ho·li·ness   (hō′ lĭ·něs)
hol·lan·daise sauce
             (hŏl′ ɑn·dāz′)
hol·low   (hŏl′ ō)
hol·ly·hock   (hŏl′ ĭ·hŏk)
hol·o·caust   (hŏl′ ō·kôst)
hol·ster   (hōl′ stěr)
ho·ly   (hō′ lĭ)
   ho·li·er   ho·li·est
   ho·li·ness
hom·age   (hŏm′ ĭj)
Hom·burg hat   (hŏm′ bûrg)
home   (hōm)
   home e·co·nom·ics
   home·made   home·mak·er
   home run   home·sick
   home·spun   home·stead
   home·ward   home·work
home·ly   (hōm′ lĭ)
   home·li·ness
home·y   (hōm′ ĭ)
hom·i·cide   (hŏm′ ĭ·sīd)
   hom·i·cid·al   (hŏm′ ĭ·sīd′ ɑl)
hom·i·let·ic   (hŏm′ ĭ·lět′ ĭk)
hom·i·ly   (hŏm′ ĭ·lĭ)
   -lies
hom·i·ny grits   (hŏm′ ĭ·nĭ)
ho·mo·ge·ne·ous
         (hō′ mō·jē′ nē·ŭs)
ho·mo·ge·ne·i·ty
            (-jē·nē′ ĭ·tĭ)
ho·mog·e·nized milk
            (hŏ·mŏj′ ĕ·nīzd)

ho·mol·o·gous   (hŏ·mŏl′ ŏ·gŭs)
hom·o·nym   (hŏm′ ŏ·nĭm)
ho·mo·sex·u·al
        (hō′ mŏ·sěk′ shŏŏ·ɑl)
Hon·du·ras,   (hŏn·dōōr′ ɑs)
   Cen. Am.
hon·es·ty   (ŏn′ ĕs·tĭ)
hon·ey   (hŭn′ ĭ)
   hon·eyed   hon·ey·bee
   hon·ey·comb
   hon·ey·dew mel·on
   hon·ey·moon   hon·ey·suck·le
Hong Kong   (hŏng′ kŏng′)
honk·y-tonk   (hŏngk′ ĭ·tŏngk′)
hon·or   (ŏn′ ēr)
   hon·or·a·ble
   hon·or·ar·y   (ŏn′ ēr·ĕr′ ĭ)
hon·o·rar·i·um   (ŏn′ ŏ·râr′ ĭ·ŭm)
hood·lum   (hōōd′ lŭm)
hoo·doo   (hōō′ dōō)
hood·wink   (hōōd′ wĭngk)
hoo·ey   (hōō′ ĭ)
hoof·er   (hōōf′ ēr)
hook·up   (hŏŏk′ ŭp′)
hook·y   (hŏŏk′ ĭ)
hoo·li·gan   (hōō′ lĭ·gɑn)
Hoo·sier   (hōō′ zhēr)
hope·ful   (hōp′ fŏŏl)
   -ful·ly   -ful·ness
hop·per   (hŏp′ ēr)
hop·scotch   (hŏp′ skŏch′)
horde   (hôrd)
ho·ri·zon   (hŏ·rī′ z'n)
hor·i·zon·tal   (hŏr′ ĭ·zŏn′ tɑl)
   -tal·ly
hor·mone   (hôr′ mōn)
hor·net   (hôr′ nĕt)
hor·o·scope   (hŏr′ ŏ·skōp)
hor·ren·dous   (hŏ·rĕn′ dŭs)
hor·ri·ble   (hŏr′ ĭ·b'l)
hor·rid   (hŏr′ ĭd)
hor·ri·fy   (hŏr′ ĭ·fī)
   -fied   -fy·ing
hor·ri·fi·ca·tion
         (hŏr′ ĭ·fĭ·kā′ shŭn)
hor·ror   (hŏr′ ēr)
hors d'oeuvre   (ôr′ dû′ vr′)
horse   (hôrs)
   horse·back   horse·fly
   horse·man·ship
   horse·pow·er   horse-rad·ish
   horse sense   horse·shoe
   hors·y
hor·ti·cul·ture   (hŏr′ tĭ·kŭl′ tûr)
ho·san·na   (hŏ·zăn′ ɑ)

ho·sier·y (hō' zhēr·ĭ)
hos·pi·ta·ble (hŏs' pĭ·tá·b'l)
  hos·pi·tal·i·ty (hŏs' pĭ·tăl' ĭ·tĭ)
hos·pi·tal (hŏs' pĭt·ǎl)
  hos·pi·tal·ize -iz·ing
hos·tage (hŏs' tĭj)
hos·tel (hŏs' tĕl)
  (inn; see *hostile*)
host·ess (hōs' tĕs)
hos·tile (hŏs' tĭl)
  (unfriendly; see *hostel*)
  hos·til·i·ty (hŏs·tĭl' ĭ·tĭ)
  -ties
hot (hŏt)
  hot·bed   hot-blood·ed
  hot dog   hot·head·ed
  hot·house   hot plate
  hot rod
ho·tel (hō·tĕl')
hour·glass (our' glás')
house (hous)
  house·boat   house·coat
  house·fly   house·ful
  house·hold   house·keep·er
  house or·gan   house par·ty
  house·top   house·warm·ing
  house·wife   -wives
  house·work
hous·ing (houz' ĭng)
hov·el (hŏv' ĕl)
hov·er·ing (hŭv' ĕr·ĭng)
how·be·it (hou·bē' ĭt)
how·ev·er (hou·ĕv' ĕr)
how·itz·er (hou' ĭt·sĕr)
howl (houl)
how·so·ev·er (hou' sŏ·ĕv' ĕr)
hub·bub (hŭb' ŭb)
huck·le·ber·ry (hŭk' 'l·bĕr' ĭ)
  -ber·ries
huck·ster (hŭk' stĕr)
hud·dle (hŭd' 'l)
  hud·dling
hue (hū)
  (color; see *hew*)
  hue and cry
huge (hūj)
  huge·ness
Hu·gue·not (hū' gē·nŏt)
hu·la (hōō' lä)
hulk·ing (hŭl' kĭng)
hul·la·ba·loo (hŭl' á·bá·lōō')
hu·man (hū' mǎn)
  hu·mane (hū·mān')
  hu·man·is·tic (hū' mǎn·ĭs' tĭk)

hu·man·i·tar·i·an
    (hū·mǎn' ĭ·târ' ĭ·ǎn)
hu·man·i·ty (hū·mǎn' ĭ·tĭ)
  -ties
hum·ble (hŭm' b'l)
  -bling
hum·bug (hŭm' bŭg')
hum·drum (hŭm' drŭm')
hu·mid (hū' mĭd)
  hu·mid·i·fy (hū·mĭd' ĭ·fĭ)
  -fied   -fy·ing
  hu·mid·i·ty (hū·mĭd' ĭ·tĭ)
hu·mi·dor (hū' mĭ·dôr)
hu·mil·i·ate (hū·mĭl' ĭ·āt)
  -at·ing
  hu·mil·i·a·tion
    (hū·mĭl' ĭ·ā' shŭn)
hu·mil·i·ty (hū·mĭl' ĭ·tĭ)
hum·ming·bird (hŭm' ĭng·bûrd')
hum·mock (hŭm' ŭk)
hu·mor (hū' mēr)
  hu·mor·ous (hū' mēr·ous)
  hu·mor·esque (hū' mēr·ĕsk')
hu·mus (hū' mŭs)
hunch·back (hŏnch' băk')
hun·dred (hŭn' drĕd)
  hun·dred·fold
  hun·dred-per·cent·er
  hun·dredth   hun·dred·weight
Hun·ga·ry (hŭng' gá·rĭ)
  Hun·gar·i·an (hŭng·gâr' ĭ·ǎn)
hun·ger (hŭng' gĕr)
hun·gry (hŭng' grĭ)
  hun·gri·ly
hunt·ress (hŭn' trĕs)
hunts·man (hŭnts' mǎn)
hur·dle (hûr' d'l)
  (a barrier; or to leap a barrier; see *hurtle*) -dling
hur·dy-gur·dy (hûr' dĭ·gûr' dĭ)
hurl (hûrl)
hur·rah (hōō·rö')
  or: hur·ray (hōō·rā')
hur·ri·cane (hûr' ĭ·kān)
hur·ry (hûr' ĭ)
  hur·ried   hur·ry·ing
hurt·ful (hûrt' fōōl)
  -ful·ly   -ful·ness
hur·tle (hûr' t'l)
  (to throw violently; see *hurdle*)
  -tling
hus·band (hŭz' bǎnd)
husk·y (hŭs' kĭ)
  hus·ki·ness
hus·sar (hōō·zär')

hus·sy   (hŭz′ ĭ)
   hus·sies
hus·tings   (hŭs′ tǐngz)
hus·tle   (hŭs′ ′l)
   -tling
hy·a·cinth   (hī′ à·sǐnth)
hy·brid   (hī′ brǐd)
   hy·brid·i·za·tion
         (hī′ brǐd·ǐ·zā′ shŭn)
hy·drant   (hī′ drănt)
hy·drate   (hī′ drāt)
   -drat·ing
   hy·dra·tion   (hī·drā′ shŭn)
hy·drau·lic   (hī·drô′ lǐk)
   -li·cal·ly
hy·dro·car·bon
         (hī′ drô·kär′ bŏn)
hy·dro·chlo·ric   (hī′ drô·klō′ rǐk)
hy·dro·dy·nam·ics
         (hī′ drô·dī·năm′ ĭks)
hy·dro·e·lec·tric
         (hī′ drô·ê·lĕk′ trĭk)
hy·dro·gen   (hī′ drô·jĕn)
   hy·dro·gen per·ox·ide
   hy·dro·gen·ate   (hī′ drô·jĕn·āt)
   -at·ing
   hy·dro·gen·a·tion
         (hī′ drô·jĕn·ā′ shŭn)
hy·drol·y·sis   (hī·drŏl′ ĭ·sĭs)
hy·drom·e·ter   (hī·drŏm′ ê·tẽr)
hy·dro·pho·bi·a
         (hī′ drô·fō′ bǐ·à)
hy·dro·ther·a·py
         (hī′ drô·thĕr′ à·pǐ)
hy·drox·ide   (hī·drŏk′ sīd)
hy·giene   (hī′ jēn)
   hy·gi·en·ic   (hī′ jī·ĕn′ ǐk)
hy·men   (hī′ mĕn)
hymn   (hǐm)
   hym·nal   (hǐm′ nàl)
   hym·nol·o·gy   (hǐm·nŏl′ ô·jǐ)
hy·per·   (hī′ pẽr)
   hy·per·a·cid·i·ty
   hy·per·ac·tive hy·per·crit·i·cal
   hy·per·sen·si·tive
   hy·per·son·ic hy·per·ten·sion
hy·per·bo·le   (hī·pûr′ bô·lē)
hy·phen   (hī′ fĕn)
   hy·phen·a·tion
         (hī′ fĕn·ā′ shŭn)
hyp·no·sis   (hĭp·nō′ sĭs)
   hyp·not·ic   (hĭp·nŏt′ ĭk)
   hyp·no·tist   (hĭp′ nô·tĭst)
   hyp·no·tize   (hĭp′ nô·tīz)
   -tiz·ing

hy·po·chon·dri·a
         (hī′ pô·kŏn′ drǐ·à)
   hy·po·chon·dri·ac   (-ăk)
hy·poc·ri·sy   (hī·pŏk′ rǐ·sǐ)
   -sies
   hyp·o·crite   (hǐp′ ô·krǐt)
   hyp·o·crit·i·cal
         (hǐp′ ô·krǐt′ ǐ·kàl)
hy·po·der·mic   (hī′ pô·dûr′ mǐk)
hy·po·ten·sion   (hī′ pô·tĕn′ shŭn)
hy·pot·e·nuse   (hī·pŏt′ ê·nūs)
hy·po·thal·a·mus
         (hī′ pô·thăl′ à·mŭs)
hy·poth·e·sis   (hī·pŏth′ ê·sĭs)
   pl. hy·poth·e·ses
   hy·poth·e·size   -siz·ing
   hy·po·thet·i·cal
         (hī′ pô·thĕt′ ǐ·kàl)
hys·sop   (hǐs′ ŭp)
hys·ter·ec·to·my
         (hǐs′ tẽr·ĕk′ tô·mǐ)
hys·te·ri·a   (hǐs·tēr′ ǐ·à)
   hys·ter·i·cal   (-tẽr′ ǐ·kàl)
   hys·ter·ics   (-tẽr′ ǐks)

I

i·am·bic   (ī·ăm′ bǐk)
i·bi·dem   (ĭ·bī′ dĕm)
   abbr. ibid.
i·bis   (ī′ bǐs)
Ib·sen, Hen·rik
         (ĭb′ s′n, hĕn′ rǐk)
ice   (īs)
   ice bag   ice·berg
   ice·boat   ice·break·er
   ice·cap   ice cream
   ice·house   ice·man
   ice pack
Ice·land   (īs′ lănd)
   Ice·lan·dic   (īs·lăn′ dǐk)
ich·thy·ol·o·gy   (ĭk′ thǐ·ŏl′ ô·jǐ)
i·ci·cle   (ī′ sǐk·′l)
ic·ing   (īs′ ĭng)
i·con   (ī′ kŏn)
   i·con·o·clast   (ī·kŏn′ ô·klăst)
   i·co·nog·ra·phy
         (ī′ kô·nŏg′ rà·fǐ)
i·cy   (ī′ sǐ)
   i·ci·ly   (ī′ sǐ·lǐ)
I·da·ho   (ī′ dà·hō)
   abbr. Ida.
   I·da·ho·an   (-hō′ ăn)
i·de·a   (ī·dē′ à)

i·de·al   (ĭ·dē′ ăl)
  i·de·al·ism
  i·de·al·is·tic   (ĭ·dē′ ăl·ĭs′ tĭk)
  i·de·al·i·za·tion
        (ĭ·dē′ ăl·ĭ·zā′ shŭn)
  i·de·al·ly
i·de·a·tion   (ĭ′ dē·ā′ shŭn)
i·den·ti·cal   (ĭ·děn′ tĭ·kăl)
i·den·ti·fy   (ĭ·děn′ tĭ·fī)
  -fied,   -fy·ing
  i·den·ti·fi·ca·tion
        (ĭ·děn′ tĭ·fī·kā′ shŭn)
id·e·ol·o·gy   (ĭd′ ê·ŏl′ ô·jĭ)
  -gies
  id·e·o·log·i·cal
        (ĭd′ ê·ô·lŏj′ ĭ·kăl)
ides of March   (īdz)
id·i·o·cy   (ĭd′ ĭ·ô·sĭ)
id·i·om   (ĭd′ ĭ·ŭm)
  id·i·o·mat·ic   (ĭd′ ĭ·ô·măt′ ĭk)
  -i·cal·ly
id·i·o·syn·cra·sy
        (ĭd′ ĭ·ô·sĭng′ krà·sĭ)
id·i·ot   (ĭd′ ĭ·ŭt)
  id·i·o·cy   (ĭd′ ĭ·ô·sĭ)
  id·i·ot·ic   (ĭd′ ĭ·ŏt′ ĭk)
i·dle   (ī′ d'l)
  (inactive; see *idol, idyl*)
  i·dle·ness
  i·dly
i·dol   (ī′ dŭl)
  (deity; see *idle, idyl*)
  i·dol·a·ter   (ī·dŏl′ à·tẽr)
  i·dol·a·trous   (ī·dŏl′ à·trŭs)
  i·dol·a·try   (ī·dŏl′ à·trĭ)
  -tries
  i·dol·i·za·tion
        (ī′ dŭl·ĭ·zā′ shŭn)
  i·dol·ize   (ī′ dŭl·īz)
  -iz·ing
i·dyl   (ī′ dĭl)
  (literary work; see *idle, idol*)
  i·dyl·lic   (ī·dĭl′ ĭk)
ig·loo   (ĭg′ lōō)
ig·ne·ous   (ĭg′ nê·ŭs)
ig·nite   (ĭg·nīt′)
  -nit·ing   ig·nit·i·ble
ig·ni·tion   (ĭg·nĭsh′ ŭn)
ig·no·ble   (ĭg·nŏ′ b'l)
ig·no·min·i·ous
        (ĭg′ nô·mĭn′ ĭ·ŭs)
ig·no·min·y   (ĭg′ nô·mĭn·ĭ)
  -min·ies
ig·no·ra·mus   (ĭg′ nô·rā′ mŭs)

ig·no·rance   (ĭg′ nô·răns)
  -rant
ig·nore   (ĭg·nōr′)
  -nor·ing
i·gua·na   (ĭ·gwä′ nà)
Il·i·ad   (ĭl′ ĭ·ăd)
ill   (ĭl)
  ill-ad·vised   ill-bred
  ill-con·ceived   ill-de·fined
  ill-fat·ed   ill-got·ten
  ill-hu·mored   ill-kept
  ill-man·nered   ill-na·tured
  ill-starred   ill tem·per
  ill-tem·pered   ill-treat·ment
  ill-us·age
il·le·gal   (ĭl·lē′ găl)
  -gal·ly
  il·le·gal·i·ty   (ĭl′ lê·găl′ ĭ·tĭ)
il·leg·i·ble   (ĭl·lĕj′ ĭ·b'l)
il·le·git·i·mate   (ĭl′ lê·jĭt′ ĭ·mĭt)
  -ma·cy
il·lib·er·al   (ĭl·lĭb′ ẽr·ăl)
il·lic·it   (ĭl·lĭs′ ĭt)
  (unlawful; see *elicit*)
il·lim·i·ta·ble   (ĭl·lĭm′ ĭt·à·b'l)
Il·li·nois   (ĭl′ ĭ·noi′)
  abbr. Ill.
  Il·li·nois·an   (-noi′ ăn)
il·lit·er·a·cy   (ĭl·lĭt′ ẽr·à·sĭ)
  -er·ate
il·log·i·cal   (ĭl·lŏj′ ĭ·k'l)
  -cal·ly
il·lume   (ĭ·lūm′)
  il·lum·ing
il·lu·mi·nate   (ĭ·lū′ mĭ·nāt)
  -nat·ing
  il·lu·mi·nant   (ĭ·lū′ mĭ·nănt)
  il·lu·mi·na·tion
        (ĭ·lū′ mĭ·nā′ shŭn)
il·lu·sion   (ĭ·lū′ shŭn)
  (misconception; see *allusion*)
  il·lu·sion·al
il·lu·sive   (ĭ·lū′ sĭv)
  (unreal; see *elusive*)
il·lu·so·ry   (ĭ·lū′ sô·rĭ)
il·lus·trate   (ĭl′ ŭs·trāt)
  -trat·ing
  il·lus·tra·tion   (ĭl′ ŭs·trā′ shŭn)
  il·lus·tra·tive   (ĭ·lŭs′ trà·tĭv)
  il·lus·tra·tor
il·lus·tri·ous   (ĭ·lŭs′ trĭ·ŭs)
im·age   (ĭm′ ĭj)
  im·age·ry   (ĭm′ ĭj·rĭ)
im·ag·ine   (ĭ·măj′ ĭn)
  -in·ing   im·ag·i·na·ble

im·ag·i·nar·y
im·ag·i·na·tion
        (ĭ·măj′ ĭ·nā′ shŭn)
im·ag·i·na·tive
        (ĭ·măj′ ĭ·nā′ tĭv)
im·bal·ance   (ĭm·băl′ ăns)
im·be·cile   (ĭm′ bê·sĭl)
  im·be·cil·i·ty (ĭm′ bê·sĭl′ ĭ·tĭ)
im·bibe   (ĭm·bīb′)
  -bib·ing
im·bro·glio (ĭm·brōl′ yō)
im·bue   (ĭm·bū′)
  -bu·ing
im·i·tate   (ĭm′ ĭ·tāt)
  -tat·ing
  im·i·ta·ble (ĭm′ ĭ·tá·b'l)
  im·i·ta·tive (ĭm′ ĭ·tā′ tĭv)
  im·i·ta·tor
im·mac·u·late (ĭ·măk′ û·lĭt)
  Im·mac·u·late Con·cep·tion
im·ma·nent (ĭm′ á·nĕnt)
  (indwelling; see *imminent*)
  im·ma·nence
im·ma·te·ri·al (ĭm′ má·tēr′ ĭ·ăl)
im·ma·ture (ĭm′ á·tūr′)
  im·ma·tu·ri·ty
im·meas·ur·a·ble
        (ĭ·mĕzh′ ēr·á·b'l)
im·me·di·ate (ĭ·mē′ dĭ·ĭt)
  im·me·di·a·cy (-dĭ·á·sĭ)
  im·me·di·ate·ly
im·me·mo·ri·al
        (ĭm′ mê·mō′ rĭ·ăl)
im·mense   (ĭ·mĕns′)
  im·men·si·ty
im·merse   (ĭ·mûrs′)
  im·mers·ing
  im·mer·sion (ĭ·mûr′ shŭn)
im·mi·grate (ĭm′ ĭ·grāt)
  (to enter a country; see *emigrate*)
  -grat·ing   im·mi·grant
  im·mi·gra·tion
        (ĭm′ ĭ·grā′ shŭn)
im·mi·nent (ĭm′ ĭ·nĕnt)
  (about to happen; see *immanent*)
  im·mi·nence
im·mo·bile (ĭm·mō′ bĭl)
  im·mo·bil·i·ty (ĭm′ ô·bĭl′ ĭ·tĭ)
  im·mo·bi·lized (ĭm·mō′ bĭ·līzd)
im·mod·er·ate (ĭm·mŏd′ ēr·ĭt)
im·mod·est (ĭm·mŏd′ ĕst)
im·mo·late (ĭm′ ô·lāt)
  -lat·ing
  im·mo·la·tion (ĭm′ ô·lā′ shŭn)

im·mor·al   (ĭm·mŏr′ ăl)
  (not moral)
  im·mo·ral·i·ty
        (ĭm′ mô·răl′ ĭ·tĭ)
im·mor·tal (ĭ·môr′ tăl)
  (deathless)
  im·mor·tal·i·ty
        (ĭm′ ôr·tăl′ ĭ·tĭ)
  im·mor·tal·ize (ĭ·môr′ tăl·īz)
  -iz·ing
im·mov·a·ble (ĭm·mōōv′ á·b'l)
im·mune   (ĭ·mūn′)
  im·mu·ni·ty (ĭ·mū′ nĭ·tĭ)
  -ties
  im·mu·ni·za·tion
        (ĭm′ û·nĭ·zā′ shŭn)
im·mu·ta·ble (ĭ·mū′ tá·b'l)
im·pact·ed (ĭm·păk′ tĕd)
  im·pac·tion (ĭm·păk′ shŭn)
im·pair·ment (ĭm·pâr′ mĕnt)
im·pale   (ĭm·pāl′)
  -pal·ing
  im·pal·pa·ble (ĭm·păl′ pá·b'l)
im·part   (ĭm·pärt′)
im·par·tial (ĭm·pär′ shăl)
  -tial·ly
  im·par·ti·al·i·ty
        (ĭm′ pär·shĭ·ăl′ ĭ·tĭ)
im·pass·a·ble (ĭm·pás′ á·b'l)
im·passe   (ĭm·pás′)
im·pas·sioned (ĭm·păsh′ ŭnd)
im·pas·sive (ĭm·pás′ ĭv)
im·pa·tient (ĭm·pā′ shĕnt)
  -tience
im·peach   (ĭm·pēch′)
im·pec·ca·ble (ĭm·pĕk′ á·b'l)
im·pe·cu·ni·ous
        (ĭm′ pê·kū′ nĭ·ŭs)
im·pede   (ĭm·pēd′)
  -ped·ing
  im·ped·i·ment (ĭm·pĕd′ ĭ·mĕnt)
im·pel   (ĭm·pĕl′)
  -pelled   -pel·ling
im·pend·ing (ĭm·pĕnd′ ĭng)
im·pen·e·tra·ble
        (ĭm·pĕn′ ê·trá·b'l)
  im·pen·e·tra·bil·i·ty
        (ĭm·pĕn′ ê·trá·bĭl′ ĭ·tĭ)
im·pen·i·tence (ĭm·pĕn′ ĭ·tĕns)
im·per·a·tive (ĭm·pĕr′ á·tĭv)
im·per·cep·ti·ble
        (ĭm′ pĕr·sĕp′ tĭ·b'l)
im·per·cep·tive (-tĭv)
im·per·fect (ĭm·pûr′ fĕkt)

im·pe·ri·al (ĭm·pēr′ ĭ·ăl)
  im·pe·ri·al·is·tic
    (ĭm·pēr′ ĭ·ăl·ĭs′ tĭk)
im·pe·ri·ous (ĭm·pēr′ ĭ·ŭs)
im·per·ish·a·ble
    (ĭm·pĕr′ ĭsh·á·b'l)
im·per·ma·nent
    (ĭm·pûr′ má·nĕnt)
  -nence
im·per·me·a·ble (ĭm·pûr′ mē·á·b'l)
im·per·son·al (ĭm·pûr′ sŭn·ăl)
  -al·ly
im·per·son·ate (ĭm·pûr′ sŭn·āt)
  -at·ing
  im·per·son·a·tion
    (ĭm·pûr′ sŭn·ā′ shŭn)
  im·per·son·a·tor
im·per·ti·nence
    (ĭm·pûr′ tĭ·nĕns)
im·per·turb·a·ble
    (ĭm′ pĕr·tûr′ bá·b'l)
im·per·vi·ous (ĭm·pûr′ vĭ·ŭs)
im·pe·ti·go (ĭm′ pē·tī′ gō)
im·pet·u·ous (ĭm·pĕt′ û·ŭs)
  (impulsive)
  im·pet·u·os·i·ty
    (ĭm·pĕt′ û·ŏs′ ĭ·tĭ)
im·pe·tus (ĭm′ pē·tŭs)
  (momentum)
im·pi·e·ty (ĭm·pī′ ĕ·tĭ)
  -ties
  im·pi·ous (ĭm·pī′ ŭs)
im·pinge (ĭm·pĭnj)
  -ping·ing
imp·ish (ĭmp′ ĭsh)
im·pla·ca·ble (ĭm·plā′ ká·b'l)
im·plant (ĭm·plănt′)
im·plau·si·ble (ĭm·plô′ zĭ·b'l)
im·ple·ment (ĭm′ plē·mĕnt)
  im·ple·men·ta·tion
    (ĭm′ plē·mĕn·tā′ shŭn)
im·pli·cate (ĭm′ plĭ·kāt)
  -cat·ing
  im·pli·ca·tion
    (ĭm′ plĭ·kā′ shŭn)
im·plic·it (ĭm·plĭs′ ĭt)
im·plore (ĭm·plōr′)
  -plor·ing
im·ply (ĭm·plī′)
  -plied   -ply·ing
im·po·lite (ĭm′ pō·līt′)
  im·po·lite·ness
im·pol·i·tic (ĭm·pŏl′ ĭ·tĭk)

im·pon·der·a·ble
    (ĭm·pŏn′ dĕr·á·b'l)
im·port (ĭm·pōrt′) v.
  (ĭm′ pōrt) n.
  im·port·a·ble (ĭm·pōr′ tá·b'l)
  im·por·ta·tion
    (ĭm′ pōr·tā′ shŭn)
im·por·tance (ĭm·pōr′ tăns)
  -tant
im·por·tu·nate (ĭm·pōr′ tŭ·nĭt)
im·por·tune (ĭm′ pōr·tūn′)
im·pos·ing (ĭm·pōz′ ĭng)
im·po·si·tion (ĭm′ pō·zĭsh′ ŭn)
im·pos·si·ble (ĭm·pŏs′ ĭ·b'l)
  -bly
  im·pos·si·bil·i·ty
    (ĭm·pŏs′ ĭ·bĭl′ ĭ·tĭ)
im·pos·tor (ĭm·pŏs′ tĕr)
im·pos·ture (ĭm·pŏs′ tŭr)
im·po·tent (ĭm′ pō·tĕnt)
  -tence
im·pound (ĭm·pound′)
im·pov·er·ish (ĭm·pŏv′ ĕr·ĭsh)
im·prac·ti·ca·ble
    (ĭm·prăk′ tĭ·ká·b'l)
im·prac·ti·cal (ĭm·prăk′ tĭ·kăl)
  im·prac·ti·cal·i·ty
    (ĭm·prăk′ tĭ·kăl′ ĭ·tĭ)
im·pre·cate (ĭm′ prē·kāt)
  -cat·ing
  im·pre·ca·tion
    (ĭm′ prē·kā′ shŭn)
im·preg·na·ble
    (ĭm·prĕg′ ná·b'l)
im·preg·nate (ĭm·prĕg′ nāt)
  -nat·ing
im·pre·sa·ri·o (ĭm′ prā·sä′ rĭ·ō)
im·press (ĭm′ prĕs) n.
im·press (ĭm·prĕs′) v.
  im·press·i·ble
  im·pres·sion (ĭm·prĕsh′ ŭn)
  im·pres·sion·a·ble
  im·pres·sion·is·tic
    (ĭm·prĕsh′ ŭn·ĭs′ tĭk)
  im·pres·sive
im·pri·ma·tur (ĭm′ prĭ·mā′ tĕr)
im·print (ĭm·prĭnt′) v.
  (ĭm′ prĭnt) n.
im·pris·on (ĭm·prĭz′'n)
  im·pris·on·ment
im·prob·a·ble (ĭm·prŏb′ á·b'l)
  im·prob·a·bil·i·ty
    (ĭm′ prŏb·á·bĭl′ ĭ·tĭ)
im·promp·tu (ĭm·prŏmp′ tū)
im·prop·er (ĭm·prŏp′ ĕr)

im·pro·pri·e·ty
     (ĭm′ prō·prī′ ĕ·tĭ)
-ties
im·prove   (ĭm·prōōv′)
-prov·ing   im·prov·a·ble
im·prove·ment
im·prov·i·dent   (ĭm·prŏv′ ĭ·dĕnt)
-dence
im·pro·vise   (ĭm′ prō·vīz)
-vis·ing
im·pro·vi·sa·tion
     (ĭm′ prō·vĭ·zā′ shŭn)
im·pru·dent   (ĭm·prōō′ dĕnt)
-dence
im·pugn   (ĭm·pūn′)
im·pulse   (ĭm′ pŭls)
im·pul·sion   (ĭm·pŭl′ shŭn)
im·pul·sive   (ĭm·pŭl′ sĭv)
im·pu·ni·ty   (ĭm·pū′ nĭ·tĭ)
im·pure   (ĭm·pūr′)
im·pu·ri·ty   -ties
im·pute   (ĭm·pūt′)
-put·ing   im·put·a·ble
im·pu·ta·tion
     (ĭm′ pū·tā′ shŭn)
in·a·bil·i·ty   (ĭn′ ȧ·bĭl′ ĭ·tĭ)
-ties
in ab·sen·ti·a   (ĭn ăb·sĕn′ shĭ·ȧ)
in·ac·ces·si·ble   (ĭn′ ăk·sĕs′ ĭ·b'l)
in·ac·cu·ra·cy   (ĭn·ăk′ û·rá·sĭ)
-cies
in·ac·cu·rate   -rate·ly
in·ac·tive   (ĭn·ăk′ tĭv)
in·ac·tiv·i·ty   (ĭn′ ăk·tĭv′ ĭ·tĭ)
in·ad·e·quate   (ĭn·ăd′ ê·kwĭt)
-qua·cy
in·ad·mis·si·ble
     (ĭn′ ăd·mĭs′ ĭ·b'l)
in·ad·vert·ence
     (ĭn′ ăd·vûr′ tĕns)
-ent
in·ad·vis·a·ble
     (ĭn′ ăd·vīz′ ȧ·b'l)
in·al·ien·a·ble   (ĭn·āl′ yĕn·ȧ·b'l)
in·al·ter·a·ble   (ĭn·ôl′ tẽr·ȧ·b'l)
in·am·o·ra·ta   (ĭn·ăm′ ô·rä′ tá)
in·ane   (ĭn·ān′)
in·an·i·ty   (ĭn·ăn′ ĭ·tĭ)
in·an·i·mate   (ĭn·ăn′ ĭ·māt)
in·ap·peas·a·ble
     (ĭn′ ȧ·pēz′ ȧ·b'l)
in·ap·pli·ca·ble
     (ĭn·ăp′ lĭ·kȧ·b'l)
in·ap·pre·ci·a·ble
     (ĭn′ ȧ·prē′ shĭ·ȧ·b'l)

in·ap·pre·ci·a·tive
     (ĭn′ ȧ·prē′ shĭ·ā′ tĭv)
in·ap·proach·a·ble
     (ĭn′ ȧ·prōch′ ȧ·b'l)
in·ar·tic·u·late
     (ĭn′ ăr·tĭk′ û·lāt)
-late·ly
in·ar·tis·tic   (ĭn′ ăr·tĭs′ tĭk)
in·as·much as   (ĭn′ ăs·mŭch′)
in·at·ten·tion   (ĭn′ ȧ·tĕn′ shŭn)
in·at·ten·tive   (ĭn′ ȧ·tĕn′ tĭv)
-tive·ly
in·au·di·ble   (ĭn·ô′ dĭ·b'l)
in·au·gu·ral   (ĭn·ô′ gû·rǎl)
in·au·gu·rate   (ĭn·ô′ gû·rāt)
-rat·ing
in·au·gu·ra·tion
     (ĭn·ô′ gû·rā′ shŭn)
in·aus·pi·cious
     (ĭn′ ôs·pĭsh′ ŭs)
in·born   (ĭn′ bôrn′)
in·cal·cu·la·ble
     (ĭn·kăl′ kû·lȧ·b'l)
in·can·des·cent
     (ĭn′ kăn·dĕs′ ĕnt)
-cence
in·can·ta·tion   (ĭn′ kăn·tā′ shŭn)
in·ca·pa·ble   (ĭn·kā′ pȧ·b'l)
in·ca·pa·cious   (ĭn′ kȧ·pā′ shŭs)
in·ca·pac·i·tate
     (ĭn′ kȧ·păs′ ĭ·tāt)
-tat·ing
in·ca·pac·i·ta·tion
     (ĭn′ kȧ·păs′ ĭ·tā′ shŭn)
in·car·cer·ate   (ĭn·kär′ sẽr·āt)
-at·ing
in·car·cer·a·tion
     (ĭn·kär′ sẽr·ā′ shŭn)
in·car·nate   (ĭn·kär′ nāt)
in·car·na·tion
     (ĭn′ kär·nā′ shŭn)
in·cau·tious   (ĭn·kô′ shŭs)
in·cen·di·ar·y   (ĭn·sĕn′ dĭ·ĕr′ ĭ)
in·cense   (ĭn·sĕns′) v.
-cens·ing   (ĭn′ sĕns) n.
in·cen·tive   (ĭn·sĕn′ tĭv)
in·cep·tion   (ĭn·sĕp′ shŭn)
in·ces·sant·ly   (ĭn·sĕs′ ănt·lĭ)
in·cest   (ĭn′ sĕst)
in·ces·tu·ous   (ĭn·sĕs′ tû·ŭs)
in·cho·ate   (ĭn·kō′ ĭt)
in·ci·dent   (ĭn′ sĭ·dĕnt)
in·ci·dence
in·ci·den·tal   (ĭn′ sĭ·dĕn′ tǎl)
-tal·ly

in·cin·er·ate (ĭs·sĭn′ ĕr·āt)
-at·ing in·cin·er·a·tor
in·cip·i·ent (ĭn·sĭp′ ĭ·ĕnt)
-ence
in·cise (ĭn·sīz′)
-cis·ing
in·ci·sion (ĭn·sĭzh′ ŭn)
in·ci·sive (ĭn·sī′ sĭv)
in·ci·sor tooth (ĭn·sī′ zĕr)
in·cite (ĭn·sīt′)
-cit·ing in·cite·ment
in·clem·ent (ĭn·klĕm′ ĕnt)
in·cline (ĭn′ klīn) n.
in·cline (ĭn·klīn′) v.
-clin·ing in·clin·a·ble
in·cli·na·tion (ĭn′ klĭ·nā′ shŭn)
in·clude (ĭn·klōōd′)
-clud·ing
in·clu·sion (ĭn·klōō′ zhŭn)
in·clu·sive -sive·ly
in·cog·ni·to (ĭn·kŏg′ nĭ·tō)
in·co·her·ent (ĭn′ kō·hēr′ ĕnt)
-ence
in·com·bus·ti·ble
     (ĭn′ kŏm·bŭs′ tĭ·b'l)
in·come (ĭn′ kŭm)
in·com·ing (ĭn′ kŭm′ ĭng)
in·com·men·su·rate
     (ĭn′ kŏ·mĕn′ shŏŏ·rĭt)
in·com·men·su·ra·ble
in·com·mo·di·ous
     (ĭn′ kŏ·mō′ dĭ·ŭs)
in·com·mu·ni·ca·ble
     (ĭn′ kŏ·mū′ nĭ·kȧ·b'l)
in·com·mu·ni·ca·tive
in·com·mu·ni·ca·do
     (ĭn′ kŏ·mū′ nĭ·kä′ dō)
in·com·pa·ra·ble
     (ĭn·kŏm′ pȧ·rȧ·b'l)
in·com·pat·i·ble
     (ĭn′ kŏm·păt′ ĭ·b'l)
in·com·pat·i·bil·i·ty
     (ĭn′ kŏm·păt′ ĭ·bĭl′ ĭ·tĭ)
in·com·pe·tence
     (ĭn·kŏm′ pĕ·tĕns)
-tent
in·com·plete (ĭn′ kŏm·plēt′)
in·com·pli·ant (ĭn′ kŏm·plī′ ȧnt)
in·com·pre·hen·si·ble
     (ĭn′ kŏm·prĕ·hĕn′ sĭ·b'l)
in·con·ceiv·a·ble
     (ĭn·kŏn·sēv′ ȧ·b'l)
in·con·clu·sive
     (ĭn′ kŏn·klōō′ sĭv)

in·con·gru·ous
     (ĭn·kŏng′ grōō·ŭs)
in·con·gru·i·ty
     (ĭn′ kŏng·grōō′ ĭ·tĭ)
-ties
in·con·se·quen·tial
     (ĭn·kŏn′ sĕ·kwĕn′ shȧl)
in·con·sid·er·ate
     (ĭn′ kŏn·sĭd′ ĕr·ĭt)
in·con·sist·ent
     (ĭn′ kŏn·sĭs′ tĕnt)
-ten·cy
in·con·sol·a·ble
     (ĭn′ kŏn·sōl′ ȧ·b'l)
in·con·so·nant (ĭn·kŏn′ sŏ·nȧnt)
-nance
in·con·spic·u·ous
     (ĭn′ kŏn·spĭk′ û·ŭs)
in·con·stant (ĭn·kŏn′ stȧnt)
-stan·cy
in·con·test·a·ble
     (ĭn′ kŏn·tĕs′ tȧ·b'l)
in·con·ti·nent (ĭn·kŏn′ tĭ·nĕnt)
-nence
in·con·tro·vert·i·ble
     (ĭn′ kŏn·trŏ·vûr′ tĭ·b'l)
in·con·ven·ient
     (ĭn′ kŏn·vēn′ yĕnt)
-ience
in·cor·po·rat·ed
     (ĭn·kôr′ pŏ·rāt′ ĕd)
in·cor·rect·ly (ĭn′ kŏ·rĕkt′ lĭ)
in·cor·ri·gi·ble
     (ĭn·kŏr′ ĭ·jĭ·b'l)
in·cor·ri·gi·bil·i·ty
     (ĭn·kŏr′ ĭ·jĭ·bĭl′ ĭ·tĭ)
in·cor·rupt·i·ble
     (ĭn′ kŏ·rŭp′ tĭ·b'l)
in·crease (ĭn′ krēs) n.
-creas·ing (ĭn·krēs′) v.
in·cred·i·ble (ĭn·krĕd′ ĭ·b'l)
in·cred·i·bil·i·ty
     (ĭn·krĕd′ ĭ·bĭl′ ĭ·tĭ)
in·cred·u·lous (ĭn·krĕd′ û·lŭs)
in·cre·du·li·ty (ĭn′ krĕ·dū′ lĭ·tĭ)
in·cre·ment (ĭn′ krĕ·mĕnt)
in·crim·i·nat·ing
     (ĭn·krĭm′ ĭ·nāt′ ĭng)
in·crus·ta·tion (ĭn′ krŭs·tā′ shŭn)
in·cu·bate (ĭn′ kû·bāt)
-bat·ing
in·cu·ba·tion (ĭn′ kû·bā′ shŭn)
in·cu·ba·tor (ĭn′ kû·bā′ tĕr)
in·cu·bus (ĭn′ kû·bŭs)

in·cul·cate   (ĭn·kŭl′ kāt)
-cat·ing
in·cul·ca·tion
         (ĭn′ kŭl·kā′ shŭn)
in·cul·pate   (ĭn·kŭl′ pāt)
-pat·ing
in·cum·bent   (ĭn·kŭm′ bĕnt)
-ben·cy
in·cur   (ĭn·kûr′)
-curred   -cur·ring
in·cur·a·ble   (ĭn·kûr′ à·b'l)
in·cur·sion   (ĭn·kûr′ zhŭn)
in·debt·ed·ness   (ĭn·dĕt′ ĕd·nĕs)
in·de·cen·cy   (ĭn·dē′ sĕn·sĭ)
in·de·ci·pher·a·ble
         (ĭn′ dē·sī′ fēr·à·b'l)
in·de·ci·sive   (ĭn′ dē·sī′ sĭv)
in·de·ci·sion   (ĭn′ dē·sĭzh′ ŭn)
in·dec·o·rous   (ĭn·dĕk′ ô·rŭs)
in·de·co·rum   (ĭn′ dē·kō′ rŭm)
in·deed   (ĭn·dēd′)
in·de·fat·i·ga·ble
         (ĭn′ dē·făt′ ĭ·gà·b'l)
in·de·fat·i·ga·bil·i·ty
         (ĭn′ dē·făt′ ĭ·gà·bĭl′ ĭ·tĭ)
in·de·fea·si·ble   (ĭn′ dē·fē′ zĭ·b'l)
in·de·fen·si·ble
         (ĭn′ dē·fĕn′ sĭ·b'l)
in·de·fin·a·ble
         (ĭn′ dē·fīn′ à·b'l)
in·def·i·nite   (ĭn·dĕf′ ĭ·nĭt)
-nite·ly
in·del·i·ble   (ĭn·dĕl′ ĭ·b'l)
in·del·i·cate   (ĭn·dĕl′ ĭ·kĭt)
-ca·cy
in·dem·ni·fy   (ĭn·dĕm′ nĭ·fī)
-fied   -fy·ing
in·dem·ni·ty   (ĭn·dĕm′ nĭ·tĭ)
-ties
in·den·ta·tion   (ĭn′ dĕn·tā′ shŭn)
in·den·ture   (ĭn·dĕn′ tûr)
in·de·pend·ence
         (ĭn′ dē·pĕn′ dĕns)
-dent
in·de·scrib·a·ble
         (ĭn′ dē·skrīb′ à·b'l)
in·de·struct·i·ble
         (ĭn′ dē·strŭk′ tĭ·b'l)
in·de·ter·mi·na·ble
         (ĭn′ dē·tûr′ mĭ·nà·b'l)
in·de·ter·mi·nate
         (ĭn′ dē·tûr′ mĭ·nàt)
in·dex   (ĭn′ dĕks)
-dex·es
In·di·a ink   (ĭn′ dĭ·à)

In·di·an·a   (ĭn′ dĭ·ăn′ à)
     abbr. Ind.
In·di·an·i·an   (ăn′ ĭ·ăn)
in·di·cate   (ĭn′ dĭ·kāt)
-cat·ing
in·di·ca·tion   (ĭn′ dĭ·kā′ shŭn)
in·dic·a·tive   (ĭn·dĭk′ à·tĭv)
in·di·ca·tor
in·dict   (ĭn·dīt′)
in·dict·ment
in·dif·fer·ence   (ĭn·dĭf′ ēr·ĕns)
in·di·gence   (ĭn′ dĭ·jĕns)
in·dig·e·nous   (ĭn·dĭj′ ê·nŭs)
in·di·ges·tion   (ĭn′ dĭ·jĕs′ chŭn)
in·di·gest·i·ble
in·dig·nant   (ĭn·dĭg′ nănt)
-nance
in·dig·na·tion
         (ĭn′ dĭg·nā′ shŭn)
in·dig·ni·ty   (ĭn·dĭg′ nĭ·tĭ)
-ties
in·di·go   (ĭn′ dĭ·gō)
in·di·rect   (ĭn′ dĭ·rĕkt′)
in·dis·cern·i·ble
         (ĭn′ dĭ·zûr′ nĭ·b'l)
in·dis·creet   (ĭn′ dĭs·krēt′)
in·dis·cre·tion
         (ĭn′ dĭs·krĕsh′ ŭn)
in·dis·crim·i·nate
         (ĭn′ dĭs·krĭm′ ĭ·nĭt)
in·dis·pen·sa·ble
         (ĭn′ dĭs·pĕn′ sà·b'l)
in·dis·posed   (ĭn′ dĭs·pōzd′)
in·dis·pu·ta·ble
         (ĭn·dĭs′ pū·tà·b'l)
in·dis·sol·u·ble
         (ĭn′ dĭ·sŏl′ û·b'l)
in·dis·tinct   (ĭn′ dĭs·tĭngkt′)
in·dis·tin·guish·a·ble
         (ĭn′ dĭs·tĭng′ gwĭsh·à·b'l)
in·di·vid·u·al   (ĭn′ dĭ·vĭd′ û·ăl)
in·di·vid·u·al·ism, -al·ist
in·di·vid·u·al·i·ty
         (ĭn′ dĭ·vĭd′ û·ăl′ ĭ·tĭ)
in·di·vid·u·al·ize, -iz·ing
in·di·vid·u·al·ly
in·di·vis·i·ble   (ĭn′ dĭ·vĭz′ ĭ·b'l)
In·do·chi·na   (ĭn′ dô·chī′ nà)
in·doc·tri·nate   (ĭn·dŏk′ trĭ·nāt)
-nat·ing
in·doc·tri·na·tion
         (ĭn·dŏk′ trĭ·nā′ shŭn)
in·do·lent   (ĭn′ dô·lĕnt)
-lence

in·dom·i·ta·ble (ĭn·dŏm′ ĭ·tá·b'l)

In·do·ne·sia (ĭn′ dô·nē′ zhá)

in·doors (ĭn′ dōrz′)

in·du·bi·ta·ble (ĭn·dū′ bĭ·tá·b'l)

in·duce (ĭn·dūs′)

-duc·ing   in·duce·ment

in·duct (ĭn·dŭkt′)

in·duc·tion (ĭn·dŭk′ shŭn)

in·duc·tive   in·duc·tor

in·due (ĭn·dū′)

-du·ing

in·dulge (ĭn·dŭlj′)

-dulg·ing

in·dul·gent   -gence

in·dus·try (ĭn′ dŭs·trĭ)

-tries

in·dus·tri·al (ĭn·dŭs′ trĭ·ál)

-al·ly   -al·ism

in·dus·tri·al·ist (ĭn·dŭs′ trĭ·ál·ĭst)

in·dus·tri·al·i·za·tion (ĭn·dŭs′ trĭ·ál·ĭ·zā′ shŭn)

in·dus·tri·ous (ĭn·dŭs′ trĭ·ŭs)

in·dwell·ing (ĭn′ dwĕl′ ĭng)

in·e·bri·at·ed (ĭn·ē′ brĭ·āt′ ĕd)

in·e·bri·a·tion (ĭn·ē′ brĭ·ā′ shŭn)

in·ed·i·ble (ĭn·ĕd′ ĭ·b'l)

in·ef·fa·ble (ĭn·ĕf′ á·b'l)

in·ef·face·a·ble (ĭn′ ĕ·fās′ á·b'l)

in·ef·fec·tive (ĭn′ ĕ·fĕk′ tĭv)

in·ef·fec·tu·al (ĭn′ ĕ·fĕk′ tū·ál)

in·ef·fec·tu·al·i·ty (ĭn′ ĕ·fĕk′ tū·ăl′ ĭ·tĭ)

in·ef·fi·ca·cious (ĭn′ ĕf·ĭ·kā′ shŭs)

in·ef·fi·ca·cy (ĭn·ĕf′ ĭ·ká·sĭ)

in·ef·fi·cient (ĭn′ ĕ·fĭsh′ ĕnt)

-cien·cy

in·e·las·tic (ĭn′ ĕ·lăs′ tĭk)

in·el·e·gance (ĭn·ĕl′ ê·găns)

in·el·i·gi·ble (ĭn·ĕl′ ĭ·jĭ·b'l)

in·el·i·gi·bil·i·ty (ĭn·ĕl′ ĭ·jĭ·bĭl′ ĭ·tĭ)

in·e·luc·ta·ble (ĭn′ ê·lŭk′ tá·b'l)

in·ept (ĭn·ĕpt′)

in·ept·i·tude (ĭn·ĕpt′ ĭ·tūd)

in·e·qual·i·ty (ĭn′ ê·kwŏl′ ĭ·tĭ)

-ties

in·eq·ui·ta·ble (ĭn·ĕk′ wĭ·tá·b'l)

in·eq·ui·ty (ĭn·ĕk′ wĭ·tĭ)

-ties

in·e·rad·i·ca·ble (ĭn′ ê·răd′ ĭ·ká·b'l)

in·e·ras·a·ble (ĭn′ ê·răs′ á·b'l)

in·ert (ĭn·ûrt′)

in·er·tia (ĭn·ûr′ shá)

in·es·cap·a·ble (ĭn′ ĕs·kăp′ á·b'l)

in·es·sen·tial (ĭn′ ĕ·sĕn′ shál)

in·es·ti·ma·ble (ĭn·ĕs′ tĭ·má·b'l)

in·ev·i·ta·ble (ĭn·ĕv′ ĭ·tá·b'l)

in·ev·i·ta·bil·i·ty (ĭn·ĕv′ ĭ·tá·bĭl′ ĭ·tĭ)

in·ex·cus·a·ble (ĭn′ ĕks·kūz′ á·b'l)

in·ex·haust·i·ble (ĭn′ ĕg·zôs′ tĭ·b'l)

in·ex·o·ra·ble (ĭn·ĕk′ sô·rá·b'l)

in·ex·pe·di·ent (ĭn′ ĕks·pē′ dĭ′·ĕnt)

in·ex·pen·sive (ĭn′ ĕks·pĕn′ sĭv)

in·ex·pe·ri·enced (ĭn′ ĕks·pēr′ ĭ·ĕnst)

in·ex·pert (ĭn′ ĕks·pûrt′)

in·ex·pli·ca·ble (ĭn·ĕks′ plĭ·ká·b'l)

in·ex·press·i·ble (ĭn′ ĕks·prĕs′ ĭ·b'l)

in·ex·pres·sive

in·ex·tri·ca·ble (ĭn·ĕks′ trĭ·ká·b'l)

in·fal·li·ble (ĭn·făl′ ĭ·b'l)

in·fal·li·bil·i·ty (ĭn·făl′ ĭ·bĭl′ ĭ·tĭ)

in·fa·mous (ĭn′ fá·mŭs)

in·fa·my (ĭn′ fá·mĭ)

in·fant (ĭn′ fănt)

in·fan·cy

in·fan·ti·cide (ĭn·făn′ tĭ·sīd)

in·fan·tile (ĭn′ făn·tīl)

in·fan·try (ĭn′ făn·trĭ)

in·fan·try·man

in·fat·u·ate (ĭn·făt′ û·āt)

-at·ing

in·fat·u·a·tion (ĭn·făt′ û·ā′ shŭn)

in·fec·tion (ĭn·fĕk′ shŭn)

in·fec·tious (ĭn·fĕk′ shŭs)

in·fer (ĭn·fûr′)

-ferred   -fer·ring

in·fer·ence (ĭn′ fĕr·ĕns)

in·fer·en·tial (ĭn′ fĕr·ĕn′ shál)

in·fe·ri·or (ĭn·fēr′ ĭ·ēr)

in·fe·ri·or·i·ty com·plex (ĭn·fēr′ ĭ·ôr′ ĭ·tĭ)

in·fer·nal (ĭn·fûr′ nál)

in·fer·no (ĭn·fûr′ nō)
in·fi·del (ĭn′ fĭ·dĕl)
in·fi·del·i·ty (ĭn′ fĭ·dĕl′ ĭ·tĭ)
in·field·er (ĭn′ fēl′ dĕr)
in·fil·trate (ĭn·fĭl′ trāt)
  -trat·ing
  in·fil·tra·tion (ĭn′ fĭl·trā′ shŭn)
in·fi·nite (ĭn′ fĭ·nĭt)
  in·fi·nite·ly
in·fin·i·tes·i·mal
      (ĭn′ fĭn·ĭ·tĕs′ ĭ·măl)
in·fin·i·tive (ĭn·fĭn′ ĭ·tĭv)
in·fin·i·ty (ĭn·fĭn′ ĭ·tĭ)
in·firm (ĭn·fûrm′)
  in·fir·ma·ry (ĭn·fûr′ mà·rĭ)
  -ries
  in·fir·mi·ty (ĭn·fûr′ mĭ·tĭ)
  -ties
in·flame (ĭn·flām′)
  -flam·ing
in·flam·ma·ble (ĭn·flăm′ à·b'l)
  in·flam·ma·to·ry
     (ĭn·flăm′ à·tō′ rĭ)
in·flam·ma·tion (ĭn′ flà·mā′ shŭn)
in·flate (ĭn·flāt′)
  -flat·ing   in·flat·a·ble
  in·fla·tion (ĭn·flā′ shŭn)
  in·fla·tion·ar·y
in·flec·tion (ĭn·flĕk′ shŭn)
  -tion·al
in·flex·i·ble (ĭn·flĕk′ sĭ·b'l)
  in·flex·i·bil·i·ty
     (ĭn·flĕk′ sĭ·bĭl′ ĭ·tĭ)
in·flict (ĭn·flĭkt′)
  in·flic·tion (ĭn·flĭk′ shŭn)
in·flu·ence (ĭn′ flōō·ĕns)
  in·flu·en·tial (ĭn′ flōō·ĕn′ shăl)
in·flu·en·za (ĭn′ flōō·ĕn′ zà)
in·flux (ĭn′ flŭks)
in·form (ĭn·fôrm′)
  in·form·ant (ĭn·fôr′ mănt)
  in·for·ma·tion
     (ĭn′ fôr·mā′ shŭn)
  in·form·a·tive (ĭn·fôr′ mà·tĭv)
  in·form·er
in·for·mal (ĭn·fôr′ măl)
  -mal·ly
  in·for·mal·i·ty
     (ĭn′ fôr·măl′ ĭ·tĭ)
in·frac·tion (ĭn·frăk′ shŭn)
in·fra·red (ĭn′ frà·rĕd′)
in·fre·quent (ĭn·frē′ kwĕnt)
  -quen·cy
in·fringe (ĭn·frĭnj′)
  -fring·ing   in·fringe·ment

in·fu·ri·ate (ĭn·fū′ rĭ·āt)
  -at·ing
in·fuse (ĭn·fūz′)
  -fus·ing
  in·fu·sion (ĭn·fū′ shŭn)
in·gen·ious (ĭn·jĕn′ yŭs)
  (clever; see *ingenuous*)
in·gé·nue (ăN′ zhā′ nū′)
in·ge·nu·i·ty (ĭn′ jĕ·nū′ ĭ·tĭ)
in·gen·u·ous (ĭn·jĕn′ û·ŭs)
  (frank; see *ingenious*)
  in·gen·u·ous·ness
in·gest (ĭn·jĕst′)
  in·ges·tion
in·glo·ri·ous (ĭn·glō′ rĭ·ŭs)
in·got i·ron (ĭng′ gŏt)
in·grained (ĭn′ grānd′)
in·grate (ĭn′ grāt)
  in·grat·i·tude (ĭn·grăt′ ĭ·tūd)
in·gra·ti·ate (ĭn·grā′ shĭ·āt)
  -at·ing
  in·gra·ti·a·tion
     (ĭn·grā′ shĭ·ā′ shŭn)
in·gre·di·ent (ĭn·grē′ dĭ·ĕnt)
in·grown (ĭn′ grōn′)
in·hab·it (ĭn·hăb′ ĭt)
  -ited   -it·ing
  in·hab·it·able
  in·hab·it·an·cy
     (ĭn·hăb′ ĭ·tăn·sĭ)
  in·hab·it·ant
in·hale (ĭn·hāl′)
  -hal·ing
  in·hal·ant (ĭn·hāl′ ănt)
  in·ha·la·tion (ĭn′ hà·lā′ shŭn)
  in·ha·la·tor (ĭn′ hà·lā′ tĕr)
in·her·ent (ĭn·hĕr′ ĕnt)
  -en·cy
in·her·it (ĭn·hĕr′ ĭt)
  -it·ed   -it·ing
  in·her·it·a·ble   in·her·it·ance
  in·her·i·tor
in·hib·it (ĭn·hĭb′ ĭt)
  -it·ed   -it·ing
  in·hi·bi·tion (ĭn′ hĭ·bĭsh′ ŭn)
  in·hib·i·tor
  in·hib·i·to·ry (ĭn·hĭb′ ĭ·tō′ rĭ)
in·hos·pi·ta·ble
     (ĭn·hŏs′ pĭ·tà·b'l)
in·hu·man (ĭn·hū′ măn)
  in·hu·man·i·ty
     (ĭn′ hū·măn′ ĭ·tĭ)
  in·hu·man·ness
in·hu·mane (ĭn′ hū·mān′)
  -mane·ly

in·hume (ĭn·hūm′)
-hum·ing
in·im·i·cal (ĭn·ĭm′ ĭ·kăl)
in·im·i·ta·ble (ĭn·ĭm′ ĭ·tá·b'l)
in·iq·ui·tous (ĭ·nĭk′ wĭ·tŭs)
in·iq·ui·ty -ties
in·i·tial (ĭ·nĭsh′ ăl)
-tialed -tial·ing
in·i·tial·ly
in·i·ti·ate (ĭ·nĭsh′ ĭ·āt)
-at·ing
in·i·ti·a·tion
(ĭ·nĭsh′ ĭ·ā′ shŭn)
in·i·ti·a·tive (ĭ·nĭsh′ ĭ·ā′ tĭv)
in·ject (ĭn·jĕkt′)
in·jec·tion in·jec·tor
in·ju·di·cious (ĭn′ jōō·dĭsh′ ŭs)
in·junc·tion (ĭn·jŭngk′ shŭn)
in·jure (ĭn′ jẽr)
-jur·ing
in·ju·ri·ous (ĭn·jōōr′ ĭ·ŭs)
in·ju·ry (ĭn′ jẽr·ĭ)
-ries
in·jus·tice (ĭn·jŭs′ tĭs)
ink·ling (ĭngk′ lĭng)
in·laid (ĭn·lād′)
in·land (ĭn′ lănd)
in·law (ĭn′ lô′)
in·lay (ĭn′ lā′) n.
in·let (ĭn′ lĕt)
in·mate (ĭn′ māt)
in·most (ĭn′ mōst)
in·nards (ĭn′ ẽrdz)
in·nate (ĭn′ nāt)
in·ner·most (ĭn′ ẽr·mōst)
in·ner·vate (ĭ·nûr′ vāt)
(to supply with nerves; see ener-
vate)
-vat·ing
in·ner·va·tion (ĭn′ ẽr·vā′ shŭn)
in·ning (ĭn′ ĭng)
inn·keep·er (ĭn′ kēp′ ẽr)
in·no·cent (ĭn′ ō·sĕnt)
-cence
in·noc·u·ous (ĭ·nŏk′ û·ŭs)
in·no·vate (ĭn′ ō·vāt)
-vat·ing
in·no·va·tion (ĭn′ ō·vā′ shŭn)
in·no·va·tor (ĭn′ ō·vā′ tẽr)
in·nu·en·do (ĭn′ û·ĕn′ dō)
-does
in·nu·mer·a·ble
(ĭ·nû′ mẽr·á· b'l)
in·oc·u·late (ĭn·ŏk′ û·lāt)
-lat·ing

in·oc·u·la·tion
(ĭn·ŏk′ û·lā′ shŭn)
in·of·fen·sive (ĭn′ ō·fĕn′ sĭv)
in·op·er·a·ble (ĭn·ŏp′ ẽr·á·b'l)
in·op·er·a·tive (ĭn·ŏp′ ẽr·ā′ tĭv)
in·op·por·tune (ĭn·ŏp′ ŏr·tūn′)
-tune·ly
in·or·di·nate (ĭn·ôr′ dĭ·nĭt)
in·or·gan·ic (ĭn′ ôr·găn′ ĭk)
in·put (ĭn′ pŏŏt′)
in·quest (ĭn′ kwĕst)
in·quire (ĭn·kwīr′)
-quir·ing
in·quir·y (ĭn·kwīr′ ĭ)
-quir·ies
in·qui·si·tion (ĭn′ kwĭ·zĭsh′ ŭn)
in·quis·i·tive (ĭn·kwĭz′ ĭ·tĭv)
in·quis·i·tor (ĭn·kwĭz′ ĭ·tẽr)
in·quis·i·to·ri·al
(ĭn·kwĭz′ ĭ·tō′ rĭ·ăl)
in·rush·ing (ĭn′ rŭsh′ ĭng)
in·sane (ĭn·sān′)
in·san·i·ty (ĭn·săn′ ĭ·tĭ)
in·sa·ti·a·ble (ĭn·sā′ shĭ·á·b'l)
in·scribe (ĭn·skrīb′)
-scrib·ing
in·scrip·tion (ĭn·skrĭp′ shŭn)
in·scru·ta·ble (ĭn·skrōō′ tá·b'l)
in·sect (ĭn′ sĕkt)
in·sec·ti·cide (ĭn·sĕk′ tĭ·sīd)
in·se·cure (ĭn′ sē·kūr′)
in·se·cu·ri·ty (ĭn′ sē·kū′ rĭ·tĭ)
in·sem·i·na·tion
(ĭn·sĕm′ ĭ·nā′ shŭn)
in·sen·sate (ĭn·sĕn′ sāt)
in·sen·si·ble (ĭn·sĕn′ sĭ·b'l)
in·sen·si·tive (ĭn·sĕn′ sĭ·tĭv)
in·sen·si·tiv·i·ty
(ĭn·sĕn′ sĭ·tĭv′ ĭ·tĭ)
in·sep·a·ra·ble (ĭn·sĕp′ á·rá·b'l)
in·sert (ĭn·sûrt′) v.
(ĭn′ sûrt) n.
in·ser·tion (ĭn·shr′ shŭn)
in·sid·i·ous (ĭn·sĭd′ ĭ·ŭs)
in·sight (ĭn′ sīt′)
in·sig·ni·a (ĭn·sĭg′ nĭ·á)
n. pl.
sing. in·sig·ne (-nē)
in·sig·nif·i·cant
(ĭn′ sĭg·nĭf′ ĭ·kănt)
-cance
in·sin·cere (ĭn′ sĭn·sẽr′)
-cere·ly
in·sin·cer·i·ty (ĭn′ sĭn·sẽr′ ĭ·tĭ)

in·sin·u·ate (ĭn·sĭn′ ū·āt)
-at·ing
in·sin·u·a·tion
    (ĭn·sĭn′ ū·ā′ shŭn)
in·sip·id (ĭn·sĭp′ ĭd)
in·sist (ĭn·sĭst′)
in·sist·ence (ĭn·sĭs′ tĕns)
-tent
in·so·far (ĭn′ sō·fär′)
in·sole (ĭn′ sōl′)
in·so·lent (ĭn′ sō·lĕnt)
-lence
in·sol·u·ble (ĭn·sŏl′ ū·b'l)
in·solv·a·ble (ĭn·sŏl′ vá·b'l)
in·sol·ven·cy (ĭn·sŏl′ vĕn·sĭ)
in·som·ni·a (ĭn·sŏm′ nĭ·á)
in·som·ni·ac (-ăk)
in·so·much as (ĭn′ sō·mŭch′)
in·sou·ci·ance (ĭn·sōō′ sĭ·áns)
in·spect (ĭn·spĕkt′)
in·spec·tion (ĭn·spĕk′ shŭn)
in·spec·tor
in·spire (ĭn·spīr′)
-spir·ing
in·spi·ra·tion·al
    (ĭn′ spĭ·rā′ shŭn·ál)
in·spir·it (ĭn·spĭr′ ĭt)
in·sta·bil·i·ty (ĭn′ stá·bĭl′ ĭ·tĭ)
in·stall (ĭn·stôl′)
in·stal·la·tion (ĭn′ stá·lā′ shŭn)
in·stall·ment
in·stant (ĭn′ stănt)
-stance
in·stan·ta·ne·ous
    (ĭn′ stăn·tā′ nē·ŭs)
in·state (ĭn·stāt′)
-stat·ing
in·stead (ĭn·stĕd′)
in·step (ĭn′ stĕp)
in·sti·gate (ĭn′ stĭ·gāt)
-gat·ing
in·sti·ga·tion (ĭn′ stĭ·gā′ shŭn)
in·sti·ga·tor
in·still (ĭn·stĭl′)
in·stinct (ĭn′ stĭngkt)
in·stinc·tive (ĭn·stĭngk′ tĭv)
in·sti·tute (ĭn′ stĭ·tūt)
-tut·ing
in·sti·tu·tion (ĭn′ stĭ·tū′ shŭn)
in·struct (ĭn·strŭkt′)
in·struc·tion (ĭn·strŭk′ shŭn)
-tion·al   in·struc·tive
in·struc·tor   in·struc·tress
in·stru·ment (ĭn′ strōō·mĕnt)

in·stru·men·tal
    (ĭn′ strōō·mĕn′ tál)
in·stru·men·tal·i·ty
    (ĭn′ strōō·mĕn·tăl′ ĭ·tĭ)
in·stru·men·ta·tion
    (ĭn′ strōō·mĕn·tā′ shŭn)
in·sub·or·di·nate
    (ĭn′ sŭ·bôr′ dĭ·nĭt)
in·sub·or·di·na·tion
    (ĭn′ sŭ·bôr′ dĭ·nā′ shŭn)
in·sub·stan·tial
    (ĭn′ sŭb·stăn′ shál)
-tial·ly
in·suf·fer·a·ble
    (ĭn·sŭf′ ĕr·á·b'l)
in·suf·fi·cient (ĭn′ sŭ·fĭsh′ ĕnt)
-cien·cy
in·su·lar (ĭn′ sŭ·lĕr)
in·su·lar·i·ty (ĭn′ sŭ·lĕr′ ĭ·tĭ)
in·su·late (ĭn′ sŭ·lāt)
-lat·ing
in·su·la·tion (ĭn′ sŭ·lā′ shŭn)
in·su·la·tor
in·su·lin (ĭn′ sŭ·lĭn)
in·sult (ĭn·sŭlt′) s.
    (ĭn′ sŭlt) n.
in·su·per·a·ble
    (ĭn·sŭ′ pĕr·á·b'l)
in·sup·port·a·ble
    (ĭn′ sŭ·pôr′ tá·b'l)
in·sure (ĭn·shōōr′)
-sur·ing   in·sur·a·ble
in·sur·ance (ĭn·shōōr′ áns)
in·sur·gent (ĭn·sûr′ jĕnt)
-gen·cy
in·sur·mount·a·ble
    (ĭn′ sûr·moun′ tá·b'l)
in·sur·rec·tion (ĭn′ sŭ·rĕk′ shŭn)
in·sus·cep·ti·ble
    (ĭn′ sŭ·sĕp′ tĭ·b'l)
in·tact (ĭn·tăkt′)
in·tagl·io (ĭn·tăl′ yō)
in·take (ĭn′ tāk′)
in·tan·gi·ble (ĭn·tăn′ jĭ·b'l)
in·te·ger (ĭn′ tē·jĕr)
in·te·gral (ĭn′ tē·grál)
-gral·ly
in·te·grate (ĭn′ tē·grāt)
-grat·ing
in·te·gra·tion (ĭn′ tē·grā′ shŭn)
in·teg·ri·ty (ĭn·tĕg′ rĭ·tĭ)
in·tel·lect (ĭn′ tĕ·lĕkt)
in·tel·lec·tu·al
    (ĭn′ tĕ·lĕk′ tū·ál)
-al·ly

in·tel·li·gent (ĭn·těl' ĭ·jĕnt)
-gence
in·tel·li·gent·si·a
(ĭn·těl' ĭ·jĕnt' sĭ·à)
in·tel·li·gi·ble (ĭn·těl' ĭ·jĭ·b'l)
in·tel·li·gi·bil·i·ty
(ĭn·těl' ĭ·jĭ·bĭl' ĭ·tĭ)
in·tem·per·ate (ĭn·těm' pẽr·ĭt)
-ance
in·tend (ĭn·těnd')
in·tense (ĭn·těns')
in·ten·si·fy -fied, -fy·ing
in·ten·si·ty
in·ten·sive -sive·ly
in·tent (ĭn·těnt')
in·ten·tion (ĭn·těn' shŭn)
-tion·al
in·ter (ĭn·tûr')
-terred -ter·ring
in·ter·ac·tion (ĭn' tẽr·ăk' shŭn)
in·ter·breed (ĭn' tẽr·brēd')
in·ter·cede (ĭn' tẽr·sēd')
-ced·ing
in·ter·cept (ĭn' tẽr·sĕpt')
in·ter·cep·tion in·ter·cep·tor
in·ter·ces·sion (ĭn' tẽr·sĕsh' ŭn)
in·ter·change (ĭn' tẽr·chānj')
-chang·ing
in·ter·change·a·ble
in·ter·com (ĭn' tẽr·kŏm')
in·ter·con·nec·tion
(ĭn' tẽr·kŏ·nĕk' shŭn)
in·ter·course (ĭn' tẽr·kōrs)
in·ter·de·pend·ence
(ĭn' tẽr·dê·pĕn' dĕns)
in·ter·dict (ĭn' tẽr·dĭkt')
in·ter·est (ĭn' tẽr·ĕst)
in·ter·est·ed·ly
in·ter·fere (ĭn' tẽr·fẽr')
-fer·ing
in·ter·fer·ence (ĭn' tẽr·fẽr' ĕns)
in·ter·im (ĭn' tẽr·ĭm)
in·te·ri·or (ĭn·tẽr' ĭ·ẽr)
in·ter·ject (ĭn' tẽr·jĕkt')
in·ter·jec·tion
in·ter·lace (ĭn' tẽr·lās')
-lac·ing
in·ter·lard (ĭn' tẽr·lärd')
in·ter·lin·ing (ĭn' tẽr·lĭn' ĭng)
in·ter·lock (ĭn' tẽr·lŏk')
in·ter·loc·u·tor
(ĭn' tẽr·lŏk' û·tẽr)
in·ter·lop·er (ĭn' tẽr·lōp' ẽr)
in·ter·lude (ĭn' tẽr·lūd)

in·ter·mar·riage
(ĭn' tẽr·măr' ĭj)
in·ter·me·di·ar·y
(ĭn' tẽr·mē' dĭ·ĕr' ĭ)
in·ter·me·di·ate
(ĭn' tẽr·mē' dĭ·ĭt)
in·ter·mez·zo (ĭn' tẽr·mĕd' zō)
in·ter·mi·na·ble
(ĭn·tûr' mĭ·nà·b'l)
in·ter·mis·sion (ĭn' tẽr·mĭsh' ŭn)
in·ter·mit·tent (ĭn' tẽr·mĭt' ĕnt)
-mit·ten·cy
in·ter·mix·ture (ĭn' tẽr·mĭks' tûr)
in·tern (ĭn' tûrn)
in·tern·ship
in·ter·nal (ĭn·tûr' năl)
-nal·ly
in·ter·na·tion·al
(ĭn' tẽr·năsh' ŭn·ăl)
in·ter·ne·cine (ĭn' tẽr·nē' sĭn)
in·tern·ment (ĭn·tûrn' mĕnt)
in·ter·phone (ĭn' tẽr·fōn')
in·ter·po·late (ĭn·tûr' pô·lāt)
-lat·ing
in·ter·po·la·tion
(ĭn·tûr' pô·lā' shŭn)
in·ter·pose (ĭn' tẽr·pōz')
-pos·ing
in·ter·pret (ĭn·tûr' prĕt)
in·ter·pre·ta·tion
(ĭn·tûr' prĕ·tā' shŭn)
in·ter·pret·er in·ter·pre·tive
in·ter·reg·num
(ĭn' tẽr·rĕg' nŭm)
in·ter·ro·gate (ĭn·tĕr' ô·gāt)
-gat·ing in·ter·ro·ga·tor
in·ter·rog·a·tive
(ĭn' tẽ·rŏg' à·tĭv)
in·ter·rog·a·to·ry
(ĭn' tẽ·rŏg' à·tō' rĭ)
in·ter·rupt (ĭn' tẽ·rŭpt')
in·ter·rup·tion
(ĭn' tẽ·rŭp' shŭn)
in·ter·sect (ĭn' tẽr·sĕkt')
in·ter·sperse (ĭn' tẽr·spûrs')
-spers·ing
in·ter·sper·sion (-spûr' shŭn)
in·ter·state (ĭn' tẽr·stāt')
in·ter·stel·lar (ĭn' tẽr·stĕl' ẽr)
in·ter·stice (ĭn·tûr' stĭs)
in·ter·sti·tial (ĭn' tẽr·stĭsh' ăl)
in·ter·val (ĭn' tẽr·văl)
in·ter·vene (ĭn' tẽr·vēn')
-ven·ing
in·ter·ven·tion (-vĕn' shŭn)

in·ter·view (ĭn' tĕr·vū)
  in·ter·view·er
in·ter·weave (ĭn' tĕr·wēv')
  -weav·ing
  in·ter·wo·ven (ĭn' tĕr·wō' vĕn)
in·tes·tate (ĭn·tĕs' tāt)
in·tes·tine (ĭn·tĕs' tĭn)
  in·tes·ti·nal (ĭn·tĕs' tĭ·nǎl)
in·ti·mate (ĭn' tĭ·māt) v.
  -mat·ing
  in·ti·ma·tion (ĭn' tĭ·mā' shŭn)
in·ti·mate (ĭn' tĭ·mĭt) adj.
  in·ti·ma·cy (ĭn' tĭ·mǎ·sǐ)
  in·ti·mate·ly (-mĭt·lǐ)
in·tim·i·date (ĭn·tĭm' ĭ·dāt)
  -dat·ing
in·tol·er·a·ble (ĭn·tŏl' ĕr·ǎ·b'l)
in·tol·er·ant (ĭn·tŏl' ĕr·ǎnt)
  -rance
in·to·na·tion (ĭn' tō·nā' shŭn)
in·tox·i·cate (ĭn·tŏk' sǐ·kāt)
  -cat·ing
  in·tox·i·cant (ĭn·tŏk' sǐ·kǎnt)
  in·tox·i·ca·tion
    (ĭn·tŏk' sǐ·kā' shŭn)
in·trac·ta·ble (ĭn·trăk' tǎ·b'l)
in·tra·mu·ral (ĭn' trǎ·mū' rǎl)
in·tran·si·gent (ĭn·trăn' sǐ·jĕnt)
  -gen·cy
in·tran·si·tive (ĭn·trăn' sǐ·tĭv)
in·tra·ve·nous (ĭn' trǎ·vē' nŭs)
in·trep·id (ĭn·trĕp' ĭd)
in·tri·cate (ĭn' trĭ·kĭt)
  -cate·ly
  in·tri·ca·cy (-kǎ·sǐ)
in·trigue (ĭn·trēg')
  -tri·guing
in·trin·sic (ĭn·trĭn' sǐk)
  in·trin·si·cal·ly
in·tro·duce (ĭn' trō·dūs')
  -duc·ing
  in·tro·duc·tion
    (ĭn' trō·dŭk' shŭn)
  in·tro·duc·to·ry
    (ĭn' trō·dŭk' tō·rǐ)
in·tro·it (ĭn' trō' ĭt)
in·tro·jec·tion (ĭn' trō·jĕk' shŭn)
in·tro·spec·tive (ĭn' trō·spĕk' tĭv)
in·tro·ver·sion (ĭn' trō·vûr' shŭn)
in·tro·vert (ĭn' trō·vûrt') n.
in·trude (ĭn·trōōd')
  -trud·ing
  in·tru·sion (ĭn·trōō' zhŭn)
  in·tru·sive (-sĭv)

in·tu·i·tion (ĭn' tū·ĭsh' ŭn)
  in·tu·i·tive (ĭn·tū' ĭ·tĭv)
  in·tu·i·tive·ness
in·un·date (ĭn' ŭn·dāt)
  -dat·ing
  in·un·da·tion (ĭn' ŭn·dā' shŭn)
in·ure (ĭn·ūr')
  -ur·ing in·ure·ment
in·vade (ĭn·vād')
  -vad·ing
in·val·id (ĭn·văl' ĭd) adj.
  (null)
  in·val·i·date (ĭn·văl' ĭ·dāt)
  in·val·i·da·tion
    (ĭn·văl' ĭ·dā' shŭn)
in·va·lid (ĭn' vǎ·lĭd)
  adj., n.; (sick) in·va·lid·ism
in·val·u·a·ble (ĭn·văl' ū·ǎ·b'l)
in·var·i·a·ble (ĭn·vâr' ĭ·ǎ·b'l)
in·va·sion (ĭn·vā' zhŭn)
in·vec·tive (ĭn·vĕk' tĭv)
in·veigh (ĭn·vā')
in·vei·gle (ĭn·vē' g'l)
  -gling
in·vent (ĭn·vĕnt')
  in·ven·tion (ĭn·vĕn' shŭn)
  in·ven·tive
in·ven·to·ry (ĭn' vĕn·tō' rǐ)
  -ries
in·verse (ĭn·vûrs')
  -verse·ly
in·ver·sion (ĭn·vûr' shŭn)
in·vert (ĭn·vûrt') v.
  (ĭn' vûrt) n.
in·ver·te·brate (ĭn·vûr' tĕ·brāt)
in·ves·ti·gate (ĭn·vĕs' tǐ·gāt)
  -gat·ing
  in·ves·ti·ga·tion
    (ĭn·vĕs' tǐ·gā' shŭn)
  in·ves·ti·ga·tive
    (ĭn·vĕs' tǐ·gā' tĭv)
  in·ves·ti·ga·tor
    (ĭn·vĕs' tǐ·gā' tĕr)
in·ves·ti·ture (ĭn·vĕs' tǐ·tûr)
in·vest·ment (ĭn·vĕst' mĕnt)
in·ves·tor (ĭn·vĕs' tĕr)
in·vet·er·ate (ĭn·vĕt' ĕr·ĭt)
in·vid·i·ous (ĭn·vĭd' ĭ·ŭs)
in·vig·or·at·ing
  (ĭn·vĭg' ĕr·āt' ĭng)
in·vin·ci·ble (ĭn·vĭn' sǐ·b'l)
  in·vin·ci·bil·i·ty
    (ĭn·vĭn' sǐ·bĭl' ĭ·tǐ)
in·vi·o·la·ble (ĭn·vī' ō·lǎ·b'l)
in·vi·o·late (ĭn·vī' ō·lāt)

in·vis·i·ble (ĭn·vĭz′ ĭ·b′l)
in·vis·i·bil·i·ty
    (ĭn·vĭz′ ĭ·bĭl′ ĭ·tĭ)
in·vi·ta·tion (ĭn′ vĭ·tā′ shŭn)
in·vite (ĭn·vīt′)
 -vit·ing
in·vo·ca·tion (ĭn′ vô·kā′ shŭn)
in·voice (ĭn′ vois)
in·voke (ĭn·vōk′)
 -vok·ing
in·vo·ca·tion (ĭn′ vô·kā′ shŭn)
in·vol·un·tar·y (ĭn·vŏl′ ŭn·tĕr′ ĭ)
in·vol·un·tar·i·ly
in·vo·lu·tion (ĭn′ vô·lū′ shŭn)
in·volve·ment (ĭn·vŏlv′ mĕnt)
in·vul·ner·a·ble
    (ĭn·vŭl′ nĕr·à·b′l)
in·vul·ner·a·bil·i·ty
    (ĭn·vŭl′ nĕr·à·bĭl′ ĭ·tĭ)
in·ward (ĭn′ wĕrd)
i·o·dide (ī′ ô·dīd)
i·o·dine (ī′ ô·dīn)
i·on (ī′ ŏn)
 i·on·ic (ī·ŏn′ ĭk)
 i·on·ize (ī′ ŏn·īz)
 i·on·o·sphere (ī·ŏn′ ô·sfēr)
i·o·ta (ī·ô′ tà)
I·O·U (ī′ ō′ ū′)
I·o·wa (ī′ ô·wä)
 abbr. Ia.
 I·o·wan
I·Q (ī′ kū′)
 I·Qs
I·ra·ni·an (ī·rā′ nĭ·ăn)
I·ra·qi (ê·rä′ kê)
i·ras·ci·ble (ī·răs′ ĭ·b′l)
i·rate (ī′ rāt)
ire·ful (īr′ fŏŏl)
ir·i·des·cent (ĭr′ ĭ·dĕs′ ĕnt)
 -cence
i·ris (ī′ rĭs)
I·rish·man (ī′ rĭsh·măn)
irk·some (ûrk′ sŭm)
i·ron (īr′ ĕrn)
 i·ron·clad i·ron cur·tain
 i·ron lung i·ron·work
i·ro·ny (ī′ rô·nĭ)
 i·ron·i·cal (ī·rŏn′ ĭ·kăl)
 -cal·ly
Ir·o·quois (ĭr′ ô·kwoi)
ir·ra·di·ate (ĭ·rā′ dĭ·āt)
 -at·ing
 ir·ra·di·a·tion (ĭ·rā′ dĭ·ā′ shŭn)
ir·ra·tion·al (ĭr·răsh′ ŭn·ăl)

ir·ra·tion·al·i·ty
    (ĭr·răsh′ ŭn·ăl′ ĭ·tĭ)
ir·re·claim·a·ble
    (ĭr′ rê·klām·′ á·b′l)
ir·rec·on·cil·a·ble
    (ĭr·rĕk′ ŏn·sĭl′ á·b′l)
ir·re·cov·er·a·ble
    (ĭr′ rê·kŭv′ ĕr·á·b′l)
ir·re·deem·a·ble
    (ĭr′ rê·dēm′ á·b′l)
ir·re·duc·i·ble (ĭr′ rê·dūs′ ĭ·b′l)
ir·ref·u·ta·ble (ĭr·rĕf′ û·tá·b′l)
ir·reg·u·lar (ĭr·rĕg′ û·lĕr)
 ir·reg·u·lar·i·ty
    (ĭr·rĕg′ û·lăr′ ĭ·tĭ)
ir·rel·e·vant (ĭr·rĕl′ ê·vănt)
 -van·cy
ir·re·li·gious (ĭr′ rê·lĭj′ ŭs)
ir·re·me·di·a·ble
    (ĭr′ rê·mê′ dĭ·á·b′l)
ir·rep·a·ra·ble (ĭ·rĕp′ á·rá·b′l)
ir·re·place·a·ble
    (ĭr′ rê·plās′ á·b′l)
ir·re·press·i·ble
    (ĭr′ rê·prĕs′ ĭ·b′l)
ir·re·proach·a·ble
    (ĭr′ rê·prōch′ á·b′l)
ir·re·sist·i·ble (ĭr′ rê·zĭs′ tĭ·b′l)
ir·res·o·lute (ĭ·rĕz′ ô·lūt)
ir·re·spec·tive (ĭr′ rê·spĕk′ tĭv)
ir·re·spon·si·ble
    (ĭr′ rê·spŏn′ sĭ·b′l)
 ir·re·spon·si·bil·i·ty
    (ĭr′ rê·spŏn′ sĭ·bĭl′ ĭ·tĭ)
ir·re·triev·a·ble
    (ĭr′ rê·trēv′ á·b′l)
ir·rev·er·ence (ĭ·rĕv′ ĕr·ĕns)
ir·re·vers·i·ble (ĭr′ rê·vûr′ sĭ·b′l)
ir·rev·o·ca·ble (ĭ·rĕv′ ô·ká·b′l)
ir·ri·gate (ĭr′ ĭ·gāt)
 -gat·ing
 ir·ri·ga·ble (ĭr′ ĭ·gá·b′l)
ir·ri·ga·tion (ĭr′ ĭ·gā′ shŭn)
ir·ri·ta·ble (ĭr′ ĭ·tá·b′l)
 ir·ri·ta·bil·i·ty
    (ĭr′ ĭ·tá·bĭl′ ĭ·tĭ)
ir·ri·tant (ĭr′ ĭ·tănt)
 -tan·cy
ir·ri·tate (ĭr′ ĭ·tāt)
 -tat·ing
ir·ri·ta·tion (ĭr′ ĭ·tā′ shŭn)
ir·rup·tion (ĭ·rŭp′ shŭn)
ir·rup·tive
i·sin·glass (ī′ zĭng·glăs′)

Is·lam (Ĭs′ lăm)
  Is·lam·ic (Ĭs·lăm′ Ĭk)
is·land (Ī′ lănd)
  is·land·er
isle (Īl)
  (small island; see *aisle*)
is·let (Ī′ lĕt)
i·so·bar (Ī′ sō·bär)
i·so·late (Ī′ sō·lāt)
  -lat·ing
i·so·la·tion (Ī′ sō·lā′ shŭn)
i·sos·ce·les (Ī·sŏs′ ě·lēz)
i·so·tope (Ī′ sō·tōp)
Is·ra·el (Ĭz′ rĭ·ěl)
  Is·rae·li (Ĭz·rā′ lĭ)
  Is·ra·el·ite (Ĭz′ rĭ·ěl·īt)
is·sue (Ĭsh′ ū)
  is·su·ing
  is·su·ance (Ĭsh′ ū·ăns)
  is·su·ant
Is·tan·bul, Turk. (Ĭs′ tăm·bōōl′)
isth·mus (Ĭs′ mŭs)
I·tal·ian (Ĭ·tăl′ yăn)
i·tal·ic (Ĭ·tăl′ Ĭk)
  i·tal·i·cize (Ĭ·tăl′ Ĭ·sīz)
  -ciz·ing
i·tem·ize (Ī′ těm·īz)
  -iz·ing
i·tin·er·ant (Ī·tĭn′ ěr·ănt)
i·tin·er·ar·y (Ī·tĭn′ ěr·ěr′ Ĭ)
  -ar·ies
its (Ĭts)
  (belonging to it)
it's (Ĭts)
  (it is, it has)
it·self (Ĭt·sělf′)
i·vor·y (Ī′ vō·rĭ)
i·vy (Ī′ vĭ)
  i·vies

J

ja·bot (zhá′ bō′)
jack (jăk)
  jack-in-the-pul·pit
  jack·knife
  jack-of-all-trades
  jack-o′ -lan·tern
  jack·pot   jack rab·bit
jack·al (jăk′ ôl)
jack·et (jăk′ ět)
jag·ged (jăg′ ěd)
jag·uar (jăg′ wär)
jail·bird (jāl′ bûrd′)

Ja·mai·ca (já·mā′ ká)
jam·bo·ree (jăm′ bô·rē′)
jan·i·tor (jăn′ Ĭ·těr)
  jan·i·to·ri·al (jăn′ Ĭ·tô′ rĭ·ăl)
Jan·u·ar·y (jăn′ û·ěr′ Ĭ)
Jap·a·nese (jăp′ á·nēz′)
jar·gon (jär′ gŏn)
jas·mine (jăz′ mĭn)
jaun·dice (jôn′ dĭs)
jaun·ty (jôn′ tĭ)
  jaun·ti·ly
jave·lin (jăv′ lĭn)
jaw·bone (jô′ bōn′)
jay·walk·er (jā′ wôk′ ěr)
jazz·y (jăz′ Ĭ)
jeal·ous·y (jěl′ ŭs·Ĭ)
  -ous·ies
jeans (jēnz)
jeep (jēp)
Jef·fer·so·ni·an (jěf′ ěr·sō′ nĭ·ăn)
Je·ho·vah (jē·hō′ vá)
je·june (jē·jōōn′)
jel·ly (jěl′ Ĭ)
  jel·lied   jel·ly·ing
  jel·ly·fish
jeop·ard·y (jěp′ ěr·dĭ)
  jeop·ard·ize -iz·ing
jer·kin (jûr′ kĭn)
jerk·y (jûr′ kĭ)
  jerk·i·ness
jer·ry-built (jěr′ Ĭ·bĭlt′)
jer·sey (jûr′ zĭ)
  -seys
Je·ru·sa·lem (jě·rōō′ sá·lěm)
jest·er (jěs′ těr)
Jes·u·it (jěz′ û·Ĭt)
jet pro·pul·sion (jět)
jet·sam (jět′ săm)
jet·ti·son (jět′ Ĭ·sŭn)
jet·ty (jět′ Ĭ)
  jet·ties
jew·el (jōō′ ěl)
  -eled   -el·ing
  jew·el·er   jew·el·ry
Jew·ry (jōō′ rĭ)
jew's-harp (jōōz′ härp′)
Jez·e·bel (jěz′ ě·běl)
jibe (jĭb)
  jib·ing
jif·fy (jĭf′ Ĭ)
jig·ger (jĭg′ ěr)
jig·saw puz·zle (jĭg′ sô′)
jin·gle (jĭng′ g′l)
  -gling

jin·go (jĭng' gō)
  -goes jin·go·ism
jin·rik·i·sha (jĭn·rĭk' shä)
jit·ney (jĭt' nĭ)
jock·ey (jŏk' ĭ)
jo·cose (jō·kōs')
  jo·cos·i·ty (jō·kŏs' ĭ·tĭ)
joc·u·lar (jŏk' û·lẽr)
  joc·u·lar·i·ty (jŏk' û·lăr' ĭ·tĭ)
joc·und (jŏk' ŭnd)
  jo·cun·di·ty (jō·kŭn' dĭ·tĭ)
jodh·purs (jŏd' pẽrz)
jog·gle (jŏg' 'l)
  jog·gling
Jo·han·nes·burg, S. Afr.
  (jō·hăn' ĭs·bûrg)
John·son City,
  N.Y., Tenn. (jŏn' s'n)
Johns·town, Pa. (jŏnz' toun)
joie de vi·vre (zhwä' dẽ·vē' vr')
joint (joint)
  join·ture (join' tụr)
jok·ing·ly (jōk' ĭng·lĭ)
jol·li·ty (jŏl' ĭ·tĭ)
  jol·li·ness
jon·quil (jŏng' kwĭl)
jos·tle (jŏs' 'l)
  -tling
jour·nal (jûr' năl)
  jour·nal·ese (jûr' năl·ēz')
  jour·nal·ism
  jour·nal·is·tic (jûr' năl·ĭs' tĭk)
jour·ney (jûr' nĭ)
  -neys
joust (jŭst)
jo·vi·al (jō' vĭ·ăl)
  -al·ly
jowl (joul)
joy·ful (joi' fŏŏl)
  joy·ous (joi' ŭs)
ju·bi·lant (jōō' bĭ·lănt)
  -lance
ju·bi·la·tion (jōō' bĭ·lă' shŭn)
ju·bi·lee (jōō' bĭ·lē)
judge (jŭj)
  judg·ing
  judg·ment
ju·di·ca·ture (jōō' dĭ·kȧ·tụr)
ju·di·cial (jōō·dĭsh' ăl)
  -cial·ly
  ju·di·ci·ar·y (jōō·dĭsh' ĭ·ĕr' ĭ)
  ju·di·cious (jōō·dĭsh' ŭs)
jug·ger·naut (jŭg' ẽr·nôt)
jug·gler (jŭg' lẽr)
jug·u·lar vein (jŭg' û·lẽr)

juice (jōōs)
  juic·i·ness juic·y
ju·jit·su (jōō·jĭt' sōō)
juke·box (jōōk' bŏks')
ju·lep (jōō' lĕp)
ju·li·enne (jōō' lĭ·ĕn')
jum·bled (jŭm' b'ld)
jum·bo (jŭm' bō)
junc·tion (jŭngk' shŭn)
junc·ture (jŭngk' tụr)
jun·gle (jŭng' g'l)
jun·ior (jōōn' yẽr)
ju·ni·per (jōō' nĭ·pẽr)
jun·ket (jŭng' kĕt)
jun·ta (jŭn' tȧ)
ju·rid·i·cal (jōō·rĭd' ĭ·kăl)
ju·ris·dic·tion (jōōr' ĭs·dĭk' shŭn)
ju·ris·pru·dence
  (jōōr' ĭs·prōō' dĕns)
ju·ry (jōōr' ĭ)
  ju·ries ju·rist
  ju·ror
jus·tice (jŭs' tĭs)
jus·ti·fy (jŭs' tĭ·fī)
  -fied, -fy·ing
  jus·ti·fi·a·ble (jŭs' tĭ·fī' ȧ·b'l)
  jus·ti·fi·ca·tion
    (jŭs' tĭ·fĭ·kā' shŭn)
ju·ve·nile (jōō' vē·nĭl)
jux·ta·pose (jŭks' tȧ·pōz')
  jux·ta·po·si·tion
    (jŭks' tȧ·pȯ·zĭsh' ŭn)

K

kai·ser (kī' zẽr)
kale (kāl)
ka·lei·do·scope (kȧ·lī' dȯ·skōp)
kan·ga·roo (kăng' gȧ·rōō')
Kan·sas (kăn' zȧs)
  abbr. Kans. or Kan.
  Kan·san
ka·pok (kā' pŏk)
ka·put (kȧ·pŏŏt')
kar·a·kul (kăr' ȧ·kŭl)
ka·ty·did (kā' tĭ·dĭd')
Kau·ai (is.) (kou' ĭ)
kay·ak (kī' ăk)
keel·boat (kēl' bōt')
keen·ness (kēn' nĕs)
keep·sake (kēp' sāk')
kelp (kĕlp)
Ken·ne·dy, John F. and
  Jac·que·line (kĕn' ĕ·dĭ)

ken·nel (kĕn′ ĕl)
Ken·tuck·y (kĕn·tŭk′ ĭ)
 abbr. Ky.
 Ken·tuck·i·an
Ken·ya (kĕn′ yȧ)
ker·chief (kûr′ chĭf)
ker·nel (kûr′ nĕl)
ker·o·sene (kĕr′ ō·sēn′)
ketch (kĕch)
ket·tle·drum (kĕt′ 'l·drŭm′)
key (kē)
 key·board key·hole
 key·note key sig·na·ture
 key·stone
khak·i (kăk′ ĭ)
khe·dive (kĕ·dēv′)
Khru·shchev, Ni·ki·ta
 (xrŏŏsh·chôf′, nyĭ·kē′ tá)
kib·itz·er (kĭb′ ĭt·sēr)
kick·back (kĭk′ băk′)
kid·nap (kĭd′ năp)
 -naped -nap·ing
 kid·nap·er
kid·ney (kĭd′ nĭ)
kill·deer (kĭl′ dēr′)
kill·joy (kĭl′ joi′)
kiln (kĭl)
ki·lo· (kĭl′ ō-)
 kil·o·cy·cle kil·o·gram
 kil·o·me·ter kil·o·watt
 kil·o·watt-hour
ki·mo·no (kĭ·mō′ nȧ)
 -nos
kin·der·gar·ten
 (kĭn′ dēr·gär′ t'n)
 kin·der·gart·ner
kind·heart·ed (kīnd′ här′ tĕd)
kin·dle (kĭn′ d'l)
 -dling
kind·ly (kīnd′ lĭ)
 kind·li·er -li·est, -li·ness
kin·dred (kĭn′ drĕd)
kin·e·scope (kĭn′ ē·skōp)
kin·es·thet·ic (kĭn′ ĕs·thĕt′ ĭk)
ki·net·ic (kĭ·nĕt′ ĭk)
king·dom (kĭng′ dŭm)
king·fish·er (kĭng′ fĭsh′ ēr)
kins·man (kĭnz′ măn)
ki·osk (kē·ŏsk′)
kirsch (kĭrsh)
kis·met (kĭz′ mĕt)
kitch·en (kĭch′ ĕn)
 kitch·en·ette (kĭch′ ĕ·nĕt′)
 kitch·en·ware
kit·ten (kĭt′ 'n)

klep·to·ma·ni·a
 (klĕp′ tō·mā′ nĭ·ȧ)
 klep·to·ma·ni·ac
 (-ăk)
klieg light (klēg)
klis·ter (klĭs′ tēr)
knack (năk)
knap·sack (năp′ săk′)
knave (nāv)
 knav·er·y (nāv′ ēr·ĭ)
 knav·ish
knead (nēd)
knee·cap (nē′ kăp′)
kneel (nēl)
 knelt (nĕlt)
knell (nĕl)
knick·ers (nĭk′ ērz)
knick·knack (nĭk′ năk′)
knife (nīf)
 pl. knives (nīvz)
knight (nīt)
 knight-er·rant knight·hood
knit (nĭt)
 knit·ting knit·wear
knob (nŏb)
 knob·by
knock (nŏk)
 knock·down knock·kneed
 knock·out
knoll (nŏl)
knot (nŏt)
 knot·ted knot·ting
 knot·hole knot·ty
know (nō)
 know·a·ble know·how
 know·ing·ly known
knowl·edge (nŏl′ ĕj)
 knowl·edge·a·ble
 (nŏl′ ĕj·ȧ·b'l)
knuck·le (nŭk′ 'l)
ko·a·la (kō·ä′ lȧ)
Ko·dak (kō′ dăk)
 Ko·da·chrome
Ko·di·ak bear (kō′ dĭ·ăk)
kohl·ra·bi (kōl′ rä′ bĭ)
ko·sher (kō′ shēr)
kow·tow (kō′ tou′)
kraft pa·per (krăft)
krem·lin (krĕm′ lĭn)
Ku·blai Khan (kū′ blī kän′)
ku·dos (kū′ dŏs)
Ku Klux Klan (kū klŭks klăn)
kum·quat (kŭm′ kwŏt)

L

la·bel (lā′ bĕl)
  -beled -bel·ing
la·bor (lā′ bĕr)
  la·bor·er
  la·bo·ri·ous (lá·bō′ rĭ·ŭs)
  la·bor·sav·ing la·bor un·ion
lab·o·ra·to·ry (lăb′ ô·rá·tô′ rĭ)
  -ries
lab·y·rinth (lăb′ ĭ·rĭnth)
lac·er·ate (lăs′ ĕr·āt)
  -at·ing
  lac·er·a·tion (lăs′ ĕr·ā′ shŭn)
lach·ry·mal (lăk′ rĭ·măl)
  lach·ry·mose (lăk′ rĭ·mōs)
lack·a·dai·si·cal
     (lăk′ á·dā′ zĭ·kăl)
lack·ey (lăk′ ĭ)
  -eys
lack·lus·ter (lăk′ lŭs′ tĕr)
la·con·ic (lá·kŏn′ ĭk)
  la·con·i·cal·ly
lac·quer (lăk′ ĕr)
la·crosse (lá·krôs′)
lac·ta·tion (lăk·tā′ shŭn)
lac·tic ac·id (lăk′ tĭk)
lac·tose (lăk′ tōs)
lac·y (lās′ ĭ)
  lac·i·ness
lad·der-back chair
     (lăd′ ĕr·băk′)
lad·en (lăd′ 'n)
lad·ing (lăd′ ĭng)
  (bill of)
la·dle (lā′ d'l)
  -dling
la·dy (lā′ dĭ)
  -dies la·dy·fin·ger
  la·dy-kill·er la·dy·like
  la·dy's-slip·per
la·ger beer (lä′ gĕr)
lag·gard (lăg′ ĕrd)
la·goon (lá·gōōn′)
lais·sez faire (lĕ′ sā′ fâr′)
la·i·ty (lā′ ĭ·tĭ)
lama (lä·má′)
  (priest; see *llama*)
La·ma·ism (lä′ má·ĭz′m)
lam·baste (lăm′ bāst′)
  -bast·ing
lamb·skin (lăm′ skĭn′)
la·mé (lá′ mā′)

la·ment (lá·mĕnt′)
  lam·en·ta·ble (lăm′ ĕn·tá·b'l)
  lam·en·ta·tion
     (lăm′ ĕn·tā′ shŭn)
  la·ment·ed (lá·mĕn′ tĕd)
lam·i·nate (lăm′ ĭ·nāt)
  -nat·ing
  lam·i·nar (lăm′ ĭ·nĕr)
  lam·i·na·tion (lăm′ ĭ·nā′ shŭn)
lamp·black (lămp′ blăk′)
lam·poon (lăm·pōōn′)
  lam·poon·er·y
lam·prey eel (lăm′ prĭ)
lance (láns)
  lanc·ing
lan·cet (lán′ sĕt)
land (lănd)
  land-grant col·lege
  land·hold·er land·lord
  land·lub·ber land·own·er
  land·scape land·slide
lan·guage (lăng′ gwĭj)
lan·guid (lăng′ gwĭd)
lan·guish·ing (lăng′ gwĭsh·ĭng)
lan·guor (lăng′ gĕr)
  lan·guor·ous (lăng′ gĕr·ŭs)
lank·y (lăngk′ ĭ)
  lank·i·ness
lan·o·lin (lăn′ ô·lĭn)
lan·tern (lăn′ tĕrn)
lan·yard (lăn′ yĕrd)
Laos (louz)
  La·o·tian (lá·ō′ shăn)
la·pel (lá·pĕl′)
lap·i·dar·y (lăp′ ĭ·dĕr′ ĭ)
lap·is laz·u·li (lăp′ ĭs lăz′ û·lĭ)
Lap·land·er (lăp′ lăn·dĕr)
  Lapp
lapse (lăps)
  laps·ing
lar·ce·ny (lär′ sĕ·nĭ)
  -nies lar·ce·nist
  lar·ce·nous
lard·er (lär′ dĕr)
large·ly (lärj′ lĭ)
large-scale (lärj′ skāl′)
lar·gess (lär′ jĕs)
lar·ghet·to (lär·gĕt′ ô)
lar·go (lär′ gō)
lar·i·at (lär′ ĭ·ăt)
lark·spur (lärk′ spûr)
lar·va (lär′ vá)
  pl. lar·vae (-vē)
  lar·vi·cide (lär′ vĭ·sĭd)
lar·yn·gi·tis (lär′ ĭn·jī′ tĭs)

lar·ynx (lăr′ ĭngks)
  pl. la·ryn·ges (lá·rĭn′ jēz)
las·civ·i·ous (lá·sĭv′ ĭ·ŭs)
las·si·tude (lăs′ ĭ·tūd)
las·so (lăs′ ō)
  las·soed   las·so·ing
  las·sos
last·ing·ly (lăst′ ĭng·lĭ)
latch·key (lăch′ kē′)
la·teen sail (lá·tēn′)
late·ly (lāt′ lĭ)
la·tent (lā′ tĕnt)
  la·ten·cy
lat·er·al (lăt′ ẽr·ál)
  -al·ly
la·tex (lā′ tĕks)
lath·work (lăth′ wûrk′)
lat·i·tude (lăt′ ĭ·tūd)
lat·i·tu·di·nal (lăt′ ĭ·tū′ dĭ·nál)
la·trine (lá·trēn′)
lat·ter·most (lăt′ ẽr·mōst)
lat·tice (lăt′ ĭs)
  lat·tice·work   lat·tic·ing
laud (lôd)
  laud·a·ble
  laud·a·to·ry (lôd′ á·tō′ rĭ)
lau·da·num (lô′ dá·nŭm)
laugh (lăf)
  laugh·a·ble   laugh·ing·stock
  laugh·ter
launch (lônch)
laun·der (lôn′ dẽr)
  laun·dress (lôn′ drĕs)
  laun·dry   -dries
  laun·dry·man
lau·re·ate (lô′ rē·āt)
lau·rel (lô′ rĕl)
lav·a·liere (lăv′ á·lĭr′)
lav·a·to·ry (lăv′ á·tō′ rĭ)
  -ries
lav·en·der (lăv′ ẽn·dẽr)
lav·ish (lăv′ ĭsh)
law (lô)
  law-a·bid·ing   law break·er
  law·ful   -ful·ly
  -ful·ness   law·giv·er
  law·less·ness   law·mak·er
  law·suit
lawn mow·er (lôn)
law·yer (lô′ yẽr)
lax·a·tive (lăk′ sá·tĭv)
lax·i·ty (lăk′ sĭ·tĭ)
lay·er (lā′ ẽr)
lay·man (lā′ măn)
lay·off (lā′ ôf′)

lay·o·ver (lā′ ō′ vẽr)
la·zy (lā′ zĭ)
  la·zi·er   -zi·est
  -zi·ly   -zi·ness
  la·zy·bones   La·zy Su·san
leach (lēch)
  (dissolve; see leech)
lead (lĕd) v.
lead (lĕd) n.
  lead·en
  lead poi·son·ing
lead·er·ship (lĕd′ ẽr·shĭp)
leaf (lēf)
  leaves
  leaf·age (lēf′ ĭj)
  leaf·hop·per   leaf·let
  leaf·y
league (lēg)
leak (lēk)
  (crack or hole; see leek)
  leak·age (lēk′ ĭj)
  leak·y
lean-to (lēn′ tōō′)
leap·frog (lēp′ frŏg′)
leap year (lēp yẽr)
learn·ed·ly (lûr′ nĕd·lĭ)
lease·hold·er (lēs′ hōl′ dẽr)
leash (lēsh)
least (lēst)
leath·er (lĕth′ ẽr)
  Leath·er·ette (lĕth′ ẽr·ĕt′)
  leath·er·y
leav·en·ing (lĕv′ ẽn·ĭng)
Leb·a·non (lĕb′ á·nŭn)
  Leb·a·nese (lĕb′ á·nēz′)
lech·er (lĕch′ ẽr)
  lech·er·ous (lĕch′ ẽr·ŭs)
  lech·er·y
lec·tern (lĕk′ tẽrn)
lec·ture (lĕk′ tûr)
  lec·tur·er
ledge (lĕj)
ledg·er (lĕj′ ẽr)
leech (lēch)
  (worm; see leach)
leek (lēk)
  (plant; see leak)
leer·ing (lĭr′ ĭng)
leer·y (lĭr′ ĭ)
lee·ward (lē′ wẽrd)
lee·way (lē′ wā′)
left-hand·ed (lĕft′ hăn′ dĕd)
left·ist (lĕf′ tĭst)
leg·a·cy (lĕg′ á·sĭ)

le·gal (lē′ gǎl)
  le·gal·i·ty (lê·gǎl′ ĭ·tĭ)
  le·gal·ize -iz·ing
  le·gal·i·za·tion
       (lē′ gǎl·ĭ·zā′ shŭn)
  le·gal·ly le·gal ten·der
leg·ate (lĕg′ ĭt)
  le·ga·tion (lê·gā′ shŭn)
leg·end (lĕj′ ĕnd)
  leg·end·ar·y (lĕj′ ĕn·dĕr′ ĭ)
leg·er·de·main (lĕj′ ĕr·dĕ·mān′)
le·ger·i·ty (lê·jĕr′ ĭ·tĭ)
leg·gings (lĕg′ ĭngz)
leg·horn (lĕg′ hôrn)
leg·i·ble (lĕj′ ĭ·b′l)
  leg·i·bil·i·ty (lĕj′ ĭ·bĭl′ ĭ·tĭ)
le·gion (lē′ jŭn)
  le·gion·naire (lē′ jŭn·âr′)
leg·is·late (lĕj′ ĭs·lāt)
  -lat·ing
  leg·is·la·tion (lĕj′ ĭs·lā′ shŭn)
  leg·is·la·tive (lĕj′ ĭs·lā′ tĭv)
  leg·is·la·tor (lĕj′ ĭs·lā′ tĕr)
  leg·is·la·ture (lĕj′ ĭs·lā′ tūr)
le·git·i·mate (lê·jĭt′ ĭ·mĭt)
  le·git·i·ma·cy
  le·git·i·ma·tion
       (lê·jĭt′ ĭ·mā′ shŭn)
  le·git·i·mize (lê·jĭt′ ĭ·mīz)
  -miz·ing
leg·ume (lĕg′ ûm)
lei·sure (lē′ zhēr)
  lei·sure·li·ness lei·sure·ly
leit·mo·tiv (līt′ mō·tēf′)
lem·ming (lĕm′ ĭng)
lem·on (lĕm′ ŭn)
  lem·on·ade (lĕm′ ŭn·ād′)
le·mur (lē′ mēr)
lend-lease (lĕnd′ lēs′)
length (lĕngth)
  length·en length·i·ness
  length·wise length·y
le·ni·ent (lē′ nĭ·ĕnt)
  -en·cy
len·i·ty (lĕn′ ĭ·tĭ)
lens (lĕnz)
  lens·es
Lent·en (lĕn′ tĕn)
len·til (lĕn′ tĭl)
leop·ard (lĕp′ ĕrd)
le·o·tard (lē′ ō·tärd)
lep·er (lĕp′ ĕr)
  lep·ro·sy (lĕp′ rō·sĭ)
  lep·rous
Les·bi·an (lĕz′ bĭ·ǎn)

le·sion (lē′ zhŭn)
less (lĕs)
  less·en·ing less·er
les·see (lĕs·ē′)
  les·sor
les·son (lĕs′ ′n)
lest (lĕst)
let·down (lĕt′ doun′)
le·thal (lē′ thǎl)
  -thal·ly
le·thar·gic (lê·thär′ jĭk)
  le·thar·gi·cal·ly
  leth·ar·gy (lĕth′ ĕr·jĭ)
let·ter·head (lĕt′ ĕr·hĕd′)
let·tuce (lĕt′ ĭs)
let·up (lĕt′ ŭp′)
leu·ke·mi·a (lù·kē′ mĭ·à)
lev·ee (lĕv′ ē)
  (dike; see levy)
lev·el (lĕv′ ĕl)
  -eled -eling
  lev·el·er lev·el·head·ed
  lev·el·ly
le·ver (lē′ vĕr)
le·ver·age (lē′ vĕr′ ĭj)
le·vi·a·than (lê·vī′ à·thǎn)
Le·vi's (lē′ vīz)
lev·i·ty (lĕv′ ĭ·tĭ)
lev·y (lĕv′ ĭ)
  (to collect; see levee)
  lev·ied lev·y·ing
lewd·ness (lūd′ nĕs)
lex·i·cog·ra·phy
       (lĕk′ sĭ·kŏg′ rà·fĭ)
lex·i·con (lĕk′ sĭ·kŏn)
li·a·ble (lī′ à·b′l)
  li·a·bil·i·ty (lī′ à·bĭl′ ĭ·tĭ)
li·ai·son (lē′ ā·zŏn′)
li·ar (lī′ ĕr)
li·ba·tion (lī·bā′ shŭn)
li·bel (lī′ bĕl)
  -beled -bel·ing
  li·bel·er li·bel·ous
lib·er·al (lĭb′ ĕr·ǎl)
  -al·ly lib·er·al·ism
  lib·er·al·i·ty (lĭb′ ĕr·ǎl′ ĭ·tĭ)
  lib·er·al·ize -iz·ing
lib·er·ate (lĭb′ ĕr·āt)
  -at·ing lib·er·a·tor
lib·er·tar·i·an (lĭb′ ĕr·târ′ ĭ·ǎn)
lib·er·tine (lĭb′ ĕr·tēn)
lib·er·ty (lĭb′ ĕr·tĭ)
  -ties
li·bi·do (lĭ′ bī′ dō)
li·bid·i·nal (lĭ·bĭd′ ĭ·nǎl)

li·bid·i·nous   (lǐ·bǐd′ ǐ·nŭs)

li·brar·y   (lī′ brĕr′ ǐ)
  -brar·ies
  li·brar·i·an   (lī·brâr′ ǐ·ăn)

li·bret·to   (lǐ·brĕt′ ō)

Lib·y·a   (lǐb′ ǐ·à)

lice   (līs)

li·cense   (lī′ sĕns)
  -cens·ing
  li·cen·see   (lī′ sĕn·sē′)

li·cen·tious   (lǐ·sĕn′ shŭs)

li·chen   (lī′ kĕn)

lic·it   (lǐs′ ǐt)

lic·o·rice   (lǐk′ ō·rǐs)

lie   (lī)
  lied   ly·ing
  li·ar

Lie·der·kranz   (lē′ dĕr·krănts′)

liege   (lēj)

lien   (lē·ĕn)

lieu   (lū)

lieu·ten·ant   (lū·tĕn′ ănt)
  -an·cy

life   (līf)
  pl. lives   life belt
  life·blood   life·boat
  life·guard   life·line
  life·long   life·sav·er
  life·sized   life·time
  life·work

lig·a·ment   (lǐg′ à·mĕnt)

lig·a·ture   (lǐg′ à·tŭr)

light   (līt)
  light-fin·gered   light·head·ed
  light·heart·ed   light·house
  light-year

light·ning   (līt′ nǐng)

like   (līk)
  lik·ing   lik·a·ble
  like·ly   -li·hood
  like·ness   like·wise

li·lac   (lī′ lăk)

lil·y   (lǐl′ ǐ)
  lil·ies
  lil·y of the val·ley

limb   (lǐm)

lim·ber   (lǐm′ bĕr)

lim·bo   (lǐm′ bō)
  -boes

Lim·burg·er   (lǐm′ bûrg·ĕr)

lime·light   (līm′ līt′)

Lim·er·ick   (lǐm′ ĕr·ǐk)

lime·stone   (līm′ stōn′)

lime·wa·ter   (līm′ wô′ tĕr)

lim·it   (lǐm′ ǐt)
  -it·ed   -it·ing
  lim·i·ta·tion   (lǐm′ ǐ·tā′ shŭn)
  lim·it·less

limn   (lǐm)

lim·ou·sine   (lǐm′ ŏŏ·zēn′)

lim·pid   (lǐm′ pǐd)

lin·age   (līn′ ǐj)
  (alignment; see *lineage*)

linch·pin   (lǐnch′ pǐn′)

lin·den tree   (lǐn′ dĕn)

lin·e·age   (lǐn′ ê·ǐj)
  (ancestry; see *linage*)

lin·e·al   (lǐn′ ê·ăl)

lin·e·a·ment   (lǐn′ ê·à·mĕnt)

lin·e·ar meas·ure
      (lǐn′ ê·ĕr)

line·man   (līn′ măn)

lin·en   (lǐn′ ĕn)

lin·ge·rie   (lăn′ zhê·rē)

lin·guist   (lǐng′ gwǐst)
  lin·guis·tics   (lǐng·gwǐs′ tǐks)

lin·i·ment   (lǐn′ ǐ·mĕnt)

lin·ing   (līn′ ǐng)

link·age   (lǐngk′ ǐj)

li·no·le·um   (lǐ·nō′ lê·ŭm)

Lin·o·type   (līn′ ô·tīp)

lin·seed oil   (lǐn′ sēd′)

li·on·ess   (lī′ ŭn·ĕs)

li·on·ize   (lī′ ŭn·īz)
  -iz·ing

liq·ue·fac·tion   (lǐk′ wê·făk′ shŭn)

liq·ue·fy   (lǐk′ wê·fī)
  -fied,   -fy·ing
  liq·ue·fi·a·ble   (lǐk′ wê·fī′ à·b'l)

li·queur   (lê·kûr′)

liq·uid   (lǐk′ wǐd)

liq·ui·date   (lǐk′ wǐ·dāt)
  -dat·ing
  liq·ui·da·tion
      (lǐk′ wǐ·dā′ shŭn)

liq·uor   (lǐk′ ĕr)

lisle   (līl)

lis·some   (lǐs′ ŭm)

lis·ten   (lǐs′ 'n)

list·less   (lǐst′ lĕs)

lit·a·ny   (lǐt′ à·nǐ)
  -nies

li·ter   (lē′ tĕr)

lit·er·a·cy   (lǐt′ ĕr·à·sǐ)

lit·er·al   (lǐt′ ĕr·ăl)
  -al·ly

lit·er·ar·y   (lǐt′ ĕr·ĕr′ ǐ)

lit·er·ate   (lǐt′ ĕr·ǐt)
  lit·er·a·ture   (lǐt′ ĕr·à·tŭr)

lithe	(lĭth)
lithe·ness	
lith·o·graph	(lĭth′ ō·grăf)
lit·i·gate	(lĭt′ ĭ·gāt)
-gat·ing	
lit·i·gant	(lĭt′ ĭ·gănt)
lit·i·ga·tion	(lĭt′ ĭ·gā′ shŭn)
li·ti·gious	(lĭ·tĭj′ ŭs)
lit·mus pa·per	(lĭt′ mŭs)
lit·ter	(lĭt′ ēr)
lit·tle·ness	(lĭt′ 'l·nĕs)
lit·ur·gy	(lĭt′ ēr·jĭ)
-gies	
li·tur·gi·cal	(lĭ·tûr′ jĭ·kăl)
live	(lĭv) v.
liv·ing	(lĭv) adj.
liv·a·ble	(lĭv′ à·b'l)
live·li·hood	(lĭv′ lĭ·hŏŏd)
live·ly	(lĭv′ lĭ)
live·li·er	-li·est
-li·ness	
liv·en	(lĭv′ ĕn)
liv·er	(lĭv′ ēr)
liv·er·wurst	(lĭv′ ēr·wûrst′)
liv·er·y sta·ble	(lĭv′ ēr·ĭ)
live·stock	(lĭv′ stŏk′)
liv·id	(lĭv′ ĭd)
liv·ing room	(lĭv′ ĭng)
liz·ard	(lĭz′ ērd)
lla·ma	(lä′ mà)
(animal; see *lama*)	
loaf	(lōf)
pl. loaves	(lōvz)
loaf·er	(lōf′ ēr)
loam	(lōm)
loathe	(lōth)
loath·ing	loath·some
lob·by	(lŏb′ ĭ)
lob·bies	lob·by·ist
lobe	(lōb)
lo·bar	(lō′ bēr)
lob·lol·ly pine	(lŏb′ lŏl′ ĭ)
lo·bot·o·my	(lō·bŏt′ ō·mĭ)
lob·ster	(lŏb′ stēr)
lob·ule	(lŏb′ ūl)
lo·cal	(lō′ kăl)
lo·cal·ism	
lo·cal·i·ty	(lō·kăl′ ĭ·tĭ)
-ties	lo·cal·ize
-iz·ing	
lo·cate	(lō′ kāt)
-cat·ing	
lo·ca·tion	(lō·kā′ shŭn)
lock·et	(lŏk′ ĕt)
lock·jaw	(lŏk′ jô′)

lo·co·mo·tion	(lō′ kō·mō′ shŭn)
lo·co·mo·tive	(lō′ kō·mō′ tĭv)
lo·co·weed	(lō′ kō·wēd′)
lo·cust	(lō′ kŭst)
lo·cu·tion	(lō·kū′ shŭn)
lode·star	(lōd′ stär′)
lode·stone	(lōd′ stōn′)
lodge	(lŏj)
lodg·ing	
loft·y	(lôf′ tĭ)
loft·i·ly	-i·ness
lo·gan·ber·ry	(lō′ găn·bĕr′ ĭ)
-ber·ries	
log·a·rithm	(lŏg′ à·rĭth′m)
log·ger·head	(lŏg′ ēr·hĕd′)
log·ging	(lŏg′ ĭng)
log·ic	(lŏj′ ĭk)
log·i·cal	-cal·ly
lo·gi·cian	(lō·jĭsh′ ăn)
lo·gis·tics	(lō·jĭs′ tĭks)
lo·gy	(lō′ gĭ)
log·i·ness	
Lo·hen·grin	(lō′ ĕn·grĭn)
loin·cloth	(loin′ klŏth′)
loi·ter·er	(loi′ tēr·ēr)
lol·li·pop	(lŏl′ ĭ·pŏp)
lone·ly	(lōn′ lĭ)
lone·li·ness	
lone·some	(lōn′ sŭm)
-some·ness	
long	(lŏng)
long·bow	long-dis·tance
long·hand	long-lived
long-play·ing	long·shore·man
long-suf·fer·ing	
long-term bond	
long-wind·ed	
lon·gev·i·ty	(lŏn·jĕv′ ĭ·tĭ)
lon·gi·tude	(lŏn′ jĭ·tūd)
lon·gi·tu·di·nal	
	(lŏn′ jĭ·tū′ dĭ·năl)
look·ing glass	(lŏŏk′ ĭng glăs)
look·out	(lŏŏk′ out′)
loom·ing	(lŏŏm′ ĭng)
loon·y	(lŏŏn′ ĭ)
loon·i·ness	
loop·hole	(lŏŏp′ hōl′)
loose	(lŏŏs)
loose-joint·ed	loose·ly
loos·en	loose·ness
loot·er	(lŏŏt′ ēr)
lop-eared	(lŏp′ ērd′)
lop·sid·ed	(lŏp′ sīd′ ĕd)
lo·qua·cious	(lō·kwā′ shŭs)
lo·quac·i·ty	(lō·kwăs′ ĭ·tĭ)

lor·do·sis   (lôr·dō′ sĭs)
lord·ship   (lôrd′ shĭp)
lore   (lōr)
Lor·e·lei   (lôr′ ĕ·lī)
lor·gnette   (lôr′ nyĕt′)
lose   (lōōz) v.
    los·ing
loss   (lôs) n.
    loss lead·er
lo·tion   (lō′ shŭn)
lot·ter·y   (lŏt′ ĕr·ĭ)
    lot·ter·ies
lo·tus   (lō′ tŭs)
loud   (loud)
    loud·mouthed   loud-speak·er
Lou·i·si·an·a   (lōō′ ĭ·zĭ·ăn′ à)
    abbr. La.
    Lou·i·si·an·i·an
    or Lou·i·si·an·an
lounge   (lounj)
    loung·ing
louse   (lous)
    pl. lice   (lĭs)
    lous·y   (lous′ ĭ)
lout·ish   (lout′ ĭsh)
lou·ver   (lōō′ vĕr)
    lou·vered
love   (lŭv)
    lov·ing   lov·a·ble
    love·bird   love·less
    love·lorn   love-mak·ing
    love·sick
love·ly   (lŭv′ lĭ)
    love·li·er   -li·est, -li·ness
low   (lō)
    low·born   low·brow
    low-pres·sure   low tide
low·er·class·man
    (lō′ ĕr·klàs′ măn)
low·ly   (lō′ lĭ)
    low·li·er   -li·est, -li·ness
loy·al   (loi′ ăl)
    loy·al·ty
Loy·o·la, St. Ig·na·ti·us
    (loi·ō′ là, Ig·nā′ shĭ·ŭs)
loz·enge   (lŏz′ ĕnj)
lub·ber·ly   (lŭb′ ĕr·lĭ)
lu·bri·cate   (lū′ brĭ·kăt)
    -cat·ing
    lu·bri·cant   (-brĭ·kănt)
    lu·bri·ca·tion   (lū′ brĭ·kā′ shŭn)
    lu·bri·ca·tor
lu·cid   (lū′ sĭd)
    lu·cid·i·ty   (lū·sĭd′ ĭ·tĭ)
luck·less   (lŭk′ lĕs)

luck·y   (lŭk′ ĭ)
    luck·i·er   -i·est
    -i·ly   -i·ness
lu·cra·tive   (lū′ krà·tĭv)
lu·cre   (lū′ kĕr)
lu·di·crous   (lū′ dĭ·krŭs)
lug·gage   (lŭg′ ĭj)
lu·gu·bri·ous   (lù·gū′ brĭ·ŭs)
luke·warm   (lūk′ wôrm′)
lull   (lŭl)
lull·a·by   (lŭl′ à·bī′)
    -bied   -by·ing
lum·ba·go   (lŭm·bā′ gō)
lum·bar   (lŭm′ bĕr)
    (vertebra; see lumber)
lum·ber   (lŭm′ bĕr)
    (timber; see lumbar)
    lum·ber·jack   lum·ber·yard
lu·mi·nar·y   (lū′ mĭ·nĕr′ ĭ)
    -nar·ies
lu·mi·nes·cent   (lū′ mĭ·nĕs′ ĕnt)
    -cence
lu·mi·nous   (lū′ mĭ·nŭs)
    lu·mi·nos·i·ty   (lū′ mĭ·nŏs′ ĭ·tĭ)
lum·mox   (lŭm′ ŭks)
lump·y   (lŭmp′ ĭ)
    lump·i·ness
lu·na·cy   (lū′ nà·sĭ)
lu·nar   (lū′ nĕr)
lu·na·tic   (lū′ nà·tĭk)
lunch·eon   (lŭn′ chŭn)
    lunch·eon·ette   (lŭn′ chŭn·ĕt′)
lunge   (lŭnj)
    lung·ing
lung·fish   (lŭng′ fĭsh′)
lu·pine   (lū′ pĭn) n.
    (flower)
lu·pine   (lū′ pĭn) adj.
    (wolfish)
lurch   (lûrch)
lu·rid   (lū′ rĭd)
lurk   (lûrk)
lus·cious   (lŭsh′ ŭs)
lus·ter·ware   (lŭs′ tĕr·wâr′)
lust·ful   (lŭst′ fŏŏl)
    -ful·ly   -ful·ness
lus·trous   (lŭs′ trŭs)
lust·y   (lŭs′ tĭ)
    lust·i·er   -i·est
    -i·ly   -i·ness
Lu·ther·an   (lū′ thĕr·ăn)
Lux·em·bourg   (lŭk′ sĕm·bûrg)
lux·u·ri·ant   (lŭks·ū′ rĭ·ănt)
    lux·u·ri·ance

lux·u·ri·ate (lŭks·ū′ rĭ·āt)
  -at·ing
lux·u·ry (lŭk′ shŏŏ·rĭ)
  -ries
  lux·u·ri·ous (lŭks·ū′ rĭ·ŭs)
ly·ce·um (lī·sē′ ŭm)
lye (lī)
ly·ing·in (lī′ ĭng·ĭn′)
lymph (lĭmf)
  lym·phat·ic (lĭm·făt′ ĭk)
lynch law (lĭnch)
lynx (lĭngks)
ly·on·naise (lī′ ŭ·nāz′)
lyr·ic (lĭr′ ĭk)
  lyr·i·cal (lĭr′ ĭ·kăl)
  lyr·i·cism (lĭr′ ĭ·sĭz′m)

M

ma'am (măm)
ma·ca·bre (mȧ·kä′ b'r)
mac·ad·am (măk·ăd′ ăm)
  mac·ad·am·ise
    (măk·ăd′ ăm·īz)
mac·a·ro·ni (măk′ ȧ·rō′ nĭ)
mac·a·roon (măk′ ȧ·rōōn′)
ma·caw (mȧ·kô′)
Mc·Coy, the (mȧ·koi′)
ma·che·te (mä·chā′ tå)
Mach·i·a·vel·li·an
    (măk′ ĭ·ȧ·vĕl′ ĭ·ăn)
mach·i·na·tion (măk′ ĭ·nā′ shŭn)
ma·chine (mȧ·shēn′)
  ma·chin·er·y ma·chine shop
  ma·chin·ist
mack·er·el (măk′ ēr·ĕl)
Mack·i·naw coat
    (măk′ ĭ·nô)
Mac·mil·lan, Har·old
    (măk·mĭl′ ăn)
mac·ro·cosm (măk′ rō·kŏz′m)
mad·am (măd′ ăm)
mad·ame (mä′ dăm′)
  pl. mes·dames (mā′ dăm′)
mad·den·ing (măd′ 'n·ĭng)
Ma·dei·ra wine (mȧ·dēr′ ȧ)
ma·de·moi·selle
    (măd′ mwá′ zĕl′)
ma·don·na (mȧ·dŏn′ ȧ)
ma·dras (mȧ·drăs′)
mad·ri·gal (măd′ rĭ·găl)
mael·strom (māl′ strŏm)
ma·e·stro (mä·ĕ′ strō)
maf·fi·a (mäf′ fè·ä)

mag·a·zine (măg′ ȧ·zēn′)
ma·gen·ta (mȧ·jĕn′ tȧ)
mag·got (măg′ ŭt)
mag·ic (măj′ ĭk)
  mag·i·cal -cal·ly
  ma·gi·cian (mȧ·jĭsh′ ăn)
mag·is·trate (măj′ ĭs·trāt)
  mag·is·te·ri·al
    (măj′ ĭs·tēr′ ĭ·ăl)
  mag·is·tra·cy (măj′ ĭs·trȧ·sĭ)
Mag·na Char·ta
    (măg′ nȧ kär′ tȧ)
mag·na cum lau·de
    (măg′ nȧ kŭm lô′ dĕ)
mag·nan·i·mous
    (măg·năn′ ĭ·mŭs)
mag·na·nim·i·ty
    (măg′ nȧ·nĭm′ ĭ·tĭ)
mag·nate (măg′ nāt)
mag·ne·sia (măg·nē′ shȧ)
  mag·ne·si·um
    (măg·nē′ shĭ·ŭm)
mag·net (măg′ nĕt)
  mag·net·ic (măg·nĕt′ ĭk)
  mag·net·ism mag·net·ize
Mag·nif·i·cat (măg·nĭf′ ĭ·kăt)
mag·ni·fi·ca·tion
    (măg′ nĭ·fĭ·kā′ shŭn)
mag·nif·i·cent (măg·nĭf′ ĭ·sĕnt)
  -cence
mag·nif·i·co (măg·nĭf′ ĭ·kō)
  -coes
mag·ni·fy (măg′ nĭ·fī)
  -fied -fy·ing
  mag·ni·fi·er
mag·ni·tude (măg′ nĭ·tūd)
mag·no·li·a (măg·nō′ lĭ·ȧ)
mag·num o·pus
    (măg′ nŭm ō′ pŭs)
mag·pie (măg′ pī)
mag·uey (măg′ wā)
Mag·yar (măg′ yär)
ma·ha·ra·ja (mȧ·hä′ rä′ jȧ)
  n. masc.
ma·ha·ra·ni (mȧ·hä′ rä′ nē)
  n. fem.
ma·hat·ma (mȧ·hăt′ mȧ)
mah-jongg (mä′ jŏng′)
ma·hog·a·ny (mȧ·hŏg′ ȧ·nĭ)
maid·en (mād′ 'n)
mail (māl)
  mail·a·ble mail·box
  mail·man
  mail-or·der house
mail·lot (mä′ yō′)

maim (măm)
Maine (mān)
  abbr. Me.
main·land (mān' lănd')
main·stay (mān' stā')
main·tain (mān·tān')
  main·tain·a·ble
  main·te·nance (mān' t'n·ăns)
maî·tre d'hô·tel (mā' trĕ dō' tĕl')
maize (māz)
  (corn; see maze)
maj·es·ty (măj' ĕs·tǐ)
  -ties
  ma·jes·tic (mà·jĕs' tǐk)
  -ti·cal·ly
ma·jor (mā' jĕr)
  ma·jor-do·mo (mā' jĕr·dō' mō)
  ma·jor·ette (mā' jĕr·ĕt')
  ma·jor league
ma·jor·i·ty (mà·jŏr' ǐ·tǐ)
  -ties
make (māk)
  mak·ing   make-be·lieve
  make·shift   make-up
mal·a·chite (măl' à·kīt)
mal·ad·justed (măl' ă·jŭs' tĕd)
mal·a·dy (măl' à·dǐ)
  -dies
ma·laise (mă·lāz')
ma·lar·i·a (mà·lâr' ǐ·à)
Ma·lay·a (mà·lā' à)
mal·con·tent (măl' kŏn·tĕnt')
mal de mer (măl' dĕ mâr')
mal·e·fac·tor (măl' ĕ·făk' tĕr)
ma·lev·o·lent (mà·lĕv' ō·lĕnt)
mal·fea·sance (măl·fē' zăns)
mal·for·ma·tion
        (măl' fôr·mā' shŭn)
mal·ice (măl' ǐs)
ma·li·cious (mà·lǐsh' ŭs)
ma·lign (mà·līn')
  ma·lig·nan·cy (mà·lǐg' năn·sǐ)
  ma·lig·nant
ma·lin·ger (mà·lǐng' gĕr)
  ma·lin·ger·er
mal·lard (măl' ĕrd)
mal·le·a·ble (măl' ĕ·à·b'l)
  mal·le·a·bil·i·ty
        (măl' ĕ·à·bǐl' ǐ·tǐ)
mal·let (măl' ĕt)
malm·sey wine (măm' zǐ)
mal·nu·tri·tion
        (măl' nŭ·trǐsh' ŭn)
mal·prac·tice (măl' prăk' tǐs)
malt (môlt)

Mal·thu·sian (măl·thū' zhăn)
malt·ose (môl' tōs)
mam·ba snake (măm' bă)
mam·mal (măm' ăl)
  mam·ma·li·an (mă·mā' lǐ·ăn)
  mam·ma·ry (măm' à·rǐ)
mam·mon (măm' ŭn)
mam·moth (măm' ŭth)
man (măn)
  manned   man·ning
  man-at-arms   man-eat·er
  man·ful   -ful·ly
  -ful·ness   man·hole
  man·hood   man·kind
  man·ly   -li·ness
  man·nish   man-of-war
  man·pow·er
man·a·cle (măn' à·k'l)
  -cling
man·age (măn' ǐj)
  -ag·ing
  man·age·a·bil·i·ty
        (măn' ǐj·à·bǐl' ǐ·tǐ)
  man·age·a·ble man·age·ment
  man·ag·er   man·ag·er·ess
  man·a·ge·ri·al
        (măn' à·jēr' ǐ·ăl)
  -al·ly
ma·ña·na (mă·nyä' nä)
man·a·tee (măn' à·tē')
man·da·mus, writ of
        (măn·dā' mŭs)
man·da·rin (măn' dà·rǐn)
man·date (măn' dāt)
man·da·to·ry (măn' dà·tō' rǐ)
man·di·ble (măn' dǐ·b'l)
man·do·lin (măn' dō·lǐn)
ma·neu·ver (mà·nōō' vĕr)
  ma·neu·ver·a·bil·i·ty
        (mà·nōō' vĕr·à·bǐl' ǐ·tǐ)
  ma·neu·ver·a·ble
man·ga·nate (măng' gà·nāt)
man·ga·nese (măng' gà·nēs)
man·gle (măng' g'l)
  -gling
man·go (măng' gō)
  -goes
man·gy (măn' jǐ)
  man·gi·ness
ma·ni·a (mā' nǐ·à)
ma·ni·ac (mā' nǐ·ăk)
  ma·ni·a·cal (mà·nī' à·kăl)
ma·nic (mā' nǐk)
  ma·nic-de·pres·sive

man·i·cure (măn' ĭ·kūr)
man·i·cur·ist
man·i·fest (măn' ĭ·fĕst)
man·i·fes·ta·tion
(măn' ĭ·fĕs·tā' shŭn)
man·i·fest·ly
man·i·fes·to (măn' ĭ·fĕs' tō)
man·i·fold (măn' ĭ·fōld)
Ma·nil·a paper (má·nĭl' á)
ma·nip·u·late (má·nĭp' û·lāt)
-lat·ing
ma·nip·u·la·tion
(má·nĭp' û·lā' shŭn)
ma·nip·u·la·tive
(má·nĭp' û·lā' tĭv)
ma·nip·u·la·tor
(-lā' tẽr)
man·na (măn' á)
man·ne·quin (măn' ĕ·kĭn)
man·ner (măn' ẽr)
(way of acting; see manor)
man·ner·ism
man·ner·ly -li·ness
man·or (măn' ẽr)
(house of an estate; see manner)
ma·no·ri·al (má·nō' rĭ·ál)
man·sard roof (măn' särd)
manse (măns)
man·sion (măn' shŭn)
man·tel (măn' t'l)
(fireplace framework; see mantle)
man·tel·piece
man·til·la (măn·tĭl' á)
man·tle (măn' t'l)
(cloak; see mantel)
man·u·al (măn' û·ál)
man·u·al·ly
man·u·fac·ture (măn' û·făk' tûr)
-tur·ing
man·u·fac·tur·er
ma·nure (má·nūr')
man·u·script (măn' û·skrĭpt)
Manx cat (măngks)
man·y·sid·ed (mĕn' ĭ·sĭd' ĕd)
Ma·o·ri (mä' ō·rĭ)
Mao Tse-tung (mä' ō·dzŭ' dŏŏng')
map (măp)
mapped map·ping
ma·ple sir·up (mā' p'l)
ma·ra·ca (mä·rä' kä)
mar·a·schi·no cher·ry
(măr' á·skē' nō)
mar·a·thon (măr' á·thŏn)
ma·raud·er (má·rôd' ẽr)

mar·ble (mär' b'l)
-bling mar·ble·ize
mar·chion·ess (mär' shŭn·ĕs)
Mar·di gras (mär' dĕ grä')
mar·ga·rine (mär' já·rĭn)
mar·gin (mär' jĭn)
mar·gin·al
mar·i·gold (măr' ĭ·gōld)
mar·i·jua·na (măr' ĭ·wä' ná)
ma·rim·ba (má·rĭm' bá)
mar·i·nade (măr' ĭ·nād')
mar·i·nate (măr' ĭ·nāt)
-nat·ing
ma·rine (má·rēn')
mar·i·ner (măr' ĭ·nẽr)
mar·i·o·nette (măr' ĭ·ô·nĕt')
mar·i·tal (măr' ĭ·tál)
(matrimonial; see martial)
mar·i·tal·ly
mar·i·time (măr' ĭ·tīm)
mar·jo·ram (măr' jô·rám)
mark·ed·ly (mär' kĕd·lĭ)
mar·ket (mär' kĕt)
-ket·ed -ket·ing
mar·ket·a·ble mar·ket·place
mar·ket val·ue
marks·man·ship
(märks' măn·shĭp)
mark·up (märk' ŭp')
marl (märl)
mar·lin (mär' lĭn)
mar·ma·lade (mär' má·lād)
mar·mo·set (mär' mō·zĕt)
mar·mot (mär' mŭt)
ma·roon (má·rōōn')
mar·quee (mär·kē')
mar·quis (mär' kwĭs)
mar·qui·sette (mär' kĭ·zĕt')
mar·riage (măr' ĭj)
mar·riage·a·bil·i·ty
(măr' ĭj·á·bĭl' ĭ·tĭ)
mar·riage·a·ble
(măr' ĭj·á·b'l)
mar·row (măr' ō)
mar·ry (măr' ĭ)
mar·ried mar·ry·ing
mar·shal (mär' shál)
-shaled -shal·ing
marsh·mal·low (märsh' măl' ō)
mar·su·pi·al (mär·sū' pĭ·ál)
mar·ten (mär' tĕn)
(mammal; see martin)
mar·tial (mär' shál)
(warlike; see marital)

Mar·ti·an (măr′ shǐ·ăn)
  (of Mars)
mar·tin (măr′ tǐn)
  (bird; see **marten**)
mar·ti·net (măr′ tǐ·nĕt′)
mar·tyr (măr′ tēr)
  mar·tyr·dom
mar·vel (măr′ vĕl)
  -veled   -vel·ing
  mar·vel·ous (măr′ vĕl·ŭs)
Marx·ist (märk′ sĭst)
Mar·y·land (mĕr′ ĭ·lănd)
  abbr. Md.   Mar·y·land·er
mas·car·a (măs·kăr′ à)
mas·cot (măs′ kŏt)
mas·cu·line (măs′ kū·lǐn)
  mas·cu·lin·i·ty
        (măs′ kū·lǐn′ ǐ·tǐ)
mas·och·ism (măz′ ŏk·ǐz′m)
  mas·och·ist (-ǐst)
ma·son (mā′ s′n)
  ma·son·ic (mà·sŏn′ ǐk)
  ma·son·ry
Ma·son-Dix·on line
mas·quer·ade (măs′ kēr·ād′)
Mas·sa·chu·setts
      (măs′ à·chōō′ sĕts)
  abbr. Mass.
mas·sa·cre (măs′ à·kēr)
  mas·sa·cred (-kērd)
  mas·sa·cring (-krǐng)
mas·sage (mà·säzh′)
  mas·sag·ing
mas·seur (mă·sûr′)
  mas·seuse (mă·sûz′) *fem.*
mas·sive (măs′ ǐv)
  mas·sive·ly
mas·ter (măs′ tēr)
  mas·ter·dom mas·ter-at-arms
  mas·ter·ful, -ful·ly, -ful·ness
  mas·ter·ly   mas·ter·piece
  mas·ter stroke mas·ter·work
  mas·ter·y
mast·head (măst′ hĕd′)
mas·ti·cate (măs′ tǐ·kāt)
  -cat·ing
mas·ti·ca·tion
      (măs′ tǐ·kā′ shŭn)
mas·tiff (măs′ tǐf)
mas·to·don (măs′ tō·dŏn)
mas·toid (măs′ toid)
mat·a·dor (măt′ à·dôr)
match·less (măch′ lĕss)
match·mak·er (măch′ māk′ ēr)

ma·te·ri·al (mà·tēr′ ǐ·ăl)
  (substance; see **matériel**)
ma·te·ri·al·ism
ma·te·ri·al·ist ma·te·ri·al·ize
ma·te·ri·al·ly
ma·té·ri·el (mà·tēr′ ǐ·ĕl′)
  (equipment; see **material**)
ma·ter·nal (mà·tûr′ năl)
  ma·ter·nal·ly
  ma·ter·ni·ty (mà·tûr′ nǐ·tǐ)
math·e·mat·ics
      (măth′ ê·măt′ ǐks)
  math·e·mat·i·cal, -cal·ly
  math·e·ma·ti·cian
      (măth′ ê·mà·tǐsh′ ăn)
mat·in (măt′ ǐn)
  mat·in·al (măt′ ǐ·năl)
mat·i·nee (măt′ ǐ·nā′)
ma·tri·arch (mā′ trǐ·ärk)
  ma·tri·arch·y (mā′ trǐ·är′ kǐ)
ma·tric·u·late (mà·trǐk′ û·lāt)
  -lat·ing
  ma·tric·u·la·tion
      (mà·trǐk′ û·lā′ shŭn)
mat·ri·mo·ny (măt′ rǐ·mō′ nǐ)
  mat·ri·mo·ni·al
      (măt′ rǐ·mō′ nǐ·ăl)
  -al·ly
ma·trix (mā′ trǐks)
  pl. ma·tri·ces (mā′ trǐ·sēz)
ma·tron (mā′ trŭn)
  ma·tron·ly -li·ness
mat·ter (măt′ ēr)
  mat·ter-of-fact *adj.*
mat·ting (măt′ ǐng)
mat·tress (măt′ rĕs)
ma·ture (mà·tūr′)
  -tur·ing
mat·u·ra·tion (măt′ û·rā′ shŭn)
ma·ture·ly
ma·tu·ri·ty (mà·tū′ rǐ·tǐ)
maud·lin (môd′ lǐn)
Mau·i Is., Ha·wai·i
      (mou′ ê)
maul·er (môl′ ēr)
Maun·dy Thurs·day
      (môn′ dǐ)
Mau·re·ta·ni·a, Afr.
      (mô′ rê·tā′ nǐ·à)
mau·so·le·um (mô′ sō·lē′ ŭm)
mauve (mōv)
mav·er·ick (măv′ ēr·ǐk)
mawk·ish (môk′ ǐsh)
max·im (măk′ sǐm)
max·i·mal (măk′ sǐ·măl)

max·i·mum (măk′ sǐ·mŭm)
  pl. max·i·ma
  max·i·mize -miz·ing
may·hem (mā′ hĕm)
may·on·naise (mā′ ŏ·nāz′)
may·or (mā′ ẽr)
  may·or·al·ty (mā′ ẽr·ăl·tǐ)
maze (māz)
  (labyrinth; see maize)
ma·zur·ka (má·zûr′ ká)
mead (mēd)
  (fermented drink; see meed)
mead·ow (mĕd′ ō)
mea·ger (mē′ gẽr)
meal·time (mēl′ tīm′)
meal·y (mēl′ ĭ)
  meal·i·ness meal·y·mouthed
mean (mēn)
  (intend; see mien)
  mean·ing·less mean·ness
  mean·time mean·while
me·an·der·ing (mē·ăn′ dẽr·ĭng)
mea·sles (mē′ z'lz)
meas·ure (mĕzh′ ẽr)
  -ur·ing
  meas·ur·a·bil·i·ty
         (mĕzh′ ẽr·á·bǐl′ ǐ·tǐ)
  meas·ur·a·ble meas·ure·less
  meas·ure·ment
meat (mēt)
  (food; see meet, mete)
meat·y (mēt′ ĭ)
  meat·i·er, -i·est, -i·ness
me·chan·ic (mē·kăn′ ĭk)
  me·chan·i·cal
  mech·a·nism (mĕk′ á·nǐz'm)
  mech·a·nis·tic (mĕk′ á·nǐs′ tǐk)
  mech·a·nize (mĕk′ á·nǐz)
med·al (mĕd′ 'l)
  med·al·ist
  me·dal·lion (mē·dăl′ yŭn)
med·dle (mĕd′ 'l)
  med·dling med·dler
  med·dle·some
me·di·a (mē′ dǐ·á)
  pl. of me·di·um
me·di·an (mē′ dǐ·ăn)
me·di·ate (mē′ dǐ·āt)
  -at·ing
  me·di·a·tion (mē′ dǐ·ā′ shŭn)
  me·di·a·tor
med·i·cal (mĕd′ ǐ·kăl)
med·i·cate (mĕd′ ǐ·kāt)
  -cat·ing

med·i·ca·tion
         (mĕd′ ǐ·kā′ shŭn)
med·i·ca·tive (mĕd′ ǐ·kā′ tǐv)
med·i·cine (mĕd′ ǐ·sǐn)
  me·dic·i·nal (mē·dǐs′ ǐ·năl)
  -nal·ly
me·di·e·val (mē′ dǐ·ē′ văl)
me·di·o·cre (mē′ dǐ·ō′ kẽr)
  me·di·oc·ri·ty (mē′ dǐ·ŏk′ rǐ·tǐ)
med·i·tate (mĕd′ ǐ·tāt)
  -tat·ing
  med·i·ta·tion (mĕd′ ǐ·tā′ shŭn)
  med·i·ta·tive (mĕd′ ǐ·tā′ tǐv)
  med·i·ta·tor
Med·i·ter·ra·ne·an (sea)
     (mĕd′ ǐ·tẽ·rā′ nē·ăn)
me·di·um (mē′ dǐ·ŭm)
  pl. me·di·ums (in general sense)
  pl. me·di·a (as in "communica-
    tions media" and in scientific
    sense)
med·ley (mĕd′ lǐ)
  -leys
Me·du·sa (mē·dū′ sá)
meed (mēd)
  (reward; see mead)
meek (mēk)
meer·schaum (mẽr′ shŭm)
meet (mēt)
  (come upon; see meat, mete)
meet·ing·house (mēt′ ĭng·hous′)
meg·a·cy·cle (mĕg′ á·sī′ k'l)
meg·a·lo·ma·ni·a
     (mĕg′ á·lō·mā′ nǐ·á)
meg·a·phone (mĕg′ á·fōn)
meg·a·ton (mĕg′ á·tŭn′)
Meis·ter·sing·er
     (mīs′ tẽr·sǐng′ ẽr)
mel·an·cho·li·a
     (mĕl′ ăn·kō′ lǐ·á)
  mel·an·chol·ic (-kŏl′ ǐk)
  mel·an·chol·y (-kŏl′ ǐ)
Mel·a·ne·sia (mĕl′ á·nē′ shá)
mé·lange (mā′ länzh′)
me·lee (mā′ lā′)
mel·lif·lu·ent (mē·lǐf′ lōō·ĕnt)
  -ence mel·lif·lu·ous
mel·low (mĕl′ ō)
mel·o·dra·ma (mĕl′ ō·drä′ má)
  mel·o·dra·mat·ic
     (mĕl′ ō·drá·măt′ ǐk)
mel·o·dy (mĕl′ ō·dǐ)
  -dies
me·lo·dic (mē·lŏd′ ǐk)
me·lo·di·ous (mē·lō′ dǐ·ŭs)

mel·on   (mĕl′ ŭn)
melt   (mĕlt)
 melt·a·ble   melt·ing pot
mem·brane   (mĕm′ brān)
 mem·bra·nous   (mĕm′ brá·nŭs)
me·men·to   (mê·mĕn′ tō)
 -tos
mem·o   (mĕm′ ō)
 -os
mem·oir   (mĕm′ wär)
mem·o·ra·ble   (mĕm′ ô·rá·b′l)
 mem·o·ra·bil·i·a
                (mĕm′ ô·rá·bĭl′ ĭ·á)
 mem·o·ra·bil·i·ty
                (mĕm′ ô·rá·bĭl′ ĭ·tĭ)
mem·o·ran·dum
                (mĕm′ ô·răn′ dŭm)
 pl. -dums or -da
me·mo·ri·al   (mê·mō′ rĭ·ál)
 me·mo·ri·al·ise
mem·o·ry   (mĕm′ ô·rĭ)
 -ries
 mem·o·ri·za·tion
                (mĕm′ ô·rĭ·zā′ shŭn)
 mem·o·rize   -iz·ing
men·ace   (mĕn′ ĭs)
 men·ac·ing·ly
mé·nage   (mâ·näzh′)
me·nag·er·ie   (mê·năj′ ēr·ĭ)
men·da·cious   (mĕn·dā′ shŭs)
 men·dac·i·ty   (mĕn·dăs′ ĭ·tĭ)
Men·del's law   (mĕn′ dĕlz)
 Men·de·li·an   (mĕn·dē′ lĭ·ăn)
men·di·cant   (mĕn′ dĭ·kánt)
 -can·cy
me·ni·al   (mē′ nĭ·ál)
 -al·ly
men·in·gi·tis   (mĕn′ ĭn·jī′ tĭs)
men·o·pause   (mĕn′ ô·pôz)
men·stru·ate   (mĕn′ strōō·āt)
 -at·ing   men·stru·al
 men·stru·a·tion
                (mĕn′ strōō·ā′ shŭn)
men·su·ra·tion
                (mĕn′ shōō·rā′ shŭn)
men·tal   (mĕn′ tál)
 men·tal·i·ty   (mĕn·tăl′ ĭ·tĭ)
 men·tal·ly
men·thol   (mĕn′ thŏl)
 men·tho·lat·ed
                (mĕn′ thô·lāt′ ĕd)
men·tion   (mĕn′ shŭn)
 men·tion·a·ble
men·tor   (mĕn′ tēr)

men·u   (mĕn′ ū)
 -us
Meph·i·stoph·e·les
                (mĕf′ ĭ·stŏf′ ĕ·lēz)
mer·can·tile   (mûr′ kăn·tĭl)
 mer·can·til·ism
                (mûr′ kăn·tĭl·ĭz′m)
mer·ce·nar·y   (mûr′ sĕ·nĕr′ ĭ)
 nari·es
mer·cer·ized thread
                (mûr′ sĕr·īzd)
mer·chan·dise   (mûr′ chăn·dīz)
mer·chant   (mûr′ chănt)
Mer·cu·ro·chrome
                (mûr·kū′ rô·krōm′)
mer·cu·ry   (mûr′ kū·rĭ)
 mer·cu·ri·al   (mûr·kū′ rĭ·ál)
 mer·cu·ric   (mûr·kū′ rĭk)
 mer·cu·ry-va·por lamp
mer·cy   (mûr′ sĭ)
 -cies
 mer·ci·ful, -ful·ly, -ful·ness
 mer·ci·less   -less·ness
mere   (mēr)
 mere·ly
mer·e·tri·cious (mĕr′ ê·trĭsh′ ŭs)
mer·gan·ser duck
                (mĕr·găn′ sēr)
merge   (mûrj)
 merg·ing   mer·gence
 merg·er
me·rid·i·an   (mê·rĭd′ ĭ·ăn)
me·ringue   (mĕ·răng′)
mer·it   (mĕr′ ĭt)
 -it·ed   -it·ing
 mer·i·to·ri·ous
                (mĕr′ ĭ·tō′ rĭ·ŭs)
mer·maid   (mûr′ mād′)
mer·ry   (mĕr′ ĭ)
 mer·ri·ment   mer·ri·ly
 mer·ry-go-round
 mer·ry-mak·er
me·sa   (mā′ sá)
Me·sa·bi (iron range)
                (mê·sä′ bĭ)
mes·cal   (mĕs·kăl′)
mes·mer·ize   (mĕz′ mēr·īz)
 -iz·ing
 mes·mer·ism   (mĕz′ mēr·ĭz′m)
mes·quite   (mĕs·kēt′)
mes·sage   (mĕs′ ĭj)
 mes·sen·ger   (mĕs′ ĕn·jēr)
Mes·si·ah   (mĕ·sī′ á)
 Mes·si·an·ic   (mĕs′ ĭ·ăn′ ĭk)
mess kit   (mĕs)

mess·mate (mĕs′ māt′)
mess·y (mĕe′ ĭ)
  mess·i·ness
mes·ti·zo (mĕs·tē′ zō)
  -zos
me·tab·o·lism (mĕ·tăb′ ô·lĭz′m)
met·a·bol·ic (mĕt′ à·bŏl′ ĭk)
met·al (mĕt′ 'l)
  (substance; see *mettle*)
me·tal·lic (mĕ·tăl′ ĭk)
met·al·lur·gist (mĕt′ 'l·ûr′ jĭst)
met·al·lur·gy (mĕt′ 'l·ûr′ jĭ)
met·al·ware   met·al·work·er
met·a·mor·pho·sis
       (mĕt′ à·môr′ fô·sĭs)
  pl. met·a·mor·pho·ses
met·a·mor·phic
    (mĕt′ à·môr′ fĭk)
met·a·phor (mĕt′ à·fêr)
  met·a·phor·i·cal
    (mĕt′ à·fôr′ ĭ·kál)
met·a·phys·ics (mĕt′ à·fĭz′ ĭks)
  met·a·phys·i·cal (-fĭz′ ĭ·kál)
  met·a·phy·si·cian (-fĭ·zĭsh′ án)
met·a·tar·sal (mĕt′ à·tär′ sál)
mete (mēt)
  (allot; see *meat*, *meet*)
  met·ing
me·te·or (mē′ tê·ẽr)
  me·te·or·ic (mē′ tê·ôr′ ĭk)
  me·te·or·ite (mē′ tê·ẽr·ĭt)
me·te·or·ol·o·gy
    (mē′ tê·ẽr·ŏl′ ô·jĭ)
  me·te·or·o·log·i·cal
    (mē′ tê·ẽr·ô·lŏj′ ĭ·kál)
  me·te·or·ol·o·gist
    (mē′ tê·ẽr·ŏl′ ô·jĭst)
me·ter (mē′ tẽr)
meth·ane (mĕth′ ān)
meth·od (mĕth′ ŭd)
  me·thod·i·cal (mĕ·thŏd′ ĭ·kál)
  meth·od·o·log·i·cal
    (mĕth′ ŭd·ô·lŏj′ ĭ·kál)
  meth·od·ol·o·gy
    (mĕth′ ŭd·ŏl′ ô·jĭ)
Meth·od·ist (mĕth′ ŭd·ĭst)
Me·thu·se·lah (mĕ·thū′ zĕ·lá)
meth·yl (mĕth′ ĭl)
  meth·yl·ene
me·tic·u·lous (mĕ·tĭk′ û·lŭs)
met·ric (mĕt′ rĭk)
  met·ri·cal
met·ro·nome (mĕt′ rô·nōm)
me·trop·o·lis (mĕ·trŏp′ ô·lĭs)

met·ro·pol·i·tan
    (mĕt′ rô·pŏl′ ĭ·tán)
met·tle (mĕt′ 'l)
  (spirit; see *metal*)
mez·za·nine (mĕz′ à·nēn)
mez·zo-so·pra·no
  (mĕd′ zō·sô·prä′ nō)
mi·as·ma (mĭ·ăz′ má)
mi·ca (mī′ ká)
Mich·i·gan (mĭsh′ ĭ·gán)
  abbr. Mich.
  Mich·i·gan·ite *or*
  Mich·i·gan·der
    (mĭsh′ ĭ·gán′ dẽr)
micro- (mī′ krô-)
mi·cro·a·nal·y·sis
mi·cro·cosm (mī′ krô·kŏz′m)
mi·cro·cos·mic
    mī′ krô·kŏz′ mĭk)
mi·cro·film   mi·cro·groove
mi·crom·e·ter (mī·krŏm′ ê·tẽr)
mi·cro·or·gan·ism
    (mī′ krô·ôr′ găn·ĭz′m)
mi·cro·phone   mi·cro·print
mi·cro·scope (mī′ krô·skōp)
mi·cro·scop·ic (-skŏp′ ĭk)
mi·cro·wave
mi·crobe (mī′ krōb)
mi·cron (mī′ krŏn)
mid- (mĭd-)
  mid-chan·nel   mid-con·ti·nent
  mid·day   mid·land
  mid-o·cean   mid·night
  mid-point   mid·riff
  mid·ship·man   mid·sum·mer
  mid·way   mid·week
  Mid·west   Mid·west·ern·er
  mid·wife   mid·win·ter
  mid·year
Mi·das (mī′ dás)
mid·dle (mĭd′ 'l)
  mid·dle age   mid·dle-aged
  mid·dle class *n.*
  mid·dle-class *adj.*
  mid·dle ear   Mid·dle East
  mid·dle·man   mid·dle·weight
  Mid·dle West
  Mid·dle West·ern·er
mid·dling (mĭd′ lĭng)
mid·dy blouse (mĭd′ ĭ)
midg·et (mĭj′ ĕt)
mid·riff (mĭd′ rĭf)
midst (mĭdst)
mien (mēn)
  (demeanor; see *mean*)

might   (mĭt)
  (strength; see *mite*)
might·y   (mīt′ ĭ)
  might·i·er, -i·est, -i·ly, -i·ness
mi·gnon·ette   (mĭn′ yŭn·ĕt′)
mi·graine head·ache
                (mī′ grān)
mi·grate   (mī′ grāt)
  -grat·ing
  mi·grant   (mī′ grănt)
  mi·gra·tion   (mī·grā′ shŭn)
  mi·gra·to·ry   (mī′ grà·tō′ rǐ)
mi·ka·do   (mĭ·kä′ dō)
mi·la·dy   (mĭ·lā′ dĭ)
mil·dew   (mĭl′ dū)
mile·age   (mĭl′ ĭj)
mile·stone   (mīl′ stōn′)
mi·lieu   (mē′ lyû′)
mil·i·tar·y   (mĭl′ ĭ·tĕr′ ĭ)
  mil·i·tan·cy   (-tăn·sĭ)
  mil·i·tant   (-tănt)
  mil·i·ta·rist   (mĭl′ ĭ·tà·rĭst)
  mil·i·ta·ris·tic
              (mĭl′ ĭ·tà·rĭs′ tĭk)
  mil·i·ta·rize   -riz·ing
  mil·i·tate   -tat·ing
  mi·li·tia   (mĭ·lĭsh′ à)
milk   (mĭlk)
  milk·man
  milk of mag·ne·sia
  milk shake   milk·sop
  milk·weed   milk·y
mil·len·ni·um   (mĭ·lĕn′ ĭ·ŭm)
  pl. mil·len·nia   mil·len·ni·al
mil·le·pede   (mĭl′ ė·pēd)
mil·let   (mĭl′ ĕt)
mil·li·me·ter   (mĭl′ ĭ·mē′ tẽr)
mil·li·ner   (mĭl′ ĭ·nẽr)
  mil·li·ner·y   (-nẽr′ ĭ)
mil·lion   (mĭl′ yŭn)
  mil·lion·aire   (mĭl′ yŭn·âr′)
  mil·lionth
mill·stone   (mĭl′ stōn′)
mill·wright   (mĭl′ rīt′)
mi·lord   (mĭ·lôrd′)
Mil·wau·kee, Wis.
             (mĭl·wô′ kė)
mime   (mīm)
  mi·met·ic   (mĭ·mĕt′ ĭk)
mim·e·o·graph   (mĭm′ ė·ō·gráf′)
mim·ic   (mĭm′ ĭk)
  mim·ick·er   mim·ic·ry
mi·mo·sa   (mĭ·mō′ sà)
min·a·ret   (mĭn′ à·rĕt′)
mince·meat   (mĭns′ mēt′)

mince·ing·ly   (mĭn′ sĭng·lĭ)
mind   (mīnd)
  mind·ful, -ful·ly, -ful·ness
  mind·less   mind read·er
  mind's eye
min·er   (mīn′ ẽr)
  (one who mines; see *minor*)
min·er·al   (mĭn′ ẽr·ăl)
  min·er·al·ize   -iz·ing
  min·er·al·og·i·cal
            (mĭn′ ẽr·ăl·ŏj′ ĭ·kăl)
  min·er·al·o·gy
            (mĭn′ ẽr·ăl′ ô·jĭ)
mi·ne·stro·ne soup
            (mē·nà·strō′ nà)
min·gle   (mĭng′ g′l)
  -gling
min·i·a·ture   (mĭn′ ĭ·à·tŭr)
min·i·mum   (mĭn′ ĭ·mŭm)
  min·i·mal   (-măl)
  min·i·mize   -mis·ing
min·ing   (mīn′ ĭng)
min·ion   (mĭn′ yŭn)
min·is·ter   (mĭn′ ĭs·tẽr)
  min·is·te·ri·al   (mĭn′ ĭs·tẽr′ ĭ·ăl)
  min·is·tra·tion   (mĭn′ ĭs·trā′ shŭn)
  min·is·try   (mĭn′ ĭs·trĭ)
  -tries
Min·ne·ap·o·lis,   (mĭn′ ė·ăp′ ô·lĭs)
  Minn.
Min·ne·so·ta   (mĭn′ ė·sō′ tà)
  abbr. Minn.   Min·ne·so·tan
min·now   (mĭn′ ō)
mi·nor   (mī′ nẽr)
  (under age; see *miner*)
mi·nor·i·ty   (mĭ·nŏr′ ĭ·tĭ)
  -ties
min·strel   (mĭn′ strĕl)
mint·age   (mĭn′ tĭj)
mint ju·lep   (mĭnt)
min·u·et   (mĭn′ û·ĕt′)
mi·nus   (mī′ nŭs)
mi·nus·cule   (mĭ·nŭs′ kŭl)
min·ute   (mĭn′ ĭt)
  (time unit)   min·ute·man
mi·nute   (mĭ·nūt′)
  (little)   mi·nute·ly
mi·nu·ti·a   (mĭ·nū′ shĭ·à)
  pl. mi·nu·tiae   (-ē)
minx   (mĭngks)
  minx·es
mir·a·cle   (mĭr′ à·k′l)
mi·rac·u·lous   (mĭ·răk′ û·lŭs)
mi·rage   (mĭ·räzh′)
mire   (mīr)

mir·ror   (mĭr′ ẽr)
  mir·rored   mir·ror·ing
mirth   (mûrth)
  mirth·ful, -ful·ly, -ful·ness
mis·al·li·ance   (mĭs′ ȧ·lī′ ȧns)
mis·an·thrope (mĭs′ ăn·thrōp)
  mis·an·throp·ic
        (mĭs′ ăn·thrŏp′ ĭk)
mis·be·got·ten (mĭs′ bē·gŏt′ 'n)
mis·cal·cu·la·tion
    (mĭs′ kăl·kū·lā′ shŭn)
mis·car·riage   (mĭs·kăr′ ĭj)
mis·ce·ge·na·tion
    (mĭs′ ē·jē·nā′ shŭn)
mis·cel·la·ne·ous
    (mĭs′ ĕ·lā′ nē·ŭs)
  mis·cel·la·ny (mĭs′ ĕ·lā′ nĭ)
mis·chief   (mĭs′ chĭf)
  mis·chie·vous (mĭs′ chĭ·vŭs)
mis·con·cep·tion
    (mĭs′ kŏn·sĕp′ shŭn)
mis·con·strue (mĭs′ kŏn·strōō′)
  -stru·ing
mis·de·mean·or
    (mĭs′ dē·mēn′ ẽr)
mi·ser   (mī′ zẽr)
mis·er·a·ble (mĭz′ ẽr·ȧ·b'l)
mis·fea·sance (mĭs·fē′ zăns)
mis·hap   (mĭs·hăp′)
mis·in·ter·pre·ta·tion
    (mĭs′ ĭn·tûr′ prē·tā′ shŭn)
mis·judgment (mĭs·jŭj′ mĕnt)
mis·man·age·ment
    (mĭs·măn′ ĭj·mĕnt)
mis·no·mer (mĭs·nō′ mẽr)
mi·sog·y·ny (mĭ·sŏj′ ĭ·nĭ)
mis·rep·re·sen·ta·tion
    (mĭs′ rĕp·rē·zĕn·tā′ shŭn)
mis·sal   (mĭs′ ȧl)
  (devotional book; see *missile*)
mis·shap·en (mĭs·shăp′ ĕn)
mis·sile   (mĭs′ ĭl)
  (self-propelling weapon; see *mis-
sal*)
mis·sion   (mĭsh′ ŭn)
mis·sion·ar·y (mĭsh′ ŭn·ĕr′ ĭ)
  -aries
Mis·sis·sip·pi (mĭs′ ĭ·sĭp′ ĭ)
  abbr. Miss.
  Mis·sis·sip·pi·an
mis·sive   (mĭs′ ĭv)
Mis·sou·ri (mĭ·zŏŏr′ ĭ)
  abbr. Mo. Mis·sou·ri·an
mis·spell   (mĭs·spĕl′)

mis·state   (mĭs·stāt′)
  mis·stat·ing
mis·step   (mĭs·stĕp′)
  mis·stepped mis·step·ping
mis·take   (mĭs·tāk′)
  -tak·ing mis·tak·a·ble
  mis·tak·en
mis·tle·toe (mĭs′ 'l·tō)
mis·tress   (mĭs′ trĕs)
mis·un·der·stand·ing
    (mĭs′ ŭn·dẽr·stănd′ ĭng)
mite   (mīt)
  (a bit; see *might*)
mi·ter   (mī′ tẽr)
mit·i·gate (mĭt′ ĭ·gāt)
  -gat·ing mit·i·gant
  mit·i·ga·tion (mĭt′ ĭ·gā′ shŭn)
  mit·i·ga·tor
mitt   (mĭt)
mit·ten   (mĭt′ 'n)
mix   (mĭks)
  mix·ture (mĭks′ tûr)
  mix-up
mne·mon·ics (nē·mŏn′ ĭks)
moat   (mōt)
  (ditch; see *mote*)
mo·bile   (mō′ bĭl) *adj.*
  mo·bil·i·ty (mō·bĭl′ ĭ·tĭ)
mo·bile   (mō′ bēl) *n.*
mo·bi·lize (mō′ bĭ·līz)
  -liz·ing
  mo·bi·li·za·tion
    (mō′ bĭ·lĭ·zā′ zhŭn)
mob·oc·ra·cy (mŏb·ŏk′ rȧ·sĭ)
moc·ca·sin (mŏk′ ȧ·sĭn)
mock   (mŏk)
  mock·er·y mock-he·ro·ic
  mock·ing·bird
mod·al   (mōd′ ȧl)
  (pertaining to mode; see *model*)
mod·el   (mŏd′ 'l)
  (design; see *modal*)
  -eled -el·ing
mod·er·ate (mŏd′ ẽr·ĭt)
  mod·er·ate·ly
  mod·er·a·tion (mŏd′ẽr·ā′shŭn)
  mod·er·a·tor (mŏd′ ẽr·ā′ tẽr)
mod·ern   (mŏd′ ẽrn)
  mod·ern·is·tic (mŏd′ ẽr·nĭs′ tĭk)
  mo·der·ni·ty (mō·dûr′ nĭ·tĭ)
  mod·ern·i·za·tion
    (mŏd′ ẽr·nĭ·zā′ shŭn)
  mod·ern·ize (mŏd′ ẽr·nīz)
  -iz·ing mod·ern·ness

mod·est   (mŏd′ ĕst)
  mod·est·ly   mod·es·ty
mod·i·cum   (mŏd′ ĭ·kŭm)
mod·i·fy   (mŏd′ ĭ·fī)
  -fied,   -fy·ing
  mod·i·fi·a·ble   (mŏd′ ĭ·fī′ ȧ·b'l)
  mod·i·fi·ca·tion
      (mŏd′ ĭ·fĭ·kā′ shŭn)
  mod·i·fi·er
mod·ish   (mŏd′ ĭsh)
mo·diste   (mō·dēst′)
mod·u·late   (mŏd′ û·lāt)
  -lat·ing
  mod·u·la·tion   (mŏd′û·lā′shŭn)
  mod·u·la·tor
mo·dus o·pe·ran·di
      (mō′ dŭs ŏp′ ĕ·răn′ dī)
mo·gul   (mō′ gŭl)
mo·hair   (mō′ hâr′)
Mo·ham·med·an
      (mō·hăm′ ĕ·dȧn)
Mo·hawk   (mō′ hôk)
moi·ré   (mwä′ rā′)
moist   (moist)
  mois·ten   (mois′ 'n)
  mois·ture   (mois′ tûr)
  mois·ture·proof
  mois·tur·ize   -iz·ing
mo·lar   (mō′ lẽr)
mo·las·ses   (mō·lăs′ ĕz)
mold   (mōld)
  mold·a·ble   mold·ing
  mold·y
mol·e·cule   (mŏl′ ê·kūl)
  mo·lec·u·lar   (mō·lĕk′ û·lẽr)
mole·hill   (mōl′ hĭl′)
mo·lest   (mō·lĕst′)
  mo·les·ta·tion
      (mō′ lĕs·tā′ shŭn)
  mo·lest·er
mol·li·fy   (mŏl′ ĭ·fī)
  -fied,   -fy·ing
  mol·li·fi·ca·tion
      (mŏl′ ĭ·fĭ·kā′ shŭn)
mol·lusk   (mŏl′ ŭsk)
mol·ly·cod·dle   (mŏl′ ĭ·kŏd′ 'l)
  -cod·dling
mol·ten   (mōl′ tĕn)
mo·lyb·de·num
      (mō·lĭb′ dê·nŭm)
mo·ment   (mō′ mĕnt)
mo·men·tar·y   (mō′ mĕn·tĕr′ ĭ)
  mo·men·tar·i·ly
mo·men·tous   (mō·mĕn′ tŭs)

mo·men·tum   (mō·mĕn′ tŭm)
  pl. mo·men·ta
Mo·na Li·sa   (mō′ nȧ lē′ zȧ)
mon·arch   (mŏn′ ẽrk)
  mo·nar·chic   (mō·när′ kĭk)
  mon·arch·y   (mŏn′ ẽr·kĭ)
  -arch·ies
mon·as·ter·y   (mŏn′ ȧs·tĕr′ ĭ)
  -ter·ies
mo·nas·tic   (mō·năs′ tĭk)
  mo·nas·ti·cism
      (mō·năs′ tĭ·sĭz'm)
mon·e·tar·y   (mŏn′ ê; tĕr′ ĭ)
  mon·e·tar·i·ly
mon·e·tize   (mŏn′ ê·tīz)
  -tiz·ing
mon·ey   (mŭn′ ĭ)
  mon·eyed
  mon·ey-chang·er
  mon·ey-lend·er
  mon·ey-mak·ing
  mon·ey or·der
mon·ger   (mŭng′ gẽr)
Mon·gol   (mŏng′ gŏl)
  Mon·go·lian   (mŏng·gōl′ yȧn)
  Mon·gol·oid   (mŏng′ gŏl·oid)
mon·goose   (mŏng′ gōōs)
mon·grel   (mŭng′ grĕl)
mon·i·ker   (mŏn′ ĭ·kẽr)
mon·i·tor   (mŏn′ ĭ·tẽr)
monk   (mŭngk)
  monk·er·y   monk·ish
mon·key   (mŭng′ kĭ)
  -keys   mon·key-shine
  mon·key wrench
mon·o·chro·ma·tic
      (mŏn′ ô·krō·măt′ ĭk)
mon·o·cle   (mŏn′ ô·k'l)
mo·nog·a·my   (mō·nŏg′ ȧ·mĭ)
  mo·nog·a·mist (-mĭst)
  mo·nog·a·mous (-mŭs)
mon·o·gram   (mŏn′ ô·grăm)
  mon·o·gram·mat·ic
      (mŏn′ ô·grȧ·măt′ ĭk)
mon·o·graph   (mŏn′ ô·grȧf)
mo·nog·y·ny   (mō·nŏj′ ĭ·nĭ)
mon·o·lith·ic   (mŏn′ ô·lĭth′ ĭk)
mon·o·logue   (mŏn′ ô·lŏg)
mon·o·man·ia   (mŏn′ ô·mā′ nĭ·ȧ)
mo·nop·o·ly   (mō·nŏp′ ô·lĭ)
  -lies
  mo·nop·o·lis·tic
      (mō·nŏp′ ô·lĭs′ tĭk)
  mo·nop·o·lize, -liz·ing

mon·o·syl·la·ble
    (mŏn′ ô·sĭl′ á·b'l)
mon·o·syl·lab·ic
    (mŏn′ ô·sĭ·lăb′ ĭk)
mon·o·the·ism
    (mŏn′ ô·thê·ĭz'm)
mon·o·the·is·tic
    (mŏn′ ô·thê·ĭs′ tĭk)
mon·o·tone   (mŏn′ ô·tōn)
mo·not·o·nous (mô·nŏt′ ô·nŭs)
  mo·not·o·ny (mô·nŏt′ ô·nĭ)
mon·ox·ide   (mŏn·ŏk′ sĭd)
mon·sieur   (mě·syû′)
mon·si·gnor (mŏn·sē′ nyôr)
mon·soon   (mŏn·sōōn′)
mon·ster   (mŏn′ stēr)
  mon·stros·i·ty (mŏn·strŏs′ ĭ·tĭ)
  -ties
  mon·strous (mŏn′ strŭs)
mon·tage   (mŏn·täzh′)
Mon·tan·a   (mŏn·tăn′ á)
  abbr. Mont. Mon·tan·an
Mon·te Car·lo (mŏn′ tê kär′ lō)
Mon·te·rey, Calif.
    (mŏn′ tẽ·rā′)
Mon·ter·rey, Mex.
    (mŏn′ tĕ·rā′)
month·ly   (mŭnth′ lĭ)
  -lies
mon·u·ment (mŏn′ û·měnt)
mon·u·men·tal
    (mŏn′ û·měn′ tǎl)
mood·y   (mōōd′ ĭ)
  mood·i·er, -i·est, -i·ly, -i·ness
moon   (mōōn)
  moon·beam moon·light
  moon·shine moon·stone
  moon·struck
moor·age   (mōōr′ ĭj)
Moor·ish   (mōōr′ ĭsh)
moose   (mōōs)
  n. sing. & pl.
moot court   (mōōt)
mope   (mōp)
  mop·ing mop·ish
mop·pet   (mŏp′ ĕt)
mo·raine   (mô·rān′)
mor·al   (mŏr′ ǎl)
  (ethical)
  mor·al·ist
  mor·al·is·tic (mŏr′ ǎl·ĭs′ tĭk)
  mor·al·i·ty (mô·rǎl′ ĭ·tĭ)
  mor·al·i·za·tion
    (mŏr′ ǎl·ĭ·zā′ shŭn)
  mor·al·i·zer mor·al·ly

mo·rale   (mô·rǎl′)
  (zeal)
mo·rass   (mô·rǎs′)
mor·a·to·ri·um
    (mŏr′ á·tō′ rĭ·ŭm)
  pl. mor·a·to·ri·a
mo·ray eel   (mô·rā′)
mor·bid   (mŏr′ bĭd)
  mor·bid·i·ty (mŏr·bĭd′ ĭ·tĭ)
mor·dant   (mŏr′ dǎnt)
  -dan·cy
more·o·ver (mōr·ō′ vēr)
mo·res   (mō′ rēz)
  (customs)
mor·ga·nat·ic (mŏr′ gá·nǎt′ ĭk)
morgue   (mŏrg)
mor·i·bund (mŏr′ ĭ·bŭnd)
Mor·mon   (mŏr′ mŭn)
morn·ing   (mŏr′ nĭng)
  (early day; see *mourning*)
  morn·ing-glo·ry
  morn·ing star
Mo·roc·can (mô·rŏk′ đn)
mo·roc·co leath·er
    (mô·rŏk′ ō)
mo·ron   (mō′ rŏn)
  mo·ron·ic (mô·rŏn′ ĭk)
mo·rose   (mô·rōs′)
  mo·rose·ly
mor·phine   (mŏr′ fēn)
mor·phol·o·gy (mŏr·fŏl′ ô·jĭ)
  mor·pho·log·i·cal
    (mŏr′ fô·lŏj′ ĭ·kǎl)
Mor·ris chair (mŏr′ ĭs)
mor·row   (mŏr′ ō)
Morse code (mŏrs)
mor·sel   (mŏr′ sěl)
mor·tal   (mŏr′ tǎl)
  mor·tal·i·ty (mŏr·tǎl′ ĭ·tĭ)
  mor·tal·ly
mor·tar   (mŏr′ tēr)
  mor·tar·board
mort·gage   (mŏr′ gǐj)
  -gag·ing
  mort·ga·gee (mŏr′ gǐ·jē′)
  mort·ga·gor
mor·ti·cian (mŏr·tĭsh′ đn)
mor·ti·fy   (mŏr′ tĭ·fĭ)
  -fied -fy·ing
  mor·ti·fi·ca·tion
    (mŏr′ tĭ·fĭ·kā′ shŭn)
mor·tise   (mŏr′ tĭs)
mor·tu·ar·y (mŏr′ tû·ěr′ ĭ)
  -ar·ies
mo·sa·ic   (mô·zā′ ĭk)

Mo·selle wine   (mô·zĕl′)
Mo·ses   (mō′ zĭz)
   Mo·sa·ic law   (mô·zā′ ĭk)
mo·sey   (mō′ zĭ)
   -sey·ing
Mos·lem   (mŏz′ lĕm)
mosque   (mŏsk)
mos·qui·to   (mŭs·kē′ tō)
   -toes
moss   (môs)
most·ly   (mōst′ lĭ)
mote   (mōt)
   (particle; see *moat*)
mo·tel   (mō·tĕl′)
mo·tet   (mō·tĕt′)
moth ball   (môth bôl)
moth·eat·en   (môth′ ēt′ 'n)
moth·er   (mŭth′ ĕr)
   Mother Goose   moth·er·hood
   moth·er-in-law   moth·ers-in-law
   moth·er·land
   moth·er·ly   -li·ness
   moth·er-of-pearl
   Moth·er's Day
   moth·er tongue
mo·tif   (mō·tēf′)
mo·tile   (mō′ tĭl)
   mo·til·i·ty   (mō·tĭl′ ĭ·tĭ)
mo·tion   (mō′ shŭn)
   mo·tion·less   mo·tion pic·ture
   mo·tion-pic·ture pro·jec·tor
mo·ti·vate   (mō′ tĭ·vāt)
   -vat·ing
   mo·ti·va·tion   (mō′ tĭ·vā′ shŭn)
mo·tive   (mō′ tĭv)
mot·ley   (mŏt′ lĭ)
mo·tor   (mō′ tĕr)
   mo·tor·boat   mo·tor·cade
   mo·tor·cy·cle   -cy·clist
   mo·tor-driv·en   mo·tor·drome
   mo·tor·ist   mo·tor·ized
   mo·tor·man
mot·tled   (mŏt′ 'ld)
mot·to   (mŏt′ ō)
   mot·toes
mound   (mound)
mount   (mount)
   mount·a·ble
moun·tain   (moun′ tĭn)
   moun·tain·eer   (moun′ tĭ·nēr′)
   moun·tain lau·rel
   moun·tain·ous   (moun′ tĭ·nŭs)
   moun·tain·side
moun·te·bank   (moun′ tē·băngk)

mourn·ful   (môrn′ fōōl)
   -ful·ly   -ful·ness
mourn·ing   (môrn′ ĭng)
   (lamentation; see *morning*)
   mourn·ing dove
mouse   (mous)
   pl. mice   (mĭs)
mousse   (mōōs)
mousse·line de soie
           (mōōs′ lēn′ dē swä′)
mous·y   (mous′ ĭ)
   mous·i·ness
mouth   (mouth)
   mouth·ful   -fuls
   mouth or·gan   mouth·piece
mou·ton coat   (mōō′ tŏn)
move   (mōōv)
   mov·ing
   mov·a·bil·i·ty
           (mōōv·à·bĭl′ ĭ·tĭ)
   mov·a·ble   (mōōv′ á·b'l)
   move·ment
mov·ie   (mōōv′ ĭ)
   mov·ing pic·ture
mow·er   (mō′ ĕr)
Mo·zam·bique,   (mō′ zăm·bēk′)
   Afr.
mu·ci·lage   (mū′ sĭ·lĭj)
   mu·ci·lag·i·nous
           (mū′ sĭ·lăj′ ĭ·nŭs)
muck·rak·er   (mŭk′ răk′ ĕr)
mu·cous mem·brane
           (mū′ kŭs)
mud·dle   (mŭd′ 'l)
   mud·dling
   mud·dle-head·ed
mud·dy   (mŭd′ ĭ)
   mud·di·ness
mud·guard   (mŭd′ gärd′)
mud·sling·er   (mŭd′ slĭng′ ĕr)
muff   (mŭf)
muf·fin   (mŭf′ ĭn)
muf·fle   (mŭf′ 'l)
   muf·fling   muf·fler
muf·ti   (mŭf′ tĭ)
mug·gy   (mŭg′ ĭ)
   mug·gi·ness
mug·wump   (mŭg′ wŭmp′)
muk·luk   (mŭk′ lŭk)
mu·lat·to   (mù·lăt′ ō)
   -lat·toes
mul·ber·ry   (mŭl′ bĕr′ ĭ)
   -ber·ries
mulch   (mŭlch)
mulct   (mŭlkt)

mule (mūl)
  mule skin·ner
  mu·le·teer (mū' lĕ·tẽr')
  mul·ish
mulled ci·der (mŭld)
mul·let (mŭl' ĕt)
mul·ti·far·i·ous (mŭl' tĭ·fâr' ĭ·ŭs)
mul·ti·fold (mŭl' tĭ·fōld)
Mul·ti·graph (mŭl' tĭ·gráf)
mul·ti·lat·er·al
        (mŭl' tĭ·lăt' ẽr·ăl)
  -al·ly
mul·ti·lin·e·ar (mŭl' tĭ·lĭn' ē·ẽr)
mul·ti·mil·lion·aire
        (mŭl' tĭ·mĭl' yŭn·âr')
mul·ti·par·tite (mŭl' tĭ·pär' tīt)
mul·ti·ple (mŭl' tĭ·p'l)
  mul·ti·ple scle·ro·sis
  mul·ti·pli·ci·ty
        (mŭl' tĭ·plĭs' ĭ·tĭ)
mul·ti·ply (mŭl' tĭ·plī)
  -plied   -ply·ing
  mul·ti·pli·cand
        (mŭl' tĭ·plĭ·kănd')
  mul·ti·pli·ca·tion
        (mŭl' tĭ·plĭ·kā' shŭn)
  mul·ti·pli·er
mul·ti·tude (mŭl' tĭ·tūd)
  mul·ti·tu·di·nous
        (mŭl' tĭ·tū' dĭ·nŭs)
mum·ble (mŭm' b'l)
  -bling
mum·bo jum·bo
        (mŭm' bō jŭm' bō)
mum·mer (mŭm' ẽr)
mum·mi·fy (mŭm' ĭ·fī)
  -fied   -fy·ing
  mum·mi·fi·ca·tion
        (mŭm' ĭ·fĭ·kā' shŭn)
mum·my (mŭm' ĭ)
  mum·mies
mumps (mŭmps)
mun·dane (mŭn' dān)
  mun·dane·ly
mu·nic·i·pal (mū·nĭs' ĭ·păl)
  mu·nic·i·pal·i·ty
        (mū·nĭs' ĭ·păl' ĭ·tĭ)
mu·nif·i·cent (mū·nĭf' ĭ·sĕnt)
  -cence
mu·ni·tions (mū·nĭsh' ŭnz)
mu·ral (mū' răl)
mur·der (mûr' dẽr)
  mur·der·er   mur·der·ess
  mur·der·ous (-ŭs)

murk·y (mûr' kĭ)
  murk·i·ness
mur·mur (mûr' mẽr)
  -mured   -mur·ing
mus·ca·tel (mŭs' kà·tĕl')
mus·cle (mŭs' 'l)
  (body tissue; see *mussel*)
  -cling   mus·cle-bound
mus·cu·lar (mŭs' kû·lẽr)
  mus·cu·lar dys·tro·phy
  mus·cu·lar·i·ty
        (mŭs' kû·lăr' ĭ·tĭ)
  mus·cu·la·ture
        (mŭs' kû·là·tûr)
muse (mūz)
  mus·ing
mu·sette bag (mū·zĕt')
mu·se·um (mū·zē' ŭm)
mush·room (mŭsh' rōōm)
mu·sic (mū' zĭk)
  mu·si·cal (mū' zĭ·kăl)
  -cal·ly
  mu·si·cale (mū' zĭ·kăl')
  mu·si·cian (mū·zĭsh' ăn)
musk deer (mŭsk)
mus·keg (mŭs' kĕg)
mus·kel·lunge (mŭs' kĕ·lŭnj)
mus·ket (mŭs' kĕt)
  mus·ket·eer (mŭs' kĕ·tẽr')
  mus·ket·ry
musk·mel·on (mŭsk' mĕl' ŭn)
musk ox (mŭsk)
musk·rat (mŭsk' răt')
mus·lin (mŭz' lĭn)
mus·sel (mŭs' 'l)
  (shellfish; see *muscle*)
mus·tache (mŭs·tàsh')
  mus·ta·chio (mŭs·tā' shō)
  -chioed
mus·tard (mŭs' tẽrd)
mus·ter (mŭs' tẽr)
mus·ty (mŭs' tĭ)
  mus·ti·ness
mu·ta·ble (mū' tà·b'l)
  mu·ta·bil·i·ty (mū' tà·bĭl' ĭ·tĭ)
mu·ti·late (mū' tĭ·lāt)
  -lat·ing
  mu·ti·la·tion (mū' tĭ·lā' shŭn)
  mu·ti·la·tor
mu·ti·ny (mū' tĭ·nĭ)
  -nies, -nied, -ny·ing
  mu·ti·neer (mū' tĭ·nẽr')
  mu·ti·nous
mutt (mŭt)
mut·ter (mŭt' ẽr)

mut·ton (mŭt′ 'n)
mu·tu·al (mū′ tụ̇· dl)
  -al·ly
  mu·tu·al·i·ty (mū′ tụ̇·ăl′ ĭ·tĭ)
muz·zle (mŭz′ 'l)
  muz·zling muz·zle-load·er
my·o·pi·a (mī·ō′ pĭ·ȧ)
  my·op·ic (mī·ŏp′ ĭk)
myr·i·ad (mĭr′ ĭ·dd)
myrrh (mûr)
myr·tle (mûr′ t'l)
my·self (mĭ·sĕlf′)
mys·te·ri·ous (mĭs·tēr′ ĭ·ŭs)
  mys·ter·y (mĭs′ tēr·ĭ)
  -ter·ies
mys·tic (mĭs′ tĭk)
  mys·ti·cal mys·ti·cism
mys·ti·fy (mĭs′ tĭ·fī)
  -fied -fy·ing
  mys·ti·fi·ca·tion
    (mĭs′ tĭ·fĭ·kā′ shŭn)
myth (mĭth)
  myth·i·cal myth·i·cal·ly
  myth·o·log·i·cal
    (mĭth′ ŏ·lŏj′ ĭ·kǎl)
  my·thol·o·gy (mĭ·thŏl′ ŏ·jĭ)
  -gies

N

na·dir (nā′ dēr)
nag·ging (năg′ ĭng)
na·ïve (nä·ēv′)
  na·ïve·ly
  na·ïve·té (nä·ēv′ tā′)
na·ked (nā′ kĕd)
  na·ked·ness
nam·by-pam·by
    (năm′ bĭ·păm′ bĭ)
name (nām)
  nam·ing nam·a·ble
  name·less name·ly
  name·sake
na·palm bomb (nä′ päm)
naph·tha (năf′ thȧ)
  naph·tha·lene (năf′ thȧ·lēn)
  naph·thol (năf′ thŏl)
nap·kin (năp′ kĭn)
Na·po·le·on Bo·na·parte
  (nȧ·pō′ lĕ·ŭn bō′ nȧ·pärt)
  Na·po·le·on·ic wars
    (nȧ·pō′ lĕ·ŏn′ ĭk)
nar·cis·sus (när·sĭs′ ŭs)
  nar·cis·sis·tic (när′ sĭ·sĭs′ tĭk)

nar·co·sis (när·kō′ sĭs)
nar·co·syn·the·sis
    (när′ kō·sĭn′ thē·sĭs)
nar·cot·ic (när·kŏt′ ĭk)
  nar·co·tize (när′ kō·tīz)
  tiz·ing
Nar·ra·gan·sett (bay)
    (năr′ ȧ·găn′ sĕt)
nar·rate (nă·rāt′)
  nar·rat·ing
  nar·ra·tion (nă·rā′ shŭn)
  nar·ra·tive (năr′ ȧ·tĭv)
  -tive·ly
  nar·ra·tor (nă·rā′ tēr)
nar·row (năr′ ō)
  nar·row-gauge
  nar·row-mind·ed
  nar·row·ness
na·sal (nā′ zǎl)
  na·sal·i·ty (nā·zăl′ ĭ·tĭ)
  na·sal·ize -iz·ing
  na·sal·ly
nas·cent (năs′ ĕnt)
Nas·sau (năs′ ô)
nas·tur·tium (năs·tûr′ shŭm)
nas·ty (năs′ tĭ)
  nas·ti·er, -ti·est, -ti·ly, -ti·ness
na·tal (nā′ tǎl)
na·ta·to·ri·um (nā′ tȧ·tō′ rĭ·ŭm)
na·tion (nā′ shŭn)
na·tion·al (năsh′ ŭn·ȧl)
  na·tion·al·ism
  na·tion·al·is·tic
    (năsh′ ŭn·ȧl·ĭs′ tĭk)
  na·tion·al·i·ty
    (năsh′ ŭn·ăl′ ĭ·tĭ)
  -ties
  na·tion·al·i·za·tion
    (năsh′ ŭn·ȧl·ĭ·zā′ shŭn)
  na·tion·al·ize (năsh′ ŭn·ȧl·īz)
  -iz·ing na·tion·al·ly
na·tive (nā′ tĭv)
  na·tive·ly
  na·tiv·is·tic (nā′ tĭv·ĭs′ tĭk)
na·tiv·i·ty (nȧ·tĭv′ ĭ·tĭ)
nat·ty (năt′ ĭ)
  nat·ti·ly
nat·u·ral (năt′ û·rǎl)
  nat·u·ral·ism nat·u·ral·ist
  nat·u·ral·is·tic
    (năt′ û·rǎl·ĭs′ tĭk)
  nat·u·ral·i·za·tion
    (năt′ û·rǎl·ĭ·zā′ shŭn)
  nat·u·ral·ize -iz·ing
  nat·u·ral·ly nat·u·ral·ness

na·ture (nā′ tŭr)
na·tur·o·path (nā′ tŭr·ŏ·păth′)
naugh·ty (nô′ tĭ)
  naugh·ti·er -ti·est
  -ti·ly -ti·ness
nau·se·a (nô′ shē·á)
  nau·se·ate (nô′ shē·āt)
  -at·ing
  nau·se·a·tion (nô′ shē·ā′ shŭn)
  nau·seous (nô′ shŭs)
nau·ti·cal (nô′ tĭ·kál)
nau·ti·lus (nô′ tĭ·lŭs)
na·val (nā′ vál)
  (of ships; see navel)
nave (nāv)
na·vel (nā′ věl)
  (umbilicus; see naval)
  na·vel or·ange
nav·i·gate (năv′ ĭ·gāt)
  -gat·ing
  nav·i·ga·bil·i·ty
      (năv′ ĭ·gá·bĭl′ ĭ·tĭ)
  nav·i·ga·ble (năv′ ĭ·gá·b′l)
  nav·i·ga·tion (năv′ ĭ·gā′ shŭn)
  -tion·al nav·i·ga·tor
na·vy (nā′ vĭ)
  -vies
Naz·a·rene (năz′ á·rēn′)
Na·zi (nä′ tsē)
  Na·zism (nä′ tsĭz′m)
Ne·an·der·thal man
      (nē·ăn′ dĕr·täl′)
Ne·a·pol·i·tan (nē′ á·pŏl′ ĭ·tăn)
neap tide (nēp)
near (nēr)
  near·by Near. East
  near·est near·ly
  near·ness
  near·sight·ed·ness
neat·ness (nēt′ něs)
neat's-foot oil (nēts′ fŏŏt′)
Ne·bras·ka (ně·brăs′ ká)
  abbr. Nebr., Neb.
  Ne·bras·kan
neb·u·la (něb′ û·lá)
  pl. neb·u·lae (-lē)
  neb·u·lar (-lĕr)
neb·u·lous (něb′ û·lŭs)
nec·es·sar·y (něs′ ě·sěr′ ĭ)
  nec·es·sar·i·ly (něs′ ě·sěr′ ĭ·lĭ)
  ne·ces·si·tate (ně·sěs′ ĭ·tāt)
  -tat·ing
  ne·ces·si·tous (ně·sěs′ ĭ·tŭs)
  ne·ces·si·ty (ně·sěs′ ĭ·tĭ)
  -ties

neck·er·chief (něk′ ēr·chĭf)
neck·lace (něk′ lĭs)
neck·tie (něk′ tī′)
ne·crol·o·gy (ně·krŏl′ ŏ·jĭ)
nec·ro·man·cy (něk′ rŏ·măn′ sĭ)
nec·tar (něk′ tēr)
nec·tar·ine (něk′ tēr·ēn′)
need (nēd)
  need·ful need·i·est
  need·less -less·ly
  need·y
nee·dle (nē′ d′l)
  nee·dle-point lace
  nee·dle·work
ne′er-do-well (nâr′ dŏŏ·wěl′)
ne·far·i·ous (ně·fâr′ ĭ·ŭs)
ne·gate (ně·gāt′)
  -gat·ing
  ne·ga·tion (ně·gā′ shŭn)
neg·a·tive (něg′ á·tĭv)
  neg·a·tive·ly neg·a·tiv·ism
neg·lect (něg·lěkt′)
  neg·lect·ful, -ful·ly, -ful·ness
neg·li·gee (něg′ lĭ·zhā′)
neg·li·gent (něg′ lĭ·jěnt)
  -gence
neg·li·gi·ble (něg′ lĭ·jĭ·b′l)
  neg·li·gi·bil·i·ty
      (něg′ lĭ·jĭ·bĭl′ ĭ·tĭ)
ne·go·ti·ate (ně·gō′ shĭ·āt)
  -at·ing
  ne·go·ti·a·bil·i·ty
      (ně·gō′ shĭ·á·bĭl′ ĭ·tĭ)
  ne·go·ti·a·ble
      (ně·gō′ shĭ·á·b′l)
  ne·go·ti·a·tion
      (ně·gō′ shĭ·ā′ shŭn)
  ne·go·ti·a·tor
Ne·gro (nē′ grō)
  -groes Ne·groid
Neh·ru, Ja·wa·har·lal
      (nā′ rŏŏ, já·wä′ hár·lăl)
neigh (nā)
neigh·bor (nā′ bĕr)
  neigh·bor·hood
  neigh·bor·ly -li·ness
nei·ther (nē′ thēr)
nem·a·tode (něm′ á·tŏd)
nem·e·sis (něm′ ě·sĭs)
  pl. nem·e·ses
ne·o- (nē′ ŏ)
  ne·o-Cath·o·lic
  ne·o·clas·sic ne·o-Goth·ic
  ne·o-Hel·len·ic
  ne·o·im·pres·sion·ism

ne·o·lith·ic   ne·o·phyte

ne·o·plasm   Ne·o·pla·ton·ic

ne·o·prene

Ne·o-Scho·las·tic

Ne·o·zo·ic

neph·ew (nĕf′ ū)

ne·phri·tis (nĕ·frī′ tĭs)

   ne·phrit·ic (nĕ·frĭt′ ĭk)

nep·o·tism (nĕp′ ŏ·tĭz′m)

Nep·tune (nĕp′ tūn)

nerve (nûrv)

   nerve·less   nerve-rack·ing

   nerv·ous   nerv·ous·ness

   nerv·y

nes·tle (nĕs′ ′l)

   -tling

neth·er·most (nĕth′ ĕr·mōst)

net·ting (nĕt′ ĭng)

net·tle (nĕt′ ′l)

net·work (nĕt′ wûrk′)

neu·ral·gia (nū·răl′ já)

neu·ras·the·ni·a

     (nū′ răs·thē′ nĭ·á)

neu·ri·tic (nū·rĭt′ ĭk)

   neu·ri·tis (nū·rī′ tĭs)

neu·rol·o·gy (nū·rŏl′ ŏ·jĭ)

   neu·ro·log·i·cal

     (nū′ rŏ·lŏj′ ĭ·kál)

neu·ro·psy·cho·sis

     (nū′ rŏ·sī·kō′ sĭs)

neu·ro·sis (nū·rŏ′ sĭs)

   pl. neu·ro·ses (-sēz)

neu·rot·ic (nū·rŏt′ ĭk)

neu·ter (nū′ tĕr)

neu·tral (nū′ trăl)

   neu·tral·i·ty (nū·trăl′ ĭ·tĭ)

   neu·tral·i·za·tion

     (nū′ trăl·ĭ·zā′ shŭn)

   neu·tral·ize   -iz·ing

   neu·tral·iz·er

neu·tron (nū′ trŏn)

Ne·va·da (nĕ·văd′ á)

   abbr. Nev.   Ne·va·dan

nev·er·the·less (nĕv′ ĕr·thĕ·lĕs′)

new (nū)

   new·born   new·com·er

   new·fan·gled   new-fash·ioned

   new·ly-wed   new·ness

new·el (nū′ ĕl)

New·found·land

     (nū′ fŭnd·lănd′)

New Guin·ea (nū gĭn′ ĭ)

New Hamp·shire

     (nū hăm(p)′ shēr)

   abbr. N.H.

New Heb·ri·des (nū hĕb′ rĭ·dēz)

New Jer·sey (nū jûr′ zĭ)

   abbr. N.J.   New Jer·sey·ite

New Mex·i·co (nū mĕk′ sĭ·kō)

   abbr. N. Mex.   New Mex·i·can

news (nūz)

   news·cast·er   news·let·ter

   news·man

   news·pa·per·man

   news·print   news·reel

   news·stand   news·y

New York (nū yôrk′)

   abbr. N.Y.

New Zea·land (nū zē′ lánd)

   abbr. N.Z.

nex·us (nĕk′ sŭs)

ni·a·cin (nī′ á·sĭn)

Ni·ag·a·ra (nī·ăg′ á·rá)

nib·ble (nĭb′ ′l)

   nib·bling

Nic·a·ra·gua (nĭk′ á·rä′ gwä)

Ni·cene (creed) (nī·sēn′)

ni·ce·ty (nī′ sĕ·tĭ)

   -ties

niche (nĭch)

nick·el (nĭk′ ĕl)

nick·el·o·de·on (nĭk′ ĕl·ŏ′ dē·ŭn)

nick·name (nĭk′ năm′)

nic·o·tine (nĭk′ ŏ·tēn)

nic·o·tin·ic ac·id

     (nĭk′ ŏ·tĭn′ ĭk)

niece (nēs)

Ni·ge·ri·a, Afr. (nī·jēr′ ĭ·á)

nig·gard·ly (nĭg′ ĕrd·lĭ)

nig·gling (nĭg′ ′lĭng)

nigh (nī)

night (nīt)

   night blind·ness

   night·cap   night club

   night crawl·er   night·fall

   night·gown   night·hawk

   night·in·gale   night·latch

   night·long   night·mare

   night owl   night·shade

   night·shirt   night·time

   night·wear

night·in·gale (nīt′ ĭn·gāl)

ni·hil·ism (nī′ ĭ·lĭz′m)

   ni·hil·ist (nī′ ĭ·lĭst)

Ni·ke mis·sile (nī′ kē)

nil (nĭl)

nim·ble (nĭm′ b′l)

   nim·ble·ness   nim·bly

nim·bus (nĭm′ bŭs)

nine (nīn)
  nine·fold   nine·pins
  ninth
nine·teen (nīn' tēn')
nine·ty (nīn' tĭ)
  -ties   nine·ti·eth
  nine·ty·fold
nip·ple (nĭp' 'l)
Nip·pon·ese (nĭp' ŏ·nēz')
nip·py (nĭp' ĭ)
  nip·pi·ness
nir·va·na (nĭr·vä' nà)
ni·sei (nē' sā')
  n. sing. & pl.
ni·trate (nī' trāt)
ni·tric ac·id (nī' trĭk)
ni·tride (nī' trĭd)
ni·tri·fy (nī' trĭ·fī)
  -fied   -fy·ing
ni·trite (nī' trīt)
ni·tro·gen (nī' trŏ·jĕn)
  ni·tro·gen·ize (nī' trŏ·jĕn·īz)
  ni·trog·e·nous (nī·trŏj' ĕ·nŭs)
ni·tro·glyc·er·in (nī' trŏ·glĭs' ĕr·ĭn)
ni·trous ox·ide (nī' trŭs)
nit·wit (nĭt' wĭt')
No·bel prize (nō· bĕl')
no·ble (nō' b'l)
  no·bil·i·ty (nō·bĭl' ĭ·tĭ)
  no·ble·man   no·ble·ness
  no·bly
no·blesse o·blige
        (nō' blĕs' ŏ' blēzh')
no·bod·y (nō' bŏd·ĭ)
noc·tur·nal (nŏk·tûr' năl)
  -nal·ly
noc·turne (nŏk' tûrn)
noc·u·ous (nŏk' ů·ŭs)
node (nōd)
nod·ule (nŏd' ūl)
no·el (nō·ĕl')
nog·gin (nŏg' ĭn)
noise (noiz)
  noise·less   noise·mak·er
  nois·y   nois·i·er
  -i·est, -i·ly, -i·ness
noi·some (noi' sŭm)
no·mad (nō' măd)
  no·mad·ic (nō·măd' ĭk)
nom de plume (nŏm' dē plōōm')
no·men·cla·ture
        (nō' mĕn·klā' tūr)
nom·i·nal (nŏm' ĭ·năl)
  -nal·ly

nom·i·nate (nŏm' ĭ·nāt)
  -nat·ing
  nom·i·na·tion
        (nŏm' ĭ·nā' shŭn)
  nom·i·na·tor
  nom·i·nee (nŏm' ĭ·nē')
nom·i·na·tive (nŏm' ĭ·ná·tĭv)
non- (nŏn)
  non·ab·sorb·ent
  non·ac·cept·ance
  non·ag·gres·sive
  non·al·co·hol·ic
  non-Ar·y·an
  non·be·liev·er
  non·bel·lig·er·ent
  non·bloom·ing
  non·cha·lance
  non-Chris·tian
  non·co·er·cive
  non·com·bat·ant
  non·com·bus·ti·ble
  non·com·mis·sioned
  non·com·mit·tal
  non·com·mu·nist
  non·com·pet·i·tive
  non·com·pli·ance
  non·con·duc·tor
  non·con·form·ist
  non·con·tro·ver·sial
  non·cor·ro·sive
  non·de·script
  non·e·lec·tive
  non·en·ti·ty
  non·es·sen·tial
  non·ex·ist·ence
  non·fea·sance
  non·fic·tion
  non·in·ter·ven·tion
  non·ir·ri·tant
  non·mem·ber
  non·me·tal·lic
  non·ob·jec·tive
  non·par·ti·san
  non·pay·ment
  non·pro·duc·tive
  non·prof·it
  non·rec·og·ni·tion
  non·re·cur·ring
  non·re·new·a·ble
  non·res·i·dent, -den·tial
  non·re·stric·tive
  non·sec·tar·i·an
  non·stra·te·gic
  non·tech·ni·cal
  non·tox·ic

non·trans·fer·a·ble

non·typ·i·cal

non·vi·o·lence

non·cha·lant   (nŏn' shȧ·lŏnt')
  -lance

non·pa·reil   (nŏn' pȧ·rĕl')

non·plus   (nŏn' plŭs')
  -plused   -plus·ing

non·sense   (nŏn' sĕns)
  -sen·si·cal

non se·qui·tur   (nŏn sĕk' wĭ·tẽr)

noo·dle   (nōō' d'l)

no one   (nō' wŭn')

noose   (nōōs)

norm   (nôrm)

nor·mal   (nôr' mȧl)
  nor·mal·cy
  nor·mal·i·ty   (nôr·măl' ĭ·tĭ)
  nor·mal·ly

nor·ma·tive   (nôr' mȧ·tĭv)

Norse·man   (nôrs' mȧn)

north   (nôrth)
  north·east   north·east·er·ly
  north·er·ly   north·ern·er
  north·ern lights
  north·ern·most
  north·land   North Pole
  north·ward
  north·west·er·ly

North Car·o·li·na
                      (nôrth kăr' ō·lī' nȧ)
  abbr. N.C.   N. Car.
  North Car·o·lin·i·an
                      (-kăr' ō·lĭn' ĭ·ăn)

North Da·ko·ta   (nôrth dȧ·kō' tȧ)
  abbr. N. Dak.
  North Da·ko·tan

Nor·we·gian   (nôr·wē' jȧn)

nose   (nōz)
  nose·bleed   nose dive
  nose-dive *v.*   nose·gay
  nose·piece   nos·y

nos·tal·gi·a   (nŏs·tăl' jĭ·ȧ)
  nos·tal·gic

nos·tril   (nŏs' trĭl)

nos·trum   (nŏs' trŭm)

no·ta·ble   (nō' tȧ·b'l)
  no·ta·bil·i·ty   (nō' tȧ·bĭl' ĭ·tĭ)

no·ta·ry   (nō' tȧ·rĭ)
  -ries   no·ta·ry pub·lic
  no·ta·rize   (nō' tȧ·rīz)
  -riz·ing

no·ta·tion   (nō·tā' shŭn)
  no·ta·tion·al

notch   (nŏch)

note·book   (nōt' bŏŏk')

note·wor·thy   (nōt' wŭr' thĭ)

no·tice   (nō' tĭs)
  -tic·ing   no·tice·a·ble

no·ti·fy   (nō' tĭ·fī)
  -fied   -fy·ing

no·ti·fi·ca·tion
                      (nō' tĭ·fĭ·kā' shŭn)
  no·ti·fi·er

no·tion   (nō' shŭn)

no·to·ri·e·ty   (nō' tō·rī' ĕ·tĭ)

no·to·ri·ous   (nō·tō' rĭ·ŭs)

No·tre Dame, U. of
                      (nō' tẽr dām')

no-trump   (nō' trŭmp')

not·with·stand·ing
                      (nŏt' wĭth·stăn' dĭng)

nou·gat   (nōō' gȧt)

nought   (nôt)

noun   (noun)

nour·ish   (nûr' ĭsh)
  nour·ish·ment

No·va Sco·tia   (nō' vȧ skō' shȧ)

nov·el   (nŏv' ĕl)
  nov·el·ette   (nŏv' ĕl·ĕt')
  nov·el·ist
  no·vel·la   (nō·vĕl' lä)
  nov·el·ty   -ties

No·vem·ber   (nō·vĕm' bẽr)

no·ve·na   (nō·vē' nȧ)
  pl. no·ve·nae   (-nē)

nov·ice   (nŏv' ĭs)
  no·vi·ti·ate   (nō·vĭsh' ĭ·ȧt)

No·vo·cain   (nō' vō·kān)

now·a·days   (nou' ȧ·dāz')

no·where   (nō' hwâr)

nox·ious   (nŏk' shŭs)

noz·zle   (nŏz' 'l)

nth de·gree   (ĕnth)

nu·ance   (nū·äns')

nub·bin   (nŭb' ĭn)

nu·bile   (nū' bĭl)
  nu·bil·i·ty   (nū·bĭl' ĭ·tĭ)

nu·cle·ar   (nū' klē·ẽr)
  nu·cle·ar en·er·gy
  nu·cle·ar fis·sion
  nu·cle·ar phys·ics

nu·cle·on   (nū' klē·ŏn)

nu·cle·us   (nū' klē·ŭs)
  pl. nu·cle·i   (-ī)

nude   (nūd)
  nud·ism   nud·ist
  nu·di·ty

nug·get   (nŭg' ĕt)

nui·sance   (nū' sȧns)

null	(nŭl)		
(and void)		**O**	
nul·li·fi·ca·tion			
	(nŭl′ ĭ·fĭ·kā′ shŭn)	oaf·ish	(ōf′ ĭsh)
nul·li·fy	(nŭl′ ĭ·fī)	O·a·hu is., Ha·wai·i	
-fied	-fy·ing		(ō·ä′ hōō)
nul·li·ty	(nŭl′ ĭ·tĭ)	oak·en	(ōk′ ĕn)
numb	(nŭm)	oars·man	(ōrz′ mǎn)
numb·ly	numb·ness	o·a·sis	(ō·ā′ sĭs)
num·ber	(nŭm′ bēr)	pl. o·a·ses	(-sēz)
num·ber·less		oath	(ōth)
nu·mer·a·ble	(nū′ mĕr·à·b′l)	oat·meal	(ōt′ mēl′)
nu·mer·al	(nū′ mĕr·ǎl)	ob·bli·ga·to	(ŏb′ lĭ·gä′ tō)
nu·mer·ate	(nū′ mĕr·āt)	ob·du·rate	(ŏb′ dû·rāt)
-at·ing		ob·du·ra·cy	
nu·mer·a·tion		o·be·di·ent	(ō·bē′ dĭ·ĕnt)
	(nū·mĕr·ā′ shŭn)	-ence	
nu·mer·i·cal	(nú·mĕr′ ĭ·kǎl)	o·bei·sance	(ō·bā′ sǎns)
-cal·ly		ob·e·lisk	(ŏb′ ĕ·lĭsk)
nu·mer·ol·o·gy	(nū′ mĕr·ŏl′ ō·jĭ)	o·bese	(ō·bēs′)
nu·mer·ous	(nū′ mĕr·ŭs)	o·bes·i·ty	(ō·bēs′ ĭ·tĭ)
nu·mis·mat·ics	(nū′ mĭz·mǎt′ ĭks)	o·bey	(ō·bā′)
num·skull	(nŭm′ skŭl′)	-beyed	-bey·ing
nun	(nŭn)	ob·fus·cate	(ŏb·fŭs′ kāt)
nun·nery		-cat·ing	
nun·ci·o	(nŭn′ shĭ·ō)	ob·fus·ca·tion	
nup·tial	(nŭp′ shǎl)		(ŏb′ fŭs·kā′ shŭn)
nurse	(nûrs)	o·bit·u·ar·y	(ō·bĭt′ û·ĕr′ ĭ)
nurs·ing	nurse·maid	-ar·ies	
nurs·er·y	(nûr′ sēr·ĭ)	ob·ject	(ŏb′ jĕkt) n.
-er·ies		ob·ject	(ŏb·jĕkt′) v.
nurs·er·y rhyme		ob·jec·ti·fy	(ŏb·jĕk′ tĭ·fī)
nur·ture	(nûr′ tûr)	-fied	
-tur·ing		ob·jec·tion	(ŏb·jĕk′ shŭn)
nut·crack·er	(nŭt′ krǎk′ ēr)	ob·jec·tion·a·ble	
nut·hatch	(nŭt′ hǎch′)	ob·jec·tive	-tive·ly
nut·meg	(nŭt′ mĕg)	ob·jec·tiv·ism	
nu·tri·a	(nū′ trĭ·à)	ob·jec·tiv·i·ty	(ŏb′ jĕk·tĭv′ ĭ·tĭ)
nu·tri·ent	(nū′ trĭ·ĕnt)	ob·jec·tor	
nu·tri·ment	(nū′ trĭ·mĕnt)	ob·jet d′art	(ŏb′ zhĕ′ dár′)
nu·tri·tion	(nū·trĭsh′ ŭn)	ob·jets d′art	(ŏb′ zhĕ′ dár′)
nu·tri·tion·al	(nū·trĭsh′ ŭn·ǎl)	ob·late	(ŏb′ lāt)
-al·ly		ob·la·tion	(ŏb·lā′ shŭn)
nu·tri·tious	(nū·trĭsh′ ŭs)	ob·li·gate	(ŏb′ lĭ·gāt)
nu·tri·tive	(nū′ trĭ·tĭv)	-gat·ing	
nut·shell	(nŭt′ shĕl′)	ob·li·ga·tion	(ŏb′ lĭ·gā′ shŭn)
nuz·zle	(nŭz′ ′l)	ob·lig·a·to·ry	(ŏb·lĭg′ à·tō′ rĭ)
nuz·zling		o·blige	(ō·blīj′)
Ny·as·a·land, Āfr.		-blig·ing	
	(nĭ·ǎs′ à·lǎnd′)	o·blique	(ŏb·lēk′)
ny·lon	(nī′ lŏn)	-blique·ly	
nymph	(nĭmf)	ob·lit·er·ate	(ŏb·lĭt′ ĕr·āt)
nym·pho·ma·ni·ac		-at·ing	
	(nĭm′ fō·mā′ nĭ·ǎk)	ob·lit·er·a·tion	
			(ŏb·lĭt′ ĕr·ā′ shŭn)

ob·liv·i·on   (ŏb·lĭv′ ĭ·ŭn)
   ob·liv·i·ous   (ŏb·lĭv′ ĭ·ŭs)
ob·long   (ŏb′ lŏng)
ob·lo·quy   (ŏb′ lŏ·kwĭ)
   -quies
ob·nox·ious   (ŏb·nŏk′ shŭs)
o·boe   (ō′ bō)
   o·bo·ist
ob·scene   (ŏb·sēn′)
   -scene·ly
   ob·scen·i·ty   (ŏb·sĕn′ ĭ·tĭ)
   -ties
ob·scur·ant·ism
           (ŏb·skūr′ ăn·tĭz′m)
ob·scure   (ŏb·skūr′)
   ob·scu·ri·ty   (ŏb·skū′ rĭ·tĭ)
ob·se·qui·ous   (ŏb·sē′ kwĭ·ŭs)
ob·se·quies   (ŏb′ sē·kwĭz)
ob·serve   (ŏb·zûrv′)
   -serv·ing   ob·serv·a·ble
   ob·serv·ant   -ance
   ob·ser·va·tion
           (ŏb′ zēr·vā′ shŭn)
   -tion·al
   ob·serv·a·to·ry
           (ŏb·zûr′ vá·tō′ rĭ)
   -ries   ob·serv·er
ob·sess   (ŏb·sĕs′)
   ob·ses·sion   ob·ses·sive
ob·sid·i·an   (ŏb·sĭd′ ĭ·ăn)
ob·so·lete   (ŏb′ sŏ·lēt)
   ob·so·les·cent   (ŏb′ sŏ·lĕs′ ĕnt)
   -cence
ob·sta·cle   (ŏb′ stá·k′l)
ob·stet·rics   (ŏb·stĕt′ rĭks)
   ob·stet·ri·cal   (ŏb·stĕt′ rĭ·kăl)
   ob·ste·tri·cian
           (ŏb′ stĕ·trĭsh′ ăn)
ob·sti·nate   (ŏb′ stĭ·nĭt)
   ob·sti·na·cy   (-ná·sĭ)
   ob·sti·nate·ly
ob·strep·er·ous
           (ŏb·strĕp′ ĕr·ŭs)
ob·struct   (ŏb·strŭkt′)
   ob·struct·er   ob·struc·tion
   ob·struc·tion·ist
ob·tain   (ŏb·tān′)
   ob·tain·a·ble
ob·trude   (ŏb·trōōd′)
   -trud·ing
   ob·tru·sion   (ŏb·trōō′ zhŭn)
   ob·tru·sive   (ŏb·trōō′ sĭv)
   -sive·ness
ob·tuse   (ŏb·tūs′)
   -tuse·ness

ob·verse   (ŏb·vûrs′)
   ob·verse·ly   ob·ver·sion
ob·vi·ate   (ŏb′ vĭ·āt)
   -at·ing
ob·vi·ous   (ŏb′ vĭ·ŭs)
oc·a·ri·na   (ŏk′ á·rē′ ná)
oc·ca·sion   (ŏ·kā′ zhŭn)
   oc·ca·sion·al   -al·ly
oc·ci·dent   (ŏk′ sĭ·děnt)
   oc·ci·den·tal   (ŏk′ sĭ·děn′ tăl)
oc·cip·i·tal   (ŏk·sĭp′ ĭ·tăl)
oc·clude   (ŏ·klōōd′)
   oc·clud·ing
   oc·clu·sion   (ŏ·klōō′ zhŭn)
oc·cult   (ŏ·kŭlt′)
   oc·cult·ism
oc·cu·pant   (ŏk′ ŭ·pănt)
   -pan·cy
oc·cu·pa·tion   (ŏk′ ŭ·pā′ shŭn)
   oc·cu·pa·tion·al, -al·ly
oc·cu·py   (ŏk′ ŭ·pĭ)
   -pied   -py·ing
oc·cur   (ŏ·kûr′)
   oc·curred   oc·cur·ring
   oc·cur·rence
o·cean   (ō′ shăn)
   o·ce·an·ic   (ō′ shē·ăn′ ĭk)
o·ce·a·nog·ra·phy
           (ō′ shē·á·nŏg′ rá·fĭ)
o·ce·lot   (ō′ sē·lŏt)
o·cher   (ō′ kēr)
o′clock   (ŏ·klŏk′)
oc·ta·gon   (ŏk′ tá·gŏn)
   oc·tag·o·nal   (ŏk·tăg′ ŏ·năl)
   -nal·ly
oc·ta·he·dron   (ŏk′ tá·hē′ drŭn)
oc·tane   (ŏk′ tān)
oc·tave   (ŏk′ tāv)
oc·tet   (ŏk·tĕt′)
Oc·to·ber   (ŏk·tō′ bēr)
oc·to·ge·nar·i·an
           (ŏk′ tŏ·jê·nâr′ ĭ·ăn)
oc·to·pus   (ŏk′ tŏ·pŭs)
   -pus·es
oc·to·roon   (ŏk′ tŏ·rōōn′)
oc·u·lar   (ŏk′ ŭ·lēr)
oc·u·list   (ŏk′ ŭ·lĭst)
odd   (ŏd)
   odd·i·ty   (ŏd′ ĭ·tĭ)
   odd·ly   odd·ment
   odds and ends
ode   (ŏd)
o·di·ous   (ō′ dĭ·ŭs)
   o·di·um   (ō′ dĭ·ŭm)
o·dom·e·ter   (ŏ·dŏm′ ê·tēr)

o·dor (ō′ dĕr)
  o·dor·if·er·ous
      (ō′ dĕr·ĭf′ ĕr·ŭs)
  o·dor·less
  o·dor·ous (ō′ dĕr·ŭs)
od·ys·sey (ŏd′ ĭ·sĭ)
Oed·i·pus com·plex
      (ĕd′ ĭ·pŭs)
oes·trus (ĕs′ trŭs)
off (ŏf)
  off and on   off·cast
  off-chance   off-col·or
  off·hand   off·ing
  off·set   off·set·ting
  off·shoot   off·shore
  off·side   off·spring
of·fal (ŏf′ ăl)
of·fend (ō·fĕnd′)
  of·fend·er
of·fense (ō·fĕns′)
  of·fen·sive -sive·ly
of·fer (ŏf′ ĕr)
  of·fer·ing
of·fer·to·ry (ŏf′ ĕr·tō′ rĭ)
of·fice (ŏf′ ĭs)
  of·fice boy
  of·fice·hold·er (ŏf′ ĭs·hōl′ dĕr)
  of·fi·cer (ŏf′ ĭ·sĕr)
of·fi·cial (ō·fĭsh′ ăl)
  of·fi·cial·dom of·fi·cial·ly
of·fi·ci·ate (ō·fĭsh′ ĭ·āt)
  -at·ing
  of·fi·ci·a·tion
      (ō·fĭsh′ ĭ·ā′ shŭn)
  of·fi·ci·a·tor
of·fi·cious (ō·fĭsh′ ŭs)
of·ten (ŏf′ ĕn)
  of·ten·er   of·ten·est
  of·ten·times
o·gre (ō′ gĕr)
  o·gre·ish (ō′ gĕr·ĭsh)
O·hi·o (ō·hī′ ō)
  abbr. O.   O·hi·o·an
ohm (ōm)
oil·skin (oil′ skĭn′)
oil·y (oil′ ĭ)
  oil·i·ness
oint·ment (oint′ mĕnt)
O.K. (ō′ kā′)
  (also okay) O.K.′ d
  O·K.′ ing
O·ki·na·wa Is. (ō′ kĭ·nä′ wä)
O·kla·ho·ma (ō′ klä·hō′ mä)
  abbr. Okla. O·kla·ho·man
o·kra (ō′ krä)

old (ōld)
  old coun·try old-fash·ioned
  old-fo·gy·ish Old Glo·ry
  old maid·ish
  Old Tes·ta·ment
  old-tim·er   old wives′ tale
  old-world adj.
old·ster (ōld′ stĕr)
o·le·ag·i·nous (ō′ lē·ăj′ ĭ·nŭs)
o·le·an·der (ō′ lē·ăn′ dĕr)
o·le·o·mar·ga·rine
      (ō′ lē·ō·mär′ jă·rĭn)
ol·fac·to·ry (ŏl·făk′ tō·rĭ)
ol·i·garch (ŏl′ ĭ·gärk)
  ol·i·gar·chic (ŏl′ ĭ·gär′ kĭk)
  -chi·cal
  ol·i·garch·y (ŏl′ ĭ·gär′ kĭ)
  -chies
O·lym·pic (ō·lĭm′ pĭk)
  O·lym·pi·an
o·me·ga (ō·mē′ gä)
om·e·let (ŏm′ ĕ·lĕt)
o·men (ō′ mĕn)
om·i·nous (ŏm′ ĭ·nŭs)
o·mis·sion (ō·mĭsh′ ŭn)
o·mit (ō·mĭt′)
  -mit·ted   -mit·ting
om·ni·bus (ŏm′ nĭ·bŭs)
om·nip·o·tent (ŏm·nĭp′ ō·tĕnt)
  -tence
om·ni·pres·ent (ŏm′ nĭ·prĕz′ ĕnt)
om·nis·cient (ŏm·nĭsh′ ĕnt)
  -cience
om·niv·o·rous (ŏm·nĭv′ ō·rŭs)
once (wŭns)
on·com·ing (ŏn′ kŭm′ ĭng)
one (wŭn)
  one-horse town one·self
  one-sid·ed   one·time
  one-track mind one-way street
on·er·ous (ŏn′ ĕr·ŭs)
on·ion·skin (ŭn′ yŭn·skĭn′)
on·look·er (ŏn′ lŏŏk′ ĕr)
on·ly (ŏn′ lĭ)
on·o·mat·o·poe·ia
      (ŏn′ ō·măt′ ō·pē′ yä)
on·set (ŏn′ sĕt′)
on·slaught (ŏn′ slôt′)
on·to (ŏn′ tōō)
on·tol·o·gy (ŏn·tŏl′ ō·jĭ)
  on·to·log·i·cal (ŏn′ tō·lŏj′ ĭ·kăl)
o·nus (ō′ nŭs)
on·ward (ŏn′ wĕrd)
on·yx (ŏn′ ĭks)

ooze (ōōz)
  ooz·ing
o·pac·i·ty (ô·păs′ ĭ·tĭ)
o·pal (ō′ pɑl)
o·pal·es·cent (ō′ pɑl·ĕs′ ĕnt)
  -cence
o·paque (ô·pāk′)
  o·paque·ness
o·pen (ō′ pĕn)
  o·pen-air *adj.*
  o·pen-and-shut case
  o·pen·er   o·pen-eyed
  o·pen·hand·ed
  o·pen house   o·pen let·ter
  o·pen-mind·ed   o·pen·work
op·er·a (ŏp′ ĕr·ȧ)
  op·er·a·tic (ŏp′ ĕr·ăt′ ĭk)
op·er·a·ble (ŏp′ ĕr·ȧ·b′l)
op·er·ate (ŏp′ ĕr·āt)
  -at·ing
  op·er·a·tion (ŏp′ ĕr·ā′ shŭn)
  -tion·al
  op·er·a·tive (ŏp′ ĕr·ā′ tĭv)
  op·er·a·tor
op·er·et·ta (ŏp′ ĕr·ĕt′ ȧ)
oph·thal·mol·o·gist
    (ŏf′ thăl·mŏl′ ô·jĭst)
o·pi·ate (ō′ pĭ·āt)
o·pine (ô·pīn′)
  -pin·ing
o·pin·ion (ô·pĭn′ yŭn)
  o·pin·ion·at·ed
    (ô·pĭn′ yŭn·āt′ ĕd)
  o·pin·ion·a·tive
    (ô·pĭn′ yŭn·ā′ tĭv)
o·pi·um (ō′ pĭ·ŭm)
o·pos·sum (ô·pŏs′ ŭm)
op·po·nent (ŏ·pō′ nĕnt)
op·por·tune (ŏp′ ôr·tūn′)
  op·por·tune·ly
op·por·tun·ism (ŏp′ ôr·tūn′ ĭz′m)
  op·por·tun·ist
  op·por·tun·is·tic
    (ŏp′ ôr·tūn·ĭs′ tĭk)
op·por·tu·ni·ty (ŏp′ ôr·tū′ nĭ·tĭ)
  -ties
op·pose (ô·pōz′)
  op·pos·ing   op·pos·a·ble
op·po·site (ŏp′ ô·zĭt)
  op·po·site·ly
  op·po·si·tion (ŏp′ ô·zĭsh′ ŭn)
op·press (ô·prĕs′)
  op·pres·sion (ô·prĕsh′ ŭn)
  op·pres·sive   op·pres·sor

op·pro·bri·ous (ô·prō′ brĭ·ŭs)
  op·pro·bri·um
op·tic (ŏp′ tĭk)
  op·ti·cal
  op·ti·cian (ŏp·tĭsh′ ăn)
op·ti·mism (ŏp′ tĭ·mĭz′m)
  op·ti·mist
  op·ti·mis·tic (ŏp′ tĭ·mĭs′ tĭk)
  -ti·cal·ly
op·ti·mum (ŏp′ tĭ·mŭm)
op·tion (ŏp′ shŭn)
  op·tion·al   -al·ly
op·tom·e·try (ŏp·tŏm′ ê·trĭ)
  op·tom·e·trist (ŏp·tŏm′ ê·trĭst)
op·u·lence (ŏp′ û·lĕns)
  -lent
o·pus (ō′ pŭs)
  pl. op·e·ra (ŏp′ ê·rȧ)
or·a·cle (ŏr′ ȧ·k′l)
  o·rac·u·lar (ô·răk′ û·lẽr)
o·ral (ō′ rɑl)
  (spoken; see *aural*)
  o·ral·ly
or·ange (ŏr′ ĕnj)
  or·ange·ade (ŏr′ ĕnj·ād′)
  or·ange pe·koe
o·rang·u·tan (ô·răng′ ōō·tăn′)
o·rate (ô·rāt′)
  -rat·ing
  o·ra·tion (ô·rā′ shŭn)
  or·a·tor (ŏr′ ȧ·tẽr)
  or·a·tor·i·cal (ŏr′ ȧ·tŏr′ ĭ·kɑl)
  or·a·to·ry (ŏr′ ȧ·tō′ rĭ)
  o·ra·to·ri·o (ŏr′ ȧ·tō′ rĭ·ō)
or·bit (ŏr′ bĭt)
  -bit·ed   -bit·ing
  or·bit·al
or·chard (ŏr′ chẽrd)
or·ches·tra (ŏr′ kĕs·trȧ)
  or·ches·tral (ŏr·kĕs′ trɑl)
  or·ches·trate (ŏr′ kĕs·trāt)
  or·ches·tra·tion
    (ŏr′ kĕs·trā′ shŭn)
or·chid (ŏr′ kĭd)
or·dain (ŏr·dān′)
or·deal (ŏr·dēl′)
or·der (ŏr′ dẽr)
  or·der·ly   -li·ness
or·di·nal (ŏr′ dĭ·nɑl)
or·di·nance (ŏr′ dĭ·năns)
  (law; see *ordnance*)
or·di·nar·y (ŏr′ dĭ·nẽr′ ĭ)
  or·di·nar·i·ly   -i·ness
or·di·nate (ŏr′ dĭ·nát)
  -nat·ing

or·di·na·tion (ôr′ dĭ·nā′ shŭn)
ord·nance (ôrd′ năns)
  (military supplies: see *ordnance*)
or·dure (ôr′ dụr)
Or·e·gon (ôr′ ê·gŏn)
  abbr. Oreg. *or* Ore.
Or·e·go·ni·an (ôr′ ê·gō′ nĭ·ăn)
or·gan (ôr′ găn)
or·gan·ic (ôr·găn′ ĭk)
or·gan·ism (ôr′ găn·ĭz′m)
or·gan·ist (ôr′ găn·ĭst)
or·gan·dy (ôr′ găn·dĭ)
  -dies
or·gan·ize (ôr′ găn·ĭz)
  -iz·ing   or·gan·iz·able
or·gan·i·za·tion
    (ôr′ găn·ĭ·zā′ shŭn)
  or·gan·iz·er
or·gan·za (ôr·găn′ ză)
or·gasm (ôr′ găz′m)
or·gy (ôr′ jĭ)
  -gies
or·gi·as·tic (ôr′ jĭ·ăs′ tĭk)
o·ri·ent (ō′ rĭ·ĕnt)
o·ri·en·tal (ō′ rĭ·ĕn′ tăl)
o·ri·en·ta·tion (ō′ rĭ·ĕn·tā′ shŭn)
or·i·fice (ôr′ ĭ·fĭs)
or·i·gin (ôr′ ĭ·jĭn)
o·rig·i·nal (ō·rĭj′ ĭ·năl)
  o·rig·i·nal·i·ty
    (ō·rĭj′ ĭ·năl′ ĭ·tĭ)
  o·rig·i·nal·ly
o·rig·i·nate (ō·rĭj′ ĭ·nāt)
  -nat·ing
  o·rig·i·na·tion
    (ō·rĭj′ ĭ·nā′ shŭn)
  o·rig·i·na·tor
o·ri·ole (ō′ rĭ·ōl)
or·i·son (ôr′ ĭ·zŭn)
or·lon (ôr′ lŏn)
or·na·ment (ôr′ nă·mĕnt)
or·na·men·tal (ôr′ nă·mĕn′ tăl)
  -tal·ly
or·na·men·ta·tion
    (ôr′ nă·mĕn·tā′ shŭn)
or·nate (ôr·nāt′)
  or·nate·ly   -nate·ness
or·ner·y (ôr′ nĕr·ĭ)
  or·ner·i·ness
or·ni·thol·o·gy (ôr′ nĭ·thŏl′ ō·jĭ)
or·phan (ôr′ făn)
  or·phan·age
or·tho·don·tist (ôr′ thô·dŏn′ tĭst)
or·tho·dox·y (ôr′ thô·dŏk′ sĭ)
  -dox·ies

or·tho·gen·ic (ôr′ thô·jĕn′ ĭk)
or·thog·ra·phy (ôr·thŏg′ ră·fĭ)
or·tho·pe·dics (ôr′ thô·pē′ dĭks)
os·cil·late (ŏs′ ĭ·lāt)
  (vibrate; see *osculate*)
  -cil·lat·ing
os·cil·la·tion (ŏs′ ĭ·lā′ shŭn)
os·cil·la·tor (ŏs′ ĭ·lā′ tẽr)
os·cu·late (ŏs′ kū·lāt)
  (to kiss; see *oscillate*)
  -lat·ing
os·cu·la·tion (ŏs′ kū·lā′ shŭn)
os·mo·sis (ŏs·mō′ sĭs)
os·mot·ic (ŏs·mŏt′ ĭk)
os·prey (ŏs′ prĭ)
  -preys
os·si·cle (ŏs′ ĭ·k′l)
os·si·fy (ŏs′ ĭ·fĭ)
  -fied   -fy·ing
  os·si·fi·ca·tion
    (ŏs′ ĭ·fĭ·kā′ shŭn)
os·ten·si·ble (ŏs·tĕn′ sĭ·b′l)
os·ten·ta·tion (ŏs′ tĕn·tā′ shŭn)
os·ten·ta·tious (-shŭs)
os·te·o·path (ŏs′ tê·ô·păth)
os·tra·cize (ŏs′ tră·sĭz)
  -ciz·ing
os·tra·cism (ŏs′ tră·sĭz′m)
os·trich (ŏs′ trĭch)
oth·er·wise (ŭth′ ẽr·wīz′)
oth·er·world·ly
    (ŭth′ ẽr·wûrld′ lĭ)
o·ti·ose (ō′ shĭ·ōs)
Ot·ta·wa, Can. (ŏt′ ă·wă)
ot·ter (ŏt′ ẽr)
Ot·to·man (ŏt′ ô·măn)
ought (ôt)
  (bound by duty; see *aught*)
Oui·ja board (wē′ jă)
ounce (ouns)
our·selves (our·sĕlvz′)
oust (oust)
  oust·er
out (out)
  out-and-out   out·bal·ance
  out·board   out·break
  out·burst   out·cast
  out·class   out·come
  out·crop   out·cry
  out·dis·tance   out·do
  out·doors   out·er·most
  out·field   out·fit·ter
  out·go·ing   out·growth
  out·land·ish   out·last
  out·law   out·let

out·line	out·look
out·ly·ing	out·ma·neu·ver
out·mod·ed	out-of-date
out-of-door	out-of-the-way
out·pa·tient	out·post
out·pour·ing	out·put
out·rage	out·ra·geous
out·reach	out·rig·ger
out·right	out·sell
out·set	out·sid·er
out·size	out·skirts
out·smart	out·spo·ken
out·spo·ken·ness	
out·spread	out·stand·ing
out·strip	out·ward
out·weigh	out·wit

o·va·ry   (ō′ vá·rǐ)
  -ries
o·va·tion   (ō·vā′ shŭn)
ov·en   (ŭv′ ĕn)
o·ver   (ō′ vĕr)

o·ver·act	o·ver·all
o·ver·alls	o·ver·awed
o·ver·bear·ing	o·ver·board
o·ver·cast	
o·ver·de·vel·op·ment	
o·ver·dose	o·ver·draft
o·ver·ex·po·sure	
o·ver·haul	o·ver·head
o·ver·lap·ping	o·ver·lay
o·ver·look	o·ver·night
o·ver·pass	
o·ver·pow·er·ing	
o·ver·pro·duc·tion	
o·ver·rate	o·ver·reach
o·ver·ride	o·ver·rul·ing
o·ver·run	o·ver·seas
o·ver·seer	o·ver·shoe
o·ver·sight	o·ver·sup·ply
o·ver-the-count·er	
o·ver·throw	o·ver·time
o·ver·tone	o·ver·ween·ing
o·ver·weight	o·ver·whelm·ing
o·ver·work	o·ver·wrought

o·vert   (ō′ vûrt)
o·ver·ture   (ō′ vĕr·tûr)
o·vip·a·rous   (ō·vĭp′ á·rŭs)
o·vum   (ō′ vŭm)
  pl. o·va
owe   (ō)
  ow·ing
owl·ish   (oul′ ĭsh)
own·er·ship   (ōn′ ĕr·shĭp)
ox   (ŏks)
  pl. ox·en

ox·al·ic   (ŏks·ăl′ ĭk)
ox·eye dai·sy   (ŏks′ ī′)
ox·i·da·tion   (ŏk′ sĭ·dā′ shŭn)
ox·ide   (ŏk′ sīd)
ox·i·dize   (ŏk′ sĭ·dīz)
  -diz·ing
ox·tail   (ŏks′ tāl′)
ox·y·gen   (ŏk′ sĭ·jĕn)
oys·ter   (ois′ tĕr)
o·zone   (ō′ zōn)

P

pab·u·lum   (păb′ û·lŭm)
pace·mak·er   (pās′ māk′ ēr)
pach·y·derm   (păk′ ĭ·dûrm)
pac·i·fy   (păs′ ĭ·fī)
  -fied   -fy·ing
  pa·cif·ic   (pá·sĭf′ ĭk)
  pac·i·fi·ca·tion
            (păs′ ĭ·fĭ·kā′ shŭn)
  pac·i·fi·er   pac·i·fist
pack·age   (păk′ ĭj)
  -ag·ing
pack·et   (păk′ ĕt)
pack·ing house   (păk′ ĭng)
pack·sack   (păk′ săk′)
pack·sad·dle   (păk′ săd′ ′l)
pact   (păkt)
pad·ding   (păd′ ĭng)
pad·dle wheel   (păd′ ′l)
pad·dock   (păd′ ŭk)
pad·lock   (păd′ lok′)
pa·dre   (pä′ drĭ)
pae·an   (pē′ ăn)
pa·gan   (pā′ găn)
  pa·gan·ism
pag·eant   (păj′ ĕnt)
  pag·eant·ry
pag·i·na·tion   (păj′ ĭ·nā′ shŭn)
pa·go·da   (pá·gō′ dá)
paid   (pād)
pail·ful   (pāl′ fōͦl)
pain   (pān)
  (punishment; see *pane*)
  pain·ful   -ful·ly
  -ful·ness   pain·less
  pains·tak·ing
paint·brush   (pănt′ brŭsh′)
paint·ing   (pănt′ ĭng)
pair   (pâr)
  (two; see *pear*)
Pais·ley print   (pāz′ lĭ)
pa·ja·ma   (pá·jä′ má)

Pak·i·stan (păk′ ĭ·stăn′)
  Pak·i·stan·i (-ĭ)
pal·ace (păl′ ĭs)
  pa·la·tial (pá·lā′ shál)
pal·a·din (păl′ á·dĭn)
pal·at·a·ble (păl′ ĭt·á·b′l)
  pal·at·a·bil·i·ty
       (păl′ ĭt·á·bĭl′ ĭ·tĭ)
pal·ate (păl′ ĭt)
  (roof of mouth; see *palette, pallet*)
pal·a·tal (păl′ á·tál)
pa·la·tial (pá·lā′ shál)
  -tial·ly
pal·a·tine (păl′ á·tīn)
pa·lav·er (pá·lăv′ ēr)
pale (pāl)
  pale·face   pale·ness
pa·le·o- (pā′ lē·ō-)
  pa·le·o·bot·a·ny
       (-bŏt′ á·nĭ)
  pa·le·o·lith·ic (-lĭth′ ĭk)
  pa·le·on·tol·o·gy
       (pā′ lē·ŏn·tŏl′ ō·jĭ)
  Pa·le·o·zo·ic era
       (-zō′ ĭk)
  pa·le·o·zo·ol·o·gy
       (-zō·ŏl′ ō·jĭ)
pal·ette (păl′ ĕt)
  (painter's board; see *palate, pallet*)
  pal·ette knife
pal·frey (pôl′ frĭ)
pal·i·sade (păl′ ĭ·sād′)
pal·la·di·um (pá·lā′ dĭ·ŭm)
Pal·las Ath·e·na
       (păl′ ás á·thē′ ná)
pall·bear·er (pôl′ bâr′ ēr)
pal·let (păl′ ĕt)
  (bed; see *palate, palette*)
pal·li·ate (păl′ ĭ·āt)
  -at·ing
  pal·li·a·tion (păl′ ĭ·ā′ shŭn)
  pal·li·a·tive (păl′ ĭ·ā′ tĭv)
pal·lid (păl′ ĭd)
  pal·lor (păl′ ēr)
pal·met·to (păl·mĕt′ ō)
palm·is·try (păm′ ĭs·trĭ)
pal·my·ra (păl·mī′ rá)
pal·o·mi·no (păl′ ō·mē′ nō)
pal·pa·ble (păl′ pá·b′l)
pal·pi·tate (păl′ pĭ·tāt)
  -tat·ing
  pal·pi·ta·tion (păl′ pĭ·tā′ shŭn)
pal·sy (pôl′ zĭ)
  -sied

pal·try (pôl′ trĭ)
  pal·tri·ness
pam·pas (păm′ páz)
pam·per (păm′ pēr)
pam·phlet (păm′ flĕt)
  pam·phlet·eer (păm′ flĕt·ēr′)
pan·a·ce·a (păn′ á·sē′ á)
Pan·a·ma (păn′ á·mô)
  Pan·a·ma hat
  Pan·a·ma·ni·an
       (păn′ á·mä′ nĭ·án)
Pan-A·mer·i·can
       (păn′ á·mĕr′ ĭ·kán)
pan·a·tel·la (păn′ á·tĕl′ á)
pan·cake (păn′ kāk′)
pan·chro·mat·ic
       (păn′ krō·măt′ ĭk)
pan·cra·ti·um (păn·krā′ shĭ·ŭm)
pan·cre·as (păn′ krē·ás)
  pan·cre·at·ic juice
       (păng′ krē·ăt′ ĭk)
pan·da (păn′ dá)
pan·dem·ic (păn·dĕm′ ĭk)
pan·de·mo·ni·um
       (păn′ dē·mō′ nĭ·ŭm)
pan·der (păn′ dēr)
  pan·der·er
Pan·do·ra's box (păn·dō′ ráz)
pan·dow·dy (păn·dou′ dĭ)
pane (păn)
  (a panel; glass; see *pain*)
pan·e·gyr·ic (păn′ ē·jĭr′ ĭk)
pan·el (păn′ ĕl)
  -eled   -el·ing
  pan·el·ist
pan·han·dle (păn′ hăn′ d′l)
  -dling
Pan·hel·len·ic (păn′ hĕ·lĕn′ ĭk)
pan·ic (păn′ ĭk)
  -icked   -ick·ing
  pan·ick·y   pan·ic-strick·en
pan·nier (păn′ yēr)
pan·o·ply (păn′ ō·plĭ)
  -plies   pan·o·plied
pan·o·ra·ma (păn′ ō·rä′ má)
  pan·o·ram·ic (-răm′ ĭk)
pan·sy (păn′ zĭ)
  -sies
pan·ta·loon (păn′ tá·lōōn′)
pan·the·ism (păn′ thē·ĭz′m)
  pan·the·is·tic (păn′ thē·ĭs′ tĭk)
pan·the·on (păn′ thē·ŏn)
pan·ther (păn′ thēr)
  pan·ther·ess
pant·ing (pănt′ ĭng)

pan·to·mime   (păn′ tŏ·mīm)
  pan·to·mim·ic
                (păn′ tŏ·mĭm′ ĭk)
  pan·to·mim·ist
pan·to·then·ic ac·id
                (păn′ tŏ·thĕn′ ĭk)
pan·try   (păn′ trĭ)
  -tries
pant·y   (păn′ tĭ)
  pant·ies   pant·y gir·dle
  pant·y·waist
Pan·zer di·vi·sion
                (păn′ tsĕr)
pa·pa·cy   (pā′ pȧ·sĭ)
  pa·pal   (pā′ pȧl)
pa·paw   (pȧ·pô′)
pa·pay·a   (pȧ·pī′ ȧ)
pa·per   (pā′ pĕr)
  pa·per·back   pa·per·board
  pa·per cut·ter pa·per knife
  pa·per-thin   pa·per·weight
  pa·per work
pa·pier-mâ·ché
                (pā′ pĕr·mȧ·shā′)
pa·pil·la   (pȧ·pĭl′ ȧ)
  pl. pa·pil·lae   (-ē)
  pap·il·lar·y   (păp′ ĭ·lĕr′ ĭ)
pa·poose   (pȧ·pōōs′)
pa·pri·ka   (pȧ·prē′ kȧ)
pa·py·rus   (pȧ·pī′ rŭs)
  pl. pa·py·ri   (-rī)
par·a·ble   (păr′ ȧ·b′l)
pa·rab·o·la   (pȧ·răb′ ȯ·lȧ)
  par·a·bol·ic   (păr′ ȧ·bŏl′ ĭk)
  -i·cal·ly
  pa·rab·o·loid (pȧ·răb′ ȯ·loid)
par·a·chute   (păr′ ȧ·shōōt)
  -chut·ist
pa·rade   (pȧ·rād′)
  -rad·ing
par·a·digm   (păr′ ȧ·dĭm)
par·a·dise   (păr′ ȧ·dīs)
par·a·dox   (păr′ ȧ·dŏks)
  par·a·dox·i·cal
                (păr′ ȧ·dŏk′ sĭ·kăl)
  -cal·ly
par·af·fin   (păr′ ȧ·fĭn)
par·a·gon   (păr′ ȧ·gŏn)
par·a·graph   (păr′ ȧ·grăf)
Par·a·guay   (păr′ ȧ·gwĭ)
par·a·keet   (păr′ ȧ·kēt)
par·al·lax   (păr′ ȧ·lăks)
  par·al·lac·tic (păr′ ȧ·lăk′ tĭk)
par·al·lel   (păr′ ȧ·lĕl)
  -al·leled   -al·lel·ing

par·al·lel·o·gram
                (păr′ ȧ·lĕl′ ȯ·grăm)
pa·ral·y·sis (pȧ·răl′ ĭ·sĭs)
  par·a·lyt·ic (păr′ ȧ·lĭt′ ĭk)
  par·a·lyze   (păr′ ȧ·līz)
  -lyz·ing
par·a·me·ci·um
                (păr′ ȧ·mē′ shĭ·ŭm)
  pl. par·a·me·ci·a
pa·ram·e·ter (pȧ·răm′ ē·tĕr)
par·a·mount   (păr′ ȧ·mount)
par·a·mour   (păr′ ȧ·mŏŏr)
par·a·noi·a   (păr′ ȧ·noi′ ȧ)
  par·a·noi·ac   (-ăk)
par·a·pet   (păr′ ȧ·pĕt)
  -pet·ed
par·a·pher·na·li·a
                (păr′ ȧ·fĕr·nā′ lĭ·ȧ)
par·a·phrase (păr′ ȧ·frāz)
  phras·ing
  par·a·phras·tic
                (păr′ ȧ·frăs′ tĭk)
par·a·ple·gi·a (păr′ ȧ·plē′ jĭ·ȧ)
  par·a·pleg·ic   (-plĕj′ ĭk)
par·a·psy·chol·o·gy
                (păr′ ȧ·sĭ·kŏl′ ȯ·jĭ)
par·a·site   (păr′ ȧ·sīt)
  par·a·sit·ic (păr′ ȧ·sĭt′ ĭk)
  -i·cal
  par·a·sit·ism (păr′ ȧ·sīt·ĭz′m)
  par·a·si·tol·o·gy
                (păr′ ȧ·sī·tŏl′ ȯ·jĭ)
par·a·sym·pa·thet·ic
                (păr′ ȧ·sĭm′ pȧ·thĕt′ ĭk)
par·a·troop·er (păr′ ȧ·trōōp′ ĕr)
par·boil   (păr′ boil)
par·cel   (păr′ sĕl)
  -celed   -cel·ing
  par·cel post
par·chee·si   (păr·chē′ zĭ)
parch·ment   (părch′ mĕnt)
par·don   (păr′ d′n)
  par·don·a·ble par·don·er
pare   (păr)
  par·ing
par·ent   (păr′ ĕnt)
  par·ent·age   (păr′ ĕn·tĭj)
  pa·ren·tal   (pȧ·rĕn′ tăl)
  par·ent·hood
pa·ren·the·sis (pȧ·rĕn′ thē·sĭs)
  pl. pa·ren·the·ses (-sēz)
  par·en·thet·ic (păr′ ĕn·thĕt′ ĭk)
  -i·cal·ly
pa·re·sis   (pȧ·rē′ sĭs)
  pa·ret·ic   (pȧ·rĕt′ ĭk)

par·ex·cel·lence
    (păr ĕk′ sĕ·läns)
par·fait (pär fā′)
pa·ri·ah (pá·rī′ á)
pa·ri·e·tal (pá·rī′ ĕ·tâl)
par·i·mu·tu·el (păr′ ĭ·mū′ tū·ĕl)
par·ish (păr′ ĭsh)
  par·ish·ion·er (pá·rĭsh′ ŭn·ĕr)
par·i·ty (păr′ ĭ·tĭ)
par·ka (păr′ ká)
park·way (pärk′ wā′)
par·lance (pär′ lăns)
par·lay (pär′ lā)
  (bet; see parley)
par·ley (pär′ lĭ)
  (conversation; see parlay)
par·lia·ment (pär′ lĭ·měnt)
  par·lia·men·tar·i·an
    (pär′ lĭ·měn·târ′ ĭ·ăn)
  par·lia·men·ta·ry
    (pär′ lĭ·měn′ tá·rĭ)
par·lor (pär′ lẽr)
  par·lor car par·lor·maid
Par·me·san cheese
    (pär′ mē·zăn′)
Par·nas·sus (pär·năs′ ŭs)
pa·ro·chi·al (pá·rō′ kĭ·ăl)
par·o·dy (păr′ ŏ·dĭ)
  -dies
  par·o·died -dy·ing
  par·o·dist
pa·role (pá·rōl′)
  pa·rol·ee (pá·rōl′ ē′)
par·ox·ysm (păr′ ŏk·sĭz'm)
par·quet (pär·kă′)
par·ri·cide (păr′ ĭ·sīd)
  -cid·al
Par·ris Is., S.C. (păr′ ĭs)
par·rot (păr′ ŭt)
  par·rot·ed par·rot·ing
par·ry (păr′ ĭ)
  par·ried par·ry·ing
parse (pärs)
  pars·ing
par·si·mo·ni·ous
    (păr′ sĭ·mō′ nĭ·ŭs)
  par·si·mo·ny (păr′ sĭ·mō′ nĭ)
pars·ley (pärs′ lĭ)
pars·nip (pärs′ nĭp)
par·son (pär′ s'n)
  par·son·age (-ĭj)
par·take (pär·tāk′)
  tak·ing
par·the·no·gen·e·sis
    (pär′ thē·nŏ·jĕn′ ĕ·sĭs)

Par·the·non (păr′ thē·nŏn)
par·tial (pär′ shăl)
  par·ti·al·i·ty (pär′ shĭ·ăl′ ĭ·tĭ)
  par·tial·ly
par·tic·i·pate (pär·tĭs′ ĭ·pāt)
  -pat·ing
  par·tic·i·pant (-pănt)
  par·tic·i·pa·tion
    (pär·tĭs′ ĭ·pā′ shŭn)
  par·tic·i·pa·tor
par·ti·ci·ple (pär′ tĭ·sĭ·p'l)
  par·ti·cip·i·al (pär′ tĭ·sĭp′ ĭ·ăl)
par·ti·cle (pär′ tĭ·k'l)
par·tic·u·lar (pär·tĭk′ û·lẽr)
  par·tic·u·lar·i·ty
    (pẽr·tĭk′ û·lăr′ ĭ·tĭ)
  par·tic·u·lar·ize
  -iz·ing par·tic·u·lar·ly
par·ti·san (pär′ tĭ·zăn)
  par·ti·san·ship
par·ti·tion (pär·tĭsh′ ŭn)
  par·ti·tion·ment
par·ti·tive (pär′ tĭ·tĭv)
part·ner (pärt′ nẽr)
  part·ner·ship
par·tridge (pär′ trĭj)
par·tu·ri·tion (pär′ tû·rĭsh′ ŭn)
par·ty (pär′ tĭ)
  -ties
par·ve·nu (pär′ vê·nū)
pas·chal lamb (păs′ kăl)
pa·sha (pá·shä′)
pasque·flow·er (păsk′ flou′ ĕr)
pass·a·ble (păs′ á·b'l)
pas·sage (păs′ ĭj)
  pas·sage·way
Pas·sa·ic, N.J. (pă·sā′ ĭk)
pass·book (păs′ bŏŏk′)
pas·sé (pă·sā′)
pas·sen·ger pi·geon
    (păs′ ĕn·jẽr)
pass·er-by (păs′ ẽr·bī′)
pas·sion (păsh′ ŭn)
  pas·sion·ate (-ĭt)
  -ate·ly pas·sion·flow·er
  pas·sion·less Pas·sion play
pas·sive (păs′ ĭv)
  pas·sive·ly
  pas·siv·i·ty (pă·sĭv′ ĭ·tĭ)
pass·key (păs′ kē′)
pass·port (păs′ pōrt)
paste (păst)
  past·ing paste·board
  past·y
pas·tel (păs·tĕl′)

pas·teur·ize   (păs' tẽr·īz)
 -iz·ing
 pas·teur·i·za·tion
                (păs' tẽr·ĭ·zā' shŭn)
pas·tiche   (păs·tēsh')
pas·time   (păs' tīm')
pas·tor   (păs' tẽr)
 pas·tor·ate   (-ĭt)
pas·to·ral   (păs' tŏ·răl)
 (rural; see *pastorale*)
pas·to·ra·le   (păs' tŏ·rä' lå)
 (music; see *pastoral*)
 pl. -ra·li   (-rä' lē)
pas·tra·mi   (păs·trä' mĭ)
pas·try   (pās' trĭ)
 -tries
pas·ture   (păs' tûr)
 -tur·ing
 pas·tur·age   (-ĭj)
patch·work   (păch' wûrk')
pâ·té de foie gras
                (pä' tā' đĕ fwä' grä')
pa·tel·la   (pȧ·tĕl' ȧ)
 pl. pa·tel·lae   (-ē)
pat·en   (păt' ĕn)
pat·ent   (păt' ĕnt)
 pat·ent·a·ble
 pat·ent·ee   (păt' ĕn·tē')
 pa·tent·ly   pat·en·tor
pa·ter·fa·mil·i·as
                (pā' tẽr·fȧ·mĭl' ĭ·ȧs)
pa·ter·nal   (pȧ·tûr' năl)
 pa·ter·nal·is·tic
                (pȧ·tûr' năl·ĭs' tĭk)
 pa·ter·ni·ty   (pȧ·tûr' nĭ·tĭ)
pa·ter·nos·ter   (pā' tẽr·nŏs' tẽr)
Pat·er·son, N. J.   (păt' ẽr·s'n)
pa·thet·ic   (pȧ·thĕt' ĭk)
 -i·cal·ly
 pa·thet·ic fal·la·cy
path·find·er   (păth' fīn' đẽr)
pa·thol·o·gy   (pȧ·thŏl' ŏ·jĭ)
 -gies
 path·o·log·i·cal
                (păth' ŏ·lŏj' ĭ·kăl)
 pa·thol·o·gist   (pȧ·thŏl' ŏ·jĭst)
pa·thos   (pā' thŏs)
pa·tient   (pā' shĕnt)
 pa·tience
pat·i·na   (păt' ĭ·nȧ)
pat·i·o   (păt' ĭ·ō)
pat·ois   (păt' wä)
pa·tri·arch   (pā' trĭ·ärk)
 pa·tri·ar·chal   (pā' trĭ·är' kăl)
 pa·tri·arch·y   -arch·ies

pa·tri·cian   (pȧ·trĭsh' ăn)
pat·ri·mo·ny   (păt' rĭ·mō' nĭ)
pa·tri·ot   (pā' trĭ·ŭt)
 pa·tri·ot·ic   (pā' trĭ·ŏt' ĭk)
 -i·cal·ly
 pa·tri·ot·ism   (pā' trĭ·ŭt·ĭz'm)
pa·trol   (pȧ·trōl')
 -trolled,   -trol·ling
 pa·trol·man   pa·trol wag·on
pa·tron   (pā' trŭn)
 pa·tron·age   (pā' trŭn·ĭj)
 pa·tron·ess   (pā' trŭn·ĕs)
 pa·tron·ize
 pa·tron·iz·ing·ly
pat·ro·nym·ic   (păt' rŏ·nĭm' ĭk)
pa·troon   (pȧ·trōōn')
pat·ter   (păt' ẽr)
pat·tern   (păt' ẽrn)
pat·ty shell   (păt' ĭ)
pau·ci·ty   (pô' sĭ·tĭ)
Paul·ist   (pôl' ĭst)
paunch·y   (pôn' chĭ)
pau·per   (pô' pẽr)
 pau·per·ize   -iz·ing
pause   (pôz)
 paus·ing
pav·an   (păv' ăn)
pave·ment   (pāv' mĕnt)
pa·vil·ion   (pȧ·vĭl' yŭn)
pav·ing   (pāv' ĭng)
pawn·bro·ker   (pôn' brō' kẽr)
Paw·nee In·di·ans
                (pô·nē')
pay   (pā)
 pay·a·ble
 pay·ee   (pā' ē')
 pay·er   pay·mas·ter
 pay·ment   pay·off
 pay·roll
peace   (pēs)
 peace·a·ble
 peace·ful, -ful·ly, -ful·ness
 peace·mak·er   peace of·fer·ing
 peace of·fi·cer
peach   (pēch)
pea·cock   (pē' kŏk')
pea·hen   (pē' hĕn')
pea jack·et   (pē)
peaked   (pēk' ĕd)
 (thin; see *peeked*)
peal·ing   (pēl' ĭng)
 (of a bell; see *peeling*)
pea·nut   (pē' nŭt')
pearl   (pûrl)
 (gem; see *purl*)

pearl·y (pûr′ lǐ)
peas·ant (pĕz′ ∂nt)
  peas·ant·ry
peb·ble (pĕb′ ′l)
  peb·bly
pe·can (pē·kăn′)
pec·ca·dil·lo (pĕk′ ∂·dĭl′ ō)
  -dil·loes
pec·ca·ry (pĕk′ ∂·rĭ)
pec·tin (pĕk′ tĭn)
  pec·tic ac·id
pec·to·ral (pĕk′ tō·r∂l)
pe·cul·iar (pē·kūl′ yēr)
  pe·cu·li·ar·i·ty
        (pē·kū′ lǐ·ăr′ ĭ·tǐ)
  -ties
pe·cu·ni·ar·y (pē·kū′ nǐ·ěr′ ǐ)
ped·a·gogue (pĕd′ ∂·gŏg)
  ped·a·gog·ic (pĕd′ ∂·gŏj′ ǐk)
  -i·cal
  ped·a·go·gy (pĕd′ ∂·gō′ jǐ)
ped·al (pĕd′ ∂l)
  (on a bike; see peddle)
  -aled   -al·ing
ped·ant (pĕd′ ∂nt)
  pe·dan·tic (pē·dăn′ tǐk)
  -ti·cal·ly
  ped·ant·ry (pĕd′ ∂nt·rǐ)
ped·dle (pĕd′ ′l)
  (sell; see pedal)
  ped·dling   ped·dler
ped·es·tal (pĕd′ ĕs·t∂l)
pe·des·tri·an (pē·dĕs′ trǐ·∂n)
pe·di·at·rics (pē′ dǐ·ăt′ rǐks)
  pe·di·a·tri·cian
       (pē′ dǐ·∂·trǐsh′ ∂n)
ped·i·cure (pĕd′ ǐ·kūr)
ped·i·gree (pĕd′ ǐ·grē)
peeked (pēkt)
  (looked; see peaked)
peel·ing (pēl′ ǐng)
  (of an apple; see pealing)
Peep·ing Tom (pēp′ ǐng)
peer (pēr)
  (an equal; see pier)
  peer·age (pēr′ ǐj)
  peer·less
peeve (pēv)
  peev·ing   pee·vish
pee·wee (pē′ wē)
Peg·a·sus (pĕg′ ∂·sŭs)
peign·oir (pān·wär′)
pe·jo·ra·tive (pē′ jō·rā′ tǐv)
  -tive·ly
Pe·king·ese (pē′ kǐng·ēz′)

pe·koe (pē′ kō)
pelf (pĕlf)
pel·i·can (pĕl′ ǐ·kǎn)
pel·la·gra (pē·lā′ grà)
pel·let (pĕl′ ĕt)
pell-mell (pĕl′ mĕl′)
pel·lu·cid (pē·lū′ sǐd)
pel·vic (pĕl′ vǐk)
  pel·vis
pem·mi·can (pĕm′ ǐ·kǎn)
pe·nal (pē′ n∂l)
  pe·nal code
  pe·nal·ize   -iz·ing
pen·al·ty (pĕn′ ∂l·tǐ)
  -ties
pen·ance (pĕn′ ∂ns)
pence (pĕns)
pen·chant (pĕn′ chǎnt)
pen·cil (pĕn′ sǐl)
  -ciled   -cil·ing
pend·ant (pĕn′ d∂nt)
  (ornament; see pendent)
pend·ent (pĕn′ dĕnt)
  (suspended; see pendant)
  pend·en·cy
pend·ing (pĕnd′ ǐng)
pen·du·lous (pĕn′ dū·lŭs)
pen·du·lum (pĕn′ dū·lŭm)
pen·e·trate (pĕn′ ē·trāt)
  -trat·ing
  pen·e·tra·ble (pĕn′ ē·trà·b′l)
  pen·e·trant (pĕn′ ē·trănt)
  pen·e·tra·tion
       (pĕn′ ē·trā′ shŭn)
  pen·e·tra·tive (pĕn′ ē·trā′ tǐv)
pen·guin (pĕn′ gwǐn)
pen·hold·er (pĕn′ hōl′ dēr)
pen·i·cil·lin (pĕn′ ǐ·sǐl′ ǐn)
pen·in·su·la (pĕn·ǐn′ sū·là)
  pen·in·su·lar (-lēr)
pen·i·tent (pĕn′ ǐ·tĕnt)
  -tence
  pen·i·ten·tial (pĕn′ ǐ·tĕn′ sh∂l)
pen·i·ten·tia·ry
      (pĕn′ ǐ·tĕn′ shà·rǐ)
  -ries
pen·knife (pĕn′ nīf′)
pen·man·ship (pĕn′ mǎn·shǐp)
pen·nant (pĕn′ ∂nt)
pen·ni·less (pĕn′ ǐ·lĕs)
Penn·syl·va·nia
      (pĕn′ sǐl·văn′ yà)
  abbr. Pa. or Penna.
  Penn·syl·va·nian

pen·ny (pĕn′ ĭ)
  pen·nies
  pen·ni·less (pĕn′ ĭ·lĕs)
  pen·ny an·te pen·ny·weight
  pen·ny-wise
pe·nol·o·gy (pē·nŏl′ ō·jĭ)
pen·sion (pĕn′ shŭn)
  pen·sion·er
pen·ta- (pĕn′ tá-)
  pen·ta·gon (pĕn′ tá·gŏn)
  pen·tag·o·nal (pĕn·tăg′ ō·nǎl)
  pen·ta·he·dron
    (pĕn′ tá·hē′ drŭn)
  pen·tam·e·ter (pĕn·tăm′ ē·tēr)
  Pen·ta·teuch (pĕn′ tá·tūk)
  pen·tath·lon (pĕn·tăth′ lŏn)
Pen·te·cos·tal (pĕn′ tē·kŏs′ tǎl)
pent·house (pĕnt′ hous′)
pe·nu·che (pē·nōō′ chē)
pe·nul·ti·mate (pē·nŭl′ tĭ·mĭt)
pe·nu·ri·ous (pē·nū′ rĭ·ŭs)
  pen·u·ry (pĕn′ û·rĭ)
pe·on (pē′ ŏn)
  pe·on·age (pē′ ŏn·ĭj)
pe·o·ny (pē′ ō·nĭ)
  -nies
peo·ple (pē′ p'l)
  -pling
pep·lum (pĕp′ lŭm)
pep·per (pĕp′ ēr)
  pep·per·corn pep·per·mint
  pep·per·y
pep·sin (pĕp′ sĭn)
pep·tic (pĕp′ tĭk)
pep·tone (pĕp′ tōn)
per·ad·ven·ture
  (pûr′ ăd·vĕn′ tûr)
per·am·bu·late
  (pĕr·ăm′ bū·lāt)
  -lat·ing
  per·am·bu·la·tion
    (pĕr·ăm′ bū·lā′ shŭn)
  per·am·bu·la·tor
    (pĕr·ăm′ bū·lā′ tēr)
per an·num (pēr ăn′ ŭm)
per·bo·rate (pûr·bō′ rāt)
per·cale (pēr·kāl′)
per cap·i·ta (pēr·kăp′ ĭ·tá)
per·ceive (pēr·sēv′)
  -ceiv·ing per·ceiv·a·ble
per cent (pēr sĕnt′)
  per·cent·age (pēr·sĕn′ tĭj)
  per·cen·tile (pēr·sĕn′ tĭl)
per·cept (pûr′ sĕpt)
per·cep·ti·ble (pēr·sĕp′ tĭ·b'l)

per·cep·tion (pēr·sĕp′ shŭn)
per·cep·tive (pēr·sĕp′ tĭv)
perch (pûrch)
per·chance (pēr·cháns′)
per·cip·i·ent (pēr·sĭp′ ĭ·ĕnt)
  -ence
per·co·late (pûr′ kō·lāt)
  -lat·ing per·co·la·tor
per·cus·sion (pēr·kŭsh′ ŭn)
per·di·tion (pēr·dĭsh′ ŭn)
per·dur·a·ble (pûr·dūr′ á·b'l)
per·e·gri·nate (pēr′ ē·grĭ·nāt)
  -nat·ing
  per·e·gri·na·tion
    (pēr′ ē·grĭ·nā′ shŭn)
per·emp·to·ry (pēr·ĕmp′ tō·rĭ)
  per·emp·to·ri·ly
per·en·ni·al (pēr·ĕn′ ĭ·ǎl)
  per·en·ni·al·ly
per·fect (pûr′ fĕkt) *adj.*
  per·fect par·ti·ci·ple
per·fect (pēr·fĕkt′) *v.*
  per·fect·i·bil·i·ty
    (pēr·fĕk′ tĭ·bĭl′ ĭ·tĭ)
  per·fect·i·ble
  per·fec·tion (pēr·fĕk′ shŭn)
  per·fec·tion·ist
per·fec·to (pēr·fĕk′ tō)
per·fi·dy (pûr′ fĭ·dĭ)
  -dies
  per·fid·i·ous (pēr·fĭd′ ĭ·ŭs)
per·fo·rate (pûr′ fō·rāt)
  -rat·ing
  per·fo·ra·tion
    (pûr′ fō·rā′ shŭn)
per·force (pēr·fōrs′)
per·form (pēr·fōrm′)
  per·form·a·ble per·form·ance
per·fume (pēr·fūm′)
  -fum·ing
per·func·to·ry (pēr·fŭngk′ tō·rĭ)
  per·func·to·ri·ly
  per·func·to·ri·ness
per·haps (pēr·hăps′)
Per·i·cles (pĕr′ ĭ·klēz)
Per·i·cle·an (pĕr′ ĭ·klē′ ǎn)
per·i·gee (pĕr′ ĭ·jē)
per·i·he·li·on (pĕr′ ĭ·hē′ lĭ·ŏn)
per·il (pĕr′ ĭl)
  -iled -il·ing
  per·il·ous (pĕr′ ĭ·lŭs)
per·im·e·ter (pē·rĭm′ ē·tēr)
per·i·ne·um (pĕr′ ĭ·nē′ ŭm)
pe·ri·od (pēr′ ĭ·ŭd)
  pe·ri·od·ic (pēr′ ĭ·ŏd′ ĭk)

pe·ri·od·i·cal (pēr′ ĭ·ŏd′ ĭ·k*a*l)
-cal·ly
pe·ri·o·dic·i·ty
        (pēr′ ĭ·ō·dĭs′ ĭ·tĭ)
per·i·os·te·um (pĕr′ ĭ·ŏs′ tē·ŭm)
per·i·pa·tet·ic (pĕr′ ĭ·pá·tĕt′ ĭk)
pe·riph·er·y (pě·rĭf′ ēr·ĭ)
-er·ies
pe·riph·er·al (pě·rĭf′ ēr·*a*l)
per·i·scope (pēr′ ĭ·skōp)
  per·i·scop·ic (pēr′ ĭ·skŏp′ ĭk)
per·ish (pēr′ ĭsh)
  per·ish·a·ble
per·i·stal·sis (pēr′ ĭ·stăl′ sĭs)
  per·i·stal·tic (-tĭk)
per·i·to·ni·tis (pēr′ ĭ·tō·nī′ tĭs)
per·i·wig (pēr′ ĭ·wĭg)
per·i·win·kle (pēr′ ĭ·wĭng′ k′l)
per·jure (pûr′ jēr)
  -jur·ing per·jur·er
  per·ju·ry
perk·y (pûrk′ ĭ)
per·ma·nent (pûr′ má·nĕnt)
  -nence
per·man·ga·nate
        (pēr·măng′ gá·nāt)
per·me·ate (pûr′ mē·āt)
  -at·ing
  per·me·a·bil·i·ty
        (pûr′ mē·á·bĭl′ ĭ·tĭ)
  per·me·a·ble (pûr′ mē·á·b′l)
per·mis·si·ble (pēr·mĭs′ ĭ·b′l)
  per·mis·si·bil·i·ty
        (pēr·mĭs′ ĭ·bĭl′ ĭ·tĭ)
per·mis·sion (pēr·mĭsh′ ŭn)
per·mis·sive (pēr·mĭs′ ĭv)
  -mis·sive·ly
per·mit (pēr·mĭt′) v.
  -mit·ted -mit·ting
per·mit (pûr′ mĭt) n.
per·mute (pēr·mūt′)
  -mut·ing
  per·mu·ta·tion
        (pûr′ mū·tā′ shŭn)
per·ni·cious a·ne·mi·a
        (pēr·nĭsh′ ŭs)
per·nick·et·y (pēr·nĭk′ ě·tĭ)
per·o·rate (pēr′ ō·rāt)
  -rat·ing
  per·o·ra·tion (pēr′ ō·rā′ shŭn)
per·ox·ide (pēr·ŏk′ sīd)
per·pen·dic·u·lar
        (pûr′ pĕn·dĭk′ ū·lēr)
per·pe·trate (pûr′ pē·trāt)
  -trat·ing

per·pe·tra·tion
        (pûr′ pē·trā′ shŭn)
per·pe·tra·tor
per·pet·u·al (pēr·pĕt′ ū·*a*l)
  -al·ly
  per·pet·u·ate (pēr·pĕt′ ū·āt)
  -at·ing
  per·pet·u·a·tion
        (pēr·pĕt′ ū·ā′ shŭn)
  per·pe·tu·i·ty (pûr′ pē·tū′ ĭ·tĭ)
per·plex (pēr·plĕks′)
per·se·cute (pûr′ sē·kūt)
  -cut·ing
  per·se·cu·tion
        (pûr′ sē·kū′ shŭn)
  per·se·cu·tor
per·se·vere (pûr′ sē·vēr′)
  -ver·ing per·se·ver·ance
Per·sian lamb (pûr′ zhǎn)
per·si·flage (pûr′ sĭ·fläzh)
per·sim·mon (pēr·sĭm′ ŭn)
per·sist (pēr·sĭst′)
  per·sis·tence -tent
per·son (pûr′ s′n)
  per·son·a·ble (pûr′ sŭn·á·b′l)
  per·son·age (-ĭj)
  per·son·al·i·ty
        (pûr′ sŭ·năl′ ĭ·tĭ)
  -ties
  per·son·al·ize, -iz·ing
  per·son·al·ly
per·so·na non gra·ta
        (pēr·sō′ ná nŏn grä′ tá)
per·son·al (pûr′ sŭn·*a*l)
  (private; see *personnel*)
per·son·i·fy (pēr·sŏn′ ĭ·fī)
  -fied -fy·ing
  per·son·i·fi·ca·tion
        (pēr·sŏn′ ĭ·fĭ·kā′ shŭn)
per·son·nel (pûr′ sō·nĕl′)
  (employees; see *personal*)
per·spec·tive (pēr·spĕk′ tĭv)
  (n.; appearance; see *prospective*)
per·spi·ca·cious
        (pûr′ spĭ·kā′ shŭs)
  per·spi·cac·i·ty
        (pûr′ spĭ·kǎs′ ĭ·tĭ)
per·spi·cu·i·ty (pûr′ spĭ·kū′ ĭ·tĭ)
per·spire (pēr·spīr′)
  -spir·ing
  per·spi·ra·tion
        (pûr′ spĭ·rā′ shŭn)
per·suade (pēr·swād′)
  -suad·ing per·suad·a·ble
  per·suad·er

per·sua·sion   (-swā′ zhŭn)
per·sua·sive
per·sua·sive·ness
per·tain   (pĕr·tān′)
per·ti·na·cious   (pûr′ tĭ·nā′ shŭs)
  per·ti·nac·i·ty   (-năs′ ĭ·tĭ)
per·ti·nent   (pûr′ tĭ·nĕnt)
  -nence
per·turb   (pĕr·tûrb′)
  per·turb·a·ble
  per·tur·ba·tion
              (pûr′ tĕr·bā′ shŭn)
pe·ruke   (pĕ·rōōk′)
pe·ruse   (pĕ·rōōz′)
  -rus·ing
  pe·rus·al   (pĕ·rōōz′ ăl)
per·vade   (pĕr·vād′)
  -vad·ing   per·va·sion
  per·va·sive
per·verse   (pĕr·vûrs′)
  per·verse·ly
per·ver·sion   (pĕr·vûr′ zhŭn)
per·vert   (pĕr·vûrt′) v.
per·vert   (pûr′ vûrt) n.
pe·so   (pā′ sō)
  -sos
pes·si·mism   (pĕs′ ĭ·mĭz′m)
  pes·ai·mist
  pes·si·mis·ti·cal·ly
              (pĕs′ ĭ·mĭs′ tĭ·kăl·ĭ)
pes·ti·cide   (pĕs′ tĭ·sīd)
pes·tif·er·ous   (pĕs·tĭf′ ĕr·ŭs)
pes·ti·lent   (pĕs′ tĭ·lĕnt)
  -lence
  pes·ti·len·tial   (pĕs′ tĭ·lĕn′ shăl)
pes·tle   (pĕs′ l)
pet·al   (pĕt′ l)
pe·tard   (pĕ·tärd′)
pet·cock   (pĕt′ kŏk′)
pe·tite   (pĕ·tēt′)
pe·ti·tion   (pĕ·tĭsh′ ŭn)
  pe·ti·tion·ar·y
  pe·ti·tion·er
pet·it ju·ry   (pĕt′ ĭ)
pe·tits fours   (pĕ·tē′ fōōr′)
pet·ri·fy   (pĕt′ rĭ·fĭ)
  -fied   -fy·ing
pe·tro·le·um   (pĕ·trō′ lē·ŭm)
pe·trol·o·gy   (pĕ·trŏl′ ō·jĭ)
pet·ti·coat   (pĕt′ ĭ·kōt)
pet·ti·fog   (pĕt′ ĭ·fŏg)
  -fogged   -fog·ging
  pet·ti·fog·ger
pet·ty   (pĕt′ ĭ)
  pet·ti·ness   pet·ty cash

pet·ty lar·ce·ny
pet·u·lant   (pĕt′ û·lănt)
  -lance   -lan·cy
pe·tu·ni·a   (pĕ·tū′ nĭ·à)
pew   (pū)
pew·ter   (pū′ tĕr)
pha·lanx   (fā′ lăngks)
  -lanx·es
phal·lus   (făl′ ŭs)
  phal·lic   (făl′ ĭk)
phan·tom   (făn′ tŭm)
Phar·aoh   (făr′ ō)
Phar·i·see   (făr′ ĭ·sē)
  phar·i·sa·i·cal   (făr′ ĭ·sā′ ĭ·kăl)
phar·ma·cy   (făr′ mà·sĭ)
  -cies
  phar·ma·ceu·ti·cal
              (fär′ mà·sū′ tĭ·kăl)
  phar·ma·cist   (făr′ mà·sĭst)
  phar·ma·col·o·gy
              (fär′ mà·kŏl′ ō·jĭ)
phar·ynx   (făr′ ĭngks)
  pl. pha·ryn·ges
phase   (fāz)
  (aspect; see faze)
pheas·ant   (fĕz′ ănt)
phe·no·bar·bi·tal
              (fē′ nō·bär′ bĭ·tôl)
phe·nom·e·non   (fē·nŏm′ ē·nŏn)
  pl. phe·nom·e·na
  phe·nom·e·nal
Phil·a·del·phi·a,
  Pa.   (fĭl′ à·dĕl′ fĭ·à)
phi·lan·der·er   (fĭ·lăn′ dēr·ēr)
phi·lan·thro·py
              (fĭ·lăn′ thrō·pĭ)
  phil·an·throp·ic
              (fĭl′ ăn·thrŏp′ ĭk)
  phil·an·throp·ist
phi·lat·e·ly   (fĭ·lăt′ ĕ·lĭ)
  phi·lat·e·list   (fĭ·lăt′ ĕ·lĭst)
phil·har·mon·ic
              (fĭl′ ĕr·mŏn′ ĭk)
Phil·ip, Prince, Duke of
  Ed·in·burgh
              (fĭl′ ĭp;
              ĕd′ 'n·bûr′ ō)
phi·lip·pic   (fĭ·lĭp′ ĭk)
Phil·ip·pine (is.)   (fĭl′ ĭ·pēn)
  But: Fil·i·pi·no
Phi·lis·tine   (fĭ·lĭs′ tĭn)
phil·o·den·dron
              (fĭl′ ō·dĕn′ drŏn)

phi·lol·o·gy   (fĭ·lŏl′ ō·jĭ)
  phi·lol·o·gist
phi·los·o·phy   (fĭ·lŏs′ ō·fĭ)
  -phies   phi·los·o·pher
  phil·o·soph·i·cal
     (fĭl′ ō·sŏf′ ĭ·kăl)
  phi·los·o·phize
phil·ter   (fĭl′ tẽr)
  (as in *love philter*; see *filter*)
phlegm   (flĕm)
  phleg·mat·ic   (flĕg·măt′ ĭk)
phlo·gis·tic   (flō·jĭs′ tĭk)
phlo·gis·ton   (flō·jĭs′ tŏn)
phlox   (flŏks)
pho·bi·a   (fō′ bĭ·à)
  pho·bic   (fō′ bĭk)
phoe·be   (fē′ bè)
Phoe·ni·cian   (fē·nĭsh′ ăn)
Phoe·nix, Ariz.   (fē′ nĭks)
pho·net·ic   (fō·nĕt′ ĭk)
  pho·net·i·cal·ly
phon·ics   (fŏn′ ĭks)
pho·no·graph   (fō′ nō·grȧf)
phos·gene   (fŏz′ jēn)
phos·phate   (fŏs′ fāt)
phos·pho·res·cence
     (fŏs′ fō·rĕs′ ĕns)
  -cent
phos·pho·rus   (fŏs′ fō·rŭs)
  phos·phor·ic   (fŏs·fŏr′ ĭk)
pho·to   (fō′ tō)
  -toed, -to·ing, -tos
pho·to·e·lec·tric
     (fō′ tō·ê·lĕk′ trĭk)
pho·to·en·grav·ing
     (fō′ tō·ĕn·grăv′ ĭng)
pho·to·flood lamp
     (fō′ tō·flŭd′)
pho·to·gen·ic   (fō′ tō·jĕn′ ĭk)
pho·to·graph   (fō′ tō·grȧf)
  pho·tog·ra·pher
     (fō·tŏg′ rȧ·fẽr)
  pho·to·graph·ic
     (fō′ tō·grȧf′ ĭk)
  pho·tog·ra·phy
     (fō·tŏg′ rȧ·fĭ)
pho·to·gra·vure   (fō′ tō·grȧ·vūr′)
pho·to·mu·ral   (fō′ tō·mū′ răl)
pho·to·off·set   (fō′ tō·ôf′ sĕt′)
pho·to·sen·si·tive
     (fō′ tō·sĕn′ sĭ·tĭv)
pho·to·sphere   (fō′ tō·sfẽr)
Pho·to·stat   (fō′ tō·stăt)
pho·to·syn·the·sis
     (fō′ tō·sĭn′ thê·sĭs)

phrase   (frāz)
  phras·ing   phras·al
phra·se·o·log·i·cal
     (frā′ zê·ō·lŏj′ ĭ·kăl)
phra·se·ol·o·gy
     (frā′ zê·ŏl′ ō·jĭ)
phre·net·ic   (frê·nĕt′ ĭk)
phre·nol·o·gy   (frê·nŏl′ ō·jĭ)
phy·log·e·ny   (fĭ·lŏj′ ê·nĭ)
phy·lum   (fī′ lŭm)
  pl. phy·la
phys·ic   (fĭz′ ĭk)
phys·i·cal   (fĭz′ ĭ·kăl)
  phys·i·cal ther·a·py
phy·si·cian   (fĭ·zĭsh′ ăn)
phys·ics   (fĭz′ ĭks)
  phys·i·cist   (fĭz′ ĭ·sĭst)
phys·i·og·no·my
     (fĭz′ ĭ·ŏg′ nō·mĭ)
  -mies
phys·i·ol·o·gy   (fĭz′ ĭ·ŏl′ ō·jĭ)
  phys·i·o·log·i·cal
     (fĭz′ ĭ·ō·lŏj′ ĭ·kăl)
phys·i·o·ther·a·py
     (fĭz′ ĭ·ō·thĕr′ ȧ·pĭ)
phy·sique   (fĭ·zēk′)
pi·a·nis·si·mo   (pê′ ȧ·nĭs′ ĭ·mō)
pi·an·o   (pĭ·ăn′ ō)
  -os
  pi·an·ist   (pĭ·ăn′ ĭst)
pi·az·za   (pĭ·ăz′ à)
pi·ca   (pī′ kȧ)
pic·a·resque   (pĭk′ ȧ·rĕsk′)
pic·a·yune   (pĭk′ ȧ·yōōn′)
  pic·a·yun·ish
Pic·ca·dil·ly   (pĭk′ ȧ·dĭl′ ĭ)
pic·ca·lil·li   (pĭk′ ȧ·lĭl′ ĭ)
pic·co·lo   (pĭk′ ō·lō)
  -los
pick·a·back   (pĭk′ ȧ·băk′)
pick·a·nin·ny   (pĭk′ ȧ·nĭn′ ĭ)
  -nin·nies
pick·ax   (pĭk′ ăks′)
  -ax·es
pick·er·el   (pĭk′ ẽr·ĕl)
  pick·er·el·weed
pick·et   (pĭk′ ĕt)
  -et·ed   -et·ing
  pick·et·er
pick·le   (pĭk′ 'l)
  -ling
pick·pock·et   (pĭk′ pŏk′ ĕt)
pick·up   (pĭk′ ŭp′)
pic·nic   (pĭk′ nĭk)
  -nicked   -nick·ing

pic·nick·er

pic·to·graph (pĭk′ tṓ·gráf)

pic·to·ri·al (pĭk·tṓ′ rĭ·ȧl)
-al·ly

pic·ture (pĭk′ tŭr)
-tur·ing

pic·tur·esque (pĭk′ tŭr·ĕsk′)

pid·dling (pĭd′ lĭng)

pidg·in Eng·lish
(pĭj′ ĭn)

pie·bald (pī′ bôld′)

piece (pēs)
piec·ing   piece·meal
piece·work

piéce de ré·sis·tance
(pyĕs′ dĕ rā′ zĕs′ täns′)

pied (pīd)

pied·mont (pēd′ mŏnt)

pier (pēr)
(breakwater; see *peer*)

pierce (pērs)
pierc·ing

pi·e·ty (pī′ ĕ·tĭ)
-ties

pig (pĭg)
pig·head·ed   pig i·ron
pig·pen   pig·skin
pig·sty   -sties
pig·tail

pi·geon (pĭj′ ŭn)
pi·geon-breast·ed
pi·geon-hole   pi·geon-toed

pig·gy bank (pĭg′ ĭ)

pig·ment (pĭg′ mĕnt)
pig·men·tar·y (pĭg′ mĕn·tĕr′ ĭ)
pig·men·ta·tion
(pĭg′ mĕn·tā′ shŭn)

pi·las·ter (pĭ·lăs′ tĕr)

pi·lau (pĭ·lō′)

pil·chard (pĭl′ chĕrd)

pile driv·er (pīl)

pil·fer (pĭl′ fĕr)
pil·fer·age   pil·fer·er

pil·grim (pĭl′ grĭm)
pil·grim·age (pĭl′ grĭ·mĭj)
Pil·grim Fa·thers

pil·ing (pĭl′ ĭng)

pil·lage (pĭl′ ĭj)

pil·lar (pĭl′ ĕr)

pill·box (pĭl′ bŏks′)

pil·lo·ry (pĭl′ ṓ·rĭ)
-ries

pil·low (pĭl′ ṓ)
pil·low·case   pil·low slip

pi·lot (pī′ lŭt)
-lot·ed   -lot·ing

Pilt·down man (pĭlt′ doun′)

pi·men·to (pĭ·mĕn′ tṓ)
-tos

pim·per·nel (pĭm′ pĕr·nĕl)

pim·ple (pĭm′ p′l)
-ply

pin·a·fore (pĭn′ ȧ·fōr′)

pin·ball ma·chine
(pĭn′ bôl′)

pince-nez (păns′ nā′)

pin·cers (pĭn′ sĕrz)

pinch hit·ter (pĭnch)

pin·cush·ion (pĭn′ kŏŏsh′ ŭn)

pin·e·al gland (pĭn′ ê·ȧl)

pine·ap·ple (pīn′ ăp′ ′l)

pin·feath·er (pĭn′ fĕth′ ĕr)

Ping-pong (pĭng′ pŏng′)

pin·hole (pĭn′ hōl′)

pin·ion (pĭn′ yŭn)

pink·eye (pĭngk′ ī′)

pin·nace (pĭn′ ĭs)

pin·na·cle (pĭn′ ȧ·k′l)

pin·nate (pĭn′ āt)

pi·noch·le (pē′ nŭk′ ′l)

pin·point (pĭn′ point′)

pin·tail duck (pĭn′ tāl′)

pin·to (pĭn′ tṓ)

pin-up (pĭn′ ŭp′)

pi·o·neer (pī′ ō·nēr′)

pi·ous (pī′ ŭs)
pi·e·ty (pī′ ĕ·tĭ)

pipe (pīp)
pip·ing   pipe dream
pipe·line   pipe or·gan

pi·pette (pĭ·pĕt′)

pi·quant (pē′ kȧnt)
pi·quan·cy (pē′ kȧn·sĭ)

pique (pēk)

pi·qué (pē·kā′)

pi·ra·nha fish (pĭ·rän′ yȧ)

pi·rate (pī′ rĭt)
pi·ra·cy (pī′ rȧ·sĭ)

pir·ou·ette (pĭr′ ŏŏ·ĕt′)
-ett·ing

pis·ca·to·ri·al (pĭs′ kȧ·tṓ′ rĭ·ȧl)

pis·tach·i·o (pĭs·tăsh′ ĭ·ō)

pis·til (pĭs′ tĭl)
(plant part; see *pistol*)

pis·tol (pĭs′ t′l)
(firearm; see *pistil*)

pis·ton ring (pĭs′ tŭn)

pitch (pĭch)
pitch-black

pitch·blende (pĭch′ blĕnd′)
pitch·er pitch·fork
pitch pipe
pit·e·ous (pĭt′ ê·ŭs)
pit·fall (pĭt′ fôl′)
pith·y (pĭth′ ĭ)
pit·i·a·ble (pĭt′ ĭ·à·b'l)
pit·i·ful (pĭt′ ĭ·fŏŏl)
-ful·ly -ful·ness
pit·i·less (pĭt′ ĭ·lĕs)
pi′ ton (pē′ tôn′)
pit·tance (pĭt′ ăns)
Pitts·burg, Kans. (pĭts′ bûrg)
Pitts·burgh, Pa. (pĭts′ bûrg)
pi·tu·i·tar·y gland
(pĭ·tū′ ĭ·tĕr′ ĭ)
pit·y (pĭt′ ĭ)
pit·ied pit·y·ing
pit·e·ous (pĭt′ ê·ŭs)
pit·i·a·ble
pit·i·ful, -ful·ly, -ful·ness
pit·i·less
piv·ot (pĭv′ ŭt)
-ot·ed -ot·ing
piv·ot·al
pix·y (pĭk′ sĭ)
pix·ies
piz·za (pēt′ sà)
piz·ze·ri·a (pēt′ sĕ·rē′ à)
plac·ard (plăk′ ărd)
pla·cate (plā′ kāt)
-cat·ing
pla·ce·bo (plà·sē′ bō)
place·ment (plās′ mĕnt)
pla·cen·ta (plà·sĕn′ tà)
pla·cen·tal
plac·er min·ing (plăs′ ēr)
plac·id (plăs′ ĭd)
pla·cid·i·ty (plà·sĭd′ ĭ·tĭ)
plack·et (plăk′ ĕt)
pla·gi·a·rism (plā′ jĭ·à·rĭz'm)
pla·gi·a·rist pla·gi·a·rize
pla·gi·ar·y
plague (plāg)
plaid (plăd)
plain (plān)
plain-clothes man
plains·man
plaint (plānt)
plain·tiff (plān′ tĭf)
plain·tive (plān′ tĭv)
plain·tive·ly
plait·ing (plăt′ ĭng)
plane (plān)
plane an·gle

plane ge·om·e·try
plan·et (plăn′ ĕt)
plan·e·tar·y (plăn′ ĕ·tĕr′ ĭ)
plan·e·tar·i·um
(plăn′ ĕ·târ′ ĭ·ŭm)
pl. plan·e·tar·i·a
plank (plăngk)
plank·ton (plăngk′ tŏn)
plank·ton·io (plăngk·tŏn′ ĭk)
pla·no·graph (plā′ nō·gráf)
plan·tain (plăn′ tĭn)
plan·ta·tion (plăn·tā′ shŭn)
plaque (plăk)
plas·ma (plăz′ mà)
plas·ter (plăs′ tĕr)
plas·ter·board plas·ter cast
plas·ter of Par·is
plas·tic (plăs′ tĭk)
plas·tic·i·ty (plăs·tĭs′ ĭ·tĭ)
plas·tic sur·ger·y
plate (plāt)
plat·ing plate·ful
plate glass plate·let
pla·teau (plà·tō′)
plat·en (plăt′ 'n)
plat·form (plăt′ fôrm′)
plat·i·num (plăt′ ĭ·nŭm)
plat·i·tude (plăt′ ĭ·tūd)
plat·i·tu·di·nous
(plăt′ ĭ·tū′ dĭ·nŭs)
Pla·ton·ic (plà·tŏn′ ĭk)
pla·toon (plà·tōōn′)
plat·ter (plăt′ ĕr)
plat·y·pus (plăt′ ĭ·pŭs)
-pus·es
plau·dit (plô′ dĭt)
plau·si·ble (plô′ zĭ·b'l)
plau·si·bil·i·ty
(plô′ zĭ·bĭl′ ĭ·tĭ)
play (plā)
play·bill play·boy
play·ful, -ful·ly, -ful·ness
play·go·er play·ground
play-off play·wright
play·writ·ing
pla·za (plä′ zá)
plea (plē)
plead (plēd)
plead·a·ble
pleas·ant (plĕz′ ănt)
pleas·ance pleas·ant·ry
-ries
please (plēz)
pleas·ing

pleas·ure   (plĕzh′ ẽr)
  pleas·ur·a·ble
pleat   (plēt)
ple·be·ian   (plė· bē′ yăn)
pleb·i·scite   (plĕb′ ĭ·sīt)
pledge   (plĕj)
  pledg·ing
  pledg·ee   (plĕj′ ē′)
Pleis·to·cene   (plīs′ tō·sēn)
ple·na·ry   (plē′ nȧ·rĭ)
plen·i·po·ten·ti·ar·y
                         (plĕn′ ĭ·pȯ·tĕn′ shĭ·ĕr′ ĭ)
plen·te·ous   (plĕn′ tė·ŭs)
plen·ti·ful   (plĕn′ tĭ·fŏŏl)
  -ful·ly   -ful·ness
pleth·o·ra   (plĕth′ ȯ·rȧ)
pleu·ri·sy   (plŏŏr′ ĭ·sĭ)
plex·us   (plĕk′ sŭs)
pli·a·ble   (plī′ ȧ·b′l)
  pli·a·bil·i·ty   (plī′ ȧ·bĭl′ ĭ·tĭ)
  pli·a·ble·ness
pli·ant   (plī′ ănt)
  pli·an·cy
pli·ers   (plī′ ẽrz)
plight   (plīt)
plinth   (plĭnth)
Pli·o·cene   (plī′ ȯ·sēn)
plod   (plŏd)
  plod·ded   plod·ding
plot·ter   (plŏt′ ẽr)
plov·er   (plŭv′ ẽr)
plow·share   (plou′ shâr′)
pluck·y   (plŭk′ ĭ)
  pluck·i·ness
plum·age   (plōōm′ ĭj)
plumb   (plŭm)
  plumb·er   plumb·ing
  plumb line
plume   (plōōm)
  plum·age
plum·met   (plŭm′ ĕt)
  plum·met·ed   plum·met·ing
plun·der   (plŭn′ dẽr)
plunge   (plŭnj)
  plung·ing
plu·per·fect   (plōō′ pûr′ fĕkt)
plu·ral   (plŏŏr′ ȧl)
  plu·ral·is·tic   (plŏŏr′ ȧl·ĭs′ tĭk)
  plu·ral·i·ty   (plŏŏ·răl′ ĭ·tĭ)
plus   (plŭs)
plu·toc·ra·cy   (plōō·tŏk′ rȧ·sĭ)
  plu·to·crat   (plōō′ tȯ·krăt)
plu·to·ni·um   (plōō·tȯ′ nĭ·ŭm)
ply   (plī)
  plied   ply·ing

ply·wood
Ply·mouth rock   (plĭm′ ŭth)
pneu·mat·ic   (nŭ·măt′ ĭk)
pneu·mo·ni·a   (nŭ·mō′ nĭ·ȧ)
poach·er   (pōch′ ẽr)
pock·et   (pŏk′ ĕt)
  -et·ed   -et·ing
  pock·et·book   pock·et·knife
  pock·et mon·ey
  pock·et ve·to
pock·mark   (pŏk′ märk′)
  pock-marked
po·di·um   (pō′ dĭ·ŭm)
  pl. po·di·a
po·et   (pō′ ĕt)
  po·em
  po·et·ic   (pō·ĕt′ ĭk)
  po·et·i·cal   (pō·ĕt′ ĭ·kȧl)
  -cal·ly   po·et·ic li·cense
  po·et lau·re·ate
  po·et·ry
po·grom   (pō·grŏm′)
poign·ant   (poin′ yȧnt)
  poign·an·cy
poin·set·ti·a   (poin·sĕt′ ĭ·ȧ)
point·less   (point′ lĕs)
poi·son   (poi′ z′n)
  poi·son i·vy   poi·son·ous
  poi·son su·mac
poke bon·net   (pōk)
po·ker face   (pō′ kẽr)
po·lar   (pō′ lẽr)
  po·lar bear
  po·lar·i·ty   (pō·lăr′ ĭ·tĭ)
Po·la·ris   (pō·lā′ rĭs)
po·lar·ize   (pō′ lẽr·īz)
  -iz·ing
  po·lar·i·za·tion
                         (pō′ lẽr·ĭ·zā′ shŭn)
Po·lar·oid   (pō′ lẽr·oid)
pole   (pōl)
  (long piece of wood; see poll)
po·lem·ic   (pō·lĕm′ ĭk)
  po·lem·i·cist   (pō·lĕm′ ĭ·sĭst)
pole·star   (pōl′ stär′)
pole vault·er   (pōl)
  pole-vault v.
po·lice·man   (pō·lēs′ mȧn)
pol·i·cy   (pŏl′ ĭ·sĭ)
  -cies   pol·i·cy·hold·er
po·li·o   (pō′ lĭ·ō)
  po·li·o·my·e·li·tis
                         (pō′ lĭ·ȯ·mī′ ĕ·lī′ tĭs)
pol·ish   (pŏl′ ĭsh)

po·lite (pṓ·līt′)
  po·lite·ly
pol·i·tics (pŏl′ ĭ·tĭks)
  po·lit·i·cal (pṓ·lĭt′ ĭ·kăl)
  pol·i·ti·cian (pŏl′ ĭ·tĭsh′ ăn)
  po·lit·i·co (pṓ·lĭt′ ĭ·kō)
  -cos
pol·i·ty (pŏl′ ĭ·tĭ)
pol·ka (pō(l)′ kȧ)
  pol·ka dot
poll (pōl)
  (survey; see pole)
  poll·ee poll·ster
  poll tax
pol·len (pŏl′ ĕn)
pol·li·nate (pŏl′ ĭ·nāt)
  -nat·ing
  pol·li·na·tion (pŏl′ ĭ·nā′ shŭn)
pol·li·wog (pŏl′ ĭ·wŏg)
pol·lute (pṓ·lūt′)
  pol·lut·ing
  pol·lu·tion (pṓ·lū′ shŭn)
Pol·ly·an·na (pŏl′ ĭ·ăn′ ȧ)
po·lo (pō′ lō)
  po·lo coat po·lo shirt
pol·o·naise (pŏl′ ȯ·nāz′)
pol·ter·geist (pŏl′ tẽr·gīst′)
pol·troon (pŏl·trōōn′)
pol·y·an·dry (pŏl′ ĭ·ăn′ drĭ)
pol·y·chro·mat·ic
  (pŏl′ ĭ·krō·măt′ ĭk)
pol·y·eth·yl·ene
  (pŏl′ ĭ·ĕth′ ĭ·lēn)
po·lyg·a·my (pṓ·lĭg′ ȧ·mĭ)
  po·lyg·a·mist po·lyg·a·mous
pol·y·glot (pŏl′ ĭ·glŏt)
pol·y·gon (pŏl′ ĭ·gŏn)
  po·lyg·o·nal (pṓ·lĭg′ ȯ·năl)
po·lyg·y·ny (pṓ·lĭj′ ĭ·nĭ)
Pol·y·ne·sian (pŏl′ ĭ·nē′ shăn)
pol·yp (pŏl′ ĭp)
pol·y·phon·ic (pŏl′ ĭ·fŏn′ ĭk)
pol·y·tech·nic (pŏl′ ĭ·tĕk′ nĭk)
po·made (pṓ·mād′)
pome·gran·ate (pŏm′ grăn′ ĭt)
pom·pa·dour (pŏm′ pȧ·dŏr)
pom·pa·no (pŏm′ pȧ·nō)
pom·pon (pŏm′ pŏn)
pomp·ous (pŏmp′ ŭs)
  pom·pos·i·ty (pŏm·pŏs′ ĭ·tĭ)
pon·cho (pŏn′ chō)
  -chos
pon·der (pŏn′ dẽr)
  pon·der·a·ble pon·der·ous
pon·gee (pŏn·jē′)

pon·tiff (pŏn′ tĭf)
  pon·tif·i·cal (pŏn·tĭf′ ĭ·kăl)
  pon·tif·i·cate (pŏn·tĭf′ ĭ·kāt)
  -cat·ing
pon·toon (pŏn·tōōn′)
po·ny (pō′ nĭ)
  -nies
poo·dle (pōō′ d’l)
pooh-pooh (pōō′ pōō′)
pope (pōp)
  pop·er·y pop·ish
pop·lar (pŏp′ lẽr)
pop·lin (pŏp′ lĭn)
pop·py (pŏp′ ĭ)
  pop·pies
pop·u·lace (pŏp′ û·lĭs)
pop·u·lar (pŏp′ û·lẽr)
  pop·u·lar·i·ty (pŏp′ û·lăr′ ĭ·tĭ)
  pop·u·lar·i·za·tion
    (pŏp′ û·lẽr·ĭ·zā′ shŭn)
  pop·u·lar·ize -izing
pop·u·late (pŏp′ û·lāt)
  -lat·ing
  pop·u·la·tion (pŏp′ û·lā′ shŭn)
Pop·u·list (pŏp′ û·lĭst)
pop·u·lous (pŏp′ û·lŭs)
por·ce·lain (pōr′ sĕ·lĭn)
por·cu·pine (pōr′ kû·pīn)
pore (pōr)
  por·ing (n.: a tiny opening;
    v.: to study; see pour)
po·ros·i·ty (pṓ·rŏs′ ĭ·tĭ)
po·rous (pō′ rŭs)
por·no·graph·ic
    (pōr′ nṓ·grăf′ ĭk)
por·poise (pōr′ pŭs)
por·ridge (pōr′ ĭj)
por·ta·ble (pōr′ tȧ·b’l)
  port·a·bil·i·ty (pōr′ tȧ·bĭl′ ĭ·tĭ)
por·tage (pōr′ tĭj)
por·tal (pōr′ tăl)
por·tend (pōr·tĕnd′)
  por·tent (pōr′ tĕnt)
  por·ten·tous (pōr·tĕn′ tŭs)
por·ter·house steak
    (pōr′ tẽr·hous′)
port·fo·li·o (pōrt·fō′ lĭ·ō)
  -os
por·ti·co (pōr′ tĭ·kō)
  -coes
por·tion (pōr′ shŭn)
port·land ce·ment
    (pōrt′ lănd)
port·ly (pōrt′ lĭ)
  port·li·ness

port·man·teau (pôrt·măn′ tō)
por·trait (pōr′ trāt)
  por·trai·ture (pōr′ trā·tŭr)
por·tray (pōr·trā′)
  por·tray·a·ble por·tray·al
Por·tu·guese (pōr′ tŭ·gēz)
pos·it (pŏz′ ĭt)
  -it·ed -it·ing
po·si·tion (pô·zĭsh′ ŭn)
pos·i·tive (pŏz′ ĭ·tĭv)
  pos·i·tive·ly -tive·ness
  pos·i·tiv·ism
pos·se (pŏs′ ē)
pos·sess (pô·zĕs′)
  pos·ses·sion pos·ses·sive
  pos·ses·sive·ness
  pos·ses·sor
pos·si·ble (pŏs′ ĭ·b′l)
  pos·si·bil·i·ty (pŏs′ ĭ·bĭl′ ĭ·tĭ)
pos·sum (pŏs′ ŭm)
post- (pŏst-)
  post·card post·date
  post ex·change
  post·grad·u·ate
  post·haste
  post·hu·mous (pŏs′ tŭ·mŭs)
  post·im·pres·sion·ism
  post·lude post·man
  post·mark post·mas·ter
  post me·rid·i·em
            (-mē·rĭd′ ĭ·ĕm)
  post·mis·tress post·mor·tem
  post·na·tal post of·fice
  post·or·bit·al post·paid
  post·pon·a·ble (pōst·pŏn′ ȧ·b′l)
  post·pone·ment
  post·Rev·o·lu·tion·ar·y
  post·script post·war
post·age (pōs′ tĭj)
post·al (pōs′ tăl)
post·er (pōs′ tēr)
pos·te·ri·or (pŏs·tēr′ ĭ·ēr)
pos·ter·i·ty (pŏs·tĕr′ ĭ·tĭ)
pos·tu·late (pŏs′ tŭ·lāt)
  -lat·ing
pos·ture (pŏs′ tŭr)
  pos·tur·al
po·sy (pō′ zĭ)
  -sies
pot· (pŏt-)
  pot·bel·ly -bel·lied
  pot·boil·er pot·hole
  pot·latch pot liq·uor
  pot·luck pot·pie
  pot shot

po·ta·ble (pō′ tȧ·b′l)
pot·ash (pŏt′ ăsh′)
po·tas·si·um (pô·tăs′ ĭ·ŭm)
  po·tas·si·um bro·mide
  car·bon·ate chlo·rate
  chlo·ride hy·drox·ide
  per·man·ga·nate
po·ta·tion (pō·tā′ shŭn)
po·ta·to (pô·tā′ tō)
  -toes po·ta·to bee·tle
  po·ta·to chips
po·tent (pō′ tĕnt)
  po·ten·cy
po·ten·tate (pō′ tĕn·tāt)
po·ten·tial (pō·tĕn′ shǎl)
  -tial·ly
  po·ten·ti·al·i·ty
        (pō·tĕn′ shĭ·ăl′ ĭ·tĭ)
pot·pour·ri (pō′ pōō′ rē′)
pot·sherd (pŏt′ shûrd′)
pot·tage (pŏt′ ĭj)
pot·ter·y (pŏt′ ēr·ĭ)
pouch (pouch)
Pough·keep·sie, (pô·kĭp′ sĭ)
  N. Y.
poul·tice (pōl′ tĭs)
poul·try (pōl′ trĭ)
pounce (pouns)
  pounc·ing
pound (pound)
  pound·age pound·cake
  pound-fool·ish
pour (pōr)
  (to flow; see *pore*)
pousse-ca·fé (pōōs′ kȧ′ fā′)
pout (pout)
pout·er pi·geon (pout′ ēr)
pov·er·ty (pŏv′ ēr·tĭ)
  pov·er·ty-strick·en
pow·der (pou′ dēr)
  pow·der horn pow·der room
pow·er (pou′ ēr)
  pow·er am·pli·fi·er
  pow·er·boat pow·er-driv·en
  pow·er·ful, -ful·ly, -ful·ness
  pow·er·less
pow·wow (pou′ wou′)
pox (pŏks)
prac·ti·ca·ble (prăk′ tĭ·kȧ·b′l)
  prac·ti·ca·bil·i·ty
       (prăk′ tĭ·kȧ·bĭl′ ĭ·tĭ)
prac·ti·cal (prăk′ tĭ·kăl)
  prac·ti·cal·i·ty
       (prăk′ tĭ·kăl′ ĭ·tĭ)
  prac·ti·cal·ly

prac·tice　(prăk′ tĭs)
　-tic·ing
prac·ti·tion·er　(prăk·tĭsh′ ŭn·ēr)
Prae·to·ri·an guard
　　　　　(prē·tô′ rĭ·ăn)
prag·mat·ic　(prăg·măt′ ĭk)
　prag·mat·i·cal·ly
　prag·ma·tism　(prăg′ mȧ·tĭz′m)
prai·rie　(prâr′ ĭ)
　prai·rie schoon·er
praise　(prāz)
　prais·ing
　praise·wor·thy, -wor·thi·ness
pra·line　(prä′ lēn)
prance　(prăns)
　pranc·ing
prank·ish　(prăngk′ ĭsh)
prate　(prāt)
　prat·ing
prat·tle　(prăt′ 'l)
　prat·tling
prawn　(prôn)
pray　(prā)
　(entreat; see prey)
prayer　(prâr)
pray·ing man·tis
　　　　　(prā′ ĭng măn′ tĭs)
preach　(prēch)
　preach·er　　preach·ment
pre·am·ble　(prē′ ăm′ b'l)
Pre-Cam·bri·an
　　　　　(prē′ kăm′ brĭ·ăn)
pre·can·cel　(prē·kăn′ sĕl)
　-celed　　-cel·ing
pre·car·i·ous　(prē·kâr′ ĭ·ŭs)
pre·cau·tion　(prē·kô′ shŭn)
　-tion·ar·y
pre·cede　(prē·sēd′)
　-ced·ing
　pre·ced·ence　(prē·sēd′ ĕns)
　pre·ced·ent　(prē·sēd′ ĕnt)
　(going before)
prec·e·dent　(prĕs′ ê·dĕnt)
　(setting an example)
pre·cept　(prē′ sĕpt)
pre·cinct　(prē′ sĭngkt)
pre·cious　(prĕsh′ ŭs)
prec·i·pice　(prĕs′ ĭ·pĭs)
pre·cip·i·tant　(prē·sĭp′ ĭ·tănt)
pre·cip·i·tate　(prē·sĭp′ ĭ·tāt)
　-tat·ing
　pre·cip·i·ta·tion
　　　　　(prē·sĭp′ ĭ·tā′ shŭn)
pre·cip·i·tous　(prē·sĭp′ ĭ·tŭs)

pré·cis　(prā·sē′)
　(summary; see precise)
pre·cise　(prē·sīs′)
　(sharply defined; se précis)
　pre·cise·ly
pre·ci·sion　(prē·sĭzh′ ŭn)
pre·clude　(prē·klōōd′)
　-clud·ing
　pre·clu·sion　(-klōō′ zhŭn)
pre·co·cious　(prē·kō′ shŭs)
pre·con·cep·tion
　　　　　(prē′ kŏn·sĕp′ shŭn)
pre·con·di·tion
　　　　　(prē′ kŏn·dĭsh′ ŭn)
　-tion·ing
pre·cur·sor　(prē·kûr′ sēr)
pred·a·tor　(prĕd′ ȧ·tēr)
　pred·a·to·ry　(prĕd′ ȧ·tô′ rĭ)
pred·e·ces·sor　(prĕd′ ê·sĕs′ ēr)
pre·des·ti·na·tion
　　　　　(prē·dĕs′ tĭ·nā′ shŭn)
pre·des·tine　(prē·dĕs′ tĭn)
　-tin·ing
pre·de·ter·mine
　　　　　(prē′ dê·tûr′ mĭn)
　-min·ing
pre·dic·a·ment
　　　　　(prē·dĭk′ ȧ·mĕnt)
pred·i·cate　(prĕd′ ĭ·kāt) v.
　-cat·ing　　(-kĭt) adj., n.
　pred·i·ca·tion
　　　　　(prĕd′ ĭ·kā′ shŭn)
pre·dict　(prē·dĭkt′)
　pre·dict·a·ble
　pre·dic·tion　(prē·dĭk′ shŭn)
　pre·dic·tive　　pre·dic·tor
pre·di·lec·tion　(prē′ dĭ·lĕk′ shŭn)
pre·dom·i·nant
　　　　　(prē·dŏm′ ĭ·nănt)
　-nance
　pre·dom·i·nate　　(-năt)
　-nat·ing
　pre·dom·i·na·tion
　　　　　(prē·dŏm′ ĭ·nā′ shŭn)
pre·em·i·nent　(prē·ĕm′ ĭ·nĕnt)
　pre·em·i·nence
pre·empt　(prē·ĕmpt′)
　pre·emp·tion　　pre·emp·tive
　pre·emp·to·ry
preen　(prēn)
pre·ex·ist·ence　(prē′ ĕg·zĭs′ tĕns)
pre·fab·ri·cate　(prē·făb′ rĭ·kāt)
　-cat·ing
　pre·fab·ri·ca·tion
　　　　　(prē′ făb·rĭ·kā′ shŭn)

pref·ace (prĕf' ĭs)
  -ac·ing
pre·fect (prē' fĕkt)
  pre·fec·ture
pre·fer (prē·fûr')
  -ferred -fer·ring
  pref·er·a·ble (prĕf' ĕr·ȧ·b'l)
  pref·er·ence (prĕf' ĕr·ĕns)
  pref·er·en·tial
    (prĕf' ĕr·ĕn' shȧl)
  pre·fer·ment (prē·fûr' mĕnt)
  pre·ferred stock (prē·fûrd')
preg·nant (prĕg' nȧnt)
  preg·nan·cy
pre·hen·sile (prē·hĕn' sĭl)
pre·his·tor·ic (prē' hĭs·tŏr' ĭk)
prej·u·dice (prĕj' ŏŏ·dĭs)
  prej·u·di·cial
    (prĕj' ŏŏ·dĭsh' ȧl)
prel·ate (prĕl' ĭt)
  prel·a·cy (-ȧ·sĭ)
  prel·a·ture (-ȧ·tŭr)
pre·lim·i·nar·y
    (prē·lĭm' ĭ·nĕr' ĭ)
  -nar·ies
  pre·lim·i·nar·i·ly
    (prē·lĭm' ĭ·nĕr' ĭ·lĭ)
prel·ude (prĕl' ūd)
pre·ma·ture (prē' mȧ·tūr')
  pre·ma·ture·ly
pre·med·i·cal (prē·mĕd' ĭ·kȧl)
pre·med·i·tate (prē·mĕd' ĭ·tāt)
  -tat·ing
  pre·med·i·ta·tion
    (prē' mĕd·ĭ·tā' shŭn)
pre·mi·er (prē' mĭ·ēr)
  (chief officer; see première)
pre·mière (prē·mēr')
  (first showing; see premier)
prem·ise (prĕm' ĭs)
pre·mi·um (prē' mĭ·ŭm)
pre·mo·lar (prē·mō' lēr)
pre·mo·ni·tion (prē' mō·nĭsh' ŭn)
  pre·mon·i·to·ry
    (prē·mŏn' ĭ·tō' rĭ)
pre·na·tal (prē·nā' tȧl)
pre·oc·cu·pa·tion
    (prē·ŏk' ū·pā' shŭn)
pre·oc·cu·py (prē·ŏk' ū·pĭ)
  -pied, -py·ing
pre·or·dain (prē' ôr·dān')
  pre·or·di·na·tion
    (prē' ôr·dĭ·nā' shŭn)
prep school (prĕp)

pre·pare (prē·pâr')
  -par·ing
  prep·a·ra·tion
    (prĕp' ȧ·rā' shŭn)
  pre·par·a·tive (prē·pǎr' ȧ·tĭv)
  pre·par·a·to·ry
    (prē·pǎr' ȧ·tō' rĭ)
  pre·par·ed·ness
    (prē·pǎr' ĕd·nĕs)
pre·pay (prē·pā')
  -paid -pay·ing
  pre·pay·ment
pre·pon·der·ance
    (prē·pŏn' dĕr·ȧns)
  -ant
prep·o·si·tion
    (prĕp' ō·zĭsh' ŭn)
  -tion·al
pre·pos·ses·sing
    (prē' pŏ·zĕs' ĭng)
pre·pos·ter·ous
    (prē·pŏs' tĕr·ŭs)
pre·req·ui·site (prē·rĕk' wĭ·zĭt)
pre·rog·a·tive (prē·rŏg' ȧ·tĭv)
pres·age (prĕs' ĭj) n.
pre·sage (prē·sāj') v.
  -sag·ing
Pres·by·te·ri·an
    (prĕz' bĭ·tēr' ĭ·ȧn)
pres·by·ter·y (prĕz' bĭ·tĕr' ĭ)
  -ter·ies
pre·school (prē·skŏŏl')
pre·sci·ence (prē' shĭ·ĕns)
pre·scind (prē·sĭnd')
pre·scribe (prē·skrīb')
  (dictate; see proscribe)
  -scrib·ing
  pre·scrip·tion (prē·skrĭp' shŭn)
pres·ence (prĕz' ĕns)
pre·sent (prē·zĕnt') v.
  pre·sent·a·ble
  pres·ent·a·tion
    (prĕz' ĕn·tā' shŭn)
pres·ent (prĕz' ĕnt) n., adj.
pre·sen·ti·ment
    (prē·zĕn' tĭ·mĕnt)
pre·sent·ment (prē·zĕnt' mĕnt)
pre·serv·a·tive (prē·zûr' vȧ·tĭv)
pre·serve (prē·zûrv')
  -serv·ing pre·serv·a·ble
  pres·er·va·tion
    (prĕz' ēr·vā' shŭn)
pre·side (prē·zīd')
  -sid·ing

pres·i·dent (prĕz′ ĭ·dĕnt)
  pres·i·den·cy
  pres·i·den·tial
    (prĕz′ ĭ·dĕn′ shǎl)
pre·si·di·o (prē·sē′ dĭ·ō)
pre·sid·i·um (prē·sĭd′ ĭ·ŭm)
press a·gent (prĕs)
pres·sure (prĕsh′ ĕr)
  pres·sur·ize -iz·ing
pres·ti·dig·i·ta·tion
    (prĕs′ tĭ·dĭj′ ĭ·tā′ shŭn)
  -ta·tor
pres·tige (prĕs·tēzh′)
pres·to (prĕs′tō)
pre·sume (prē·zūm′)
  -sum·ing pre·sum·a·ble
  pre·sum·ed·ly
  pre·sump·tion
    (prē·zŭmp′ shŭn)
  pre·sump·tive (-zŭmp′ tĭv)
  pre·sump·tu·ous
    (-zŭmp′ tū·ŭs)
pre·sup·pose (prē′ sŭ·pōz′)
  -sup·pos·ing
  pre·sup·po·si·tion
    (prē′ sŭp·ō·zĭsh′ ŭn)
pre·tend (prē·tĕnd′)
  pre·tend·er
  pre·tense (prē·tĕns′)
  pre·ten·sion (prē·tĕn′ shŭn)
  pre·ten·tious (prē·tĕn′ shŭs)
pre·ter·nat·u·ral
    (prē′ tĕr·nǎt′ û·rǎl)
pre·text (prē′ tĕkst)
pret·ti·fy (prĭt′ ĭ·fī)
  -fied -fy·ing
pret·ty (prĭt′ ĭ)
  pret·ti·er pret·ti·est
  pret·ti·ly pret·ti·ness
pre·vail (prē·vāl′)
  -vailed -vail·ing
prev·a·lent (prĕv′ ă·lĕnt)
pre·var·i·cate (prē·văr′ ĭ·kāt)
  -cat·ing pre·var·i·ca·tor
pre·vent (prē·vĕnt′)
  pre·vent·a·tive
    (prē·vĕn′ tă·tĭv)
  pre·ven·tive (prē·vĕn′ tĭv)
pre·view (prē′ vū′)
pre·vi·ous (prē′ vĭ·ŭs)
prey (prā)
  (victim; see *pray*)
price·less (prīs′ lĕs)
prick·le (prĭk′ 'l)
  -ling prick·ly heat

pride·ful (prīd′ fŏŏl)
  -ful·ly -ful·ness
priest (prēst)
  priest·ess priest·hood
  priest·ly -li·ness
prig (prĭg)
  prig·gish
pri·ma·cy (prī′ mă·sĭ)
pri·ma don·na (prē′ mă dŏn′ ă)
pri·ma-fa·ci·e ev·i·dence
    (prī′ mă fā′ shĭ·ē)
pri·mal (prī′ mǎl)
pri·ma·ry (prī′ mĕr·ĭ)
  -ries
  pri·ma·ri·ly (prī′ mĕr·ĭ·lĭ)
pri·mate (prī′ mĭt)
prim·er (prĭm′ ĕr)
  (book)
pri·me·val (prī·mē′ vǎl)
prim·i·tive (prĭm′ ĭ·tĭv)
pri·mo·gen·i·ture
    (prī′ mō·jĕn′ ĭ·tūr)
pri·mor·di·al (prī·môr′ dĭ·ǎl)
prim·rose (prĭm′ rōz′)
prince·ly (prĭns′ lĭ)
prin·cess (prĭn′ sĕs)
prin·ci·pal (prĭn′ sĭ·pǎl)
  (adj., highest-ranking;
  n., school official; see *principle*)
  prin·ci·pal·i·ty
    (prĭn′ sĭ·pǎl′ ĭ·tĭ)
  prin·ci·pal·ly
prin·ci·ple (prĭn′ sĭ·p'l) n.
  (rule; see *principal*)
  prin·ci·pled
print·a·ble (prĭnt′ ă·b'l)
pri·or (prī′ ĕr)
  pri·or·ess
  pri·or·i·ty (prī·ŏr′ ĭ·tĭ)
  -ties
prism (prĭz′m)
  pris·mat·ic (prĭz·măt′ ĭk)
pris·on (prĭz′ 'n)
  pris·on·er
pris·sy (prĭs′ ĭ)
pris·tine (prĭs′ tēn)
prith·ee (prĭth′ ē)
pri·vate (prī′ vĭt)
  pri·va·cy (-vă·sĭ)
pri·va·tion (prī·vā′ shŭn)
priv·i·lege (prĭv′ ĭ·lĭj)
priv·y coun·cil (prĭv′ ĭ)
prize (prīz)
  priz·ing prize fight·er

prob·a·ble   (prŏb′ a·b'l)
  prob·a·bil·i·ty
                    (prŏb′ a·bĭl′ ĭ·tĭ)
  prob·a·bly
pro·bate   (prō′ bāt)
  pro·ba·tion   (prō·bā′ shŭn)
  pro·ba·tion·er
                    (prō·bā′ shŭn·ẽr)
probe   (prōb)
  prob·ing
prob·i·ty   (prŏb′ ĭ·tĭ)
prob·lem   (prŏb′ lĕm)
  prob·lem·at·i·cal
                    (prŏb′ lĕm·ăt′ ĭ·kăl)
pro·bos·cis   (prō·bŏs′ ĭs)
pro·caine   (prō·kān′)
pro·ce·dure   (prō·sē′ dŭr)
  pro·ce·dur·al
pro·ceed   (prō·sēd′) v.
pro·ceeds   (prō′ sēdz) n.
proc·ess   (prŏs′ ĕs)
pro·ces·sion   (prō·sĕsh′ ŭn)
  -ces·sion·al
pro·claim   (prō·klām′)
  proc·la·ma·tion
                    (prŏk′ la·mā′ shŭn)
pro·cliv·i·ty   (prō·klĭv′ ĭ·tĭ)
  -ties
pro·con·sul   (prō·kŏn′ sŭl)
pro·cras·ti·nate
                    (prō·krăs′ tĭ·nāt)
  -nat·ing
  pro·cras·ti·na·tion
                    (prō·krăs′ tĭ·nā′ shŭn)
  pro·cras·ti·na·tor
pro·cre·ate   (prō′ krē·āt)
  -at·ing
  pro·cre·a·tion
                    (prō′ krē·ā′ shŭn)
  pro·cre·a·tor
proc·tor   (prŏk′ tẽr)
proc·u·ra·tor   (prŏk′ û·rā′ tẽr)
  proc·u·ra·cy   (prŏk′ û·rá·sĭ)
pro·cure   (prō·kūr′)
  -cur·ing   pro·cure·ment
  pro·cur·er
prod·i·gal   (prŏd′ ĭ·găl)
  prod·i·gal·i·ty
                    (prŏd′ ĭ·găl′ ĭ·tĭ)
pro·di·gious   (prō·dĭj′ ŭs)
prod·i·gy   (prŏd′ ĭ·jĭ)
  -gies
pro·duce   (prō·dūs′) v.
  -duc·ing   pro·duc·er
  pro·duc·i·ble

prod·uce   (prŏd′ ūs) n.
prod·uct   (prŏd′ ŭkt)
  pro·duc·tion   (prō·dŭk′ shŭn)
  pro·duc·tive   (prō·dŭk′ tĭv)
  pro·duc·tiv·i·ty
                    (prō′ dŭk·tĭv′ ĭ·tĭ)
pro·fane   (prō·fān′)
  -fan·ing
  prof·a·na·tion
                    (prŏf′ a·nā′ shŭn)
  pro·fan·i·ty   (prō·făn′ ĭ·tĭ)
pro·fess   (prō·fĕs′)
  pro·fess·ed·ly
  pro·fes·sion   (prō·fĕsh′ ŭn)
  pro·fes·sion·al
  pro·fes·sor   (prō·fĕs′ ẽr)
  pro·fes·sor·ate   (prō·fĕs′ ẽr·ĭt)
  pro·fes·so·ri·al
                    (prō′ fĕ·sō′ rĭ·ăl)
prof·fer   (prŏf′ ẽr)
  prof·fered   prof·fer·ing
pro·fi·cient   (prō·fĭsh′ ĕnt)
  pro·fi·cien·cy
pro·file   (prō′ fĭl)
prof·it   (prŏf′ ĭt)
  (gain; see prophet)
  -it·ed   -it·ing
  prof·it·a·ble
  prof·it-and-loss state·ment
  prof·it·eer   (prŏf′ ĭ·tẽr′)
  prof·it·less
prof·li·gate   (prŏf′ lĭ·găt)
  prof·li·ga·cy   (-gá·sĭ)
pro·found   (prō·found′)
  pro·fun·di·ty   (prō·fŭn′ dĭ·tĭ)
  -ties
pro·fuse   (prō·fūs′)
  pro·fuse·ly
  pro·fu·sion   (-fū′ zhŭn)
pro·gen·i·tor   (prō·jĕn′ ĭ·tẽr)
prog·e·ny   (prŏj′ ĕ·nĭ)
prog·no·sis   (prŏg·nō′ sĭs)
  pl. prog·no·ses   (-sēz)
  prog·nos·tic   (prŏg·nŏs′ tĭk)
  prog·nos·ti·cate
                    (prŏg·nŏs′ tĭ·kāt)
  -cat·ing
pro·gram   (prō′ grăm)
  pro·gram·mat·ic
                    (prō′ grá·măt′ ĭk)
prog·ress   (prŏg′ rĕs) n.
pro·gress   (prō·grĕs′) v.
  pro·gres·sion   (prō·grĕsh′ ŭn)
  pro·gres·sive   -sive·ly

pro·hib·it (prō·hĭb′ ĭt)
-it·ed -it·ing
pro·hi·bi·tion (prō′ ĭ·bĭsh′ ŭn)
pro·hib·i·tive (prō·hĭb′ ĭ·tĭv)
pro·hib·i·to·ry
(prō·hĭb′ ĭ·tō′ rĭ)
pro·ject (prō·jĕkt′) v.
pro·jec·tile (prō·jĕk′ tĭl)
pro·jec·tion (prō·jĕk′ shŭn)
pro·jec·tive (prō·jĕk′ tĭv)
pro·jec·tor (prō·jĕk′ tēr)
proj·ect (prŏj′ ĕkt) n.
pro·lac·tin (prō·lăk′ tĭn)
pro·le·tar·i·an (prō′ lē·târ′ ĭ·ăn)
pro·le·tar·i·at
pro·lif·er·ate (prō·lĭf′ ēr·āt)
-at·ing
pro·lif·er·a·tion
(prō·lĭf′ ēr·ā′ shŭn)
pro·lif·ic (prō·lĭf′ ĭk)
pro·lif·i·cal·ly
pro·lix (prō·lĭks′)
pro·lix·i·ty (prō·lĭk′ sĭ·tĭ)
pro·logue (prō′ lŏg)
pro·long (prō·lŏng′)
prom·e·nade (prŏm′ ē·nād′)
prom·i·nence (prŏm′ ĭ·nĕns)
-nent
pro·mis·cu·ous (prō·mĭs′ kū·ŭs)
prom·is·cu·i·ty
(prŏm′ ĭs·kū′ ĭ·tĭ)
prom·ise (prŏm′ ĭs)
-is·ing
prom·is·so·ry (prŏm′ ĭ·sō′ rĭ)
prom·on·to·ry (prŏm′ ŭn·tō′ rĭ)
-ries
pro·mote (prō·mōt′)
-mot·ing pro·mot·er
pro·mo·tion
prompt (prŏmpt)
prompt·ness
pro·mul·gate (prō·mŭl′ gāt)
-gat·ing
pro·mul·ga·tion
(prō′ mŭl·gā′ shŭn)
pro·mul·ga·tor
prone (prōn)
prone·ness
prong·horn (prŏng′ hôrn′)
pro·noun (prō′ noun)
pro·nounce (prō·nouns′)
-nounc·ing
pro·nounce·a·ble
pro·nounc·ed·ly
pro·nounce·ment

pro·nun·ci·a·tion
(prō·nŭn′ sĭ·ā′ shŭn)
proof (prōōf)
proof·read·er
prop·a·gan·da (prŏp′ à·găn′ dà)
prop·a·gan·dist
prop·a·gan·dise
-diz·ing
prop·a·gate (prŏp′ à·gāt)
-gat·ing
prop·a·ga·tion
(prŏp′ à·gā′ shŭn)
prop·a·ga·tor
pro·pane (prō′ pān)
pro·pel (prō·pĕl′)
-pelled -pel·ling
pro·pel·lant (prō·pĕl′ ănt)
pro·pel·ler
pro·pen·si·ty (prō·pĕn′ sĭ·tĭ)
-ties
prop·er (prŏp′ ēr)
prop·er·ty (prŏp′ ēr·tĭ)
-ties
prop·er·tied
proph·e·cy (prŏf′ ē·sĭ) n.
-cies
proph·e·sy (prŏf′ ē·sĭ) v.
-sied -sy·ing
proph·e·si·er
proph·et (prŏf′ ĕt)
(seer; see *profit*)
proph·et·ess
pro·phet·ic (prō·fĕt′ ĭk)
pro·phy·lac·tic
(prō′ fĭ·lăk′ tĭk)
pro·phy·lax·is (-lăk′ sĭs)
pro·pin·qui·ty (prō·pĭng′ kwĭ·tĭ)
pro·pi·ti·ate (prō·pĭsh′ ĭ·āt)
-at·ing
pro·pi·ti·a·tion
(prō·pĭsh′ ĭ·ā′ shŭn)
pro·pi·tious (prō·pĭsh′ ŭs)
pro·pi·tious·ness
pro·po·nent (prō·pō′ nĕnt)
pro·por·tion (prō·pôr′ shŭn)
pro·por·tion·al
pro·por·tion·ate
(-ĭt)
pro·pose (prō·pōz′)
-pos·ing pro·pos·al
prop·o·si·tion (prŏp′ ò·zĭsh′ ŭn)
-tion·al
pro·pound (prō·pound′)
pro·pri·e·tor (prō·prī′ ē·tēr)
pro·pri·e·tar·y
(prō·prī′ ē·tĕr′ ĭ)

pro·pri·e·ty (prō·prī′ ĕ·tĭ)
  -ties
pro·pul·sion (prō·pŭl′ shŭn)
  pro·pul·sive
pro·rate (prō′ rāt′)
  -rat·ing
  pro·ra·tion (prō·rā′ shŭn)
pro·sa·ic (prō·zā′ ĭk)
  pro·sa·i·cal·ly
pro·sce·ni·um (prō·sē′ nĭ·ŭm)
pro·scribe (prō·skrīb′)
  (condemn; see *prescribe*)
  pro·scrip·tion (-skrĭp′ shŭn)
pros·e·cute (prŏs′ ê·kūt)
  -cut·ing
  pros·e·cu·tion
        (prŏs′ ê·kū′ shŭn)
  pros·e·cu·tor
pros·e·lyte (prŏs′ ĕ·līt)
pro·slav·er·y (prō·slāv′ ẽr·ĭ)
pros·o·dy (prŏs′ ô·dĭ)
pros·pect (prŏs′ pĕkt)
pro·spec·tive (prō·spĕk′ tĭv)
  adj. (confidently expected; see
  perspective)
pro·spec·tus (prō·spĕk′ tŭs)
pros·per (prŏs′ pẽr)
  pros·per·i·ty (prŏs·pĕr′ ĭ·tĭ)
  pros·per·ous
pros·tate gland (prŏs′ tāt)
pros·ti·tute (prŏs′ tĭ·tūt)
  pros·ti·tu·tion
        (prŏs′ tĭ·tū′ shŭn)
pros·trate (prŏs′ trāt)
  pros·tra·tion (prŏs·trā′ shŭn)
pros·y (prŏz′ ĭ)
pro·tag·o·nist (prō·tăg′ ô·nĭst)
pro·tect (prō·tĕkt′)
  pro·tec·tion (prō·tĕk′ shŭn)
  pro·tec·tion·ism
  pro·tec·tive tar·iff
  pro·tec·tor   pro·tec·tress
  pro·tec·tor·ate
        (prō·tĕk′ tẽr·ĭt)
pro·té·gé (prō′ tĕ·zhā)
pro·te·in (prō′ tē·ĭn)
pro tem·po·re (prō tĕm′ pô·rĕ)
pro·test (prō·tĕst′) *v.*
        (prō′ tĕst) n.
  prot·es·ta·tion
        (prŏt′ ĕs·tā′ shŭn)
Prot·es·tant (prŏt′ ĕs·tănt)
pro·to·col (prō′ tô·kŏl)
pro·ton (prō′ tŏn)
pro·to·plasm (prō′ tô·plăz′m)

pro·to·type (prō′ tô·tīp)
pro·to·zo·an (prō′ tô·zō′ ăn)
  pro·to·zo·ic (-ĭk)
pro·trude (prō·trōōd′)
  -trud·ing
  pro·tru·sion (prō·trōō′ zhŭn)
pro·tu·ber·ance
        (prō·tū′ bẽr·ăns)
  -ant
proud (proud)
prove (prōōv)
  prov·ing   prov·a·ble
  prov·en
prov·en·der (prŏv′ ĕn·dẽr)
prov·erb (prŏv′ ûrb)
  pro·ver·bi·al (prō·vûr′ bĭ·ăl)
pro·vide (prō·vīd′)
  -vid·ing   pro·vid·er
prov·i·dence (prŏv′ ĭ·dĕns)
  -dent
  prov·i·den·tial
        (prŏv′ ĭ·dĕn′ shăl)
prov·ince (prŏv′ ĭns)
  pro·vin·cial (prō·vĭn′ shăl)
  -cial·ism
pro·vi·sion (prō·vĭzh′ ŭn)
  pro·vi·sion·al, -al·ly
  pro·vi·sion·er
pro·vi·so (prō·vī′ zō)
  -sos
pro·voke (prō·vōk′)
  -vok·ing
  prov·o·ca·tion
        (prŏv′ ô·kā′ shŭn)
  pro·voc·a·tive (prō·vŏk′ ă·tĭv)
  -tive·ly   pro·vok·er
pro·vost mar·shal
        (prō′ vō)
prow·ess (prou′ ĕs)
prowl·er (proul′ ẽr)
prox·im·i·ty (prŏks·ĭm′ ĭ·tĭ)
prox·y (prŏk′ sĭ)
  prox·ies
prude (prōōd)
  prud·er·y   prud·ish
pru·dent (prōō′ dĕnt)
  -dence
prun·ing hook (prōōn′ ĭng)
pru·ri·ent (prōōr′ ĭ·ĕnt)
  -ence
Prus·sian blue (prŭsh′ ăn)
prus·sic ac·id (prŭs′ ĭk)
pry (prī)
  pried   pry·ing
  pry·er

psalm (säm)
psalm·ist
psal·mo·dy (säl′ mò·dï)
Psal·ter (sôl′ tër)
pseu·do·nym (sü′ dò·nïm)
pso·ri·a·sis (sò·rï′ á·sïs)
psy·chi·a·try (aī·kī′ á·trï)
  psy·chi·at·ric (aī′ kī·ät′ rïk)
  psy·chi·a·trist (aī·kī′ á·trïst)
psy·chic (aī′ kïk)
psy·cho- (aī′ kò-)
  psy·cho·a·nal·y·sis
  psy·cho·an·a·lyt·i·cal
  psy·cho·an·a·lyze, -lyz·ing
  psy·cho·dra·ma
  psy·cho·mo·tor
  psy·cho·neu·ro·sis
  psy·cho·neu·rot·ic
  psy·cho·path·ic
  psy·cho·so·mat·ic
  psy·cho·sur·ger·y
  psy·cho·ther·a·peu·tics
  psy·cho·ther·a·py
psy·chol·o·gy (aī·kŏl′ ò·jï)
  psy·cho·log·i·cal
(aī′ kò·lŏj′ ï·kǎl)
psy·chom·e·try (aī·kŏm′ ê·trï)
psy·cho·sis (aī·kŏ′ sïs)
  pl. -ses
ptar·mi·gan (tär′ mï·gǎn)
pter·o·dac·tyl (tër′ ò·dǎk′ tïl)
Ptol·e·my (tŏl′ ê·mï)
  Ptol·e·ma·ic (tŏl′ ê·mā′ ïk)
pto·maine (tō′ mān)
pu·ber·ty (pū′ bër·tï)
pu·bic (pū′ bïk)
pub·lic (pŭb′ lïk)
  pub·lic·ad·dress sys·tem
  pub·lic·ly
pub·li·ca·tion (pŭb′ lï·kā′ shǔn)
pub·li·cize (pŭb′ lï·sïz)
  -ciz·ing
  pub·li·cist (pŭb′ lï·sïst)
  pub·lic·i·ty (pŭb·lïs′ ï·tï)
pub·lish (pŭb′ lïsh)
  pub·lish·a·ble pub·lish·er
puck·er (pŭk′ ër)
puck·ish (pŭk′ ïsh)
pud·ding (pŏŏd′ ïng)
pud·dle (pŭd′ 'l)
pudg·y (pŭj′ ï)
pueb·lo (pwĕb′ lō)
  -los
pu·er·ile (pū′ ër·ïl) -
  pu·er·il·i·ty (pū′ ër·ïl′ ï·tï)

Puer·to Ri·co (pwĕr′ tú rē′ kō)
  Puer·to Ri·can
puf·fin (pŭf′ ïn)
puff·y (pŭf′ ï)
  puff·i·ness
Pu·get (sound) (pū′ jĕt)
pu·gil·ist (pū′ jï·lïst)
pug·na·cious (pŭg·nā′ ahǔs)
  pug·nac·i·ty (pŭg·nǎs′ ï·tï)
pu·is·sance (pū′ ï·sǎns)
  pu·is·sant
pul·chri·tude (pŭl′ krï·tūd)
  pul·chri·tu·di·nous
(pŭl′ krï·tū′ dï·nǎs)
pul·let (pŏŏl′ ĕt)
pul·ley (pŏŏl′ ï)
Pull·man car (pŏŏl′ mǎn)
pull·o·ver (pŏŏl′ ō′ vër)
pul·mo·nar·y (pŭl′ mò·nĕr′ ï)
Pul·mo·tor (pŭl′ mō′ tër)
pul·pit (pŏŏl′ pït)
pulp·wood (pŭlp′ wŏŏd′)
pul·que (pŏŏl′ kǎ)
pul·sate (pŭl′ sāt)
  -sat·ing
  pul·sa·tion (pŭl·sā′ shǔn)
pul·ver·ize (pŭl′ vër·ïz)
  -iz·ing
pu·ma (pū′ mǎ)
pum·ice (pŭm′ ïs)
pum·per·nick·el
(pŭm′ për·nïk′ 'l)
pump·kin (pŭmp′ kïn)
punch·ing bag (pŭnch′ ïng)
punc·til·i·ous (pŭngk·tïl′ ï·ǔs)
punc·tu·al (pŭngk′ tú·ǎl)
  -al·ly
  punc·tu·al·i·ty
(pŭngk′ tú·ǎl′ ï·tï)
punc·tu·ate (pŭngk′ tú·āt)
  -at·ing
  punc·tu·a·tion
(pŭngk′ tú·ā′ shǔn)
punc·ture (pŭngk′ tŭr)
  -tur·ing
  punc·tur·a·ble
pun·dit (pŭn′ dït)
pun·gent (pŭn′ jĕnt)
  pun·gen·cy
pun·ish (pŭn′ ïsh)
  pun·ish·a·ble pun·ish·ment
pu·ni·tive (pū′ nï·tïv)
pun·ster (pŭn′ stër)
pu·pa (pū′ pǎ)
  pl. pu·pae (-pē)
pu·pil (pū′ p'l)

pup·pet   (pŭp′ ĕt)
   pup·pet·ry
pup·py   (pŭp′ ĭ)
   pup·pies
pur·blind   (pûr′ blīnd′)
pur·chase   (pûr′ chĭs)
   -chas·ing   pur·chas·a·ble
Pur·due (univ.)   (pĕr·dū′)
pure   (pŭr)
   pure·bred   pure·ly
   pu·ri·fi·ca·tion
           (pū′ rĭ·fĭ·kā′ shŭn)
   pu·ri·fi·er   pu·ri·fy
   -fied, -fy·ing   pu·ri·ty
pu·rée   (pū·rā′)
pur·ga·tive   (pûr′ gȧ·tĭv)
pur·ga·to·ry   (pûr′ gȧ·tō′ rĭ)
   pur·ga·to·ri·al
           (pûr′ gȧ·tō′ rĭ·ȧl)
purge   (pûrj)
   purg·ing
Pu·ri·tan   (pū′ rĭ·tăn)
   pu·ri·tan·i·cal
           (pū′ rĭ·tăn′ ĭ·kăl)
purl   (pûrl)
   (knitting stitch; see *pearl*)
pur·lieu   (pûr′ lū)
pur·loin   (pûr·loin′)
pur·ple   (pûr′ p'l)
pur·port   (pûr·pôrt′) v.
           (pûr′ pôrt) n.
pur·pose   (pûr′ pŭs)
   pur·pose·ful, -ful·ly, -ful·ness
   pur·pose·less   pur·pose·ly
   pur·pos·ive
purr   (pûr)
purse   (pûrs)
purs·lane   (pûrs′ lān)
pur·sue   (pĕr·sū′)
   -su·ing
   pur·su·ance   (pĕr·sū′ ȧns)
   pur·su·ant   pur·su·er
   pur·suit   (pĕr·sūt′)
pur·vey   (pûr·vā′)
   pur·vey·ance   pur·vey·or
pur·view   (pûr′ vū)
pus   (pŭs)
   pus·sy
push   (pŏŏsh)
   push-but·ton *adj.*
   push·cart   push·o·ver
pu·sil·lan·i·mous
           (pū′ sĭ·lăn′ ĭ·mŭs)
   pu·sil·la·nim·i·ty
           (pū′ sĭ·lȧ·nĭm′ ĭ·tĭ)

puss·y·foot   (pŏŏs′ ĭ·fŏŏt′)
pus·tule   (pŭs′ tūl)
pu·tre·fy   (pū′ trė·fī)
   -fied   -fy·ing
   pu·tre·fac·tion
           (pū′ trė·făk′ shŭn)
pu·tres·cent   (pū·trĕs′ ĕnt)
pu·trid   (pū′ trĭd)
putt   (pŭt)
put·tee   (pŭt′ ĭ)
   (legging; see *putty*)
put·ty   (pŭt′ ĭ)
   (cement; see *puttee*)
puz·zle   (pŭz′ 'l)
   puz·zling   puz·zle·ment
Pyg·my   (pĭg′ mĭ)
py·lon   (pī′ lŏn)
py·lo·rus   (pī·lō′ rŭs)
   py·lor·ic   (pī·lôr′ ĭk)
py·or·rhe·a   (pī′ ô·rē′ ȧ)
pyr·a·mid   (pĭr′ ȧ·mĭd)
pyre   (pīr)
Py·rex   (pī′ rĕks)
py·ri·tes   (pī·rī′ tēz)
py·ro·ma·ni·ac
           (pī′ rō·mā′ nĭ·ăk)
py·ro·tech·nics
           (pī′ rō·tĕk′ nĭks)
Pyr·rhic vic·to·ry
           (pĭr′ ĭk)
py·thon   (pī′ thŏn)

Q

quack   (kwăk)
   quack·er·y   quack grass
quad·ran·gle   (kwŏd′ răng′ g'l)
quad·rant   (kwŏd′ rănt)
quad·ri·lat·er·al
           (kwŏd′ rĭ·lăt′ ĕr·ȧl)
quad·roon   (kwŏd·rōōn′)
quad·ru·ped   (kwŏd′ rŏŏ·pĕd)
quad·ru·ple   (kwŏd′ rŏŏ·p'l)
quad·ru·plet   (kwŏd′ rŏŏ·plĕt)
quad·ru·pli·cate
           (kwŏd·rōō′ plĭ·kāt)
quaff   (kwáf)
quag·mire   (kwăg′ mīr)
quail   (kwāl)
quaint   (kwānt)
Quak·er   (kwāk′ ĕr)
qual·i·fy   (kwŏl′ ĭ·fī)
   -fied   -fy·ing

qual·i·fi·ca·tion (kwŏl' ĭ·fĭ·kā' shŭn)
qual·i·fi·er
qual·i·ty (kwŏl' ĭ·tĭ)
 -ties
qual·i·ta·tive (kwŏl' ĭ·tā' tĭv)
qualm (kwäm)
quan·da·ry (kwŏn' dá·rĭ)
 -ries
quan·ti·fy (kwŏn' tĭ·fī)
 -fied -fy·ing
quan·ti·ty (kwŏn' tĭ·tĭ)
 -ties
quan·ti·ta·tive (kwŏn' tĭ·tā' tĭv)
quan·tum theory (kwŏn' tŭm)
quar·an·tine (kwŏr' ăn·tēn)
quar·rel (kwŏr' ĕl)
 quar·reled quar·rel·ing
 quar·rel·some
quar·ry (kwŏr' ĭ)
 quar·ried quar·ry·ing
quar·ter (kwŏr' tẽr)
 quar·ter·back quar·ter-deck
 quar·ter·mas·ter
quar·ter·ly (kwŏr' tẽr·lĭ)
 -lies
quar·tet (kwŏr·tĕt')
quar·to (kwŏr' tō)
 -tos
quartz (kwôrts)
quartz·ite (kwôrts' ĭt)
qua·si-ju·di·cial (kwā' sĭ·jōō·dĭsh' ăl)
quat·rain (kwŏt' răn)
quat·re·foil (kăt' ẽr·foil')
qua·ver (kwā' vẽr)
quay (kwā)
quea·sy (kwē' zĭ)
 quea·si·ness
queen (kwēn)
 queen·ly -li·ness
queer (kwẽr)
quell (kwĕl)
quench (kwĕnch)
quer·u·lous (kwĕr' ū·lŭs)
que·ry (kwẽr' ĭ)
 -ries
quest (kwĕst)
ques·tion (kwĕs' chŭn)
 ques·tion·a·ble
 ques·tion·er ques·tion·ing·ly
 ques·tion·naire (kwĕs' chŭn·âr')
quet·zal (kĕt·säl')

queue (kū)
 (waiting line; see cue)
 queu·ing
quib·ble (kwĭb' 'l)
 quib·bling
quick (kwĭk)
 quick·en quick-fir·ing
 quick-freeze quick·sand
 quick·sil·ver quick-wit·ted
quid·di·ty (kwĭd' ĭ·tĭ)
quid pro quo (kwĭd prō kwō)
quies·cent (kwĭ·ĕs' ĕnt)
 quies·cence
qui·et (kwī' ĕt)
 qui·et·er qui·et·ly
 qui·e·tude (kwī' ĕ·tūd)
 qui·e·tus (kwī·ē' tŭs)
quill (kwĭl)
quilt (kwĭlt)
quince (kwĭns)
qui·nine (kwī' nīn)
quin·sy (kwĭn' zĭ)
quint·es·sence (kwĭnt·ĕs' ĕns)
quin·tet (kwĭn·tĕt')
quin·til·lion (kwĭn·tĭl' yŭn)
quin·tu·ple (kwĭn' tū·p'l)
quin·tu·plet (kwĭn' tū·plĕt)
quin·tu·pli·cate
 (kwĭn·tū' plĭ·kāt)
quip (kwĭp)
 quipped quip·ping
 quip·ster
quire (kwīr)
quirk (kwûrk)
quirt (kwûrt)
quis·ling (kwĭz' lĭng)
quit (kwĭt)
 quit·ting quit·tance
 quit·ter
quite (kwīt)
quiv·er (kwĭv' ẽr)
Quix·ote, Don (kē·hō' tā, dŏn)
 quix·ot·ic (kwĭks·ŏt' ĭk)
quiz (kwĭz)
 quizzed quiz·zing
 quiz·zes
quiz·zi·cal (kwĭz' ĭ·kăl)
 quiz·zi·cal·ly
quoits (kwoits)
quon·dam (kwŏn' dăm)
quo·rum (kwō' rŭm)
quo·ta (kwō' tá)
quote (kwōt)
 quot·ing quot·a·ble
 quo·ta·tion (kwō·tā' shŭn)

quoth (kwŏth)
quo·tid·i·an (kwō·tĭd′ ĭ·ăn)
quo·tient (kwō′ shĕnt)

R

rab·bet joint (răb′ ĕt)
rab·bi (răb′ ī)
  rab·bin·i·cal (ră·bĭn′ ĭ·kăl)
rab·bit (răb′ ĭt)
  rab·bit fe·ver   rab·bit punch
rab·ble (răb′ ′l)
Rab·e·lai·si·an
        (răb′ ě·lā′ zĭ·ăn)
rab·id (răb′ ĭd)
ra·bies (rā′ bēz)
rac·coon (ră·kōōn′)
ra·cial (rā′ shăl)
rac·ism (răs′ ĭz′m)
  rac·ist
rack·et (răk′ ĕt)
  rack·et·eer (răk′ ě·tēr′)
rac·on·teur (răk′ ŏn·tûr′)
rac·y (rās′ ĭ)
  rac·i·ness
ra·dar (rā′ där)
  ra·dar·scope
Rad·cliffe (coll.) (răd′ klĭf)
ra·di·ant (rā′ dĭ·ănt)
ra·di·ance
ra·di·ate (rā′ dĭ·āt)
  -at·ing
  ra·di·a·tion (rā′ dĭ·ā′ shŭn)
  ra·di·a·tor (rā′ dĭ·ā′ tēr)
rad·i·cal (răd′ ĭ·kăl)
  rad·i·cal·ism   rad·i·cal·ly
ra·di·o·ac·tive (rā′ dĭ·ō·ăk′ tĭv)
  ra·di·o·ac·tiv·i·ty
        (-ăk·tĭv′ ĭ·tĭ)
ra·di·ol·o·gy (rā′ dĭ·ŏl′ ō·jĭ)
ra·di·o·log·i·cal
     (rā′ dĭ·ō·lŏj′ ĭ·kăl)
ra·di·o·sen·si·tive
     (rā′ dĭ·ō·sĕn′ sĭ·tĭv)
ra·di·o·sonde (rā′ dĭ·ō·sŏnd′)
ra·di·o·tel·e·gram
     (rā′ dĭ·ō·tĕl′ ě·grăm)
ra·di·o·ther·a·py
     (rā′ dĭ·ō·thĕr′ ă·pĭ)
rad·ish (răd′ ĭsh)
ra·di·um (rā′ dĭ·ŭm)
ra·di·us (rā′ dĭ·ŭs)
  pl. ra·di·i (-ī)
raf·fi·a (răf′ ĭ·ă)

raff·ish (răf′ ĭsh)
raf·fle (răf′ ′l)
  raf·fling
raft·er (răf′ tēr)
rag·a·muf·fin (răg′ ă·mŭf′ ĭn)
rag·ged (răg′ ĕd)
rag·lan (răg′ lăn)
ra·gout (ră·gōō′)
rag·weed (răg′ wēd′)
raid·er (rād′ ēr)
rail·ing (rāl′ ĭng)
rail·ler·y (rāl′ ēr·ĭ)
rail·road (rāl′ rōd′)
rail·way (rāl′ wā′)
rai·ment (rā′ mĕnt)
rain (rān)
  (falling drops of water; see *reign,*
  rein)
  rain·bow   rain·coat
  rain·drop   rain·fall
  rain gauge   rain·proof
  rain·storm   rain wa·ter
  rain·y
Rai·nier, Mt. (ră·nēr′)
raise (rāz)
  (awaken; see *raze*)
  rais·ing
rai·sin (rā′ z′n)
ra·ja (rā′ jă)
rak·ish (răk′ ĭsh)
ral·ly (răl′ ĭ)
  ral·lied   ral·ly·ing
ram·bler (răm′ blēr)
ram·e·kin (răm′ ě·kĭn)
ram·i·fi·ca·tion
     (răm′ ĭ·fĭ·kā′ shŭn)
ram·jet en·gine (răm′ jĕt′)
ram·page (răm·pāj′)
  -pag·ing
ramp·ant (răm′ pănt)
ram·part (răm′ pärt)
ram·rod (răm′ rŏd′)
ram·shack·le (răm′ shăk′ ′l)
ranch house (rănch)
ran·cid (răn′ sĭd)
ran·cor (răng′ kēr)
  ran·cor·ous (răng′ kēr·ŭs)
ran·dom (răn′ dŭm)
range (rānj)
  rang·ing   rang·er
  rang·y, rang·i·er, -i·est, -i·ness
ran·kle (răng′ k′l)
  -kling
ran·sack (răn′ săk)
ran·som (răn′ sŭm)

rant (rănt)
xa·pa·cious (rá·pā′ shŭs)
  ra·pac·i·ty (rá·păs′ ĭ·tĭ)
rap·id (răp′ ĭd)
  rap·id-fire
  ra·pid·i·ty (rá·pĭd′ ĭ·tĭ)
ra·pi·er (rā′ pĭ·ēr)
xap·ine (răp′ ĭn)
Rap·pa·han·nock (riv.)
        (răp′ á·hăn′ ŭk)
rap·port (ră′ pôr′)
rapt (răpt)
xap·ture (răp′ tŭr)
  rap·tur·ous (răp′ tŭr·ŭs)
xar·e·fy (rār′ ê·fī)
  -fied   -fy·ing
rare·ly (rār′ lĭ)
rar·i·ty (rār′ ĭ·tĭ)
  -ties
ras·cal (răs′ kăl)
  ras·cal·i·ty (răs·kăl′ ĭ·tĭ)
  ras·cal·ly
rash·er (răsh′ ēr)
rasp·ber·ry (răz′ bĕr′ ĭ)
  -ber·ries
rasp·ing (răs′ pĭng)
ratch·et (răch′ ĕt)
xate (rāt)
  rat·ing   rat·a·ble
rath·skel·ler (räts′ kĕl′ ēr)
rat·i·fy (răt′ ĭ·fī)
  -fied   -fy·ing
  rat·i·fi·ca·tion
      (răt′ ĭ·fĭ·kā′ shŭn)
  rat·i·fi·er
ra·tio (rā′ shō)
  ra·ti·oc·i·na·tion
    (răsh′ ĭ·ŏs′ ĭ·nā′ shŭn)
ra·tion·al (răsh′ ŭn·ăl)
  ra·tion·al·is·tic
    (răsh′ ŭn·ăl·ĭs′ tĭk)
  ra·tion·al·i·ty
    (răsh′ ŭn·ăl′ ĭ·tĭ)
ra·tion·ale (răsh′ ŭn·ăl′)
ra·tion·al·ize (răsh′ ŭn·ăl·īs)
  -iz·ing
  ra·tion·al·i·za·tion
    (răsh′ ŭn·ăl·ĭ·zā′ shŭn)
rat·tan (ră·tăn′)
rat·tle (răt′ ĭ)
  rat·tling   rat·tle-brained
  rat·tle·snake
rat·trap (răt′ trăp′)
rau·cous (rô′ kŭs)

rav·age (răv′ ĭj)
  -ag·ing
rav·el (răv′ ĕl)
  -eled   -el·ing
rav·en·ing (răv′ ĕn·ĭng)
rav·en·ous (răv′ ĕn·ŭs)
ra·vi·o·li (rä·vyô′·lê)
rav·ish·ing (răv′ ĭsh·ĭng)
raw (rô)
  raw·boned   raw·hide
  raw ma·te·ri·al
ray·on (rā′ ŏn)
xaze (rāz)
  (demolish; see raise)
  raz·ing
ra·zor (rā′ zēr)
re·ab·sorb (rē′ ăb·sôrb′)
reach (rēch)
re·act (rē·ăkt′)
  re·ac·tion (rē·ăk′ shŭn)
  re·ac·tion·ar·y
    (rē·ăk′ shŭn·ăr′ ĭ)
  re·ac·tor (rē·ăk′ tēr)
read (rēd)
  (peruse; see reed)
read·a·ble (rēd′ á·b'l)
  read·a·bil·i·ty (rēd′ á·bĭl′ ĭ·tĭ)
read·er·ship (rēd′ ēr·ship)
read·i·ly (rēd′ ĭ·lĭ)
read·i·ness (rēd′ ĭ·nĕs)
re·ad·just·ment (rē′ á·jŭst′ mĕnt)
re·ad·mis·sion (rē′ ăd·mĭsh′ ŭn)
re·ad·mit (rē′ ăd·mĭt′)
  -mit·ted   -mit·ting
  re·ad·mit·tance
      (rē′ ăd·mĭt′ ăns)
read·y (rĕd′ ĭ)
  read·ied   read·y·ing
  read·i·er, -i·est, -i·ly, -i·ness
  read·y-made   read·y-to-wear
re·af·firm (rē′ á·fŭrm′)
  re·af·fir·ma·tion
      (rē′ ăf·ēr·mā′ shŭn)
re·a·gent (rē·ā′ jĕnt)
re·al (rē′ ăl)
  (actual; see reel)
  re·al es·tate
  re·al·is·tic (rē′ ăl·ĭs′ tĭk)
  re·al·i·ty (rē·ăl′ ĭ·tĭ)
re·al·ize (rē′ ăl·īz)
  -iz·ing   re·al·iz·a·ble
  re·al·i·za·tion
      (rē′ ăl·ĭ·zā′ shŭn)
re·al·lo·ca·tion
      (rē′ ăl·ô·kā′ shŭn)

re·al·ly (rē′ ăl·ĭ)
realm (rĕlm)
re·al·ty (rē′ ăl·tĭ)
  re·al·tor (rē′ ăl·tĕr)
ream (rēm)
reap·er (rēp′ ĕr)
re·ap·pear·ance
         (rē′ ă·pēr′ ŭns)
re·ap·point (rē′ ă·point′)
re·ar·ma·ment (rē·är′ mȧ·mĕnt)
re·ar·range·ment
         (rē′ ȧ·rānj′ mĕnt)
rea·son (rē′ z'n)
  -soned   -son·ing
  rea·son·a·ble
re·as·sem·ble (rē′ ȧ·sĕm′ b'l)
  -bling
re·as·sign (rē′ ȧ·sīn′)
re·as·sure (rē′ ȧ·shōōr′)
  -as·sur·ing
re·a·wak·en (rē′ ȧ·wāk′ ĕn)
re·bate (rē′ bāt)
  -bat·ing
re·bel (rē·bĕl′) v.
  -belled   -bel·ling
reb·el (rĕb′ ĕl) n., adj.
re·bel·lion (rē·bĕl′ yŭn)
re·bel·lious (rē·bĕl′ yŭs)
re·birth (rē·bûrth′)
re·bound (rē·bound′)
re·buff (rē·bŭf′)
re·buke (rē·būk′)
re·bus (rē′ bŭs)
re·but (rē·bŭt′)
  -but·ted   -but·ting
  re·but·tal (rē·bŭt′ ăl)
re·cal·ci·trant (rē·kăl′ sĭ·trănt)
  -trance
re·call·a·ble (rē·kôl′ ȧ·b'l)
re·cant (rē·kănt′)
re·cap (rē·kăp′)
  -capped   -cap·ping
  re·cap·pa·ble
re·ca·pit·u·late
         (rē′ kȧ·pĭt′ ū·lāt)
  -lat·ing
  re·ca·pit·u·la·tion
         (rē′ kȧ·pĭt′ ū·lā′ shŭn)
re·cede (rē·sēd′)
  -ced·ing
re·ceipt (rē·sēt′)
re·ceive (rē·sēv′)
  -ceiv·ing   re·ceiv·a·ble
  re·ceiv·er·ship

re·cent (rē′ sĕnt)
re·cen·cy   re·cent·ly
re·cep·ta·cle (rē·sĕp′ tȧ·k'l)
re·cep·tion (rē·sĕp′ shŭn)
  re·cep·tion·ist
re·cep·tive (rē·sĕp′ tĭv)
  re·cep·tive·ness
  re·cep·tiv·i·ty (rē′ sĕp·tĭv′ ĭ·tĭ)
re·cep·tor (rē·sĕp′ tĕr)
re·ces·sion (rē·sĕsh′ ŭn)
  re·ces·sion·al   re·ces·sive
rec·i·pe (rĕs′ ĭ·pē)
re·cip·i·ent (rē·sĭp′ ĭ·ĕnt)
  -ence
re·cip·ro·cal (rē·sĭp′ rō·kăl)
re·cip·ro·cate, -cat·ing
re·cip·ro·ca·tion
         (rē·sĭp′ rō·kā′ shŭn)
rec·i·proc·i·ty (rĕs′ ĭ·prŏs′ ĭ·tĭ)
re·cite (rē·sīt′)
  -cit·ing   re·cit·al
  rec·i·ta·tion (rĕs′ ĭ·tā′ shŭn)
reck·less (rĕk′ lĕs)
reck·on (rĕk′ ŭn)
  reck·on·ing
re·claim (rē·klām′)
  re·claim·a·ble
  rec·la·ma·tion
         (rĕk′ lȧ·mā′ shŭn)
re·clin·er (rē·klīn′ ĕr)
re·cluse (rē·klōōs′)
rec·og·ni·tion (rĕk′ ŏg·nĭsh′ ŭn)
rec·og·nize (rĕk′ ŏg·nīz)
  -niz·ing   rec·og·niz·a·ble
re·coil (rē·koil′)
  -coiled   -coil·ing
re·col·lect (rĕk′ ŏ·lĕkt′)
rec·om·mend (rĕk′ ŏ·mĕnd′)
  rec·om·men·da·tion
         (rĕk′ ŏ·mĕn·dā′ shŭn)
re·com·mit (rē′ kŏ·mĭt′)
  -com·mit·ted   -com·mit·ting
  re·com·mit·ment
rec·om·pense (rĕk′ ŏm·pĕns)
rec·on·cile (rĕk′ ŏn·sīl)
  -cil·ing   rec·on·cil·a·ble
  rec·on·cil·i·a·tion
         (rĕk′ ŏn·sĭl′ ĭ·ā′ shŭn)
rec·on·dite (rĕk′ ŭn·dĭt)
re·con·di·tioned
         (rē′ kŏn·dĭsh′ ŭnd)
re·con·nais·sance
         (rē·kŏn′ ĭ·sȧns)
rec·on·noi·ter (rĕk′ ŏ·noi′ tĕr)
re·con·sid·er (rē′ kŏn·sĭd′ ĕr)

re·con·sti·tute   (rē·kŏn′ stĭ·tūt)
   -tut·ing
re·con·struc·tion
       (rē′ kŏn·strŭk′ shŭn)
re·con·vene   (rē′ kŏn·vēn′)
   -ven·ing
re·con·vert   (rē′ kŏn·vûrt′)
   re·con·ver·sion
       (rē′ kŏn·vûr′ shŭn)
re·cord   (rē·kôrd′) v.
rec·ord   (rĕk′ ẽrd) n.
re·coup   (rē·kōōp′)
re·course   (rē·kōrs′)
re·cov·er   (rē·kŭv′ ẽr)
   re·cov·er·a·ble
   re·cov·er·y
rec·re·ant   (rĕk′ rē·ănt)
rec·re·a·tion   (rĕk′ rē·ā′ shŭn)
re·crim·i·na·tion
       (rē·krĭm′ ĭ·nā′ shŭn)
re·cru·des·cence
       (rē′ krōō·dĕs′ ĕns)
re·cruit   (rē·krōōt′)
   re·cruit·er   re·cruit·ment
rec·tal   (rĕk′ tăl)
rec·tan·gle   (rĕk′ tăng′ g'l)
   rec·tan·gu·lar
       (rĕk·tăng′ gŭ·lẽr)
rec·ti·fy   (rĕk′ tĭ·fī)
   -fied   -fy·ing
   rec·ti·fi·a·ble
rec·ti·lin·e·ar   (rĕk′ tĭ·lĭn′ ē·ẽr)
rec·ti·tude   (rĕk′ tĭ·tūd)
rec·tor   (rĕk′ tẽr)
   rec·tor·ies   -tor·ies
rec·tum   (rĕk′ tŭm)
re·cum·bent   (rē·kŭm′ bĕnt)
   -ben·cy
re·cu·per·ate   (rē·kū′ pẽr·āt)
   -at·ing
re·cu·per·a·tion
       (rē·kū′ pẽr·ā′ shŭn)
re·cu·per·a·tive
       (rē·kū′ pẽr·ā′ tĭv)
re·cur   (rē·kûr′)
   -curred   -cur·ring
   re·cur·rence   re·cur·rent
red   (rĕd)
   red-blood·ed   red·coat
   red·den   red·dish
   red-hand·ed   red·head
   red-hot   red-let·ter day
   red o·cher   red·skin
   red tape

re·deem   (rē·dēm′)
   re·deem·a·ble   re·deem·er
re·demp·tion   (rē·dĕmp′ shŭn)
re·demp·tive   (rē·dĕmp′ tĭv)
re·de·vel·op·ment
       (rē′ dē·vĕl′ ŭp·mĕnt)
red·in·gote   (rĕd′ ĭng·gōt)
re·dis·cov·er·y
       (rē′ dĭs·kŭv′ ẽr·ĭ)
red·o·lent   (rĕd′ ō·lĕnt)
   -lence
re·dou·ble   (rē·dŭb′ 'l)
   -bling
re·doubt·a·ble   (rē·dout′ à·b'l)
re·dound   (rē·dound′)
re·dress   (rē·drĕs′)
re·duce   (rē·dūs′)
   -duc·ing   re·duc·i·ble
   re·duc·tion   (rē·dŭk′ shŭn)
re·dun·dant   (rē·dŭn′ dănt)
   -dan·cy
re·du·pli·ca·tion
       (rē·dū′ plĭ·kā′ shŭn)
re-ech·o   (rē·ĕk′ ō)
reed   (rēd)
   (grass; see read)
re-ed·u·ca·tion
       (rē·ĕd′ û·kā′ shŭn)
reef   (rēf)
reek   (rēk)
reel   (rēl)
   (dance; see real)
re-e·lect   (rē′ ē·lĕkt′)
re-e·mer·gence   (rē′ ē·mûr′ jĕns)
re-em·ploy   (rē′ ĕm·ploi′)
re-en·act   (rē′ ĕn·ăkt′)
re-en·gage   (rē′ ĕn·gāj′)
   -gag·ing
re-en·list·ment   (rē′ ĕn·lĭst′ mĕnt)
re-en·ter   (rē·ĕn′ tẽr)
   re-en·try   -tries
re-es·tab·lish   (rē′ ĕs·tăb′ lĭsh)
re-ex·am·ine   (rē′ ĕg·zăm′ ĭn)
   -in·ing
re·fer   (rē·fûr′)
   -ferred   -fer·ring
   ref·er·a·ble   (rĕf′ ẽr·à·b'l)
   re·fer·ral
ref·er·ee   (rĕf′ ẽr·ē′)
ref·er·ence   (rĕf′ ẽr·ĕns)
ref·er·en·dum   (rĕf′ ẽr·ĕn′ dŭm)
re·fill·a·ble   (rē·fĭl′ à·b'l)
re·fine   (rē·fīn′)
   -fin·ing   re·fine·ment
   re·fin·er·y   -er·ies

re·flect (rĕ·flĕkt′)
  re·flec·tion   re·flec·tive
  re·flec·tive·ness
  re·flec·tor
re·flex (rē′ flĕks)
re·for·est·a·tion
       (rē′ fôr·ĕs·tā′ shŭn)
re·form (rē·fôrm′)
  re·form·a·ble
  ref·or·ma·tion
       (rĕf′ ŏr·mā′ shŭn)
re·form·a·to·ry
       (rē·fôr′ má·tō′ rĭ)
  -ries
re·fract (rē·frăkt′)
  re·frac·tion   re·frac·tive
re·frac·to·ry (rē·frăk′ tō·rĭ)
re·frain (rē·frān′)
re·fresh·ment (rē·frĕsh′ mĕnt)
re·frig·er·ate (rē·frĭj′ ĕr·āt)
  -at·ing   re·frig·er·a·tor
  re·frig·er·a·tion
       (rē·frĭj′ ĕr·ā′ shŭn)
ref·uge (rĕf′ ūj)
ref·u·gee (rĕf′ ū·jē′)
re·fund (rē·fŭnd′)
re·fur·bish (rē·fûr′ bĭsh)
re·fuse (rē·fūz′) v.
  -fus·ing
  re·fus·al (rē·fūz′ ăl)
ref·use (rĕf′ ūs) adj., n.
re·fute (rē·fūt′)
  -fut·ing
  ref·u·ta·ble (rĕf′ ū·tá·b′l)
  ref·u·ta·tion (rĕf′ ū·tā′ shŭn)
re·gal (rē′ găl)
  -gal·ly
re·gale (rē·gāl′)
  -gal·ing   re·gale·ment
re·ga·li·a (rē·gā′ lĭ·á)
re·gard·ing (rē·gärd′ ĭng)
re·gat·ta (rē·găt′ á)
re·gen·er·a·tion
       (rē·jĕn′ ĕr·á′ shŭn)
re·gent (rē′ jĕnt)
  -gen·cy
re·gime (rā·zhēm′)
reg·i·men (rĕj′ ĭ·mĕn)
reg·i·ment (rĕj′ ĭ·mĕnt)
  reg·i·men·tal (rĕj′ ĭ·mĕn′ tăl)
  reg·i·men·ta·tion
       (rĕj′ ĭ·mĕn·tā′ shŭn)
re·gion (rē′ jŭn)
  re·gion·al

reg·is·ter (rĕj′ ĭs·tĕr)
  reg·is·trant (-trănt)
  reg·is·trar (-trär)
  reg·is·tra·tion (rĕj′ ĭs·trā′ shŭn)
  reg·is·try
re·gress (rē·grĕs′)
  re·gres·sive   re·gres·sion
re·gret (rē·grĕt′)
  -gret·ted   -gret·ting
  re·gret·ful, -ful·ly, -ful·ness
  re·gret·ta·ble
reg·u·lar (rĕg′ ū·lĕr)
  reg·u·lar·i·ty (rĕg′ ū·lăr′ ĭ·tĭ)
  reg·u·lar·ize -iz·ing
reg·u·late (rĕg′ ū·lāt)
  -lat·ing
  reg·u·la·tion (rĕg′ ū·lā′ shŭn)
  reg·u·la·tive (rĕg′ ū·lā′ tĭv)
  reg·u·la·tor (rĕg′ ū·lā′ tĕr)
  reg·u·la·to·ry (rĕg′ ū·lá·tō′ rĭ)
re·gur·gi·tate (rē·gûr′ jĭ·tāt)
  -tat·ing
re·ha·bil·i·tate
       (rē′ há·bĭl′ ĭ·tāt)
  -tat·ing
  re·ha·bil·i·ta·tion
       (rē′ há·bĭl′ ĭ·tā′ shŭn)
re·hearse (rē·hûrs′)
  -hears·ing   re·hears·al
Reich (rīk)
reign (rān)
  (royal authority; see *rain*, *rein*)
re·im·burse·ment
       (rē′ ĭm·bûrs′ mĕnt)
rein (rān)
  (bridle strap; see *rain*, *reign*)
re·in·car·na·tion
       (rē′ ĭn·kär·nā′ shŭn)
rein·deer (rān′ dēr′)
re·in·force·ment
       (rē′ ĭn·fōrs′ mĕnt)
re·in·sert (rē′ ĭn·sûrt′)
re·in·state·ment
       (rē′ ĭn·stāt′ mĕnt)
re·in·te·grate (rē·ĭn′ tē·grāt)
  -grat·ing
re·in·tro·duce (rē′ ĭn·trō·dūs′)
  -duc·ing
re·in·vest (rē′ ĭn·vĕst′)
re·is·sue (rē·ĭsh′ ū)
  -is·su·ing
re·it·er·ate (rē·ĭt′ ĕr·āt)
  -at·ing
  re·it·er·a·tion
       (rē·ĭt′ ĕr·ā′ shŭn)

re·ject (rĕ·jĕkt′)
  re·jec·tion (rĕ·jĕk′ shŭn)
re·joice (rĕ·jois′)
  -joic·ing
re·join·der (rĕ·join′ dĕr)
re·ju·ve·nate (rĕ·jōō′ vĕ·nāt)
  -nat·ing
  re·ju·ve·na·tion
        (rĕ·jōō′ vĕ·nā′ shŭn)
re·kin·dle (rĕ·kĭn′ d′l)
  -dling
re·lapse (rĕ·lăps′)
  -laps·ing
re·late (rĕ·lāt′)
  -lat·ing
re·la·tion (rĕ·lā′ shŭn)
  re·la·tion·ship
rel·a·tive (rĕl′ á·tĭv)
  rel·a·tiv·i·ty (rĕl′ á·tĭv′ ĭ·tĭ)
re·lax (rĕ·lăks′)
  re·lax·a·tion (rē′ lăk·sā′ shŭn)
  re·lax·er
re·lay (rĕ·lā′)
  -layed -lay·ing
re·lease (rĕ·lēs′)
  -leas·ing
rel·e·gate (rĕl′ ê·gāt)
  -gat·ing
  rel·e·ga·tion (rĕl′ ê·gā′ shŭn)
re·lent (rĕ·lĕnt′)
  re·lent·less
rel·e·vant (rĕl′ ê·vănt)
  -vance, -van·cy
re·li·a·ble (rĕ·lī′ á·b′l)
  re·li·a·bil·i·ty (rĕ·lī′ á·bĭl′ ĭ·tĭ)
re·li·ant (rĕ·lī′ ănt)
  re·li·ance
rel·ic (rĕl′ ĭk)
re·lief (rĕ·lēf′)
re·lieve (rĕ·lēv′)
  -liev·ing re·liev·a·ble
re·li·gion (rĕ·lĭj′ ŭn)
  re·li·gious
re·lin·quish (rĕ·lĭng′ kwĭsh)
rel·ish (rĕl′ ĭsh)
re·lo·ca·tion (rē′ lô·kā′ shŭn)
re·luc·tant (rĕ·lŭk′ tănt)
  -tance
re·ly (rĕ·lī′)
  -lied -ly·ing
Rem·brandt van Rijn
      (rĕm′ brănt văn rīn′)
re·main (rĕ·mān′)
  re·main·der
re·mand (rĕ·mănd′)

re·mark·a·ble (rĕ·mär′ ká·b′l)
re·mar·riage (rĕ·măr′ ĭj)
rem·e·dy (rĕm′ ê·dĭ)
  -died, -dies, -dy·ing
re·me·di·a·ble (rĕ·mē′ dĭ·á·b′l)
re·me·di·al (rĕ·mē′ dĭ·ăl)
  rem·e·di·less
re·mem·ber (rĕ·mĕm′ bĕr)
  re·mem·brance (-brăns)
re·mind·er (rĕ·mīn′ dĕr)
rem·i·nisce (rĕm′ ĭ·nĭs′)
  -nis·cing rem·i·nis·cence
  rem·i·nis·cent
re·miss (rĕ·mĭs′)
re·mis·sion (rĕ·mĭsh′ ŭn)
re·mit (rĕ·mĭt′)
  -mit·ted -mit·ting
  re·mit·ta·ble re·mit·tal
  re·mit·tance re·mit·tent
  re·mit·tor
rem·nant (rĕm′ nănt)
re·mod·el (rĕ·mŏd′ ′l)
  -eled -el·ing
re·mon·strate (rĕ·mŏn′ strāt)
  -strat·ing
  re·mon·strance
      (rĕ·mŏn′ străns)
re·morse (rĕ·môrs′)
  re·morse·ful, -ful·ly, -ful·ness
  re·morse·less
re·mote (rĕ·mōt′)
  re·mote·ly -mote·ness
re·move (rĕ·mōōv′)
  -mov·ing re·mov·a·ble
  re·mov·al
re·mu·ner·a·tion
      (rĕ·mū′ nĕr·ā′ shŭn)
re·mu·ner·a·tive
      (rĕ·mū′ nĕr·ā′ tĭv)
ren·ais·sance (rĕn′ ĕ·zäns′)
  Ren·ais·sance art
ren·der (rĕn′ dĕr)
ren·dez·vous (rän′ dĕ·vōō)
ren·di·tion (rĕn·dĭsh′ ŭn)
ren·e·gade (rĕn′ ê·gād)
re·nege (rĕ·nĕg′)
  -neg·ing
re·ne·go·ti·ate
      (rē′ nê·gō′ shĭ·āt)
  -at·ing
  re·ne·go·ti·a·ble
      (rē′ nê·gō′ shĭ·á·b′l)
re·new·al (rĕ·nū′ ăl)
ren·net (rĕn′ ĕt)

re·nom·i·nate   (rē·nŏm′ ĭ·nāt)
  -nat·ing
re·nounce   (rē·nouns′)
  -nounc·ing   re·nounce·ment
ren·o·vate   (rĕn′ ō·vāt)
  -vat·ing
ren·o·va·tion   (rĕn′ ō·vā′ shŭn)
re·nown   (rē·noun′)
  re·nowned   (-nound)
rent·al   (rĕn′ tăl)
re·nun·ci·a·tion
              (rē·nŭn′ sĭ·ā′ shŭn)
re·oc·cu·py   (rē·ŏk′ û·pĭ)
  -pied   -py·ing
re·oc·cu·pa·tion
              (rē′ ŏk·û·pā′ shŭn)
re·o·pen   (rē·ō′ pĕn)
re·or·der   (rē·ôr′ dĕr)
re·or·gan·i·za·tion
              (rē′ ôr·găn·ĭ·zā′ shŭn)
re·pair   (rē·pâr′)
rep·a·ra·tion   (rĕp′ à·rā′ shŭn)
rep·ar·tee   (rĕp′ ĕr·tē′)
re·past   (rē·păst′)
re·pay   (rē·pā′)
  -paid   -pay·ing
re·pay·a·ble   re·pay·ment
re·peal   (rē·pēl′)
  -pealed   -peal·ing
  re·peal·a·ble
re·peat   (rē·pēt′)
  re·peat·ed·ly   re·peat·er
re·pel   (rē·pĕl′)
  -pelled   -pel·ling
  re·pel·lent
re·pent   (rē·pĕnt′)
  re·pent·ance
re·per·cus·sion
              (rē′ pĕr·kŭsh′ ŭn)
rep·er·toire   (rĕp′ ĕr·twär)
rep·er·to·ry   (rĕp′ ĕr·tō′ rĭ)
rep·e·ti·tion   (rĕp′ ê·tĭsh′ ŭn)
  rep·e·ti·tious
re·pet·i·tive   (rē·pĕt′ ĭ·tĭv)
re·place   (rē·plās′)
  -plac·ing   re·place·a·ble
  re·place·ment
re·plen·ish   (rē·plĕn′ ĭsh)
re·plete   (rē·plēt′)
  re·ple·tion   (rē·plē′ shŭn)
rep·li·ca   (rĕp′ lĭ·kà)
rep·li·ca·tion   (rĕp′ lĭ·kā′ shŭn)
re·ply   (rē·plī′)
  -plied   -ply·ing

re·port   (rē·pōrt′)
  re·port·a·ble   re·port·er
  rep·or·to·ri·al   (rĕp′ ôr·tō′ rĭ·ăl)
re·pose   (rē·pōz′)
  -pos·ing   re·pose·ful
re·pos·i·to·ry   (rē·pŏz′ ĭ·tō′ rĭ)
  -ries
re·pos·sess   (rē′ pŏ·zĕs′)
  re·pos·ses·sion
rep·re·hend   (rĕp′ rē·hĕnd′)
rep·re·hen·si·ble
              (rĕp′ rē·hĕn′ sĭ·b′l)
rep·re·sent   (rĕp′ rē·zĕnt′)
  rep·re·sent·a·ble
  rep·re·sen·ta·tion
              (rĕp′ rē·zĕn·tā′ shŭn)
  rep·re·sent·a·tive
              (rĕp′ rē·zĕn′ tà·tĭv)
re·press   (rē·prĕs′)
  re·pres·sion   (rē·prĕsh′ ŭn)
  re·pres·sive
re·prieve   (rē·prēv′)
  -priev·ing
rep·ri·mand   (rĕp′ rĭ·mănd)
re·pris·al   (rē·prīz′ ăl)
re·proach·ful   (rē·prōch′ fŏŏl)
  -ful·ly   -ful·ness
rep·ro·bate   (rĕp′ rō·bāt)
  rep·ro·ba·tion
              (rĕp′ rō·bā′ shŭn)
re·pro·duce   (rē′ prō·dūs′)
  -duc·ing   re·pro·duc·i·ble
  re·pro·duc·tion
              (rē′ prō·dŭk′ shŭn)
  re·pro·duc·tive
              (rē′ prō·dŭk′ tĭv)
re·proof   (rē·prōōf′) n.
re·prove   (rē·prōōv′) v.
  -prov·ing
rep·tile   (rĕp′ tĭl)
  rep·til·i·an   (rĕp·tĭl′ ĭ·ăn)
re·pub·lic   (rē·pŭb′ lĭk)
  re·pub·li·can
re·pu·di·ate   (rē·pū′ dĭ·āt)
  -at·ing
  re·pu·di·a·tion
              (rē·pū′ dĭ·ā′ shŭn)
re·pug·nant   (rē·pŭg′ nănt)
  -nance
re·pulse   (rē·pŭls′)
  -puls·ing
  re·pul·sion   (rē·pŭl′ shŭn)
  re·pul·sive   -sive·ness
rep·u·ta·ble   (rĕp′ û·tà·b′l)

rep·u·ta·bil·i·ty
(rĕp′ ū·tȧ·bĭl′ ĭ·tĭ)
rep·u·ta·tion (rĕp′ ū·tā′ shŭn)
re·put·ed·ly (rē·pūt′ ĕd·lĭ)
re·quest (rē·kwĕst′)
re·qui·em (rē′ kwĭ·ĕm)
re·quire·ment (rē·kwīr′ mĕnt)
req·ui·site (rĕk′ wĭ·zĭt)
req·ui·si·tion (rĕk′ wĭ·zĭsh′ ŭn)
re·quite (rē·kwīt′)
re·quit·al
re·sale (rē·sāl′)
re·sal·a·ble
re·scind (rē·sĭnd′)
re·scis·sion (rē·sĭzh′ ŭn)
res·cue (rĕs′ kū)
-cu·ing
re·search (rē·sûrch′)
re·sem·ble (rē·zĕm′ b'l)
-bling
re·sem·blance (rē·zĕm′ blȧns)
re·sent (rē·zĕnt′)
re·sent·ful, -ful·ly, -ful·ness
re·sent·ment
res·er·va·tion (rĕz′ ĕr·vā′ shŭn)
re·serve (rē·zûrv′)
-serv·ing re·serv·ed·ly
re·serv·ist
res·er·voir (rĕz′ ĕr·vwôr′)
re·set·tle·ment (rē·sĕt′ 'l·mĕnt)
re·side (rē·zīd′)
-sid·ing
res·i·dent (rĕz′ ĭ·dĕnt)
res·i·dence
res·i·den·tial (rĕz′ ĭ·dĕn′ shȧl)
res·i·due (rĕz′ ĭ·dū)
re·sid·u·al (rē·zĭd′ ū·ȧl)
re·sign (rē·zīn′)
res·ig·na·tion (rĕz′ ĭg·nā′ shŭn)
re·sign·ed·ly (rē·zīn′ ĕd·lĭ)
re·sil·i·ent (rē·zĭl′ ĭ·ĕnt)
re·sil·i·ence
res·in (rĕz′ ĭn)
res·in·ous (rĕz′ ĭ·nŭs)
re·sist (rē·zĭst′)
re·sis·tance (rē·zĭs′ tȧns)
re·sis·tant re·sist·i·ble
re·sis·tive re·sis·tor
res·o·jet en·gine
(rĕz′ ō·jĕt′)
res·o·lute (rĕz′ ō·lūt)
-lute·ly
res·o·lu·tion (rĕz′ ō·lū′ shŭn)
re·solve (rē·zŏlv′)
-solv·ing re·solv·a·ble

res·o·nant (rĕz′ ō·nȧnt)
-nance res·o·na·tor
re·sort (rē·zôrt′)
re·sound (rē·zound′)
re·source (rē·sōrs′)
re·source·ful, -ful·ly, -ful·ness
re·spect (rē·spĕkt′)
re·spect·a·bil·i·ty
(rē·spĕk′ tȧ·bĭl′ ĭ·tĭ)
re·spect·a·ble (rē·spĕk′ tȧ·b'l)
re·spect·er
re·spect·ful, -ful·ly, -ful·ness
re·spect·ing
re·spec·tive -tive·ly
res·pi·ra·tion (rĕs′ pĭ·rā′ shŭn)
res·pi·ra·tor (rĕs′ pĭ·rā′ tĕr)
re·spir·a·to·ry (rē·spĭr′ ȧ·tō′ rĭ)
res·pite (rĕs′ pĭt)
re·splend·ent (rē·splĕn′ dĕnt)
-ence
re·spond·ent (rē·spŏn′ dĕnt)
re·sponse (rē·spŏns′)
re·spon·si·ble (rē·spŏn′ sĭ·b'l)
re·spon·si·bil·i·ty
(rē·spŏn′ sĭ·bĭl′ ĭ·tĭ)
re·spon·sive (rē·spŏn′ sĭv)
-sive·ness
res·tau·rant (rĕs′ tō·rȧnt)
res·tau·ra·teur (rĕs′ tō·rȧ·tûr′)
(NOTE: no n)
rest·ful (rĕst′ fŏŏl)
-ful·ly -ful·ness
res·ti·tu·tion (rĕs′ tĭ·tū′ shŭn)
res·tive (rĕs′ tĭv)
rest·less (rĕst′ lĕs)
res·to·ra·tion (rĕs′ tō·rā′ shŭn)
re·stor·a·tive (rē·stôr′ ȧ·tĭv)
re·strain (rē·strān′)
re·strain·a·ble re·straint
re·strict (rē·strĭkt′)
re·stric·tion (rē·strĭk′ shŭn)
re·stric·tive (rē·strĭk′ tĭv)
re·sult (rē·zŭlt′)
re·sult·ant
re·sume (rē·zūm′) v.
-sum·ing
ré·su·mé (rā′ zŭ·mā′) n.
re·sump·tion (rē·zŭmp′ shŭn)
re·sur·gent (rē·sûr′ jĕnt)
-gence
res·ur·rect (rĕz′ ŭ·rĕkt′)
res·ur·rec·tion
(rĕz′ ŭ·rĕk′ shŭn)
re·sus·ci·tate (rē·sŭs′ ĭ·tāt)
-tat·ing

re·sus·ci·ta·tion
(rĕ·sŭs′ ĭ·tā′ shŭn)
re·sus·ci·ta·tor
(rĕ·sŭs′ ĭ·tā′ tēr)
re·tail (rē′ tāl)
re·tail·er
re·tain (rē·tān′)
re·tain·a·ble   re·tain·er
re·tal·i·ate (rē·tăl′ ĭ-āt)
-at·ing
re·tal·i·a·tion
(rē·tăl′ ĭ·ā′ shŭn)
re·tal·i·a·tive (rē·tăl′ ĭ·ā′ tĭv)
re·tal·i·a·to·ry
(rē·tăl′ ĭ·à·tō′ rĭ)
re·tard (rē·tärd′)
re·tar·da·tion (rē′ tär·dā′ shŭn)
retch (rĕch)
(vomit; see *wretch*)
re·ten·tion (rē·tĕn′ shŭn)
re·ten·tive
ret·i·cent (rĕt′ ĭ·sĕnt)
-cence
ret·i·na (rĕt′ ĭ·nà)
ret·i·nue (rĕt′ ĭ·nū)
re·tire (rē·tīr′)
-tir·ing   re·tire·ment
re·tort (rē·tôrt′)
re·touch (rē·tŭch′)
re·tract (rē·trăkt′)
re·tract·a·ble   re·trac·tion
re·tread (rē·trĕd′)
re·treat (rē·trēt′)
re·trench·ment (rē·trĕnch′ mĕnt)
re·tri·al (rē·trī′ ăl)
ret·ri·bu·tion (rĕt′ rĭ·bū′ shŭn)
re·trieve (rē·trēv′)
-triev·ing   re·triev·a·ble
re·triev·er
ret·ro·ac·tive (rĕt′ rō·ăk′ tĭv)
ret·ro·ces·sion (rĕt′ rō·sĕsh′ ŭn)
ret·ro·gres·sion
(rĕt′ rō·grĕsh′ ŭn)
ret·ro·spect (rĕt′ rō·spĕkt)
ret·ro·ver·sion (rĕt′ rō·vûr′ shŭn)
re·turn (rē·tûrn′)
re·turn·a·ble
re·un·ion (rē·ūn′ yŭn)
re·u·nite (rē′ ū·nīt′)
-nit·ing
rev (rĕv)
revved   rev·ving
re·vamp (rē·vămp′)
re·veal (rē·vēl′)
-vealed   -veal·ing

re·veal·a·ble   re·veal·ment
rev·eil·le (rĕv′ ĕ·lĭ)
rev·el (rĕv′ ĕl)
-eled   -el·ing
rev·el·ry
rev·e·la·tion (rĕv′ ĕ·lā′ shŭn)
re·venge (rē·vĕnj′)
-veng·ing   re·venge·ful
rev·e·nue (rĕv′ ĕ·nū)
re·ver·ber·ate (rē·vûr′ bĕr·āt)
-at·ing
re·ver·ber·a·tion
(rē·vûr′ bĕr·ā′ shŭn)
re·vere (rē·vēr′)
-ver·ing
rev·er·end (rĕv′ ēr·ĕnd)
rev·er·ent (rĕv′ ēr·ĕnt)
rev·er·ence
rev·er·ie (rĕv′ ēr·ĭ)
re·verse (rē·vûrs′)
-vers·ing   re·ver·sal
re·vers·i·ble
re·ver·sion (rē·vûr′ shŭn)
re·vert (rē·vûrt′)
re·vert·i·ble
re·view (rē·vū′)
(survey; see *revue*)
re·vile (rē·vīl′)
-vil·ing   re·vile·ment
re·vise (rē·vīz′)
-vis·ing
re·vi·sion (rē·vĭzh′ ŭn)
re·vi·tal·ize (rē·vī′ tăl·ĭz)
-iz·ing
re·vi·tal·i·za·tion
(rē′ vĭ·tăl·ĭ·zā′ shŭn)
re·viv·al (rē·vīv′ ăl)
re·viv·al·ist
re·vive (rē·vīv′)
-viv·ing
re·viv·i·fy (rē·vĭv′ ĭ·fĭ)
-fied,   -fy·ing
re·voke (rē·vōk′)
-vok·ing
rev·o·ca·ble (rĕv′ ō·kà·b'l)
re·volt·ing (rē·vōl′ tĭng)
rev·o·lu·tion (rĕv′ ō·lū′ shŭn)
rev·o·lu·tion·ar·y
rev·o·lu·tion·ize, -iz·ing
re·volv·er (rē·vŏl′ vēr)
re·vue (rē·vū′)
(burlesque; see *review*)
re·vul·sion (rē·vŭl′ shŭn)
re·ward (rē·wôrd′)

rhap·so·dy (răp′ sŏ·dĭ)
  -dies
  rhap·so·dize -diz·ing
Rhen·ish (rĕn′ ĭsh)
rhe·o·stat (rē′ ŏ·stăt)
rhet·o·ric (rĕt′ ŏ·rĭk)
  rhe·tor·i·cal (rē·tŏr′ ĭ·kăl)
  rhet·o·ri·cian (rĕt′ ŏ·rĭsh′ ăn)
rheu·ma·tism (rōō′ mă·tĭz′m)
  rheu·mat·ic (rōō·măt′ ĭk)
  rheu·ma·toid ar·thri·tis
    (rōō′ mă·toid)
Rh fac·tor (är′ ăch′)
  Rh-neg·a·tive Rh-pos·i·tive
rhine·stone (rīn′ stōn′)
Rhine wine (rīn)
rhi·ni·tis (rī·nī′ tĭs)
rhi·noc·er·os (rī·nŏs′ ĕr·ŏs)
Rhode Is·land (rōd ī′ lănd)
  abbr. R. I.
  Rhode Is·land·er
Rho·de·sia (rō·dē′ zhă)
Rhodes schol·ar·ship
  (rōdz)
rhom·bus (rŏm′ bŭs)
rhu·barb (rōō′ bärb)
rhyme (rīm)
  rhym·ing
rhythm (rĭth′m)
  rhyth·mic (rĭth′ mĭk)
  -mi·cal
Ri·al·to (rī·ăl′ tō)
rib·ald (rĭb′ ăld)
  rib·ald·ry (-rĭ)
rib·bing (rĭb′ĭng)
rib·bon (rĭb′ŭn)
ri·bo·fla·vin (rī′ bŏ·flā′ vĭn)
rich·es (rĭch′ ĕz)
rick·ets (rĭk′ ĕts)
rick·et·y (rĭk′ ĕ·tĭ)
rick·ey (rĭk′ ĭ)
rick·rack (rĭk′ răk′)
rick·sha (rĭk′ shä)
ric·o·chet (rĭk′ ŏ·shā′)
  -cheted -chet·ing
rid·dance (rĭd′ ăns)
rid·dle (rĭd′ ′l)
  rid·dling
ride (rīd)
  rid·ing
  rid·den (rĭd′ ′n)
ridge (rĭj)
rid·i·cule (rĭd′ ĭ·kūl)
  -cul·ing
ri·dic·u·lous (rĭ·dĭk′ û·lŭs)

rife (rīf)
rif·fle (rĭf′ ′l)
  (shuffle; see *rifle*)
  rif·fling
riff·raff (rĭf′ răf′)
ri·fle (rī′ f′l)
  (gun; see *riffle*)
  -fling ri·fle·man
rift (rĭft)
rig·ging (rĭg′ ĭng)
right (rīt)
  (correct; see *rite, wright, write*)
  right an·gle right-an·gled
  right·eous (rī′ chŭs)
  right·ful, -ful·ly, -ful·ness
  right-hand·ed
  right of way (pl. rights of way)
rig·id (rĭj′ ĭd)
  ri·gid·i·ty (rĭ·jĭd′ ĭ·tĭ)
rig·ma·role (rĭg′ mă·rōl)
rig·or (rĭg′ ĕr)
  ri·gor mor·tis (rĭg′ ĕr môr′ tĭs)
  rig·or·ous (rĭg′ ĕr·ŭs)
ring (rĭng)
  ring·lead·er ring·mas·ter
  ring·side ring·worm
rinse (rĭns)
  rins·ing
Rio de Ja·nei·ro,
  Bra·zil (rē′ ŏ dē jă·nā′ rō)
Ri·o Grande (riv.)
  (rē′ ŏ grănd′)
ri·ot (rī′ ŭt)
  -ot·ed -ot·ing
  ri·o·ter ri·ot·ous
rip·cord (rĭp′ kôrd′)
rip·en (rĭp′ ĕn)
rip·ple (rĭp′ ′l)
  rip·pling
rip-roar·ing (rĭp′ rôr′ ĭng)
Rip van Win·kle
  (rĭp′ văn wĭng′ k′l)
rise (rīz)
  ris·ing
  ris·en (rĭz′ ′n)
risk·y (rĭs′ kĭ)
  risk·i·ness
ri·sot·to (rē·sôt′ tō)
ris·qué (rĭs·kā′)
rite (rīt)
  (liturgy; see *right, wright, write*)
rit·u·al (rĭt′ û·ăl)
rit·u·al·is·tic (rĭt′ û·ăl·ĭs′ tĭk)
rit·u·al·ly

ri·val (rī′ vəl)
  -valed -val·ing
  ri·val·ry
Ri·vie·ra (rĕ·vyä′ rä)
riv·u·let (rĭv′ û·lĕt)
roach (rōch)
road (rōd)
  road·bed road·block
  road·house road run·ner
  road·way
roam (rōm)
roan (rōn)
Ro·a·noke, Va. (rō′ à·nōk)
roar·ing (rōr′ ĭng)
roast (rōst)
rob·ber·y (rŏb′ ĕr·ĭ)
  rob·ber·ies
rob·in (rŏb′ ĭn)
Rob·in·son Cru·soe
                    (rŏb′ ĭn·s'n krōō′ sō)
ro·bot (rō′ bŏt)
ro·bust (rō·bŭst′)
rock (rŏk)
  rock bot·tom n.
  rock-bot·tom adj.
  rock gar·den rock-ribbed
  rock salt
Rock·e·fel·ler, John
                    (rŏk′ ĕ·fĕl′ ĕr)
rock·er (rŏk′ ĕr)
rock·et (rŏk′ ĕt)
  rock·et launch·er
  rock·et·ry
rock·y (rŏk′ ĭ)
  rock·i·er, -i·est, -i·ly, -i·ness
  Rock·ies (mts.)
ro·co·co (rō·kō′ kō)
ro·dent (rō′ dĕnt)
ro·de·o (rō′ dĕ·ō)
roe (rō)
  (doe; eggs; see row)
roent·gen (rŭnt′ gĕn)
rogue (rōg)
  ro·guer·y (rō′ gĕr·ĭ)
  rogues′ gal·ler·y
  ro·guish
roil (roil)
  roil·ing
roist·er (rois′ tĕr)
role (rōl)
  (actor's part; see roll)
roll (rōl)
  (revolve; see role)
  roll·back roll call

roll·er (rōl′ ĕr)
  roll·er bear·ing
  roll·er coast·er
  roll·er skate
rol·lick·ing (rŏl′ ĭk·ĭng)
rol·y-pol·y (rō′ lĭ·pō′ lĭ)
ro·maine let·tuce
                    (rō·mān′)
Ro·man Cath·o·lic (church)
                    (rō′ mən kăth′ ō·lĭk)
ro·mance (rō·măns′)
Ro·man·esque (rō′ mən·ĕsk′)
Ro·ma·nia (rō·mān′ yà)
ro·man·tic (rō·măn′ tĭk)
  ro·man·ti·cal·ly
  ro·man·ti·cize (-tĭ·sīz)
Ro·me·o (rō′ mĕ·ō)
romp·er (rŏmp′ ĕr)
ron·do (rŏn′ dō)
  -dos
roof·ing (rōōf′ ĭng)
rook·er·y (rōōk′ ĕr·ĭ)
  -er·ies
rook·ie (rōōk′ ĭ)
room (rōōm)
  room·ette (rōōm·ĕt′)
  room·ful room·i·ness
  room·mate room·y
Roo·se·velt, Frank·lin D.
                    (rō′ zĕ·vĕlt)
roost·er (rōōs′ tĕr)
root (rōōt)
  (stem; see rout, route)
  root beer root·er
  root·less
rop·y (rōp′ ĭ)
  rop·i·ness
Roque·fort cheese
                    (rōk′ fĕrt)
Ror·schach test (rôr′ shäk)
ro·sa·ry (rō′ zà·rĭ)
  -ries
rose (rōz)
  rose·bud rose-col·ored
  rose·mar·y rose wa·ter
  rose·wood
ro·se·ate (rō′ zĕ·ăt)
Ro·set·ta stone (rō·zĕt′ à)
ro·sette (rō·zĕt′)
Rosh Ha·sha·na
                    (rōsh hä·shä′ nä)
ros·in (rŏz′ ĭn)
ros·ter (rŏs′ tĕr)
ros·trum (rŏs′ trŭm)
  pl. ros·tra

ros·y (rōz′ ĭ)
  ros·i·er, -i·est, -i·ly, -i·ness
ro·ta·ry (rō′ tȧ·rĭ)
ro·tate (rō′ tāt)
  -tat·ing
  ro·ta·tion (rȯ·tā′ shŭn)
  ro·ta·tor
ro·te·none (rō′ t'n·ōn)
ro·tis·se·rie (rō′ tĕs′ rē′)
ro·to·gra·vure (rō′ tō·grȧ·vūr′)
ro·to sec·tion (rō′ tō)
rot·ten (rŏt′ 'n)
  rot·ten·ness
ro·tund (rȯ·tŭnd′)
  ro·tun·di·ty (rȯ·tŭn′ dĭ·tĭ)
ro·tun·da (rȯ·tŭn′ dȧ)
rou·é (rōō·ā′)
rouge (rōōzh)
rough (rŭf)
  rough·age
  rough-and-read·y
  rough·hew   rough·house
  rough·neck   rough·rid·er
  rough·shod
rou·lette (rōō·lĕt′)
round (round)
  round·a·bout   round rob·in
  round-shoul·dered
  round steak   Round Ta·ble
  round trip   round·up
roun·de·lay (roun′ dĕ·lā)
rouse (rouz)
  rous·ing
Rous·seau, Jean Jacques
              (rōō′ sō′)
roust·a·bout (roust′ ȧ·bout′)
rout (rout)
  (conquer; see route)
route (rōōt)
  (path; see root, rout)
  rout·ing
rou·tine (rōō·tēn′)
rov·er (rōv′ ẽr)
row (rō)
  (propel with oars; see roe)
row·boat (rō′ bōt′)
row·dy (rou′ dĭ)
  row·dy·ish
roy·al (roi′ ăl)
  roy·al·ist   roy·al·ty
rub·ber (rŭb′ ẽr)
  rub·ber·neck   rub·ber-stamp
rub·bish (rŭb′ ĭsh)
rub·ble (rŭb′ 'l)
rub·down (rŭb′ doun′)

ru·bel·la (rōō·bĕl′ ȧ)
Ru·bi·con (rōō′ bĭ·kŏn)
ru·bric (rōō′ brĭk)
ruche (rōōsh)
  ruch·ing
ruck·sack (rŭk′ săk′)
ruc·tion (rŭk′ shŭn)
rud·der (rŭd′ ẽr)
rud·dy (rŭd′ ĭ)
  rud·di·ness
rude (rōōd)
  rude·ly   rude·ness
ru·di·ment (rōō′ dĭ·mĕnt)
  ru·di·men·ta·ry
              (rōō′ dĭ·mĕn′ tȧ·rĭ)
rue (rōō)
  ru·ing
  rue·ful, -ful·ly, -ful·ness
ruffed grouse (rŭft)
ruf·fi·an (rŭf′ ĭ·ǎn)
ruf·fle (rŭf′ 'l)
  ruf·fling   ruf·fly
Rug·by foot·ball
              (rŭg′ bĭ)
rug·ged (rŭg′ ĕd)
ru·in (rōō′ ĭn)
  ru·in·a·tion (rōō′ ĭ·nā′ shŭn)
  ru·in·ous (rōō′ ĭ·nŭs)
rul·er (rōōl′ ẽr)
rul·ing (rōōl′ ĭng)
rum·ba (rōōm′ bä)
rum·ble (rŭm′ b'l)
  -bling
ru·mi·nant (rōō′ mĭ·nǎnt)
ru·mi·nate (rōō′ mĭ·nāt)
  -nat·ing
  ru·mi·na·tion
              (rōō′ mĭ·nā′ shŭn)
rum·mage (rŭm′ ĭj)
rum·my (rŭm′ ĭ)
ru·mor (rōō′ mēr)
rum·ple (rŭm′ p'l)
  -pling
rum·pus room (rŭm′ pŭs)
rum·run·ner (rŭm′ rŭn′ ẽr)
run (rŭn)
  ran   run·ning
  run·a·way   run-down
  run-on   run·way
run·ci·ble spoon
              (rŭn′ sĭ·b'l)
rune (rōōn)
  ru·nic
run·ner-up (rŭn′ ẽr·ŭp′)
rup·ture (rŭp′ tựr)

ru·ral (rōŏr′ ăl)
ruse (rōōz)
rus·set (rŭs′ ĕt)
Rus·sian (rŭsh′ ăn)
rus·tic (rŭs′ tĭk)
rus·tle (rŭs′ 'l)
  -tling   rus·tler
rust·y (rŭs′ tĭ)
  rust·i·ness
ru·ta·ba·ga (rōō′ tá·bā′ gá)
ruth·less (rōōth′ lĕs)
rye (rī)
Ryu·kyu (is.) (rĭ·ōō′ kū)

S

Sab·bath (săb′ ăth)
sab·bat·i·cal (să·băt′ ĭ·kăl)
sa·ber (sā′ bēr)
sa·ble (sā′ b'l)
sab·o·tage (săb′ ŏ·täzh′)
  sab·o·teur (săb′ ŏ·tûr′)
sac·cha·rine (săk′ á·rĭn)
sac·er·do·tal (săs′ ēr·dō′ tăl)
sa·chem (sā′ chĕm)
sa·chet (să·shā′)
sack·cloth (săk′ klŏth′)
sa·cral (sā′ krăl)
sac·ra·ment (săk′ rá·mĕnt)
  sac·ra·men·tal
     (săk′ rá·mĕn′ tăl)
sa·cred (sā′ krĕd)
sac·ri·fice (săk′ rĭ·fīs)
  -fic·ing
  sac·ri·fi·cial (săk′ rĭ·fĭsh′ ăl)
  sac·ri·fi·cial·ly
sac·ri·lege (săk′ rĭ·lĕj)
  sac·ri·le·gious (săk′ rĭ·lĕj′ jŭs)
sa·cro·il·i·ac (sā′ krō·ĭl′ ĭ·ăk)
sac·ro·sanct (săk′ rō·săngkt)
sad·den (săd′ 'n)
sad·dle (săd′ 'l)
  sad·dling   sad·dle·bag
  sad·dle soap
sad·ism (săd′ ĭz'm)
  sad·ist
  sa·dis·tic (sá·dĭs′ tĭk)
  -ti·cal·ly
sa·fa·ri (sá·fä′ rĭ)
safe (sāf)
  safe·break·er   safe·con·duct
  safe·de·pos·it box
  safe·guard   safe·keep·ing

safe·ty (sāf′ tĭ)
  safe·ty belt   safe·ty ra·zor
  safe·ty valve   safe·ty zone
saf·fron (săf′ rŭn)
sa·ga (sä′ gá)
sa·ga·cious (sá·gā′ shŭs)
  sa·gac·i·ty (sá·găs′ ĭ·tĭ)
sage·brush (sāj′ brŭsh′)
sa·hib (sä′ ĭb)
sail (sāl)
  sailed   sail·ing
  sail·boat   sail·or
saint·ed (sān′ tĕd)
St. John (riv., Me.)
     (sānt jŏn′)
St. Johns (riv., Fla.)
     (sānt jŏnz′)
St. Law·rence (sānt lô′ rĕns)
Saint Pat·rick's (sānt păt′ rĭks)
St. Vi·tus's dance
     (sānt vī′ tŭs·ĭz)
sa·laam (sá·läm′)
sa·la·cious (sá·lā′ shŭs)
sal·ad (săl′ ăd)
sal·a·man·der (săl′ á·măn′ dēr)
sa·la·mi (sä·lä′ mē)
sal·a·ry (săl′ á·rĭ)
  -ried   -ries
sale (sāl)
  sal·a·ble   sales·man
  sales tax
sa·li·ent (sā′ lĭ·ĕnt)
  sa·li·ence
sa·line (sā′ līn)
  sa·lin·i·ty (sá·lĭn′ ĭ·tĭ)
sa·li·va (sá·lī′ vá)
  sal·i·var·y (săl′ ĭ·vĕr′ ĭ)
  sal·i·vate (săl′ ĭ·vāt)
  -vat·ing
  sal·i·va·tion (săl′ ĭ·vā′ shŭn)
sal·low (săl′ ŏ)
sal·ma·gun·di (săl′ má·gŭn′ dĭ)
salm·on (săm′ ŭn)
sa·lon (sá·lŏn′)
  (drawing room; see *saloon*)
sa·loon (sá·lōōn′)
  (alehouse; see *salon*)
sal so·da (săl′ sō′ dá)
salt·cel·lar (sôlt′ sĕl′ ēr)
salt·pe·ter (sôlt′ pē′ tēr)
salt·y (sôl′ tĭ)
  salt·i·ness
sa·lu·bri·ous (sá·lū′ brĭ·ŭs)
sal·u·tar·y (săl′ ú·tĕr′ ĭ)

sa·lu·ta·to·ri·an
    (sȧ·lū′ tȧ·tō′ rĭ·ăn)
sa·lute   (sȧ·lūt′)
  -lut·ing
sal·u·ta·tion   (săl′ ū·tā′ shŭn)
sal·vage   (săl′ vĭj)
  (save; see *salvage*)
  -vag·ing
sal·va·tion   (săl·vā′ shŭn)
salve   (săv)
sal·vo   (săl′ vō)
  -vos
Sa·mar·i·tan   (sȧ·măr′ ĭ·tăn)
same·ness   (sām′ nĕs)
Sa·mo·a   (sȧ·mō′ ȧ)
sam·o·var   (săm′ ō·vär)
sam·pan   (săm′ păn)
sam·ple   (săm′ p'l)
  -pling   sam·pler
sam·u·rai   (săm′ ōō·rī)
san·a·to·ri·um   (săn′ ȧ·tō′ rĭ·ŭm)
  pl. san·a·to·ri·a
sanc·ti·fy   (săngk′ tĭ·fī)
  -fied,   -fy·ing
sanc·ti·mo·ni·ous
    (săngk′ tĭ·mō′ nĭ·ŭs)
sanc·tion   (săngk′ shŭn)
sanc·ti·ty   (săngk′ tĭ·tĭ)
  -ties
sanc·tu·ar·y   (săngk′ tū·ĕr′ ĭ)
  -ar·ies
sanc·tum sanc·to·rum
    (săngk′ tŭm săngk·tō′ rŭm)
sand   (sănd)
  sand·bag   sand bar
  sand·blast   sand·bur
  sand-lot base·ball
  sand·pa·per   sand·stone
  sand·storm
san·dal   (săn′ dăl)
  san·dal·wood
sand·wich   (sănd′ wĭch)
sane   (sān)
  sane·ly
San·for·ized   (săn′ fĕr·īzd)
San Fran·cis·co,
  Calif.   (săn′ frăn·sĭs′ kō)
sang-froid   (săn′ frwä′)
san·guine   (săng′ gwĭn)
  san·gui·nar·y   (săng′ gwi·nĕr′ ĭ)
  san·guin·e·ous
    (săng·gwĭn′ ê·ŭs)
san·i·tar·i·um   (săn′ ĭ·târ′ ĭ·ŭm)
san·i·tar·y   (săn′ ĭ·tĕr′ ĭ)
san·i·ta·tion   (săn′ ĭ·tā′ shŭn)

san·i·ty   (săn′ ĭ·tĭ)
San·skrit   (săn′ skrĭt)
sans-ser·if   (sănz′ sĕr′ ĭf)
San·ta Claus   (săn′ tȧ klôz)
San·ti·a·go, Chile
    (săn′ tĭ·ä′ gō)
São Pau·lo, Bra·zil
    (souɴm pou′ lōō)
sa·pi·ent   (sā′ pĭ·ĕnt)
  -ence
sap·o·dil·la   (săp′ ō·dĭl′ ȧ)
sap·phire   (săf′ īr)
sap·sa·go   (săp′ sȧ·gō)
Sar·a·cen   (săr′ ȧ·sĕn)
sar·casm   (sär′ kăz'm)
  sar·cas·tic   (sär·kăs′ tĭk)
sar·coph·a·gus
    (sär·kŏf′ ȧ·gŭs)
  pl. sar·coph·a·gi   (-jī)
sar·dine   (sär·dēn′)
sar·don·ic   (sär·dŏn′ ĭk)
  sar·don·i·cal·ly
sar·gas·so   (sär·găs′ ō)
sa·ri   (sä′ rē)
sa·rong   (sȧ·rŏng′)
sar·sa·pa·ril·la
    (săs′ pȧ·rĭl′ ȧ)
sar·to·ri·al   (sär·tō′ rĭ·ăl)
Sas·katch·e·wan,
  Can.   (săs·kăch′ ê·wŏn)
sas·sa·fras   (săs′ ȧ·frăs)
Sa·tan   (sā′ tăn)
  sa·tan·ic   (sȧ·tăn′ ĭk)
satch·el   (săch′ ĕl)
sate   (sāt)
  sat·ing
sa·teen   (sȧ·tēn′)
sat·el·lite   (săt′ ĕ·līt)
sa·ti·ate   (sā′ shĭ·āt)
  -at·ing
  sa·ti·a·ble   (sā′ shĭ·ȧ·b'l)
  sa·ti·e·ty   (sȧ·tī′ ĕ·tĭ)
sat·in   (săt′ ĭn)
sat·ire   (săt′ īr)
  sa·tir·ic   (sȧ·tĭr′ ĭk)
  sat·i·rist   (săt′ ĭ·rĭst)
  sat·i·rize   (săt′ ĭ·rīz)
  -riz·ing
sat·is·fac·tion   (săt′ ĭs·făk′ shŭn)
sat·is·fac·to·ry
    (săt′ ĭs·făk′ tō·rĭ)
  sat·is·fac·to·ri·ly, -i·ness
sat·is·fy   (săt′ ĭs·fī)
  -fied   -fy·ing

sat·u·rate (săt′ û·rāt)
  -rat·ing
  sat·u·ra·tion (săt′ û·rā′ shŭn)
sat·ur·nine (săt′ ēr·nīn)
sat·yr (săt′ ēr)
sauce (sôs)
  sauce·pan   sau·cer
  sau·cy
Sa·u·di A·ra·bi·a
  (sä·ōō′ dĭ á·rā′ bĭ·á)
sauer·kraut (sour′ krout′)
Sault Sainte Ma·rie,
  Mich. (sōō′ sânt má·rē′)
saun·ter (sôn′ tēr)
sau·sage (sô·sĭj)
sau·té (sō·tā′)
  sau·téed   sau·té·ing
sau·terne (sō·tûrn′)
sav·age (săv′ ĭj)
  sav·age·ly
  sav·age·ry (săv′ ĭj·rĭ)
sa·van·na (sá·văn′ á)
Sa·van·nah, Ga.
  (sá·văn′ á)
sa·vant (sá·vänt′)
sav·ior (săv′ yēr)
sa·voir-faire (sá′ vwár′ fâr′)
sa·vor (sā′ vēr)
  -vored   -vor·ing
  sa·vor·less   sa·vor·y
sa·voy cab·bage
  (sá·voi′)
saw·mill (sô′ mĭl′)
saw-toothed (sô′ tōōtht′)
saw·yer (sô′ yēr)
sax·o·phone (săk′ sô·fōn)
scab·bard (skăb′ ērd)
sca·brous (skā′ brŭs)
scaf·fold·ing (skăf′ ŭld·ĭng)
scal·a·wag (skăl′ á·wăg)
scald (skôld)
scale (skāl)
  scal·ing   scal·a·ble
scal·lion (skăl′ yŭn)
scal·lop (skŏl′ ŭp)
  scal·loped
scalp (skălp)
scal·pel (skăl′ pĕl)
scal·y (skāl′ ĭ)
  scal·i·ness
scam·per (skăm′ pēr)
scan (skăn)
  scanned   scan·ning
scan·dal (skăn′ dăl)
  scan·dal·ize   -iz·ing

scan·dal·mon·ger (-mŭng′ gēr)
scan·dal·ous (-ŭs)
Scan·di·na·vi·an
  (skăn′ dĭ·nā′ vĭ·án)
scant·y (skăn′ tĭ)
  scant·i·ly   -i·ness
scape·goat (skāp′ gōt′)
scar (skär)
  scarred   scar·ring
scarce (skârs)
  scarce·ly
  scar·ci·ty (skâr′ sĭ·tĭ)
scare (skâr)
  scar·ing   scare·crow
  scar·y
scarf (skärf)
  pl. scarves
scar·let (skär′ lĕt)
scathe (skāth)
  scath·ing·ly
scat·ter·brain (skăt′ ēr·brān′)
scav·enge (skăv′ ĕnj)
  -eng·ing   scav·en·ger
sce·nar·i·o (sē·nâr′ ĭ·ō)
sce·nar·ist (sē·nâr′ ĭst)
scene (sēn)
scen·er·y (sēn′ ēr·ĭ)
sce·nic (sē′ nĭk)
scent (sĕnt)
scep·ter (sĕp′ tēr)
sched·ule (skĕd′ ŭl)
  -ul·ing
scheme (skēm)
  schem·ing
sche·mat·ic (skē·măt′ ĭk)
  schem·er
Sche·nec·ta·dy, (skĕ·nĕk′ tá·dĭ)
  N. Y.
scher·zo (skĕr′ tsō)
schism (sĭz′m)
schis·mat·ic (sĭz·măt′ ĭk)
schist (shĭst)
schiz·oid (skĭz′ oid)
schiz·o·phre·ni·a
  (skĭz′ ô·frē′ nĭ·á)
  schiz·o·phren·ic (-frĕn′ ĭk)
schmaltz (shmôlts)
schnapps (shnăps)
schnau·zer (shnou′ zēr)
schol·ar (skŏl′ ēr)
  schol·ar·ship
scho·las·tic (skô·lăs′ tĭk)
  scho·las·ti·cism
  (skô·lăs′ tĭ·sĭz′m)

school (skōōl)
  school·boy   school·house
  school·mas·ter school·room
  school·teach·er
  school·work
schoon·er (skōōn′ ẽr)
schot·tische (shŏt′ ĭsh)
schuss (shŏōs)
Schwei·tzer, Al·bert
    (shvī′ tsẽr)
sci·at·i·ca (sī·ăt′ ĭ·kȧ)
  sci·at·ic nerve
sci·ence (sī′ ĕns)
  sci·en·tif·ic (sī′ ĕn·tĭf′ ĭk)
  -i·cal·ly   sci·en·tist
scim·i·tar (sĭm′ ĭ·tẽr)
scin·til·late (sĭn′ tĭ·lāt)
  -til·lat·ing
  scin·til·la·tion (sĭn′ tĭ·lā′ shŭn)
sci·on (sī′ ŭn)
scia·sors (sĭz′ ẽrz)
scle·ro·sis (sklē·rō′ sĭs)
scoff (skŏf)
scone (skōn)
scoot·er (skōōt′ ẽr)
scope (skōp)
scorch (skôrch)
scorn·ful (skôrn′ fŏŏl)
  -ful·ly   -ful·ness
Scor·pi·o (skôr′ pĭ·ō)
scor·pi·on (skôr′ pĭ·ŭn)
Scotch (skŏch)
scot-free (skŏt′ frē′)
Scots·man (skŏts′ mȧn)
Scot·tish (skŏt′ ĭsh)
scoun·drel (akoun′ drĕl)
  scoun·drel·ly
scour (skour)
scourge (skûrj)
scout·mas·ter (skout′ măs′ tẽr)
scowl (skoul)
  scowled   scowl·ing
scrab·ble (skrăb′ ′l)
scrag·gy (skrăg′ ĭ)
scram·ble (skrăm′ b′l)
  -bling
scrap·book (skrăp′ bŏŏk′)
scrap·py (skrăp′ ĭ)
scratch (skrăch)
scrawl (skrôl)
  scrawl·y
scraw·ny (skrô′ nĭ)
scream (skrēm)
screech (skrēch)
screen·play (akrēn′ plā′)

screw (skrōō)
scrib·ble (skrĭb′ ′l)
  scrib·bling
scribe (skrīb)
scrim·mage (skrĭm′ ĭj)
  scrim·mag·ing
scrimp (skrĭmp)
scrip (skrĭp)
  (money; see script)
script (skrĭpt)
  (manuscript; see scrip)
  script-writ·er
scrip·ture (skrĭp′ tûr)
  scrip·tur·al
scroll (skrōl)
scrounge (skrounj)
  scroung·ing
scrub·by (skrŭb′ ′l)
scruff (skrŭf)
scru·ple (skrōō′ p′l)
scru·pu·lous (skrōō′ pŭ·lŭs)
scru·ti·ny (skrōō′ tĭ·nĭ)
  -nies
  scru·ti·nize -niz·ing
scuff (skŭf)
scuf·fle (skŭf′ ′l)
  scuf·fling
scul·ler·y (skŭl′ ẽr·ĭ)
scul·lion (skŭl′ yŭn)
sculp·tor (skŭlp′ tẽr)
  sculp·tress sculp·ture
  sculp·tur·al
scum (skŭm)
  scum·my
scup·per·nong (skŭp′ ẽr·nŏng)
scur·ril·ous (skûr′ ĭ·lŭs)
scur·ry (skûr′ ĭ)
  scur·ried scur·ry·ing
scur·vy (skûr′ vĭ)
scut·tle (skŭt′ ′l)
  scut·tling
  scut·tle·butt (skŭt′ ′l·bŭt′)
scythe (sīth)
sea (sē)
  sea·board   sea·coast
  sea·far·ing   sea·go·ing
  sea gull   sea·man
  sea·plane   sea·scape
  sea·shore   sea·sick·ness
  sea·side   sea ur·chin
  sea wall   sea·ward
  sea·wor·thy
seal·skin (sēl′ skĭn′)
seam (sēm)
  seam·less   seam·y

seam·stress   (sēm′ strĕs)
sé·ance   (sā′ äns′)
sear   (sēr)
search   (sûrch)
  search·light   search war·rant
sea·son   (sē′ z′n)
  sea·son·a·ble
  sea·son·al   -al·ly
  sea·son·ing   sea·son tick·et
Se·at·tle, Wash.   (sē·ăt′ ′l)
se·cede   (sē·sēd′)
  -ced·ing
se·ces·sion   (sē·sĕsh′ ŭn)
  se·ces·sion·ist
se·clude   (sē·klōōd′)
  -clud·ing
se·clu·sion   (-klōō′ zhŭn)
sec·ond   (sĕk′ ŭnd)
  sec·ond·ar·y   sec·ond-class
  sec·ond fid·dle   sec·ond·hand
  sec·ond na·ture
  sec·ond-rate   sec·ond sight
se·cret   (sē′ krĕt)
  se·cre·cy   (sē′ krĕ·sĕl)
  se·cre·tive   (sē·krē′ tĭv)
sec·re·tar·i·at   (sĕk′ rē·târ′ ĭ·ăt)
sec·re·tar·y   (sĕk′ rē·tĕr′ ĭ)
  -tar·ies
  sec·re·tar·i·al   (sĕk′ rē·târ′ ĭ·ăl)
  sec·re·tar·y·ship
se·crete   (sē·krēt′)
  -cret·ing
  se·cre·tion   (sē·krē′ shŭn)
  se·cre·tive   (sē·krē′ tĭv)
sect   (sĕkt)
sec·tar·i·an   (sĕk·târ′ ĭ·ăn)
sec·tion   (sĕk′ shŭn)
  sec·tion·al
sec·tor   (sĕk′ tĕr)
sec·u·lar   (sĕk′ û·lĕr)
  sec·u·lar·ize   -iz·ing
se·cure   (sē·kūr′)
  -cur·ing
  se·cure·ly   -cure·ness
  se·cu·ri·ty   -ties
se·dan   (sē·dăn′)
se·date   (sē·dāt′)
  se·date·ly
se·da·tion   (sē·dā′ shŭn)
sed·a·tive   (sĕd′ à·tĭv)
sed·en·tar·y   (sĕd′ ĕn·tĕr′ ĭ)
sedge   (sĕj)
sed·i·ment   (sĕd′ ĭ·mĕnt)
  sed·i·men·ta·ry
                       (sĕd′ ĭ·mĕn′ tà·rĭ)

sed·i·men·ta·tion
                       (sĕd′ ĭ·mĕn·tā′ shŭn)
se·di·tion   (sē·dĭsh′ ŭn)
se·di·tious   (-ŭs)
se·duce   (sē·dūs′)
  -duc·ing   se·duce·ment
  se·duc·i·ble
se·duc·tion   (sē·dŭk′ shŭn)
  se·duc·tive   -tive·ly
  se·duc·tress
sed·u·lous   (sĕd′ û·lŭs)
seed·ling   (sēd′ lĭng)
seed·y   (sēd′ ĭ)
  seed·i·ness
see·ing   (sē′ ĭng)
seem·ing·ly   (sēm′ ĭng·lĭ)
seem·ly   (sēm′ lĭ)
  seem·li·ness
seep·age   (sēp′ ĭj)
se·er   (sē′ ĕr)
  seer·suck·er   (sēr′ sŭk′ ĕr)
see·saw   (sē′ sô′)
seeth   (sēth)
  seeth·ing
seg·ment   (sĕg′ mĕnt)
  seg·men·tar·y
  seg·men·ta·tion
                       (sĕg′ mĕn·tā′ shŭn)
seg·re·gate   (sĕg′ rē·gāt)
  -gat·ing
  seg·re·ga·tion   (sĕg′ rē·gā′ shŭn)
seine   (sān)
  sein·ing
seis·mo·graph   (sīz′ mô·grăf)
seize   (sēz)
  seiz·ing   seiz·a·ble
  sei·zure   (sē′ zhĕr)
sel·dom   (sĕl′ dŭm)
se·lect   (sē·lĕkt′)
  se·lec·tee   (sē·lĕk′ tē′)
  se·lec·tion   se·lec·tive
  se·lec·tiv·i·ty   (sē·lĕk′ tĭv′ ĭ·tĭ)
se·le·ni·um   (sē·lē′ nĭ·ŭm)
self   (sĕlf)
  self-a·base·ment
  self-ad·dressed
  self-cen·tered
  self-con·fi·dence
  self-con·scious
  self-con·trol
  self-de·ni·al
  self-dis·ci·pline
  self-ev·i·dent
  self-ex·plan·a·to·ry
  self-ex·pres·sion

self-ful·fill·ment
self-in·dul·gence
self-made
self-pit·y
self-pres·er·va·tion
self-pro·tec·tion
self-re·li·ance
self-re·spect·ing
self-right·eous
self-sac·ri·fice
self·same
self-sat·is·fied
self-styled
self-sup·port·ing
sell·out (sĕl′ out′)
Selt·zer wa·ter (sĕlt′ sĕr)
sel·vage (sĕl′ vĭj)
(fabric edge; see *salvage*)
se·man·tics (sĕ·măn′ tĭks)
sem·a·phore (sĕm′ à·fōr)
sem·blance (sĕm′ blăns)
se·men (sē′ mĕn)
se·mes·ter (sĕ·mĕs′ tēr)
sem·i· (sĕm′ ĭ-)
sem·i·au·to·mat·ic
sem·i·cir·cle   sem·i·co·lon
sem·i·fi·nal·ist
sem·i·month·ly
sem·i·pre·cious
sem·i·week·ly
sem·i·nal (sĕm′ ĭ·năl)
sem·i·nar (sĕm′ ĭ·när′)
sem·i·nar·y (sĕm′ ĭ·nĕr′ ĭ)
-nar·ies
Sem·i·nole (sĕm′ ĭ·nōl)
Se·mit·ic (sĕ·mĭt′ ĭk)
sem·o·li·na (sĕm′ ō·lē′ ná)
sen·ate (sĕn′ ĭt)
sen·a·tor (sĕn′ à·tēr)
sen·a·to·ri·al (sĕn′ à·tō′ rĭ·ăl)
send-off (sĕnd′ ôf′)
Sen·e·gal, (sĕn′ ĕ·gôl′)
Repub. of
se·nile (sē′ nīl)
se·nil·i·ty (sĕ·nĭl′ ĭ·tĭ)
sen·ior (sēn′ yēr)
sen·ior·i·ty (sĕn·yôr′ ĭ·tĭ)
sen·na (sĕn′ à)
se·ñor (sā·nyôr′)
sen·sa·tion (sĕn·sā′ shŭn)
sen·sa·tion·al
sense (sĕns)
sens·ing   sense·less
sen·si·ble (sĕn′ sĭ·b′l)
sen·si·bil·i·ty (sĕn′ sĭ·bĭl′ ĭ·tĭ)

sen·si·tive (sĕn′ sĭ·tĭv)
sen·si·tive·ness
sen·si·tiv·i·ty (sĕn′ sĭ·tĭv′ ĭ·tĭ)
sen·si·tize (sĕn′ sĭ·tīz)
-tiz·ing
sen·so·ry (sĕn′ sō·rĭ)
sen·su·al (sĕn′ shŏŏ·ăl)
-al·ly
sen·su·al·i·ty
(sĕn′ shŏŏ·ăl′ ĭ·tĭ)
sen·su·ous
sen·tence (sĕn′ tĕns)
sen·ten·tious (sĕn·tĕn′ shŭs)
sen·tient (sĕn′ shĕnt)
sen·ti·ence (sĕn′ shĭ·ĕns)
sen·ti·ment (sĕn′ tĭ·mĕnt)
sen·ti·men·tal (sĕn′ tĭ·mĕn′ tăl)
sen·ti·men·tal·i·ty
(sĕn′ tĭ·mĕn·tăl′ ĭ·tĭ)
sen·ti·nel (sĕn′ tĭ·nĕl)
sen·try (sĕn′ trĭ)
-tries
sep·a·ra·ble (sĕp′ à·rá·b′l)
sep·a·ra·bil·i·ty
(sĕp′ à·rà·bĭl′ ĭ·tĭ)
sep·a·rate (sĕp′ à·rāt)
-rat·ing   sep·a·rate·ly
sep·a·ra·tion (sĕp′ à·rā′ shŭn)
sep·a·ra·tist (sĕp′ à·rā′ tĭst)
sep·a·ra·tor (sĕp′ à·rā′ tēr)
se·pi·a (sē′ pĭ·á)
Sep·tem·ber (sĕp·tĕm′ bēr)
sep·tet (sĕp·tĕt′)
sep·tic (sĕp′ tĭk)
sep·tu·a·ge·nar·i·an
(sĕp′ tŏŏ·à·jĕ·nâr′ ĭ·ăn)
sep·tum (sĕp′ tŭm)
pl. sep·ta
sep·ul·cher (sĕp′ ŭl·kēr)
se·pul·chral (sĕ·pŭl′ krăl)
se·quel (sē′ kwĕl)
se·quence (sē′ kwĕns)
se·quen·tial (sĕ·kwĕn′ shăl)
se·ques·ter (sĕ·kwĕs′ tēr)
se·ques·tra·tion
(sē′ kwĕs·trā′ shŭn)
se·quin (sē′ kwĭn)
se·quoi·a (sĕ·kwoi′ à)
se·ragl·io (sĕ·răl′ yō)
se·ra·pe (sĕ·rä′ pā)
ser·a·phim (sĕr′ à·fĭm)
ser·e·nade (sĕr′ ĕ·nād′)
-nad·ing
ser·en·dip·i·ty (sĕr′ ĕn·dĭp′ ĭ·tĭ)

se·rene (sĕ·rēn')
  se·rene·ly
  se·ren·i·ty (sĕ·rĕn' ĭ·tĭ)
seri·dom (sûrf' dŭm)
serge (sûrj)
  (fabric; see surge)
ser·geant (sär' jĕnt)
  ser·geant at arms
se·ri·al (sēr' ĭ·ăl)
  (in a series; see cereal)
se·ri·al·i·za·tion
        (sēr' ĭ·ăl·ĭ·zā' shŭn)
  se·ri·al·ize -iz·ing
se·ries (sēr' ēz)
  n. sing. & pl.
ser·if (sĕr' ĭf)
se·ri·ous (sēr' ĭ·ŭs)
ser·mon (sûr' mŭn)
  ser·mon·ize -iz·ing
ser·pent (sûr' pĕnt)
  ser·pen·tine (sûr' pĕn·tēn)
ser·rat·ed (sĕr' āt·ĕd)
se·rum (sēr' ŭm)
serv·ant (sûr' vănt)
serv·ice (sûr' vĭs)
  -ic·ing
  serv·ice·a·bil·i·ty
        (sûr' vĭs·à·bĭl' ĭ·tĭ)
  serv·ice·a·ble (sûr' vĭs·à·b'l)
  serv·ice·man serv·ice sta·tion
ser·vile (sûr' vĭl)
  ser·vil·i·ty (sĕr·vĭl' ĭ·tĭ)
ser·vi·tude (sûr' vĭ·tūd)
ses·a·me seed (sĕs' á·mē)
ses·qui·cen·ten·nial
        (sĕs' kwĭ·sĕn·tĕn' ĭ·ăl)
ses·sion (sĕsh' ŭn)
  (meeting; see cession)
set (sĕt)
  set·back set·ter
  set·ting set-to
  set-up
set·tee (sĕ·tē')
set·tle (sĕt' 'l)
  set·tling set·tle·ment
  set·tler
sev·en·fold (sĕv' ĕn·fōld')
sev·en·teen (sĕv' ĕn·tēn')
sev·en·ty (sĕv' ĕn·tĭ)
  -ties sev·en·ti·eth
sev·er (sĕv' ĕr)
  -ered -er·ing
sev·er·al (sĕv' ĕr·ăl)
  sev·er·al·ly
sev·er·ance (sĕv' ĕr·ăns)

se·vere (sĕ·vēr')
  se·vere·ly
  se·ver·i·ty (sĕ·vĕr' ĭ·tĭ)
sew·age (sū' ĭj)
sew·er (sū' ĕr)
sewn (sōn)
sex·tet (sĕks·tĕt')
sex·ton (sĕks' tŭn)
sex·u·al (sĕk' shŏŏ·ăl)
  -al·ly
  sex·u·al·i·ty
        (sĕk' shŏŏ·ăl' ĭ·tĭ)
shab·by (shăb' ĭ)
  shab·bi·ly shab·bi·ness
shack·le (shăk' 'l)
  shack·ling
shad·dock (shăd' ŭk)
shad·ow (shăd' ō)
  shad·ow·box shad·ow·y
shad·y (shād' ĭ)
  shad·i·ness
shaft (shäft)
shag (shăg)
  shag·gy shag rug
shah (shä)
shake (shāk)
  shak·ing shak·a·ble
  shake·down shake-up
Shake·speare, Wil·liam
        (shāk' spēr)
  Shake·spear·e·an
        (shāk·spēr' ê·ăn)
shak·y (shāk' ĭ)
  shak·i·ness
shale (shāl)
shal·lot (shà·lŏt')
shal·low (shăl' ō)
sha·man (shä' măn)
sham·bles (shăm' b'lz)
shame (shām)
  sham·ing shame·faced
  shame·fac·ed·ly
  shame·ful, -ful·ly, -ful·ness
  shame·less
sham·poo (shăm·pŏŏ')
  -pooed -poo·ing
sham·rock (shăm' rŏk)
shang·hai (shăng·hī')
  -haied -hai·ing
Shan·gri-La (shăng' grē·lä')
Shan·tung (shăn·tŭng')
shan·ty (shăn' tĭ)
  -ties
shape·less (shāp' lĕs)

shape·ly (shāp'lǐ)
  shape·li·ness

share·crop·per (shâr' krŏp' ẽr)
share·hold·er (shâr' hōl' dẽr)
shark·skin (shärk' skǐn')
sharp (shärp)
  sharp·en·er sharp-eyed
  sharp·shoot·er sharp-sight·ed
  sharp-wit·ted
Shas·ta dai·sy (shăs' tả)
shat·ter (shăt' ẽr)
Sha·vi·an (shā' vǐ·ản)
shawl (shôl)
Shaw·nee (shô·nē')
sheaf (shēf)
  pl. sheaves (shēvz)
shear (shēr)
  (to cut; see sheer)
  shorn
sheath (shēth) n.
sheathe (shēthɇ) v.
  sheath·ing
shed (shĕd)
  shed·ding
sheen (shēn)
sheep (shēp)
  sheep·herd·er sheep·ish
  sheep·shank sheeps·head
  sheep·shear·ing
  sheep·skin
sheer (shēr)
  (transparent; see shear)
sheet (shēt)
sheik (shēk)
  sheik·dom
shelf (shĕlf)
  pl. shelves
shell (shĕl)
  shell·fire shell·fish
  shell shock
shel·lac (shĕ·lăk')
  shel·lacked shel·lack·ing
shel·ter (shĕl' tẽr)
shelve (shĕlv)
  shelv·ing
Shen·an·do·ah riv.
  (shĕn' ản·dō' ả)
she·nan·i·gans (shē·năn' ĭ·gảnz)
shep·herd (shĕp' ẽrd)
sher·bet (shûr' bĕt)
sher·iff (shĕr' ĭf)
sher·ry (shĕr' ĭ)
  sher·ries

Shet·land po·ny (shĕt' lǎnd)
shib·bo·leth (shǐb' ô·lĕth)
shield (shēld)
shift·less (shǐft' lĕs)
shift·y (shǐf' tǐ)
  shift·i·ness
shil·le·lagh (shǐ·lā' lē)
shil·ling (shǐl' ĭng)
shil·ly-shal·ly (shǐl' ǐ·shăl' ǐ)
shim·mer (shǐm' ẽr)
shim·my (shǐm' ǐ)
shine (shīn)
  shin·ing shin·y
  shone
shin·gle (shǐng' g'l)
  -gling
Shin·to (shǐn' tō')
  Shin·to·ist
ship (shǐp)
  shipped ship·ping
  ship·board ship·load
  ship·mate ship·pa·ble
  ship·shape ship·wreck
shirk (shûrk)
  shirk·er
shirr (shûr)
shirt·waist (shûrt' wāst')
shiv·er (shǐv' ẽr)
  -ered, -er·ing shiv·er·y
shoal (shōl)
shock (shŏk)
  shock ab·sorb·er
  shock ther·a·py
shod·dy (shŏd' ǐ)
  shod·di·ness
shoe (shōō)
  shoe·ing shoe·horn
  shoe·lace shoe·mak·er
  shoe·shop shoe·string
  shoe tree
shop (shŏp)
  shopped shop·ping
  shop·keep·er shop·lift·er
  shop·walk·er shop·win·dow
  shop·worn
shorn (shōrn)
short (shōrt)
  short·cake short·change
  short cir·cuit short·com·ing
  short cut short·hand
  short·hand·ed Short·horn
  short-lived (shôrt' lǐvd')
  short shrift short·sight·ed
  short·stop short sto·ry

short-tem·pered

short-term — short-wave *adj.*

short-wind·ed

short·age (shôrt' ĭj)

short·en·ing (shôr' t'n·ĭng)

shot·gun (shŏt' gŭn')

shot-put (shŏt' poŏt')

should (shoŏd)

should·n't

shoul·der (shōl' dĕr)

shout (shout)

shove (shŭv)

shov·ing

shov·el (shŭv' 'l)

-eled — -el·ing

show (shō)

show bill — show·boat

show·case — show·down

show·man·ship

show-off — show·room

show·er (shou' ĕr)

show·er·y

show·y (shō' ĭ)

show·i·ly — -i·ness

shrank (shrăngk)

shriek (shrĭk)

shrap·nel (shrăp' nĕl)

shred (shrĕd)

shred·ded — shred·ding

shred·der

shrew (shrōō)

shrew·ish

shrewd (shrōōd)

shriek (shrĕk)

shrift (shrĭft)

shrike (shrīk)

shrill (shrĭl)

shrimp (shrĭmp)

shrine (shrīn)

Shrin·er

shrink (shrĭngk)

shrink·age (shrĭngk' ĭj)

shrunk·en

shriv·el (shrĭv' 'l)

-eled — -el·ing

shroud (shroud)

shrub (shrŭb)

shrub·ber·y

shrunk·en (shrŭngk' ĕn)

shuck (shŭk)

shud·der (shŭd' ĕr)

shuf·fle (shŭf' 'l)

shuf·fling — shuf·fle·board

shun (shŭn)

shunned — shun·ning

shunt (shŭnt)

shut·down (shŭt' doun')

shut-in (shŭt' ĭn')

shut·out (shŭt' out')

shut·ter (shŭt' ĕr)

shut·tle·cock (shŭt' 'l·kŏk')

shy (shī)

shied — shy·ing

shi·er — shy·ly

shy·ness

shy·ster (shī' stĕr)

Si·a·mese cat (sī' ȧ·mēz')

sib·i·lant (sĭb' ĭ·lȧnt)

-lance

sib·ling (sĭb' lĭng)

sick (sĭk)

sick·bed — sick·en·ing

sick·ly — -li·ness

sick·ness

side (sīd)

sid·ing — side·board

side·burns — side·car

side is·sue — side·light

side·long — side·split·ting

side-step — side stroke

side·swipe — side·track

side·walk — side·ways

side·wind·er

si·de·re·al (sī·dēr' ē·ǎl)

si·dle (sī' d'l)

-dling

siege (sēj)

si·er·ra (sī·ĕr' ȧ)

si·es·ta (sī·ĕs' tȧ)

sieve (sĭv)

sift (sĭft)

sigh (sī)

sight (sīt)

(view; see *cite, site*)

sight bill — sight·less

sight·ly — -li·ness

sign (sīn)

sign·board — sign·post

sig·nal (sĭg' nȧl)

sig·nal·ize — -iz·ing

sig·nal·man

sig·na·to·ry (sĭg' nȧ·tō' rĭ)

sig·na·ture (sĭg' nȧ·tụr)

sig·net ring (sĭg' nĕt)

sig·nif·i·cant (sĭg·nĭf' ĭ·kȧnt)

-cance

sig·ni·fi·ca·tion

(sĭg' nĭ·fĭ·kā' shȧn)

sig·ni·fy (sĭg' nĭ·fī)

-fied — -fy·ing

si·lage (sī' lĭj)

si·lence (sī′ lĕns)
  si·lenc·er   si·lent
sil·hou·ette (sĭl′ ŏŏ·ĕt′)
sil·i·ca gel (sĭl′ ĭ·kə)
sil·i·cate (sĭl′ ĭ·kāt)
sil·i·con (sĭl′ ĭ·kŏn)
silk·en (sĭl′ kĕn)
silk·y (sĭl′ kĭ)
  silk·i·ly   -i·ness
sil·ly (sĭl′ ĭ)
  sil·li·ness
si·lo (sī′ lō)
  -los
sil·ver·ware (sĭl′ vĕr·wâr′)
sim·i·an (sĭm′ ĭ·ən)
sim·i·lar (sĭm′ ĭ·lēr)
  sim·i·lar·i·ty (sĭm′ ĭ·lăr′ ĭ·tĭ)
sim·i·le (sĭm′ ĭ·lē)
si·mil·i·tude (sĭ·mĭl′ ĭ·tūd)
sim·mer (sĭm′ ēr)
sim·o·ny (sĭm′ ō·nĭ)
sim·ple (sĭm′ p′l)
  sim·plic·i·ty (sĭm·plĭs′ ĭ·tĭ)
  sim·pli·fi·ca·tion
      (sĭm′ plĭ·fĭ·kā′ shŭn)
  sim·pli·fy, -fied, -fy·ing
  sim·ply
sim·u·late (sĭm′ û·lāt)
  -lat·ing
  sim·u·la·tion (sĭm′ û·lā′ shŭn)
si·mul·ta·ne·ous
      (sī′ mŭl·tā′ nĕ·ŭs)
since (sĭns)
sin·cere (sĭn·sēr′)
  sin·cere·ly
  sin·cer·i·ty (sĭn·sĕr′ ĭ·tĭ)
si·ne·cure (sī′ nĕ·kūr)
sin·ew (sĭn′ û)
  sin·ew·y
sin·ful (sĭn′ fŏŏl)
  -ful·ly   -ful·ness
sing (sĭng)
  sing·a·ble
singe (sĭnj)
  singe·ing
sin·gle (sĭng′ g′l)
  sin·gle-breast·ed
  sin·gle file   sin·gle-hand·ed
  sin·gle-mind·ed
  sin·gle·ness   sin·gly
sin·gle·ton (sĭng′ g′l·tŭn)
sing·song (sĭng′ sông′)
sin·gu·lar (sĭng′ gû·lēr)
  sin·gu·lar·i·ty
      (sĭng′ gû·lăr′ ĭ·tĭ)

sin·is·ter (sĭn′ ĭs·tēr)
sink·age (sĭngk′ ĭj)
sin·ner (sĭn′ ēr)
sin·u·ous (sĭn′ û·ŭs)
si·nus (sī′ nŭs)
  si·nus·i·tis (sī′ nŭs·ī′ tĭs)
Sioux Cit·y, Ia. (sōō)
si·phon (sī′ fŏn)
si·ren (sī′ rĕn)
sir·loin (sûr′ loin′)
si·roc·co (sĭ·rŏk′ ō)
sir·up (sĭr′ ŭp)
  sir·up·y
si·sal (sī′ sǎl)
sis·ter-in-law (sĭs′ tēr·ĭn·lô′)
  pl. sis·ters-in-law
site (sīt)
  (location; see sight, cite)
sit·ter (sĭt′ ēr)
sit·u·ate (sĭt′ û·āt)
  -at·ing
  sit·u·a·tion (sĭt′ û·ā′ shŭn)
sitz bath (sĭts)
six·pence (sĭks′ pĕns)
six·teenth (sĭks′ tēnth′)
sixth (sĭksth)
six·ty (sĭks′ tĭ)
  -ties   six·ti·eth
size (sīz)
siz·ing (sīz′ ĭng) siz·a·ble
siz·zle (sĭz′ ′l)
  siz·zling
skate (skāt)
  skat·ing
skeet (skēt)
skein (skān)
skel·e·ton (skĕl′ ē·tŭn)
  skel·e·tal
sketch (skĕch)
  sketch·book   sketch·y
skew·er (skū′ ēr)
ski (skē)
  skied   ski·ing
  ski·er
skill (skĭl)
  skill·ful, -ful·ly, -ful·ness
skim milk (skĭm)
skimp·y (skĭmp′ ĭ)
  skimp·i·ness
skin (skĭn)
  skinned,   skin·ning
  skin-deep   skin div·ing
  skin·flint   skin·tight
skin·ny (skĭn′ ĭ)
  skin·ni·ness

skip·per   (skĭp′ ĕr)
skir·mish   (skûr′ mĭsh)
skirt   (skûrt)
skit·tish   (skĭt′ ĭsh)
skit·tles   (skĭt′ 'lz)
skul·dug·ger·y   (skŭl·dŭg′ ĕr·ĭ)
skulk   (skŭlk)
skull   (skŭl)
  skull·cap
skunk   (skŭngk)
sky   (skī)
  skies   sky·lark
  sky·light   sky line
  sky·scrap·er   sky·ward
  sky·writ·ing
slack   (slăk)
  slack·en
slake   (slāk)
  slak·ing
sla·lom   (slä′ lŭm)
slan·der   (slăn′ dĕr)
  slan·der·er   slan·der·ous
slant·wise   (slănt′ wīz′)
slap·dash   (slăp′ dăsh′)
slap·stick   (slăp′ stĭk′)
slat·tern·ly   (slăt′ ĕrn·lĭ)
slaugh·ter   (slô′ tĕr)
  slaugh·ter·house
Slav   (släv)
slave   (släv)
  slav·ing   slave·hold·er
  slav·er·y   slav·ey
  slav·ish
slay·er   (slā′ ĕr)
slea·zy   (slē′ zĭ)
sled·ding   (slĕd′ ĭng)
sledge ham·mer
                  (slĕj)
sleek   (slēk)
sleep   (slēp)
  sleep·walk·er   sleep·i·ly
  sleep·i·ness   sleep·y
sleet   (slēt)
sleeve   (slēv)
  sleeve·less
sleigh   (slā)
sleight of hand   (slīt)
slen·der·ize   (slĕn′ dĕr·īz)
  -iz·ing
sleuth   (slooth)
slew   (sloo)
  (killed; see *slough*)
slice   (slīs)
  slic·ing
slick·er   (slĭk′ ĕr)

slight   (slīt)
slime   (slīm)
  slim·y
sling·shot   (slĭng′ shŏt′)
slink·y   (slĭngk′ ĭ)
slip·knot   (slĭp′ nŏt′)
slip·page   (slĭp′ ĭj)
slip·per·y   (slĭp′ ĕr·ĭ)
  slip·per·i·ness
slip·shod   (slĭp′ shŏd′)
sliv·er   (slĭv′ ĕr)
sloe-eyed   (slō′ īd′)
sloe gin   (slō)
slo·gan   (slō′ găn)
sloop   (sloop)
slope   (slōp)
  slop·ing
slop·py   (slŏp′ ĭ)
  slop·pi·ly   slop·pi·ness
sloth·ful   (slŏth′ fōōl)
slouch   (slouch)
slough
  (when pron. slŭf, means to cast
  off; when pron. sloo, means
  swamp or inlet; see *slew*)
Slo·vak   (slō′ văk)
slov·en·ly   (slŭv′ ĕn·lĭ)
  slov·en·li·ness
slow·down   (slō′ doun′)
sludge   (slŭj)
slug·gard   (slŭg′ ĕrd)
slug·gish   (slŭg′ ĭsh)
sluice   (sloos)
  sluic·ing
slum·ber   (slŭm′ bĕr)
  slum·ber·ous
slur   (slûr)
  slurred   slur·ring
sly   (slī)
  sli·est   sly·ness
smack   (smăk)
small   (smôl)
  small change   small-mind·ed
  small·pox   small talk
smart   (smärt)
smash·up   (smăsh′ ŭp′)
smat·ter·ing   (smăt′ ĕr·ĭng)
smear   (smēr)
smel·ling salts   (smĕl′ ĭng)
smelt   (smĕlt)
smelt·er   (smĕl′ tĕr)
smile   (smīl)
  smil·ing
smirch   (smûrch)
smirk   (smûrk)

smite (smīt)
  smit·ing
  smit·ten (smĭt' 'n)
smith·er·eens (smĭth' ĕr·ēnz')
smock (smŏk)
smog (smŏg)
smoke (smōk)
  smok·ing smoke·house
  smoke screen smoke·stack
  smok·y
smol·der (smōl' dĕr)
smooth (smōōth)
smor·gas·bord (smôr' gäs·bôrd')
smoth·er (smŭth' ĕr)
smudge (smŭj)
  smudg·ing smudg·y
smug (smŭg)
  smug·gest smug·ly
smug·gle (smŭg' 'l)
  smug·gling smug·gler
smut (smŭt)
  smut·ty
snack (snăk)
sna·fu (snă·fōō')
  -fued -fu·ing
snail (snāl)
  snail-paced
snap·drag·on (snăp' drăg' ŭn)
snap·per (snăp' ĕr)
snap·shot (snăp' shŏt')
snare drum (snâr)
snarl·ing (snärl' ĭng)
sneak·ers (snēk' ĕrz)
sneak·y (snēk' ĭ)
  sneak·i·ly
sneer·ing (snēr' ĭng)
sneeze (snēz)
  sneez·ing
snick·er (snĭk' ĕr)
snif·fle (snĭf' 'l)
  snif·fling
snip·pet (snĭp' ĕt)
snitch (snĭch)
sniv·el (snĭv' 'l)
  -eled -el·ing
snob (snŏb)
  snob·ber·y snob·bish
snoop·y (snōōp' ĭ)
snooze (snōōz)
  snooz·ing
snore (snōr)
  snor·ing
snor·kel (snôr' kĕl)
snout (snout)

snow (snō)
  snow·ball snow·bound
  snow-blind snow-capped
  snow·drift snow·flake
  snow·plow snow·shoe
  snow·storm snow·y
snug·gle (snŭg' 'l)
  snug·gling
so-and-so (sō' ănd·sō')
soap (sōp)
  soap·box soap op·e·ra
  soap·suds
soar·ing (sōr' ĭng)
so·be·it (sō·bē' ĭt)
so·ber (sō' bĕr)
so·bri·e·ty (sō·brī' ĕ·tĭ)
so·bri·quet (sō' brĭ·kā)
so-called (sō' kôld')
soc·cer (sŏk' ĕr)
so·cia·ble (sō' shá·b'l)
  so·cia·bil·i·ty (sō' shá·bĭl' ĭ·tĭ)
so·cial (sō' shăl)
  so·cial·ism
  so·cial·is·tic (sō' shăl·ĭs' tĭk)
  so·cial·ite (sō' shăl·īt)
  so·cial·ized
so·ci·e·ty (sō·sī' ĕ·tĭ)
  -ties
  so·ci·e·tal (sō·sī' ĕ·tăl)
so·ci·ol·o·gy (sō' sĭ·ŏl' ō·jĭ)
  so·ci·o·log·i·cal
      (sō' sĭ·ō·lŏj' ĭ·kăl)
  so·ci·ol·o·gist (sō' sĭ·ŏl' ō·jĭst)
sock·et (sŏk' ĕt)
Soc·ra·tes (sŏk' rá·tēz)
  So·crat·ic (sō·krăt' ĭk)
so·dal·i·ty (sō·dăl' ĭ·tĭ)
  -ties
sod·den (sŏd' 'n)
  sod·den·ness
so·di·um (sō' dĭ·ŭm)
  so·di·um bi·car·bon·ate
  so·di·um car·bon·ate
  so·di·um chlo·ride
  so·di·um hy·drox·ide
  so·di·um ni·trate
Sod·om (sŏd' ŭm)
  (and Gomorrah)
sod·om·y (sŏd' ŭm·ĭ)
soft (sôft)
  soft·ball soft-heart·ed
  soft-ped·al soft-shell
  soft-soap soft-spo·ken
sog·gy (sŏg' ĭ)
  sog·gi·ness

soil·age   (soil′ ĭj)
soi·ree   (swä·rā′)
so·journ   (sṓ·jûrn′)
sol·ace   (sŏl′ ĭs)
so·lar   (sō′ lẽr)
   so·lar·i·um   (sō·lăr′ ĭ·ŭm)
   so·lar plex·us
sol·der·ing i·ron
         (sŏd′ ẽr·ĭng)
sol·dier   (sōl′ jẽr)
sole   (sōl)
   sole·ly
sol·e·cism   (sŏl′ ė·sĭs′m)
sol·emn   (sŏl′ ĕm)
   so·lem·ni·ty   (sō·lĕm′ nĭ·tĭ)
   -ties
   sol·em·nize   (sŏl′ ĕm·nĭz)
   -niz·ing
so·lic·it   (sō·lĭs′ ĭt)
   -it·ed   -it·ing
   so·lic·i·ta·tion
         (sō·lĭs′ ĭ·tā′ shŭn)
   so·lic·i·tor
so·lic·it·ous   (sō·lĭs′ ĭ·tŭs)
so·lic·i·tude   (sō·lĭs′ ĭ·tūd)
sol·id   (sŏl′ ĭd)
   sol·i·dar·i·ty   (sŏl′ ĭ·dăr′ ĭ·tĭ)
   so·lid·i·fy   (sō·lĭd′ ĭ·fĭ)
   -fied   -fy·ing
   so·lid·i·ty   (sō·lĭd′ ĭ·tĭ)
so·lil·o·quy   (sō·lĭl′ ō·kwĭ)
   pl. -quies
   so·lil·o·quize   (sō·lĭl′ ō·kwĭz)
   -quiz·ing
sol·i·taire   (sŏl′ ĭ·târ)
sol·i·tar·y   (sŏl′ ĭ·tĕr′ ĭ)
   sol·i·tar·i·ness
sol·i·tude   (sŏl′ ĭ·tūd)
so·lo   (sō′ lō)
   -los   so·lo·ist
Sol·o·mon   (sŏl′ ō·mŭn)
sol·stice   (sŏl′ stĭs)
sol·u·ble   (sŏl′ ū·b′l)
   sol·u·bil·i·ty   (sŏl′ ū·bĭl′ ĭ·tĭ)
so·lu·tion   (sō·lū′ shŭn)
solve   (sŏlv)
   solv·ing
   solv·a·bil·i·ty   (sŏl′ vȧ·bĭl′ ĭ·tĭ)
   solv·a·ble
sol·vent   (sŏl′ vĕnt)
   sol·ven·cy
So·ma·li·land, Afr.
         (sō·mä′ lė·lănd′)
so·mat·ic   (sō·măt′ ĭk)
som·ber   (sŏm′ bẽr)

som·bre·ro   (sŏm·brâr′ ō)
some   (sŭm)
   some·bod·y   some·one
   some·thing   some·times
   some·where
som·er·sault   (sŭm′ ẽr·sŏlt)
som·nam·bu·list
         (sŏm·năm′ bū·lĭst)
so·nar   (sō′ när)
so·na·ta   (sō·nä′ tȧ)
song·ster   (sŏng′ stẽr)
   song·stress
son·ic   (sŏn′ ĭk)
son-in-law   (sŭn′ ĭn·lô′)
   pl. sons-in-law
son·net   (sŏn′ ĕt)
   son·net·eer   (sŏn′ ė·tẽr′)
so·no·rous   (sō·nō′ rŭs)
so·nor·i·ty   (sō·nŏr′ ĭ·tĭ)
soothe   (sōōth)
   sooth·ing
sooth·say·er   (sōōth′ sā′ ẽr)
soot·y   (sōōt′ ĭ)
   soot·i·ness
soph·ism   (sŏf′ ĭz′m)
so·phis·ti·cat·ed
         (sō·fĭs′ tĭ·kăt′ ĕd)
   so·phis·ti·ca·tion
         (sō·fĭs′ tĭ·kā′ shŭn)
soph·ist·ry   (sŏf′ ĭs·trĭ)
   -ries
soph·o·more   (sŏf′ ō·mōr)
   soph·o·mor·ic   (sŏf′ ō·mŏr′ ĭk)
so·po·rif·ic   (sō′ pō·rĭf′ ĭk)
so·pran·o   (sō·prăn′ ō)
   -os
Sor·bonne   (sôr·bŏn′)
sor·cer·y   (sôr′ sẽr·ĭ)
   sor·cer·er   sor·cer·ess
sor·did   (sôr′ dĭd)
sore·ly   (sōr′ lĭ)
sor·ghum   (sôr′ gŭm)
so·ror·i·ty   (sō·rŏr′ ĭ·tĭ)
   -ties
sor·rel   (sôr′ ĕl)
sor·row   (sôr′ ō)
   sor·row·ful, -ful·ly, -ful·ness
sor·ry   (sôr′ ĭ)
   sor·ri·er   sor·ri·est
sor·tie   (sôr′ tē)
sot·tish   (sŏt′ ĭsh)
sou·brette   (sōō·brĕt′)
souf·flé   (sōō′ flā′)
sought   (sôt)

soul (sōl)
  soul·ful, -ful·ly, -ful·ness
  soul·less
sound (sound)
  sound·proof
soup (sōōp)
soup·çon (sōōp' sŏɴ')
sour (sour)
  sour·dough
source (sōrs)
souse (sous)
south (south)
  south·east
  south·er·ly (sŭth' ĕr·lĭ)
  south·ern·er (sŭth' ĕr·nēr)
  south·ern·most
    (sŭth' ĕrn·mōst)
  south·paw   South Pole
  south·ward   south·west·ern
South Car·o·li·na
  (south kăr' ô·lĭ' nà)
  abbr. S. C.
South Car·o·lin·i·an
  (-kăr' ô·lĭn'ĭ·ăn)
South Da·ko·ta (south dà·kō' tá)
  abbr. S. Dak.
  South Da·ko·tan
sou·ve·nir (sōō' vĕ·nēr')
sou'west·er (sou' wĕs' tēr)
sov·er·eign (sŏv' ĕr·ĭn)
  sov·er·eign·ty
so·vi·et (sō' vĭ·ĕt)
soy·bean (soi' bēn')
space·ship (spās' shĭp')
spa·cious (spā' shŭs)
spa·ghet·ti (spá·gĕt' ĭ)
span·gle (spăng' g'l)
Span·iard (spăn' yērd)
span·iel (spăn' yĕl)
Span·ish (spăn' ĭsh)
span·ner (spăn' ēr)
spare (spâr)
  spar·ing   spare·ness
  spare·ribs
spar·kle (spär' k'l)
  -kling
spar·row (spăr' ō)
sparse (spärs)
  sparse·ly
Spar·tan (spär' t'n)
spasm (spăz'm)
  spas·mod·ic (spăz·mŏd' ĭk)
spas·tic (spăs' tĭk)
spa·tial (spā' shǎl)
  spa·tial·ly

spat·ter (spăt' ēr)
spat·u·la (spăt' û·là)
spawn (spôn)
speak·eas·y (spēk' ēz' ĭ)
spear·mint (spēr' mĭnt')
spe·cial (spĕsh' ǎl)
  spe·cial·ist
  spe·cial·i·za·tion
  (spĕsh' ǎl·ĭ·zā' shŭn)
  spe·cial·ize -iz·ing
  spe·cial·ty
spe·cie (spē' shĭ)
  (coin; see *species*)
spe·cies (spē' shĭz)
  (kind, variety; see *specie*)
spe·cif·ic (spē·sĭf' ĭk)
  spe·cif·i·cal·ly
spec·i·fy (spĕs' ĭ·fĭ)
  -fied   -fy·ing
  spec·i·fi·a·ble (spĕs' ĭ·fĭ' à·b'l)
  spec·i·fi·ca·tion
  (spĕs' ĭ·fĭ·kā' shŭn)
spec·i·men (spĕs' ĭ·mĕn)
spe·cious (spē' shŭs)
speck·led (spĕk' 'ld)
spec·ta·cle (spĕk' tà·k'l)
spec·tac·u·lar (spĕk·tăk' û·lēr)
spec·ta·tor (spĕk·tă' tēr)
spec·ter (spĕk' tēr)
spec·tral (spĕk' trǎl)
spec·tro·scope (spĕk' trô·skōp)
spec·trum (spĕk' trŭm)
  pl. spec·tra
spec·u·late (spĕk' û·lāt)
  -lat·ing
  spec·u·la·tion
  (spĕk' û·lā' shŭn)
  spec·u·la·tive (spĕk' û·lā' tĭv)
  spec·u·la·tor
speech (spēch)
speed (spēd)
  speed·boat   speed·i·ly
  speed in·di·ca·tor
  speed lim·it
  speed·om·e·ter
  (spēd·ŏm' ê·tēr)
  speed·way   speed·y
spell·bound (spĕl' bound')
spell·ing (spĕl' ĭng)
spend·thrift (spĕnd' thrĭft')
sperm (spûrm)
sper·ma·ce·ti (spûr' má·sē' tĭ)
spew (spū)
sphag·num (sfăg' nŭm)

sphere	(sfēr)
spher·al	spher·i·cal
sphinc·ter	(sfĭngk′ tēr)
sphinx	(sfĭngks)
spick-and-span	(spĭk′ ănd·spăn′)
spic·y	(spīs′ ĭ)
spic·i·er, -i·est, -i·ly, -i·ness	
spi·der	(spī′ dĕr)
spiel	(spēl)
spig·ot	(spĭg′ ŭt)
spike·let	(spīk′ lĕt)
spill·age	(spĭl′ ĭj)
spin·ach	(spĭn′ ĭch)
spi·nal	(spī′ năl)
spin·dle	(spĭn′ d′l)
spin·dly	
spine·less	(spīn′ lĕs)
spin·et	(spĭn′ ĕt)
spin·ner·et	(spĭn′ ĕr·ĕt)
spin·ning wheel	
	(spĭn′ ĭng)
spin·ster	(spĭn′ stēr)
spin·y	(spīn′ ĭ)
spi·ral	(spī′ răl)
-raled	-ral·ing
spi·ral·ly	
spir·it	(spĭr′ ĭt)
spir·it·ed	spir·it·less
spir·it·u·al	(spĭr′ ĭt·û·ăl)
spir·it·u·al·i·ty	
	(spĭr′ ĭt·û·ăl′ ĭ·tĭ)
spite·ful	(spīt′ fŏŏl)
-ful·ly	-ful·ness
spit·fire	(spĭt′ fīr′)
spit·tle	(spĭt′ 'l)
spit·toon	(spĭ·tōōn′)
spleen	(splēn)
splen·did	(splĕn′ dĭd)
splen·dor	(splĕn′ dĕr)
splice	(splīs)
splic·ing	
splin·ter	(splĭn′ tēr)
split-lev·el	(splĭt′ lĕv′ ĕl)
spoil	(spoil)
spoiled	spoil·ing
spoil·age	(spoil′ ĭj)
spo·ken	(spō′ kĕn)
spokes·man	(spōks′ măn)
sponge	(spŭnj)
spong·ing	sponge·cake
spon·gy	
spon·sor	(spŏn′ sēr)
spon·ta·ne·ous	(spŏn·tā′ nē·ŭs)
spon·ta·ne·i·ty	
	(spŏn′ tá·nē′ ĭ·tĭ)

spoof	(spōōf)
spoon·ful	(spōōn′ fŏŏl)
spoon·fuls	
spoor	(spŏŏr)
(animal track; see spore)	
spo·rad·ic	(spō·răd′ ĭk)
spore	(spōr)
(germ; see spoor)	
sport	(spōrt)
spor·tive	sports·man·like
sports·wear	sport·y
spot·light	(spŏt′ līt′)
spot·ty	(spŏt′ ĭ)
spouse	(spous)
spout	(spout)
sprain	(sprān)
sprawl·ing	(sprôl′ ĭng)
spread	(sprĕd)
spright·ly	(sprīt′ lĭ)
spright·li·ness	
spring	(sprĭng)
spring·board	spring·time
sprin·kle	(sprĭng′ k′l)
-kling	
sprint	(sprĭnt)
sprite	(sprīt)
sprock·et wheel	(sprŏk′ ĕt)
sprout	(sprout)
spruce	(sprōōs)
spry	(sprī)
spri·est	spri·ness
spu·ri·ous	(spū′ rĭ·ŭs)
spurn	(spûrn)
spurt	(spûrt)
sput·nik	(spŏŏt′ nĭk)
sput·ter	(spŭt′ ĕr)
spu·tum	(spū′ tŭm)
spy·glass	(spī′ glás′)
squab	(skwŏb)
squab·ble	(skwŏb′ 'l)
squab·bling	
squad	(skwŏd)
squad·ron	(skwŏd′ rŭn)
squal·id	(skwŏl′ ĭd)
squall	(skwôl)
squal·or	(skwŏl′ ĕr)
squan·der	(skwŏn′ dĕr)
square	(skwâr)
squar·ing	square dance
square·ly	square-rig·ger
squash	(skwŏsh)
squat	(skwŏt)
squatted	squat·ting
squat·ter	
squaw	(skwô)

squawk (skwôk)
squeak (skwēk)
squeal (skwēl)
  squeal·er
squeam·ish (skwēm′ ĭsh)
squee·gee (skwē′ jē)
squeeze (skwēz)
  squeez·ing
squelch (skwĕlch)
squib (skwĭb)
squid (skwĭd)
squint (skwĭnt)
squire (skwīr)
  squir·ing
squirm (skwûrm)
squir·rel (skwûr′ ĕl)
squirt (skwûrt)
sta·ble (stā′ b'l)
  sta·bil·i·ty (stå·bĭl′ ĭ·tĭ)
  sta·bil·ize -iz·ing
  sta·bly
stac·ca·to (stå·kä′ tō)
sta·di·um (stā′ dĭ·ŭm)
staff (stăf)
stage (stāj)
  stag·ing stage·coach
  stage fright stage·hand
  stage man·ag·er
  stage-struck stag·y
stag·ger (stăg′ ĕr)
stag·nant (stăg′ nănt)
stag·nate (stăg′ nāt)
  -nat·ing
  stag·na·tion (stăg·nā′ shŭn)
staid (stād)
stain·less (stān′ lĕs)
stair·way (stâr′ wā′)
stake (stāk)
  (post; see steak)
sta·lac·tite (stå·lăk′ tīt)
sta·lag·mite (stå·lăg′ mīt)
stale·mate (stāl′ māt′)
Sta·lin·ist (stä′ lĭn·ĭst)
stalk (stôk)
stall (stôl)
stal·lion (stăl′ yŭn)
stal·wart (stôl′ wĕrt)
sta·men (stā′ mĕn)
stam·i·na (stăm′ ĭ·nå)
stam·mer (stăm′ ĕr)
stam·pede (stăm·pēd′)
  -ped·ing
stance (stăns)
stan·chion (stăn′ shŭn)

stand (stănd)
  stand·ee (stăn·dē′)
  stand-in stand·out
  stand·still
stand·ard (stăn′ dĕrd)
  stand·ard-bear·er
  stand·ard·i·za·tion
    (stăn′ dĕr·dĭ·zā′ shŭn)
  stand·ard·ize -iz·ing
stan·za (stăn′ ză)
sta·ple (stā′ p'l)
star (stär)
  star·board star·fish
  star·let star·light
  star·lit star·ry
  star sap·phire
starch (stärch)
star·ling (stär′ lĭng)
star·tle (stär′ t'l)
  -tling
starve (stärv)
  starv·ing
star·va·tion (stär·vā′ shŭn)
state (stāt)
  stat·ing state·hood
  state·house state·less
  state·ly -li·ness
  state·ment states′ rights
  state·room
  state's at·tor·ney
  state's ev·i·dence
  states·man·like
stat·ic (stăt′ ĭk)
sta·tion (stā′ shŭn)
  sta·tion·mas·ter
  sta·tion wag·on
sta·tion·ar·y (stā′ shŭn·ĕr′ ĭ)
  (unmoving; see stationery)
sta·tion·er·y (stā′ shŭn·ĕr′ ĭ)
  (paper; see stationary)
sta·tis·tics (stå·tĭs′ tĭks)
stat·u·ar·y (stăt′ û·ĕr′ ĭ)
stat·ue (stăt′ û)
stat·u·esque (stăt′ û·ĕsk′)
stat·u·ette (stăt′ û·ĕt′)
stat·ure (stăt′ ûr)
sta·tus (stā′ tŭs)
stat·ute (stăt′ ût)
stat·u·to·ry (stăt′ û·tō′ rĭ)
stead·fast (stĕd′ fást)
stead·y (stĕd′ ĭ)
  stead·i·ness
steak (stāk)
  (meat; see stake)

steal (stēl)
  (take feloniously; see *steel*)
  stole   steal·ing
stealth·y (stĕl′ thĭ)
  stealth·i·ness
steam (stēm)
  steam·boat   steam en·gine
  steam-roll·er   steam·ship
steel (stēl)
  (metal; see *steal*)
  steel·head   steel wool
  steel·y
steep (stēp)
stee·ple (stē′ p′l)
  stee·ple·chase stee·ple jack
steer (stēr)
steer·age (stēr′ ĭj)
stein (stīn)
stel·lar (stĕl′ ēr)
stench (stĕnch)
sten·cil (stĕn′ sĭl)
  -ciled   -cil·ing
ste·nog·ra·pher
      (stĕ·nŏg′ rȧ·fēr)
  sten·o·graph·ic
      (stĕn′ ō·grăf′ ĭk)
  sten·o·type (stĕn′ ō·tīp)
sten·to·ri·an (stĕn·tō′ rĭ·ȧn)
step (stĕp)
  (pace; see *steppe*)
  stepped,   step·ping
  step·child   step·fa·ther
  step·par·ent step·ping·stone
steppe (stĕp)
  (Russian plains; see *step*)
ster·e·o·phon·ic
      (stĕr′ ê·ō·fŏn′ ĭk)
ster·e·op·ti·con
      (stĕr′ ê·ŏp′ tĭ·kŏn)
ster·e·o·scope (stĕr′ ê·ō·skōp′)
ster·e·o·type (stĕr′ ê·ō·tīp′)
ster·ile (stĕr′ ĭl)
  ste·ril·i·ty (stĕ·rĭl′ ĭ·tĭ)
  ster·i·li·za·tion
      (stĕr′ ĭ·lĭ·zā′ shŭn)
  ster·i·lize   -iz·ing
ster·ling (stûr′ lĭng)
stern (stûrn)
  stern·ness
ster·num (stûr′ nŭm)
steth·o·scope (stĕth′ ō·skōp)
  steth·o·scop·ic
      (stĕth′ ō·skŏp′ ĭk)
ste·ve·dore (stē′ vĕ·dōr′)

Ste·ven·son, Ad·lai E.
      (stē′ vĕn·s′n, ăd′ lā)
stew·ard (stū′ ērd)
  stew·ard·ess
stick·ler (stĭk′ lēr)
stick·pin (stĭk′ pĭn′)
stick-to-it·ive·ness
      (stĭk′ tōō′ ĭt·ĭv·nĕs)
stiff·en (stĭf′ ĕn)
sti·fle (stī′ f′l)
  -fling
stig·ma (stĭg′ mȧ)
  stig·ma·tize   -tiz·ing
stig·ma·tism (stĭg′ mȧ·tĭz′m)
stilt·ed (stĭlt′ tĕd)
stim·u·late (stĭm′ û·lāt)
  -lat·ing
  stim·u·lant (-lȧnt)
  stim·u·la·tion
      (stĭm′ û·lā′ shŭn)
  stim·u·la·tive (stĭm′ û·lā′ tĭv)
  stim·u·la·tor
stim·u·lus (stĭm′ û·lŭs)
  pl. stim·u·li (-lī)
sting·y (stĭn′ jĭ)
  sting·i·ness
sti·pend (stī′ pĕnd)
stip·ple (stĭp′ ′l)
  stip·pling
stip·u·late (stĭp′ û·lāt)
  -lat·ing
  stip·u·la·tion (stĭp′ û·lā′ shŭn)
stir·rup (stĭr′ ŭp)
stitch (stĭch)
stock (stŏk)
  stock·bro·ker stock ex·change
  stock·hold·er stock mar·ket
  stock·pile
stock·ade (stŏk·ād′)
stock·i·net (stŏk′ ĭ·nĕt′)
stock·ing (stŏk′ ĭng)
stodg·y (stŏj′ ĭ)
  stodg·i·ness
sto·gie (stō′ gĭ)
sto·ic (stō′ ĭk)
  sto·i·cal·ly
stok·er (stōk′ ēr)
sto·len (stō′ lĕn)
stol·id (stŏl′ ĭd)
  sto·lid·i·ty (stō·lĭd′ ĭ·tĭ)
stom·ach (stŭm′ ȧk)
stone (stōn)
  stone·cut·ter stone-deaf
  stone·mas·on·ry
  stone·ware   ston·y

stooge	(stōōj)	strength	(strĕngth)
stool pi·geon	(stōōl)	strength·ened	
stop	(stŏp)	stren·u·ous	(strĕn′ û·ŭs)
stopped	stop·ping	strep·to·coc·cus	
stop·cock	stop·gap		(strĕp′ tô·kŏk′ ŭs)
stop light	stop·o·ver	pl. strep·to·coc·ci	(-kŏk′ sī)
stop·page	stop·per	strep·to·my·cin	
stor·age	(stôr′ ĭj)		(strĕp′ tô·mī′ sĭn)
store·keep·er	(stôr′ kēp′ ēr)	stress	(strĕs)
sto·ry	(stō′ rĭ)	stretch	(strĕch)
-ries		stretch·a·ble	
(story of a building sometimes		strewn	(strōōn)
spelled storey)		stri·at·ed	(strī′ āt·ĕd)
sto·ried	sto·ry·tell·er	stri·a·tion	(strī·ā′ shŭn)
stout·heart·ed	(stout′ här′ tĕd)	strick·en	(strĭk′ ĕn)
stove·pipe	(stōv′ pīp′)	strict	(strĭkt)
stow·a·way	(stō′ á·wā′)	stric·ture	(strĭk′ tūr)
strad·dle	(străd′ 'l)	stri·dent	(strī′ dĕnt)
strad·dling		-dence	-den·cy
strag·gly	(străg′ lĭ)	strife	(strīf)
straight	(strāt)	strike	(strīk)
(without curves; see strait)		strik·ing	strike·break·er
straight·a·way straight·en		strin·gent	(strĭn′ jĕnt)
straight·for·ward		-gen·cy	
strain·er	(strān′ ēr)	string·y	(strĭng′ ĭ)
strait	(strāt)	striped	(strīpt)
(tight, narrow; see straight)		strip·ling	(strĭp′ lĭng)
strait·jack·et strait-laced		stroke	(strōk)
strange	(strānj)	strok·ing	
strange·ly	strange·ness	stroll·er	(strōl′ ēr)
stran·gle	(străng′ g'l)	strong	(strŏng)
-gling	stran·gle hold	strong-arm	strong·box
stran·gu·la·tion		strong-willed	
	(străng′ gû·lā′ shŭn)	stron·ti·um	(strŏn′ shĭ·ŭm)
strap·ping	(străp′ ĭng)	struc·ture	(strŭk′ tūr)
strat·e·gy	(străt′ ė·jĭ)	struc·tur·al	
-gies		stru·del	(shtrōō′ dĕl)
strat·a·gem	(străt′ á·jĕm)	strug·gle	(strŭg′ 'l)
stra·te·gic	(strá·tē′ jĭk)	strug·gling	
strat·e·gist	(străt′ ė·jĭst)	strum	(strŭm)
strat·i·fy	(străt′ ĭ·fī)	strummed	strum·ming
-fied	-fy·ing	strum·pet	(strŭm′ pĕt)
strat·i·fi·ca·tion		strych·nine	(strĭk′ nĭn)
	(străt′ ĭ·fĭ·kā′ shŭn)	stub·ble	(stŭb′ 'l)
strat·o·sphere	(străt′ ô·sfēr)	stub·bly	
stra·tum	(strā′ tŭm)	stub·born	(stŭb′ ērn)
pl. -ta		stub·born·ly	stub·born·ness
stra·tus	(strā′ tŭs)	stuc·co	(stŭk′ ō)
pl. -ti	(-tī)	stu·dent	(stū′ dĕnt)
straw·ber·ry	(strô′ bĕr′ ĭ)	stu·di·o	(stū′ dĭ·ō)
-ber·ries		-os	
streak·y	(strēk′ ĭ)	stu·di·ous	(stū′ dĭ·ŭs)
streak·i·ness		stud·y	(stŭd′ ĭ)
stream·lined	(strēm′ līnd′)	stud·ied	stud·ies
street·car	(strēt′ kär′)	stud·y·ing	

stuff·ing   (stŭf' ĭng)
stuff·y   (stŭf' ĭ)
  stuff·i·ly   -i·ness
stul·ti·fy   (stŭl' tĭ·fī)
  -fied   -fy·ing
  stul·ti·fi·ca·tion
                   (stŭl' tĭ·fĭ·kā' shŭn)
stum·ble   (stŭm' b'l)
  -bling
stun·ning   (stŭn' ĭng)
stu·pe·fy   (stū' pē·fī)
  -fied   -fy·ing
  stu·pe·fac·tion
                   (stū' pē·făk' shŭn)
stu·pen·dous   (stū·pĕn' dŭs)
stu·pid   (stū' pĭd)
  stu·pid·i·ty   (stū·pĭd' ĭ·tĭ)
stu·por   (stū' pĕr)
  stu·por·ous
stur·dy   (stûr' dĭ)
  stur·di·ly   -di·ness
stur·geon   (stûr' jŭn)
stut·ter   (stŭt' ĕr)
sty   (stī)
  sties
style   (stīl)
  styl·ing   styl·ish
  styl·ist
  sty·lis·tic   (stī·lĭs' tĭk)
  styl·ize   -iz·ing
sty·lus   (stī' lŭs)
sty·mie   (stī' mĭ)
  -mied   -my·ing
styp·tic   (stĭp' tĭk)
suave   (swäv)
  suave·ly   suave·ness
  suav·i·ty   (swäv' ĭ·tĭ)
sub·al·tern   (sŭ·bôl' tĕrn)
sub·com·mit·tee
                   (sŭb' kŏ·mĭt' ē)
sub·con·scious   (sŭb·kŏn' shŭs)
sub·con·trac·tor
                   (sŭb·kŏn' trăk·tĕr)
sub·due   (sŭb·dū')
  -du·ing
sub·ject   (sŭb·jĕkt') v.
                   (sŭb' jĕkt) adj.,n.
  sub·jec·tive   (sŭb·jĕk' tĭv)
  -tive·ly
  sub·jec·tiv·i·ty
                   (sŭb' jĕk·tĭv' ĭ·tĭ)
sub·ju·gate   (sŭb' jŏŏ·gāt)
  -gat·ing
sub·junc·tive   (sŭb·jŭngk' tĭv)

sub·lease   (sŭb' lēs')
  -leas·ing
sub·li·mate   (sŭb' lĭ·māt)
  -mat·ing
  sub·li·ma·tion
                   (sŭb' lĭ·mā' shŭn)
sub·lime   (sŭb·līm')
  sub·lime·ly
  sub·lim·i·ty   (sŭb·lĭm' ĭ·tĭ)
sub·lim·i·nal   (sŭb·lĭm' ĭ·năl)
  -nal·ly
sub·mar·gin·al   (sŭb·mär' jĭ·năl)
  -al·ly
sub·ma·rine   (sŭb' má·rēn')
sub·merge   (sŭb·mûrj')
  -merg·ing
sub·mer·gence   (sŭb·mûr' jĕns)
sub·merse   (sŭb·mûrs')
  -mers·ing   sub·mers·i·ble
sub·mis·sion   (sŭb·mĭsh' ŭn)
sub·mis·sive   (sŭb·mĭs' ĭv)
  sub·mis·sive·ness
sub·mit   (sŭb·mĭt')
  -mitted   -mit·ting
sub·nor·mal   (sŭb·nôr' măl)
  sub·nor·mal·i·ty
                   (sŭb' nôr·măl' ĭ·tĭ)
sub·or·di·nate   (sŭ·bôr' dĭ·nĭt)
                   adj., n
                   (-năt) v.
  -nat·ing
  sub·or·di·na·tion
                   (sŭ·bôr' dĭ·nā' shŭn)
sub·orn   (sŭb·ôrn')
sub·poe·na   (sŭb·pē' ná)
sub·scribe   (sŭb·skrīb')
  -scrib·ing
  sub·scrip·tion
                   (sŭb·skrĭp' shŭn)
sub·se·quent   (sŭb' sē·kwĕnt)
  -quence
sub·ser·vi·ent   (sŭb·sûr' vĭ·ĕnt)
  -ence
sub·side   (sŭb·sīd')
  -sid·ing
sub·sid·i·ar·y   (sŭb·sĭd' ĭ·ĕr' ĭ)
  -ar·ies
sub·si·dy   (sŭb' sĭ·dĭ)
  -dies
  sub·si·di·za·tion
                   (sŭb' sĭ·dĭ·zā' shŭn)
  sub·si·dize   -diz·ing
sub·sist·ence   (sŭb·sĭs' tĕns)
sub·soil   (sŭb' soil')
sub·spe·cies   (sŭb·spē' shĭz)

sub·stance   (sŭb′ stăns)
sub·stand·ard   (sŭb·stăn′ dĕrd)
sub·stan·tial   (sŭb·stăn′ shăl)
  -tial·ly
sub·stan·ti·ate   (sŭb·stăn′ shĭ·āt)
  -at·ing
  sub·stan·ti·a·tion
                    (sŭb·stăn′ shĭ·ā′ shŭn)
sub·stan·tive   (sŭb′ stăn·tĭv)
sub·sti·tute   (sŭb′ stĭ·tūt)
  -tut·ing
sub·stra·tum   (sŭb·strā′ tŭm)
sub·struc·ture   (sŭb·strŭk′ tŭr)
sub·ter·fuge   (sŭb′ tĕr·fūj)
sub·ter·ra·ne·an
                    (sŭb′ tĕ·rā′ nē·ăn)
sub·tle   (sŭt′ ′l)
  sub·tle·ness
  sub·tle·ty, -ties (sŭt′ ′l·tĭ)
  sub·tly   (sŭt′ lĭ)
sub·tract   (sŭb·trăkt′)
  sub·trac·tion
sub·trop·i·cal   (sŭb·trŏp′ ĭ·kăl)
sub·urb   (sŭb′ ŭrb)
  sub·ur·ban   (sŭb·ûr′ băn)
  sub·ur·ban·ite   (sŭb·ûr′ băn·īt)
  sub·ur·bi·a   (sŭb·ûr′ bĭ·ă)
sub·ver·sive   (sŭb·vûr′ sĭv)
  sub·ver·sion
sub·vert   (sŭb·vûrt′)
  sub·vert·er
suc·ceed   (sŭk·sēd′)
suc·cess   (sŭk·sĕs′)
  suc·cess·ful, -ful·ly, -ful·ness
suc·ces·sion   (sŭk·sĕsh′ ŭn)
suc·ces·sive   (sŭk·sĕs′ ĭv)
  suc·ces·sive·ly suc·ces·sor
suc·cinct   (sŭk·sĭngkt′)
suc·cor   (sŭk′ ĕr)
suc·co·tash   (sŭk′ ŏ·tăsh)
suc·cu·lent   (sŭk′ ū·lĕnt)
  -lence
suc·cumb   (sŭ·kŭm′)
suck·ling   (sŭk′ lĭng)
suc·tion   (sŭk′ shŭn)
sud·den   (sŭd′ ′n)
  sud·den·ly   sud·den·ness
suds·y   (sŭd′ zĭ)
sue   (sū)
  su·ing
suède   (swād)
su·et   (sū′ ĕt)
suf·fer   (sŭf′ ĕr)
  suf·fer·ance   (sŭf′ ĕr·ăns)

suf·fice   (sŭ·fīs′)
  suf·fic·ing
suf·fi·cient   (sŭ·fĭsh′ ĕnt)
  -cien·cy
suf·fix   (sŭf′ ĭks)
suf·fo·cate   (sŭf′ ŏ·kāt)
  -cat·ing
  suf·fo·ca·tion   (sŭf′ ŏ·kā′ shŭn)
suf·frage   (sŭf′ rĭj)
suf·fra·gette   (sŭf′ ră·jĕt′)
suf·fuse   (sŭ·fūz′)
  suf·fus·ing
  suf·fu·sion   (sŭ·fū′ zhŭn)
sug·ar   (shŏŏg′ ĕr)
  sug·ar-coat   sug·ar·plum
  sug·ar·y
sug·gest   (sŭg·jĕst′)
  sug·gest·i·ble
  sug·ges·tion   (sŭg·jĕs′ chŭn)
  sug·ges·tive   -tive·ness
su·i·cide   (sū′ ĭ·sīd)
  su·i·cid·al   (sū′ ĭ·sīd′ ăl)
suit·a·ble   (sūt′ ă·b′l)
  suit·a·bil·i·ty   (sūt′ ă·bĭl′ ĭ·tĭ)
suit·case   (sūt′ kās′)
suite   (swēt)
  (retinue; see sweet)
suit·or   (sūt′ ĕr)
sul·fa   (sŭl′ fă)
sul·fa·nil·a·mide
                    (sŭl′ fă·nĭl′ ă·mīd)
sul·fate   (sŭl′ fāt)
sul·fide   (sŭl′ fīd)
sul·fite   (sŭl′ fīt)
sul·fur   (sŭl′ fĕr)
  sul·fur di·ox·ide
  sul·fu·ric ac·id (sŭl·fū′ rĭk)
  sul·fu·rous
sulk·y   (sŭl′ kĭ)
  sulk·i·ness
sul·len   (sŭl′ ĕn)
  sul·len·ly   sul·len·ness
sul·tan   (sŭl′ tăn)
  sul·tan·a   (sŭl·tăn′ ă)
sul·try   (sŭl′ trĭ)
  sul·tri·ness
su·mac   (shŏŏ′ măk)
sum·ma·ry   (sŭm′ ă·rĭ)
  -ries
  sum·ma·ri·ly   (sŭm′ ă·rĭ·lĭ)
  sum·ma·ri·za·tion
                    (sŭm′ ă·rĭ·zā′ shŭn)
  sum·ma·rize   -riz·ing
sum·mer   (sŭm′ ĕr)
  sum·mer·house

sum·mer·time sum·mer·y
sum·mit (sŭm' ĭt)
sum·mon (sŭm' ŭn)
sum·mon·er
sump·tu·ous (sŭmp' tū̇·ŭs)
sun (sŭn)
  sunned sun·ning
  sun bath sun·burn
  sun·di·al sun·dried
  sun·fast sun·flow·er
  sun·glass·es sun lamp
  sun·light sun·ny
  sun·rise sun·set
  sun·shade sun·shine
  sun·stroke sun·up
sun·dae (sŭn' dĭ)
sun·der (sŭn' dẽr)
sunk·en (sŭngk' ĕn)
su·per (sō̇' pẽr)
su·per·a·bun·dance
  (sō̇' pẽr·ȧ·bŭn' dȧns)
su·per·an·nu·ate
  (sō̇' pẽr·ăn' ū̇·āt)
su·perb (sō̇·pûrb')
su·per·car·go (sō̇' pẽr·kär' gō)
su·per·cil·i·ous
  (sō̇' pẽr·sĭl' ĭ·ŭs)
su·per·e·go (sō̇' pẽr·ē' gō)
su·per·fi·cial (sō̇' pẽr·fĭsh' ăl)
  -cial·ly
su·per·fi·ci·al·i·ty
  (sō̇' pẽr·fĭsh' ĭ·ăl' ĭ·tĭ)
  -ties
su·per·flu·ous (sō̇·pûr' flōō·ŭs)
su·per·flu·i·ty
  (sō̇' pẽr·flōō' ĭ·tĭ)
  -ties
su·per·high·way
  (sō̇' pẽr·hī' wā̇')
su·per·hu·man
  (sō̇' pẽr·hū' măn)
su·per·im·pose (sō̇' pẽr·ĭm·pōz')
  -pos·ing
su·per·in·tend (sō̇' pẽr·ĭn·tĕnd')
  su·per·in·tend·ent
su·pe·ri·or (sō̇·pẽr' ĭ·ẽr)
  su·pe·ri·or·i·ty
  (sō̇·pẽr' ĭ·ŏr' ĭ·tĭ)
su·per·la·tive (sō̇·pûr' lȧ·tĭv)
  -tive·ly
su·per·mar·ket
  (sō̇' pẽr·mär' kĕt)
su·per·nu·mer·ar·y
  (sō̇' pẽr·nū' mẽr·ĕr' ĭ)
  -ar·ies

su·per·sat·u·rate
  (sō̇' pẽr·săt' ū̇·rāt)
  -rat·ing
su·per·sede (sō̇' pẽr·sēd')
  -sed·ing
su·per·ses·sion (-sĕsh' ŭn)
su·per·son·ic (sō̇' pẽr·sŏn' ĭk)
su·per·sti·tion (sō̇' pẽr·stĭsh' ŭn)
  su·per·sti·tious
su·per·struc·ture
  (sō̇' pẽr·strŭk' tūr)
su·per·vise (sō̇' pẽr·vīz')
  -vis·ing su·per·vi·sor
  su·per·vi·so·ry
  (sō̇' pẽr·vī' zō·rĭ)
su·pine (sō̇·pīn')
sup·per (sŭp' ẽr)
sup·plant (sŭ·plȧnt')
sup·ple (sŭp' 'l)
  sup·ple·ness
sup·ple·ment (sŭp' lê·mĕnt)
  sup·ple·men·tal
  (sŭp' lê·mĕn' tăl)
  sup·ple·men·ta·ry
  (sŭp' lê·mĕn' tȧ·rĭ)
sup·pli·ant (sŭp' lĭ·ȧnt)
  -ance
sup·pli·cant (sŭp' lĭ·kȧnt)
sup·pli·cate (sŭp' lĭ·kāt)
  -cat·ing
sup·ply (sŭ·plī')
  sup·plied sup·ply·ing
  sup·pli·er sup·plies
sup·port (sŭ·pōrt')
  sup·port·a·ble sup·port·er
sup·pose (sŭ·pōz')
  sup·pos·ing sup·pos·a·ble
  sup·pos·ed·ly
sup·po·si·tion (sŭp' ō·zĭsh' ŭn)
  sup·po·si·tion·al
sup·pos·i·to·ry (sŭ·pŏz' ĭ·tō' rĭ)
  -ries
sup·press (sŭ·prĕs')
  sup·press·i·ble
  sup·pres·sion (-prĕsh' ŭn)
  sup·pres·sive
su·preme (sō̇·prēm')
  su·prem·a·cy (sō̇·prĕm' ȧ·sĭ)
  su·preme·ly
sur·cease (sûr·sēs')
sur·charge (sûr' chärj') n.
sure·ly (shōōr' lĭ)
sure·ty (shōōr' tĭ)
  -ties

sur·face	(sûr′ fĭs)	su·ze·rain·ty	(sū′ zĕ·rän·tĭ)
-fac·ing		svelte	(svĕlt)
surf·board	(sûrf′ bōrd′)	swab·ber	(swŏb′ ĕr)
sur·feit	(sûr′ fĭt)	swad·dling clothes	
-feit·ed			(swŏd′ lĭng)
surge	(sûrj)	swag·ger	(swăg′ ĕr)
(to swell; see *serge*)		Swa·hi·li	(swä·hē′ lè)
surg·ing		swain	(swān)
sur·geon	(sûr′ jŭn)	swal·low	(swŏl′ ō)
sur·ger·y	(sûr′ jĕr·ĭ)	swa·mi	(swä′ mĭ)
sur·gi·cal	(sûr′ jĭ·kăl)	swank·y	(swăngk′ ĭ)
-cal·ly		swan's-down	(swŏnz′ doun′)
sur·ly	(sûr′ lĭ)	swarth·y	(swôr′ thĭ)
sur·li·ness		swarth·i·ness	
sur·mise	(sûr·mĭz′)	swash·buck·ler	(swŏsh′ bŭk′ lĕr)
-mis·ing		swas·ti·ka	(swŏs′ tĭ·ká)
sur·mount	(sûr·mount′)	swatch	(swŏch)
sur·mount·a·ble		swat·ter	(swŏt′ ĕr)
sur·name	(sûr′ nām)	sway-backed	(swā′ băkt′)
sur·pass	(sẽr·pás′)	Swa·zi·land	(swä′ zĕ·länd′)
sur·pass·a·ble		swear	(swâr)
sur·plice	(sûr′ plĭs)	sweat	(swĕt)
(vestment; see *surplus*)		sweat·i·ness sweat shirt	
sur·plus	(sûr′ plŭs)	sweat·shop	
(excess; see *surplice*)		sweat·er	(swĕt′ ĕr)
sur·prise	(sẽr·prīz′)	Swede	(swēd)
-pris·ing		Swed·ish	
sur·re·al·ism	(sŭ·rē′ ăl·ĭz′m)	sweep·stake	(swēp′ stāk′)
sur·ren·der	(sŭ·rĕn′ dẽr)	sweet	(swĕt)
sur·rep·ti·tious	(sûr′ ĕp·tĭsh′ ŭs)	(agreeable; see *suite*)	
sur·rey	(sûr′ ĭ)	sweet·bread sweet·bri·er	
sur·ro·gate	(sûr′ ō·gāt)	sweet·en·ing sweet·meats	
sur·round	(sŭ·round′)	sweet po·ta·to sweet Wil·liam	
sur·tax	(sûr′ tăks′)	swel·ter·ing	(swĕl′ tẽr·ĭng)
sur·veil·lance	(sûr·văl′ dns)	swept	(swĕpt)
sur·vey	(sẽr·vā′) v.	swerve	(swûrv)
	(sûr′ vă) n.	swerv·ing	
sur·vey·or	(sẽr·vā′ ẽr)	swill	(swĭl)
sur·vive	(sẽr·vīv′)	swim	(swĭm)
-viv·ing sur·viv·al		swam swim·ming	
sur·vi·vor		swim·mer	
sus·cep·ti·ble	(sŭ·sĕp′ tĭ·b′l)	swin·dler	(swĭn′ dlẽr)
sus·cep·ti·bil·i·ty		swine	(swīn)
	(sŭ·sĕp′ tĭ·bĭl′ ĭ·tĭ)	swin·ish	
sus·pect	(sŭs′ pĕkt) n.	swirl	(swûrl)
	(sŭs·pĕkt′)	switch	(swĭch)
	adj., v.	switch·back switch·board	
sus·pend	(sŭs·pĕnd′)	switch·man	
sus·pend·er	(sŭs·pĕn′ dẽr)	swiv·el	(swĭv′ ′l)
sus·pen·sion	(sŭs·pĕn′ shŭn)	-eled, -el·ing	
sus·pi·cious	(sŭs·pĭsh′ ŭs)	swol·len	(swōl′ ĕn)
sus·pi·cion	(sŭs·pĭsh′ ŭn)	sword	(sōrd)
sus·tain·ing	(sŭs·tān′ ĭng)	sword·fish swords·man	
sus·te·nance	(sŭs′ tē·ndns)	syc·a·more	(sĭk′ á·mōr)
su·ture	(sū′ tûr)		

syc·o·phant (sĭk′ ŏ·fănt)
-phan·cy
syl·la·ble (sĭl′ ȧ·b'l)
syl·lab·ic (sĭ·lăb′ ĭk)
syl·lab·i·ca·tion (sĭ·lăb′ ĭ·kā′ shŭn)
syl·lab·i·fy (sĭ·lăb′ ĭ·fī)
-fied -fy·ing
syl·la·bus (sĭl′ ȧ·bŭs)
-bus·es
syl·lo·gism (sĭl′ ŏ·jĭz'm)
syl·lo·gis·tic (sĭl′ ŏ·jĭs′ tĭk)
sylph (sĭlf)
sylph·like
syl·van (sĭl′ vȧn)
sym·bi·o·sis (sĭm′ bĭ·ō′ sĭs)
sym·bi·ot·ic (-ŏt′ ĭk)
sym·bol (sĭm′ bŭl)
(emblem; see *cymbal*)
sym·bol·ic (sĭm·bŏl′ ĭk)
sym·bol·i·cal (sĭm·bŏl′ ĭ·kȧl)
-cal·ly sym·bol·ism
sym·bol·ize -iz·ing
sym·met·ri·cal (sĭ·mĕt′ rĭ·kȧl)
-cal·ly
sym·me·try (sĭm′ ė·trĭ)
sym·pa·thy (sĭm′ pȧ·thĭ)
-thies
sym·pa·thet·ic (sĭm′ pȧ·thĕt′ ĭk)
sym·pa·thize -thiz·ing
sym·pho·ny (sĭm′ fō·nĭ)
-nies
sym·phon·ic (sĭm·fŏn′ ĭk)
sym·po·si·um (sĭm·pō′ zĭ·ŭm)
pl. sym·po·si·a
symp·tom (sĭmp′ tŭm)
symp·to·mat·ic (sĭmp′ tō·măt′ ĭk)
syn·a·gogue (sĭn′ ȧ·gŏg)
syn·chro·mesh (sĭng′krō·mĕsh′)
syn·chro·nize (sĭng′ krō·nīz)
-niz·ing
syn·chro·ni·za·tion (sĭng′ krō·nĭ·zā′ shŭn)
syn·co·pa·tion (sĭng′ kŏ·pā′ shŭn)
syn·di·cate (sĭn′ dĭ·kāt) *n.*
-cat·ing (-kāt) *v.*
syn·drome (sĭn′ drōm)
syn·od (sĭn′ ŭd)
syn·o·nym (sĭn′ ŏ·nĭm)
syn·on·y·mous (sĭ·nŏn′ ĭ·mŭs)

syn·op·sis (sĭ·nŏp′ sĭs)
pl. -ses
syn·op·tic (sĭ·nŏp′ tĭk)
syn·tax (sĭn′ tăks)
syn·the·sis (sĭn′ thė·sĭs)
pl. -ses
syn·the·size (sĭn′ thė·sīz)
-siz·ing
syn·thet·ic (sĭn·thĕt′ ĭk)
syn·thet·i·cal·ly
syph·i·lis (sĭf′ ĭ·lĭs)
sy·rin·ga (sĭ·rĭng′ gȧ)
syr·inge (sĭr′ ĭnj)
sy·rin·ge·al (sĭ·rĭn′ jė·ȧl)
syr·inx (sĭr′ ĭngks)
pl. syr·in·ges (sĭ·rĭn′ jēz)
sys·tem (sĭs′ tĕm)
sys·tem·at·ic (sĭs′ tĕm·ăt′ ĭk)
-i·cal·ly
sys·tem·a·tize (sĭs′ tĕm·ȧ·tīz)
-tiz·ing

T

Ta·bas·co (tȧ·băs′ kō)
tab·er·nac·le (tăb′ ēr·năk′l)
tab·leau (tăb′ lō)
pl. tab·leaux (-lōz)
ta·ble·cloth (tā′ b'l·klŏth′)
ta·ble d'hôte (tā′ blĕ dōt′)
ta·ble·spoon (tā′ b'l·spōōn′)
ta·ble·spoon·ful, -fuls
tab·let (tăb′ lĕt)
tab·loid (tăb′ loid)
ta·boo (tȧ·bōō′)
-booed -boo·ing
ta·bor (tā′ bēr)
tab·u·late (tăb′ ū·lāt)
-lat·ing
tab·u·lar (tăb′ ū·lēr)
tab·u·la·tion (tăb′ ū·lā′ shŭn)
tab·u·la·tor
tac·it (tăs′ ĭt)
tac·i·turn (tăs′ ĭ·tûrn)
tac·i·tur·ni·ty (tăs′ ĭ·tûr′ nĭ·tĭ)
tack·le (tăk′l)
-ling
tact (tăkt)
tact·ful, -ful·ly, -ful·ness
tact·less -less·ness
tac·tics (tăk′ tĭks)
tac·ti·cal (tăk′ tĭ·kȧl)
-cal·ly
tac·ti·cian (tăk·tĭsh′ ȧn)

tac·tile (tăk′ tĭl)
tad·pole (tăd′ pōl′)
taf·fe·ta (tăf′ ê·tá)
Ta·hi·ti·an (tá·hē′ tĭ·án)
tail (tāl)
  tailed, tail·ing
  tail·first tail·less
  tail·piece tail spin
  tail wind
tai·lor (tā′ lẽr)
  tai·lor·ing tai·lor·made
taint (tānt)
Tai·wan (tĭ·wän′)
  (also Formosa)
Taj Mahal (täj má·häl′)
talc (tălk)
tal·cum pow·der
  (tăl′ kŭm)
tal·ent (tăl′ ĕnt)
tale·tell·er (tāl′ tĕl′ ẽr)
tal·is·man (tăl′ ĭs·măn)
talk·a·tive (tôk′ á·tĭv)
  -tive·ness
Tal·la·has·see, Fla.
  (tăl′ á·hăs′ ê)
tal·low (tăl′ ō)
tal·ly·ho (tăl′ ĭ·hō′)
Tal·mud (tăl′ mŭd)
tal·on (tăl′ ŭn)
tam·a·rack (tăm′ á·răk)
tam·bou·rine (tăm′ bŏŏ·rēn′)
tame (tām)
  tam·ing tam·a·ble
  tame·ly
Tam·ma·ny Hall (tăm′ á·nĭ)
tamp·er (tăm′ pẽr)
tam·pon (tăm′ pŏn)
tan·a·ger (tăn′ á·jẽr)
tan·dem (tăn′ dĕm)
Tan·gan·yi·ka (tăn′ găn·yē′ ká)
tan·gent (tăn′ jĕnt)
  tan·gen·tial (tăn·jĕn′ shăl)
tan·ge·rine (tăn′ jẽ·rēn′)
tan·gi·ble (tăn′ jĭ·b′l)
tan·gle (tăng′ g′l)
  -gling
tang·y (tăng′ ĭ)
  tang·i·ness
tank·ard (tăngk′ ẽrd)
tan·ner·y (tăn′ ẽr·ĭ)
  tan·ner·ies
tan·nic ac·id (tăn′ ĭk)
tan·ta·lize (tăn′ tá·līz)
  -liz·ing
tan·ta·mount (tăn′ tá·mount′)

tan·trum (tăn′ trŭm)
Tao·ism (tou′ ĭz′m)
ta·pa cloth (tä′ pä)
ta·per (tā′ pẽr)
  (candle; see tapir)
tap·es·try (tăp′ ĕs·trĭ)
  -tries
tape·worm (tăp′ wûrm′)
tap·i·o·ca (tăp′ ĭ·ō′ ká)
ta·pir (tā′ pẽr)
  (animal; see taper)
tap·ster (tăp′ stẽr)
tar·an·tel·la (tăr′ ăn·tĕl′ á)
  (dance)
ta·ran·tu·la (tá·răn′ tū·lá)
  (spider)
tar·dy (tär′ dĭ)
  tar·di·ly -i·ness
tar·get (tär′ gĕt)
tar·iff (tär′ ĭf)
tar·nish (tär′ nĭsh)
  tar·nish·a·ble
ta·ro root (tä′ rō)
tar·pau·lin (tär·pô′ lĭn)
tar·pon (tär′ pŏn)
tar·ra·gon (tăr′ á·gŏn)
tar·ry (tăr′ ĭ)
  tar·ried tar·ry·ing
tar·tan (tär′ tăn)
tar·tar (tär′ tẽr)
  (cream of tartar)
tar·tare sauce (tär′ tẽr)
task·mas·ter (täsk′ măs′ tẽr)
tas·sel (tăs′ ′l)
  tas·seled tas·sel·ing
taste (tāst)
  tast·ing
  taste·ful, -ful·ly, -ful·ness
  taste·less
  tast·i·ly -i·ness
  tast·y
tat·tered (tăt′ ẽrd)
tat·tle (tăt′ ′l)
  tat·tling tat·tle·tale
tat·too (tă·tōō′)
  tat·tooed tat·too·ing
taught (tôt)
  (instructed; see taut)
taunt (tônt)
taupe (tōp)
taut (tôt)
  (tight; see taught)
tau·tol·o·gy (tô·tŏl′ ō·jĭ)
  -gies

tau·to·log·i·cal
        (tô′ tô·lŏj′ ĭ·kǎl)
tav·ern   (tăv′ ẽrn)
taw·dry   (tô′ drĭ)
  taw·dri·ness
taw·ny   (tô′ nĭ)
  taw·ni·ness
tax   (tăks)
  tax·a·ble
  tax·a·tion   (tăks·ā′ shŭn)
  tax-ex·empt   tax·gath·er·er
  tax·pay·er
tax·i   (tăk′ sĭ)
  tax·is   tax·i·cab
tax·i·der·mist   (tăk′ sĭ·dûr′ mĭst)
Tchai·kov·sky, Pe·ter Il·ich
        (chī·kôf′ skĭ)
teach   (tēch)
  teach·a·bil·i·ty
        (tēch′ á·bĭl′ ĭ·tĭ)
  teach·a·ble   teach·er
tea·cup·ful   (tē′ kŭp·fŏŏl′)
  -fuls
teak·wood   (tēk′ wŏŏd′)
team   (tēm)
  team·mate   team·ster
  team·work
tea·pot   (tē′ pŏt′)
tear·ful   (tẽr′ fŏŏl)
  -ful·ly   -ful·ness
tease   (tēz)
  teas·ing
tea·spoon·ful   (tē′ spŏŏn·fŏŏl′)
  -fuls
teat   (tāt)
tech·ni·cal   (těk′ nĭ·kǎl)
  -cal·ly
  tech·ni·cal·i·ty
        (těk′ nĭ·kǎl′ ĭ·tĭ)
  tech·ni·cian   (těk·nĭsh′ ăn)
Tech·ni·col·or   (těk′ nĭ·kŭl′ ẽr)
tech·nique   (těk·nēk′)
tech·nol·o·gy   (těk·nŏl′ ô·jĭ)
  -gies
  tech·no·log·i·cal
        (těk′ nô·lŏj′ ĭ·kǎl)
  -cal·ly
  tech·nol·o·gist   (těk·nŏl′ ô·jĭst)
te·di·ous   (tē′ dĭ·ŭs)
  te·di·um   (tē′ dĭ·ŭm)
teem·ing   (tēm′ ĭng)
  (crowded)
teen·ag·er   (tēn′ āj′ ẽr)
tee shirt   (tē)
teeth   (tēth) n. pl.

teethe   (tēth) v.
  teeth·ing
tee·to·tal·er   (tē·tō′ t′lẽr)
Te·hran, I·ran   (tě·hrän′)
Tel A·viv, Is·ra·el
        (těl′ á·vēv′)
tel·e·cast   (těl′ ê·kást′)
  tel·e·cast·er
tel·e·graph   (těl′ ê·gráf)
tel·e·ol·o·gy   (těl′ ê·ŏl′ ô·jĭ)
te·lep·a·thy   (tê·lěp′ á·thĭ)
tel·e·phone   (těl′ ê·fōn)
tel·e·scope   (těl′ ê·skōp)
  tel·e·scop·ic   (těl′ ê·skŏp′ ĭk)
tel·e·type   (těl′ ê·tīp)
tel·e·vi·sion   (těl′ ê·vĭzh′ ŭn)
  tel·e·view·er
tel·e·vise   -vis·ing
tell·tale   (těl′ tāl′)
te·mer·i·ty   (tê·měr′ ĭ·tĭ)
tem·per   (těm′ pẽr)
tem·per·a   (těm′ pẽr·á)
tem·per·a·ment
        (těm′ pẽr·á·měnt)
  tem·per·a·men·tal
        (těm′ pẽr·á·měn′ tǎl)
  -tal·ly
tem·per·ance   (těm′ pẽr·ðns)
tem·per·ate   (těm′ pẽr·ĭt)
  -ate·ly
tem·per·a·ture   (těm′ pẽr·á·tûr)
tem·pest   (těm′ pěst)
  tem·pes·tu·ous
        (těm·pěs′ tû·ŭs)
tem·plate   (těm′ plĭt)
tem·ple   (těm′ p′l)
tem·po·ral   (těm′ pô·rǎl)
  tem·po·ral·ly
tem·po·rar·y   (těm′ pô·rěr′ ĭ)
  tem·po·rar·i·ly
        (těm′ pô·rěr′ ĭ·lĭ)
tem·po·rize   (těm′ pô·rīz)
  -riz·ing
tempt   (těmpt)
  tempt·a·ble
  temp·ta·tion   (těmp·tā′ shŭn)
  tempt·er   tempt·ress
ten·a·ble   (těn′ á·b′l)
te·na·cious   (tê·nā′ shŭs)
te·nac·i·ty   (tê·năs′ ĭ·tĭ)
ten·ant   (těn′ ǎnt)
  -an·cy
tend·en·cy   (těn′ děn·sĭ)
  -cies
ten·den·tious   (těn·děn′ shŭs)

tend·er (tĕn′ dĕr)
  ten·der·foot ten·der·heart·ed
  ten·der·loin
ten·don (tĕn′ dŭn)
ten·dril (tĕn′ drĭl)
Ten·e·brae (tĕn′ ĕ·brē)
ten·e·ment (tĕn′ ĕ·mĕnt)
ten·et (tĕn′ ĕt)
ten·fold (tĕn′ fōld′)
Ten·nes·see (tĕn′ ĕ·sē′)
  abbr. Tenn.
  Ten·nes·see·an (-sē′ ăn)
ten·nis (tĕn′ ĭs)
ten·or (tĕn′ ĕr)
ten·pins (tĕn′ pĭnz′)
tense (tĕns)
  tense·ly tense·ness
  ten·si·ty (tĕn′ sĭ·tĭ)
ten·sile strength (tĕn′ sĭl)
ten·sion (tĕn′ shŭn)
ten·sor (tĕn′ sĕr)
ten·ta·cle (tĕn′ tá·k′l)
ten·ta·tive (tĕn′ tá·tĭv)
  ten·ta·tive·ly, -tive·ness
ten·ter·hooks (tĕn′ tĕr·hŏŏks′)
ten·u·ous (tĕn′ û·ús)
ten·ure (tĕn′ ûr)
te·pee (tē′ pē)
tep·id (tĕp′ ĭd)
te·qui·la (tá·kē′ lä)
ter·ma·gant (tûr′ má·gănt)
ter·mi·na·ble (tûr′ mĭ·ná·b′l)
ter·mi·nal (tûr′ mĭ·nál)
ter·mi·nate (tûr′ mĭ·nāt)
  -nat·ing
  ter·mi·na·tion
    (tûr′ mĭ·nā′ shŭn)
ter·mi·nol·o·gy
    (tûr′ mĭ·nŏl′ ō·jĭ)
  ter·mi·no·log·i·cal
    (tûr′ mĭ·nô·lŏj′ ĭ·kál)
ter·mi·nus (tûr′ mĭ·nŭs)
  pl. ter·mi·ni (-nĭ)
ter·mite (tûr′ mīt)
tern (tûrn)
  (bird; see *turn*)
ter·race (tĕr′ ĭs)
ter·ra cot·ta (tĕr′ á·kŏt′ ă) *n.*
  ter·ra-cot·ta *adj.*
ter·rain (tĕ·rān′)
ter·ra·pin (tĕr′ á·pĭn)
ter·raz·zo (tĕr·răt′ tsō)
ter·res·tri·al (tĕ·rĕs′ trĭ·ál)
ter·ri·ble (tĕr′ ĭ·b′l)
  ter·ri·ble·ness ter·ri·bly

ter·ri·er (tĕr′ ĭ·ĕr)
ter·rif·ic (tĕ·rĭf′ ĭk)
  ter·rif·i·cal·ly
ter·ri·fy (tĕr′ ĭ·fĭ)
  -fied, -fy·ing
ter·ri·to·ri·al (tĕr′ ĭ·tō′ rĭ·ál)
  ter·ri·to·ry (tĕr′ ĭ·tō′ rĭ)
ter·ror (tĕr′ ĕr)
  ter·ror·ize -iz·ing
ter·ry cloth (tĕr′ ĭ)
terse (tûrs)
  terse·ness
ter·ti·ar·y (tûr′ shĭ·ĕr′ ĭ)
tes·ta·ment (tĕs′ tá·mĕnt)
tes·ti·cle (tĕs′ tĭ·k′l)
tes·ti·fy (tĕs′ tĭ·fĭ)
  -fied, -fy·ing
  tes·ti·fi·er
tes·ti·mo·ny (tĕs′ tĭ·mō′ nĭ)
  -nies
  tes·ti·mo·ni·al
    (tĕs′ tĭ·mō′ nĭ·ál)
tet·a·nus (tĕt′ á·nŭs)
tête-à-tête (tāt′ á·tāt′)
teth·er (tĕth′ ĕr)
tet·ra·chlo·ride (tĕt′ rá·klō′ rīd)
tet·ra·he·dron (tĕt′ rá·hē′ drŭn)
tet·ral·o·gy (tĕ·trăl′ ô·jĭ)
  -gies
te·tram·e·ter (tĕ·trăm′ ĕ·tĕr)
te·trarch (tē′ trärk)
Teu·ton·ic (tū·tŏn′ ĭk)
Tex·as (tĕk′ sás)
  abbr. Tex.
  Tex·an (tĕk′ sán)
text·book (tĕkst′ bŏŏk′)
tex·tile (tĕks′ tĭl)
tex·tu·al (tĕks′ tû·ál)
tex·ture (tĕks′ tûr)
  tex·tur·al
Thai·land (tī′ lănd)
than (t͟hăn)
  (other, else; "none other than
  yourself"; see *then*)
thank (thăngk)
  thank·ful, -ful·ly, -ful·ness
  thank·less
Thanks·giv·ing (thănks·gĭv′ ĭng)
thatched (thăcht)
the·a·ter (thē′ á·tĕr)
  the·a·ter-in-the-round
  the·at·ri·cal (thē·ăt′ rĭ·kál)
  -cal·ly
theft (thĕft)

their   (thâr)
   (of them; see *there*)
   theirs
the·ism   (thē' ĭz'm)
   the·is·tic   (thē·ĭs' tĭk)
theme   (thēm)
   the·mat·ic   (thē·măt' ĭk)
them·selves   (thĕm·sĕlvz')
then   (thĕn)
   (at that time; see *than*)
thence   (thĕns)
   thence·forth   thence·for·ward
the·oc·ra·cy   (thē·ŏk' ró·sĭ)
the·ol·o·gy   (thē·ŏl' ô·jĭ)
   the·o·lo·gi·an   (thē' ô·lō' jĭ·ăn)
   the·o·log·i·cal   (thē' ô·lŏj' ĭ·kăl)
   -cal·ly
the·o·rem   (thē' ô·rĕm)
the·o·ry   (thē' ô·rĭ)
   -ries
   the·o·ret·i·cal   (thē' ô·rĕt' ĭ·kăl)
   -cal·ly
   the·o·re·ti·cian
                         (thē' ô·rē·tĭsh' ăn)
   the·o·rist   (thē' ô·rĭst)
   the·o·rize   -riz·ing
the·os·o·phy   (thē·ŏs' ô·fĭ)
ther·a·peu·tic   (thĕr' á·pū' tĭk)
   ther·a·peu·ti·cal·ly
ther·a·py   (thĕr' á·pĭ)
there   (thâr)
   (in that place; see *their*)
   there·a·bouts   there·aft·er
   there·by   there·fore
   there·in   there·in·aft·er
   there·in·to   there·of
   there·on   there·un·der
   there·un·to   there·up·on
   there·with
ther·mal   (thûr' măl)
ther·mo·dy·nam·ics
                         (thûr' mō·dĭ·năm' ĭks)
ther·mom·e·ter
                         (thĕr·mŏm' ê·tēr)
ther·mo·nu·cle·ar
                         (thûr' mō·nū' klē·ēr)
Ther·mos bot·tle
                         (thûr' mŏs)
ther·mo·stat   (thûr' mō·stăt)
   ther·mo·stat·i·cal·ly
                         (thûr' mō·stăt' ĭ·kăl·ĭ)
the·sau·rus   (thē·sô' rŭs)
these   (thēz)
the·sis   (thē' sĭs)
   pl. the·ses   (-sēz)

Thes·pi·an   (thĕs' pĭ·ăn)
thi·a·mine   (thī' á·mēn)
thick·ened   (thĭk' ĕnd)
thick·et   (thĭk' ĕt)
thick-skinned   (thĭk' skĭnd')
thief   (thēf) *n.*
   pl. thieves   (thēvz)
thieve   (thēv) *v.*
   thiev·ing   thiev·er·y
   thiev·ish
thigh·bone   (thī' bōn')
thim·ble·ful   (thĭm' b'l·fŏŏl)
thin   (thĭn)
   thin·ly   thin·ness
   thin·ner   thin·ning
   thin-skinned
think·a·ble   (thĭngk' á·b'l)
third   (thûrd)
   third class
   third-class *adj. & adv.*
   third de·gree   third-rate
thirst·y   (thûrs' tĭ)
   thirst·i·er, -i·est, -i·ly, -i·ness
thir·teen   (thûr' tēn')
thir·ty   (thûr' tĭ)
   -ties   thir·ti·eth
this·tle   (thĭs' 'l)
thith·er   (thĭth' ēr)
thong   (thŏng)
tho·rax   (thō' răks)
   tho·rac·ic   (thō·răs' ĭk)
tho·ri·um   (thō' rĭ·ăm)
thor·ough   (thûr' ō)
   thor·ough·bred
   thor·ough·go·ing
   thor·ough·ness
though   (thō)
thought   (thôt)
   thought·ful, -ful·ly, -ful·ness
   thought·less, -less·ly, -less·ness
thou·sand   (thou' zănd)
   thou·sand·fold thou·sandth
thrall·dom   (thrôl' dŭm)
thread·bare   (thrĕd' bâr')
threat·en   (thrĕt' 'n)
three   (thrē)
   three-di·men·sion·al
   three-pen·ny
   three-point land·ing
   three·some
thresh·er   (thrĕsh' ēr)
thresh·old   (thrĕsh' ōld)
thrice   (thrīs)
thrift·y   (thrĭf' tĭ)
   thrift·i·er, -i·est, -i·ly, -i·ness

thrill·ing (thrĭl′ ĭng)
thriv·ing (thrĭv′ ĭng)
throat (thrōt)
throes (thrōz)
throm·bo·sis (thrŏm·bō′ sĭs)
throt·tle (thrŏt′ ′l)
through (thrōō)
  through·out
throw (thrō)
  throw·a·way throw·back
thug (thŭg)
  thug·gish
thumb (thŭm)
  thumb·nail thumb·tack
thun·der (thŭn′ dẽr)
  thun·der·bird thun·der·bolt
  thun·der·clap thun·der·cloud
  thun·der·head thun·der·ous
  thun·der·show·er
  thun·der·struck
thwart (thwôrt)
thyme (tīm)
  (seasoning; see *time*)
thy·mus gland (thī′ mŭs)
thy·roid gland (thī′ roid)
thy·self (thī·sĕlf′)
ti·ar·a (tĭ·âr′ ȧ)
Ti·bet·an (tĭ·bĕt′ ǎn)
tic (tĭk)
  (twitching; see *tick*)
tick (tĭk)
  (parasite; see *tic*)
tick·et (tĭk′ ĕt)
tick·le (tĭk′ ′l)
  -ling
  tick·lish (tĭk′ lĭsh)
tick·tack·toe (tĭk′ tăk·tō′)
tid·bit (tĭd′ bĭt′)
tid·dly·winks (tĭd′ ′l·ĭ·wĭngks′)
tide (tīd)
  tid·al (tīd′ ăl)
  tide·wa·ter
ti·dy (tī′ dĭ)
  -died -dy·ing
  ti·di·er, -i·est, -i·ly, -i·ness
tie (tī)
  tied ty·ing
  tie-up
tier (tēr)
  (row)
tiff (tĭf)
tight (tīt)
  tight·en tight·fist·ed
  tight-lipped tight·rope
ti·gress (tī′ grĕs)

Ti·jua·na, Mex. (tē·hwä′ nä)
tile (tīl)
  til·ing
till (tĭl)
  till·a·ble
  till·age (tĭl′ ĭj)
tim·bale (tĭm′ bȧl)
tim·ber (tĭm′ bẽr)
  (wood; see *timbre*)
tim·bre (tĭm′ bẽr)
  (tone; see *timber*)
Tim·buk·tu (tĭm·bŭk′ tōō)
time (tīm)
  (period, occasion; see *thyme*)
  tim·ing time-hon·ored
  time·keep·er time·less
  time·li·ness time·ly
  time·piece time·sav·ing
  time·ta·ble time·worn
  time zone
tim·id (tĭm′ ĭd)
  ti·mid·i·ty (tĭ·mĭd′ ĭ·tĭ)
tim·or·ous (tĭm′ ẽr·ŭs)
tim·pa·ni (tĭm′ pȧ·nē)
tinc·ture (tĭngk′ tŭr)
tin·der·box (tĭn′ dẽr·bŏks′)
tine (tīn)
tin (tĭn)
  tin foil tin·ny
  tin-pan al·ley tin·type
tinge (tĭnj)
  tinge·ing
tin·gle (tĭng′ g′l)
  -gling
tin·sel (tĭn′ sĕl)
  -seled
ti·ny (tī′ nĭ)
  ti·ni·er, -i·est, -i·ness
tip-off (tĭp′ ôf′)
Tip·pe·rar·y (tĭp′ ĕ·râr′ ĭ)
tip·pler (tĭp′ lẽr)
tip·ster (tĭp′ stẽr)
tip·toe (tĭp′ tō′)
  -toe·ing
ti·rade (tī′ rād)
tire (tīr)
  tir·ing tired·ness
  tire·less
  tire·some -some·ly
tis·sue (tĭsh′ ū)
Ti·tan·ic (tī·tăn′ ĭk)
tithe (tītħ)
  tith·ing
ti·tian (tĭsh′ ăn)

tit·il·late (tĭt' ĭ·lāt)
-il·lat·ing
tit·il·la·tion (tĭt' ĭ·lā' shŭn)
ti·tle (tī' t'l)
-tling ti·tle·hold·er
ti·tlist (tī' tlĭst)
tit·mouse (tĭt' mous')
ti·trate (tī' trāt)
-trat·ing
ti·tra·tion (tī·trā' shŭn)
tit·u·lar (tĭt' û·lẽr)
to (tōō)
(toward; see too, two)
toad·stool (tōd' stōōl')
toad·y (tōd' ĭ)
toad·ied toad·y·ing
to-and-fro (tōō' ănd·frō')
toast·mas·ter (tōst' măs' tẽr)
to·bac·co (tȯ·băk' ō)
-bac·cos
to·bog·gan (tȯ·bŏg' ăn)
to·day (tōō·dā')
tod·dy (tŏ' dĭ)
(hot toddy) tod·dies
to-do (tōō·dōō')
toe (tō)
toe·ing toe dance n.
toe hold toe·nail
to·ga (tō' gȧ)
to·geth·er (tōō·gĕth' ẽr)
togged (tŏgd)
tog·gle switch (tŏg' 'l)
toil (toil)
toil·er toil·worn
toi·let (toi' lĕt)
toi·lette (toi·lĕt')
To·kay wine (tȯ·kā')
to·ken (tō' kĕn)
tol·er·a·ble (tŏl' ẽr·ȧ·b'l)
tol·er·ant (tŏl' ẽr·ănt)
-ance
tol·er·ate (tŏl' ẽr·āt)
-at·ing
tol·er·a·tion (tŏl' ẽr·ā' shŭn)
toll (tōl)
toll booth toll·gate
toll·keep·er toll road
Tol·stoy, Le·o (tŏl·stoi')
tom·a·hawk (tŏm' ȧ·hôk)
to·ma·to (tȯ·mā' tō)
-toes
tomb·stone (tōōm' stōn')
tom·boy·ish (tŏm' boi' ĭsh)
tome (tōm)
tom·fool·er·y (tŏm' fōōl' ẽr·ĭ)

to·mor·row (tōō·mŏr' ō)
tom-tom (tŏm' tŏm')
ton·al (tōn' ăl)
to·nal·i·ty (tȯ·năl' ĭ·tĭ)
tone·less (tōn' lĕs)
tongue (tŭng)
tongue-tied
ton·ic (tŏn' ĭk)
to·nic·i·ty (tȯ·nĭs' ĭ·tĭ)
to·night (tōō·nīt')
ton·nage (tŭn' ĭj)
ton·sil (tŏn' sĭl)
ton·sil·lec·to·my
(tŏn' sĭ·lĕk' tȯ·mĭ)
ton·sil·li·tis (tŏn' sĭ·lī' tĭs)
ton·sure (tŏn' shẽr)
ton·so·ri·al (tŏn·sō' rĭ·ăl)
too (tōō)
(also; see to, two)
tool·mak·er (tōōl' māk' ẽr)
tooth (tōōth)
tooth·ache tooth·brush
tooth·less tooth·pick
top (tŏp)
top·coat top·flight
top hat top-heav·y
top·most top·notch
top·per top·sail
top se·cret top ser·geant
top·soil
to·paz (tō' păz)
top·ic (tŏp' ĭk)
top·i·cal (tŏp' ĭ·kăl)
to·pog·ra·phy (tȯ·pŏg' rȧ·fĭ)
to·pol·o·gy (tȯ·pŏl' ȯ·jĭ)
top·ple (tŏp' 'l)
top·pling
top·sy-tur·vy (tŏp' sĭ·tûr' vĭ)
toque (tōk)
to·rah (tō' rä)
torch·bear·er (tôrch' bâr' ẽr)
tor·e·a·dor (tŏr' ê·ȧ·dôr')
tor·ment (tôr' mĕnt') v.
(tôr' mĕnt) n.
tor·men·tor (tôr·mĕn' tẽr)
tor·na·do (tôr·nā' dō)
-does
tor·pe·do (tôr·pē' dō)
-does
tor·por (tôr' pẽr)
tor·pid (tôr' pĭd)
torque (tôrk)
tor·rent (tŏr' ĕnt)
tor·ren·tial (tȯ·rĕn' shăl)
tor·rid (tŏr' ĭd)

tor·sion (tôr′ shŭn)
tor·so (tôr′ sō)
  -sos
tor·til·la (tôr·tē′ yä)
tor·toise (tôr′ tŭs)
tor·tu·ous (tôr′ tŭ·ŭs)
tor·ture (tôr′ tûr)
  -tur·ing tor·tur·er
To·ry (tō′ rĭ)
  -ries
toss·up (tŏs′ ŭp′)
to·tal (tō′ tăl)
  to·tal·i·ty (tō·tăl′ ĭ·tĭ)
  -ties
  to·tal·ize -iz·ing
  to·tal·ly
to·tal·i·tar·i·an
    (tō·tăl′ ĭ·târ′ ĭ·ăn)
to·tem (tō′ těm)
  to·tem·ic (tō·těm′ ĭk)
tou·can (tōō·kän′)
touch (tŭch)
  touch·a·ble touch·down
  touch·y
tou·ché (tōō′ shā′)
tough (tŭf)
  tough·ened
tou·pee (tōō′ pā′)
tour de force (tōōr′ dĕ fôrs′)
tour·ist (tōōr′ ĭst)
  tour·ism
tour·na·ment (tōōr′ ná·měnt)
tour·ney (tōōr′ nĭ′)
  -neys
tour·ni·quet (tōōr′ nĭ·kĕt)
tou·sled (tou′ z′ld)
to·ward (tō′ ĕrd)
tow·el (tou′ ĕl)
  -eled -el·ing
tow·er (tou′ ĕr)
  -ered -er·ing
tow·head (tō′ hĕd′)
tow·line (tō′ līn′)
town (toun)
  town cri·er town hall
  town·ship towns·peo·ple
tox·ic (tŏk′ sĭk)
  tox·ic·i·ty (tŏks·ĭs′ ĭ·tĭ)
tox·in (tŏk′ sĭn)
trace (trās)
  trac·ing trace·a·ble
  trac·er·y
tra·che·a (trā′ kĕ·á)
trac·ta·ble (trăk′ tá·b′l)

trac·ta·bil·i·ty
    (trăk′ tá·bĭl′ ĭ·tĭ)
trac·tion (trăk′ shŭn)
trac·tor (trăk′ tĕr)
trade (trād)
  trad·ing trade-in
  trade·mark trade name
  trade school trades·man
  trade wind
tra·di·tion (trá·dĭsh′ ŭn)
  tra·di·tion·al, -al·ly
  tra·di·tion·al·ist
traf·fic (trăf′ ĭk)
  traf·ficked traf·fick·ing
trag·e·dy (trăj′ ĕ·dĭ)
  -dies
tra·ge·di·an (trá·jē′ dĭ·ăn)
trag·ic (trăj′ ĭk)
  trag·i·cal·ly
  trag·i·com·ic (trăj′ ĭ·kŏm′ ĭk)
trail·er (trāl′ ĕr)
train (trān)
  train·a·ble
  train·ee (trăn·ē′)
trait (trāt)
trai·tor (trā′ tĕr)
  trai·tor·ous
tra·jec·to·ry (trá·jĕk′ tô·rĭ)
tram·meled (trăm′ ĕld)
tram·ple (trăm′ p′l)
  -pling
tram·po·line (trăm′ pŏ·lĭn)
tram·way (trăm′ wā′)
trance (trăns)
tran·quil (trăng′ kwĭl)
  tran·quil·iz·er
  tran·quil·li·ty (trăn·kwĭl′ ĭ·tĭ)
  tran·quil·ly
trans·act (trăns·ăkt′)
  trans·ac·tion
trans·at·lan·tic
    (trăns′ ăt·lăn′ tĭk)
tran·scend (trăn·sĕnd′)
  tran·scend·ent (trăn·sĕn′ dĕnt)
  -ence
  tran·scen·den·tal
    (trăn′ sĕn·dĕn′ tăl)
tran·scribe (trăn·skrīb′)
  -scrib·ing
  tran·scrip·tion
    (trăn·skrĭp′ shŭn)
tran·sept (trăn′ sĕpt)
trans·fer (trăns·fûr′)
  -ferred -fer·ring
  trans·fer·a·ble

trans·fer·ence   (trăns·fûr' ĕns)
trans·fig·u·ra·tion
        (trăns·fĭg' ū·rā' shŭn)
trans·fixed   (trăns·fĭkst')
trans·for·ma·tion
        (trăns' fôr·mā' shŭn)
trans·form·er   (trăns·fôr' mēr)
trans·fu·sion   (trăns·fū' zhŭn)
trans·gress   (trăns·grĕs')
  trans·gres·sion (-grĕsh' ŭn)
  trans·gres·sor   (-grĕs' ēr)
tran·sience   (trăn' shĕns)·
  -sient
tran·sis·tor   (trăn·zĭs' tēr)
trans·it   (trăn' sĭt)
tran·si·tion   (trăn·zĭsh' ŭn)
  tran·si·tion·al
tran·si·tive   (trăn' sĭ·tĭv)
tran·si·to·ry   (trăn' sĭ·tō' rĭ)
trans·late   (trăns·lāt')
  -lat·ing   trans·lat·a·ble
  trans·la·tion   trans·la·tor
trans·lit·er·a·tion
        (trăns·lĭt' ēr·ā' shŭn)
trans·lu·cent   (trăns·lū' sĕnt)
  -cence
trans·mi·gra·tion
        (trăns' mĭ·grā' shŭn)
trans·mit   (trăns·mĭt')
  -mit·ted   -mit·ting
  trans·mit·tal   (trăns·mĭt' ăl)
  trans·mit·ter
trans·mute   (trăns·mūt')
  -mut·ing
tran·som   (trăn' sŭm)
trans·par·ent   (trăns·pâr' ĕnt)
  -en·cy
tran·spire   (trăn·spīr')
  -spir·ing
trans·plant   (trăns·plănt')
trans·port   (trăns·pōrt')
  trans·port·a·ble
  trans·por·ta·tion
        (trăns' pôr·tā' shŭn)
trans·pose   (trăns·pōz')
  -pos·ing
  trans·po·si·tion
        (trăns' pô·zĭsh' ŭn)
Trans·vaal, S. Afr.
        (trăns·väl')
trans·verse   (trăns·vûrs')
tra·peze   (trȧ·pēz')
trap·per   (trăp' ēr)
Trap·pist   (trăp' ĭst)

trau·ma   (trô' mȧ)
  trau·mat·ic   (trô·măt' ĭk)
trav·ail   (trăv' āl)
trav·el   (trăv' ĕl)
  -eled   -el·ing
  trav·el·er
  trav·e·logue   (trăv' ĕ·lŏg)
trav·erse   (trăv' ērs)
  -vers·ing   trav·ers·a·ble
trav·es·ty   (trăv' ĕs·tĭ)
  -ties
trawl·er   (trôl' ēr)
treach·er·y   (trĕch' ēr·ĭ)
  -er·ies   treach·er·ous
trea·cle   (trē' k'l)
  trea·cly
trea·dle   (trĕd' 'l)
tread·mill   (trĕd' mĭl')
trea·son   (trē' z'n)
  trea·son·a·ble   trea·son·ous
treas·ure   (trĕzh' ēr)
  treas·ur·er   treas·ur·y
treat   (trēt)
  treat·a·ble   treat·ment
trea·tise   (trē' tĭs)
trea·ty   (trē' tĭ)
  -ties
tre·ble   (trĕb' 'l)
  tre·ble clef
tree·top   (trē' tŏp')
tre·foil   (trē' foil)
trek   (trĕk)
  trekked   trek·king
trel·lis   (trĕl' ĭs)
trem·ble   (trĕm' b'l)
  -bling
tre·men·dous   (trē·mĕn' dŭs)
trem·o·lo   (trĕm' ô·lō)
trem·or   (trĕm' ēr)
trem·u·lous   (trĕm' û·lŭs)
trench·ant   (trĕn' chȧnt)
trep·i·da·tion   (trĕp' ĭ·dā' shŭn)
tres·pass·er   (trĕs' păs·ēr)
tres·tle   (trĕs' 'l)
tri·ad   (trī' ăd)
tri·al   (trī' ăl)
tri·an·gle   (trī' ăng' g'l)
  tri·an·gu·lar   (trī·ăng' gû·lēr)
Tri·as·sic   (trī·ăs' ĭk)
tribe   (trīb)
  trib·al   tribes·man
trib·u·la·tion   (trĭb' û·lā' shŭn)
trib·une   (trĭb' ûn)
tri·bu·nal   (trī·bū' năl)

trib·u·tar·y (trĭb′ ŭ·tĕr′ ĭ)
-tar·ies

trib·ute (trĭb′ ŭt)

trice (trīs)

tri·ceps (trī′ sĕps)

tri·chi·na (trĭ·kī′ nà)
trich·i·no·sis (trĭk′ ĭ·nō′ sĭs)

trick·er·y (trĭk′ ĕr·ĭ)

trick·le (trĭk′ 'l)
-ling

tri·col·or (trī′ kŭl′ ẽr)

tri·cot (trē′ kō)

tri·cy·cle (trī′ sĭk·'l)

tri·dent (trī′ dĕnt)

tri·en·ni·al (trī·ĕn′ ĭ·ăl)

tri·fling (trī′ flĭng)

trig·ger (trĭg′ ẽr)

tri·lin·gual (trī·lĭng′ gwăl)

tril·lion (trĭl′ yŭn)
(number)

tril·li·um (trĭl′ ĭ·ŭm)
(flower)

tril·o·gy (trĭl′ ō·jĭ)
-gies

trim·ming (trĭm′ ĭng)

trin·i·ty (trĭn′ ĭ·tĭ)

trin·ket (trĭng′ kĕt)

tri·o (trē′ ō)
-os

tri·par·tite (trī·pär′ tīt)

tri·ple (trĭp′ 'l)
-pling
tri·plet (trĭp′ lĕt)
tri·ply
trip·li·cate (trĭp′ lĭ·kāt)

tri·pod (trī′ pŏd)

trip·tych (trĭp′ tĭk)

trite (trīt)
trite·ness

tri·umph (trī′ ŭmf)
tri·um·phal (trī·ŭm′ făl)
tri·um·phant (trī·ŭm′ fănt)
tri·um·vi·rate (trī·ŭm′ vĭ·rāt)

triv·et (trĭv′ ĕt)

triv·i·a (trĭv′ ĭ·à)

triv·i·al (trĭv′ ĭ·ăl)
triv·i·al·i·ty (trĭv′ ĭ·ăl′ ĭ·tĭ)
triv·i·al·ly

trod·den (trŏd′ 'n)

troi·ka (troi′ kà)

trol·ley (trŏl′ ĭ)
trol·leys

trol·lop (trŏl′ ŭp)

trom·bone (trŏm′ bōn)

troop (trōōp)
(boy scouts, soldiers; see troupe)

tro·phy (trō′ fĭ)
-phies

trop·ic (trŏp′ ĭk)
trop·i·cal

tro·pism (trō′ pĭz'm)

trop·o·sphere (trŏp′ ō·sfēr)

trot·ter (trŏt′ ẽr)

trou·ba·dour (trōō′ bà·dōōr)

trou·ble (trŭb′ 'l)
-bling   trou·ble·some
trou·blous

trough (trôf)

troupe (trōōp)
(actors; see troop)

trou·sers (trou′ zẽrs)

trous·seau (trōō′ sō′)
pl. trous·seaux (-sō′)

trout (trout)

trow·el (trou′ ĕl)
-eled   -el·ing

tru·ant (trōō′ ănt)
-an·cy

truce (trōōs)

truck·age (trŭk′ ĭj)

truck·le (trŭk′ 'l)
-ling

truc·u·lence (trŭk′ ŭ·lĕns)

trudge (trŭj)
trudg·ing
trudg·en stroke (trŭj′ ĕn)

true (trōō)
true·love   true·ness
tru·ism   tru·ly

truf·fle (trŭf′ 'l)

trum·pet·er (trŭm′ pĕt·ẽr)

trun·cate (trŭng′ kāt)
-cat·ing

trun·dle bed (trŭn′ d'l)

trun·nion (trŭn′ yŭn)

truss (trŭs)

trus·tee (trŭs·tē′)
(one holding property in trust;
see trusty)
trus·tee·ship

trust·ful (trŭst′ fŏŏl)
-ful·ly   -ful·ness

trust·wor·thy (trŭst′ wûr′ thĭ)
-wor·thi·ness

trust·y (trŭs′ tĭ)
(convict allowed special privi-
leges; see trustee)
trust·ies

truth·ful (trōōth′ fŏŏl)
　-ful·ly -ful·ness
fry (trī)
　tried try·ing
　try·out
tryst·ing place (trĭs′ tĭng)
tsar (zär)
　(or czar)
tset·se fly (tsĕt′ sē)
tu·ba (tū′ bá)
　pl. tu·bae (-bē)
tub·ba·ble (tŭb′ á·b′l)
tu·ber·cu·lar (tū·bûr′ kū·lĕr)
　tu·ber·cu·lo·sis
　　　(tū·bûr′ kū·lō′ sĭs)
tu·ber·ous (tū′ bĕr·ŭs)
tub·ing (tūb′ ĭng)
tu·bu·lar (tū′ bū·lĕr)
Tuc·son, Ariz. (tōō·sŏn′)
Tu·dor (tū′ dĕr)
Tues·day (tūz′ dĭ)
tuft·ed (tŭf′ tĕd)
tu·i·tion (tū·ĭsh′ ŭn)
tu·la·re·mi·a (tōō′ lá·rē′ mĭ·á)
tu·lip (tū′ lĭp)
tum·ble-down (tŭm′ b′l·doun′)
tum·ble·weed (tŭm′ b′l·wēd′)
tu·mor (tū′ mĕr)
tu·mult (tū′ mŭlt)
　tu·mul·tu·ous (tū·mŭl′ tū·ŭs)
tu·na fish (tōō′ ná)
tun·dra (tŏŏn′ drá)
tune·ful (tūn′ fŏŏl)
　-ful·ly -ful·ness
　tune·less
tung·sten (tŭng′ stĕn)
tu·nic (tū′ nĭk)
tun·ing fork (tūn′ ĭng)
Tu·ni·si·a (tū·nĭzh′ ĭ·á)
tun·nel (tŭn′ ĕl)
　tun·neled tun·nel·ing
tur·ban (tûr′ bán)
　(headdress)
tur·bine (tûr′ bĭn)
　(rotary engine)
tur·bo·jet en·gine
　　　(tûr′ bō·jĕt′)
tur·bu·lent (tûr′ bū·lĕnt)
　-lence
tu·reen (tū·rēn′)
turf (tûrf)
tur·gid (tûr′ jĭd)
　tur·gid·i·ty (tûr·jĭd′ ĭ·tĭ)
tur·key (tûr′ kĭ)
　-keys

Turk·ish (tûr′ kĭsh)
tur·mer·ic (tûr′ mĕr·ĭk)
tur·moil (tûr′ moil)
turn (tûrn)
　(revolve; see *tern*)
　turn·a·bout turn·coat
　turn·key turn·out
　turn·o·ver turn·pike
　turn·plate turn·stile
　turn·ta·ble
tur·nip (tûr′ nĭp)
tur·pen·tine (tûr′ pĕn·tĭn)
tur·pi·tude (tûr′ pĭ·tūd)
tur·quoise (tûr′ koiz)
tur·ret (tûr′ ĕt)
　tur·ret·ed
tur·tle (tûr′ t′l)
　tur·tle·back tur·tle-neck *adj.*
tus·sle (tŭs′ ′l)
　tus·sling
tu·te·lage (tū′ tĕ·lĭj)
tu·te·lar·y (tū′ tĕ·lĕr′ ĭ)
tu·tor (tū′ tĕr)
　tu·tor·age (tū′ tĕr·ĭj)
　tu·to·ri·al (tū·tō′ rĭ·ál)
tux·e·do (tŭk·sē′ dō)
　-dos
twad·dle (twŏd′ ′l)
twain (twān)
twang (twăng)
tweak (twēk)
tweed (twēd)
tweet·er (twēt′ ĕr)
tweez·ers (twēz′ ĕrz)
twelfth (twĕlfth)
twen·ty (twĕn′ tĭ)
　-ties twen·ti·eth
　twen·ty-twen·ty
twice (twīs)
twi·light (twī′ līt′)
twinge (twĭnj)
　twing·ing
twin·kle (twĭng′ k′l)
　-kling
twirl (twûrl)
twist·er (twĭs′ tĕr)
twitch (twĭch)
two (tōō)
　(pair; see *to, too*)
　two-by-four two-faced
　two-fist·ed two-fold
　two·some two-way
ty·coon (tī·kōōn′)
ty·ing (tī′ ĭng)
tyke (tīk)

tym·pan·ic (tĭm·păn′ ĭk)
type (tīp)
  typ·ing   type·script
  type·set·ter   type·writ·er
ty·phoid (tī′ foid)
ty·phoon (tī·fōōn′)
ty·phus (tī′ fŭs)
typ·i·cal (tĭp′ ĭ·kəl)
  typ·i·cal·ly   -cal·ness
typ·i·fy (tĭp′ ĭ·fī)
  -fied   -fy·ing
typ·ist (tĭp′ ĭst)
ty·pog·ra·phy (tī·pŏg′ rə·fĭ)
  ty·po·graph·i·cal
             (tī′ pō·grăf′ ĭ·kəl)
tyr·an·ny (tĭr′ ə·nĭ)
  -an·nies
  ty·ran·ni·cal (tĭ·răn′ ĭ·kəl)
  tyr·an·nize   -an·niz·ing
  tyr·an·nous
ty·rant (tī′ rănt)
ty·ro (tī′ rō)
  -ros

U

u·biq·ui·tous (ū·bĭk′ wĭ·tŭs)
  u·biq·ui·ty (-tĭ)
U-boat (ū′ bōt′)
ud·der (ŭd′ ər)
ugh (ŭ)
ug·ly (ŭg′ lĭ)
  ug·li·er, -li·est, -li·ness
u·ku·le·le (ū′ kŭ·lā′ lĕ)
ul·cer (ŭl′ sĕr)
  ul·ce·ra·tion (ŭl′ sĕr·ā′ shŭn)
  ul·cer·ous
ul·te·ri·or (ŭl·tēr′ ĭ·ĕr)
ul·ti·mate (ŭl′ tĭ·mĭt)
  -mate·ly
ul·ti·ma·tum (ŭl′ tĭ·mā′ tŭm)
ul·tra- (ŭl′ trə-)
  ul·tra·con·serv·a·tive
  ul·tra·lib·er·al ul·tra·ma·rine
  ul·tra·mod·ern
  ul·tra·vi·o·let
U·lys·ses (ū·lĭs′ ēz)
um·ber (ŭm′ bĕr)
um·bil·i·cal cord
           (ŭm·bĭl′ ĭ·kəl)
um·brage (ŭm′ brĭj)
um·brel·la (ŭm·brĕl′ ə)
um·laut (ōōm′ lout)
um·pire (ŭm′ pīr)

un·a·ble (ŭn·ā′ b'l)
un·a·bridged (ŭn′ ə·brĭjd′)
un·ac·count·a·ble
         (ŭn′ ə·koun′ tə·b'l)
un·ac·cus·tomed
         (ŭn′ ə·kŭs′ tŭmd)
un·af·fect·ed (ŭn′ ə·fĕk′ tĕd)
un·A·mer·i·can
         (ŭn′ ə·mĕr′ ĭ·kăn)
u·na·nim·i·ty (ū′ nə·nĭm′ ĭ·tĭ)
  u·nan·i·mous (ū·năn′ ĭ·mŭs)
un·as·sum·ing (ŭn′ ə·sŭm′ ĭng)
un·a·void·a·ble
         (ŭn′ ə·void′ ə·b'l)
un·be·com·ing
         (ŭn′ bē·kŭm′ ĭng)
un·be·knownst (ŭn′ bē·nōnst′)
un·bi·ased (ŭn·bī′ əst)
un·bid·den (ŭn·bĭd′ 'n)
un·bri·dled (ŭn·brī′ d'ld)
un·can·ny (ŭn·kăn′ ĭ)
un·cer·e·mo·ni·ous
         (ŭn′ sĕr·ə·mō′ nĭ·ŭs)
un·cer·tain·ty (ŭn·sûr′ tĭn·tĭ)
  -ties
un·chris·tian (ŭn·krĭs′ chăn)
un·civ·i·lized (ŭn·sĭv′ ĭ·līzd)
un·clas·si·fi·a·ble
         (ŭn·klăs′ ĭ·fī′ ə·b'l)
un·cle (ŭng′ k'l)
un·com·fort·a·ble
         (ŭn·kŭm′ fẽrt·ə·b'l)
un·com·mit·ted (ŭn′ kə·mĭt′ ĕd)
un·com·mon (ŭn·kŏm′ ŭn)
  un·com·mon·ly
  un·com·mon·ness
un·com·mu·ni·ca·tive
         (ŭn′ kə·mū′ nĭ·kā′ tĭv)
un·com·pro·mis·ing
         (ŭn·kŏm′ prō·mīz′ ĭng)
un·con·cern·ed·ly
         (ŭn′ kŏn·sûr′ nĕd·lĭ)
un·con·di·tion·al
         (ŭn′ kŏn·dĭsh′ ŭn·əl)
un·con·scion·a·ble
         (ŭn·kŏn′ shŭn·ə·b'l)
un·con·scious (ŭn·kŏn′ shŭs)
un·con·sti·tu·tion·al
         (ŭn′ kŏn·sti·tū′ shŭn·əl)
un·couth (ŭn·kōōth′)
unc·tion (ŭngk′ shŭn)
unc·tu·ous (ŭngk′ tū·ŭs)
un·daunt·ed (ŭn·dôn′ tĕd)
un·de·mon·stra·tive
         (ŭn′ dē·mŏn′ strə·tĭv)

un·de·ni·a·ble (ŭn′ dē·nī′ á·b'l)
un·der (ŭn′ dẽr)
  un·der·brush   un·der·clothes
  un·der·cur·rent
  un·der·es·ti·mate
  un·der·ex·po·sure
  un·der·grad·u·ate
  un·der·hand·ed
  un·der·lie   -ly·ing
  un·der·neath
  un·der·nour·ished
  un·der·pin·ning
  un·der·priv·i·leged
  un·der·rate   un·der·signed
  un·der·stand·a·ble
  un·der·stood   un·der·tow
  un·der·weight un·der·writ·er
un·de·sir·a·ble
        (ŭn′ dē·zīr′ á·b'l)
un·do·ing (ŭn·dōō′ ĭng)
un·doubt·ed·ly
un·du·la·tion (ŭn′ dū·lā′ shŭn)
un·du·ly (ŭn·dū′ lĭ)
un·dy·ing (ŭn·dī′ ĭng)
un·eas·i·ness (ŭn·ēz′ ĭ·nĕs)
un·em·ploy·a·ble
        (ŭn′ ĕm·ploi′ á·b'l)
un·e·qual (ŭn·ē′ kwăl)
  -qualed   un·e·qual·ly
un·e·quiv·o·cal
       (ŭn′ ē·kwĭv′ ô·kăl)
  -cal·ly
un·err·ing (ŭn·ûr′ ĭng)
un·e·ven·ness (ŭn·ē′ vĕn·nĕs)
un·ex·pur·gat·ed
       (ŭn·ĕks′ pẽr·gāt′ ĕd)
un·faith·ful (ŭn·fāth′ fool)
  -ful·ly,   -ful·ness
un·fa·mil·i·ar·i·ty
      (ŭn′ fá·mĭl′ ĭ·ăr′ ĭ·tĭ)
un·fas·ten (ŭn·fás′ 'n)
un·fa·vor·a·ble
      (ŭn·fā′ vẽr·á·b'l)
un·feigned (ŭn·fānd′)
un·fet·tered (ŭn·fĕt′ ẽrd)
un·flinch·ing (ŭn·flĭn′ chĭng)
un·for·get·ta·ble
      (ŭn′ fôr·gĕt′ á·b'l)
un·for·tu·nate·ly
      (ŭn·fôr′ tū·nĭt·lĭ)
un·friend·li·ness
      (ŭn·frĕnd′ lĭ·nĕs)
un·furled (ŭn·fûrld′)

un·gain·li·ness
      (ŭn·gān′ lĭ·nĕs)
un·grace·ful (ŭn·grās′ fool)
un·grate·ful (ŭn·grāt′ fool)
un·hap·pi·ness (ŭn·hăp′ ĭ·nĕs)
un·har·nessed (ŭn·här′ nĕst)
un·hinged (ŭn·hĭnjd′)
un·hur·ried (ŭn·hûr′ ĭd)
u·ni·cam·er·al
      (ū′ nĭ·kăm′ ẽr·ăl)
u·ni·corn (ū′ nĭ·kôrn)
u·ni·fi·ca·tion (ū′ nĭ·fĭ·kā′ shŭn)
u·ni·form·i·ty (ū′ nĭ·fôr′ mĭ·tĭ)
u·ni·fy (ū′ nĭ·fĭ)
  -fied,   -fy·ing
u·ni·lat·er·al (ū′ nĭ·lăt′ ẽr·ăl)
un·im·peach·a·ble
      (ŭn′ ĭm·pēch′ á·b'l)
un·ion·ize (ūn′ yŭn·īz)
  -iz·ing
u·nique (ū·nēk′)
  -nique·ly
u·ni·son (ū′ nĭ·sŭn)
u·nit (ū′ nĭt)
u·ni·tar·y (ū′ nĭ·tĕr′ ĭ)
u·nite (ū·nīt′)
  -nit·ing
u·ni·ty (ū′ nĭ·tĭ)
  -ties
u·ni·ver·sal (ū′ nĭ·vûr′ săl)
  -sal·ly
u·ni·ver·sal·i·ty
      (ū′ nĭ·vûr·săl′ ĭ·tĭ)
u·ni·verse (ū′ nĭ·vûrs)
u·ni·ver·si·ty (ū′ nĭ·vûr′ sĭ·tĭ)
  -ties
un·kempt (ŭn·kĕmpt′)
un·know·a·ble (ŭn·nō′ á·b'l)
un·leash (ŭn·lēsh′)
un·less (ŭn·lĕs′)
un·like·ly (ŭn·līk′ lĭ)
  un·like·li·hood
un·lim·it·ed (ŭn·lĭm′ ĭ·tĕd)
un·men·tion·a·ble
      (ŭn·mĕn′ shŭn·á·b'l)
un·mer·ci·ful (ŭn·mûr′ sĭ·fool)
un·mis·tak·a·ble
      (ŭn·mĭs·tāk′ á·b'l)
un·mit·i·gat·ed
      (ŭn·mĭt′ ĭ·gāt′ ĕd)
un·named (ŭn·nāmd′)
un·nat·u·ral (ŭn·năt′ û·răl)
un·nec·es·sar·y
      (ŭn·nĕs′ ĕ·sĕr′ ĭ)
un·nerv·ing (ŭn·nûrv′ ĭng)

un·num·bered (ŭn·nŭm′ bĕrd)
un·oc·cu·pied (ŭn·ŏk′ û·pĭd)
un·par·al·leled (ŭn·păr′ ă·lĕld)
un·plumbed (ŭn·plŭmd′)
un·prec·e·dent·ed
    (ŭn·prĕs′ ê·dĕn′ tĕd)
un·prej·u·diced
    (ŭn·prĕj′ ŏŏ·dĭst)
un·prin·ci·pled
    (ŭn·prĭn′ sĭ·p'ld)
un·pro·nounce·a·ble
    (ŭn′ prô·nouns′ ă·b'l)
un·qual·i·fied (ŭn·kwŏl′ ĭ·fīd)
un·ques·tion·a·ble
    (ŭn·kwĕs′ chŭn·ă·b'l)
un·rav·eled (ŭn·răv′ ĕld)
un·re·al·i·ty (ŭn′ rē·ăl′ ĭ·tĭ)
un·rea·son·a·ble
    (ŭn·rē′ z'n·ă·b'l)
un·re·con·struct·ed
    (ŭn′ rē·kŏn·strŭk′ tĕd)
un·re·lent·ing (ŭn·rē·lĕn′ tĭng)
un·re·mit·ting (ŭn′ rē·mĭt′ ĭng)
un·right·eous (ŭn·rī′ chŭs)
un·ri·valed (ŭn·rī′ văld)
un·ruf·fled (ŭn·rŭf′ 'ld)
un·rul·y (ŭn·rōōl′ ĭ)
  un·rul·i·ness
un·sat·u·rat·ed
    (ŭn·săt′ û·rāt′ ĕd)
un·sa·vor·y (ŭn·sā′ vĕr·ĭ)
  un·sa·vor·i·ness
un·sea·son·a·ble
    (ŭn·sē′ z'n·ă·b'l)
un·seem·ly (ŭn·sēm′ lĭ)
un·shack·led (ŭn·shăk′ 'ld)
un·sheathe (ŭn·shēth′)
  -sheath·ing
un·skill·ful (ŭn·skĭl′ fŏŏl)
un·so·cia·ble (ŭn·sō′ shá·b'l)
un·so·phis·ti·cat·ed
    (ŭn′ sô·fĭs′ tĭ·kāt′ ĕd)
un·spar·ing (ŭn·spâr′ ĭng)
un·speak·a·ble (ŭn·spēk′ ă·b'l)
un·spot·ted (ŭn·spŏt′ ĕd)
un·sub·stan·tial
    (ŭn′ sŭb·stăn′ shăl)
un·suit·a·ble (ŭn·sūt′ á·b'l)
un·tan·gled (ŭn·tăng′ g'ld)
un·tie (ŭn·tī′)
  -tied   -ty·ing
un·til (ŭn·tĭl′)
un·time·ly (ŭn·tīm′ lĭ)
un·ti·tled (ŭn·tī′ t'ld)
un·touch·a·ble (ŭn′ tŭch′ á·b'l)

un·to·ward (ŭn·tō′ ĕrd)
un·tram·meled (ŭn·trăm′ ĕld)
un·truth·ful (ŭn·trōōth′ fŏŏl)
un·tu·tored (ŭn·tō′ tĕrd)
un·u·su·al (ŭn·û′ zhŏŏ·ăl)
  un·u·su·al·ly
un·ut·ter·a·ble (ŭn·ŭt′ ĕr·á·b'l)
un·want·ed (ŭn·wŏnt·ĕd)
  (not desired; see *unwonted*)
un·war·rant·a·ble
    (ŭn·wŏr′ ăn·tá·b'l)
un·war·y (ŭn·wâr′ ĭ)
  -war·i·ness
un·whole·some
    (ŭn·hōl′ săm)
un·wield·y (ŭn·wēl′ dĭ)
un·wit·ting (ŭn·wĭt′ ĭng)
un·wont·ed (ŭn·wŭn′ tĕd)
  (unaccustomed; see *unwanted*)
un·world·li·ness
    (ŭn·wûrld′ lĭ·nĕs)
up (ŭp)
  up·braid·ing   up·date
  up·grade   up·heav·al
  up·hol·ster·y   up·lift·ing
  up·right   up·roar·i·ous
  up·stairs   up-to-date *adj.*
  up·town   up·ward
up·per (ŭp′ ĕr)
  up·per-class   up·per·most
u·ra·ni·um (û·rā′ nĭ·ŭm)
ur·ban (ûr′ băn)
  ur·ban·i·za·tion
    (ûr′ băn·ĭ·zā′ shŭn)
  ur·ban·ize   -iz·ing
ur·bane (ŭr·băn′)
  ur·bane·ly
ur·chin (ûr′ chĭn)
urge (ûrj)
  urg·ing
ur·gent (ûr′ jĕnt)
  -gen·cy
u·ri·nal (û′ rĭ·năl)
  u·ri·nar·y (û′ rĭ·nĕr′ ĭ)
urn (ûrn)
Ur·sa Ma·jor (ûr′ sá mā′ jĕr)
U·ru·guay (û′ rŭ·gwī)
  U·ru·guay·an
use (ūs) *n.*
  (ūz) *v.*
  us·ing
  us·a·ble (ūz′ á·b'l)
  us·age (ūs′ ĭj)
  use·ful (ūs′ fŏŏl)
  -ful·ly   -ful·ness

use·less	(ūs′ lĕs)
ush·er	(ŭsh′ ĕr)
u·surp	(û·zûrp′)
u·surp·a·tion	(ū′ zẽr·pā′ shŭn)
u·su·ry	(ū′ zhōō·rǐ)
u·su·rer	(ū′ zhōō·rẽr)
u·su·ri·ous	(û·su·rī·ŭs)
U·tah	(ū′ tô)
U·tah·an	
u·ten·sil	(û·tĕn′ sĭl)
u·ter·ine	(ū′ tẽr·ĭn)
u·til·i·tar·i·an	(û·tĭl′ ĭ·târ′ ĭ·ăn)
u·til·i·ty	(û·tĭl′ ĭ·tĭ)
-ties	
u·ti·lize	(ū′ tǐ·līz)
-liz·ing u·ti·liz·a·ble	
u·ti·li·za·tion	
	(ū′ tǐ·lǐ·zā′ shŭn)
ut·most	(ŭt′ mōst)
U·to·pi·an	(û·tō′ pǐ·ăn)
ut·ter	(ŭt′ ẽr)
ut·ter·a·ble ut·ter·ance	
ut·ter·ly ut·ter·most	
u·vu·la	(ū′ vū·lȧ)

V

va·cant	(vā′ kănt)
va·can·cy	
va·cate	(vā′ kāt)
-cat·ing	
va·ca·tion	(vå·kā′ shŭn)
vac·ci·nate	(văk′ sǐ·nāt)
-nat·ing	
vac·ci·na·tion	
	(văk′ sǐ·nā′ shŭn)
vac·cine	(văk′ sēn)
vac·il·late	(văs′ ǐ·lāt)
-il·lat·ing	
vac·il·la·tion	(văs′ ǐ·lā′ shŭn)
vac·u·ous	(văk′ û·ŭs)
va·cu·i·ty	(vå·kū′ ǐ·tǐ)
vac·u·um clean·er	
	(văk′ û·ŭm)
vag·a·bond	(văg′ ȧ·bŏnd)
va·gar·y	(vȧ·gâr′ ǐ)
gar·ies	
va·gi·na	(vȧ·jī′ nȧ)
va·gran·cy	(vā′ grăn·sǐ)
vague	(vāg)
vague·ly	
vain	(văn)
(empty; conceited; see vane, vein)	
vain·glo·ri·ous	(văn′ glō′ rǐ·ŭs)

val·ance	(văl′ ăns)
(drapery; see valence)	
val·e·dic·to·ry	(văl′ ê·dǐk′ tô·rǐ)
val·e·dic·to·ri·an	
	(văl′ ê·dǐk·tō′ rǐ·ăn)
va·lence	(vā′ lĕns)
(of chemical elements; see valance)	
val·en·tine	(văl′ ĕn·tīn)
val·et	(văl′ ĕt)
val·iant	(văl′ yănt)
-iance	
val·id	(văl′ ĭd)
val·i·date	-dat·ing
va·lid·i·ty	(vȧ·lĭd′ ǐ·tǐ)
va·lise	(vȧ·lēs′)
Val·kyr·ie	(văl·kĭr′ ĭ)
val·ley	(văl′ ĭ)
val·or	(văl′ ẽr)
val·or·ous	
Val·pa·rai·so, Chile	(văl′ på·rā′ zō)
val·ue	(văl′ û)
-u·ing	
val·u·a·ble	(văl′ û·ȧ·b'l)
val·u·a·tion	(văl′ û·ā′ shŭn)
val·ue·less	
vam·pire	(văm′ pīr)
van·dal	(văn′ dăl)
Van·der·bilt (univ.)	
	(văn′ dẽr·bĭlt)
Van·dyke (beard)	
	(văn·dīk′)
vane	(văn)
(weathercock; see vain, vein)	
van·guard	(văn′ gärd′)
va·nil·la	(vȧ·nĭl′ ȧ)
van·ish	(văn′ ĭsh)
van·i·ty	(văn′ ǐ·tǐ)
-ties	
van·quish	(văng′ kwĭsh)
van·tage	(văn′ tĭj)
vap·id	(văp′ ĭd)
va·por	(vā′ pẽr)
va·por·ize	-iz·ing
va·por·ous	
var·i·a·ble	(vâr′ ǐ·ȧ·b'l)
var·i·a·bil·i·ty	
	(vâr′ ǐ·ȧ·bǐl′ ǐ·tǐ)
var·i·ant	(vâr′ ǐ·ănt)
-ance	
var·i·a·tion	(vâr′ ǐ·ā′ shŭn)
var·i·cose vein	(văr′ ǐ·kōs)
var·ied	(vâr′ ĭd)
var·i·e·gat·ed	(vâr′ ǐ·ê·gāt′ ĕd)

va·ri·e·ty (vá·rī′ ĕ·tĭ)
-ties
var·i·ous (vâr′ ĭ·ŭs)
var·let (vär′ lĕt)
var·si·ty (vär′ sĭ·tĭ)
var·y (vâr′ ĭ)
var·ied, var·ies, var·y·ing
vas·cu·lar (văs′ kū·lẽr)
vas·o·mo·tor (văs′ ò·mō′ tẽr)
vas·sal (văs′ ăl)
vas·sal·age
Vas·sar (coll.) (văs′ ẽr)
Vat·i·can (văt′ ĭ·kăn)
vau·de·ville (vô′ dĕ·vĭl)
vault·ed (vôl′ tĕd)
veal (vēl)
vec·tor (vĕk′ tẽr)
veer·ing (vēr′ ĭng)
veg·e·ta·ble (vĕj′ ĕ·tà·b′l)
veg·e·tar·i·an (vĕj′ ĕ·târ′ ĭ·ăn)
veg·e·tate (vĕj′ ĕ·tāt)
-tat·ing
veg·e·ta·tion (vĕj′ ĕ·tā′ shŭn)
veg·e·ta·tive (vĕj′ ĕ·tā′ tĭv)
ve·he·ment (vē′ ĕ·mĕnt)
-mence
ve·hi·cle (vē′ ĭ·k′l)
ve·hic·u·lar (vē·hĭk′ ū·lẽr)
veil·ing (vāl′ ĭng)
vein (vān)
(fissure; see vain, vane)
vel·lum (vĕl′ ŭm)
ve·loc·i·pede (vē·lŏs′ ĭ·pĕd)
ve·loc·i·ty (vē·lŏs′ ĭ·tĭ)
-ties
ve·lours (vē·lōōr′)
vel·vet (vĕl′ vĕt)
vel·vet·een (vĕl′ vĕ·tēn′)
ve·nal (vē′ năl)
(mercenary; see venial)
ve·nal·i·ty (vē·năl′ ĭ·tĭ)
ven·det·ta (vĕn·dĕt′ à)
ven·dor (vĕn′ dẽr)
ven·due (vĕn′ dū)
ve·neer (vē·nēr′)
ven·er·ate (vĕn′ ẽr·āt)
-at·ing
ven·er·a·ble (vĕn′ ẽr·à·b′l)
ven·er·a·tion (vĕn′ ẽr·ā′ shŭn)
ve·ne·re·al (vē·nēr′ ĕ·ăl)
ven·er·y (vĕn′ ẽr·ĭ)
Ve·ne·tian (vē·nē′ shăn)
venge·ance (vĕn′ jăns)
venge·ful (vĕnj′ fŏŏl)
-ful·ly -ful·ness

ve·ni·al (vē′ nĭ·ăl)
(excusable; see venal)
ven·i·son (vĕn′ ĭ·z′n)
ven·om (vĕn′ ŭm)
ven·om·ous (vĕn′ ŭm·ŭs)
ve·nous (vē′ nŭs)
(of veins; see Venus)
ven·ti·late (vĕn′ tĭ·lāt)
-lat·ing
ven·ti·la·tion (vĕn′ tĭ·lā′ shŭn)
ven·ti·la·tor
ven·tral (vĕn′ trăl)
ven·tril·o·quist
(vĕn·trĭl′ ò·kwĭst)
ven·ture (vĕn′ tûr)
-tur·ing ven·ture·some
ven·tur·ous
ven·ue (vĕn′ ū)
Ve·nus (vē′ nŭs)
(goddess of beauty; planet; see venous)
ve·ra·cious (vē·rā′ shŭs)
ve·rac·i·ty (vē·răs′ ĭ·tĭ)
ve·ran·da (vē·răn′ dà)
ver·bal (vûr′ băl)
-bal·ly
ver·bal·i·za·tion
(vûr′ băl·ĭ·zā′ shŭn)
ver·bal·ize -iz·ing
ver·ba·tim (vûr′ bă′ tĭm)
ver·be·na (vēr·bē′ nà)
ver·bi·age (vûr′ bĭ·ĭj)
ver·bose (vûr·bōs′)
ver·bos·i·ty (vûr·bŏs′ ĭ·tĭ)
ver·bo·ten (fẽr·bō′ tĕn)
ver·dant (vûr′ dănt)
-dan·cy
ver·dict (vûr′ dĭkt)
ver·dure (vûr′ dūr)
verge (vûrj)
verg·ing
ver·i·fy (vĕr′ ĭ·fī)
-fied -fy·ing
ver·i·fi·a·ble (vĕr′ ĭ·fī′ à·b′l)
ver·i·ly (vĕr′ ĭ·lĭ)
ver·i·si·mil·i·tude
(vĕr′ ĭ·sī·mĭl′ ĭ·tūd)
ver·i·ta·ble (vĕr′ ĭ·tà·b′l)
ver·i·ty (vĕr′ ĭ·tĭ)
-ties
ver·mi·cel·li (vûr′ mĭ·sĕl′ ĭ)
ver·mil·ion (vēr·mĭl′ yŭn)
ver·min (vûr′ mĭn)
Ver·mont (vēr·mŏnt′)
abbr. Vt. Ver·mont·er

ver·mouth   (vĕr·mōōth′)
ver·nac·u·lar   (vĕr·năk′ ů·lẽr)
ver·nal e·qui·nox
       (vûr′ nål)
Ver·sailles   (vĕr·sälz)
ver·sa·tile   (vûr′ så·tĭl)
   ver·sa·til·i·ty   (vûr′ så·tĭl′ ĭ·tĭ)
verse   (vûrs)
   vers·ing
   ver·si·fi·ca·tion
       (vûr′ sĭ·fĭ·kā′ shŭn)
   ver·si·fy   (vûr′ sĭ·fĭ)
   -fied   -fy·ing
ver·sion   (vûr′ shŭn)
ver·sus   (vûr′ sŭs)
ver·te·bra   (vûr′ tê·brȧ)
   pl. ver·te·brae   (-brē)
   ver·te·bral   (vûr′ tê·brȧl)
ver·te·brate   (vûr′ tê·brȧt)
ver·tex   (vûr′ tĕks)
ver·ti·cal   (vûr′ tĭ·kȧl)
ver·ti·go   (vûr′ tĭ·gō)
ves·pers   (vĕs′ pẽrz)
ves·sel   (vĕs′ 'l)
ves·tal   (vĕs′ tȧl)
vest·ee   (vĕs′ tē′)
ves·ti·bule   (vĕs′ tĭ·būl)
ves·tige   (vĕs′ tĭj)
   ves·tig·i·al   (vĕs·tĭj′ ĭ·ȧl)
vest·ment   (vĕst′ mĕnt)
ves·try   (vĕs′ trĭ)
   -tries
ves·ture   (vĕs′ tûr)
vetch   (vĕch)
vet·er·an   (vĕt′ ẽr·ȧn)
vet·er·i·nar·i·an
       (vĕt′ ẽr·ĭ·nâr′ ĭ·ȧn)
   vet·er·i·nar·y   (vĕt′ ẽr·ĭ·nĕr′ ĭ)
ve·to   (vē′ tō)
   -toes
vex·a·tion   (vĕks·ā′ shŭn)
   vex·a·tious   (vĕks·ā′ shŭs)
vi·a   (vī′ ȧ)
vi·a·ble   (vī′ ȧ·b'l)
vi·a·duct   (vī′ ȧ·dŭkt)
vi·al   (vī′ ȧl)
vi·and   (vī′ ȧnd)
vi·brant   (vī′ brȧnt)
   -bran·cy
vi·brate   (vī′ brȧt)
   -brat·ing
   vi·bra·tion   (vī·brā′ shŭn)
   vi·bra·tor   (vī′ brā·tẽr)
vi·bra·to   (vê·brä′ tō)

vic·ar   (vĭk′ ẽr)
   vic·ar·age   (-ĭj)
   vic·ar·ate   (vĭk′ ẽr·åt)
vi·car·i·ous   (vī·kâr′ ĭ·ŭs)
vice   (vīs)
   (in the place of; evil; see *viss*)
vice-   (vīs)
   vice-ad·mi·ral   vice-chan·cel·lor
   vice·ge·rent   (vīs′ jẽr′ ĕnt)
   vice-pres·i·dent
   vice·roy
vice ver·sa   (vī′ sê vûr′ så)
vi·cin·i·ty   (vī·sĭn′ ĭ·tĭ)
   -ties
vi·cious   (vĭsh′ ŭs)
vi·cis·si·tude   (vī·sĭs′ ĭ·tūd)
vic·tim   (vĭk′ tĭm)
   vic·tim·i·za·tion
       (vĭk′ tĭm·ĭ·zā′ shŭn)
   vic·tim·ize   -iz·ing
vic·tor   (vĭk′ tẽr)
   vic·to·ri·ous   (vĭk·tō′ rĭ·ŭs)
   vic·to·ry   -ries
Vic·tro·la   (vĭk·trō′ lȧ)
vict·ual   (vĭt′ 'l)
vi·cu·ña   (vī·kōōn′ yȧ)
vid·e·o   (vĭd′ ê·ō)
vie   (vī)
   vied   vy·ing
Vi·et·nam·ese   (vê·ĕt′ nä·mēz′)
view·point   (vū′ point′)
vig·il   (vĭj′ ĭl)
   vig·i·lance   (vĭj′ ĭ·lȧns)
   -lant
   vig·i·lan·te   (vĭj′ ĭ·lăn′ tê)
vi·gnette   (vĭn·yĕt′)
vig·or   (vĭg′ ẽr)
   vig·or·ous   (vĭg′ ẽr·ŭs)
vi·king   (vī′ kĭng)
vile   (vīl)
   vile·ness
vil·i·fy   (vĭl′ ĭ·fī)
   -fied   -fy·ing
   vil·i·fier
vil·la   (vĭl′ ȧ)
vil·lage   (vĭl′ ĭj)
vil·lain   (vĭl′ ĭn)
   (scoundrel; see *villein*)
   vil·lain·ous
vil·lein   (vĭl′ ĭn)
   (serf; see *villain*)
   vil·len·age
vin·ai·grette sauce
       (vĭn′ å·grĕt′)

Vin·ci, da, Le·o·nar·do
   (dä věn′ chē, lā·ô·när′ dô)
vin·ci·ble (vĭn′ sĭ·b'l)
vin·di·cate (vĭn′ dĭ·kāt)
  -cat·ing
vin·di·ca·tion
        (vĭn′ dĭ·kā′ shŭn)
vin·dic·tive (vĭn·dĭk′ tĭv)
vin·e·gar (vĭn′ ê·gēr)
vine·yard (vĭn′ yērd)
vin·tage (vĭn′ tĭj)
vi·nyl (vī′ nĭl)
vi·o·la (vê·ô′ lä)
vi·o·la·ble (vī′ ô·lä·b'l)
vi·o·late (vī′ ô·lāt)
  -lat·ing
vi·o·la·tion (vī′ ô·lā′ shŭn)
vi·o·lence (vī′ ô·lĕns)
  -lent
vi·o·let (vī′ ô·lĕt)
vi·o·lin (vī′ ô·lĭn′)
vi·o·lin·ist
vi·o·lon·cel·lo
     (vē′ ô·lŏn·chĕl′ ô)
vi·per (vī′ pēr)
vi·ra·go (vĭ·rä′ gō)
  -goes
vir·e·o (vĭr′ ê·ô)
  -os
vir·gin (vûr′ jĭn)
vir·gin·al (vûr′ jĭ·năl)
vir·gin·i·ty (vēr·jĭn′ ĭ·tĭ)
Vir·gin·ia (vēr·jĭn′ yä)
  abbr. Va.
Vir·gin·ian (vēr·jĭn′ yŭn)
  Vir·gin·ia reel
vir·ile (vĭr′ ĭl)
vi·ril·i·ty (vĭ·rĭl′ ĭ·tĭ)
vir·tu·al (vûr′ tũ·ăl)
  -al·ly
vir·tue (vûr′ tũ)
vir·tu·ous (vûr′ tũ·ŭs)
vir·tu·os·i·ty (vûr′ tũ·ŏs′ ĭ·tĭ)
vir·tu·o·so (vûr′ tũ·ô′ sō)
vir·u·lence (vĭr′ û·lĕns)
  -lent
vi·rus (vī′ rŭs)
vi·sa (vē′ zä)
vis·age (vĭz′ ĭj)
vis-à-vis (vē′ zä·vē′)
vis·cer·al (vĭs′ ēr·ăl)
vis·cose (vĭs′ kōs)
vis·cos·i·ty (vĭs·kŏs′ ĭ·tĭ)
vis·cous (vĭs′ kŭs)
vis·count (vī′ kount′)

vise (vīs)
  (device for holding work; see vice)
vis·i·ble (vĭz′ ĭ·b'l)
vis·i·bil·i·ty (vĭz′ ĭ·bĭl′ ĭ·tĭ)
vi·sion (vĭzh′ ŭn)
vi·sion·al   vi·sion·ar·y
vis·it (vĭz′ ĭt)
  -it·ed   vis·it·a·ble
  vis·it·ant (vĭz′ ĭ·tănt)
  vis·it·a·tion (vĭz′ ĭ·tā′ shŭn)
  vis·i·tor
vi·sor (vī′ zēr)
  (front of a cap; see vizier)
vis·ta (vĭs′ tä)
vis·u·al (vĭzh′ û·ăl)
  vis·u·al·ize   -iz·ing
vi·tal (vī′ tăl)
  vi·tal·i·ty (vī·tăl′ ĭ·tĭ)
  vi·tal·ize   -iz·ing
  vi·tal·ly
vi·ta·min (vī′ tä·mĭn)
vi·ti·ate (vĭsh′ ĭ·āt)
  -at·ing
vit·re·ous (vĭt′ rê·ŭs)
vit·ri·fy (vĭt′ rĭ·fī)
  -fied   -fy·ing
vit·ri·ol (vĭt′ rĭ·ŭl)
vi·tu·per·ate (vĭ·tū′ pēr·āt)
  -at·ing
vi·tu·per·a·tion
        (vĭ·tū′ pēr·ā′ shŭn)
vi·tu·per·a·tive
        (vĭ·tū′ pēr·ā′ tĭv)
vi·va·cious (vĭ·vā′ shŭs)
  vi·vac·i·ty (vĭ·văs′ ĭ·tĭ)
viv·id (vĭv′ ĭd)
viv·i·sec·tion (vĭv′ ĭ·sĕk′ shŭn)
vix·en·ish (vĭk′ s'n·ĭsh)
vi·zier (vĭ·zēr′)
  (high official; see visor)
vo·cab·u·lar·y (vô·kăb′ û·lĕr′ ĭ)
  -lar·ies
vo·cal (vō′ kăl)
  vo·cal·ist
  vo·cal·ize   -iz·ing
  vo·cal·ly
vo·ca·tion (vô·kā′ shŭn)
  vo·ca·tion·al
vo·cif·er·ous (vô·sĭf′ ēr·ŭs)
vod·ka (vŏd′ kä)
vogue (vōg)
voice (vois)
  voic·ing   voice·less
void (void)
  void·a·ble

voile	(voil)
vol·a·tile	(vŏl' à·tĭl)
vol·a·til·i·ty	(vŏl' à·tĭl' ĭ·tĭ)
vol·a·til·ize	-ĭz·ing
vol·ca·no	(vŏl·kā' nō)
-noes	
vol·can·ic	(vŏl·kăn' ĭk)
vo·li·tion	(vō·lĭsh' ŭn)
Volks·wa·gen	(fōlks' vä' gĕn)
vol·ley	(vŏl' ĭ)
vol·leys	vol·ley·ball
volt·age	(vŏl' tĭj)
vol·u·ble	(vŏl' ū·b'l)
vol·u·bil·i·ty	(vŏl' ū·bĭl' ĭ·tĭ)
vol·ume	(vŏl' yŭm)
vo·lu·mi·nous	(vō·lū' mĭ·nŭs)
vol·un·tar·y	(vŏl' ŭn·tĕr' ĭ)
vol·un·tar·i·ly	
vol·un·teer	(vŏl' ŭn·tēr')
vo·lup·tu·ous	(vō·lŭp' tū·ŭs)
vo·lup·tu·ar·y	(vō·lŭp' tū·ĕr' ĭ)
vom·it	(vŏm' ĭt)
-it·ed	-it·ing
voo·doo	(vōō' dōō)
vo·ra·cious	(vō·rā' shŭs)
vo·rac·i·ty	(vō·răs' ĭ·tĭ)
vor·tex	(vôr' tĕks)
-tex·es	
vor·ti·cal	(vôr' tĭ·kăl)
vo·ta·ry	(vō' tà·rĭ)
-ries	
vot·ing ma·chine	
	(vōt' ĭng)
vo·tive	(vō' tĭv)
vouch·er	(vouch' ēr)
vouch·safe	(vouch·sāf')
vow·el	(vou' ĕl)
voy·age	(voi' ĭj)
voy·a·ger	
vul·can·ize	(vŭl' kăn·ĭz)
-iz·ing	
vul·gar	(vŭl' gēr)
vul·gar·i·an	(vŭl·gâr' ĭ·ăn)
vul·gar·i·ty	(vŭl·găr' ĭ·tĭ)
-ties	
vul·gar·ize	-iz·ing
Vul·gate	(vŭl' gāt)
vul·ner·a·ble	(vŭl' nĕr·à·b'l)
vul·ner·a·bil·i·ty	
	(vŭl' nĕr·à·bĭl' ĭ·tĭ)
vul·ture	(vŭl' tûr)
vy·ing	(vī' ĭng)

W

wad·dle	(wŏd' 'l)
wad·dling	
wa·fer	(wā' fēr)
waf·fle	(wŏf' 'l)
waft	(wàft)
wa·ger	(wā' jēr)
-gered	-ger·ing
wag·gish	(wăg' ĭsh)
Wag·ne·ri·an	(väg·nēr' ĭ·ăn)
wag·on	(wăg' ŭn)
waif	(wāf)
Wai·ki·ki beach	
	(wī' kĭ·kē')
wail	(wāl)
(to lament; see wale, whale)	
wail·ing	
wain·scot	(wān' skŭt)
-scot·ing	
waist·line	(wāst' līn')
wait·ress	(wāt' rĕs)
waive	(wāv)
(to forgo)	waiv·ing
waiv·er	
wake·ful	(wāk' fŏŏl)
-ful·ly	-ful·ness
wak·en	(wāk' ĕn)
wale	(wāl)
(rib in fabric; see wail, whale)	
walk·ie-talk·ie	(wôk' ĭ·tôk' ĭ)
walk·out	(wôk' out')
wal·la·by	(wŏl' à·bĭ)
-bies	
wal·let	(wŏl' ĕt)
wall·eyed pike	(wôl' īd')
wall·flow·er	(wôl' flou' ēr)
wal·lop·ing	(wŏl' ŭp·ĭng)
wal·low	(wŏl' ō)
wall·pa·per	(wôl' pā' pēr)
wal·nut	(wôl' nŭt)
wal·rus	(wôl' rŭs)
waltz	(wôlts)
wam·pum	(wŏm' pŭm)
wan·der·er	(wŏn' dēr·ēr)
wan·der·lust	(wŏn' dēr·lŭst')
wane	(wān)
wan·ing	
wan·gle	(wăng' g'l)
-gling	
wan·ton	(wŏn' tŭn)
wan·ton·ly	wan·ton·ness
war	(wôr)
war·fare	war·head

war·mon·ger war·time

war·bler (wôr′ blĕr)

war·den (wôr′ d'n)

ward·robe (wôrd′ rōb′)

ware·house (wâr′ hous′)

war·i·ness (wâr′ ĭ·nĕs)

warm (wôrm)
  warm-blood·ed warm·heart·ed
  warmth

warn·ing (wôrn′ ĭng)

war·rant (wôr′ ănt)
  war·rant·a·ble war·rant·ed
  war·rant·y (wôr′ ăn·tĭ)
  war·rant·ies

war·ri·or (wôr′ ĭ·ĕr)

war·y (wâr′ ĭ)
  war·i·er, -i·est, -i·ly, -i·ness

wash (wŏsh)
  wash·board wash·cloth
  washed-up
  wash·er·wom·an
  wash·out wash·room

wasp·ish (wŏsp′ ĭsh)

was·sail (wŏs′ 'l)

Was·ser·mann test
          (wŏs′ ĕr·măn)

waste (wāst)
  wast·ing wast·age
  waste·bas·ket
  waste·ful, -ful·ly, -ful·ness
  waste·pa·per

wast·rel (wās′ trĕl)

watch (wŏch)
  watch·dog
  watch·ful, -ful·ly, -ful·ness
  watch·mak·er watch·man
  watch·word

wa·ter (wô′ tĕr)
  wa·ter-cooled wa·ter·course
  wa·ter·fall wa·ter·fowl
  wa·ter·front wa·ter lil·y
  wa·ter·line
  wa·ter·log -logged
  wa·ter main wa·ter·mel·on
  wa·ter me·ter wa·ter·proof
  wa·ter·side wa·ter·sol·u·ble
  wa·ter·spout wa·ter sup·ply
  wa·ter·tight wa·ter tow·er
  wa·ter va·por wa·ter·way
  wa·ter·y

watt (wŏt)
  watt·age (wŏt′ ĭj)
  watt-hour

wat·tle (wŏt′ 'l)

wa·ver·ing (wā′ vĕr·ĭng)

wav·y (wāv′ ĭ)
  wav·i·ness

wax·en (wăk′ sĕn)

wax·wing (wăks′ wĭng′)

wax·work (wăks′ wûrk′)

wax·y (wăk′ sĭ)
  wax·i·ness

way (wā)
  way·far·er (wā′ fâr′ ĕr)
  way·far·ing way·laid
  way·lay way·side
  way·ward·ness

weak (wēk)
  weak·ened weak-kneed
  weak·ling

wealth (wĕlth)
  wealth·i·ly -i·ness

wean (wēn)

weap·on (wĕp′ ŭn)

wea·ri·some (wĕr′ ĭ·sŭm)
  -some·ly

wea·ry (wĕr′ ĭ)
  -ried, -ry·ing
  wea·ri·ly wea·ri·ness

wea·sel (wē′ z'l)

weath·er (wĕth′ ĕr)
  weath·er-beat·en
  weath·er·cock weath·er gauge
  weath·er·man weath·er·proof
  weath·er vane weath·er-wise

weave (wēv)
  weav·ing

web·bing (wĕb′ ĭng)

wed·ding (wĕd′ ĭng)

wedge (wĕj)
  wedg·ing

Wedg·ie (wĕj′ ĭ)

Wedg·wood ware
        (wĕj′ wŏŏd)

wed·lock (wĕd′ lŏk)

Wednes·day (wĕnz′ dĭ)

week (wēk)
  week·day week end
  week-end adj. week·ly, -lies

wee·vil (wē′ v'l)

weigh (wā)
  weight·y

weird (wērd)

wel·come (wĕl′ kŭm)

weld (wĕld)

wel·fare (wĕl′ fâr′)

well (wĕl)
  (NOTE: When "well" combinations come before a noun, they
  are usually hyphenated, as in

"*well-acted* play.") When "well" combinations come after a verb, the hyphen is usually dropped, as in "The play was *well acted.*"

well-be·ing	well·born
well-bred	well-fa·vored
well-found·ed	well-groomed
well-known	well-mean·ing
well-nigh	well off
well-read	well·spring
well-thought-of	well-to-do
well-wish·er	

Welsh rab·bit   (wĕlsh răb' ĭt)
  (*often incorrectly written* Welsh rarebit)
wel·ter·weight   (wĕl' tẽr·wāt')
wench   (wĕnch)
wept   (wĕpt)
weren't   (wûr' 'nt)
were-wolf   (wēr' wŏŏlf')
Wes·ley·an   (wĕs' lĭ·ăn)
west·er·ly   (wĕs' tẽr·lĭ)
  -lies
west·ern·er   (wĕs' tẽr·nẽr)
west·ern·most   (wĕs' tẽrn·mōst)
West·min·ster Ab·bey
       (wĕst' mĭn' stẽr)
West Vir·gin·ia
       (wĕst vẽr·jĭn' yá)
  abbr. W. Va.
  West Vir·gin·ian
west·ward   (wĕst' wẽrd)
whale   (hwāl)
  (cetacean; see *wail, vale*)
whale·bone   (hwāl' bōn')
wharf   (hwôrf)
  pl. wharves
what   (hwŏt)
  what·ev·er   what·not
  what-so·ev·er
wheat   (hwēt)
whee·dle   (hwē' d'l)
  -dling
wheel   (hwēl)
  wheel·bar·row   wheel base
  wheel chair   wheel·wright
wheeze   (hwēz)
  wheez·ing   wheez·i·ness
  wheez·y
whelp   (hwĕlp)
when   (hwĕn)
  when·ev·er   when-so·ev·er
whence   (hwĕns)
where   (hwâr)
  where·a·bouts   where·as

where·at	where·by
where·fore	where·from
where·in	where·in·to
where·of	where·on
where·so·ev·er	where·to
where·un·to	where·up·on
wher·ev·er	where·with
where·with·al	

wher·ry   (hwĕr' ĭ)
  wher·ries
wheth·er   (hwĕth' ẽr)
  (either, if; see *whither*)
whet·stone   (hwĕt' stōn')
which   (hwĭch)
  which·ev·er
whiff   (hwĭf)
Whig   (hwĭg)
  Whig·gish
while   (hwīl)
  whilst   (hwīlst)
whim·per   (hwĭm' pẽr)
whim·sey   (hwĭm' zĭ)
  whim·si·cal   (hwĭm' zĭ·kăl)
whine   (hwīn)
  whin·ing   whin·y
whin·ny   (hwĭn' ĭ)
  whin·nied   whin·ny·ing
whip   (hwĭp)
  whipped   whip·ping
  whip·cord   whip·stitch
whip·per·snap·per
       (hwĭp' ẽr·snăp' ẽr)
whip·pet   (hwĭp' ĕt)
whip·poor·will   (hwĭp' pŏŏr·wĭl')
whirl   (hwûrl)
  whirl·a·bout
  whirl·i·gig   (hwûr' lĭ·gĭg')
  whirl·pool   whirl·wind
whisk broom   (hwĭsk)
whis·ky   (hwĭs' kĭ)
  -kies
whis·per·ing   (hwĭs' pẽr·ĭng)
whist   (hwĭst)
whis·tle   (hwĭs' 'l)
  -tling
white   (hwīt)
  white·cap   white-col·lar *adj.*
  whit·ed sep·ul·cher
  white·fish   white-head·ed
  white lie   whit·en·er
  white·ness   white oak
  white sauce   white·wash
whith·er   (hwĭth' ẽr)
  (to what place; see *whether*)

whit·tle   (hwĭt' 'l)
  whit·tling
whiz   (hwĭz)
  whizzed   whiz·zing
whoa   (hwō)
who·dun·it   (hōō' dŭn' ĭt)
who·ev·er   (hōō·ĕv' ẽr)
whole   (hōl)
  whole·heart·ed   whole·ness
  whole·sale   whole·some
  whole-wheat adj.
  whol·ly
whom   (hōōm)
whoop·ee   (hwōōp' ē)
whoop·ing cough
        (hōōp' ĭng)
whop·per   (hwŏp' ẽr)
whore   (hōr)
  whore·mon·ger   whor·ish
whorl   (hwûrl)
who's   (hōōz)
  (contraction of who is: "Look
  who's here!")
whose   (hōōz)
  (possessive of who: "Whose coat
  is this?")
who·so   (hōō' sō)
who·so·ev·er   (hōō' sō·ĕv' ẽr)
Wich·i·ta, Kan.   (wĭch' ĭ·tô)
wick·ed   (wĭk' ĕd)
  wick·ed·ness
wick·er   (wĭk' ẽr)
wick·et   (wĭk' ĕt)
wide   (wīd)
  wide-an·gle lens
  wide-a·wake   wide·ly
  wid·en·ing   wide-o·pen
  wide·spread
wid·ow   (wĭd' ō)
  wid·ow·er
width   (wĭdth)
wield·y   (wēl' dĭ)
wife   (wīf)
  pl. wives   wife·ly
wig·gle   (wĭg' 'l)
  wig·gling   wig·gly
wig·wam   (wĭg' wŏm)
wild·cat   (wīld' kăt')
  wild·cat·ter
wil·der·ness   (wĭl' dẽr·nĕs)
wild·fire   (wīld' fīr')
wile   (wīl)
  wil·i·ness   wil·y
Wilkes-Bar·re, Pa.
        (wĭlks' băr' ē)

Wil·lam·ette   (wĭ·lăm' ĕt)
  (riv., Ore.)
will·ful   (wĭl' fōōl)
  -ful·ly   -ful·ness
will-o'-the-wisp (wĭl' ŏ·thē· wĭsp')
wil·low·y   (wĭl' ō·ĭ)
wil·ly-nil·ly   (wĭl' ĭ·nĭl' ĭ)
Wil·mette, Ill.   (wĭl·mĕt')
wim·ple   (wĭm' p'l)
wince   (wĭns)
  winc·ing
winch   (wĭnch)
Win·ches·ter   (wĭn' chĕs' tẽr)
wind   (wĭnd)
  wind-blown   wind·fall
  wind·jam·mer   wind·lass
  wind·pipe   wind·shield
  wind-swept   wind tun·nel
win·dow   (wĭn' dō)
  win·dow·pane   win·dow sill
Wind·sor tie   (wĭn' zẽr)
wine   (wĭn)
  wine·bib·ber   (wĭn' bĭb' ẽr)
  wine cel·lar   wine·glass
  win·er·y   -er·ies
  wine·skin   win·y
wing·spread   (wĭng' sprĕd')
Win·ni·peg, Can.
        (wĭn' ĭ·pĕg)
win·now   (wĭn' ō)
win·some   (wĭn' sŭm)
win·ter   (wĭn' tẽr)
  win·ter·green
  win·ter·ize   -iz·ing
  win·ter·time   win·ter wheat
  win·try
wip·er   (wīp' ẽr)
wire   (wīr)
  wir·ing   wire-haired
  wire·less   Wire·pho·to
  wire tap·per   wir·y
Wis·con·sin   (wĭs·kŏn' s'n)
  abbr. Wis.   Wis·con·sin·ite
wis·dom   (wĭz' dŭm)
wise·a·cre   (wĭz' ā' kẽr)
wise·crack   (wĭz' krăk')
wish·ful   (wĭsh' fōōl)
  -ful·ly   -ful·ness
wis·ta·ri·a   (wĭs·tā' rĭ·à)
wist·ful   (wĭst' fōōl)
  -ful·ly   -ful·ness
witch   (wĭch)
  witch·craft   witch doc·tor
  witch·er·y   witch ha·zel

with (wĭth)
  with·al (wĭth·ôl′)
  with·draw   with·hold·ing
  with·in   with·out
  with·stand
with·er (wĭth′ ẽr)
wit·ness (wĭt′ nĕs)
wit·ti·cism (wĭt′ ĭ·sĭz'm)
wiz·ard (wĭz′ ẽrd)
wiz·ened (wĭz′ 'nd)
wob·ble (wŏb′ 'l)
  wob·bling   wob·bly
woe·be·gone (wō′ bē·gŏn′)
woe·ful (wō′ fŏŏl)
  -ful·ly   -ful·ness
wol·ver·ine (wŏŏl′ vẽr·ēn′)
wom·an (wŏŏm′ ăn)
  pl. wom·en
  wom·an·hood   wom·an·ish
  wom·an·kind   wom·an·li·ness
  wom·an·ly   wom·en·folk
womb (wŏŏm)
wom·bat (wŏm′ băt)
won·der (wŭn′ dẽr)
  won·der·ful, -ful·ly, -ful·ness
  won·der·land   won·der·ment
  won·der-strick·en
won·drous (wŭn′ drŭs)
wont (wŭnt)
won't (wŏnt)
woo (wŏŏ)
  wooed   woo·ing
wood·bine (wŏŏd′ bīn′)
wood·craft (wŏŏd′ krăft′)
wood·en (wŏŏd′ 'n)
  wood·en·ness
wood·peck·er (wŏŏd′ pĕk′ ẽr)
woods·man (wŏŏdz′ măn)
woof·er (wŏŏf′ ẽr)
wool·en (wŏŏl′ ĕn)
wool·ly (wŏŏl′ ĭ)
  wool·li·ness
wooz·y (wŏŏz′ ĭ)
Worces·ter, Mass.
              (wŏŏs′ tẽr)
Worces·ter·shire sauce
        (wŏŏs′ tẽr·shir)
word·y (wûr′ dĭ)
  word·i·ness
work (wûrk)
  work·a·ble   work·a·day
  work·bench   work·day
  work·house   work·man·ship
  work·out   work·shop
  work·week

world (wûrld)
  world·ling   world-wea·ry
  world-wide
world·ly (wûrld′ lĭ)
  world·li·ness   world·ly-wise
worm·wood (wûrm′ wŏŏd′)
worn-out (wŏrn′ out′)
wor·ry (wûr′ ĭ)
  wor·ried   wor·ry·ing
  wor·ri·er   wor·ri·ment
  wor·ri·some
worse (wûrs)
  wors·en
wor·ship (wûr′ shĭp)
  -shiped   -ship·ing
  wor·ship·er   wor·ship·ful
worst (wûrst)
wor·sted (wŏŏs′ tĕd)
worth·while (wûrth′ hwīl′)
wor·thy (wûr′ thĭ)
  wor·thi·er, -i·est, -i·ly, -i·ness
would (wŏŏd)
  would-be   would·n't
wound (wŏŏnd)
  (injury; pron. *wound* when past of
  wind)
wo·ven (wō′ vĕn)
wraith (rāth)
wran·gler (răng′ glẽr)
wrap·per (răp′ ẽr)
wrath·ful (răth′ fŏŏl)
  -ful·ly   -ful·ness
wreak (rēk)
  (give free play to)
wreath (rēth) *n.*
wreathe (rēth) *v.*
  wreath·ing
wreck (rĕk)
  (ruin)   wreck·age
wren (rĕn)
wrench (rĕnch)
wrest (rĕst)
wres·tler (rĕs′ lẽr)
wretch (rĕch)
  (miserable person; see *retch*)
wretch·ed (rĕch′ ĕd)
  wretch·ed·ness
wrig·gle (rĭg′ 'l)
  wrig·gling   wrig·gly
wright (rīt)
  (workman; see *right, rite, write*)
wrin·kle (rĭng′ k'l)
  -kling
wrist (rĭst)
  wrist·band   wrist watch

writ	(rĭt)	yolk	(yōk)
write	(rīt)	(yellow of an egg; see *yoke*)	
(inscribe; see *right, rite, wright*)		yon·der	(yŏn′ dĕr)
writ·ing		York·shire pud·ding	
writ·er's cramp			(yôrk′ shĭr)
write-up		young	(yŭng)
writ·ten	(rĭt′ 'n)	yours	(yŏŏrz)
writhe	(rīth)	your·self	(yŏŏr·sĕlf′)
writh·ing		your·selves	
wrong	(rŏng)	youth·ful	(yŏōth′ fŏŏl)
wrong·do·er wrong·ful		-ful·ly -ful·ness	
wrought	(rôt)	yowl	(youl)
wry	(rī)	yuc·ca plant	(yŭk′ ȧ)
wry·ly wry·ness		Yu·go·sla·vi·a	(yōō′ gō·slä′ vĭ·ȧ)
Wy·o·ming	(wī·ō′ mĭng)	Yu·go·slav	
abbr. Wyo. Wy·o·ming·ite		yule·tide	(yōōl′ tīd′)

X

xen·o·pho·bi·a	(zĕn′ ō·fō′ bĭ·ȧ)
X ray	(ĕks′ rā′)
X-ray ther·a·py	
xy·lo·phone	(zī′ lō·fōn)

Y

yachts·man	(yŏts′ mȧn)
Yan·kee	(yăng′ kė)
yard·age	(yär′ dĭj)
yard·stick	(yärd′ stĭk′)
yarn-dyed	(yärn′ dīd′)
yawn	(yôn)
year	(yēr)
year·book year·ling	
year·long year·ly	
yearn·ing	(yûr′ nĭng)
yeast	(yēst)
yel·low	(yĕl′ ō)
yelp	(yĕlp)
yen	(yĕn)
yeo·man	(yō′ mȧn)
yes·ter·day	(yĕs′ tēr·dĭ)
yew tree	(yōō)
Yid·dish	(yĭd′ ĭsh)
yield	(yēld)
yo·del	(yō′ d'l)
-deled -del·ing	
yo·ga	(yō′ gȧ)
yo·ghurt	(yō′ gŏŏrt)
yo·gi	(yō′ gē)
yoke	(yōk)
(frame; see *yolk*)	
yo·kel	(yō′ kĕl)

Z

za·ny	(zā′ nĭ)
za·ni·ness	
Zan·zi·bar	(zăn′ zĭ·bär)
zeal	(zēl)
zeal·ot	(zĕl′ ŭt)
zeal·ous	(zĕl′ ŭs)
ze·bra	(zē′ brȧ)
ze·nith	(zē′ nĭth)
zep·pe·lin	(zĕp′ ĕ·lĭn)
ze·ro	(zēr′ ō)
-ros	
zest·ful	(zĕst′ fŏŏl)
-ful·ly -ful·ness	
Zeus	(zūs)
zig·gu·rat	(zĭg′ ŏŏ·răt)
zig·zag	(zĭg′ zăg′)
-zagged -zag·ging	
zinc ox·ide	(zĭngk)
zin·ni·a	(zĭn′ ĭ·ȧ)
Zi·on·ism	(zī′ ŭn·ĭz'm)
zip·per	(zĭp′ ēr)
zir·con	(zûr′ kŏn)
zith·er	(zĭth′ ēr)
zo·di·ac	(zō′ dĭ·ăk)
zom·bi	(zŏm′ bĭ)
-bis	
zone	(zōn)
zon·ing zon·al	
zo·ol·o·gy	(zō·ŏl′ ō·jĭ)
zo·o·log·i·cal	(zō′ ō·lŏj′ ĭ·kȧl)
Zo·ro·as·tri·an	(zō′ rō·ăs′ trĭ·ȧn)
zuc·chi·ni	(zōō·kē′ nē)
Zu·lu	(zōō′ lōō)
zwie·back	(tsvē′ bäk′)